D0948743

Gift of Nathan Lyons
(1930–2016)

Gift of Nathan Lyons
(1930–2016)

Semiotics and Language

ADVANCES IN SEMIOTICS

General Editor, Thomas A. Sebeok

SEMIOTICS

AND

LANGUAGE

An Analytical Dictionary

A. J. Greimas and J. Courtés

TRANSLATED BY
Larry Crist and Daniel Patte
and James Lee, Edward McMahon II,
Gary Phillips, Michael Rengstorf

INDIANA UNIVERSITY PRESS
Bloomington

Copyright© by Librairie Hachette 1979
English translation copyright © 1982 by Indiana University Press

All rights reserved

No part of this book may be reproduced or utilized in any form or
by any means, electronic or mechanical, including photocopying
and recording, or by any information storage and retrieval system,
without permission in writing from the publisher. The Association
of American University Presses' Resolution on Permissions constitutes the only exception to this prohibition.

Manufactured in the United States of America

Library of Congress Cataloging in Publication Data

Greimas, Algirdas Julien.
   Semiotics and language: an analytical dictionary.

   (Advances in semiotics)
   Translation of: Sémiotique.
   Bibliography: p.
   Includes index.
   1. Semiotics—Dictionaries. I. Courtés, Joseph,
1936-   . II. Title. III. Series.
P99.G6913   401'.41   81-47828
ISBN 0-253-35169-3   AACR2
1 2 3 4 5 86 85 84 83 82

GIFT OF NATHAN LYONS
2017

CONTENTS

TRANSLATORS' NOTE

This English version of the Greimas-Courtés work is the result of teamwork that involved a number of stages. At the very first level, Michael Rengstorf, with some help from Daniel Patte, established English equivalents for the headwords of each entry in the French version; these are found in italics following the French headword in that text. As work on the full translation proceeded, some of these equivalents were changed (the list of changes appears at the end of this preface).

Working from the dittographed form from which the French version was printed, each of the translators produced an English version of one-sixth of the dictionary. The two principal translators then had the task of integrating these six parts. This work was done in two stages.

First, each, once again beginning from the French text—that of the printed version now—read approximately half the entries and made extensive revisions. They then each read the translation as revised by the other and made further revisions thereon. Second, Crist, the primarily Anglophone translator, read the extensively revised translation aloud while Patte, the primarily Francophone translator, followed in the original French text. This part of the process took the most time. Quarrels erupted, cruces were agonized over, but agreement always ensued. In a limited number of cases it seemed that there were errors in the French text. All corrections made to that text were submitted to the authors for final judgments.

The revised text ensuing from the oral process was then retyped and was read once more in its entirety by each of the two principal translators for consistency of terminology and style. In a last series of meetings, they made final decisions concerning their revisions. It should be understood that the principal translators—who perhaps should be called "revisers"—did not bring to the six portions (two of them, of course, from their own hands) a set of preconceived notions. Rather, they were able to profit from what was best in each individual translation so as to arrive at a version that, they hope, is more felicitous than what they could have achieved by themselves.

With regard to the syntax of the original sentences, we have consciously over-translated. As anyone who has glanced at the French version can testify, the sentences are frequently quite long and extremely convoluted. We chose a considerably simpler style, in the conviction that clarifying the development of the discussion was our most-important goal. Most of the choices in translating key terms were obvious, but certain changes from the originally proposed English equivalents had to be made: changes required by the very discussion in the article for which such a word was the headword.

On the other hand, we have under-translated many of the terms, often at the risk of giving the impression that by using expressions on the borderline of acceptable English, what we have produced is more a simple transposition than a translation. Such was the case with the modalities. The infinitives of the French modal verbs (*vouloir, savoir, pouvoir, devoir*) can correspond to English gerunds (*Savoir nager est important* = Knowing how to swim is important). With an article, they can also serve as nouns (*Le devoir est souvent pénible* = Duty is often painful). Although the purely nominal form is probably more common in English (will, knowledge, power, duty), we opted to keep the form that maintained a verbal sense, at the risk of some awkwardness. Thus, "The subject's knowing qualifies it as cognitively competent" is not the same as the "ordinary-language" form: "John's knowledge helps him to do things." In so doing, we aimed at underlining the very specific use of these terms in the semiotic theory proposed.

In addition, many concepts found in this work have English equivalents used by linguists, logicians, anthropologists, sociologists, etc., but in a different sense; we often refrained from using them because these concepts were redefined by being inserted in the wider framework of the general semiotic theory proposed herein. That is, in fact, the great contribution of this work. It brings together in a consistent theoretical framework many very disparate partial theories and proposals stemming from a great variety of fields, which until now have been perceived as discrete or even divergent aspects of semiotic research. But to do so it was necessary for the authors to establish a terminology that would transcend all these projects, a terminology that is tantamount to a metalanguage.

To give some specific examples: The pair "Sender/Receiver" was used for the more parallel pair *Destinateur/Destinataire,* rather than the equally parallel "Addresser/Addressee" so as to avoid confusion with the Jakobsonian theory of communication, given that the pair being translated belongs to the more abstract category of actants. "Engagement/Disengagement" was used instead of the more "mechanical" "shifting in/shifting out" in order to avoid confusion with the equally Jakobsonian (from Jesperson) "shifter." This latter choice was also supported by the term's greater facility of use (no particles to move about in the sentence [*e.g.,* *"The discourse shifts the enunciator in"]).

A loss of symmetry was regretfully agreed to in rendering the set of parallel pairs *énonciation/énoncé* and *énonciatif/énoncif.* For the first pair the translation "enunciation/enunciate" had originally been proposed so as to keep the parallelism. But we had to abandon this proposal. On the one hand, the adjectival derivative from the originally proposed neologism *enunciate would perforce have had to be *enunciative; but that is already the adjectival form corresponding to enunciation (unless, of course, we were to propose *enunciationative). On the other hand, the translation "utterance" for *énoncé* was already in use. Unfortunately it generated the cacophonous adjectival neologism "utterative" in place of the more euphonic "enuncive" (note that this form does not derive from *enunciate, but from the real parallel in French, *énoncif*), but that is a consequence we have, albeit heavy-heartedly, accepted.

A last remark. For the translation of the term *sémiotique* we used two terms: "semiotics" when the French term designates a semiotic theory; and "semiotic system" (as shorthand for "semiotic system and process") when the French term designates a signifying whole.

Since we are dealing here with a sort of metalanguage, the most profitable way of using the dictionary is perhaps to plunge in, according to one's own needs, curiosity, or simple hazard, and then follow the authors' suggestions concerning their system of cross-references.

If one wishes a more reasoned method of proceeding, we would suggest that the dictionary be entered through one of the principal articles. Perhaps the most logical place to begin would be the entry **SEMIOTICS** or the equally programmatic **STRUCTURE.** In this latter connection, it should be pointed out—something not quite clear in the text—that the different levels of structure are lucidly schematized at the end of the entry **GENERATIVE TRAJECTORY.** Consequently, one could get an overview of the theory by reading the entries corresponding to each of the terms in this schema: **SYNTAX, FUNDAMENTAL; SYNTAX, NARRATIVE; SYNTAX, DISCOURSIVE; SEMANTICS, FUNDAMENTAL; SEMANTICS, NARRATIVE; SEMANTICS, DISCOURSIVE.**

The following English equivalents have been changed from those proposed in the French edition:

ACTE DE LANGAGE: language act → speech act
AGRESSEUR: aggressor → villain [combined article]
AVOIR: to have → having
BINARITÉ: binarity → binarism
COMBINATOIRE: tactics → combinatory principle or arrangement
DÉBRAYAGE: shifting out → disengagement
DÉNÉGATION: denegation → denial
DÉNOMINATION: denomination → name, naming
DÉPOSSESSION: depossession → dispossession
DESTINATEUR/DESTINATAIRE: addresser/addressee → sender/receiver
DÉTENSIVITÉ: detensiveness → detensivity
DURATIVITÉ: durativeness → durativity
EMBRAYAGE: shifting in → engagement
ÉMETTEUR: sender → source
ENCATALYSER: to encatylize → encatylizing
ÉNONCÉ: enunciate → utterance

INSTANCE: instance → domain
OPÉRATOIRE: instrumental → operational
PARENTHÉTISATION: parenthetization → bracketing
PERSONNAGE: personage → character
PERTINENCE: relevance → pertinence
PROPOSITION: proposition → clause/proposition (two separate entities)
RÉCEPTEUR: receiver → destination
SCIENTIFICITÉ: scientificity → scientificness
STRUCTURATION: structuralization → structuring
TRAÎTRE: traitor → villain
TROMPERIE: deceit → trickery

PREFACE

1. An Inventory of Current Views Concerning Language

The analytical dictionary that we here propose is a *dictionnaire raisonné,* that is, a systematic presentation, in the form of concise and up-to-date reflections, of all aspects of language in its very broadest sense, as semiotic system(s) and/or process(es). Its goal is to review and evaluate the various theories of language, and simultaneously to present a synthesis—or at least a partial one—of the various attempts that have been made to establish this field of knowledge as a coherent theory. It is widely known that, for about a decade and a half, the "semiotic enterprise" has given rise to different directions. Now it is perhaps time to make an inventory of these various theoretical proposals, to homologate them one with another, and to evaluate them. Semiotics can certainly be seen as a pioneering undertaking. However, we have constantly attempted to define semiotics with respect to linguistics, that is, as a project located within linguistics, or beside it, or above it. Now, linguistics itself, enriched by a tradition developed over more than a century, was, during that time, striving toward a logico-mathematical rigor which led to the elaboration of progressively more refined procedures. This development in linguistic research engendered a number of certitudes, but, often, at the expense of theoretical reflection and thus of creative questioning. It was not at all an easy task to establish a convincing exchange between an approach characterized by epistemological laxity and another, based on a set of methodological techniques, each of which approaches was ignorant of the other.

A new situation is coming into being, because, as could be expected, the semiotic movements inspired by metaphysical or ideological concerns have progressively exhausted themselves, and, above all, because promising research areas have developed, implicitly or explicitly concerned with the problems of signification. Such are generative semantics, Anglo-American logic, or American pragmatics. These research projects echo our own relentlessly pursued interests despite their quite different backgrounds. The moment thus seemed right to us to attempt, not a unification, but rather a homogenization (of the various linguistic and semiotic theories) by establishing—of course, on the basis of certain options—a common ground upon which these theories could be brought together, compared and evaluated. The present dictionary is a tentative expression of that effort.

2. Why a Dictionary

The above does not yet explain the choice of a dictionary form. Indeed, while there are two possible modes of presentation—a syntagmatic and a paradigmatic mode—at first glance a theoretical discourse would seem to be the usual and most appropriate form. Yet such a discourse would have required an effort of discoursive strategy all out of proportion with our present goal. Such a presentation might have been more effective in the long run but it would have had only a very limited impact upon research now going on. Convinced as we are that a scientific project is meaningful only when it becomes the object of a collective quest, we are prepared to sacrifice to that end some of the rigor and coherence which is our aim.

A dictionary form has both the advantages and the disadvantages of a paradigmatic approach and of a discontinuous presentation. The advantages of the dictionary form are obvious. It gives immediate access to the entire terminology presently used. It will make it easier, later on, to introduce additional information which progress in research will certainly bring about. Above all, it allows us to set side by side metalinguistic segments which have quite unequal degrees of elaboration and formulation. Thus rigorous definitions, incomplete proposals, and suggestions concerning problematic domains which still need to be explored can be juxtaposed. The major disadvantage of the dictionary form is the alphabetical dispersion of the body of concepts, making it difficult to control the taxonomic coherence which is supposed to undergird it. Yet we hope that the twofold system of cross-references that we have used (cf. # 6 below) will manifest what is our main concern: contributing—by means of a terminology which might appear to some to be grossly oversophisticated, not to say repulsive—to the elaboration of a rigorous conceptual metalanguage which is a necessary preliminary toward the establishment of any language theory as formal language.

3. An "Analytical Dictionary"

Yet aiming at such a coherence is inevitably opposed to the common conception of a specialized lexicon, viewed as a heterogeneous list of entries, each of which refers, in the most extreme cases, to a different conceptual background and, ultimately, to divergent theoretical foundations. Our determination to avoid such an eclecticism is based first of all upon the conviction that "objective" or neutral dictionaries do not exist in the humanities and in the social sciences. The presence of the redactors is felt therein, whether they will it or not, by the choice of the terms included or excluded, by the way in which these terms are received and treated. The situation being what it is, it is better to opt for a self-conscious attitude and thus to make our preferences explicit and to explain systematically the reasons for our choices.

This deliberate option for "reasoning," for reflecting upon the concepts—which first shows the place of each concept in its own theoretical context, which then raises the question of knowing to which extent these concepts are comparable and whether or not they can be homologated with each other—involves a number of risks. Indeed, there is the risk of overlooking the originality of particular theoretical contributions in favor of a certain middle of the road position made up of perennial problems and issues—without necessarily even speaking of perennially proposed solutions—which the theory of language has raised for about a century and a half. Consequently our goal was twofold: we aimed at unsettling the reader by showing that there is no finished science made up of certitudes; and at the same time, we aimed at reassuring the reader by disclosing the assured permanence of certain perspectives. In so doing we have attempted to serve, in our own way, a specific ideology of knowing.

4. Lexicographic Bricolage

As is, this dictionary is open to criticism both because of what it includes and because of what it does not mention, as well as, quantitatively, because of what it overemphasizes and what it treats insufficiently. Some of these disproportions, especially the part that treats of semiotics in the strictest sense, seem justified. Research in progress on a specific point is governed by its own strategy which favors, at any stage in its development, a particular domain or a particular approach rather than others. The preference shown these days for the analysis of discursive organizations and of individual texts, rather than for taxonomic coherence and collective corpora, is a striking example of this disequilibrium. No wonder therefore that such a preference is reflected at the level of the metalanguage and that it causes an unbalance in the organization of this dictionary. These are merely the result of the paradigmatic oscillations which mark stages in the history of any discipline. They are both legitimate and rewarding.

But the case of faddish phenomena is quite different. We refer to philosophical fashions, which often remain on the epistemological surface without influencing the scientific endeavor in itself, as well as to scientific fashions—if we can use the expression—which are manifested, for instance, in the priority given to certain formalization procedures or to certain representation systems. Since in such a case we are both judges and judged, it is difficult for us to be rather sure of the solidity of our selection criteria.

Operativity is such a criterion. Because of it we have been led at times to emphasize certain barely elaborated hypotheses or certain models which have a very local usage. Yet, we have emphasized these hypotheses and models insofar as they seemed to us to have been tried and proven, in that they have established one or another semiotic procedure which is iterative or which can be generalized. Here also our judgment rests in most cases upon intuition. The most perceptive beholder can see only what is already in his/her eye!

We have based the exclusions upon somewhat different criteria. Certain concepts or conceptual fields have been omitted, not because we question their interest or value, but simply because their integration in the overall theory proved to be difficult, and even impossible. This waiting list, which, we hope, will only be temporary, is made up of blind spots which may denote either the immaturity of certain concepts or the flaws—indeed, the many flaws, of our competence. The reader will agree that the choice between impoverishment and incoherence is often difficult to make.

5. Lacunae

Some of the lacunae, more apparent than real, need to be noted. Such is the case, for instance, of the space given to Anglo-American logic. If that space may appear insufficient, it is, in part, because the set of problems concerning speech acts has been homologated to the theory of enunciation which was formulated, as is well known, by E. Benveniste under the influence of J. L. Austin's work, and which was then developed as an integrated part of general semiotic theory. The second and main reason why we have given a limited place to Anglo-American logic is that its purely logical contributions could only have been introduced in the framework of a quite thorough presentation of the languages of logic. Such a presentation, legitimate in itself, would have greatly transformed the general organization and aim of the present work.

The case of our treatment of American pragmatics is somewhat similar. Its field of research corresponds, in part, to the theory of modal competence which we have developed. The reasons for our reservations are clear. Either its approach to problems is an integral part of language theory, and then the translation of its contribution into a semiotic form goes without saying, or pragmatics is, according to its own definition, nothing but a non-semiotic appendix to semiotics, using heterogeneous categories—psychological and sociological categories, for instance—and then it cannot claim a place in a dictionary of semiotics.

Another omission, perhaps more serious, is that of rhetoric. Because we are dealing only with the language theories which are directly linked to linguistic research with a scientific aim, it was impossible for us to account for the earlier rhetorical and poetic theories which are, in large measure, marked by a Western ethnocentrism. In saying this, we are confessing, first of all, our own limitations: since we were unable to convert their fundamental notions into semiotic concepts, we were unable to assign them a place in the overall theoretical organization. This is also to confess the limitations of semiotic theory at the present time. Despite significant contributions—which are nevertheless far from converging with each other (especially the works of G. Genette, of the Liège Group, of textual linguistics)—it appears that discursive semiotics of a figurative character remains to be constructed.

Finally, certain readers may deplore the small space given to particular, local semiotic theories, which courageously strive to open new fields of research and strive to elaborate new disciplines in the context of the "human sciences." From one domain to the next one can observe very different degrees of progress in research. Furthermore, their specialized terminologies have a tendency to be centrifugal and often highly metaphorical. These observations have led us to be prudent. Instead of recording, and thus of giving established status to what might only be ephemeral, we have thought it would be better to aim at promoting an effort toward a more homogeneous conceptualization, even if its scope has to be more limited.

Our wish is, indeed, that this dictionary be the place where progress in semiotics might be recorded, *i.e.,* that the provisional inventory of concepts which it forms be viewed as open to new and better formulations.

6. How to Use This Dictionary

In order to maintain an equilibrium between the alphabetical dispersion and the taxonomic organization which undergirds it, in order to make this dictionary an immediately accessible research tool which can simultaneously serve as a more general introduction to language theory, we have been led to establish a system of cross-references involving several levels.

—At the risk of repeating ourselves, we have regularly included in each article a brief definition, even when it is an antonym or hyponym of a concept studied in greater detail. In this way, readers who want to obtain a piece of information rapidly do not have to lose time in pursuing meaning from one cross-reference to another.

—The references found at the end of each article are intended to gather together the main conceptual interrelations. In this way, they provide the semantic context of the term under study.

—The asterisks, first designed to indicate, within each article, the terms defined elsewhere in the dictionary, were to meet the requirement for interdefinition of terms; in this way, they would test the theoretical coherence toward which we are striving. Very soon we discovered the pleonastic character of such an endeavor. With the exception of the function words and of some verbs, almost all the terms of our text had an asterisk. We have therefore limited the use of this sign. It is almost exclusively used to remind the reader of broader conceptual fields which permit a better situating of the term under definition (or of one of its constitutive elements), either within an autonomous component of the theory or by linking it to a circumscribed epistemological locus.

Such a cross-reference system, by inscribing each term of the dictionary within three concentric configurations, makes possible, therefore, a threefold reading of the dictionary, starting from any one of its articles.

7. Acknowledgments

Built on the basis of the systematic and comprehensive study of a small number of semioticians and linguists whose names, frequently mentioned, constitute a final system of references, this dictionary is nevertheless a witness and an expression of collective and anonymous research. To those whose intuitions and work have been used, we want to express our gratitude for the debt that we as their spokesmen have toward them.

Historians of lexicography well know that dictionaries are made up out of other dictionaries. Such has been our practice: we have delved abundantly into works like ours, seeking therein a starting point, a confirmation, or simply an occasion for making our position clear by opposing other positions. We want especially to thank Philippe Hamon, author of a first lexicon of semiotics, who convinced us of the necessity of giving an analytical form to our undertaking.

Our thanks go in advance to all those who, by their remarks, their criticism, and their additions, are willing to confirm the usefulness of this effort to bring semiotic research into focus.

Analytical Dictionary

ABCDEFGHIJKLMN OPQRSTUVWXYZ

ABSENCE
(absence)

Absence is one of the terms in the category* *presence/absence* which articulates the mode of semiotic existence of the objects of knowing.* "In absentia" existence, which characterizes the paradigmatic* axis of language, is called virtual* existence.—PRESENCE; EXISTENCE, SEMIOTIC

ABSTRACT
(abstrait)

Any term, whether belonging to a natural language or a metalanguage, is said to be **abstract** either because its semic density* is low, in which case it is opposed to concrete,* or because it does not have exteroceptive* semes in its sememic* composition, in which case it is opposed to figurative.* At the level of discoursive semantics,* a distinction is drawn between the abstract (or thematic) component and the figurative component.—INTEROCEPTIVITY; THEMATIZATION

ACCEPTABILITY
(acceptabilité)

1. **Acceptability** is one of the concepts of generative grammar* that have not been defined. It would seem to depend on the notion of intention,* among others. Intention is itself a notion which is questionable and vague in that, for instance, it implies consciousness, and thus would exclude dream discourse at the least. Intention is often linked with communication*: the intention of the speaker presupposes not only the competence* of the enunciator,* but also that of the enunciatee, which can accept or reject the proposed utterances. From this point of view, acceptability should be the essential basis for the definition of linguistic competence.

2. Acceptability is the basic concept of an ideal competence, postulated as being equal for everybody—a proposition which obviously cannot be verified. At the same time it defines linguistic performance,* which can be understood from this point of view as the generation and/or effective recognition* of acceptable utterances. Thus acceptability involves constraints, of an internal or external nature, which limit the speaking subject's exercise of competence.

3. Insofar as there is any attempt to make an instrumental* concept out of acceptability, it must be stressed that it essentially belongs to the performance of the enunciatee. Acceptability is thus seen as a relative judgment, not expressed in terms of definite categories. Sentences (or discourses) are not

1

acceptable/non-acceptable, but more or less acceptable. The reasons for these partial or total limitations of performance are both multiple and extra-linguistic. They may be of a psychological order, for example, (a) the finite characteristic of memory, which cannot retain more than a limited number of degrees of embedding,* or, (b) the varying degree of attention paid. They may also be of a physiological order, for example, the noise during the communication process or the receiver's physical condition, etc. Clearly this opens up research possibilities outside the field of semiotics.

4. Insofar as acceptability is situated in the domain of the enunciatee, where it appears as an epistemic* judgment based on the modality of *being-able-to-do* ("acceptable" being "that which one can accept"), the criteria which allow this judgment to be exercised are not to be sought at the level of realized* utterances. They are criteria of grammaticality and semanticity. —COMPETENCE; PERFORMANCE; GRAMMATICALITY; SEMANTICITY; INTERPRETATION; NORM

ACCOMPLISHED
(accompli)

Accomplished/unaccomplished is another name for the aspectual semic category* *perfectiveness/imperfectiveness.* —PERFECTIVENESS; ASPECTUALIZATION

ACHRONY
(achronie)

The term **achrony** is opposed to the two concepts of synchrony and diachrony, which for F. de Saussure meant two almost autonomous dimensions of linguistic research. Achrony affirms the atemporal nature of logico-semantic structures at the same time as it indicates the non-pertinence of Saussure's dichotomy. For, indeed, on the one hand, everything is temporal in semiotics (beginning with the language act) but duration plays no part therein. Only a second is needed for the production of the "spontaneous," individual metaphor, whereas the same metaphor takes several centuries to make its presence felt "in language": for example, from late Latin, *testa* ("clay pot") to French *tête* ("head"). On the other hand, logical calculation does take place in time, but time plays no part in the substitution operations that are carried out. Consequently, from the point of view of semiotic theory, we can consider that deep* semiotic structures are achronic, whereas more superficial, discoursive structures call for temporalization.*—DIACHRONY; SYNCHRONY

ACQUISITION
(acquisition)

Situated at the figurative* level, and paradigmatically opposed to deprivation,* **acquisition** represents the transformation* that establishes the conjunction* between subject* and object.* It corresponds to realization* and is brought about either in a transitive way (attribution*) or a reflexive way (appropriation*). When inscribed in the narrative schema,* acquisition is the positive form of consequence and thus falls under that discoursive figure known as test. —REALIZATION; COMMUNICATION; CONSEQUENCE; TEST

ACT
(acte)

1. In the philosophical tradition which stretches back to scholasticism,

an **act** is identified with "causing to be" and corresponds to the passage from potentiality to existence. This sort of definition, whose intuitive nature does not pass unnoticed, is extremely general. Not only can all the "events" which make up the web of narrative discourses be interpreted as acts, but discourse itself is an act, an organized sequence of cognitive acts. Consequently, it is essential to establish a model for the representation* of the act that can be used in semiotic analysis and that can eventually form the starting point for a semiotics of action.*

2. The intuitive definition of acting as "causing to be" shows that it contains two predicates that are in hypotactic* relation. Its syntactic representation will thus assume the form of two utterances*: an utterance pertaining to doing* (= causing) and an utterance pertaining to state* (= being). The former will govern the latter, which will be the object of doing. The canonical representation of an act may be formulated by a modal structure* either of the type $F [S_1 \rightarrow 0_1 (S_2 \cup 0_2)]$ or of the type $F [S_1 \rightarrow 0_1 (S_2 \cap 0_2)]$ and is recognizable at the level of surface narrative grammar.

3. The interpretation of this formula is simple: to act presupposes the existence of a subject and is identified with the modality of "doing," producing a state (or a change of state) that is formulated as the junction* of an object with the subject, which may or may not be in syncretism* with the subject of doing. Thus, to act partially corresponds to performance* and presupposes a modal competence,* considered as the potentiality of doing. This explains why an act is defined as the passage from competence to performance, with "passage" being interpreted syntactically

as the modality* of doing, which is the conversion, at the level of anthropomorphic* syntax, of the concept of transformation.*

—DOING; ACT, SPEECH

ACT, SPEECH
(acte de langage)

1. The general definition of act* also applies to **speech act** when understood as "taking the floor" (and thus initiating a speech) either as described and situated in the pragmatic dimension of discourse, or observed within the "pragmatic" framework of communication. Whether it is understood in the first sense or the second, the speech act should be considered first as a meaningful gestural aspect of doing. As such it can be incorporated into the paradigm of other, comparable, sound gestures (such as singing, whistling, belching, stuttering). It should also be considered as part (one of the terms) of an appropriate semantic category: for example, "speaking"/"keeping quiet." Furthermore, it should be seen as occupying various syntagmatic positions within the strategy of communication: for example, "beginning to speak," "giving someone the right to speak," "taking the right to speak back from someone" (see note at the end of the article). In all this, no recourse need be made to the content of the particular locution. The term **speech act** should be reserved for this significant somatic* activity. This activity could be studied in the framework of the categorization* of the world by natural languages; such a study leads to the establishment of comparative ethno-taxonomies of speech. As a somatic activity, it should be included in the pragmatic* dimension of discourse and should be dealt

with in the more general framework of narrative grammar.

2. Considered as a specific type of doing,* the speech act at first appears to be a form of "causing to know," *i.e.,* as a form of doing which brings about the conjunction* of the enunciatee*-subject with an object* of knowing. From this point of view, and in order to be effective, or simply possible, it presupposes a set of semiotic conditions which will ensure the transmission of the object of knowing. In other words, if every occurrence of speech act, accomplished *hic et nunc,* can be envisaged as a particular performance,* it presupposes, under the general title of competence,* the existence of a semiotic system in which, either wholly or partially, both the enunciator* and the enunciatee participate. The fact that the speech act presupposes a semiotic system* which is also a process* (a putting into discourse*) implies that both the semiotic form* (or schema*) and the semiotic substance* are taken up by it. The speech act is not a creation *ex nihilo* to be located at the starting point of any semiotic reflection. It is rather a particular event which is part of a system of multiple constraints.*

3. From another point of view, the speech act is, as a form of doing, a "causing to be" what it brings into being is signification.* In its pragmatic aspect it is identified with semiosis,* in uniting, at the two poles of enunciation, the signifier* and the signified.* In its cognitive aspect, it is signification, *i.e.,* the production and apprehension of significant differences.

4. Finally, the speech act can be considered as a "causing to do," *i.e.,* as a form of manipulation*: a manipulation through speech, of one subject by another. Here, obviously, we are not dealing with the problem of the imperative and the vocative, which has always been known to linguists, but rather with the question of the general properties of the discoursive organization, which can be grouped together under the term modalization of discourse. These general properties can be recognized not only as particular forms of discoursive programming, such as persuasive* doing or interpretive* doing, but also as implicit and presupposed forms, which constitute the modal competence of subjects in the domain of contractual and/or polemical communication. It is enough to postulate that the subjects participating in communication (and it matters little whether they are part of figurative discourses and can be analyzed as "subjects on paper" or "real subjects" producing discourses themselves) are invested with modal competence, so that the speech acts which they produce as performances can be interpreted as modal performances of a cognitive order. These modal performances can form the object of a semiotics of manipulation. It is within this frame of reference that analyses of the philosophy of language, which are still only partial, should be included (Austin, Searle, and to a certain extent, G. Ducrot).

5. The set of problems raised by an examination of speech acts is similar in part to that raised by enunciation.

—ENUNCIATION; PRAGMATIC(S); COMMUNICATION

(Translators' note)
The French *"prendre la parole," "donner la parole," "retirer la parole"* refers, in its restricted sense, to a quasi-parliamentary situation, where—as we have translated above—*"prendre la parole"* = *"to take the floor," "donner la*

parole" = *"to give someone the floor,"* *"retirer la parole"* = *"to take the floor from someone,"* i.e., *"to interrupt/stop someone's speech."*

ACTANT
(actant)

1. An **actant** can be thought of as that which accomplishes or undergoes an act,* independently of all other determinations. Thus, to quote L. Tesnière, from whom this term is borrowed, "actants are beings or things that participate in processes in any form whatsoever, be it only a walk-on part and in the most passive way." From this point of view, "actant" designates a type of syntactic unit,* properly formal in character, which precedes any semantic and/or ideological investment.*

2. The term "actant" is linked with a particular conception of the syntax* which interrelates the functions of the elementary utterance.* These functions, such as subject, object, predicate,* are defined independently of their realization in syntagmatic units (for example, nominal and verbal syntagms). This syntax also poses the predicate as the nucleus of the utterance. All this is to say that the actants are to be considered as the resultant terms of the relation known as the function. This concept of actant is likewise to be interpreted in the framework of case grammar (Fillmore), where each case can be considered as the representation of an actantial position. In this respect, **actantial grammar,** which is semiotic in nature, is seen as a more abstract formulation of case grammar. At a deeper* level, actantial grammar, not subject to phrase linguistic form, is able to account for the organization of narrative dis-

courses at the level of narrative syntax* (called the surface level), thanks to functional, syntactic categories* —subject, object, predicate, etc.— which it makes explicit in view of its own construction. From this point of view, it is distinguished from categorial grammars, which operate with morphological classes, and from syntagmatic grammars, which rely on distributional classes.

3. The concept of actant has the advantage of replacing, especially in literary semiotics, the term of character* as well as that of "dramatis persona" (V. Propp), since it applies not only to human beings but also to animals, objects, or concepts. Furthermore, the term character remains ambiguous since it also corresponds in part to the concept of actor* (where syncretism* of actants may occur), which is defined as the figure and/or the empty locus wherein are invested syntactic and semantic forms.

4. Typologically, the following are distinguished within the uttered discourse: (a) **The actants of communication** (or of the enunciation), which are not only the narrator* and narratee,* but also the interlocutor* and interlocutee (which participate in the structure of second degree interlocution, the dialogue*). (b) **The actants of narration** (or of the utterance*): subject/object, sender/ receiver. From the grammatical point of view, the **syntactic actants** (inscribed in a given narrative program) such as the subject of state* and the subject of doing,* are opposed here to the **functional** (or syntagmatic) **actants,** which subsume the actantial* roles in a determined narrative* trajectory. Bearing in mind the two dimensions* recognized in discourse, we distinguish between, for example, pragmatic* subjects and cognitive* subjects. The

latter appear either in syncretism with the pragmatic subjects, or as autonomous actors, in the case of the informant,* for example; or, in the case of the observer actant, they are recognizable at least as implicit positions. Since at the level of discoursive semantics, the actant is taken in charge by the procedure of figurativization,* it is then termed either individual, dual, or collective.

5. Any actant may be projected onto the semiotic square and thus articulated in at least four actantial positions (actant, antactant, negactant, negantactant). When articulated in this way, the actant is known as the **proto-actant*** and is transformed into an **actantial category.***

6. As the narrative discourse progresses, the actant may assume a certain number of actantial roles,* defined both by the position of the actant in the logical sequence of the narration (its syntactic definition) and by its modal* investment (its morphological definition). Thus the hero will be the hero* only in certain parts of the narrative—s/he was not the hero before and s/he may well not be the hero afterwards.

—FUNCTION; UTTERANCE; NARRATIVE TRAJECTORY; SYNTAX, NARRATIVE SURFACE; ACTANTIAL; ACTOR

ACTANTIAL
(ROLE, STATUS)
(actantiel [rôle, statut—])

1. As it progresses through its narrative trajectory,* an actant* can be united with a certain number of narrative states or **actantial roles.** These are defined both in terms of the actant's position within the narrative trajectory, and the particular modal investment of the actant. Thus, the subject-actant, for example, will be endowed successively with modalities* such as those of

wanting-to-do, knowing-how-to-do, or *being-able-to-do.* In this case, the subject assumes those actantial roles which manifest the subject in terms of wanting, the subject in terms of knowing, and the subject in terms of being able to do, and which then indicate the three stages in the acquisition of its modal competence (which is a necessary step towards its performance*). From the paradigmatic point of view, actantial roles are to be considered as a category* (in the sense used by Hjelmslev). Indeed, they constitute a paradigm whose elements are defined by the position they can occupy in the narrative trajectory.

2. While the **actantial status** is that which defines the actant at a given moment of the narrative trajectory, taking into account the totality of its previous trajectory (manifested or simply presupposed), the actantial role is simply the surplus which is added, at a particular point of the trajectory, to what already constitutes the actant within the syntagmatic progression of the discourse.

3. Thus defined morphologically* (by their modal content), and syntactically (by the position of the actant in the narrative trajectory), the actantial roles belong to surface narrative syntax.* When associated with one or more thematic roles (which structure the semantic component of the discourse), they allow for the constitution of actors,* as loci where narrative and discoursive structures converge and are invested.

—ACTANT; NARRATIVE TRAJECTORY; ROLE; PSYCHO-SEMIOTICS

ACTION
(action)

1. **Action** can be defined as a syntagmatic* organization of acts,*

without our having to make any *a priori* decision about the nature of this organization, whether it be an ordered or stereotyped sequence, or programmed by a competent subject.

2. In syntagmatic semiotics, action can be considered as the result of the conversion,* at a given moment of the generative* trajectory, of a narrative program,* either simple or complex. In the case of a complex program, the various pragmatic narrative programs which compose it correspond to the acts which constitute the action. That is to say that an action is a filled-out narrative program, with the subject represented by an actor* and the doing converted into a process.*

3. Narrative semiotics does not study actions as such, but actions "on paper," *i.e.,* descriptions of actions. The analysis of narrated actions enables us to recognize stereotypes of human activities and to construct typological and syntagmatic models which take account of them. The extrapolation of such procedures and such models can form the basis for a **semiotics of action.**
—ACT; NARRATIVE TRAJECTORY; PERFORMANCE

ACTOR

(acteur)

1. Historically the term **actor** has gradually replaced character (and dramatis persona), indicating thereby a greater desire for precision and generalization—a magic carpet or a business firm, for example, are actors—thus extending its use outside the purely literary.

2. Obtained by procedures of engagement* and disengagement* (which belong to the domain of enunciation*), the actor is a lexical unit, nominal in type, which, once incorporated into the discourse, may receive, at the moment of its manifestation, investments* of surface narrative syntax* and discursive semantics.* Its semantic content proper seems to consist essentially in the presence of the seme of individuation,* which gives it the appearance of an autonomous figure* in the semiotic universe. An actor may be **individual,** (for example, Peter), or **collective** (for example, a crowd), **figurative*** (anthropomorphic or zoomorphic), or **nonfigurative** (for example, fate). The individuation of an actor is often marked by the attribution of a proper noun, though that does not in any way constitute a *sine qua non* of its existence—a vague thematic* role, "father," for example, may often be used to denote the actor. Thus, onomastics,* included under discursive semantics, is complementary to actorialization,* which is one of the procedures of discoursive syntax.*

3. At first, the term actor was linked and opposed to the term actant.* From a comparative point of view, when dealing with a corpus of tale variants, it can be noted that a single subject-actant, for example, can be manifested by several occurrence-actors. Nevertheless, distributional* analysis, used in this manner, underlines particularly the invariant* nature of the actant, while not giving thereby any information on the nature of the actor. It should also be borne in mind that the actor goes beyond the limits of the sentence and, thanks to anaphora,* is maintained throughout the discourse—or at least throughout a discoursive sequence—in keeping with the principle of identity.* It ceases, at that point, to be the variable* of a single, invariant actant, and successively assumes various actantial*

roles. In the same way, since discourse is the unfolding of semantic values, the actor may receive one or more different thematic* roles.

4. Thus a more precise definition may be established by viewing the actor as the point of convergence and investment of both the syntactic and semantic components. In order to be designated actor, a lexeme should have at least one actantial role and at least one thematic role. It should be further noted that the actor is not only the point of investment of these roles, but also of their transformations, since discourse consists essentially of the interplay of successive acquisition and loss of values.*

5. At the surface level of the text, then, is seen an **actorial structure** which is nothing else than a topological structure. The various actors are built up into a network of loci which, while empty by nature, are the loci where narrative and discoursive structures are manifested.

6. From the point of view of the production* of discourse, a distinction can be made between the subject of the enunciation (which is an implicit actant logically presupposed by the utterance*) and the **actor of the enunciation.** An example of the latter case would be, for example, "Baudelaire" as defined by the totality of his discourses.
—INDIVIDUATION; IDENTITY; ACTORIALIZATION

ACTORIALIZATION
(actorialisation)

1. Along with temporalization* and spatialization,* **actorialization** is one of the components of discoursivization,* and, like these two, is based on the implementation of the operations of engagement* and disengagement.* What characterizes the procedure of actorialization is that it aims at establishing the actors* of the discourse by uniting different elements of the semantic and syntactic components. These two components, the syntactic and the semantic, can be analyzed separately; on the discursive plane, they unfold their actantial and thematic trajectories in an autonomous manner, and are joined term by term. At least one actantial* role and at least one thematic* role constitute the actors, which are thus endowed at one and the same time with a *modus operandi* and a *modus essendi.*

2. Pragmatic* values* may be either objective* or subjective* and thereby manifested either as intrinsic properties of subjects or as independent thematized objects (for example, "to be strong" or "to possess an army"). Furthermore, a given actantial role may either be interiorized and then presented in syncretism* with the subject, or may gain autonomy and appear in the form of separate actors (the helper* or opponent, for example, representing modal structures of the competence of subjects; the informant* or the observer,* embodying, for their part, autonomous cognitive subjects). Consequently, each narrative discourse displays an **actorial distribution** proper to it. This is why the generative* trajectory, which is characterized among other things by the establishment of a structure of actors, can form the basis for an **actorial typology** of narrative discourses. The two poles of this typology would present, for the first, a varied actantial and thematic distribution, yet located within a single actor; by contrast, the second would be characterized by an organization of different and autonomous actors. A typology of this nature would consequently be located between two

kinds of distributions of actors—the one tending to the psychological, the other to the sociological.

—ACTOR; DISCOURSIVIZA-TION; SYNTAX, DISCOURSIVE

ACTUALIZATION
(actualisation)

1. From the point of view of the modes of semiotic existence, and within the linguistic framework, **actualization** corresponds to the passage from system* to process.* Thus, language* is a virtual* system which is actualized in speech* and in discourse. In the same way, it can be said that a lexeme,* which is characterized as a mere virtuality, is actualized thanks to the context in which it occurs in the form of a sememe.* Used within the framework of the *virtual/actual* category,* actualization is an operation by which a unit of language is rendered present* in a given linguistic context; the actual existence ("in praesentia") thus obtained is inherent in the syntagmatic* axis of language.

2. Narrative semiotics has found it necessary to substitute for the traditional *virtual/actual* pair, the ternary articulation *virtual/actual/realized,* so that a better account can be given of narrative organizations. Thus, subjects* and objects* prior to their junction* are in a virtual position; their actualization and their realization* take place in accordance with the two types of characteristic relations of the function*; disjunction* actualizes subjects and objects, conjunction realizes them.

3. From this point of view, actualization as an operation may correspond—insofar as it is brought about from a prior realization—to a transformation* which effects the disjunction between subject and ob-

ject. On the figurative* level, it is, then, equivalent to privation.* Depending on whether at the actorial level the subject of doing is different or not from the subject, in a situation of lack there will be either a transitive* actualization (figurativized by dispossession*) or a reflexive* actualization (renunciation*). The term **actualized value** refers to any value* invested in the object at the moment, or in the syntactic position, when the object is in a disjunctive relation with the subject.

—EXISTENCE, SEMIOTIC; VALUE

ADDRESSER/ADDRESSEE
(destinateur/destinataire)

—SENDER/RECEIVER

ADEQUATION
(adéquation)

1. The term **adequation** refers to the conformity that can be seen between two semiotic entities.* The concept of adequation varies according to the way in which the relation between these entities is envisaged.

2. The term **vertical adequation** is used when the conformity between two distinct levels of language is postulated or required: between the object semiotic* system and its descriptive* metalanguage*; between the conceptualized theory* and the formal* language which axiomatizes it; between the deep* structures and the surface* structures (although the term equivalence* is more appropriate in this latter case).

3. The term **horizontal adequation** is reserved for the conformity that needs to be established between the project and its realization, *i.e.,* between the theory and its application. Indeed, since all theory is arbi-

trary,* and does not depend on the data of experience, the need for adequation at the theoretical level occurs only at the moment of application. From a different point of view, the construction of a theory can only have its application as its goal, and must consequently be subject to certain postulates (L. Hjelmslev's theory of empiricism*) which guarantee in advance the conditions of its adequation.
—THEORY; VERIFICATION; VALIDATION

AFFIRMATION
(affirmation)

1. Traditional grammar generally distinguishes four classes of clauses*: affirmative, negative, interrogative, and imperative. Whereas the latter two have to do with the interlocutor and seek to elicit his/her verbal* and/or somatic doing, affirmative and negative clauses are only statements concerning the mere fact of existence, addressed to the interlocutor, whose intervention is not requested. These are generally put together under the title of declarative clauses. (The first generative* grammars engendered only affirmative declarative clauses, affirmation being considered to be the characteristic of base sentences.) We prefer to consider them as informative* (or non-modalized) utterances, their production presupposing an "I say that," and nothing more.

2. In the Port-Royal tradition, it is said that a statement concerning the mere fact of existence which this type of utterance contains is manifested by the simple act of predication, since the copula to be* is an unparalleled instrument for making an affirmation. It is more or less in the same way that we distinguish **utterances* of state*** on the one hand, bearers of this statement of semiotic existence and characterized by the relation of junction between a subject* and an object* (that is, "affirmation," in the weakened sense of mere statement), and, on the other hand, utterances of doing* (whose two contradictory* terms are assertion* and negation*). It would seem that we should avoid the term affirmation, ambiguous as it is.
—ASSERTION; JUNCTION

AGRAMMATICALITY
(agrammaticalité)

Generative* and transformational linguistics depend on the enunciatee's competence* in order to distinguish what is grammatical from what is not. In contrast, by **agrammaticality** we understand the impossibility for two elements of the syntactic plane to be present* together in a hierarchically higher unit: in that case it is one of the possible forms of incompatibility.—GRAMMATICALITY; INCOMPATIBILITY

AGGRESSOR
(aggresseur)
—VILLAIN

ALETHIC MODALITIES
(aléthiques [modalités—])

From the semiotic point of view, the modal structure* known as **alethic** is produced when the modal utterance, with having-to-do* as its predicate, overdetermines and governs the utterance of state,* which has being* as its predicate. The mapping of this structure onto the semiotic square* permits the formulation of the alethic modal category:

Each of the terms of the square may be manifested as a noun:

necessity ⟶ impossibility

possibility ⟶ contingency

It can be seen that each modal term can then be treated either as a modal structure*, which is its syntactical definition, or as a modal value,* which is its taxonomic definition. While modal logic uses exclusively modal values (or names), modal semiotics attaches to each name its syntactic definition.—HAVING-TO-DO; MODALITY

ALGORITHM
(algorithme)

1. By **algorithm** is meant the prescription of a fixed order* in the execution of a number of explicit* instructions aiming at the solution of a certain type of problem. In scientific meta-semiotics,* which sets itself the task of representing the functioning of a semiotic system in the form of a system of rules,* the algorithm corresponds to a syntagmatic* knowing*-how-to-do, which can program, in the form of instructions, the application of appropriate rules. This knowing-how-to-do is also found in narrative discourses of all types in the form of a programmatic doing.* It varies according to the kind of competence of the operator subjects, and may either succeed or fail. It is "neutralized" by the clarification of all the rules and by the setting up of an operator subject known as the automaton.* The establishment and proper use of such a neutral operator is one of the conditions of scientificness.

2. It is obvious that the algorithmic presentation of sequences of rules can be accomplished only progressively: the algorithmic organization can only be conferred at first by certain analytical procedures.* Thus, in narrative semiotics, complex narrative programs,* for example, can already undergo an algorithmic formulation. In similar fashion, we have proposed that any ordered sequence of operations permitting passage from the initial stage to the final stage of a closed narrative* be considered as a **transformational*** **algorithm.** When an algorithm carries instructions providing for the passage, on the semiotic square,* from a primitive term (s1), to its contradictory (s$\bar{1}$), and thence, by implication,* to the contrary of the first term (s2), it can be said to be **dialectical.**

3. Sometimes the name **algorithmic linguistics** designates a branch of linguistics which deals particularly with the automation of the procedures of linguistic analyses for automatic processing, or, more generally, with the languages of documentation and programming. —RULE

ALPHABET
(alphabet)

In scientific meta-semiotics,* the term **alphabet** designates the finite inventory of symbols chosen to furnish the description* of a semiotic object, at the same time allowing expressions* to be constructed. The term structure is sometimes erroneously used in this sense. The main criticism which can be leveled against such a view of metalanguage is that insufficient attention is paid to the paradigmatic* aspect of any language, and that the alphabet is represented merely by a non-structured, simple inventory.—SYMBOL; EXPRESSION

ALTERITY
(altérité)

Alterity is a non-definable concept,* which is in opposition to another concept of the same sort, identity: this pair can at least be inter-defined by relations of reciprocal presupposition.* In the same way that identification permits a decision concerning the identity of one or several objects, so distinction* is the process by which their alterity is recognized.—IDENTITY; DIFFERENCE

AMBIGUITY
(ambiguité)

1. Ambiguity is that property of utterances* which simultaneously presents several possible readings or interpretations,* with no single one dominating the other.

2. Ambiguity may be of the lexical type, along with the phenomena of homophony or homography: it is then provoked by the pluri-semic nature of the lexemes.*

3. Syntactical ambiguity is seen when, at the level of surface syntactical structures, there is a correspondence between two or several semantic representations.*
—DISAMBIGUIZATION; HOMONYMY; UNEQUIVOCALNESS

ANALOGY
(analogie)

1. In its strict meaning, analogy is the identity* of the relation which unites two or more pairs of terms,* each one separately. Analogy is thus synonymous with mathematical proportion. If, instead of recording such relations, we try to establish them, the knowledge of three terms in a proportion of two couples enables the fourth one to be determined. Such a cognitive operation is often called reasoning by analogy. Since the neogrammarians, linguistic tradition has attributed an important role to analogical activity in the working of natural languages. The observance or the imitation of analogical models—which correspond to implicit reasoning—is clearly seen in individual practice ("I done it" instead of "I did it") and in the diachronic transformations of languages. Since the term analogy has been generalized and has thereby lost its strict meaning, it has had to be replaced by the term homology*; homologation is used to designate analogical activity.

2. In its common, loose meaning, analogy designates a more or less distant resemblance between one or several entities* between which an essential difference is implicitly acknowledged. Used in semiotics as a non-defined concept, the term analogy can be of help insofar as the established existence of analogy is prolonged by an attempt to determine its structure.

3. Thus analogy is often spoken of in reference to the relations that a semiotic system may hold with its external referent,* i.e., with the natural world. This problem is limited to the status of onomatopeia (cf. motivation*) as far as natural languages are concerned; analogy is a crucial issue when we are dealing with visual semiotics, where iconicity* is considered by some as a characteristic of this type of semiotics.

4. Analogy also acts as a starting point in the explanation of the constitution and unfolding of meta-

phoric isotopies* which seem capable of homologation among themselves.
—HOMOLOGATION; ICONICITY

ANALYSIS
(analyse)

Apart from its various colloquial uses, the term **analysis** has, since Hjelmslev, designated in semiotics the overall procedures used in the description* of a semiotic object.* In particular, these consider, from the outset, the object in question as a signifying whole (*cf.* signification*). In addition, they aim at establishing relations among the parts of this object on the one hand, and, on the other, between the parts and the whole which it constitutes. This process repeats itself until the object is depleted, *i.e.,* until indecomposable minimal units are recorded. Such a description is sometimes termed descending, by contrast with synthesis,* which is termed ascending. Different types of analysis are possible, depending on the level of pertinence chosen: for example, at the syntactic level we have distributional* and syntagmatic* analyses, and semic* or componential analysis at the semantic level.—PROCEDURE; CONTENT

ANAPHORA
(anaphore)

1. **Anaphora** is a relation of partial identity between two terms* which is established, in discourse, on the syntagmatic* axis, and thus serves to link two utterances, two paragraphs, etc.
2. Anaphora is said to be **grammatical** when it uses as a means of identification the semantic categories* which are part of the explicit frame of the grammar of any natural language (for example: pronouns, the verb to do, etc.).
3. Anaphora is **semantic** (in the narrow sense) when a condensed term or name* reexpresses a previous syntagmatic expansion.* From the terminological point of view, a distinction can be made between the **anaphorized** (a term coming in first place in the utterance, and in expansion) and the **anaphorizer,** which takes the term up again in a condensed form. This same relation is called **cataphora** when the term which is reexpressed (the cataphorizer) precedes, in the discourse, the term being expanded (the cataphorized).
4. Identity, established by recognition* or identification, is a formal anaphoric relation between two terms, one of which is present or real, and the other, which is absent, elsewhere, or past. In this sense, we can speak of **cognitive** anaphora.

5. **Anaphorization** is one of the main procedures that enable the enunciator* to establish and maintain the discursive isotopy,* *i.e.,* the interphrastic relations.
—REFERENCE; CO-REFERENCE; IDENTITY; REFERENT

ANCHORING
(ancrage)

1. By **historical anchoring** is meant the setting up, in the domain of the figurativization* of discourse, of a set of spatio-temporal indices and, more especially, of toponyms* and chrononyms,* whose aim is to constitute the simulacrum of an external referent* and to produce the meaning effect* of "reality."
2. The term **anchoring** sometimes also designates the establishment of relation(s) among semiotic entities belonging either to two different semiotic systems* (photo-

graphs and their legends in advertising; a picture and its title), or to two distinct discoursive phenomena (text and title). The effect of anchoring is to transform one of the entities into a contextual reference, thus allowing the second to be disambiguated. —HISTORY

ANTERIORITY
(antériorité)

1. **Anteriority** is one of the two terms of the logico-temporal category* *anteriority/posteriority*, which, starting from a temporal point zero, is defined by means of temporal disengagement,* as the time of **then** or **now**. It permits the construction of a framework of temporal localization of narrative programs.*

2. By **logical anteriority** is meant the characteristic of a presupposed semiotic entity,* by contrast to a presupposing entity. —LOCALIZATION, SPATIO-TEMPORAL; PRESUPPOSITION

ANTHROPOMORPHIC SYNTAX
(anthropomorphe [syntaxe-])

By contrast with fundamental syntax, which is conceived in the form of logical operations carried out in the framework of an established micro-universe, surface narrative syntax is said to be **anthropomorphic** since, after conversion,* it replaces the logical operations by the subjects of doing* and defines the subjects of state* by their junction with objects that can be invested with values that determine them. In the same way, the concepts of modal competence* and of performance which it establishes have meaning only when they refer to human subjects. Thus, applied to narrative syntax, the anthropomor-

phic qualifier bears no relation to the anthropomorphism which characterizes certain narrative discourses—particularly the ethno-literary—and which often attributes the status of subject of doing to things or to non-human beings.— SYNTAX, SURFACE NARRATIVE; PERSONIFICATION

ANTHROPONYM
(anthroponyme)

Anthroponyms—as the designation of actors* by proper nouns—are part of the onomastic sub-group of figurativization.* Combined with toponyms* and chrononyms,* they permit historical anchoring,* which aims at constituting the simulacrum of an external referent and at producing the meaning effect "reality."—ONOMASTICS, FIGURATIVIZATION; REFERENT

ANTI-DONOR
(anti-donateur)

Paradigmatically opposed to the donor* in the framework of the polemical structure of discourse, the **anti-donor** can be homologated with the opponent.—OPPONENT; DONOR; POLEMIC

ANTIPHRASIS
(antiphrase)

Antiphrasis, formerly a figure* of rhetoric, can be rigorously defined in semiotic terms. Within the framework of a given syntagmatic unit, antiphrasis corresponds to the substitution of one sign* by another, these signs being in contradictory* opposition through at least one of their semes.*—ANTITHESIS; RELATION; METAPHOR

ANTI-SENDER
(anti-destinateur)

Projected onto the semiotic square,* the sender—thereby considered as a proto-actant*—gives at least four actantial positions (sender, anti-sender, non-sender, non-anti-sender). The most used pair—sender/**anti-sender**—correlative to subject/anti-subject, is obviously linked to the polemic structure of narrative discourses.—SENDER: PROTO-ACTANT; POLEMIC

ANTITHESIS
(antithèse)

Antithesis, formerly a figure* of rhetoric, can be defined more precisely in semiotics as the manifestation, on the syntagmatic* axis, of antiphrasis; it thus manifests in combination two signs* having at least two contradictory—or sometimes contrary*—semes.—ANTIPHRASIS; RELATION

ANTONYMY
(antonymie)

1. In lexicology it is traditional to oppose to the relations of synonymy* (recognizable between two or more lexemes*) those of **antonymy,** which make it possible to couple terms in spite of (and because of) their differences. Two lexemes belonging to the same morphological class ("hot"/"cold"; "ascend"/ "descend") are thus brought together because they have a certain number of common semes* and because they are distinguished by other semes which differ among themselves.

2. It is clear that the problem of antonymy is not lexical in nature, or rather that the lexematic level only manifests underlying semic oppositions*; for, once the existence of a semantic axis* linking the two lexemes is recognized, it remains to be seen what the semic oppositions distinguishing them consist of, and whether it is possible to establish a logical typology of these oppositive relations. The problem of lexical antonymy can be resolved only within the framework of reflection on the nature of the elementary structures* of signification.

3. The definitions and classifications of antonyms vary from one lexicology to another. There is a difference, for example, between **polar antonyms,** which are categorical and allow of no intermediate terms ("husband"/"wife"), and **scalar antonyms,** which do allow gradations and are often linked to the processes of comparison ("large"/"medium"/"small"; "hot"/"lukewarm"/"cold"). Depending on the type of logical relation recognized between them, antonyms are known as **contradictory** ("single"/"married"), **contrary** ("ascend"/"descend"), **reciprocal** ("buy"/"sell"), etc. —STRUCTURE

APHORIA
(aphorie)

Aphoria is the neutral* term of the thymic category* articulated into *euphoria/dysphoria.*—THYMIC CATEGORY

APPROPRIATION
(appropriation)

Appropriation is located at the figurative* level and characterizes the position of the subject of an utterance of state,* when it has acquired an object* of value by its own action. Thus it corresponds to the reflexive* realization* of an object of value, effected at any moment of the narrative trajectory.* Together with attribution,* appropriation is one of the two forms of acquisition, which can be seen as subcomponents of the test,* as its consequence.*— ACQUISITION; REALIZATION

ARBITRARINESS
(arbitraire)

1. The term **arbitrariness** (of the sign*) is somewhat imprecise in Saussurian theory. It designates the character of the relation which unites the signifier* and the signified.* This relation, which constitutes the linguistic sign, is nonfounded and unmotivated (*i.e.,* impossible to interpret in terms of causality). This conception has played an important role historically, allowing F. de Saussure, among other things, to found the autonomy of (natural) language* considered as form.*

Though there exists no causal or "natural" relation between the signified "table" and the signifier "table," it is nonetheless impossible, when considering how language (or any semiotic system) functions, not to recognize the existence of a **necessary** relation (E. Benveniste)—or of a reciprocal presupposition* (L. Hjelmslev)—between the signifier and the signified. This relation is called the semiotic function* (L. Hjelmslev) and its establishment (or semiosis) defines first and foremost the language act. Thus, logically this relation is necessary. It is also necessary from the social point of view: although the signs of a natural language are **conventional** (another term proposed by Saussure), they are not arbitrary, since speaking subjects cannot by themselves substitute* either the signifiers or the signifieds.

2. The arbitrary or somewhat motivated character of signs is not a result of their nature as sign, but of its interpretation, *i.e.,* of the feeling or attitude that a linguistic community or an individual has with respect to the signs they use. In this case we are dealing with meta-semiotic, and not semiotic, facts.

3. Another type of confusion can be avoided by situating the question of the arbitrariness of the sign only within the framework of bi-planar* semiotic systems, to the exclusion of mono-planar semiotic systems, the units of minimal manifestation of which are not signs but signals* (L. Hjelmslev).

4. The question of the arbitrariness of the sign, which deals with relations internal to semiotic systems, is bound up with the very different question of the external relations between a given semiotic system and the "reality" of the outside world, or of the relations between two different semiotic systems (for example, the problem of the "nameable" in pictorial semiotics). In the first case, we are dealing with problems concerning the status of the referent,* in the second with the peculiarity of natural languages.*

5. In somewhat the same way, L. Hjelmslev introduces the dichotomy **arbitrariness/adequacy.*** He uses the term arbitrariness to designate theory—and more particularly semiotic theory—to the extent that, as a pure, coherent construction, it does not depend on the data of experience. By contrast, when a theory, or some of its premises, is applicable to the data of experience, it is known as adequate (or consistent with its goal).

6. Finally, the question of the arbitrariness of the sign comes up once more when we deal with the construction of a meta-language* (or a meta-semiotic system): the units, recognized and defined during semiotic description, are pure rela-

tional networks, and the names which may be conferred on them are arbitrary. However, if such a metalanguage is applied to an object semiotic system, the names chosen should carry as much information as possible about the manifestation.* —MOTIVATION; NAMING

ARCHILEXEME
(archilexème)

An **archilexeme** is a lexeme* of a given natural language under study, which is used to designate, by subsuming it, a taxonomic microsystem. In the well-known example of B. Pottier, "seat" is the archilexeme which subsumes the lexemes "chair," "sofa," "armchair," etc. While this term is useful, it is not entirely satisfactory: on the one hand, since a taxonomy is a hierarchy,* an archilexeme may have an archilexeme of a higher order (for example, "furniture" for "seat"); on the other hand, there are "archilexemes" which are not part of natural language, but of the metalanguage* used to study it (for example, "manufactured object" for "furniture"). A parallel term should be proposed to designate these "constructed archilexemes."—TAXONOMY

ARMATURE
(armature)

Used metaphorically by C. Lévi-Strauss, the term **armature** means for him a non-determined group of formal properties, of a syntactic* and/or semantic* order, which remain invariant* in two or more myths. When used in other domains, this term is often synonymous with structure,* in the broadest sense of the word.

ARTICULATION
(articulation)

1. In phonetics,* the first meaning of **articulation** is the physiological functioning of the "speech organs"; secondly, it is the capacity of this phonatory apparatus to produce a combinative arrangement of the "sounds of language" necessary to constitute a plane of expression.* Depending on the particular domain* in which the phonic data is observed, we can speak of **articulatory** phonetics (at the level of emission), **acoustic** phonetics (at the level of transmission), and **auditory** phonetics (at the level of reception).

2. By extension, articulation generally indicates all semiotic* activity on the part of the enunciator* or, by considering the results of this activity, all forms of semiotic organization which create distinct and combinable units. Used in this way, articulation seems both sufficiently general and neutral, i.e., most detached in relation to the various linguistic theories.

3. L. Hjelmslev gives the term articulation a more restricted meaning, designating thereby the analysis* of a system,* as opposed to division,* which designates the analysis of a process.*

4. By **double articulation,** A. Martinet attempts to define the specificity of natural languages* compared to other "means of communication": the first articulation is situated at the level of morpheme*-signs, the second at that of phonemes,* which constitute formants* for the morphemes. As an application of the principle of combinative arrangement, such an interpretation is not inadequate, but appears nowadays to be insufficient: in fact, it corresponds to the state of linguistics prior to recent developments in syntactic and semantic research.

ASEMANTICITY
(asémanticité)

Unlike generative* and transformational linguistics, in which a sentence is said to be asemantic when it can be given no semantic interpretation,* **asemanticity,** from an operational* point of view, is defined by us as the impossibility for two elements at the semantic level—such as two semes* or two sememes*—to be present* together in a hierarchically superior unit: we are thus talking about possible forms of incompatibility.—SEMANTICITY; INCOMPATIBILITY

ASPECTUALIZATION
(aspectualisation)

1. Within the framework of the generative* trajectory, **aspectualization** is taken to mean the establishment, at the point of the temporalization of discourse, of a system of aspectual categories* by which the implicit presence of an observer* actant is revealed. This procedure seems to be general and to characterize the three components, actorialization,* spatialization,* and temporalization,* which constitute the mechanisms of disengagement.* However, only the aspectualization of temporality has so far given rise to fuller theorizations which are worth being retained, interpreted, and filled out.

2. All temporalized discourse has two kinds of new investments which produce the two meaning effects of temporality and **aspectuality.** While the effect of temporality is linked to the establishment of a group of temporal categories which, belonging as they do to the domain of enunciation,* project a temporal organization of topological nature onto the utterance, the effect of aspectuality results from the investments of aspectual categories which convert the functions* (or predicates) of narrative utterances* into a process*; aspectuality thus appears relatively independent of enunciation.

3. Historically, **aspect** is presented in linguistics as "the way in which the action is viewed," and can be manifested in the form of autonomous grammatical morphemes.* Attempts to clarify the actantial structure* underlying the manifestation of different "aspects" have led to the introduction within this discursive configuration of an **observer** actant for which the action performed by a subject installed within the discourse appears as a process, *i.e.*, as a step or as an unfolding. From this point of view, the aspectualization of an utterance (sentence, sequence, or discourse) corresponds to a double disengagement*: the enunciator* delegates two subjects within the discourse. One of these is a subject-actant of doing, the other is a cognitive* subject. This latter subject observes and decomposes the doing of the former by transforming it into a process, which is characterized by the semes of durativeness* or punctuality,* perfectiveness* or imperfectiveness* (completed/incompleted), inchoateness* or terminativeness.*

4. The establishment of an actantial structure of this kind accounts for the different articulations* of the process (or of its aspects), but tells us nothing about the nature of the process itself. By situating aspectualization in time, we can claim that it is an overdetermination of temporality and that the process, while remaining temporal, can only be recognized by its aspectual articulations.

5. The convertability of narrative utterances, of a logical nature,

into processual utterances, of a temporal nature, enables us to understand in a general way the relation which exists between diachronic* transformations and their temporal, or historical, manifestations. Transformation is categorical (in old French, for example, we go from a two-case declension to its absence) whereas its temporal manifestation is seen as a process, having inchoative, durative, and terminative aspects. In textual analysis, such an interpretation facilitates the recognition of narrative organizations, underlying processual formations.

6. Much work remains to be done on the elaboration of the theory of aspects, and at the present time it is useless to propose, except in very general terms, an "aspectual system."

7. By **aspectual configuration** is understood an arrangement of aspectual semes set up to account for a process. Thus, for example, the inscription in an discourse-utterance of a succession of aspectual semes such as *inchoativeness* → *durativeness* → *terminativeness,* while temporalizing an utterance of state* or doing,* represents them, or allows them to be represented, as a process. Obviously, an aspectual configuration can be manifested inside a sentence, sequence, or discourse, and only certain semes of this configuration may sometimes be made explicit. Corresponding to the aspectual system, which remains to be elaborated as a taxonomy of aspects, are aspectual configurations, which are their syntagmatic organizations.

—TEMPORALIZATION; PROCESS; OBSERVER

ASSERTION
(assertion)

1. **Assertion** is, together with negation,* one of the two terms in the category* of transformation*; this latter is in turn considered to be the abstract formulation of the factitive* modality, such as it is manifested in "causing to be" or "causing to do."

2. Assertion is to be distinguished from affirmation, which is simply the taking note of semiotic existence,* informative in nature, and can be represented in utterances of state* by the relation of junction (conjunction or disjunction). Transformation—*i.e.,* assertion and/or negation—is, on the contrary, the function of utterances of doing* which govern, by overdetermining them, utterances of state, or, in the case of manipulation,* modal structures of the type "causing to be." This distinction accounts for the fact that only contents posited beforehand can be asserted or denied; it also allows us, if need be, to postulate distinct subjects for assertion and affirmation (the doing of S1 capable of affecting the being of S2).

3. Paradigmatically, assertion is defined as the contradictory* of negation. However, at the level of fundamental syntax* (or of the elementary operations carried out on the semiotic square*) assertion occupies a definite syntagmatic position and appears as an oriented* operation:

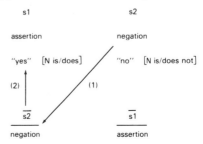

[N] "certainly"   [is/does]

Following the operation of negation which transforms s2 into $\overline{s2}$, assertion is seen as the calling-up of the term $\overline{s2}$, which, instead of reconvert-

ing $\overline{s2}$ into s2, on the contrary provokes the appearance of the term s1.
The effect of syntagmatic assertion
is then to actualize the relation of
implication (if "certainly," then
"yes") on condition that s1 is the
presupposed term and $\overline{s2}$ the presupposing term. Simple assertion
(that of classical logic) must then be
distinguished from syntagmatic assertion, which could also be called
denial* and which establishes the relation of complementarity between
the two terms. The difference between simple and syntagmatic assertion, which lies only in formulation
so long as categories of contradictories are concerned, becomes clear
when the category is constituted by
the axis of the contraries, where, for
example, the complementarity of the
terms *non-death* and *life* bring distinct
contents into play.
—AFFIRMATION; NEGATION;
SQUARE, SEMIOTIC; SYNTAX,
FUNDAMENTAL

ATTRIBUTION
(attribution)

Located at the figurative* level,
attribution corresponds to the position of the subject of an utterance of
state,* when it acquires an object* of
value thanks to a subject of doing*
other than itself. Thus, it represents
the transitive* realization* of the object, effected at any moment in the
narrative* trajectory.* Together
with appropriation,* attribution is
one of the possible forms of acquisition, which may be considered, in
terms of their consequence,* as
sub-components of the test.—AC-
QUISITION

AUTOMATON
(automate)

In scientific meta-semiotics, the
name **automaton** is given to any

(neutral) operator subject in possession of a group of explicit rules* and
an order* requiring the application
of these rules or the carrying out of
instructions. The automaton is thus
a semiotic domain constructed like a
simulacrum of the programmatic
doing and can be used as a model
either for the human subject carrying out a reproducible scientific activity, or for the construction of a
machine. The concept of automaton
has an obvious use, even if only because it orients the attitude of re-
searchers by inviting them to make
their overall analytical procedures as
clear as possible.—ALGORITHM;
PROCEDURE; SCIENTIFICNESS

AUTONOMY
(autonomie)

1. In paradigmatics, **autonomy**
is taken to mean the relation* shared
by two or more semantic categories,*
or two or more semic micro-systems,
when there exists no presupposition
between them. The relation between
two autonomous categories or systems is consequently one of simple
opposition,* of the type "either . . .
or."

2. In syntagmatics, two levels of
language are said to be autonomous
in respect to each other if they each
possess their own structural organization: while they are isotopic,* they
are not isomorphic.*

AUXILIANT
(auxiliant)

The **auxiliant,** which refers to
the modal competence* of the subject, is equivalent to the modality* of
being able to do or *not being able to do,*
whether it be manifested by the
same actor* as the subject itself or by
a different actor. In the latter case,
the individualized actor will, in its
status as an auxiliant and depending

on whether it corresponds to positive or negative deixis,* be designated sometimes as the helper,* sometimes as the opponent.*—BEING-ABLE

AXIOLOGY
(axiologie)

1. **Axiology** is generally taken to mean the theory and/or the description of value systems—moral, logical, or aesthetic.

2. In semiotics, the term axiology designates the paradigmatic* mode of existence of values,* in contrast to ideology, which assumes the form of their syntagmatic* and actantial arrangement. It is possible to consider that every semantic category,* represented on the semiotic square* (for example, life/death), can be axiologized thanks to the investment of positive and negative deixes* by the thymic category *euphoria/dysphoria*. Axiologies (or micro-systems of values) of this kind can be abstract* (life/death) or figurative* (the traditional four natural elements, for example). Insofar as we are dealing with general categories—which can be considered, as a working hypothesis,* as semantic universals—that can be articulated according to the semiotic square, a distinction can be drawn between **elementary axiological structures** (of an abstract nature) and **figurative axiological structures.**
—IDEOLOGY; STRUCTURE

AXIOMATIC
(axiomatique)

The term **axiomatic** is applied to a body of non-definable concepts and/or a group of non-demonstrable propositions which, by an arbitrary decision, are said to be interdefined and demonstrated. Contrary to traditional scientific practice, which, starting from a set of hypotheses,* aims at verifying them through confrontation with the data of experience, an axiomatic concept of this nature permits the construction of a theory by deductive steps.—THEORY; FORMAL; META-LANGUAGE

AXIS
(axe)

1. By contrast with L. Hjelmslev, for whom the syntagmatic* and the paradigmatic* are based on logical relations ("both . . . and", "either . . . . or"), many linguists, in an attempt to visualize in some way the Saussurian opposition between syntagmatic and associative relations, use the expressions **syntagmatic axis** (thus introducing a linear* consecution on a horizontal axis) and **paradigmatic axis** (a vertical axis of commutations* and substitutions*).

2. By **semantic axis** is meant a relation between two terms,* the logical nature of which is indeterminate: we are dealing here with a pre-operational concept. As the analysis progresses, this concept can be replaced, for instance, by that of semic category,* which is articulated logically (according to the elementary structure of signification).

3. **Axis** also designates one of the dimensions* of the semiotic square,* which has two fundamental axes: the primary axis, whereon are established the contraries,* and the secondary axis, reserved for the subcontraries.

ABCDEFGHIJKLMN OPQRSTUVWXYZ

BACK-READING
(rétro-lecture)

In the course of a syntagmatic analysis, which takes the sequences* in order, certain elements may be temporarily left aside because they do not seem, at the outset, to have a place in the organization of the discourse under study. On the basis of subsequent parts of the discourse (as one reads "normally," from beginning towards end), isotopic connectors prompt **back-reading,** which reconsiders these suspended elements in view of the results already obtained. This "going back" should be acknowledged as one of the possible forms of reading (understood, in its semiotic meaning, as the syntactic and semantic construction of the discourse-utterance).—CONNECTOR, ISOTOPIC; READING

BASE
(base)

1. In generative grammar, the **base** (component), which generates deep* structures, contains: (a) a categorial* sub-component which includes both syntagmatic and morphological classes* established by syntagmatic grammar (or the syntagmatic model), as well as the overall rules incurred; (b) the lexicon,* in the generativist sense, which supplies indications on the syntactic, semantic, and phonological traits of the morpheme*-signs.

2. The **basic sentence** or **basic form** is that which is generated by syntagmatic grammar and on which it is possible to carry out the transformations* (which lead to the establishment of surface structures*). —GENERATIVE GRAMMAR

BEING
(être)

Outside of its ordinary use, the lexeme **being** is used, in semiotics, with at least three different meanings: (a) It serves as copula in utterances of state*; thus, by predication,* it joins to the object properties considered "essential." On the level of semantic representation,* such properties are interpreted as subjective values* in junction* with the subject of state; (b) It is used as well to name the modal category of veridiction*: *being/seeming;* (c) Finally, it designates the positive term of the immanence* schema*: it is then in a relation of contrariety* with seeming*—VALUE; VERIDICTORY MODALITIES; HAVING/TO HAVE

BEING-ABLE
(TO DO or TO BE)
(pouvoir)

1. In the framework of a theory of modalities, **being-able** (*to do* or *to be*) can be considered as the name of one of the possible predicates of the modal* utterance governing a descriptive* utterance of doing* or of state.* Although it is a concept which cannot be defined, it nonetheless can be interdefined in a chosen and axiomatically postulated system of modal values.

2. As modal utterances are intended by definition to govern other utterances, two modal structures* of being-able are to be considered: the one comprises an utterance of state and is called for convenience's sake *being-able-to-be*; the other has for its object an utterance of doing: *being-able-to-do*. These two structures can in turn be projected onto the semiotic square* and produce corresponding modal categories, either:

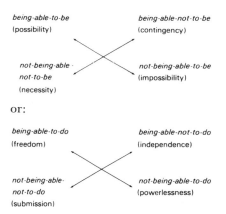

being-able-to-be (possibility) — being-able-not-to-be (contingency)

not-being-able-not-to-be (necessity) — not-being-able-to-be (impossibility)

or:

being-able-to-do (freedom) — being-able-not-to-do (independence)

not-being-able-not-to-do (submission) — not-being-able-to-do (powerlessness)

The names given to the terms of each of the modal categories, although intuitively motivated on the semantic plane, are nevertheless arbitrary by definition and can be easily replaced by others judged more adequate.

3. Even though these names are based only on semantic intuition, they cannot but demonstrate the affinities which exist between the modal structures of being-able and those of having-to* (-do or -be). Thus a confrontation of the semiotic squares of *having-to-be* and of *being-able-to-be*

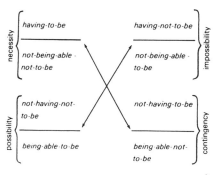

shows that one and the same name, referring to the system of alethic modalities, subsumes two modal structures, those of *having-to-be* and of *being-able-to-be*. The two terms stand each time in a relation of complementarity* (*i.e.*, the one presupposes the other). Two types of interpretations are then possible: either the alethic modalities are complex* terms subsuming the modalities of having-to and of being-able-to in a relation of complementarity (necessity, for example, would be a *not-being-able-not-to-be* presupposing a *having-to-be*), or else there is reason to distinguish two autonomous modal categories and to construct two interdependent alethic logics.

4. In parallel fashion one can envisage a confrontation between

modal structures of *having-to-do* and of *being-able-to-do*. The absence of common names for them does not lessen their interest:

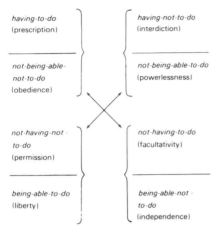

having-to-do
(prescription)

not-being-able-
not-to-do
(obedience)

not-having-not-
to-do
(permission)

being-able-to-do
(liberty)

having-not-to-do
(interdiction)

not-being-able-to-do
(powerlessness)

not-having-to-do
(facultativity)

being-able-not-
to-do
(independence)

In spite of the difference of names—and perhaps because of them—the complementary character of the terms belonging to the two modal categories is self-evident. The categories are organized as if obedience, for example, as a modal value defining a certain competence of the subject, presupposed the other modal value, prescription. Moreover, it would even seem that the definition of the hierarchical* relations of dominant/dominated needs to take this modal complementarity into account.

5. This leads us to consider the modalities of having-to- and of being-able-to- as two autonomous and complementary domains of modalization—one being called virtualizing, the other actualizing.
—MODALITY; HAVING-TO-DO or TO-BE

BELIEVING
(croire)

1. As a subject's* acceptance of an utterance of state,* **believing** is seen as a cognitive act overdetermined by the modal category* of *certainty.** This category can have a twofold interpretation in contemporary writings on logic and on semiotics. At times it is taken as an alethic* category: believing as a synonym of "possibility" is then identified with its term *not-having-not-to-be.* At other times, certainty is taken as an autonomous epistemic* category, believing-to-be, with its term *certitude.* On the basis of the distinction between the schema* *possible/impossible* (which constitutes a categorical opposition excluding any third term) and the schema *probable/improbable,* which allows for a gradation, we propose to view believing as the natural language name for the epistemic category.

2. On the axis of communication* (real or "imaginary" communication in the case of interiorized discourse), "believing" is opposed to "causing-to-believe" (or persuasion). As such, "believing" corresponds to the domain of the enunciatee* which carries out its interpretive* doing, while "causing-to-believe" is brought about by the enunciator* in charge of the persuasive* doing. Even though it is not yet possible to define believing satisfactorily, viewing it in the framework of interpretive doing, as the result and final sanction of interpretive doing, allows us to circumscribe a little better the set of issues related to it. Indeed, believing is not merely the basis of religious faith. It also constitutes the crucial domain of scientific discourse—as recent analyses have shown—as well as of other discourses. More generally, causing-to-believe as persuasive doing, which cannot be treated independently from believing, constitutes one of the main forms of manipulation.* Thus believing ap-

pears as one of the major questions semiotic research has to address in the coming years.
—EPISTEMIC MODALITIES

BINARITY
(binarité)

1. A structure* is said to be **binary** when it is defined as a relation* between two terms.*

2. A set of historical and pragmatic factors has given binary structures a privileged place in linguistic methodology. This may be due to the successful practice of the binary coupling of phonological oppositions established by the Prague School, or due to the importance gained by binary arithmetical systems (0/1) in automatic calculus, or to the operative simplicity of binary analysis in comparison with more complex structures, since every complex structure can be formally represented in the guise of hierarchy* of binary structures, etc. **Binarization,** as a linguistic practice, should be distinguished from binarism, which is an epistemological postulate according to which the binary articulation or grasp of phenomena is one of the characteristics of the human mind. The name of R. Jakobson is linked, rightly or wrongly, to this claim: he gave a binary formulation to the phemic* categories which he defined as phonological universals* of natural languages.

3. Binary formulation remains valid so long as no attempt is made to define the type of relation which joins the terms: indeed Jakobson himself recognized the existence of two types of binary opposition, which we interpret as contradiction* and contrariety.* It is this sort of typology which has enabled us to postulate the existence, beyond the realm of binarity, of a more complex elementary structure* of signification.

4. Binarity characterizes only one type of structure: it is possible to consider as binary categories only those whose constitutive relation is contradiction* (for example, *assertion/negation; conjunction/disjunction*).
—SEMIOTIC SQUARE; CATEGORY

BI-PLANAR SEMIOTIC SYSTEMS
(biplane [sémiotique—])

Bi-planar semiotic systems—or, according to L. Hjelmslev, semiotics proper—are those which contain two (language*) levels which differ in their paradigmatic articulations* and/or syntagmatic divisions.* Such is the case in natural languages.*—SEMIOTICS; CONFORMITY; UNEQUIVOCALNESS

BRACKETING
(parenthétisation)

Bracketing, as the utilization of parentheses or brackets, is a particular form of the representation of analysis* in linguistics (and generally in semiotics) and is equivalent (homologable and translatable) to that of representation by tree graphs. In this sense it constitutes a homogeneous "writing" which should not be confused with the accidental or specific use of parentheses in another system of representation (for example, in generative* grammar, the parentheses serve as a symbol* in order to indicate the optional character of a constituant*).—REPRESENTATION; TREE

ABCDEFGHIJKLMN OPQRSTUVWXYZ

CAMOUFLAGE
(camouflage)

Camouflage is a discoursive figure,* located on the cognitive dimension, and corresponds to a logical operation* of negation on the axis of the contradictories, *seeming/not-seeming,* of the semiotic square* of veridictory modalities.* The true,* defined as the conjunction of *being* and *seeming,* serves as a starting point. The operation of the negation of the term *seeming,* carried out by a given subject, produces the state of secret* and is known as camouflage. It is thus diametrically opposed to deception,* which, taking as its starting point falsity (= *non-being + non-seeming*) and denying the *non-seeming,* establishes the state of lie.* In both of these cases, we are dealing with an operation of negation, carried out on the schema* of manifestation.*—VERIDICTORY MODALITIES; SIMULATED TEST

CATALYSIS
(catalyse)

By **catalysis,** elliptical elements which are missing in the surface structure are made explicit.* This procedure is carried out with the help of manifested contextual* elements and thanks to the relations of presupposition* which they have with implicit elements. Thus, if we take the example given by L. Hjelmslev, who proposed the term, the Latin preposition *sine* presupposes an ablative, but the inverse is not true; we are dealing with the "interpolation of a reason behind a consequence," made possible "in accordance with the generalization principle." The same procedure of catalysis can be applied to the analysis of narrative discourses—where the manifestation of the consequence* of the test* enables the overall test to be made explicit—and to the semantic analysis of discourse. —ELLIPSIS; IMPLICIT

CATAPHORA
(cataphore)

Cataphora and anaphora express the same relation of partial identity* between two terms inscribed on the syntagmatic axis of a discourse. But cataphora is characterized, inversely from anaphora, by the fact that the condensed term precedes the expanded term.— ANAPHORA

CATEGORIZATION
(catégorisation)

1. The expression **categorization of the world** was introduced by E. Benveniste to designate the application of a natural language to the world, in its overall perception by our senses. From the ontogenic

point of view, in fact, the part played by natural languages—and probably by semiotic systems in general—in the child's construction of the world of common sense is doubtlessly considerable even if it cannot be determined with precision. The role of "giving form" to the world is taken up by natural languages. It is to this role that reference is made when we say, for example, that "worldview" is determined by a given cultural context: tangible proof is offered by ethno-taxonomical studies. C. Lévi-Strauss used the expression **conceptual segmentation** of the world in the same sense, and reference is often made thereto in linguistics, as also to the Sapir-Whorf hypothesis. In our view, the world of common sense, given form by semiotic systems, corresponds to natural* semiotics.

2. In a completely different domain, the term **categorization** is used to designate the projection onto the semiotic square of a specific entity, considered as a semantic axis.* This projection, as it articulates the entity, makes of it a category.*

—SEGMENTATION; REFERENT; WORLD, NATURAL; ETHNO-SEMIOTICS

CATEGORY
(catégorie)

1. The term **category** is seen in linguistics as one of the most dangerous legacies of a long tradition which intermingles philosophical, logical and grammatical considerations. Since by categories is meant the fundamental concepts* of every grammar* or of every semiotic* theory, the choice of what is considered to be fundamental necessarily determines the form of the theory it is intended to elaborate.

2. Simplifying a great deal, it is possible first to distinguish, under the term category, grammatical objects which are also designated as **classes,*** and which are paradigmatic in nature and obtained by the substitution,* in the syntagmatic chain, of units of a chosen type. We thus have: (a) "**morphological**" classes or parts of speech (nouns, adjectives, verbs, etc.); (b) "**syntactic**" or functional* classes (subject, object, predicate, predicate adjective, etc.); (c) "**syntagmatic**" classes or syntagms (nominal, verbal). The meaning of the term category thus depends on the choice of classes taken into consideration for the construction of the grammar. Thus, when in generative* grammar one speaks of the **categorial component** as forming part of the base* of the syntactic component, the categories —which enter into its composition —are essentially the "syntagmatic classes"* (within which are introduced "morphological classes," without any particular attention to the heterogeneity* of these two types of category). **Categorial grammars,** inspired by logics (Adjukiewicz, Bar-Hillel) operate, on the contrary, with categories which correspond to the "morphological classes." Actantial* grammar, which we advocate, for its part favors the "functional classes."

3. In an effort of synthesis, L. Hjelmslev defines category as a paradigm* the elements of which can be introduced only at certain positions* of the syntagmatic* chain, to the exclusion of others; we are dealing consequently with a paradigm endowed with a determined function. Thus the category of "morphological" entity receives at the same time a "syntactic" definition. The vowel, for example, is a category: (a) it is the paradigm constituted by the

phonemes *a, e, i, u,* etc.; (b) it is defined by its central position in the syllable.

It is in the same way, as a paradigm of modal* values and by its specific position in the narrative* trajectory, that we define the actantial* role, which is a category in the Hjelmslevian sense of the term.

4. In traditional grammar, the term **grammatical categories** covers the entities of the signified,* which can be recognized within the flexional morphemes* (for example, the categories of gender, number, person, case, etc.), where it is clearly a matter of semantic categories assuming grammatical functions. Recent developments of various linguistic theories—which converge on this point—have made it possible to recognize the semantic nature of all grammatical entities and at the same time to generalize the concept of category.

5. The strict application of the structural attitude inherited from F. de Saussure, according to which—and as opposed to atomism—all language is by nature relational and not substantial, obliges us to use the term category only to designate relations* (*i.e.,* semantic axes) and not the end elements of these relations. It is then possible to speak of the category of gender as, for example, being articulated by *masculine/feminine,* but it is not possible to speak of the category *feminine.* In like manner, it is not the noun which is a category, but the opposition noun/verb, for example.

6. Since all semiotic* systems are relational networks, the elementary structures* which organize these relations may be considered as **semantic categories:** depending on the plane of language which they help to constitute, they are sometimes called **semic* categories** and

sometimes **phemic* categories.** Both can be used as grammatical categories—intonation* or word order, for example, are phemic categories or grammatical functions.
—CLASS

CERTAINTY
(certitude)

Certainty is the name of the positive term* of the epistemic modal category the syntactic definition of which is *believing to be.* As opposed to evidence,* certainty presupposes the exercise of interpretive* doing, of which it is one of the possible consequences.—EPISTEMIC MODALITIES

CHANNEL
(canal)

1. The term **channel** is borrowed from information theory and designates the material or sensory medium used for the transmission of messages.* In L. Hjelmslev's terminology, it could correspond partially, in linguistics, to the expression* substance,* though in fact it is limited to semiotic theories which emphasize the structure of communication.*

2. The most common classification of semiotic systems operates according to the **channels of communication** or, which amounts to the same thing, according to the sensory orders on which the signifier* is founded (textual semiotics, the semiotics of space, pictorial semiotics, etc.). This distribution is far from satisfactory: meaningful groups as vast as the cinema, the theatre, urban space, are in fact loci where there is an overlapping of several manifestation languages,* tightly interwoven so as to produce global meanings.
—SYNCRETISM

CHARACTER
(personnage)

One of several terms used in literature and reserved for human beings, the term **character** has been progressively replaced by two other concepts, more rigorously defined in semiotics: actant and actor.—ACTANT; ACTOR

CHARGE, SEMANTIC
(charge sémantique)

By the term **semantic charge** is understood the set of semantic investments which may be distributed, at the time of realization* in a natural language, among the various constituent elements of a linguistic utterance.* In this way it is possible to consider that in sentences such as "The cook is working," "Mary is cooking," "Mary is doing some cooking," etc., although the semantic charge is displaced, it remains a constant. This bracketing of the phenomenon of lexicalization* authorizes semiotic or narrative grammar to separate the syntactic and semantic components* and to join, within the narrative utterance, the set of semantic investments in the form of values,* to the single object-actant of the utterance of state.* This also enables us to understand the various possibilities of the semantization of discourse, with the semantic charges being concentrated at times on the subject, and at other times on the expanding function, depending on the enunciator's choice.—INVESTMENT, SEMANTIC

CHRONONYM
(chrononyme)

Certain semioticians (G. Combet) have proposed to introduce alongside toponym* and anthroponym* the term **chrononym** to designate specific lengths of time, such as "day," "spring," "coffee break." This word can advantageously replace that of "period." Together with anthroponyms and toponyms, chrononyms help to establish a historical anchoring which aims at constituting the simulacrum of an external referent and to produce the meaning effect "reality."—FIGURATIVIZATION; REFERENT

CLASS
(classe)

1. **Class** is generally defined as a set of entities which have one or more distinctive* features in common.

2. In linguistics, class is taken to mean more precisely a set of entities which can be substituted for each other in a given syntagmatic* position and a given context. Class is in this sense synonymous with paradigm.

3. In grammar, the term class is partly in competition with that of category. Thus it is possible to distinguish the following classes or categories: "morphological," *i.e.,* the parts of a discourse; "syntactic" or functional, *i.e.,* subject, object, predicate, etc.; and "syntagmatic," *i.e.,* nominal or verbal syntagms, etc.—PARADIGM; UNIT; CATEGORY

CLASSEME
(classème)

1. In the terminology proposed by B. Pottier, by **classème** is understood the sub-set of generic semes which, with the semanteme* (sub-set of specific semes) and the virtueme* (sub-set of connotative semes) constitutes the sememe.*

2. A. J. Greimas uses this term in a slightly different sense. He des-

ignates contextual semes as classemes, that is to say, those semes which are recurrent in the discourse and which guarantee its isotopy. Recurrent and discernable as bundles of semic categories, classemes, although constituting syntagmatic mechanisms, are nonetheless constituted by paradigmatic analysis and can be arranged in taxonomic classes: whence the partial motivation for their name. It is difficult at present to define the limits of the semantic domain covered by classemes. At the moment, we can make only a few suggestions:

(a) As recurrent semes, classemes, theoretically, must constitute very general categories: it is in the list of classemes that the concepts that are not defined in semiotic theory (such as "religion," "term," etc.) should be found, as well as the so-called grammatical semes (which serve to constitute grammatical categories or classes). The problem of language universals is linked to the classematic inventory; (b) The list of classemes includes, on the other hand, the "generic semes" which serve as a framework for the categorization* of the world by language and which constitute classes of beings or of things (for example: animate/inanimate, animal/plant, etc.) the articulations of which vary from one culture to another; (c) If the grammatical semes guarantee the permanence of communication insofar as it concerns ordinary language, the secondary systems which develop within natural languages (such as poetic discourse) can set up classematic categories which are peculiar to them, thereby freeing—at least partially—speech from its syntactic constraints.
—SEME; ISOTOPY; MARKER (syntagmatic)

CLASSIFICATION
(classification)

1. By **classification** is generally meant the distribution of a given set of elements* into a certain number of coordinated or subordinated sub-sets. The representation,* according to a chosen system of notation, of the results of such an operation is called the taxonomy.

2. As often happens in semiotics, the theoretical question of knowing whether priority should be given to the elements or to the relations* also arises with classifications. It is often noted, for example, that the decomposing of a set and its representation by a tree* requires us to foresee, at different levels, nodes* which are specified only later and consequently are not prime "elements" that can be distributed. In this view, classification is seen as a taxonomic, cognitive activity, or as a procedure which consists in applying to an object submitted to analysis a succession of discriminatory categories,* the effect of which is to bring to light the elements composing the set and thus to construct the definition of the object considered.
—TAXONOMY; ELEMENT; RELATION

CLAUSE
(proposition)

In traditional grammar the term **clause** is used to designate either a self-sufficient syntactic unit—in which case it is called an independent clause and is identified with the simple sentence—or to designate a unit having the same structure but integrated into the complex sentence where the principal clause governs the subordinate clause. After L. Tesnière and N. Chomsky, the issues concerning the complex sentence have been absorbed by postulating a single mechanism of phrastic (sentence) production (*cf.* embedding*). On the terminological plane utterance usefully replaces the term of sentence as well as that of clause.—SENTENCE; UTTERANCE; PROPPOSITION

CLOSURE
(*clôture*)

1. On the semantic plane, **closure** can be envisaged from two different points of view. Paradigmatically, any use or articulation of a semantic universe* by a culture or person is seen as the realization of a relatively low number of the possibilities offered by the combinatory principle. The semantic schema* or structure of this universe is then said to be open, whereas its use* (or its realizations in history) at any time brings about its closure. Syntagmatically, the discursive manifestation of any semantic set (the experience of non-directive interviews is conclusive on this point) shows, sooner or later, signs of depletion and, when an attempt is made to uphold it, redundance* appears. It is thus realized that all discourse, inasmuch as it is representative of a micro-universe, can be considered semantically closed.

2. From the point of view of narrative semiotics, the problem of closure appears in very different aspects. Thus, in the ethno-literary domain, it is just as frequent to note the existence of particular classes of discourse ("genres") that are closed (the Russian folktale, for example, characterized by the reestablishment of the initial axiological state) as well as of those that are open (reciprocal and successive trickery reproduced, so to speak, to infinity).

3. Given that narrative discourses most often use only a section of the canonical narrative* schema, the fact that they are thus limited and, as it were, closed at a given moment of this schema, suspends the normally foreseeable development. In this case, the closure of the discourse is the very condition for its opening considered as potentiality.

4. The closure can also be the act of the enunciatee* (reader or analyst). For example, the Bible, considered as a collection of texts, is syntagmatically closed at different moments, thus forming a Jewish corpus and a Christian corpus, and because of this giving rise to sometimes divergent* readings. In the same way, the extraction of a micro-narrative, inserted in a larger discourse, produces by closing it a different reading from that which would be obtained by maintaining it in its context.

5. It can be generally stated that any momentary halt in reading forms a provisional closure which, according to the degree of complexity of the text, causes a range of virtual meanings to arise. This "richness" of the text does not thereby contradict the principle of its isotopy,* or of its pluri-isotopy.

CODE
(*code*)

1. The term **code** was first used in information theory, where it designates an inventory of arbitrarily chosen symbols,* accompanied by a group of rules* for the composition of coded "words," and often compared to a dictionary* or lexicon of the natural language (*cf.* the Morse code). We are dealing here, in its simple form, with a derived artificial

language.* In this sense, the alphabet, together with spelling rules, can be considered as a code.

2. In the automatic treatment of information, the code splits into a set of symbols containing instructions and capable of being understood by a machine (*cf.* machine language), and into the automatic code proper, which is by nature binary (current on/current off) and allows the data to be recorded in the memory bank and to be processed, and enables information to be supplied on demand.

3. The naïve application of the concept of code to the problems of communication (in the well-known statement of Wiener, Chinese is only American coded into Chinese) and the fleeting success of research into the field of automatic translation have generalized the use of this term in linguistics.

4. The theory of linguistic communication has attempted to exploit the opposition code/ message* (R. Jakobson), which is no more than a new way of formulating the Saussurian dichotomy (natural) language/speech.* Code is then taken to mean not only a limited set of signs or units (belonging to a morphology*), but also the procedures by which they are arranged (their syntactic organization). The articulation of these two components enables messages to be produced.

5. If language is considered as the combinatory* arrangement of minimal pertinent features (semes and/or phemes) it can be seen that the inventory of semic categories,* for example, together with rules of sememic* construction and of the projection of discursive isotopies,* forms a **semantic code** which will be manifested at the level of linguistic signs* in a lexematic dictionary. In certain cases it is even possible to

speak of a **partial code** to designate a particular semic system, a sort of sub-code the constituent elements of which enter into the composition of different sememes.

6. As a borderline case, some semioticians use the term code to cover an undefined set of units which have only a slender tie with each other, based on association, with no appeal made to an underlying logico-taxonomic organization (*cf.* R. Barthes in *S/Z*).
—COMMUNICATION; INFORMATION

COGNITIVE
(cognitif)

1. The adjective **cognitive** is used, in semiotics, as a specifying term by reference to various forms of articulation of knowing*—production, manipulation, organization, reception, assumption, etc.

2. Hierarchically superior to the pragmatic* dimension which acts as its internal referent,* the **cognitive dimension** of the discourse is developed in parallel fashion with the increase in knowing (as a cognitive activity) attributed to the subjects* installed in the discourse.* If the pragmatic dimension—along with the sequence of programmed actions* proper to it—does not necessarily imply the cognitive dimension, the reciprocal is not true: the cognitive dimension, which can be defined as the taking in charge, by knowing, of pragmatic actions, presupposes them. Furthermore, in extreme cases the pragmatic dimension in a given discourse may be nothing but the pretext for cognitive activities, as often happens in certain trends of modern literature. The proliferation—on the two axes of being* and doing*—of questions such as "What do I know?," "What have I

done?," "What have I succeeded at?," etc., goes together with the atrophy of the "What is happening" of the pragmatic component. The expansion of the cognitive dimension in narrative discourses helps, then, in the transition from the figurative* to the abstract,* between which there is no clear gap. We thus arrive at discourses that are apparently less figurative, or are characterized by a different sort of figurativity, *i.e.,* **cognitive discourses** (*cf. infra,* 6).

3. The autonomy of the cognitive dimension is made even clearer by the fact that it develops its own level of cognitive activities:

(a) **Cognitive doing*** corresponds to a transformation* which modifies the relation of a subject with the known object by establishing either a disjunction* or a conjunction.* The cognitive states*—or **cognitive positions**—thus obtained thanks to the interplay of being* and seeming* are articulated, in compliance with the semiotic square* of veridictory* modalities, into true/false/secret/lie. As for the transmission itself of the object of knowing, it can at least initially be qualified as simple. In this case we are dealing with **informative*** doing which, taking into account the communication* schema, is seen either as **emissive*** doing or as **receptive*** doing. Most frequently, if not always, however, the transfer of knowing is modalized from the veridictory point of view: considering the sender/receiver axis, we have, respectively, **persuasive*** doing and **interpretive*** doing, which bring an intersubjective fiduciary* relation into play. Given that the structure of narrative discourses is at once both contractual* and polemical,* the introduction of a persuasive doing evokes a corresponding interpretive doing: to the extent that narration

can cause two subjects to intervene with, alternately, their two forms of doing, the persuasive and the interpretive, it can bring into play, for example, the well-known structure of swindler tales, where the two actantial positions of trickster/tricked are interchangeable and the narrative endless. Of course the two forms of doing—the persuasive and the interpretative—can be attributed, by syncretism,* to one and the same actor* (for example, the subject of the enunciation) who then takes on the actantial roles of enunciator* and enunciatee.

(b) The **cognitive subject*** is that which is endowed by the enunciator with a knowing (partial or total) and installed by it in the discourse. Such an actant* allows the communication of knowing to be mediatized between the enunciator and the enunciatee in quite variable forms, depending on whether that actant is supposed to know or to be unaware of many or of a few things. At the actorial level, the role of the cognitive subject can be manifested in syncretism with that of the pragmatic* subject; inversely, the cognitive subject can be different from the pragmatic subject and give rise to the appearance of an autonomous actor such as the informant.* Finally, in certain cases, it is simply recognizable, as at least an implicit position, in the form of the observer.*

(c) Within the framework of the narrative schema,* it is possible in a certain manner to oppose the trajectory of the Sender, which unfolds in the cognitive dimension, to that of the subject-Receiver, which takes place above all in the pragmatic dimension. The Sender, in fact, manifests itself as the one which at the beginning of the narrative communicates in the form of a contract* the program to be realized. At the end, the Sender will have the task of exercising **cognitive sanction*** by the recognition* of the hero* and the undoing of the villain.* As for the subject-Sender, even if it is characterized mainly by pragmatic doing, it is also inscribed, by the fact of its relation to the Sender, in the cognitive dimension; the glorifying test*, in which it succeeds thanks to its persuasive being-able-to-do (represented by the mark*), can be considered as a **cognitive performance,*** calling forth, of course, a corresponding **cognitive competence.***

4. Taking the definition of space* as the locus of the manifestation of the overall sensitive qualities of the world, the concept of **cognitive space** can be accounted for. Indeed, the cognitive relations between subjects—but also between subjects and objects—are relations located in space (cf. seeing, touching, hearing, etc.). In the same way it can be said that, by considering the generative* trajectory of the discourse, these cognitive relations are seen, at a given moment, to be spatialized. They form, between the different subjects, proxemic* spaces, which are simply spatial representations of cognitive spaces. Within the framework of discursive semiotics, it is thus possible to speak of the **overall cognitive space** which is established in the form of an implicit contract between the enunciator and the enunciatee, and is characterized by a generalized knowing of the actions described. This space may be in turn either **absolute,** when the two protagonists of the discourse share the same omniscience concerning the related actions, or **relative,** when the enunciatee acquires the knowledge only progressively. It is also possible to take note of **partial cognitive spaces,** when the enunciator disen-

gages the structure of the enunciation* and installs it in the discourse or when it delegates its knowing to a cognitive subject.

5. **Cognitive disengagement*** is performed in two ways: (a) **Utterative** cognitive disengagement is the operation by which the enunciator establishes a gap between its own knowing and that which it attributes to the subjects installed in the discourse: this delegation* of knowing then functions for the benefit of the cognitive subjects; (b) **Enunciative** cognitive disengagement happens when, for example, the narrator,* installed in the discourse, does not share the same knowing as the enunciator that delegates it. In both cases the cognitive position of the enunciator characterized by the veridictory modalities truth, falsity, secrecy, and lie, differs from that of the actants of the narration or from that of the narrator.

6. Bearing in mind the cognitive activity of the enunciator (specified among other things by persuasive doing) and that of the enunciatee (with its interpretive doing), we can attempt to outline a **typology*** **of cognitive discourses** by distinguishing: (a) interpretive discourses, such as literary criticism, history as the interpretation of series of events, exegesis, fine arts criticism—of painting, music, architecture, etc.; (b) persuasive discourses such as those in pedagogy, politics, or advertising; (c) scientific* discourses which play on both the persuasive (with the whole range of demonstration) and the interpretive (which exploits previous discourses considered at that moment as referential discourses) with knowing-to-be-true as the project and object* of value aimed for.

—KNOWING (or KNOWLEDGE)

COHERENCE
(cohérence)

1. The term **coherence** is used colloquially to characterize a doctrine, a thought system, or a theory, all of the parts of which hold solidly together.

2. Some attempt can be made to define coherence negatively, as submission to the principle of non-contradiction, and positively, as the postulate upon which meta-logic is based and which also underlies all semiotic systems and all systems of constructed logic. L. Hjelmslev considers coherence as one of the three fundamental criteria of the scientificness of a theory.

3. In semiotic* theory, it is not only a matter of appealing to coherence but also, indeed primarily, of being able to test it in descriptions* and models.* The surest means seems to be the transcription of the theory itself into a formal* language. the insufficient development of semiotic theory lends itself, however, only partially to such a procedure. Thus we must often be content to verify the coherence of a theory at the level of its conceptual formulation, in particular, by proceeding to the comparative semantic analysis of the definitions of the concepts concerned: the establishment of a network of exhaustively interdefined concepts largely guarantees their coherence.
—SCIENTIFICNESS; THEORY

COLLECTIVE
(collectif)

1. The semantic universe* is said to be **collective** when it is articulated, at its base, by the semantic category* *nature/culture*. It is thus opposed to the individual* universe founded on the pair *life/death*.

2. An actant is said to be collective, on the basis of a collection of individual actors,* when it is endowed with a common modal competence* and/or a form of doing* common to all the actors it subsumes.

3. As opposed to the individual actant, the collective actant is necessarily either of the syntagmatic type or of the paradigmatic type. The **syntagmatic collective actant** is one where the actor-units, arranged like ordinal numbers, take over from each other—by substitution—in the execution of a single program, like the succession of different groups of craftsmen in the building of a house. The **paradigmatic collective actant,** like the senior class in a school or a social group in society, is not, however, the simple addition of cardinal numbers, but forms an intermediate totality between a collection of units and the totality which transcends it. It depends, in fact, on the classificatory division of a greater and hierarchically superior collection (for example, school, national community), a division that is effected on the basis of determination-criteria that the actors have in common, *i.e.*, their functional field or their specific qualifications.
—ACTANT; PSYCHO-SEMIOTICS; SOCIO-SEMIOTICS

COMBINATION
(combinaison)

1. A **combination** is a formation constituted by the presence of several elements,* as produced, by means of a combinatory principle, from simple elements. It can be considered that combinations of various dimensions form the syntagmatic axis* of language. Thus by the term combination are designated

the overall constituent relations* of a syntagm (relations of the type "both . . . and" according to L. Hjelmslev), in contrast to the relations of choice or opposition which characterize the paradigmatic* axis.

2. The term combination was introduced by Hjelmslev to designate the absence of presupposition between two terms. The presence of two terms in a semiotic unit* forms for him a relation without presupposition between these terms.

—COMBINATORY; PRESUPPOSITION

COMBINATORY
(PRINCIPLE or ARRANGEMENT)
(combinatoire)

1. Derived from the medieval *ars combinatoria,* the **combinatory principle** is seen as a discipline, or rather as a mathematical calculation, which enables a large number of combinations* of elements* to be formed from a small number of simple elements. Leibniz applied it to the calculation of concepts and considered it thereby the synthetic part of logic; the combinatory principle could not fail to arouse the interest of twentieth-century linguistics, the epistemological ties of which with the philosophy of the eighteenth century are well known.

2. The concept of a combinatory principle is in some way related to that of generation,* since it designates a procedure whereby complex units are generated from simple units. The product obtained is seen as a hierarchy* that theoretically corresponds to the paradigmatic* organization of a semiotic system: it is in this sense that we can state that the combinatory arrangement of a score of semic categories* can produce a very great number of sememes* (in the order of several

million), certainly sufficient to take care of the articulation of any semantic universe* coextensive with a given natural language.*

3. The introduction in the procedure of **combinatory arrangement** of a rule of order* according to which the units derived are defined not only by the co-presence of simple elements but also by the linear order of their disposition, further increases the number of possible combinations. We see, however, that the recourse in the calculation to the principle of order (organizing the derived units) already corresponds in semiotics to the appearance of the syntagmatic* axis of language.

4. It is this ability of the elements of the expression* plane as well as of those of the content* plane to inter-combine by forming increasingly complex syntagmatic units that is often designated as the **combinatory function** of language, in contrast to the distinctive* function (the function of opposition* or selection*), which characterizes the paradigmatic axis. Taken thus, the combinatory function refers to the procedure of "ascending" description,* which proceeds from minimal units to complex units and which is opposed to the "descending" procedure—that of L. Hjelmslev, for example, which starts from a "meaningful whole" and decomposes it by successive segmentation until minimal signs are obtained.

5. The principle of order— which brings linearity* into play—is not the only principle that organizes syntagmatic units (in view of the existence of disjunctive units such as "did [you/they . . .] go" or "have [you/they . . .] gone," even its universality can be questioned). In semiotics, just as much attention should be paid to the compatibility* and incompatibility* that certain

elements, units, or classes display in their ability to combine together. By considering the combinatory principle no longer as a procedure for the production of semiotic units, but as the state resulting from this procedure, the name **syntactical combinatory arrangement** and/or **semantic combinatory arrangement** designates the network of constituent relations of syntagmatic units, based on the principle of compatibility.

6. The definition of **combinatory variant,*** a term of distributional* analysis, designating a variant compatible with a given context, is in line with the foregoing remarks.

COMMENTARY
(commentaire)

1. **Commentary,** a colloquial term, is used to designate a certain type of interpretive discourse which has no scientific aim.

2. As a discursive unit, interpretive* and thematic* in nature, a commentary is obtained by utterative or enunciative disengagement.* —UNIT

COMMUNICATION
(communication)

1. Parallel and closely related to information theory,* a **schema of linguistic communication** has been developed. It remains bound to a theory quite mechanistic in character, even though it claims to be more respectful of intersubjective verbal exchanges. According to the psychologist Bühler, linguistic activity can be defined by its three functions*: expression* (from the addresser's viewpoint), appeal (from the addressee's viewpoint), and representation (which has to do with the referent* or the context*). Roman Jakobson has taken over and com-

pleted this triadic schema, using a new terminology. For him, verbal communication is based on six factors: the addresser and the addressee, the message* transmitted from one to the other, the context (or referent)—verbal or verbalizable —with which the message is concerned, the code* (more or less common to the actants of the communication) thanks to which the message is communicated, and finally the contact, which is based on both a physical channel and a psychological connection. To each of these different elements there corresponds a particular linguistic function, respectively: emotive (or expressive*), conative,* poetic,* referential,* metalinguistic,* phatic.*

2. It goes without saying that the Jakobsonian functions of language* do not exhaust their object, and that such an articulation, however suggestive it may be, does not lay the basis of a methodology for discourse analysis. The six function schema is both too general to allow for an appropriate taxonomy and an appropriate syntax and at the same time too specific in that it deals only with verbal communication—and even then it does not take the syncretic* aspect into account—to the exclusion of all other semiotic systems. Thus, for example, this schema seems to deal only with informative* doing, which can be articulated, according to the addresser/addressee relationship, as emissive* doing/receptive* doing. Now, there are other ways in which the transmission of knowing may be conceived, particularly when it is modalized: such is the case with persuasive* doing and interpretive* doing, which depend more on manipulation* than on "communication."

3. It is clear, on the other hand, that if language is communication, it

is also production of meaning,* of signification.* It cannot be reduced to a simple transmission of knowing on the "I"/"you" axis, as a certain brand of functionalism would have it. Furthermore, it develops, so to speak, for itself, for what it is, with its own internal organization that the theory of communication alone— taking a somewhat external viewpoint—does not seem able to account for.

4. Although independent from Bühler, Jakobson, Martinet and all the functionalist trend, English philosophy of language, with J. L. Austin, shares—beyond differences in terminology and preoccupations— the same concern, that of accounting for language as an intersubjective operation, even though it attempts to integrate a greater part of human activity. J. R. Searle's notion of "speech act," which has been progressively elaborated, and, beyond it, the theory of pragmatics (in the American sense), transcend the limits of simple "communication" by focusing upon the conditions of its exercise; despite a certain lack of coherence in terminology arising from a philosophico-linguistic amalgam, their contribution to the study of linguistic activity should not be ignored.

5. To avoid a conception of communication that would be too mechanistic (which goes back to the information model), or one that would be too restrictive by confining itself to "extralinguistic" parameters, it is essential to place this key notion in a larger context. Human activities as a whole are generally considered as taking place along two main axes: that of action on things, by which human beings transform nature— the axis of production*—and that of action on other persons, which creates intersubjective relations, the foundations of society—the axis of **communication.** The concept of exchange* in the French anthropological tradition which, especially since M. Mauss, covers this second sphere of activities, can be interpreted in two different ways, either as the transfer* of objects* of value, or as communication between subjects. The transfers of objects that are manifested as acquisitions* and deprivations can only affect the subjects and constitute, insofar as they take canonical forms, certain systems of interhuman relations, regulating the desires and duties of human beings. Lévi-Strauss has proposed that three fundamental dimensions of these communication-transfers be distinguished: to the exchanges of women, considered as a process, there correspond kinship structures, which have the form of systems; to the exchange of goods and services there correspond economic structures; and to the exchange of messages correspond linguistic structures. This very general schema can of course be modified or refined: in place of linguistic structures particularly, it is advantageous to register wider semiotic organizations. From the concept of exchange, on the other hand, should be taken away the euphoric connotations which allude to a universal good will among humans in their mutual relations. For indeed, it is difficult, if not impossible, to establish clear distinctions between contractual* structures and polemical structures which govern communication. Nevertheless, it remains true that such a conception of communication enables us to establish a strictly semiotic approach to the problem, which is quite different from those of economic theories, on the one hand, and from the theory of communication, on the other.

6. Insofar as communication takes place between subjects and insofar as values* invested in the objects put into circulation (pragmatic* or cognitive* values, descriptive* or modal* values) are considered as constituents of the being of the subject (constantly undergoing increases or decreases of its being), it is clear that the sender and the receiver can no longer be treated as abstractions, as the empty positions of source* and destination.* They are, on the contrary, competent* subjects, considered at a particular moment of their becoming, each inscribed in its own discourse. It can also be understood why a dialogue that appears inside a narrative discourse seems to give us a more correct representation of the process of communication than a artifact constructed on the basis of the extra-linguistic "structure of communication," and furthermore why we propose to interpret an "exchange of messages," at least at the semantic level, as a discourse with two, or several, voices.

7. This "humanization" of communication, a preoccupation of most of the recent theories in this field, does, however, raise new problems for which as yet there are no definitive solutions. Let us first note the problem of **participative communication.** Contrary to what happens during ordinary communication, where the attribution* of an object of value is concomitant with renunciation,* discourses that are in nature ethno-literary, philosophical, or juridical (cf. constitutional law), display communication structures where the transcendent Sender (absolute, sovereign, original, ultimate, etc.) offers values* that are modal (being able, for example) as well as descriptive (material goods), without really renouncing them and

without any loss of its being. This case of the transcendent Sender must obviously be distinguished from that of the giver of knowledge which, during communication, transmits a cognitive object while its own knowledge is not in any way diminished. This peculiarity is explained by the fact that the subject of the enunciation is a syncretic* actor, subsuming the two actants, enunciator* and enunciatee*; in other words, it is its own enunciatee and thus regains what it had given out as enunciator.

8. Another question, still unanswered, is that raised by the distinction—fairly easy to recognize but difficult to explain—between received communication and **appropriated communication.** Psychoanalytical discourse has brought to light the distance between mechanisms which insure that the signification will be grasped, and the little-known procedures governing its appropriation, its integration into the already-existing axiology. It is as though the receiver subject cannot gain full possession of the meaning unless it is previously equipped with a form of wanting and of being-able-to-accept; unless, in other words, the receiver subject can be defined by a certain type of receptive competence that in turn constitutes the first and last aim of the enunciator's discourse. If to appropriate another person's word is believing in it to some extent, then causing to appropriate is speaking in order to be believed. Considered in this way, communication is far less causing-to-know—as it is too hastily conceived—than causing-to-believe and causing-to-do.

9. Another of the many possible problems is that of the frequent concomitance, and resulting confusion, of productive doing (which can

be formulated as narrative doing*) and **communicative doing.** A ritual is programmed doing, whose goal is its own signification: the installation of an observer (the public, for example), perverts it not only because it transforms it into a spectacle, but also because the behavior of the observed becomes equivocal and splits into two. The conversation of two people ceases to be what it is if the participants know they are being listened to. We are not dealing here merely with the issues of the semiotics of the theatre but more widely with the "spectacular" dimension of our cultures and our signs, the study of which has been poorly approached and about which little is as yet known.

—INFORMATION; FACTITIVE-NESS; PERSUASIVE DOING; INTERPRETIVE DOING: CONTRACT; DISCOURSE; IMPLICIT; SOCIO-SEMIOTICS

COMMUTATION
(commutation)

1. **Commutation** is simply the explicit form of the relation of solidarity* (= reciprocal presupposition*) between the expression* plane and the content* plane of a semiotic system, according to which a change of content must correspond to every change of expression, and inversely. Thus, to use L. Hjelmslev's terminology, if there is a correlation* (*i.e.,* an "either . . . or" relation) between two entities* of expression—for instance, "bat" and "bit"—a correlation should also be recorded between the two entities of the content "bat" (animal) and "bit" (verb = "performed the action of biting" or noun = "small portion"): there is, then, a relation (of the type "both . . . and") between the two correlations located on each of the two planes of language.

2. Commutation may then become a procedure for the recognition* of discrete units* of either plane of language. It is thanks to this that the Prague School was able to elaborate the concepts of phoneme* and distinctive* feature, or pheme.* Though the replacement of one phoneme* by another in a given context causes a difference of content ("bat"/"bit"), the same cannot be said of the changing of one phoneme variant* for another (for example, front *a*/back *a*): the phoneme is an invariant, a phonological unit, by contrast with the variables which the different possible phonetic occurrences are. It should be further noted that the correlation ("either . . . or"), on the expression plane, between "pin" and "bin" is established not by the difference between the phonemes but between the distinctive features or, more precisely, between the two terms of the phemic category* voiced/ unvoiced.

3. The same procedure of commutation, when applied to the content plane, contributes to the elaboration of the concepts of seme* and sememe.*

—PERMUTATION; SUBSTITUTION; INVARIANT; VARIABLE

COMPARATIVE LINGUISTICS
(comparative ou comparée [linguistique—])

1. This name is used to designate nineteenth-century linguistics (formerly called **comparative** and/or **historical grammar**) as it was founded at the beginning of the last century by Franz Bopp and Rasmus Rask, and continued in the second half of the century by August Schleicher and the neo-grammarians. In the last years of the nineteenth century it was given its

most perfected formulation by F. de Saussure; its theoretical evaluation was made in the 1940s by L. Hjelmslev.

2. From the viewpoint of the history of sciences, the appearance of **comparative linguistics** marks the accession of the first of the human sciences to scientific status. Under the influence of the surrounding episteme of the time, which sought to explore every object of knowledge in its temporal dimension, linguistics also strove to be historical: the origin of languages, their relations, their organization into families, were for a considerable time the explicit key words of its research. And yet, under this theoretical appearance, the weaknesses of which never cease to amaze us, a strict comparative methodology was gradually worked out. The "archeological" attempt to reconstitute an "original" Indo-European language changed, with Saussure's formulation, into the construction of a typological* model that showed Indo-European to be—on the expression* plane—no longer like a genealogical tree, but rather like a network of formal correlations articulating the different phonological systems of particular languages. Hjelmslev sees this model as the result of the elaboration of a genetic typology which is different from the structural typology because of restrictions stemming from the fact that it takes into consideration corpora* made out of morphemes* (or words) of each language—a formal criterion which takes the place of the historicity of the evaluation. This Hjelmslevian interpretation of Saussure's model gives comparative linguistics its distinguishing scientific status as well as its specific approach.

3. Thus, comparative linguistics is not merely, as some people believe, an outmoded historical period marking one of the stages in the development of linguistics. It is rather a theory and an effective method which explore new linguistic fields and can be applied, after the necessary transpositions, to other semiotic domains.

—COMPARATIVISM; TYPOLOGY

COMPARATIVE MYTHOLOGY
(comparée [mytholigie–])

1. Understood as the study of myths, mythology* has progressed, like linguistics, from a genetic approach to comparativism.* Like comparative linguistics, which went from a deliberate historical approach to a formal methodology, mythology seems able to take on the form of a scientific discipline only when it partially renounces a historico-genetic approach (which certain research trends nevertheless consider the only fruitful one).

2. Between the views of J. Frazer, dreaming of a universal mythology, and those of certain other scholars, who hold that each myth has a unique character, a middle road has been opened up thanks to the work of G. Dumézil and C. Lévi-Strauss. For them, the comparative approach is practiced within a particular socio-cultural world the entire ideological content of which it attempts to examine, without needing to state what is properly mythic and what is not. Thus Dumézil has completely renewed research on Indo-European mythology, particularly by passing from phonetic comparativism (located on the signifier* level), a dead end, to semantic comparativism (focussed on the signified*). Thus, for example, comparisons between divinities are no

longer made merely at the level of their names, but also at that of the content* features through which they are primarily defined as the intersecting points of semantic networks. This methodological innovation has enabled Dumézil, among others, to provide a solid foundation for a description of the ideology of the Indo-European peoples, that he conceives as involving the articulation of three functions.

3. In parallel research on American Indian mythology, Lévi-Strauss has set up a comparative study which is analogous, even though it is presented in a more formal or more abstract way. Working also at the content level, he has tried to elucidate the organization of mythic* discourse by showing in particular that one myth can be translated into another (or one fragment of a myth into another) thanks to the interplay of transformations* or changes in the possible semantic codes. An underlying logical structure, based on a system of oppositions,* then becomes apparent. This structure, since it encompasses and certainly transcends the limits of the corpora under study, refers us back to the nature of the "human mind" and to the way it functions.

4. Using essentially the methodology of Lévi-Strauss for the analysis of Greek myths, M. Détienne works also in a comparative perspective. By broadening the concept of mythology to encompass the entire culture, he opens up particularly promising research possibilities in this domain.

5. These various explorations in comparative mythology—and more particularly those of Lévi-Strauss, the methodological basis of which is made more explicit—are, in large part, at the very source of

French semiotics, which is continually being enriched by contact with them.
—MYTHOLOGY;   COMPARATIVISM; TRANSFORMATION

COMPARATIVISM
(comparatisme)

1. **Comparativism** is a set of cognitive procedures aiming at establishing formal correlations between two or more semiotic objects and eventually at constituting a typological* model of these semiotic objects which then are only variables of this model. If **comparative doing,** which is characteristic of certain discourses with a scientific aim, can be considered as a part of taxonomic doing in the broad sense, it is nonetheless located on a hierarchically superior level, since to a large extent it presupposes that the objects are already constructed by taxonomic doing.

2. As a methodology, comparativism was elaborated by the **comparative linguistics*** (also known as comparative grammar) of the nineteenth century, by being applied to the expression* plane of language. On the content* plane, it has been extended to comparative mythology* thanks to the work of G. Dumézil and of C. Lévi-Strauss. Its application to **comparative literature** is still awaited: it is not beyond the bounds of possibility that the notion of intertextuality,* once it has been more rigorously elaborated, might bring comparativism into literary semiotics.

3. As a rather simplistic illustration of the comparative method, we can take what the nineteenth century considered as "phonetic laws." In the Romance field one of these laws stated that: "the tonic free Latin vowel *a* becomes *e* in French." This

was written: Latin á[> Fr. e. A formulation of this kind summarizes and subsumes a complex set of comparative procedures: (a) it presupposes a homogenous description of the phonological systems of Latin and French, making it possible to identify the two phonemes as syntagmatic units; (b) it depends on the recognition of contextual environments, considered as conditions necessary for the establishment of the correlation. Furthermore, it concerns on the one hand the position of the phoneme *a* in the larger unit of expression of the syllable (the correlation exists only if the vowel is "free," *i.e.*, if it is not followed in the same syllable by a consonant), and on the other hand, the position of the Latin phoneme in the morphosyntactical unit belonging to the sign plane—the word*—defined and marked in Latin by the accent (only those *a* vowels which are tonic in Latin come into French as the vowel *e*).

4. The example proposed clearly shows both the formal and achronic* nature of the established correlation. Although this law was considered a "historical" law, nothing in its formulation has anything to do with historicity. On the contrary, this correlation can be usefully compared to the one which can be formulated between two linguistic systems considered simultaneously, for example, the *langue d'oc* and the *langue d'oïl* [very approximately, vernacular in medieval France north of the Loire river, and south of it]. The correlation between these two systems can be stated as the correlation between the Old Occitan vowel *a*, (tonic and free) and the Old French vowel *e*. If such correlations are called transformations,* it should simply be added that in the first case the transformation is

oriented (the rules for the passage from French to Latin not being made explicit), whereas in the second case it is **neutral** (or not oriented). The distinction between the two types of transformation in no way prejudices their spatial or temporal localization, which depends on a different approach.
—TYPOLOGY; COMPARATIVE LINGUISTICS; COMPARATIVE MYTHOLOGY; INTERTEXTUALITY; TRANSFORMATION

COMPATIBILITY
(*compatibilité*)

1. The numerous combinations* produced by the combinatory principle from a small number of elements may be considered from the semiotic viewpoint as units of varied dimensions, whether they belong to the expression* plane or the content* plane. Their organization is based on the principle of **compatibility** according to which only certain elements can combine with certain others, to the exclusion of other combinations judged to be incompatible. This, accordingly, restricts the theoretical combinatory arrangement.

2. The reasons for incompatibility are difficult to discern. **Phonological incompatibility** seems to be the best studied, and it is possible to distinguish causes of an extrinsic nature (for example, distance between the points of articulation)—or of an intrinsic nature (for example, the phenomena of contiguity producing assimilation or dissimilation). The production of a theory from phonological data could perhaps permit the construction of models* which, once applied by extrapolation to the content plane, would account for the conditions of **syntactical incompatibility**—a con-

cept that is closely related to agrammaticality* (an intuitive notion)—and those of **semantic incompatibilities,** which correspond to unacceptability (in generative grammar).

3. In practice, it is sufficient that compatibility be taken to mean the possibility for two semiotic elements to contract a relation* (to be present together in a hierarchically superior unit or in a position of contiguity* on the syntagmatic axis). —COMBINATORY PRINCIPLE OR ARRANGEMENT; GRAMMATICALITY; ACCEPTABILITY; SEMANTICITY; INTERPRETATION

COMPETENCE
(compétence)

1. The concept of **competence,** introduced into linguistics by N. Chomsky, goes back epistemologically to the 17th-century psychology of the "faculties," whereas the concept of natural language (which competence seeks to replace by borrowing certain of its essential parameters), elaborated by F. de Saussure, refers back to the reflection made by the 18th century on "systems" and "mechanisms." Language and competence are considered as endowed with virtual* existence and they are opposed (and are logically anterior) the former to speech* and the latter to performance,* both speech and performance being conceived as actualizations* of preexisting potentialities. Just as the Saussurian "language" is the sole object of linguistics, "competence," described by the linguist, is the grammar* of this language. The difference in point of view appears when one attempts to spell out the "content" of this virtual domain. For Saussure language is essentially a system which is paradigmatic* by nature. Chomsky, on the contrary, in his formulation of competence insists on the aptitude for producing and for understanding an infinite number of utterances, that is, on the properly syntactic* aspect. Such a polarization is, yet, a bit artificial, for many strict Saussurian linguists (Hjelmslev or Benvéniste, to mention only the best known) had already integrated the syntagmatic* process into the sphere of "language." Chomsky's insistence on the fact that competence consists in producing "an infinite number of utterances" seems to us excessive. The combinatory* principle has been known longer than the adage according to which "no one has knowledge except of what is general." One may wonder whether it is not just as reasonable to limit the ambitions of syntax to a combinatory set of classes*—even though this entails then envisioning that other components will have to take over at a given time—rather than postulating, as does generative grammar,* a syntactic imperialism that semantic complexities risk putting into question at any moment. Chomsky's novel contribution seems to us to be the "dynamization" of the concept of language which remained too static for Saussure and his followers. A conception of language as a productive process—and no longer as a state of which competence would be one of the oriented domains, certainly constitutes a new approach. All the theoretical possibilities offered by this approach are still far from being exploited.

2. It is clear, however, that an examination of the "content" of **linguistic competence** does not exhaust the concept of competence. By contrast to performance, which is a doing* that produces utterances,

competence is a knowing-how-to-do, it is "that something" which makes doing possible. Moreover, this knowing-how-to-do, insofar as it is a "potential act," is separable from the doing on which it bears. Besides a knowing-how-to-do which manipulates the rules of grammar, there exists another which manipulates, for example, the rules of etiquette. In other words, linguistic competence is not a thing in itself, but a particular case of a much larger phenomenon which, under the generic heading of competence, belongs to the study of human action and sets up the subject as actant* (whatever might be the domain where this competence is exercised). From another point of view, competence, as it is defined by the Chomskyans, is a knowing, that is, an implicit knowledge which the subject has of his/her language (and on which the concept of grammaticality is based). It will be noted, however, that this knowing is not concerned with knowing-how-to-do, but bears on a *having-to-be,* that is, on the "content" of competence, considered as a system of constraints (set of positive and negative injunctions).

3. The distinction between what competence is and what it bears on (that is, its object, which, in the case of linguistic competence, is identified, once it has been described, with grammar) allows us to consider competence as a modal structure.* As is clear, here we return to the whole set of problems concerning act.* If act is a "causing-to-be," competence is *"that* which causes to be," that is, all the prerequisites and presuppositions which make action possible. Thus, if the problem of competence in the (vast, but nonetheless limited) linguistic domain is transposed to that of semiotics, it can be said that every sensible

behavior or every sequence of behavior presupposes, on the one hand, a virtual narrative program* and, on the other, a particular competence which makes its carrying out possible. Competence, thus conceived, is a **modal competence** which can be described as a hierarchical organization of modalities* (it will be based, for example, on a willing-to-do or a having-to-do, governing a being-able or a knowing-how-to-do). It must be distinguished from **semantic competence** (in the broadest sense of the word semantic, the one which is used, for example, when it is said that the deep structure of a language is logico-semantic in nature) the simplest form of which is the virtual narrative program. Once joined, these two forms of competence constitute what can be called the **subject's competence.**

4. The consequences drawn from such a definition concern semiotic theory in its totality. Analysis of narrative discourses makes us encounter, at every moment, in their pragmatic* and cognitive* dimensions, performing subjects (that is, subjects carrying out sequences of programmed behavior) which, in order to act, need to possess, or first to acquire, the necessary competence. The narrative trajectory* of the subject is thus composed of two syntagms, bearing the names of competence and of performance. Semiotics is thus brought to construct models of modal competence, which, based on the analysis of narrative discourses, are applicable to the non-linguistic semiotics of the natural world* (on the plane of "psycho-social reality") and must serve as premises for a semiotics of action.* Then the typology of semantic competences may be considered as one of the possible defi-

nitions of the semantic universe,*
whether collective or individual.

5. It can be seen, on the other
hand, how, in this perspective, the
concept of **communication competence,** set out by Dell Hymes, can be
confirmed and strenthened. Dell
Hymes's theory about implicit or
explicit knowledge of the psychological, cultural, and social rules presupposed by communication,* is
none other than the confrontation—
contractual* or polemical*—of two
competent subjects. Their competence—unequal, positive, or negative
—is, on the one hand, modal (and
gives rise to manipulation* operations) and, on the other, semantic
(and accounts for the reciprocal
communication of knowing and of
its misunderstandings and ambiguities).

6. If one should wish to insert
competence into the general
processs of signification,* it would
have to be conceived as a domain
situated higher than enunciation.*
The subject of the enunciation
modalizes the semiotic and narrative
structures* by giving them a status
of *having-to-be* (that is, of a system of
constraints), and takes them on as a
knowing-how-to-do, as a virtual
process. In other words, modal
competence manipulates semantic
competence by giving it, so to speak,
the status of "competence," *i.e.,* by
transforming a grammar given as a
description into a normative system
and into an operating process. As
for semantic competence—considered as "content," as the modalizable
and modalized object—its articulations merge eventually with the
levels* and the components* which
semiotic theory has been thought to
distinguish while seeking to give a
coherent representation of the
generative* trajectory. Nothing then
prohibits us from distinguishing a

semio-narrative competence, taken
over by the enunciation, and a discoursive and textual competence,
defining enunciation itself as a domain of mediation which makes performance possible, that is, the realization of the utterance-discourse.
—LANGUAGE; ACT; MODAL-
ITY; NARRATIVE TRAJECTO-
RY; SYNTAX; SURFACE NAR-
RATIVE; GENERATIVE TRA-
JECTORY; DISCOURSE; NAR-
RATIVITY

COMPLEMENTARITY
(complémentarité)

1. **Complementarity** is one of
the constituent relations* of the
semantic category* contracted by the
subcontrary* and contrary* of the
same deixis,* either positive (s1 +
$\overline{s2}$) or negative s2 + $\overline{s1}$), in the
semiotic square. Complementarity is
seen as a particular case of the
oriented relation that proceeds from
the presupposing term to the presupposed term. To be complementary, such a relation should be
isotopic* with the category of which
it is a part. In other words, implication,* by asserting the subcontrary
(the "if"; as in "if not white") should
lead to the contrary (the "then"; as
in "then black") as a presupposed
term of the same category. The relation of complementarity is said to
subsume two **complementary terms.**
However, the relation itself can, at a
hierarchically superior level, be used
as a term to constitute a new category. The relation itself is in this
case called a **complementary
metaterm.***

2. Some linguists (for example,
J. Lyons) define the complementarity of two terms by the fact that the
negation of one implies at least the
implicit affirmation of the other.
The example chosen by Lyons

(married/single) clearly shows that complementarity corresponds here to what is for us contradiction.*

3. In distributional analysis,* distribution is said to be **complementary** when two linguistic units do not appear in any common context.* The concept of complementarity in this case corresponds partly to Lyon's definition by the fact that the two units are mutually exclusive, but it also corresponds to our own definition provided that they both belong to the same level of derivation.* The two classes* to which they belong can in fact be in a relation of implication.
—SQUARE, SEMIOTIC; PRESUPPOSITION; IMPLICATION

COMPLEX TERM
(complexe [terme—])

Derived from the elementary structure* of signification, the **complex** term is defined by the "both . . . and" relation that the terms s1 and s2 of the axis of contradictories* in the semiotic square contract, after preliminary syntactic operations. The complex term can be **positive** or **negative,** depending on which of the two terms entering into its composition is dominant. The "coexistence of contraries" is an arduous problem, inherited from a long philosophical and religious tradition. V. Brøndal introduced it into linguistics, recognizing the existence of complex terms in the articulation of the grammatical categories* of certain natural languages. The problem of how such terms are generated has not yet received a satisfactory solution.—SQUARE, SEMIOTIC; TERM

COMPONENT
(composante)

The term **component** designates a constructed semiotic object—or one in the process of being constructed—not so much defined so as to show its internal organization but rather to emphasize its autonomy within the larger set where it is found. This term is most often applied to what were formerly known as the different disciplines of a science and what are now considered as the components of a theory* (for example, the semantic component, the phonological component, etc.).

COMPONENTIAL ANALYSIS
(componentielle [analyse—])

Of American origin, **componential analysis** is by its taxonomic procedures linked to semic analysis, even though it is distinguished from it through its terminology, its objectives, and its fields of application.— SEMIC ANALYSIS

COMPREHENSION
(compréhension)

1. In logic, **comprehension** is taken to mean the set of characteristics (or properties, attributions, determinations, etc.), that belong to a concept* and/or define it. As the organization of underlying qualities of the concept, comprehension is opposed to extension, which envisages quantitatively the set of objects it covers.

2. In semiotics, and in that branch of linguistics inspired by Saussure, where extension is considered as non-pertinent for analysis, comprehension may be identified

with the definition* of the concept, itself assimilated to name.* In this case, it is legitimate to start with the comprehension of a sememe,* specifying, however, that it may equally well contain negative semes (= the absent properties), in view of the fact that signification is a matter of grasping differences—a point which the concept does not traditionally admit in its comprehension. —EXTENSION

CONATIVE FUNCTION
(conative [fonction—])

In the triadic schema of verbal communication proposed by the psychologist K. Bühler (taken up and augmented by R. Jakobson), the **conative*** function is that which concerns the receiver,* as opposed to the expressive* functions, centered on the sender, and the referential function, relative to what is being spoken about. It finds its grammatical expression, for example, in the vocative or the imperative.—FUNCTION; COMMUNICATION

CONCEPT
(concept)

1. As a philosophical term, **concept** carries numerous and varied definitions, which all refer, more or less, to entities* of the signified* (= ideas) that can organize the data of experience.

2. F. de Saussure used the term to designate—in a first approximation—the signified, the sole determination of which is to participate in the constitution of the sign* (the concept of a tree and the acoustic image of a tree constitute the sign "tree"). Later, he eliminated this notion in favor of signifying form.*

3. In semiotic theory, the term concept can be kept in the sense of name* (the signification of which is clarified by its definition*). The clarification of concepts by successive definitions then becomes the major preoccupation of all the metalinguistic* constructions of the theoretician. For indeed, it appears that linguistic or semiotic theories contain many **non-defined concepts.** These are borrowed from natural languages, and, more particularly, from often implicit philosophical doctrines. While these concepts are frequently strongly suggestive, and can cover crucial sets of issues, they are not thereby integrated into the overall theory. The construction of a theory* should then involve a **conceptual phase,** where the concepts are called upon to be replaced by definitions and interdefinitions whose constituent elements are more abstract and more general than the original concepts. It is only at the top of such a conceptual hierarchy that we find **non-definable concepts** (such as "relation," "object," "description," etc.) that form an inventory which helps to establish an axiomatic* system.

4. In such a perspective, inspired by Hjelmslev, the term concept, as an element of the metalanguage,* helps to name classes of objects (the semiotic units) as well as procedures* and models.* It is in this sense that within a theory, a distinction is drawn between concepts that are "real," i.e., integrated into scientific metasemiotics,* and operational concepts, which are the bases for procedures or models that seem effective but which, because they are not integrated within the theories, can only be considered provisional. —THEORY

CONCOMITANCE
(concomitance)

By **concomitance** is meant the co-presence of two or more entities,* registered either inside a given state* or after the transformation* of one state into another (*cf.*, for example, concomitant variations). The relation of concomitance (of the type "both . . . and") accounts for, in narrative semiotics, the co-presence of two or more narrative programs*; at the stage where it is put into discourse, it is temporalized and/or spatialized with the help of the procedures of localization and nesting. —NESTING; LOCALIZATION, SPATIO-TEMPORAL

CONCRETE
(concret)

A term is said to be **concrete,** as opposed to abstract, if its semic density is relatively high.—DENSITY, SEMIC; ABSTRACT

CONDENSATION
(condensation)

The elasticity of discourse is shown both by **condensation** and expansion. The recognition* of a semantic equivalence between discoursive units of different dimensions (for example, the fact that the lexeme "discussion" sometimes summarizes the discoursive unit called "dialogue") makes, on the one hand, any analysis of the "text"— considered as rough data—completely impossible; on the other hand, it forces discoursive semiotics to elaborate an ideal hierarchy* of discoursive forms, made up of unequally complex levels* of analysis, and to consider the manifested text as a rather undistinguishable "leveling" of heteroplanar forms.— ELASTICITY OF DISCOURSIVE; EXPANSION

CONDITION
(condition)

A non-defined concept according to L. Hjelmslev, yet necessary for the definition of presupposition,* the term **condition** can be considered as the name for "if" in the relation "if . . . then." The concept of condition plays a determining role in the formulation of semiotic constraints.*

CONFIGURATION
(configuration)

1. At first, **discoursive configurations** seem to be kinds of micronarratives with an autonomous syntactic-semantic structure, which can be integrated in larger discoursive units and acquire thereby functional significations corresponding to their positions in these larger units.

2. The issues raised by these configurations are linked to those raised by motifs,* such as they have been formulated within the methodological tradition of the nineteenth century, in the domains of folklore (for example, J. Bédier), art history (Panofsky, among others), etc. Seen in the framework of the "theory of influences," motifs are viewed as forms that are narrative and/or figurative, autonomous, and mobile, able to pass from one culture to another, to be integrated into larger sets, with the partial or total loss of their former significations in favor of deviant or new semantic investments. Such trajectories of the motifs constitute a general history of forms. The French *fabliaux* of the Middle Ages were thus viewed as a collection of quite different forms that were gathered together from various cultural settings, and that had a single original creative birthplace, readily identified with ancient India.

3. The historical perspective, which predominated at the time, led scholars to take a prime interest in the provenance of recognized forms, and thereby to neglect the receptive structures (discourses, texts) in which the "borrowed" forms were included. The subsequent change in perspective has led us to recognize the existence of receptive forms—syntactic and semantic—that can receive, in invariant frameworks, new forms considered as variables. There is consequently no alternative but to distinguish, on the one hand, encompassing discursive structures and, on the other, micro-structures called motifs, of which a larger discoursive framework could take charge.

4. There is no need to return here to the criticism of the "theory of influences," which has long been tried and found wanting. In semiotics, comparative* methodology, which utilizes the procedures of oriented transformations,* can be substituted for it. It is true, nevertheless, that even within the universe of a given discourse (for example, French ethno-literary discourse), the mobility of motifs is a recognized fact. Motifs such as "marriage" or "equitable sharing" are found at the beginning, as well as at the middle or the end of a tale, thus enabling us to maintain the distinction between receiving structures (of the works receiving new forms) and received structures (of the motifs).

5. However strange it may appear at first sight, this phenomenon is not without analogy with the grammatical facts that phrastic linguistics finds at another level. We are thinking here of the difficulties raised by the non-concomitance, in a great number of natural languages, of morphological and syntagmatic classes.* While one can theoretically construct a categorial grammar operating with morphological* classes alone, or, on the contrary, a purely syntagmatic grammar that would have to manipulate only syntagmatic classes, in the practice of a language such as English, one finds quite often, alongside the facts of concomitance (verb and predicate in the case of "to fear"), situations of grammatical divergency ("to be afraid") or semantic "deviation" (In "sports clothes" "sports" loses its noun character). It is just as though, all due proportions considered, a narrative grammar of the syntagmatic type should contain, in an annex, a "morphological" sub-component that would account for the organization and the procedures of integration of discoursive configurations. Thus, narrative logic, as conceived by C. Bremond, for example, seems to us, in its deep intentions, to be more a "configurative" semiotics than a narrative semiotics strictly speaking.

6. The study of discoursive configurations remains to be done and surely constitutes one of the most urgent tasks in discoursive semiotics. Two sets of problems arise here: those relating to the internal organization of discoursive configurations and those relating to their integration into larger discoursive contexts.

7. Discoursive configurations, we have said, appear to be micro-narratives. This means that a configuration does not depend on its context, that it can be extracted from it and manifested in the form of a self-sufficient discourse. The analysis of a configuration can therefore be expected to identify therein all the levels and all the components of a discourse examined through the different domains of its generative trajectory. Thus it is easy

to identify **thematic configurations** and also **figurative configurations** (to which motifs belong). In the same way, their discoursive manifestation already presupposes an underlying narrative organization; it is not in the least surprising, then, that an inventory can be drawn up of discoursive configurations as stereotypes representing canonical modal structures, a typology of which could be undertaken (*cf.* the contractual and modal structures of manipulation*).

8. The integration of a configuration into a discourse under production can be formulated, in its simplest procedure, as the investment, during enunciation,* of the narrative* trajectory of the receiving discourse (or of one of its constituent narrative programs*) by one of the potential trajectories of the configuration. In this way, a thematic or figurative role, chosen from within the configuration, is identified with an actantial role of the narrative discourse. This identification sets in motion the distribution of **configurative roles** on the actantial disposition of the discourse, giving rise to the appearance of local or generalized isotopies. Clearly, an intervention of this nature presupposes a subject of the enunciation, endowed not only with narrative competence, but also with a supply of discoursive configurations and, so to speak, their *modus operandi.*
—MOTIF; SEMIOTICS, DISCOURSIVE

CONFORMITY
(conformité)

1. In the strict sense of the word, **conformity** means the one-to-one correspondence among the units belonging either to two comparable semiotic objects, or to two planes* or two levels* of language in such a way that, after verification, the units of every rank can be identified both as isomorphic and isotopic. Such a definition enables us to decide whether we are dealing or not with monoplanar* semiotics (or a system of symbols* in the terminology of L. Hjelmslev). Nonconformity, on the contrary, characterizes bi-planar* semiotics (or semiotics proper, according to Hjelmslev).

2. In its broadest sense, the concept of conformity approaches that of equivalence*: certain criteria of conformity, not all, are retained.
—ADEQUATION

CONFRONTATION
(confrontation)

1. Located at the figurative* level, **confrontation** corresponds to the position of the subject of an utterance of doing,* when the aim of its narrative program* is contrary* or contradictory* to that of the program of the anti-subject. Confrontation thus represents the superposition or meeting of the two narrative* trajectories, each one characterizing one of the subjects s1 or s2; consequently, it forms one of the pivots* of the narrative* schema.

2. Confrontation can be either **polemical** or **contractual,** being manifested in narratives sometimes by a struggle (ending in the domination* of one subject over another), at other times by an exchange* or, more generally, by a contract.* This distinction enables us to recognize two sociological conceptions of interhuman relations (class struggle/social contract) and, according to this criterion, to divide narratives into two main classes.

3. Polemical confrontation, on the discoursive plane, corresponds to the first of the three constituent utterances of the test.

—POLEMIC; CONTRACT; TEST

CONJUNCTION
(conjonction)

1. In traditional grammar, the term **conjunction** designates a class of morphemes* used in order to establish the relation of "conjunction" among various units at the syntagmatic level. Two sub-classes are distinguished: the conjunctions of **coordination** and those of **subordination.** It can be said that the conjunctions of subordination establish hypotactic* relations among utterances. Generative* and transformational grammar accounts for these relations by means of embedding* rules. On the other hand, the conjunctions of coordination point out, often emphatically, the relations of combination among syntagmatic units belonging to the same level.*

2. In research aimed at defining the concept of elementary structure* as the relation between two terms, it appears that this relation is both a conjunction and a disjunction. In other words, it is simultaneously a relation of combination (of the type "both . . . and") and a relation of opposition* (of the type "either . . . or") and thus it gathers together the relational properties which define each of the two axes of language (the syntagmatic and the paradigmatic axes).

The more abstract category "identity"/"alterity" appears to us to be the most adequate for expressing the universal* character of the relation (consequently the use of the terms conjunction and disjunction in this sense seems superfluous).

3. In narrative semiotics, the term conjunction needs to be kept in order to designate paradigmatically one of the two terms (the other being disjunction*) of the category **junction.** On the syntagmatic plane this category is the function* (*i.e.,* the relation between subject and object) through which utterances of state are constituted. By contrast to what is found on the paradigmatic plane, where conjunction and disjunction* are contradictory, on the syntagmatic plane the relation of these two terms can be represented by the following semiotic square:

Non-disjunction between a subject and an object* of value (keeping something for oneself) is to be distinguished from conjunction (having something).

—JUNCTION

CONNECTOR, ISOTOPIC
(connecteur d'isotopies)

1. An **isotopic connector** (also termed **shifter**) is a unit of the discoursive level, which introduces either a single reading* or several different ones. This phenomenon corresponds, for instance, to the "rhetorical coding" found by Lévi-Strauss in myths which simultaneously play upon the "literal meaning" and the "figurative meaning." In the case of pluri-isotopy,* it is the polysemic* character of the discoursive unit functioning as connector which permits the superposition of different isotopies.

2. From a typological perspective, one can distinguish, for instance, between (among others) **metaphoric connectors,** which permit the passage from an abstract* (or thematic*) isotopy to a figurative* one—the relation is then oriented: what is said on the second isotopy

can be interpreted on the first, and not vice-versa—and **anti-phrastic connectors,** which manifest on a second isotopy terms which are contrary* to those expected on the first one, etc. According to their position in the text's linearity,* **antecedent connectors,** which explicitly indicate the beginning of a new reading, can be opposed to **subsequent connectors,** which demand a back-reading.* Thus, for instance, when the two friends (in Maupassant's tale) are executed by the Prussian firing squad, their bodies fall one upon the other in the figure of the "cross"; from this figure, a new figurative isotopy—concerning Christian representation—can then be recognized. Not only are the death (with "blood gushing forth") and the previous silence of the two friends comparable to the last moments of Jesus, but the whole first part of the story as well (which includes the roles of "fishermen" and the figure of "fish") can be related, by back-reading, to the community of Christ's disciples.
—ISOTOPY; PLURI-ISOTOPY; BACK-READING; METAPHOR

CONNOTATION
(connotation)

1. A term is said to be **connotative** if, when one of the features of the concept considered in terms of its comprehension* is named, that term points to the concept as a whole (*cf.* J. S. Mill). Since the feature(s) taken into consideration has(have) been selected either through a subjective choice, or because of social convention, **connotation** is a process which it is difficult to define with precision. This explains why it has given rise to such a diversity of definitions and why the use of this term is often confusing.

2. From a semantic perspective, connotation could be interpreted as the establishment of a relation among one or more semes* located on a surface* level and the semene* to which they belong, which must be read at a deeper level (*cf.* deep structure*). Their connotation is akin to metonymy, the well-known rhetorical figure. The relation established by connotation could be either hypotactic* or hyponymic.* It would then be a case of the so-called oblique definition,* studied elsewhere.

3. In his typology of semiotic systems, Hjelmslev made room for a specific class of **connotative semiotics.*** The only common point between the connotation of concepts (located at the lexematic level) and the languages of connotation (which overdetermine discourses) is found in the rather intuitive recognition of a gap or of an oblique relation which would exist between a primary, "denotative," signified,* and a secondary, "connotative," signified. However, in order to postulate the existence of a plane of connotative content,* one needs to introduce the semiotic function (or semiosis*) which would connect it to an expression* plane. The latter cannot be considered as identical to the expression plane which is correlated with the denotative signified, for that would leave only one content plane. Thus Hjelmslev postulates an expression plane which is itself a semiotic system (for example, a natural language). The connotative semiotic system would then be a particular kind of meta-semiotic system.

4. The main difficulties appear when an attempt is made at analyzing such a connotative semiotic system. In order to identify the units of the connotative signifier, one must begin with the description of the semiotic system in question, viewed

as "denotative": the units which will be found here can, alone, eventually be bi-valent and belong simultaneously to both semiotic systems. Account must then also be taken of the fact that the role of the connotative signifiers can be fulfilled by the signs* of the semiotic system under analysis as well as by the figures* of its expression and/or content planes, and also by the two substances* which constitute its form* (for example, a Southern accent is recognized through its phonetic, and not phonological particularities). Moreover, not all the units of these various planes have connotative properties. As a result, the listing of the signifier-connotators can be performed only by extraction*—a process which, according to Hjelmslev, is not scientific. Thus he classifies connotative semiotic systems among non-scientific* semiotic systems.

5. Yet, the existence of semiotic connotations cannot be doubted, and their importance has been clearly shown in the work of R. Barthes. For him, "ideology would be, after all, the form of the connotation signifieds, while rhetoric would be the form of the connotators." The urgent need for a theory of connotative semiotic systems is thus apparent.

6. While, in Hjelmslev's perspective, the description of a connotative semiotic system must begin by the study of its expression plane (a study which, because of the principle of commutation,* would be expected progressively to elucidate the form of the connotative content), one wonders whether theoretical research should not first be focused upon the substance of this content. This would then allow us to begin by the identification of the main topical spaces where connotative activity takes place. A socio-semiotic* approach (cf. the "external linguistics" of F. de Saussure) which would elaborate tentative models of the possible loci of the manifestations of connotation, would help better to circumscribe the connotative phenomenon and to show, in part, the interrelations among **social connotations.** Such research would have to deal with and integrate problems concerning the categorization* of the world (the hypothesis of Humboldt, Sapir, and Whorf), concerning the functions of language according to Jakobson, concerning genre* typology, etc. Simultaneously, psycho-semiotics would need to deal with **individual connotations,** as Hjelmslev himself suggested. The inverse approach, elucidation of the connotative forms, would be taken up only at a later stage of research.

—DENOTATION; SEMIOTIC SYSTEM AND/OR PROCESS; SEMIOLOGY; PSYCHO-SEMIOTICS; SOCIO-SEMIOTICS

CONSEQUENCE
(conséquence)

In narrative semiotics, the term **consequence** designates the last of the three utterances constituting a test. Situated on the axis of consecution, after confrontation* and domination,* consequence (which presupposes them) can be either negative (in the case of deprivation,* which is manifested either as renunciation,* if it is reflexive, or as dispossession* if it is transitive) or positive (acquisition,* which can take two forms: attribution* and appropriation*).—TEST

CONSTANT
(constante)

The term **constant,** synonymous with invariant,* is used in semiotics to designate an entity* the presence* of which is the necessary condition of another entity to which it is linked by a relation.* The constant is thus the presupposed term of a binary structure, while the variable is the presupposing term.—VARIABLE; PRESUPPOSITION

CONSTITUENT
(constituant)

1. In linguistics a **constituent** is any unit*—from the morpheme* to the syntagm*—which participates in a larger construction.

2. **Immediate constituent** analysis. With the aim of elaborating the taxonomic part of linguistics, American linguists, following Bloomfield, have proceeded to the segmentation* of sentences into units according to the hierarchical order of the elements. The segmentation, of a binary* type, starts with the highest level (the nominal syntagm and the verbal syntagm, for instance, can be the immediate constituents of the highest level) and proceeds toward the lowest level at which the morphemes as ultimate units are identified (for instance, "fighter" includes two immediate constituents: "fight" and "er"). This kind of segmentation makes use of the procedures of substitution* and reduction,* and presupposes all the contributions of the distributional* method. Thus immediate constituent analysis proposes the structural description* of the utterance,* which can be represented as a syntagmatic tree* or by means of parentheses.* It is based, as is the distributional approach, on the principle of linearity* (as its name indicates).

As such, immediate constituent analysis is confronted by the problem of **discontinuous constituent** (for instance, "(I) do (not) like . . . "). Furthermore, it is unable to account for the phenomena of ambiguity.* Even though it has been severely criticized, it has served as the starting point for generative* and transformational grammar, which considers, perhaps a bit too hastily, that the taxonomic stage of research in linguistics is over.

CONSTITUTIVE MODEL
(constitutionnel [modèle-])

The elementary structure* of signification can be viewed as a **constitutive model** in that it represents the *ab quo* domain of the overall generative trajectory.*—STRUCTURE; MODEL; SQUARE, SEMIOTIC

CONSTRAINT
(contrainte)

1. In general terms, **constraint** is understood as any limitation of individual freedom resulting from a person's involvement in social life. In a more specific sense, **semiotic constraints** can be tentatively defined as a set of obligations—voluntary or involuntary, conscious or unconscious—to which a person is submitted by virtue of participation in one or another semiotic practice.* In an individualistic and voluntarist perspective, constraint is metaphorically identifiable with accepting the "rules of the game": the sociological approach to language, in the European tradition following Durkheim, restricts itself to defining constraint as a "social fact."

2. The contractual participation of the individual in the practice of constructed semiotic systems (such as group games or documentary lan-

guages) does not seem—at least not at first glance—to raise too many problems. By contrast, it is quite difficult to specify a person's relationship to natural* semiotic systems. Without raising the question of knowing whether the basic semiotic structures are innate or acquired—which is not directly a semiotic question—it must nevertheless be recognized that human beings "enter language" and that they are inscribed in it without being able to escape from it. All the attempts to escape from language which can be imagined, necessarily take place in the framework of these constraints. Consequently it can be said, from a modal* perspective, that semiotic constraints belong neither to the *wanting-to-do*, nor to the *having-to-do* of the subject, but much rather to a *wanting-to-have-to-be*.

3. In the semiotic perspective, it might be proper to distinguish two aspects of this notion of constraint: the very commitment which characterizes the participation of the subject in a semiotic system; and that to which the subject is committed by using this semiotic system. Commitment is, indeed, what is fundamentally presupposed by the structure of interpersonal communication.* The difficulty one experiences when attempting to name this structure (for Jakobson, the phatic function; "charity" or "good will" for certain logicians; "sympathy" for some philosophers, etc.) clearly shows that we are confronting a concept that is perhaps undefinable. We consider it as an **implicit contract,*** with the thought that a typology of intersubjective relations—from "good will" contractual structures* to polemical* structures—should progressively clarify the understanding of this inter-human relation.

4. By taking on the attitude of semiotic "charity," the subject is committed to practice a kind of "etiquette," whatever its name might be. The subject just aims at practicing a sort of "etiquette," at producing and recognizing differences,* at postulating and apprehending compatibilities* and incompatibilities. Understood in this way, semiotic constraints are nothing else than the minimal conditions necessary for the production and the apprehension of signification.*

—NORM; CONTRACT

CONSTRUCTION
(construction)

1. **Constructed,** as synonymous with artificial, is opposed to natural and refers to human action transforming nature.*

2. In a narrower sense, the term **construction** designates a programmed semiotic activity belonging to the theoretical realm and meeting the conditions of scientificness.* Thus, in order to be in a position to describe a semiotic system, one needs to construct an appropriate metalanguage (involving models, procedures, etc.).

3. On the epistemological plane, construction and structure* are often opposed. Structures are considered to be immanent and thus call for analytical procedures of recognition* and of description.* By contrast, construction is considered as the independent and arbitrary doing of the scientific subject. In fact, such a polarized distinction is excessive. The two terms are related because they merely designate different focalizations*: in the case of construction, the scientific doing is considered from the perspective of the enunciator*; in the case of de-

scription, it is considered from the perspective of the enunciatee. We are dealing here with a gnoseological set of problems according to which knowing subject and object of knowledge are necessarily bound up together. In the context of semiotic theory, the description of the object, which progressively reveals the immanent* order of the significations, cannot ultimately be distinguished from the construction by the collective epistemic subject of a language aimed at accounting for it. In both cases we are dealing with human beings and their signifying universe.
—IMMANENCE

CONTENT
(contenu)

1. **Content** is for L. Hjelmslev one of the two planes* of language (or, more generally, of any semiotic system), the other being the expression plane. The union of the two planes (or semiosis*) accounts for the existence of "meaningful" utterances* (sentences or discourses). The term content is thus synonymous with Saussure's overall signified.* The difference between the two linguistic theories only appears in the way in which linguistic form* is conceived. For Saussure linguistic form is explained by the indissoluble link between signifier and signified, which "inform" each other and produce, by dint of the union of two substances,* a single linguistic form. By contrast Hjelmslev distinguishes on each of the planes of language an autonomous form and an autonomous substance. It is the union of the two forms, of the expression and of the substance—and not of two substances as for Saussure—which constitutes, in his view, semiotic form.

2. This theoretical difference involves important consequences. For Saussure, semiology* is the study of "sign systems" because for him signs are the locus of the manifestation of semiotic form. By contrast, for Hjelmslev, the level of signs needs to be analyzed only in order to allow the study of a realm beyond the signs, the realm of figures* (of the expression and of the content plane). The plane of the **content form** which can then be analyzed (as the figures of the expression are analyzed by phonology*) becomes consequently the realm of semantics* and is the epistemological basis of the latter's autonomy. The semiotics derived from Hjelmslev's theory thus does not correspond to the semiology envisioned by Saussure. A semiotic system is neither merely a "system" (because it is at once system* and process*) nor a "system of signs" (because it deals with units—semic and phemic categories*—which are smaller than the signs and which belong to either one of the two planes of language but not to both as in the case of signs). When the content plane is considered in and of itself, its study in the Saussurian tradition takes the form of a lexicology,* while for Hjelmslev's successors it can be the domain of semantics.

3. **Content analysis,** viewed as a technique derived from sociology and psychosociology, was more or less developed in parallel with linguistic research, but without any real link with it. The linguist can only be dismayed by its basic procedure, which involves applying to the text (or to the corpus of texts) a grid of *a priori* categories which often do not even obey principles of logico-taxonomic organization. Attempts at

quantifying certain data, such as calculations of frequencies, which are closely related to linguistic statistics, or methods of "evaluative association" (Osgood) which use factorial analysis, merely provide partial results that cannot be clearly interpreted. Therefore, the present tendency, aimed at progressively transforming content analysis into discourse analysis—whether it is the analysis of the uttered discourse in itself, or an analysis dealing with data of the enunciation,* which can be explicited*—should be encouraged.
—EXPRESSION; FORM; SIGNIFIED; SUBSTANCE

CONTEXT
(contexte)

1. The **context** is the entire text* which precedes and/or accompanies the syntagmatic unit under consideration and upon which the signification depends. The context can be explicit*; it is then called **linguistic.** It can also be implicit*; in this case it is qualified as **extra-linguistic** or **situational.** The implicit context can be called upon in the semantic interpretation, because (a) the situational context can always be made explicit, since it is a living natural language producing an unlimited text (Hjelmslev); (b) the implicit elements of a linguistic text can eventually be reestablished through the homologation* of this text with the non-linguistic text which belongs to the semiotic system of the natural world.*

2. In his model of communication,* R. Jakobson posits the **context** as one of the factors of the linguistic activity and identifies it with the referent (it is the referential function* of language). Whether it is verbal or can be made so, the context is con-

sidered as necessary for making the message explicit.

3. The phrase **contextual semes*** (or classemes) is used to designate the semes or bundle of semes which are recurrent* in the unit under study and in its context. The contextual semes participate in the composition of a sememe* (which can be related with the "word in its context").
—REFERENT; WORLD, NATURAL; CLASSEME

CONTINGENCY
(contingence)

The term **contingency** designates the modal structure corresponding, from the perspective of its syntaxic definition, to the modal predicate *not-having-to* governing the utterance of state *being*. It presupposes, on the semiotic square* of the alethic modalities, the existence of necessity, of which it is the negation. As a term in logic, contingency is semiotically ambiguous because it also designates the modal structure *being-able-not-to-be*.—ALETHIC MODALITIES

CONTINUOUS
(continu)

1. The undefinable category* *continuous/discontinuous* must be included in the epistemological* inventory of the "primitive" terms. In semiotics, any entity* is considered to be continuous prior to analysis (*cf.* Saussure's "nebula") which, alone, permits the construction of discontinuous or discrete units.

2. In discoursive semiotics, the opposition *continuous/discontinuous* is manifested as an aspectual category which subdivides the durative* aspect into *continuous durative/ discontinuous durative.*
—DISCONTINUOUS; DISCRETE; UNIT; ASPECTUALIZATION

CONTRACT
(contrat)

1. In a very general sense, **contract** can be understood as the fact of establishing, of "contracting" an intersubjective relationship which has as its effect the modification of the status (being and/or seeming) of each of the subjects involved. Even though this intuitive notion cannot be defined rigorously, we need nevertheless to posit the term contract so as to determine progressively what are the minimal conditions under which the establishment of "entering into a contract" between two subjects takes place. These conditions can be viewed as being presupposed by the establishment of the structure of semiotic communication.* It is indeed necessary to recognize, hidden under the contract, this "phatic* communication" which constitutes the necessary and preliminary undergirding for any communication and which seems to involve both a tension (a well-disposed or a mistrustful expectation*) and a relaxing (as a kind of response to the expectation). Indeed, the establishment of the intersubjective structure is at once, on the one hand, an opening toward the future and toward possibilities for action, and, on the other hand, a constraint* which somehow limits the freedom of each of the subjects. We propose to use the term **implicit contract** to designate this set of preliminary components on which the intersubjective structure is based.

2. In the semiotic perspective, it does not seem appropriate to opt for either one of the two opposed ideological attitudes which consider social life respectively as made up of confrontations and struggles or as based upon "charity" and "well-intentioned" conventions. On the contrary, the structural approach demands that both the positive and the negative terms of a category* be considered together. In other words, the polemical* structures (given *a priori* or resulting from breaches) must be viewed as constituting the opposite pole of the contractual structures (*stricto sensu*). Actually, these two types of structures belong to the same contractual organization of intersubjectivity.

3. At first glance, two kinds of contract can be distinguished. A contract is said to be **unilateral** when one of the subjects makes a "proposal" and the other makes a "commitment" to that proposal. A contract is **bilateral** or **reciprocal** when "proposals" and "commitments" are interwoven. Yet such a definition, borrowed from common dictionaries, shows the modal* nature of the contractual structure. The "proposal" can be interpreted as the *wanting* of subject S1 that the subject S2 do (or be) something. "Commitment" is nothing else than the *wanting* or the *having-to* of S2 taking upon itself the suggested doing. In this perspective, the contract appears as an organization of reciprocal cognitive activities which bring about the transformation of the modal competence* of the subjects involved.

4. The preceding remarks may seem to be inspired by philosophical or sociological preoccupations. But this is not the case. They are developed exclusively and above all on the basis of a growing number of concrete analyses of discourses, and, more specifically, of narrative discourses. Such discourses involve numerous descriptions of contractual structures and thus they constitute the main source that semioticians can exploit in their effort to establish a typology of contractual structure. Thus, for instance, the

canonic narrative* schema derived from V. Propp's descriptions appears, in one of its aspects, as the syntagmatic projection of the contractual structure. In this narrative schema, the contract, established from the beginning between the Sender* and the subject-Receiver, governs the overall narrative development. What follows it in the narrative appears as its execution* by the two contracting parties: the trajectory of the subject, which is the Receiver's contribution, is followed by the sanction,* both pragmatic* (retribution*) and cognitive (recognition*) by the Sender. It is clear that this syntagmatic organization, based upon the articulation of the contract, can be broken up into a series of contractual units such as the establishment, the breaking, the re-establishment, and the execution of the contract.

5. The concept of contract must be related to that of **exchange,*** the theory of which has been elaborated by M. Mauss. In such a case, the contract appears, at first, as a delayed exchange: the distance which separates its conclusion from its execution is filled up by a tension which is both like a credit and a debit, like a confidence and an obligation. Yet a closer look shows that a simple operation involving the exchange of two objects of value is not a mere pragmatic activity. Rather, it takes place essentially on the cognitive* level. For indeed, in order that the exchange might take place, it is necessary that the two parties be assured of the "value" of the value of the object to be received as counterpart for the object given. In other words, it is necessary that a **fiduciary* contract** (often preceded by a persuasive* and by an interpretive* doing of both the subjects) be established prior to the actual pragmatic operation.

6. Such a fiduciary contract can be called **utterative** in so far as it is inscribed within the utterance-discourse and as it involves pragmatic values.* Yet it is manifested as well on the level of the structure of enunciation* where it is seen to be an **enunciative contract** (a term proposed by F. Nef), or a **veridiction* contract,** since it aims at establishing a fiduciary convention between the enunciator* and the enunciatee involving the veridictory status (on saying-the-truth) of the utterance-discourse. The fiduciary contract which is thus established can be based upon evidence* (*i.e.,* upon a self-evident certainty*) or it can be preceded by a persuasive doing (causing-to-believe) of the enunciator to which the enunciatee responds by way of an interpretive doing (a believing).
—CONSTRAINT; EXCHANGE; NARRATIVE SCHEMA; VERIDICTION

CONTRADICTION
(contradiction)

1. The relation of **contradiction** is the relation* which exists between two terms* of the binary category* *assertion/negation.** Since the names "relations," "term," "assertion," and "negation" refer to non-defined and non-definable concepts,* the above definition is located on the deepest and most abstract level of the semiotic network.

2. Contradiction is the relation which is established, as a result of the cognitive act of negation,* between two terms of which the previously-posited first one is made absent* by this operation while the second term becomes present.*

Thus it is a relation of presupposition* at the level of the posited contents*: the presence of one term presupposes the absence of the other, and vice-versa.

3. As one of the constitutive relations of the semantic category, contradiction defines the two schemas* (s1 - s̄1, s2 - s̄2) of the semiotic square. The terms of a schema are said to be contradictory to each other.
—SQUARE, SEMIOTIC

CONTRARIETY
(contrariété)

1. **Contrariety** is the relation* of reciprocal presupposition* which exists between the two terms* of a semantic axis* when the presence* of one of them presupposes that of the other, and, conversely, when the absence of the one presupposes that of the other.

2. Contrariety is the constitutive relation of the semantic category.* The two terms of a semantic axis can be said to be **contrary** if, and only if, the contradictory term of each of them implies the contrary of the other. The semantic axis is then named axis of contraries.
—SQUARE, SEMIOTIC; PRESUPPOSITION

CONTRAST
(contraste)

Certain linguists use the term **contrast** in order to designate the relation* of the type "both . . . and" which compatible units of the same rank have among themselves on the syntagmatic axis. This axis is then called the **axis of contrast** so as to be distinguished from the paradigmatic axis or axis of opposition.* These names can be homologated with axis of combination/axis of selection* (Jakobson) or with the pair com-

binatory function/distinctive* function. It should be noted that the relation of contrast (called by L. Hjelmslev "relation") is solely discriminatory* and does not imply any *a priori* judgement concerning the type of specific relation (for example, solidarity,* selection, or combination, in Hjelmslev) that the units have among themselves.—COMBINATORY PRINCIPLE or ARRANGEMENT; COMBINATION; SYNTAGMATIC

CONVERSION
(conversion)

1. L. Hjelmslev designates by the term **conversion** a set of procedures which corresponds—to a certain extent—to the concept of transformation* elaborated later on in generative* grammar. The Danish linguist uses the term conversion in order to account for the fact that natural language—or, better, a natural language state*—is not, or at least is not merely, a static structure. For indeed it also involves a dynamic aspect, having certain "transformations" which, because they are found within a state, should not be assimilated to the properly diachronic* transformations that affect the natural language state as a whole. As illustration of this point, Hjelmslev proposes the following metaphor: When Danes are drafted for military service, they remain Danes even though they are "transformed" into soldiers.

2. We use the term conversion in its Hjelmslevian sense, but apply it to the syntagmatic and discursive dimension of semiotics. As a consequence, this concept is closely related to discourse* understood and defined as an in-depth superimposing of levels. This way of envisioning discourse permits the elaboration of

autonomous descriptions—on the syntactic and semantic planes—of each of the levels of depth which correspond to the various domains proposed in the model of the generative* trajectory. Such a view of discourse necessarily raises the problem of the passage from one level to another and of the procedures to be set up in order to account for these conversions. It is clear that our approach is diametrically opposed to that of generative grammar, which first sets out more or less refined rules of transformation* and then has to struggle to define the nature and the number of levels of depth—for instance, it does not know exactly where semantic interpretation* fits. Our point is that the rules of conversion can only be conceived on the basis of equivalences; in other words, it must be admitted that two or more syntactic forms (or two or more semantic formulations) can be referred to a constant topic. Let us note furthermore that equivalence is not identity.* It is necessary to keep in mind that the generation of signification, by introducing new articulations at each stage of its trajectory, brings about at the same time an "enrichment" or an "augmentation" of meaning, since signification* is nothing else than articulation. Consequently, any conversion must be viewed both as equivalence and as surplus of signification.

3. The identification of the procedures of conversion and the establishment of the rules which would formulate them have barely begun, because research was until now primarily devoted to the study of the principles and forms of discursive organization. Nevertheless one can see, for instance, how operations* upon relational terms,* which are at the basis of fundamental syntax,*

can be converted, in passing to the narrative syntax, into utterances of doing* governing the utterances of state* (in which the transformations modify the junctions*: disjunctions being converted into conjunctions, and vice-versa). Similarly, in the semantic component, one can see how the terms of the semantic categories* are converted into values* invested in the syntactic objects, and how the syntactic objects—semantically empty loci—can be converted into figures* and into icons* of the world. As can be expected, the elaboration of conversion rules will be one of the fundamental tests of the coherence of semiotic theory.

—TRANSFORMATION; EQUIVALENCE; GENERATIVE TRAJECTORY; ANTHROPOMORPHIC SYNTAX

CO-OCCURRENCE
(co-occurrence)

Closely related to contrast,* the term **co-occurrence** designates the presence on the syntagmatic* axis of at least two semiotic entities* which are compatible with each other. This concept—which is somewhat vague since it does not specify the nature of the relation* among the co-occurrent terms—is at the very basis of distributional* analysis, for it provides the means to determine the settings or contexts of the elements which are set out.

CO-REFERENCE
(co-référence)

1. **Co-reference** is the relation existing between two linguistic signs* (whether identical or different), located at two places (whether contiguous or separated) of the spoken chain,* when these signs refer to the same extra-linguistic object. As is clear, this definition is linked to a

conception of the referent according to which the linguistic units would be merely labels of the natural world.

2. Insofar as one dissociates natural language* from the natural world* as semiotic system (a view which demands, of course, that the problem of inter-semioticity be raised, in which the referent is nothing more than the correlation between two semiotic systems), co-reference as such vanishes, making room for **anaphora**. Thus, for instance, the relation pronoun/antecedent is reduced to a syntactic anaphora; while this type of anaphora can easily be interpreted by generative* grammar, it is not so easy for generative grammar to interpret semantic anaphora (for instance, when a name* takes on a former definition) because no formal syntactic index is there to justify the relation of partial identity between two terms. More generally, by definition the anaphorization procedures which guarantee the discoursive isotopy* (relations between sentences) are difficult to integrate in a phrase*-structure linguistics.
—REFERENT; ANAPHORA

CORPUS
(corpus)

1. In the tradition of descriptive* linguistics, a **corpus** is understood as a finite set of utterances* constituted for the sake of analysis. The completed analysis is supposed to account for this set in an exhaustive and adequate way.

2. The elaboration of the concept of corpus is an attempt at defining rigorously a natural language as object of knowledge. The demands of exhaustivity* (as a rule for the constitution of the set and an instruction for the analyst) and of adequation* (as a condition for the

"truth" of the performed analysis) are set forth in order to guarantee the scientificness* of the description.* (For indeed, such a description is applied to "dead languages" and to languages without writing and for which it is difficult or even impossible to verify or to complement the available data.) This attempt is deficient because of its positivist presuppositions which can be seen in the way in which the relation between the knowing subject and the object of knowledge is determined: the corpus is viewed as "objective," as a thing in itself which has its own laws, whereas contemporary epistemology gives at least as much importance to the subject as constructing his/her own object.

3. It is against this epistemological background and taking into account the historical conditions (the interest of linguists shifting toward living languages) that several years ago the "anti-corpus" campaign developed under the leadership of Chomsky's followers. By emphasizing the constructing character of scientific doing, generative grammar*—which is called itself projective—proposed to invert, at least in appearance, the procedure. It claimed to elaborate, on the basis of a small number of data, a set of rules* which could be projected onto a larger set of utterances (either realized or potential). Such an approach, which gives priority to metalanguage over against the object-language, corresponds to the broad trends of contemporary science. Yet the "small number of data" which permits the analyst to construct a model,* is nothing other than a limited representative corpus constituted in a more or less intuitive way. Furthermore, the criteria of grammaticality* and of acceptability* which govern the projection of the rules do not seem more valid

than those of exhaustivity and of adequation that they are supposed to replace. What is actually at stake is the epistemological evaluation of two attitudes viewed as wholes, and not a secondary dispute over terminology. As J. Lyons emphasizes about the concept of corpus, there is no basic contradiction between the descriptive and the generative approaches.

4. The problem of corpus has to be raised in a different way when it is no longer a matter of collections of sentences but of collections of discourses, and when the linguist has not only a syntactic goal but also a semantic one. Corpus as an operational* concept can again be used in the implicit "generativist" sense. Thus one can speak of **syntagmatic corpora** (sets of texts of an author) or of **paradigmatic corpora** (sets of variants of a folktale), while taking into account the fact that they are never closed nor exhaustive, but merely representative and that the models that will be used in an attempt to account for them are hypothetical, projective, and predictive.

5. Semantic* analysis, as far as the concept of corpus is concerned, is in a quasi-paradoxical situation. While the choice of a limited, open, and representative corpus is for generative grammar a deliberate theoretical position, it is presented as a necessity for semantic analysis. Whether it be a case of the study of a semantic field* or of a given discourse, the corpus which is the starting point of the analysis is always tentative: the model constructed is indeed rarely coextensive with the initial corpus, and the linguistic objects taken up by the model are in part to be found outside of the boundaries of the corpus.

6. It might not be impossible to propose a number of practical rules for a "good choice" of corpus. Elsewhere we have attempted to define the concept of **representativity,** envisaging two ways to reach it: the representativity of the corpus can be obtained either by statistic sampling or by saturation of the model. In the latter case, the model, constructed on the basis of a segment chosen intuitively, is later on applied for confirmation, complement, or rejection to other segments until all the data are used (this procedure is related, as is clear, to the projections of rules).
—GENERATION;   LEXICON; VERIFICATION

CORRELATION
(corrélation)

1. L. Hjelmslev uses the term **correlation** to designate the relation "either . . . or" which exists among the elements of a paradigm,* by contrast with the term relation (of the "both . . . and" form) reserved for the syntagmatic* chain. Function* is the generic term which subsumes correlation and relation.

2. Because the term relation is commonly used in a very general sense, the term correlation most often designates in semiotics the relation among relations, whether they belong to paradigms or to syntagms.
—RELATION

COSMOLOGICAL
(cosmologique)

1. When the set of semic categories* which articulate the semantic universe* is subdivided into two subsets—the set of exteroceptive* categories and that of interoceptive* categories—the classificatory category itself (the category *exteroceptivity/interoceptivity*) must be viewed as a classematic* category which can allow the establishment of a distinc-

tion between two classes of discourses* (or between two isotopies* for the reading of a single discourse). Yet a terminology still had to be found, of which the names,* however arbitrary they might be, would not hinder semiotic research by their connotations. It has been proposed, going back to the work of Ampère and Cournot, to give the name **cosmological** to the discourse or the discursive dimension which is entirely undergirded by the classeme *exteroceptivity*, by contrast with the noological* discourse or discursive dimension characterized by the classeme *interoceptivity*. Thus a distinction could be made between discourses about the "world" and discourses about the "mind."

2. This opposition is closely related to another dichotomy, resulting from reflection on the status of mythical discourses. In them two dimensions have been recognized. The practical* dimension of the discourse recounts events and actions of human beings. Beneath this practical dimension is a mythical* dimension, which under the guise of these figurative* appearances, deals with abstract* problems involving the fate of humans and of the culture in which they live.

3. Homologating these two dichotomies was problematic, until new developments in discursive semiotics clarified the situation. At the present stage of research, it seems that the main reason for the confusion was the non-distinction between two different sets of issues. The first concerns the recognition of the levels* of depth in the generative* trajectory of the discourse. The figurative* discursive component corresponds approximately to the previously recognized practical dimension, but only accounts for a part of cosmological discourses (which can be figurative but also

thematic* and abstract as, for instance, in the case of discourses in the social sciences). The distinction between the pragmatic* and cognitive* dimensions is quite different. These dimensions are indeed viewed as distinct and hierarchically ordered levels on which are located the actions and events described by the discourses.

4. The qualifying adjective **cosmological** is, therefore, to be translated either as figurative or as pragmatic, according to its use.
—EXTEROCEPTIVITY; FIGURATIVE; PRAGMATIC

CREATIVITY
(créativité)

1. **Creativity** is a psychological concept which N. Chomsky has introduced into linguistics, giving it a precise definition: the faculty of producing and understanding new sentences* as a result of the recursive* character of syntactic constructions. Understood in this way, creativity must be considered to be a property of the speaking subject's competence. The operational* character of this concept is obviously weak or non-existent. Since the combinatory* possibilities of a natural language are quasi-infinite, this roughly amounts to saying that the "human mind" is creative. Yet the very introduction of this single term into linguistics has already had devastating effects in semiology, where it characterizes many kinds of psychologizing excesses. It is rather on the basis of the incompatibilities between categories* and between structures,* on the basis of the constraints which social epistemes impose, that one can hope progressively to define originality.*

2. Creativity could also be conceived as the result of the interaction of natural language (social) and speech* (individual). The individual

variations (phonological, syntactic, semantic variations) accumulated and spread out, seem able to account for modifications on the level of natural language. The variations belonging to performance* would then explain the diachronic transformations* of competence.
—ORIGINALITY, SEMANTIC; IDIOLECT; COMPETENCE

CULTURE
(culture)

1. From the semiotic point of view, the concept of **culture** can be viewed as coextensive with the concept of the semantic* universe,* as related to a given socio-semiotic community. The project of a **semiotics of culture** (as proposed by J. Lotman, for instance) has thus the task of dealing with the semantic universe—and, primarily, with its two macro-semiotic* components, viz., natural language* and natural world.* It has also to deal with the semantic universe as an object-semiotic system in order to construct a meta-semiotic system termed "culture." This is a huge task, since it would correspond to the description of the whole set of axiologies, ideologies, and signifying social practices. Consequently, research is usually limited to those constructions—more modest in scope and more ambitious in terms of quality—which constitute the descriptions of epistemes.* In such cases epistemes are viewed either as hierarchies of semiotic systems or as connotative meta-semiotic* systems.

2. The concept of culture is both relative and universal. While in most instances, culture is viewed as belonging to an autonomous linguistic community, there exist also **cultural regions** which transcend linguistic frontiers, as well as a world with **human culture,** characterized by certain scientific and technological practices and even, in part, by common ideologies. A distinction between micro-societies (or archaic societies) and macro-societies (or developed societies) provides a basis for two different approaches: an ethnosemiotic* approach and a sociosemiotic* approach.

3. Lévi-Straussian anthropology has introduced and generalized the use of the *nature/culture* dichotomy (which leaves little room for the seemingly more specific opposition *culture/barbarity* proposed more recently in U.S.S.R. by Lotman). This *nature/culture* dichotomy must be used with caution. It is clear that in itself the category is semantic and cultural since it is placed directly in specific cultural contexts. In this sense nature is not nature in itself but rather what is viewed in a given culture as belonging to nature, by opposition to what is perceived as culture. It is, so to speak, a "cultural nature." On the other hand, the category *nature/culture* must be viewed as a metalinguistic conceptual category belonging to anthropological theory (which needs to be evaluated as a whole). As such this category has an operational* value which permits the introduction of a first set of relations when one studies a given culture.

4. It is in this latter sense that we adopt Lévi-Strauss' dichotomy. We view, *a priori,* the opposition *nature/culture* as the first elementary investment of the social semantic universe—in the same way that the category *life/death* characterizes the individual semantic universe. Thus the category *nature/culture* can serve as a universal* which can be postulated when one begins the analysis of any micro-universe* of this type.
—UNIVERSE; SOCIO-SEMIOTICS

ABCDEFGHIJKLMN OPQRSTUVWXYZ

DEATH
(mort)

Death is the negative* term of the category *life/death* taken as a hypothetical universal* and capable by this very fact of being used as an initial articulation of the individual semantic universe.* Just like the category *culture/nature,* called upon to play the same role in the collective universe, the category *life/death* is deprived of all other semantic investment.—LIFE; UNIVERSE; STRUCTURE

DECEIVER
(décepteur)

1. **Deceiver**—a term which originally corresponded to "trickster" of native American mythology —designates the subject which can assume several actantial* roles on the veridiction* plane. A deceiver is somebody who passes himself/ herself off as somebody else (for instance, in a folktale from India, a cat wears a set of beads so as to make believe he is a Buddhist monk). Consequently, because of the mask worn, a deceiver can be viewed either in terms of its "being"—it belongs then to the domains of the lie* (since it presents itself as what it is not) but also of the secret* (it hides what it is)—or in terms of its "doing"—vis-a-vis the addressee, it performs a persuasive* cognitive doing.

2. As actor,* the deceiver is also defined by its specific semantic investments, that is, by its thematic roles which it takes on and which refer back to the organization of the undergirding axiological universe. From this point of view, the deceiver seems to be invested with contrary contents which are present in the form of complex* terms. C. Lévi-Strauss had already shown its ambiguous and equivocal character, while emphasizing its "mediating" role. The use of figurative* expression often permits the hiding of one and/or the other pole of the undergirding semantic axis,* which the deceiver sporadically assumes. —DECEPTION

DECEPTION
(déception)

1. **Deception**—or trickery—is a discursive figure* which is located on the cognitive* dimension and corresponds to a logical operation* of negation on the axis of the contradictories* *seeming/non-seeming* of the semiotic square* of the veridictory* modalities. The negation of the term *non-seeming*—starting from false* (defined as the conjunction of *non-being* and *non-seeming*) has the effect of producing the state of lie.* When this operation, carried out by

the deceiver,* is followed by a performance, the syntagmatic unit which is thus constituted is called **deceptive test.** Deception is thus diametrically opposed to camouflage* which, starting from true* and negating *seeming,* produces the state of secret.* When it is followed by a performance, camouflage constitutes a syntagmatic unit with deception, named simulated* test (this is the case, for instance, when the sender hides itself during the qualifying test under the mask of the adversary).

2. As discoursive form, the deceptive test can be invested by different figurative contents (numerous are the forms of trickery!) which are none other than the translation of the thematic* roles that the deceiver takes on.

—VERIDICTORY MODALITIES

DECISION
(décision)

The modal* structure of doing* is called **decision** when the performance is located on the cognitive dimension. It is opposed to execution,* which is located on the pragmatic* dimension.—PERFORMANCE

DECISIVE TEST
(décisive [épreuve—])

A discoursive figure* linked with the canonic narrative* schema, the **decisive test**—located on the pragmatic* dimension—corresponds to the performance. Logically presupposed by the glorifying* test, it itself presupposes the qualifying test. From the point of view of the surface narrative syntax, the decisive test represents the basic narrative program* bringing about the conjunction* of the subject* with the

sought-for object* of value (or object of the quest*).—TEST; PERFORMANCE; NARRATIVE SCHEMA

DECODING
(décodage)

1. In information* theory, **decoding,** designates the operation— or rather the program of operations—which involves recognizing, with the help of a code, the symbolic* elements constituting the message* and identifying them with the discrete units of the natural language* on the basis of which the code has been elaborated.

2. When the term code is used in the linguistic sense, decoding is an operation aiming at recognizing the code on the basis of the message (natural language* on the basis of speech*), at elucidating the (semic or phemic) structure undergirding the two planes* of language, in terms of the message which is manifested at the sign level. In this case, for instance, the number of decoding operations corresponds to the number of semes which compose the signified* of a sign.*

3. Although it applies to phrase-structure linguistics, such a representation is much less adequate in discoursive linguistics, where the term decoding should be replaced by the more appropriate term of interpretation.

—CODE; INTERPRETATION

DEDUCTION
(déduction)

1. The **deductive method** can be viewed as a succession of cognitive operations leading to a "rigorous conclusion." It is traditionally identified with syllogism. As such, deductive method is characterized by its "downward" movement, pass-

ing from the general to the particular, from the class to its components, etc., and, more specifically, by its character as a construction,* which avoids constantly calling upon "experiential data."

2. Two kinds of deductive approach can be distinguished. The **categorico-deductive** approach posits, as a starting point, a set of propositions declared to be true. The **hypothetico-deductive** approach merely presumes that these propositions are true. The latter is usually the approach followed in contemporary semiotic and linguistic research.

3. The traditional opposition between **deduction** and induction seems to be outdated. It is indeed true that the deductive approach presides over the construction of a theory* and over the establishment of its general framework; yet it is well known that limited operations of an inductive character are often used in this process in order to elaborate concepts and models of a wider scope, whose initial data are nothing more than a variable or a particular case (*cf.*, for example, the "corpus" which the generativist sets for his/her use).
—INDUCTION; HYPOTHESIS; CONSTRUCTION

DEEP STRUCTURE
(profonde [structure—])

1. **Deep structures*** are customarily opposed in semiotics to surface* (or superficial) structures. While the latter ostensibly belong to the sphere of the observable, the former are considered as underlying the utterance. However, it will be observed that the term **deep** is tainted with ideological connotations, because of the allusion to depth psychology, and that its mean-

ing is often approximate to that of authenticity.

2. Depth at the same time is linked implicitly to semantics and suggests a certain "quality" of signification and/or the difficulty of deciphering it. While readily admitting that there exist different levels of signification (or different isotopies*), it does not seem that the problem of deep structures can be reduced solely to the semantic dimension nor can semantic interpretation* be linked solely to deep structures, as standard generative* grammar so linked them.

3. In linguistics the distinction made between these two types of structures by generative and transformational grammar clearly leaves aside the meanings alluded to above in (1) and (2). The distinction takes into account only the syntactic* dimension of natural language and is based on the relation of transformation*—or of a series of transformations—which can be recognized (and made explicit under the form of rules*) between two analyses of the same sentence, the more simple and abstract of which is located at the deep level. Clearly this is not to say that in the case of surface structures one is dealing with "real" or realized sentences whereas alone the deep structures would be virtual.* Both depend on the model of competence* (or of natural language*) and are tributaries of the linguistic theory which has formulated them and of the formal* system which has made them explicit.

4. This leads us to say that these two types of structures are metalinguistic* constructions ("deep" and "surface" are two spatial metaphors, relating to the axis of verticality). The one serves to designate the position of departure, the other the point of arrival of a string

of transformations which is presented as a process of generation,* as a generative* trajectory of the whole, within which can be distinguished as many stages and headings as are necessary for the clarity of the explanation. The purely operational* character of these structural stages moreover justifies and authorizes the arranging and the questioning that the theory is then led to carry out.

5. In semiotics the use of this dichotomy is necessarily set in the general theory of the generation of signification. It accounts essentially for both the generative principle according to which complex structures are produced starting from more simple structures (*cf.* combinatory* principle) and the principle of "growth of meaning" according to which every complexification of the structures produces an extension of signification. That is why each domain of the generative trajectory must include the two components, syntax and semantics, (which the expanded generative theory is about to admit). The notion of depth being relative, each domain of the generation of discourse refers back to a "deeper" domain and so on until the deep structure par excellence, which is the elementary structure* of signification, is reached. It is this point from which the generative trajectory originates.

—SURFACE STRUCTURE; LEVEL; STRUCTURE

DEFINITION
(*définition*)

1. Identified with paraphrasing,* **definition** corresponds to a metalinguistic operation (or its result) which either passes from a term to its definition (in expansion) or passes from a syntagm (or a textual unit) to its name.* This movement (with a twofold orientation) is related to the activity of language, which plays on the elasticity* of discourse as a result of the relation *expansion/condensation.*

2. Definition, in the narrow sense, usually is limited to a sentence or syntagm (either nominal or verbal). At least three classes of definitions can be found in the natural languages*: the **taxonomic** definitions, constituted by the set of qualifications*; the **functional** definitions which, by specifying, for instance, what is the use of something, refer to its instrumental value (or to the corresponding instrumental narrative program*); and the **definitions according to generation** which explain objects by their mode of production.* From the semantic point of view, defining a sememe* consists in deconstructing it into semes* and describing their reciprocal relations. Following tradition, B. Pottier posits a distinction between generic semes and specific semes: when the generic basis is too weak or too broad—that is, when for this reason equivalence can only be based upon specific semes—we shall speak of **oblique definition.**

3. As paraphrase, definition is either scientific or non-scientific. Non-scientific paraphrasing characterizes the ordinary functioning of discourse, in which the relation between name and definition is a simple equivalence (partial semic identity*). By contrast, scientific paraphrasing is located on the level of metalanguage* and calls for complete identity.

4. In the broad and scientific sense, definition is ultimately identified with description.* For instance, a narrative is only defined following the elucidation of all the variables and the establishment of

their correlations. This is why, in terms of the practical approach, definition does not precede but follows analysis.

5. For L. Hjelmslev, definition is a partition* (division*) of a sign* content* or of a sign expression.* He proposes to distinguish: (a) **formal definitions,** which do not aim at exhausting "the intensional nature of the objects, or even [at] delimiting them extensionally on all sides, but only [at] anchoring them relatively in respect to other objects, similarly defined or *premised* as basic"; and (b) **operational definitions,** used provisionally: only some of them, at "a latter stage may be transformed into formal definitions."

6. Any theory* involves a number of non-defined (or non-definable) concepts,* or postulates, which are necessary for its organization and its coherence.* Yet, as Hjelmslev reminds us, one needs to "define as much as possible and to introduce premised definitions before those that premise them". The concepts which are at first posited as postulates must at least be integrated in a network of inter-definitions, which guarantees the internal coherence of the system. Thus, for instance, *expression* and *content* are in solidarity,* for they necessarily presuppose each other in the semiotic function.*

—PARAPHRASING

DEICTIC
(déictique)

1. By contrast with anaphoras* (or cataphoras*) which, within the discourse, refer to given units or segments, **deictics** (or **markers,** for E. Benveniste) are linguistic elements which refer to the domain of the enunciation and to its spatio-temporal coordinates: I, here, now.

Thus pronouns ("I," "you") can serve as deictics, as well as adverbs (or adverbial phrases), demonstrative adjectives, etc. It is clear that we are here dealing with **uttered enunciation** as it is manifested by the interplay of procedures of disengagement* and engagement* which simulate the establishment or the abolition of a distance between the discourse's utterance and the domain of its uttering.

2. It can be further noted that the use of deictics permits the referentialization of the discourse—that is, a simulation of the linguistic existence of an external referent which actually is a correlation between the specific semiotic system that natural language* is and the semiotic system of the natural world,* both having their specific organizations.

—ENUNCIATION; REFERENCE; REFERENT

DEIXIS
(déixis)

1. The **deixis** is one of the fundamental dimensions* of the semiotic square; by the relation of implication* it links one of the terms of the axis of the contraries* with the contradictory* of the other contrary term. Two deixes can thus be recognized: the one (s1 - $\overline{s2}$) is called **positive;** the other (s2 - $\overline{s1}$) **negative,** although these qualifications do not involve an axiologic investment. This investment only appears following the projection of the thymic* category, *euphoria/dysphoria,* upon the semiotic square.

2. In a given narrative, temporal positions (now/then) or spatial positions (here/there) can be postulated as **deixes of reference** on the basis of which temporal, aspectual, and spatial categories can develop. Thus, what is sometimes termed the

"time of the narrative" appears as a present (identifiable with a "then" deixis) by relation to which a past and a future can be installed, conforming to the logical system *anteriority/concomitance/posteriority.* —SQUARE; SPATIALIZATION; TEMPORALIZATION; SEMIOTIC

DELEGATION
(délégation)

The concept of **delegation,** very helpful but still poorly defined, refers to a procedure of transfer of competence* which, while specifying the modalities* involved (knowing or being-able-to-do, for instance), confers on the subject concerned a certain margin of autonomy for the performance. In the case of **enunciative delegation,** the procedure thus established can be, at least in part, identified with actantial disengagement.* **Utterative delegation,** for its part, seems to rest upon an implicit contract* and is related, on the figurative* level, to the gift of competence which governs the relations between Sender* and Receiver.

DEMARCATOR
(démarcateur)

The term **demarcator** designates a semiotic entity* which, while keeping its own value, is used as criterion for the delimitation of a syntagmatic unit.—SEGMENTATION; DISJUNCTION

DENIAL
(dénégation)

While negation* is paradigmatically the contrary* of assertion, the operation of **denial** presupposes the existence of a preceding utterance of assertion or of negation. Thus denial implies a syntagmatic perspective in which the relation of implication is actualized. —ASSERTION

DENOTATION
(dénotation)

1. A term is said to be **denotative** when it encompasses a definition* which aims at exhausting a concept as far as its extension* is concerned (*cf.* J. S. Mill). Thus, for instance, a linguistic unit is denotative when it subsumes all its occurrences.*

2. More broadly speaking, a denotative character is attributed to semiotic* systems, complex objects that they are, insofar as these systems fulfill the demands of the principle of empiricism* (and, more specifically, the requirement of exhaustivity*). A **denotative semiotic system** is, for L. Hjelmslev—and merely in a preliminary attempt of definition—a system none of the planes* of which is itself a semiotic system. When one of the two planes is itself composed of an expression* plane and a content* plane, such a semiotic system can no longer be viewed as denotative.

3. Such a definition adds nothing to the definition of a bi-planar* semiotic system (that is, a "semiotic" properly speaking in the terminology of the famous Danish linguist). Thus Hjelmslev completely abandons this definition of denotative semiotic system so as to propose a new distinction between scientific* and non-scientific* semiotic systems. He himself explains this shift of terminology by noting that in order to establish his definition of a semiotic system he had presupposed an ideal text* and postulated that it was characterized by structural homogeneity.* But no such text exists. Any text, as product, belongs to several different systems. Consequently, (a) a text cannot be viewed *a priori* as a homogeneous entity.* On the contrary, it is constructed in terms of the level of pertinence*

chosen, as the analysis* progresses; (b) a natural language* is not a denotative semiotic system, and the manifested discourse belongs to several systems (a semiotic system, a number of connotative semiotic systems, of non-scientific meta-semiotic systems, etc.); (c) "everyday language" is not a semiotic concept. Consequently, it can in no case be identified with the concept of denotative semiotic system which, taken as a whole to be a "signifier," would have a signified, which would make of it a connotative semiotic system (or language of connotation).
—CONNOTATION; SEMIOTICS

DENSITY, SEMIC
(densité sémique)

Semic density can be determined according to the larger or smaller number of semes* making a sememe.* This is a quantitative semantic criterion which allows the degree of abstraction of a "concept" to be evaluated. B. Pottier points out that the semic comprehension* of a concept varies in inverse proportion to the extension* of its use.—ABSTRACT

DEONTIC MODALITIES
(déontiques [modalités—])

1. From the semiotic point of view, the **deontic** modal structure appears when the modal utterance which has having-to* as predicate, overdetermines and governs the utterance of doing.* The binary projection of this structure onto the semiotic square* permits the formulation of the deontic modal category.

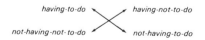

Each of the terms of the square can receive a noun as name:

It shall be noted that in deontic logic the term *obligation* is often substituted for *prescription* (this substitution is unjustified semantically, since prohibition is itself an obligation).

2. It might be useful to emphasize that the deontic modalities are part of the definition of the subject's modal competence.* Consequently, they do not govern the Sender*'s universe together with the axiology to which it belongs by transforming this universe into a system of norms. Rather, the Sender performs a causing-to-have-to-do. It does not prescribe specific doings.

3. A **deontic logic** can be recognized, based upon the modal mechanism coming from having-to-do. More generally speaking, a **deontic semiotics** can be anticipated: it would take into account the relations of having-to-do with the other modalities* such as knowing-how-to-do and being-able-to-do.
—HAVING-TO-DO or TO-BE; MODALITY

DEONTOLOGY
(déontologie)

The term **deontology** is used to designate the system of rules for conduct that one is supposed to follow in the practice of a profession or an activity. This is also called professional ethics. **Scientific deontology** demands, among other things, that research be conducted according to the criteria of scientificness.
—SCIENTIFICNESS

DEPRIVATION
(privation)

Located on the figurative* level, **deprivation,** which is opposed paradigmatically to acquisition,* represents the transformation* which establishes a disjunction* between subject* and object,* given their previous conjunction.* It is carried out in either a transitive* mode (dispossession*) or a reflexive (renunciation*) mode. When set in the narrative* schema, deprivation is the negative form of the consequence and by virtue of this can be considered as one of the possible components of the test as discoursive figure.—CONSEQUENCE; TEST; COMMUNICATION

DERIVATION
(dérivation)

1. When **derivation** is used in its common meaning—"having its origin in"—the question arises, for instance, as to whether or not written language is derived from oral language.

2. From the morphological* point of view, **derivation**—often opposed to composition (*i.e.,* formation of compound words)—deals with the distribution of affixes (prefixes and suffixes). It is seen as a system of classification* of lexical units. Thus, for instance, during the eighteenth century a whole lexicon of technological activities was elaborated in French. Starting from the name of the tool (or of the raw material), a system of names provided designations for the producer, the producing activity, the process and the place of production.

3. In a syntactic sense, derivation is an application—or its result—of analytical* procedures (for Hjelmslev) or of rewriting rules* (for Chomsky) on the basis of a class* (Hjelmslev) or of an axiom* (Chomsky). In the first case, derivation is based upon the concept of hierarchy (defined by Hjelmslev as the class of classes), and in the sec-

ond case upon the logical concept of substitution (which spells out the logical calculation and accounts for its fundamentally tautological character: a complex proposition remains true by virtue of its very form, whatever the truth value of its components might be).
—WRITING; HIERARCHY; SUBSTITUTION

DESCRIPTION
(description)

1. The term **description** was adopted in linguistics during the nineteenth century when a clear opposition was established between descriptive linguistics and normative linguistics (or grammar). Only descriptive linguistics claims a scientific status. Yet it was suspect to structural linguistics because of its implicit positivist presuppositions and was called into question again with the rise of generative* grammar because it was identified with the description of closed corpora.* Consequently, descriptive linguistics, insofar as it is the name for a scientific approach, has progressively lost its *raison d'être* and has dropped progressively from use.

2. The concept of description was thus freed from its relation with a specific methodology. It nevertheless remains one of the problematic concepts* of any theory* of language because it is used to designate the totality, the essential of scientific semiotic practice. In the Hjelmslevian tradition—according to which description is the very best example of an undefinable concept—the name description should be kept exclusively for those procedures* which satisfy the criteria of scientificness*—which procedures are in turn defined as classes of operations* that have established orders.

3. Another way of dealing with the concept of description involves opposing **description procedures** and **discovery* procedures.** This is done by asking about the heuristic value of the former, and thereby putting it into question. Yet one could argue in their defense that the strength of logic (or of the sundry types of logic) rests in large part on logical calculation, which is a description procedure; at the same time one would be emphasizing the real danger of confusing operational techniques (rewriting rules, trees,* graphs, etc.), with scientific doing itself.

4. The term description, as used above, is viewed as the designation of a process,* an activity which involves the construction of a descriptive language (of a metalanguage). Yet such terms are ambiguous in natural languages such as French and English because they are also used to name the result of the process, that is, in this case, the completed representation of the object being described. It is in this latter sense that, in generative* grammar, the phrase **structural description of the sentence** must be understood. This is the representation obtained at the end of a procedure according to which, beginning from a nuclear* sentence which has been posited axiomatically and to which the rules of rewriting have been applied, one is led to give it a semantic and phonetic interpretation.*

5. The term description is also applied, at the level of discoursive organization, to a surface* sequence which is opposed to dialogue,* narrative,* tableau, etc., by implicitly postulating that its formal characteristics allow it to be submitted to qualificative* analysis. In this sense, description must be viewed as a tentative naming of an object which remains to be defined.

—MARKER, SYNTAGMATIC; SEQUENCE; UNIT

DESCRIPTIVE
(descriptif)

1. When compared with modal* values, **descriptive values** are viewed as belonging to G. Dumezil's third function, which designates, for instance, objects which can be used or kept for later use (objective* values) as well as states such as pleasure or "states of mind" (subjective* values). Similarly, one needs to distinguish **descriptive utterances** (involving the descriptive values) from modal utterances (which govern other utterances).

2. When semiotic* theory is envisioned as a hierarchic superposition of languages in which each superior level assumes the role of examining the immediately inferior level—one can term **descriptive level** the level where the results of the analysis of the object language (or of the semiotic object* chosen for the purpose of description) are gathered (in the form of semiotic representation*).
—VALUE; UTTERANCE; MODALITY; LEVEL; DESCRIPTION; METALANGUAGE

DESEMANTIZATION
(désémantisation)

1. **Desemantization** is the loss of certain partial contents* for the benefit of the overall signified* of a larger discoursive unit. Far from being merely a linguistic phenomenon (as, for instance, in "killing time"), desemantization is a very general semiotic phenomenon. For example, "knotting one's tie" is the signified of a complex gestual process whose constitutive utterances are desemanticized. Resemantization* is the inverse procedure

(for example: "I was burdened with more tasks . . . ").

2. Desemantization is found in oral literature as one of the elements that explain the "degradation" of a mythical narrative into a folkloric narrative. Many mythical fragments which have been desemanticized are found in folkloric narratives as mere instrumental narrative programs.*

3. From the axiological perspective, desemantization is an ambiguous phenomenon. It allows human beings to live by reducing to the state of pure automatisms thousands of their programmed attitudes. Yet desemantization is also a source of alienation (for example: work on an assembly line).

DESIGNATION
(désignation)

The term **designation** is sometimes used as a synonym for denotation* or for reference*—expressing, in this case, the establishment or the existence of a relation between a linguistic sign* and the natural world* (or between signs belonging to two different semiotic systems). At other times, it is used to note the equivalence* between two linguistic units having different syntagmatic dimensions or belonging to distinct linguistic levels.—NAME/NAMING; DEFINITION

DESIRE
(désir)

1. **Desire** is a psychological term often opposed to will. Properly speaking, it therefore does not belong to semiotic terminology. From the semantic perspective, it can, with fear,* constitute a pair of contraries—the category called by R. Blanché *philia/phobia*—in which fear is not a non-wanting but a contrary wanting. On the figurative* plane

the two terms can be formulated in various ways. Thus, for instance, desire is often expressed by a forward movement (a quest* for the object of value) while fear is manifested by a backward movement (running away).

2. Semiotics, far from denying the "reality" of desire, views it as one of the lexicalizations of the modality of wanting.* Thus semiotic research should involve the development of a logic of wanting (parallel to deontic logic), in which the terms desire and will would designate the variables of wanting, and which would then be correlated with more complex semantic structures.
—WANTING

DETENSIVENESS
(détensivité)

The term **detensiveness** designates the overdetermining relation which the durative* seme* of a process* contracts with the inchoate* seme, within an aspectual configuration. Detensivity is paradigmatically opposed to tensivity.*
—ASPECTUALIZATION

DEVICE, STYLISTIC
(procédé stylistique)

A term of stylistics which designates the "way of performing" of the enunciator* during the production* of discourse, a **stylistic device** is recognizable at least intuitively on a certain level of the text's surface.* This notion takes over the old rhetorical figures,* linking them to the domain of the enunciation.* The absence of recognition* procedures for these devices, as well as the absence of any structural description which might permit the establishment of their taxonomy has so far been the principal reason for the failure of stylistics.—STYLISTICS

DIACHRONY
(diachronie)

1. Ferdinand de Saussure introduced the dichotomy *synchrony/diachrony* in order to designate two distinct ways of approaching linguistic phenomena. In actual fact, only the notion of synchrony was of consequence to Saussure, for it allowed him to establish linguistics as the study of coherent systems.* The term **diachrony** came then to designate the area of studies in historical grammar. Thus, the opposition between synchrony and diachrony, which Saussure set forth as two interrelated temporal dimensions for research, has nonetheless been taken for a long time to be an opposition between a structural attitude and an atomistic approach with regard to language facts.

2. The initially categorical opposition between the two terms of the Saussurian dichotomy has been progressively softened. Given the fact that a semiotic system* is not defined by the synchronization of the elements constituting it but by their internal, logical coherence, it was possible to interpret diachrony as a set of transformations* which are located and recognizable between two systems taken as wholes (or between two given states* of a natural language considered as the loci wherein two distinct systems are set). Such a conception, which likens the distance between two states of a language to that which exists between two related languages, in fact does away with diachrony and allows for the practice of an achronic* comparativism.*

3. Instead of making use of the questionable procedure which consists in postulating *a priori* the existence of two states of a language before knowing the transformations which alone could define these states, we can conceive of diachrony in terms of transformations located within a semiotic system (or natural language) provided that we then would identify the original states and the results of these transformations as semiotic (or linguistic) states.* This approach can be illustrated by two examples.

4. While associated with the Prague School, Roman Jakobson offered an interpretation, which according to him stems from **diachronic philology,** of changes in the expression* form of grammatical categories. These changes would be due to the redundant overdetermination of the morphemes* manifesting the grammatical categories. So, for example, the disappearance of Latin declension endings can be explained by the redundant and prolonged coexistence of superfluous morphemes which denoted the same grammatical categories (such as determinants, prepositions, etc.). It can be said that the establishment of this secondary, emphatic, system resulted in the withering of these now useless flexional morphemes.

5. Other linguists (Martinet, Haudricourt) who begin with the postulate of equilibrium* (which every semiotic system must maintain in order to be able to function) conceive of the diachronic process as chain-reaction transformations. These transformations are induced by the intrusion of a foreign element within a system (the vowel system, for example); these are transformations which seek to reestablish the lost equilibrium and succeed in constructing a new system based on a new equilibrium. This is a particularly interesting approach, for, instead of starting with states of language seeking to undergo possible

transformations, it first describes the transformations which alone can define these states.

6. If we agree to consider such transformations as **diachronic transformations,** there is no reason not to use the same nomenclature for the transformations that we recognize in the unfolding of the narrative discourse (admittedly at the level of the content* form). This discourse, which locates its performances* between two structural states (initial and final), is comparable, due allowances being made, to the linguistic process that a linguistic community accomplishes between two states of a natural language.
—SYNCHRONY; TRANSFORMATION; ACHRONY

DIALOGUE
(dialogue)

1. The term **dialogue** designates the discursive unit, enunciative* in nature, which is obtained by projecting the structure of communication* within an utterance-discourse. Its actants—sender* and receiver—are then together called interlocutors or, separately, interlocutor and interlocutee. They are distinct from narrator* and narratee because they are not the enunciator*'s and the enunciatee's direct delegates installed in the discourse. Interlocutor and interlocutee are rather narrative actants endowed with linguistic competence. Dialogue is thus linked to the narrative* schema by the syncretism which exists between the interlocutors and other actants of the narrative.

2. Reported dialogue often involves a framing. The **framing** element, whose main function is to signal the speech act as a semiotic act ("he said," "she replied"), frequently includes information about the mood of the dialogue ("anxiously,"

"with an emotion-tinged voice"). Consequently the framing must be taken into account in the analysis. The **framed** element is made up/out of intertwined response-segments, which maintain anaphoric* relations among themselves on the discursive plane (following linguistic parameters of the type question/ answer, assertion/negation, etc.). On the narrative plane the framed dialogue, as a surface phenomenon, can encompass narrative programs* or be crisscrossed by them.

3. Dialogue is the reported simulacrum of a two-voiced discourse. It is not surprising then that it can be widened to reach the dimensions of a literary discourse (example: a play).
—DISENGAGEMENT; UNIT (#7)

DICHOTOMY
(dichotomie)

A **dichotomy** is a pair of terms—usually belonging to the epistemological* level of the metalanguage—which are simultaneously posited, with an emphasis upon the relation of opposition* that allows them to be linked the one with the other. The classical example is that of the Saussurian dichotomies: language*/speech*; signifier*/signified*; synchrony/diachrony.* Such an approach is characteristic of the structural attitude, which prefers to posit the differences—viewed as more enlightening—before examining and defining the concepts.

DICTIONARY
(dictionnaire)

1. A **dictionary** is usually understood to be an inventory* of the lexemes* (and, in some cases, of the paralexemes*) of a natural language* organized in a conventional

order (usually alphabetical order). The lexemes (or paralexemes), taken as names, are given either definitions* or parasynonymic* equivalents.

2. In informatics dictionary designates the list of lexical units previously codified and entered into a computer's memory.

3. Any semantic universe,* divided up into lexemes, can take the form of a dictionary. Each lexeme, conceived as a virtuality of significations, can become the object of a semic representation subdivided, through the addition of contextual* semes, into so many sememic* trajectories. The semes, which are necessary for the description of such a dictionary, constitute its semantic code.
—INVENTORY; LEXICOGRAPHY; CODE

DIEGESIS
(diégèse)

By contrast with description* (which primarily belongs to qualificative* analysis), **diegesis** (from the Greek *diegesis*, narrative)—a term taken over from the Greek tradition and used by G. Genette—designates the narrative aspect of discourse. In this sense, the notion is related to the concepts of story* and narrative.* For the literary semiotician Genette, narration and description constitute the "narrated," which is thus distinguished from the "discourse" (understood as the way in which the narrated is presented).
—NARRATIVITY

DIFFERENCE
(différence)

The intuitive* grasp of the **difference**—that is, of a certain gap between two or more entities*— constitutes, for the post-Saussurian

semiotic tradition, the first condition for the appearance of meaning. Yet, a difference can only be recognized over against a supporting background of resemblance. Thus it is by postulating that difference and resemblance are relations*—which are apprehended and/or produced by the knowing subjects—which can be gathered together and formulated into a specific category, *alterity/identity*, that one can construct the elementary structure* of signification as a logical model.—RESEMBLANCE; ALTERITY

DIMENSION
(dimension)

1. **Dimension** is a spatial figurative* term borrowed from geometry and used to name various operational* concepts in semiotics. As a name it is very weakly motivated* and becomes suggestive only because of the qualifications added to it.

2. When it is used absolutely, *i.e.*, without qualification, **dimension** designates, in the framework of the constitutional model,* each of the binary relations* which constitute the semiotic square.* The fundamental dimensions of the square are the axes (axes of contraries* and of subcontraries*), the schemas* (positive and negative), and the deixes* (positive and negative).

3. At the level of the discourse manifested in the form of signs,* dimension means the syntagmatic "size" of the linguistic units. The issue of the dimension of the units is raised when the isomorphism* of the units belonging to the two planes* of language is studied. For instance, it can be said that the phoneme* and the sememe* can be considered to be isomorphic due to their structure but not due to their

dimensions (at the moment of mani-festation*).

4. In semantics, we proposed some time ago a distinction between the **noological*** **dimension** and the **cosmological*** **dimension,** respectively determined by the presence of the classemes* *interoceptivity* and *exteroceptivity* which thus locate the discourse (or one of its segments) on one or the other dimension. Example: "a heavy bag"/"a heavy conscience." For this meaning, we now prefer the term isotopy.*

5. At a superficial level of narrativity, the **pragmatic*** and **cognitive*** **dimensions** are distinguished as two distinct levels which are hierarchically organized and on which are located the actions and events described by the discourses.
—DIMENSIONALITY

DIMENSIONALITY
(*dimensionnalité*)

1. **Dimensionality** is the characteristic of spatiality* when the latter is interpreted through a dimensional taxonomic model, exclusive of any other spatial property. This taxonomic model is itself the result of the articulation of three spatial categories called dimensions*: *horizontality/verticality/prospectivity.* The intersection of these dimensions forms a deixis* of reference permitting the location, by relation to it, of the various entities found in a given space. A single dimension is enough to locate a punctual entity. Two dimensions, which form a plane, allow a realm of surface to be located. Finally, three dimensions locate volumes in relation to the reference volume.

2. In discursive semiotics, the dimensional model permits—during the procedure of spatialization* of the discourse—the construction of a frame of spatial localization. This is so because the dimensional model identifies the zero point of the dimensionality either with the elsewhere space or the here space—these spaces being obtained by means of spatial disengagement.*

3. The number of dimensions accounted for during the construction of the signifier* of a visual semiotic system (or during the description of a natural* semiotic system) can constitute its specific character. Thus, the planar semiotic system has a bi-dimensional signifier, whereas the spatial* semiotic system has a signifier with three dimensions.

4. Because of the important role of the procedures of visual representation in the development of the natural sciences, it is common, frequent, and normal that the terms belonging to dimensionality—such as dimension,* plane,* level,* axis,* etc.—be used metaphorically outside of the field of spatiality on condition, of course, that they be redefined in their new settings.
—LOCALIZATION, SPATIO-TEMPORAL; PLANAR SEMIOTICS

DISAMBIGUIZATION
(*désambiguisation*)

The term **disambiguization** designates the procedure* which eliminates lexical or syntactic ambiguities. This procedure permits the establishment of an isotopic* reading* of a discursive sequence. Disambiguization demands that the semantic unit which can receive several simultaneous readings be set in a wider, explicit* (or explicitable), context.*
—AMBIGUITY; UNEQUIVOCALNESS

DISCONTINUOUS
(discontinu)

1. The undefinable category* *continuous/discontinuous* belongs to the epistemological* inventory of non-defined concepts.

2. It is often said that the projection of the **discontinuous** upon the continuous is the first condition required for understanding the world. The set of problems concerning this "projection" belongs to general epistemology, and is not only a semiotic issue. In order to establish the terminology, it might be useful to emphasize here that in semiotics any entity* is viewed as continuous prior to its articulation,* *i.e.,* prior to the identification* of the variant-occurrences, which allows these latter to be organized in classes* (which alone can be viewed as discontinuous units*). Yet since the term discontinuous is related only to the syntagmatic organization, it is better to use the qualificative "discrete" in defining a semiotic unit.

3. In discursive semiotics the opposition *continuous/discontinuous* reappears in the form of an aspectual category which articulates the durative* aspect. The discontinuous aspect is thus called iterative or frequentative.

4. In linguistics, **discontinuous constituents*** designate morphemes* whose formants* can appear in two or more places in the chain, without thereby affecting the unity of the corresponding signified. The French negation "ne ... pas" is an example: it represents, from a diachronic point of view, a phenomenon of overdetermination which allows for the passage from one structure ("ne") to the other ("pas"), interrupted and frozen in its intermediary stage. We point this out in order to suggest the explanation of comparable cases in other semiotic systems.

—CONTINUOUS; DISCRETE; ASPECTUALIZATION

DISCOURSE
(discours)

1. In a first perspective, the concept of **discourse** can be identified with that of semiotic process.* In this way the totality of the semiotic facts (relations, units, operations, etc.) located on the syntagmatic* axis of language* are viewed as belonging to the theory of discourse. When one has in mind the existence of two macrosemiotic* systems—the "verbal world" manifested in the form of natural languages, and the "natural world" as the source of non-linguistic semiotic systems—the semiotic process appears as a set of **discursive practices:** linguistic practices (verbal behavior) and non-linguistic practices (signifying somatic behavior manifested by the sensory orders). When linguistic practices alone are taken into consideration, one can say that discourse is the object of knowledge considered by **discursive linguistics.** In this sense discourse is synonymous with text.* For indeed, certain European languages which do not have an equivalent for the French and English word "discours(e)" have been led to substitute for it the word "text" and to speak of textual linguistics. On the other hand—by extrapolation and as an hypothesis which seems to be fruitful—the terms discourse and text have also been used to designate certain non-linguistic semiotic processes (a ritual, a film, a comic strip are then viewed as discourses or texts). The use of these terms postulates the existence of a syntagmatic

organization undergirding these kinds of manifestations.

2. In a somewhat different theoretical framework—but one which is not contradictory with the preceding one—discourse can be identified with utterance.* The more or less implicit way in which the utterance (= what is uttered) is conceived determines two theoretical attitudes and two different types of analysis. For phrastic linguistics, the basic unit of the utterance is the sentence.* The discourse is then viewed as the result (or the operation) of the concatenation of sentences. By contrast, discoursive linguistics—as we conceive it—takes as its basic unit the discourse viewed as a signifying whole. Consequently, sentences are only segments (or broken-up parts) of the **discourse-utterance.** Of course, this does not exclude the possibility that a discourse might have at times the dimensions of a sentence, as a consequence of the procedure of condensation.*

3. When analysis of discourse is located in the wake of phrastic grammars, it seeks to recognize— and to construct models of—the discoursive sequences viewed as series of sentence-utterances. To this end, various procedures are devised or proposed, such as: (a) the establishment of an equivalence network among sentences and/or series of sentences (Z. Harris); (b) the formulation of rules—either logical or rhetorical rules—of sentence concatenation; (c) the determination of grammatical isotopies* of the sequences (taking anaphorization* into account); (d) the elaboration of deeper representations accounting for the series of surface sentences, etc. Although such procedures are pertinent, they remain nonetheless partial and do not seem to be based on any general theory of discourse.

They remind us too much of those tasks of "paragraph construction" set down in programs for secondary education in France and could be followed, in the same turn, by the equally classic "discourse construction" with its three points . . .

4. When, by contrast, it is postulated from the outset that the utterance-discourse forms a whole, then the procedures to be set up must be deductive—and no longer inductive. The procedures must consist of the analytic separation of the discoursive whole into its components. When, furthermore, a generative approach complements these procedures, semiotic theory is led to conceive of the discourse as a multilayered organization constituted by a number of depth levels,* superposed on each other. Only the last one—the most superficial one— can receive a semantic representation* which is approximately comparable to the "deep" linguistic structures (in the Chomskian perspective). Thus it appears that phrastic grammar is the natural sequel to discourse grammar.

5. For such a conception of discourse to be integrated into the general theory of language, it needs, on the one hand, to be homologated with the fundamental dichotomies *language/speech, system/process, competence/performance* (see these terms), and on the other hand, to be related to the domain of the enunciation.* Keeping the term competence* to designate all the necessary conditions for the exercise of the enunciation, a distinction between two autonomous configurations of this competence will be noted: semionarrative competence and discoursive competence (in the strict sense). Semio-narrative competence is situated upstream, being anterior to the enunciation as such. In agree-

ment with Hjelmslev and Chomsky, one can conceive of it as made up of articulations which are both taxonomic and syntactic—and not as a merely paradigmatic* organization, as "language" is for Saussure. In agreement with Saussure, semio-narrative competence can be viewed as having a transcendental status: the semio-narrative forms are postulated as being universal—found in all linguistic and translinguistic communities—and persevere in the translations from one language to another; they are also recognizable in non-linguistic semiotic systems. Thus semio-narrative competence corresponds to what could be termed classificatory and programming forms of human intelligence: but this would be an irresponsible formulation. As competence, it can be described as a fundamental grammar* of the discourse-utterance, preceding the enunciation and presupposed by it. By contrast, **discursive competence** is located downstream from semio-narrative competence: it is constituted during the enunciation, and governs, by molding them, the uttered discursive forms.

6. These brief remarks about the twofold nature of competence were necessary in order to establish a new meaning and a more restricted definition of discourse. For indeed, if enunciation is, according to Benveniste, the "putting into discourse" of language, then discourse is precisely what is put in place by the enunciation. When we substitute in Benveniste's definition the concept of semio-narrative competence for the concept of "language," we can then say that putting into discourse—or **discoursivization***—consists in taking over the semio-narrative structures and in transforming them into discursive struc-

tures. The discourse is the result of this manipulation of the deep forms, which brings about a surplus of signifying articulations. A **discursive analysis,** distinct from the narrative analysis that it presupposes, can then be envisaged.

7. Such a conception of discourse nullifies the traditional opposition between discourse (as transphrastic monologue) and communication (as dialogue and phrastic exchange). Thus communication* ceases to be an extra-linguistic structure which serves as a basis for the exchange of messages. Communication appears rather as a domain, a stage on the generative* trajectory of the discourse. At times, it brings about the appearance of a single subject-actor of the enunciation, which assumes and projects beyond itself various actantial* roles. At other times it manifests a bipolar actorial* structure which produces a two-voice discourse (= "communication") but which is nevertheless located on a homogeneous semantic isotopy and the syntactic forms of which are comparable to those of the dialogue* installed, after having been enunciated, in the discourse-utterance. Furthermore, the structure of communication no longer needs an exterior pragmatics* (in the American sense) in order to be understood and described. The actants* of the enunciation, because they assume a semio-narrative competence which transcends them and causes them to participate in the semiotic universe, are by definition competent: they "know how to communicate" without the help of any psycho-sociological factors.

8. The fact that the term discourse is progressively identified with semiotic process and that it is even used to designate, metonymically, one or the other entire semio-

tic system or semiotic process, raises the problem of the definition of the semiotic* system (as both object of knowledge and object constructed by the description). Indeed, we must keep in mind that linguistics is at the origin of semiotic research. We must also remember that natural language* is not merely defined as a semiotic system (as a language) but is also viewed, explicitly or implicitly, as a model according to which the other semiotic systems can and must be conceived. Yet, natural language, semantically coextensive with culture, is a huge domain. We consider it to be a macrosemiotic system which can only be compared with another macrosemiotic system having the same dimensions: that of the signifying natural world.* Consequently the other semiotic systems appear as "minisemiotic systems" located or constructed within these universes. Soviet semioticians were perhaps the first to raise this possibility when proposing the ill-defined but quite suggestive concept of "secondary modeling systems" to designate these "minisemiotic systems" which, even though they belong to the "macrosemiotic systems," are presumed to have an autonomy of operation and/or of signification. The Soviet concept of "secondary system" (a metonym including process) approximately corresponds to the concept of discourse (a concept which was developed in the French context and which must be interpreted as a process which presupposes a system).

9. In this new meaning, the term discourse nevertheless remains ambiguous. A semiotic domain can be named discourse (for example: literary discourse, philosophical discourse) because of its social connotation* related to a given cultural context (J. Lotman says, for instance, that a medieval sacred text is viewed by us as literary) independently from and prior to its syntactic or semantic analysis. The **typology of discourses** which can be elaborated in this perspective is therefore connotative, that is, it is specific to a given cultural localization (circumscribed both geographically and historically) and it does not have any relation with the semiotic status of these discourses.

10. Even when one leaves aside the connotative definitions of discourse (according to which, for instance, literary discourse is defined by literarity*), the problem of knowing what discourse is—in the semiotic sense—remains unresolved. When one examines the various semiotic systems from the point of view of their syntactic and semantic components, one notices that some of them—for instance, literary* semiotic systems—are indifferent vis-à-vis their invested contents, while, by contrast, others are indifferent to the syntactic organizations they might have—for example, the "feminine narrative" formulated by C. Chabrol, viewed as a universal articulation of contents, can be invested in quite different discursive forms. Since any content, whatever its nature, can be taken over as "literary" content, literary discourse can only base such specificity it might have upon the syntactic forms which it manifests. Yet, the variety of forms is so broad that literary semiotics appears mainly as a vast repertory of discursive forms and not as a syntactic structure which could be defined. While there are "many" literary discourses one cannot speak of "the" literary discourse. On the other hand when thinking about the "feminine narrative"—and also about the semantic fields called "political discourse," "religious dis-

course," etc.—one can say that there exist deep organizations of content which can be formulated as systems of values* or as epistemes* (i.e., as combinatory hierarchies). But, once more, these axiologies* can be manifested in many kinds of discourses. This amounts to saying that the general semantic theory of discourses must be dealt with independently of their syntactic typology which, when it will have been further developed, will certainly appear as very far removed from the present connotative typology of discoursive genres.*

11. Coming back to the domain of the enunciation, which is the locus of the generation of discourse, one can then say that the form of the produced discourse is dependent upon the twofold selection taking place in it. When the semio-narrative structures are viewed as the repertory of the forms which can be altered, the enunciation has then as its task the selection of those forms it needs "to make a discourse." Thus, the choice between the pragmatic* or cognitive* dimensions of the envisaged discourse, the choice between the forms which are appropriate for a discourse characterized by the construction of a subject (cf. the Bildungsroman) and those which are necessary for a discourse characterized by the construction of an object (cf. for example, the recipe for vegetable soup), etc., determine in advance the type of discourse which will finally be manifested. On the other hand, the use of the mechanisms of disengagement* and of engagement,* which define the enunciation as an activity of production, can only be viewed as a selective operation which chooses, within the combinatory set of discoursive units* which these mechanisms are able to produce, certain preferred units and/or a specific preferred ar-

rangement of units. In both cases, and whether one is dealing with semio-narrative competence or with discoursive competence (properly speaking), the production of a discourse appears to be a continuous selection of possibilities, making its way through networks of constraints.

—UTTERANCE; COMPETENCE; GENERATIVE TRAJECTORY; DISCOURSIVIZATION; SEMIOTICS; TEXUALIZATION; LITERARY SEMIOTICS; RHETORIC

DISCOURSIVIZATION
(discursivisation)

1. The recognition of two depth levels and of two types of structures*—semio-narrative and discoursive structures—which govern the organization of the discourse prior to its manifestation* in a given natural language* (or in a non-linguistic semiotic system), forces us to envisage **procedures of setting into discourse.** These procedures, together with discoursive semantics,* have to bridge the gap between, on the one hand, narrative syntax and narrative semantics (which constitute the surface level of semiotic structures) and, on the other hand, the semantico-syntactic representation* of the text. After its textualization,* this representation can serve as deep level for the linguistic structures which generate the surface linguistic structures (in Chomsky's sense). A satisfactory description of the process of production* of discourse is far from possible at the present stage of semiotic research. Thus we think it better to limit ourselves to sketching out the main features of the general economy of these procedures. We will attempt to distinguish, as far as possible, the various components of those procedures. It

is only when many partial analyses have been organized into a general strategy that a less intuitive reformulation of the structures and operations involved will be possible.

2. The procedures of **discoursivization**—destined to be constituted into a discursive syntax—have in common the possibility of being defined as the putting to work of certain operations of disengagement* and of engagement.* As such they belong to the domain of the enunciation. They need to be subdivided into at least three subcomponents: actorialization,* temporalization,* and spatialization,* the effect of which is to produce an organized group of actors* and a framework, both temporal and spatial, in which will be inscribed the narrative programs* originating in the semiotic (or narrative) structures.

3. In the same broad sense, discoursivization must be distinguished from textualization,* which, for us, is a deviation of the discourse. This deviation can theoretically originate in any domain of the generative* trajectory. Textualization tends toward its manifestation and is defined in terms of that manifestation. One of the procedures of textualization is linearization,* that is, the deconstruction of the discourse, due to the constraints of linearity of the text, and its reconstruction according to the new rules which are imposed upon it. The result is a new textual segmentation, which produces textual units* of a new kind. Textualization has the effect of producing a linear discourse which is segmented into units of various dimensions, and which can be formulated as a deep representation ready to be realized as a manifested discourse by passing to the level of the surface linguistic structures.

—DISCOURSE; GENERATIVE TRAJECTORY; ACTORIALIZATION; TEMPORALIZATION; SPATIALIZATION; SYNTAX, DISCOURSIVE; TEXTUALIZATION

DISCOVERY PROCEDURE
(découverte [procédure de—])

1. A **discovery procedure** is the explicit* formulation of the cognitive operations which permit the description* of a semiotic object and which satisfy the conditions of scientificness.* The act of making this set of procedures explicit can result in the formulation of a semiotic (or linguistic) methodology and theory. This pragmatic way of raising the issue of the relations between theory and practice can find its partial explanation in the attitude of nineteenth-century linguistics—the activities of which produced many results—that had left implicit a large part of its procedures.

2. Among the discovery procedures dating from the nineteenth century which structural linguistics formulated explicitly, mention should first be made of operations of segmentation,* of substitution,* and of commutation.* These operations account for linguistics having been constituted as a science at the beginning of the nineteenth century and are the basis of any logical language. The American structuralists' mistake was to believe (because of an excessive formalism) that these discovery procedures could take the place of a general theory and that, by being substituted for intuition,* they would permit linguistics to be conceived of as a "discovery ma-

chine." This is sufficient to justify the criticism formulated by N. Chomsky against these discovery procedures, without thereby condoning another naïve attitude, namely that grammar can be viewed as "pure description."

3. Inverting the relation between theory* and practice, one must require that the theory be applicable, *i.e.*, that it seek to produce and explain discovery procedures. Besides simplicity,* applicability seems to us to be a second criterion that can provide the foundation for **evaluation procedures** for theories (or grammars).

4. Yet, it is on the basis of concrete analyses of research and discovery discourses that the semiotician can hope to have a clearer view of the operations which are used in semiotic practices that are scientific in character.

—PROCEDURE;   THEORY; METHODOLOGY

DISCRETE
(discret)

1. As a non-defined concept, **discrete** is to be set in the epistemological* inventory of undefinable terms. Nevertheless, the semantic analysis of this inventory permits it to be interdefined, that is, to be included in the relational network of comparable concepts. Thus, following V. Brøndal, we have inscribed it as a sub-articulation of the quantitative* category of totality. This category is constituted by the opposition of the integral (totus) and the universal (omnis). Integrality is, in turn, articulated into **discreteness** (which characterizes an entity* as distinct from everything which it is not) and wholeness (allowing an entity to be apprehended in its indivisibility).

2. In semiotics, discreteness plays the same role that it does in logics or in mathematics. It serves to define the semiotic unit, which is constructed with the help of the concepts of identity* and alterity.* A **discrete unit** is characterized by a break in continuity with neighboring units. Consequently such a discrete unit can serve as a constituting element of other units, etc. Yet it must be noted that, while the concept of discreteness is indispensable for defining syntagmatic units, it is not sufficient for specifying the paradigmatic categories which can be either discrete (possible/impossible) or gradual (probable/improbable).

3. In metalanguage,* discrete is synonymous with discontinuous.

—TOTALITY; UNIT; DISCONTINUOUS; CATEGORY

DISCRIMINATORY
(discriminatoire)

A semic category* is said to be **discriminatory** when it is desemanticized* in order to serve as a formal criterion in the construction of a scientific taxonomy,* for instance. Such is the case in the pairing of terms in a naming syntagm of the type *determining + determined,* as well as in the case of the classifying or specifying terms used.

DISENGAGEMENT
(débrayage)

(A) We can try to define **disengagement** as the operation by which the domain of the enunciation* disjuncts and projects forth from itself, at the moment of the language act and in view of manifestation,* certain terms bound to its base structure, so as thereby to constitute the foundational elements of the discourse-utterance. For example, if

we take the domain of the enunciation as a syncretism* of "I-here-
now," disengagement, as one of the
constitutive aspects of the primordial
language act, will consist in inau-
gurating the utterance by articulating at the same time and as an implicit consequence the domain of the
enunciation itself. The language act
thus appears as a split which creates,
on the one hand, the subject, the
place, and the time of the enunciation and, on the other, the actantial,
spatial, and temporal representation
of the utterance. From another
point of view, which would give
dominance to the systematic and social nature of semiotic systems, it can
just as well be said that the enunciation, as a mechanism of mediation
between natural language and discourse, works in the paradigmatic
categories of person, space, and
time, with a view to situating the
explicit discourse. **Actantial disengagement,** then, in its first steps, will
consist in disjuncting a "not-I" from
the subject of the enunciation and
projecting it into the utterance, **temporal disengagement** in postulating
a "not-now" distinct from the time of
the enunciation, **spatial disengagement** in opposing a "not-here" to the
place of the enunciation.

(B) **Actantial disengagement.**

1. In order to give a representation* of the mechanics of disengagement, it will first be necessary
to insist on the fact that the subject
of the enunciation, responsible for
producing the utterance, is always
implicit and presupposed, that this
subject is never manifested inside
the discourse-utterance. (No "I" encountered in the discourse can be
considered as subject of the enunciation strictly speaking, nor identified
with that subject: in such a case
there is only a semblance of enunci-

ation, a case of uttered or reported
enunciation).

2. The category of person,
which is fundamental to the mechanics of actantial disengagement, can
be divided roughly (according to
Benveniste) into *person/non-person.*
The personal morphemes "I" and
"you" correspond to the first term;
they serve as names, in natural language (English, here), for the two
actants of the enunciation (enunciator* and enunciatee), provided
that the fact that enunciation is an
intersubjective structure be taken
into account. The actants of the utterance correspond to the term of
non-person.

3. Beginning with the subject of
the enunciation, implicit but productive of the utterance, either the
actants of the enunciation or the
actants of the utterance can be projected by their installation in the
discourse, at the moment of the language act or of its semblance within
the discourse. In the first case, an
enunciative disengagement is carried out, in the second, an **utterative
disengagement.** According to the
type of disengagement used, two
discursive forms and even two
broad types of discursive units* can
be distinguished. In the first case,
there will be the forms of the uttered (or reported) enunciation;
such is the case of narratives in "I,"
but also of dialogue* sequences. In
the second, there are found the
forms of uttered (or objectified) utterance: as in narrations which have
commonplace subjects, in so-called
objective discourse, etc.

4. Recognizing these simulacra,
i.e., the enunciators installed in the
discourse, permits an understanding
of the functioning of **internal disengagement** (of the second or of the
third degree), frequently encoun-

tered in figurative discourse of a literary nature. Beginning with a dialogue structure, one of the interlocutors* can easily "disengage" a narrative which, in turn, beginning with an actant of the utterance, will install a second-level dialogue, etc. It can be seen that the procedure of disengagement, used by the enunciator as a component of its strategy,* allows the figurative discourse in (surface) discursive units to be accounted for (units such as "narrative," "dialogue," etc.) It will be noted here that each internal disengagement produces a referentialization* effect: a second-degree discourse, installed inside the narrative, gives the impression that this narrative constitutes the "real situation" of the discourse: it referentializes this dialogue.

5. A small terminological problem arises in regard to the uttered enunciation, installed in the discourse. To the degree to which it is simulacra of the enunciator and of the enunciatee which are installed there—both of them (whether "I" or "you," the "author" or the "reader" named in the utterance) anxious to participate in that intersubjective communication which the totality of the discourse is—they can be called, respectively, narrator* and narratee. But, when there is a second-degree interlocution structure (in the dialogue*), we will speak rather of interlocutor* and of interlocutee.

6. A comparable problem arises in regard to the actants of the utterance (or actants of the narration properly speaking). The development of narrative semiotics has obliged us to recognize the existence of two autonomous dimensions of the narration: the pragmatic* dimension and the cognitive* dimension; by this very fact, we are moved to distinguish two types of subject

actants. Alongside of pragmatic subjects,* cognitive subjects are encountered in the discourse, at times producers of signification, at times interpreters of it. These cognitive subjects appear either in syncretism with pragmatic subjects, or in the form of autonomous actors (as the informant,* for example), or, finally, recognizable only as implicit positions (as the observer* actant, the role of which has so far been underestimated). **Cognitive* disengagement** thus permits the installation of a separation between the enunciator's cognitive position and those either of the actors of the narration or of the narrator.

7. The concept of disengagement owes as much to Benveniste as to Jakobson, whose "shifter" (Eng.) was rendered by N. Ruwet as "engager" (*embrayeur*, Fr.). The term of **disengager** appears to us to be more adapted to the generative approach, which moves from the enunciation to the utterance, all the more so since a dichotomization of Jakobson's concept seems to us to be necessary. By opposing the term of engagement* (designating the return of forms already disengaged to the enunciator) to that of disengagement, a bit more clarity is introduced into this mechanism which is simultaneously elementary and highly complex.

(C) **Temporal disengagement.**

1. Parallel to actantial disengagement, temporal disengagement can be understood as a procedure of projecting the term *not-now* at the moment of the language act, out from the domain of the enunciation. It has as its effect, on the one hand, the institution, by presupposition, of the *now* time of the enunciation. On the other hand, this projection permits the construction of an "objective" time beginning from the

position that can be called the *then time*. By considering the *then time* as a zero time, and by applying, beginning from that zero point, the topological category

$$
\begin{array}{c}
\textit{concomitance} \;/\; \textit{non-concomitance} \\
\diagup \qquad \diagdown \\
\textit{anteriority} \;/\; \textit{posteriority}
\end{array}
$$

it is possible to construct a simple model of the utterative time which, as a reference system, will permit localization of the different narrative programs* of the discourse.

2. To the extent to which the domain of the enunciation, taken as a whole, can be uttered and can constitute, as a simulacrum, the enunciative structure of the discourse, the *now time*, taken separately, can be disengaged and inscribed in the discourse as reported enunciative time. The *now time*, thus uttered, is articulated in turn according to the same topological category and constitutes, within the discourse, a second system of temporal reference. The utilization of these two reference systems is one of the factors for segmenting the discourse into sequence units.

3. By an inverse procedure, the disengaged utterative and enunciative procedures can, thereafter, be engaged so as to produce the illusion of their identification with the domain of the enunciation: this is temporal engagement.*

(D) **Spatial disengagement.**

1. Just like actantial or temporal disengagement, spatial disengagement appears as a procedure having as its effect the expulsion out from the domain of the enunciation of the term *not-here* of the spatial category and of thereby founding at the same time both the "objective" space of the utterance (the *elsewhere* space) and the primordial space—

which is recognizable only as a topic presupposition—of the enunciation. If *elsewhere* space is considered as an utterative space, it is apparent that the projection of the term *here*, simulating the locus of the enunciation, is equally possible, and that, beginning from this position, a *here* space, enunciative in nature, can be constituted.

2. A topological category which articulates spatiality is necessary in order to institute, beginning from the two benchmarks of the *elsewhere* and the *here*, two systems of spatial reference, which permit the establishment of two networks of positions to which the different narrative programs of the spatialized discourse can be referred. Such a topological category can be envisaged, in a first step, as a three-dimensional articulation of space, containing the axes of horizontality, verticality, and prospectivity, whose meeting point would be represented by the spatial position zero. It is evident, nonetheless, that this category of dimensionality* which we have proposed is insufficient and that there exist other categories, relating, for example, to volumes (of the type *containing/contained*) or to surfaces (*surrounding/surrounded*), which enter into play. At a time when there is much talk about spatial language, it is regrettable that logicians have not yet—so far as we know—concerned themselves with the construction of spatial logics.

3. Taking into account the fact that the domain of the enunciation can be installed in the utterance in the form of a simulacrum the space of *here*, taken separately, can be disengaged and inscribed in the discourse as reported enunciative space. It could then be articulated with respect to the chosen topological category, thus giving rise to a

secondary referential system for the localization of narrative programs. —ENGAGEMENT; TEMPORALIZATION; ENUNCIATION; DISCOURSE; SPATIALIZATION; LOCALIZATION, SPATIO-TEMPORAL

DISEQUILIBRIUM
(déséquilibre)

The positive and negative complex terms forming the axis of the contraries* and subcontraries* are said, in V. Brøndal's terminology, to be **in disequilibrium.**—EQUILIBRIUM; COMPLEX TERM; SQUARE, SEMIOTIC

DISJUNCTION
(disjonction)

1. In narrative semiotics the name **disjunction** is kept for designating paradigmatically one of the two terms (the other being conjunction*) of the category **junction.** This category is defined on the syntagmatic plane as the relation between subject* and object,* that is, as the function* constitutive of utterances of state.*

2. While, paradigmatically, disjunction and conjunction are contradictory,* such is not the case on the syntagmatic level where, according to the semiotic square*

conjunction   disjunction

non-disjunction   non-conjunction

disjunction ("not having something") must be distinguished from non-conjunction ("not having something any longer").

3. In segmentation procedures, the term disjunction is used to name the criteria making it possible to introduce discontinuity* into the syntagmatic continuity of the discourse.

Thus one speaks of **graphic, spatial, temporal, actorial, logical, topic, thymic,** etc., **disjunctions.**
—JUNCTION; SEGMENTATION

DISPOSSESSION
(dépossession)

Located on the figurative* level, **dispossession** represents the situation of the subject* of an utterance of state* when that subject is deprived of the object* of value by a subject of doing* other than itself. Thus it corresponds to a transitive* disjunction* from the object, taking place at any point in the narrative* trajectory.

Together with renunciation,* dispossession is one of the two possible forms of deprivation, which can be viewed, taken as consequence,* as sub-components of a test.
—DEPRIVATION; TEST

DISQUALIFICATION
(disqualification)

Disqualification designates the negative consequence* of the qualifying test* (example: the disqualification of the king in the myth of sovereignty).—QUALIFYING TEST

DISTINCTION
(distinction)

1. **Distinction** is a non-defined concept which is to be included in the epistemological* inventory. This is an operation which establishes alterity,* by opposition to identification, which aims at recognizing identity.*

2. Distinction is related to difference. Yet while difference, as a foundational concept of semiotics, is viewed as the property of the object,* distinction is the cognitive act

of the subject which establishes difference. Thus the two terms correspond to two different epistemological approaches.

—DIFFERENCE; DISTINCTIVE

DISTINCTIVE
(distinctif)

1. The term **distinctive feature** designates the figure* of either of the two planes* (expression*/content*) of language which is considered as minimal according to the chosen level of pertinence* and which is recognized as different by comparison with at least one other figure. The distinctive feature is called seme* (on the content plane) or pheme* (on the expression plane) only when it has been integrated into the appropriate semic or phemic category.*

2. Some linguists find it useful to introduce the notion of **distinctive function** to name the "ability" which semiotic elements have of differentiating among themselves. The distinctive function characterizes the paradigmatic* axis, by opposition to the combinatory* function, which is that of the elements located on the syntagmatic* axis.

—DISTINCTION; CATEGORY; COMBINATORY PRINCIPLE

DISTRIBUTION
(distribution)

1. **Distribution** is the set of contexts (or settings) in which a previously identified unit* can be found. When two or more units are found in the same contexts, they are called **distributionally equivalent** units. By contrast, when units have no common context, they are said to be in **complementary distribution.** In between these two extreme cases, the most frequent one is, of course, the case of a partially equivalent distribution such as the partial synonymy* (or parasynonymy*) among lexemes* found in lexicography.

2. By showing that two or several units can appear in identical contexts, distribution permits the analyst to affirm the existence, at the level of the content,* of common semes* and then to go on to semantic reduction.* Furthermore, when a given unit keeps one or more semes in all the possible contexts, these semes can then be viewed as its semic kernel,* as contrasted with the contextual* semes (which vary according to the sub-sets of contexts) which are in "complementary distribution."

3. **Distributional analysis** (L. Bloomfield, Z. S. Harris) is primarily based upon the linearity of the signifier.* Such analysis has an inductive* and descriptive character. Its main goal is the elucidation of distributions, that is, of the set of contexts in which a given linguistic unit can be found. This procedure, which theoretically avoids the necessity of calling upon meaning* as a criterion, is based upon co-occurrence.* By elucidating relations of compatibility* or of incompatibility among elements on the syntagmatic* axis, distributional analysis allows the establishment of **distributional classes,** once the recognized combinations* and restrictions* have been taken into account. This type of approach, which is taxonomic* in nature, leads to a segmentation of the sentence and ultimately to an analysis in terms of immediate constituents* (which served as the starting point for generative grammar*).

4. The methods of distributional analysis can be used in semiotics either as discovery* procedures or as verification* procedures. As discovery procedures these methods permit the analyst to infer semantic

oppositions* and to name semic categories*—on the basis of the recognition of discriminatory* criteria which permit a distinction among various contexts. As verification procedures these methods start from a previously established unit—a pheme* or a seme*—and proceed to verify its presence in a given language or discourse. As a discovery procedure this approach is called inductive, while as a verification procedure it is called deductive.*
—LINEARITY; CONSTITUENT; SYNTAGMATIC; TAXONOMY; ORDER

DIVISION
(division)

L. Hjelmslev uses the term **division** to designate the analysis* of the process,* that is, of the syntagmatic* dimension of a semiotic* system. Division is opposed to articulation (a term reserved for the analysis of the system*).—ARTICULATION

DOING/CAUSING
(faire)

1. The distinction that we have established between utterances* of **doing** and utterances of state,* even if it refers intuitively to the dichotomy change/permanence, is an *a priori* and arbitrary formulation, which permits the construction of a surface narrative syntax.* As the predicate-function of such an utterance, doing is to be considered, in an anthropomorphic* syntactic language, as the conversion* of the transformation* relation.

2. The modal character of doing needs to be recognized. According to our definition—which seems to us to be the least restrictive—a modality* is a predicate* governing and modifying another predicate (or an utterance which has as

object-actant another predicate). In this perspective, any case of doing—whether it be a case of an instrumental doing (causing-to-be), or a manipulative doing (causing-to-do), of a doing which constructs, transforms, and destroys things, or of a factitive* doing which manipulates beings—appears as the predicate-function of a modal utterance governing another utterance.

3. Along the two dimensions of narrativity* (and of the activities that it is supposed to describe and organize), the pragmatic* dimension and the cognitive* dimension, two sorts of doing will be distinguished: **pragmatic doing** and **cognitive doing.** This opposition, which at first appears to be self-evident, is nonetheless not syntactic in nature and asserts itself only at more superficial levels of language. Thus, pragmatic doing seems to be distinguished from cognitive doing by the somatic and gestual nature of its signifier, and also by the nature of the semantic investments that the objects concerned by the doing receive (the objects of pragmatic doing being descriptive values, cultural values, in a word, non-modal values). However, the somatic or gestual signifier is sometimes placed at the service of cognitive activities (in the communication or construction of objects, for example). Thus, it is G. Dumézil's third function* which best describes pragmatic doing.

4. The distinction, in the cognitive dimension, between **narrative doing** and **communicative doing** is syntactic in nature. Communicative doing is a "causing-to-know," that is, a doing which has cognition as the object of value that it aims to bring into conjunction with the receiver.* When the axis of communication* has thus been recognized, it is then

possible to introduce new distinctions—the proliferation of which must not exceed the real needs of the analysis—founded on semantico-syntactic criteria. Thus, first of all, an **informative* doing** will be recognized, defined by the absence of any modalization, as the communication of the object of cognition in its (theoretically) pure state. The informative doing can then be viewed as the articulation of an **emissive* doing** and a **receptive* doing.** The latter can be either **active** (listening, looking-at) or **passive** (hearing, seeing). It is along the same axis of communication that the distinction—which seems to us fundamental for a typology of discourse —between **persuasive* doing** and **interpretive* doing** appears, thanks to the modalizations and complexifications of the programs of doing which are its result.

5. Narrative doing—which corresponds, in our view, with what could improperly be designated as a "syntagmatic understanding"—constitutes a vast and open field for analysis and reflection, whose importance, through its relations with cognitive psychology, can only increase. Preliminary studies, in the area of discourse concerning scientific topics, have led to a distinction between a **taxonomic doing** (with its **comparative** and **taxonomic** aspects) and a **programmatic doing.**
—SYNTAX, SURFACE NARRATIVE

DOMAIN
(instance)

By **domains of substance** is meant the modes of presence for the knowing subject—modes taken over by that subject—of the substance insofar as the latter is an object of cognition. Thus, for the phonic substance, three domains are rec-ognized: the **articulatory domain,** physiological in nature, where the substance is a sort of gestuality of the muscles; the **acoustic domain,** physical in nature, where it is received in the form of waves; finally, the **auditive domain,** psycho-physiological in nature, where the substance manifests itself in both wave and quantum form. Domain and substance must therefore not be confused: it is always the same substance which is present in different ways, even if the correlation between the different domains—*e.g.,* between articulatory and acoustic analyses—is difficult to establish. In every case, the substance seems to be a continuum the segmentation of which raises enormous difficulties. Therefore, it will be understood that the commutation test—which relies on the discriminatory signified*—aided by graphic transcoding* (even though the invention of writing presupposes implicit commutation operations), remains the surest means for establishing phonic units. It is not surprising, then, that difficulties crop up when an attempt is made to recognize discrete units in non-linguistic semiotic systems (in gestuality, in painting, etc.): the disappointment felt by too hasty semioticians is equaled only by their ignorance of the problems encountered by linguists, even if the latter do not always publicize them.—SUBSTANCE

DOMINANCE
(dominance)

1. The term* which, during the operation of neutralization, is kept to manifest the entire category,* is called **dominant.** When, for instance, the opposition of masculine with feminine in French is neutralized by the apparition of the

anaphoric "ils," there is a neutralization with **dominance** of the masculine. ("They" [ils]; referring to two or more entities, at least one of which is of masculine gender.)

2. Following V. Brøndal, a distinction is made between varieties of the complex* term (which holds together the two contrary terms of the semiotic square): the complex term with a **positive dominance,** when the dominating term belongs to the positive deixis,* and the complex term with a **negative dominance,** in the opposite case. Since the complex terms are the results of the third generation of the elementary terms, this particularity of their articulation must be interpreted as the effect of syntagmatic constraints encountered along their trajectory.
—NEUTRALIZATION; SQUARE, SEMIOTIC; COMPLEX TERM

DOMINATION
(domination)

Located on the figurative* level, and in the framework of the polemical* structure, **domination** characterizes the position of the subject* of an utterance of doing* when the subject exercises its being-able-to-do* and thus makes impossible any contrary action by the anti-subject. Since it presupposes confrontation* (of a polemical type), domination is followed by its consequence,* that is, the attribution of the object* of value. With these two components —a preceding and a following component—domination is one of the three elements which constitute the test.—CONFRONTATION; ATTRIBUTION; TEST

DONOR
(donateur)

In V. Propp's terminology, the **donor** is one of the seven characters of the folktale whose "sphere of action" includes "the preparation for the transmission of a magical object, and the provision of the hero with a magical object" (p. 79). In narrative semiotics this role—together with that of Propp's "auxiliary" character—is substumed by the term helper. The **anti-donor,** a term used by some semioticians, can similarly be related to the role of opponent.*—HELPER

DUPLICATION
(duplication)

The term **duplication** designates the repetition, within the narrative schema,* of a given narrative program* with figurative* manifestations, which may differ among themselves. Duplication is characterized by the failure of the first program and the success of the second. Duplication's signification is that of emphasis*: the failure shows the difficulty of the test and underscores the importance of the success.—TRIPLICATION; TEST

DURATIVENESS
(durativité)

Durativeness is an aspectual seme* indicating, on the syntagmatic axis,* that a temporal interval situated between the inchoative* term and the terminative* term is entirely filled by a process.* Paradigmatically this seme is part of the aspectual category *durativeness/ punctuality.* The same temporal interval can be filled with identical or comparable entities located on the same level of derivation.* In such a case one speaks of **discontinuous durativeness** (or iterativeness), by contrast with **continuous durativeness** which characterizes a single process.—ASPECTUALIZATION; ITERATIVENESS

DYSPHORIA
(dysphorie)

Dysphoria is the negative term of the thymic category which serves to valorize the semantic micro-universe*—by establishing the negative values*—and to transform them into axiologies.* The thymic category is articulated as *euphoria/dysphoria,* and includes, as a neutral term, *aphoria.*—THYMIC CATEGORY

ABCD**E**FGHIJKLMN OPQRSTUVWXYZ

ECONOMY
(économie)

1. The term **economy** usually refers, in a very broad sense, to the organization of the various elements of a set* which can be broken down into its components.*

2. More precisely, the term economy is used to designate the organization of a theory* or of a semiotic* system according to the principles of coherence* and simplicity.* According to Hjelmslev, the principle of economy can be deduced from the principle of simplicity, just as the principle of reduction can.

3. In the domain of diachronic research, the term "economy of a semiotic system" is understood to mean the temporary equilibrium* which can be upset as a consequence of the action of praxis, carried out in divergent or opposed directions. A. Martinet has defined this concept in linguistics.

4. In information* theory the principle of economy governs the relations between the tendency toward a minimum in the transmission of messages,* and the amount of information actually transmitted once the relation noise*/redundance* has been taken into account.
—DIACHRONY

EFFECT, MEANING
(effet de sens)

Meaning effect (a phrase borrowed from G. Guillaume) is the impression of "reality" produced by our senses when confronted with meaning, that is with an undergirding semiotic system. It can be said, for instance, that the world* of common sense is the meaning effect produced by the encounter of the human subject with the world as object. Similarly, an "understood" sentence is the meaning effect of a specific syntagmatic organization of several sememes.* Thus, when it is affirmed, in Bloomfieldian tradition, that meaning exists but that one cannot say anything about it, the word "meaning" must be understood as "meaning effect," which is the only reality which can be grasped, but which cannot be directly apprehended. Consequently semantics* is not the description of meaning. It is rather the construction which, aiming at producing a representation* of signification,* will be validated only insofar as this representation can engender a comparable meaning effect. Located in the domain of reception, meaning effect corresponds to semiosis*—an act located at the level of enunciation—and to the manifestation which the discourse utterance is.—MEANING; SIGNIFICATION

EFFICIENCY
(efficacité)

1. In common usage, **efficiency** is the ability to produce a maximum of results with a minimum of efforts (*Petit Robert* dictionary). A semiotic theory* and the models* it allows to be constructed are said to be efficient when, in addition to obeying the principles of simplicity* and of economy,* they are also projective —that is, when they permit the anticipation and accounting for of a great number of facts.

2. As concerns a formalized* theory, it can be said to be efficient when the rules* it formulates are operational, that is, when these rules can be implemented by an automaton.* As is well known, the concept of efficiency takes, at least in part, the place of truth criteria in formal languages.
—OPERATIONAL

ELASTICITY OF DISCOURSE
(élasticité du discours)

1. **Elasticity of discourse** is probably—and at least as much as what is termed double articulation* —one of the specific properties of natural languages.* It consists in the aptitude of the discourse to flatten out, in a linear way, semiotic hierarchies,* successively to set out discoursive segments belonging to very different levels of a given semiotic system. The production of the discourse is thus characterized by two kinds of apparently contradictory activities: **expansion** and **condensation.**

2. The grammarians who adhere to a linguistics limited to the sentence* are mainly struck by the phenomenon of expansion traditionally viewed, at the level of the sentence-units, as iterations resulting from coordination and subordination. This view has been taken up again today, in a form both more precise and more general, by the concept of recursivity.* By contrast, the activity of condensation, the manifestations of which are visible in the construction of many kinds of metalanguages* (documentary languages, grammars, logical languages, etc.), has so far not been much studied with precision. It is nevertheless just as correct to affirm that an elementary utterance* (or a logical proposition) is the result of a condensation of syntax as we can affirm that the discourse is the expansion of elementary syntactic units.

3. In semantics, accounting for the elasticity of discourse becomes a must. For indeed one observes that discoursive units* of various dimensions can be recognized as semantically equivalent. The metalinguistic activity which can be recognized within the discourse, and the phe-

nomenon of paraphrasing* (considered in principle) belong to this elasticity of discourse, the most striking example of which is the interplay of linguistic names* (terms) (= condensations) and of linguistic definitions* (= expansions).
—CONDENSATION; EXPANSION; PARAPHRASING

ELEMENT
(élément)

1. Generally speaking, the term **element** designates a constitutive part of a unit* which can be broken down. In logic, in the same sense but more precisely, each individual belonging* to a class (or set) is called an element of this class (or set).

2. In a deductive* type of theory,* the elements are the primary concepts,* often undefinable, which are its foundation. It is sometimes in this sense that in semiotics the term elementary (*i.e.,* fundamental) structures* or elementary utterance* is used.

3. By bringing together the two meanings of this word, one ends up viewing the element as a substance which cannot be broken down and, in linguistics and in semiotics, as the minimal unit of the object under consideration. Such a conception is obviously unacceptable for the structural approach, which considers it atomistic. It is the relation*—and the category* viewed as relational network—which is the primary elementary unit. In this perspective, element is used to designate each of the terms* of the category.
—UNIT; CLASS; ELEMENTARY; RELATION; CATEGORY

ELEMENTARY
(élémentaire)

1. The qualificative adjective **elementary** is used, by opposition to complex, in order to characterize the simplest aspects, reduced to the essential, of a phenomenon (*cf.* elementary structure* of signification, elementary axiological structures, elementary utterance*).

2. **Elementary** must be distinguished, on the other hand, from fundamental. While fundamental specifies what is the starting point of the deductive* operations, what constitutes the first level* of a theory,* elementary qualifies the simplest form which, as such, can be recognized at any level of analysis.
—ELEMENT

ELIMINATION
(élimination)

The procedure of **elimination** is correlative to that of extraction in the analysis of a corpus* and the elaboration of models.*—EXTRACTION

ELLIPSIS
(ellipse)

1. A figure of rhetoric, **ellipsis** is the relation posited, in a text as occurrence, between a unit of the deep* structure* and a unit the manifestation of which in the surface* structure is not realized. The element which is absent on the surface is nevertheless recognizable because of the relational network in which it is inscribed and which constitutes its context.* In a narrative, the accumulation of ellipses often creates an effect of "acceleration," as F. Rastier notes.

2. According to generative* grammar, ellipsis must be viewed as the result of erasing* rules which, thanks to one or several transformations,* suppress, at the level of the manifestation, the elements which are present at the level of the deep structure. From this point of

view, ellipsis belongs to a more general process, the process of implication.

3. There is ellipsis only when the omission which characterizes it does not hinder the understanding of the utterance, whether it be phrastic or discoursive. This presupposes that the missing units can be reconstituted with the help of the presupposing elements which are present. The procedure of explicitation which is then activated is called catalysis by L. Hjelmslev.
—IMPLICIT; CATALYSIS

EMBEDDING
(enchâssement)

1. In generative and transformational grammar, **embedding** is an operation of insertion through which a constituent* of the nuclear* sentence is replaced by another element, usually a new sentence. This is a procedure of substitution* comparable to L. Tesnière's concept of "second degree translation"; it makes it possible, for example, to account for the relation which exists between a principal clause* and its subordinate clause.

2. In narrative semiotics, the term embedding is sometimes used in order to designate the insertion of a narrative* into a larger narrative, yet without specifying the nature or precise function of the micronarrative. This is a metaphoric use of the term embedding, which alludes more to its common meaning (insertion of one element into another) than to its meaning in generative grammar. Thus it is better to use the term *intercalation*.

EMISSIVE DOING
(émissif [faire—])

In the transmission of knowledge,* informative **emissive doing** characterizes the sender*'s cognitive activity, as contrasted with receptive* doing, correlatively performed by the receiver.* Insofar as it is very little modalized—if only by affirmation* (as recognition of existence)—emissive doing is opposed to persuasive* doing (which, because it belongs to the domain of the sender, plays upon the categories being* and seeming* and thus activates the veridictory* modalities).—INFORMATIVE DOING; COGNITIVE

EMPHASIS
(emphase)

By **emphasis** is understood the supplementary investment of a linguistic unit by the seme *intensivity*. This investment is done either through rhetorical means (for example, the replacement of a neutral element by a figurative element of which only the seme ("intensity" is kept) or through syntactic means (by using "accenting" phrases, such as "It is I who . . . " or *"We* did . . . "). Generative* grammar attempts to account for emphatic syntactic forms either by speaking of emphatic transformations* or by recognizing the emphasis, at the level of deep* structures, as an optional "sentence constituant."

EMPIRICISM
(empirisme)

1. The principle of **empiricism** is viewed by L. Hjelmslev as the fundamental criterion of the scientificness* of a theory.* From the gnoseological perspective, the Danish linguist thus refuses to assign primacy either to the knowing subject (or to the laws of the mind) or to the object of knowledge (the order of things), by postulating the identity of these two domains. For him, functions* undergird relations* and

relations must be brought back, during the description,* to functions. Thus, structure* can be defined as both immanent and logical.

2. Deducing all the consequences from this principle, Hjelmslev distinguishes the theory of language from the philosophy of language, by submitting the theory to the principle of empiricism which demands that it fulfill three hierarchically organized conditions: the condition of non-contradiction (or of coherence), the condition of exhaustibility, and the condition of simplicity.

—COHERENCE; EXHAUSTIVITY; SIMPLICITY

ENCATALYZING
(encatalyser)

Encatalyzing is making explicit, by means of appropriate procedures, elements* of a sentence or segments of a discursive sequence, which had remained implicit.*— CATALYSIS; ELLIPSIS; EXPLICIT

ENCODING
(encodage)

1. In information* theory, **encoding** designates the set of operations which, by the use of a given code, permit the construction of a message.*

2. This term is sometimes used in semiotics to name the operations (without specifying them) carried out during the sending of a message. The complexity of these operations appears with the concepts of language act* and of enunciation.*

—CODE

ENGAGEMENT
(embrayage)

1. **Engagement** is the inverse of disengagement.* The latter is the effect of the expulsion from the domain of the enunciation* of the category* terms which serve as support for the utterance, whereas engagement designates the effect of a return to the enunciation. This effect is produced by the suspension* of the opposition between certain terms belonging to the categories of actor and/or of space and/or of time, as well as by a negation of the domain of the utterance. Every engagement thus presupposes a disengagement operation which logically precedes it. When, for example, the American president utters: "America is a beautiful country," he operates an utterative disengagement which installs in the discourse a distinct subject, distant with regard to the domain of the enunciation. On the other hand, if the same person said: "The American president thinks that . . . ," it is still formally an utterative disengagement, but one which is supplemented by a set of procedures which we call engagement and which, although they remain implicit, aim at producing, among other things, an effect of identification* between the subject of the utterance and the subject of the enunciation.

2. Just like disengagement, engagement can be divided into **actorial, temporal,** and **spatial engagement.** Each of these procedures can be considered separately, but they are often united and put into place concomitantly, in syncretism.* Thus, for example, the memories of the pleasant fishing expedition, in Maupassant's *Two Friends,* evoked, when the two friends recognize each other, in besieged Paris, put the syncretic spatio-temporal engagement into action. Total engagement cannot be conceived, since it would completely efface any trace of the

discourse; it would be a return to the "ineffable." Just as there is no secret as long as someone can allusively suspect its existence or its eventual unveiling, engagement must leave some discursive mark of the preceding disengagement.

3. It is by beginning from the "disengaged" discourse that the procedures of disambiguization carrying forth the logical presuppositions of the utterance can be imagined. Thus an utterance of the type: "You're working well, my boy," can have a double reading. In one case, there is a simple enunciative disengagement (the enunciator compliments an industrious boy). In the other, the disengagement is followed by engagement (the enunciator addresses itself in "interior discourse"): it is the "you" which works well and compliments itself. It is not simple to explain this second reading. It will be said that the double reading can come only from the existence, in "deep structure," of two distinct utterances, and the second one, installing the subject "you" in the place of the forseeable "I," can be described as an implicit disengagement projecting the "I." This procedure would be followed by the suspension of the categoric opposition "I"/"you," which would permit the production of the "you." However, such an interpretation, correct though it may be, does not seem completely satisfying: it does not account for the essential, for the illusory impression produced, according to which the uttered "you" belongs to the domain of the enunciation. On the other hand, the suspension (or the neutralization) of the categoric opposition "I"/"you" cannot be decreed in an arbitrary fashion: it can take place only if the existence of a common base, of a relation which can subsume the two terms of the cate-

gory, is admitted. Now this common base is constituted by the term *not-I* to which we had to have recourse in order to account for the primordial operation which instituted the disengagement. In this latter procedure, the domain of the enunciation is negated, which produces a *not-I* which can be defined as the actantial domain of the utterance. This being the case, it seems that we can interpret engagement as the negation of the *not-I* (a term which arose at the moment of the first negation, this negation creating the space of the utterance), carried out by the subject of the enunciation, and which aims at an (impossible) return to the source of the enunciation. Creating all the while the enunciative illusion, engagement does not halt the disengagement operation already begun: the "not-I," expelled, can then be manifested in the form of one of the two terms it subsumes, whether as an uttered "I" or "you," and leaving a certain margin for play within the semiotic constraints. This degree of latitude can vary. The use which M. Butor makes of the plural form of "you" in *La Modification,* for example, takes account of a prolonged suspensive trajectory in the framework of the category of person projected out of the enunciation. The "I," at first installed in the trajectory aimed at generating the subject of the utterance, is supposed first to be transformed into an inclusive "we" (subsuming the "I" and the "others" comparable to me) and only thereafter to pass to an exclusive plural form "you" (the "others" as metonym of the "not-I"). Only at this point does the engaging negation, at the same time that it manifests this plural "you," reverse the path followed, back to that "I" already disengaged, creator of the enunciative illusion.

4. We do not underestimate the difficulties presented by the construction of a model that can account for the complex procedures implied by engagement. Others will certainly do better than we. We will stick to what we deem essential: engagement is both a goal of the domain of the enunciation and it is a sort of failure, an impossibility of reaching that goal. The two "references" with the aid of which a way out of the closed world of language is sought, are a means of pinning this universe onto a totally distinct exteriority—reference to the subject (to the domain of the enunciation) and reference to the object (to the world which surrounds human beings as referent*). These references succeed only, in the final analysis, in producing illusions: the referential illusion and the enunciative illusion.

5. This is doubtless not the proper place, within the limits of this entry, to attempt to develop a typology of engagements. This will be done in its proper time, when it can be based on a sufficient number of concrete analyses. Just as for disengagement, a distinction is made between **utterative engagement** (*cf.,* above, the example of the American president) and the **enunciative engagement** (the industrious boy). This is a distinction between, on the one hand, the engagement which aims at a return to the domain of the enunciation and, on the other hand, second-degree—or **internal**—engagement, which is carried out within the discourse, where the subject aimed at is already installed (*cf.* Maupassant's "two friends," whose "interiority" is constructed by engaging their memories). It is also a distinction between **homo-categoric engagement,** when the disengagement and the engagement which follows it both concern the same cate-

gory, that of actor, of space, or of time, and **hetero-categoric engagement,** when the disengaging and engaging categories are distinct, as, for example, in the case of Baudelaire, who utters: "I am the boudoir. . . ." Contrary to what happens at the moment of disengagement, the effect of which is to referentialize the domain where its operation begins, engagement produces a de-referentialization of the utterance that it concerns. It is in this latter fashion that description of nature is transformed into "mood": Proust's narrator's childhood, memorized (that is, having undergone temporal engagement), ceases being a series of "events" and becomes a figurative organization of "memories," etc. We do not believe that engagement procedures can exhaustively treat the question of symbolism, but they can nonetheless account in part for the way multiple aspects of "interior life" are put into discourse.

6. The typology of engagement procedures that we await—and for which we have just sketched out a few axes—joined to a typology of disengagement procedures which is inseparable from it, is alone capable of founding the definition—and the typology—of discursive units* and of throwing new light on the concept of writing.*
—DISENGAGEMENT

ENTITY
(grandeur)

By **entity** is designated that "existant" the semiotic existence of which is presumed (prior to the analysis* which will recognize therein a discrete unit) and the comparability of which with other entities of the same order is alone postulated.—UNIT

ENUNCIATION
(énunciation)

1. According to either implicit or explicit epistemological presuppositions **enunciation** will be defined in one of two different ways: either (a) as the non-linguistic (referential) structure which underlines linguistic communication, or (b) as a linguistic domain which is logically presupposed by the very existence of the utterance (which contains traces or markers of the enunciation). In the first case, the expressions "communication situation," or "psycho-sociological context" are used to designate the production of utterances; such a situation (or referential* context) allows for the actualization of the production of the utterance. In the second case, since the utterance is considered to be the result attained by enunciation, the latter appears as the domain of mediation* that guarantees the process by which language virtualities become discourse utterances. According to the first definition, the concept of enunciation tends to approximate the concept of speech acts,* considered individually. According to the second definition, enunciation must be conceived of as an autonomous component of language theory, *i.e.*, as a domain which governs the passage from (linguistic) competence to (linguistic) performance, from virtual semiotic structures (to be actualized by the enunciations) to structures that are realized in the form of discourse. We will retain the second definition. Since it is not in contradiction with the semiotic theory that we propose to develop, only this second notion of enunciation enables us to integrate this domain into our overall view of semiotics.

2. Emile Benveniste gave the first formulation of enunciation as a process by which natural language (Saussure's *langue*) is turned into discourse. In between language (conceived of as a paradigmatic* system) and speech*—already interpreted by Hjelmslev as a syntagmatic* system and now specified in its status as discourse—it is indeed necessary to supply mediating structures and to imagine how it is that language as social system can be assumed by the individual realm without as a result being scattered into an infinite number of examples of speech (Saussure's *parole*), outside all scientific cognizance. It is true that Benveniste's innovative contribution gave rise to a number of exegeses of a metaphysical or psychoanalytic bent, all of them exalting the unexpected reappearance of the subject and permitting the suppression of an "anonymous" conception of language credited—and discredited—for being a collective system of constraints. By restoring things to more moderate proportions, it does not appear impossible to integrate this new approach to the issue into the broader context of the Saussurian tradition.

3. If enunciation is conceived of as a domain of mediation by which discourse is produced, we must attempt to define just what it is that is mediated by this domain: what are the virtual structures that constitute that which is prior to enunciation? The debate concerning these issues is far from complete and the positions taken spread out to include the affirmation of the basically paradigmatic nature of language (which is a satisfying position, strictly speaking, for certain rigorous phonologists), the Hjelmslevian concept according to which language is both system and process, and the Chomskian attitude that sees in the rules of sentential formation (by occa-

sionally reducing the paradigmatic side to a simple alphabet*) the essence of linguistic competence.* For our part, since we are called upon to account for the differnt domains—organized as a series of strata—of the total generative trajectory, we will consider the place of the semiotic virtualities that the enunciator is called upon to actualize as the place where the semionarrative structures* reside. These are forms which, by becoming actualized as operations, make up the **semiotic competence** of the subject of the enunciation.

4. On the other hand, if the enunciation is the place where semiotic competence is exercised, it is at the same time the domain of the establishment of the subject (of the enunciation). Prior to its articulation, the place that we can label the "ego hic et nunc" is semiotically empty though (as a reservoir of meaning) semantically too full. It is the projection (along with the processes that we bring together under the name of disengagement*), outside of this domain, both of the actants of the utterance and of the spatio-temporal coordinates, which constitutes the subject of the enunciation by everything which it is not. It is the rejection (along with the processes that we call engagement*) of the same categories that are intended to hide the imaginary place of the enunciation, which confers upon the subject the illusory status of being. The set of processes that can institute the discourse as a space and time, populated with subjects other than the enunciator, thus constitutes for us *discoursive competence* in the strictest sense. If we add to this the reservoir of figures* of the world and discoursive configurations,* which enable the subject of the enunciation to exercise its figurative knowing-how-

to-do, the contents of discoursive competence in the broad sense of the term are tentatively sketched out.

5. The mechanism of enunciation, which in the unsettled state of current research can only be evoked in broad strokes, runs the risk of remaining useless if we do not include therein its essential feature, what sets it going, what makes enunciation one act* among others, namely intentionality. We refuse to use the notion of intention* (with which some have tried to ground the act of communication as being based upon an "intention to communicate"), because, among other things, it reduces signification* solely to the dimension of the conscious (what then becomes of dream discourse?). We prefer to speak of intentionality,* which we interpret as a vision of the world, as an oriented, transitive* relation owing to which the subject constitutes the world as an object while constituting it thereby. Therefore, in order to express, in a canonical form, what enunciation is, we shall say that it is an utterance the predicate-function of which we can call "intentionality" and the object of which is the discourse-utterance.

6. Finally, we must add one last comment regarding what follows an enunciation. As an act, enunciation has the effect of producing semiosis, or, to be more specific, that continuous sequence of semiotic acts that we can call manifestation.* The act of signifying involves here the constraint upon the substance of the expression* which forces us to set up textualization* processes (unidimensional and linear, but also two-dimensional and planar, etc.). It is obvious that, when considered from the point of view of the enunciatee, enunciation operates in an opposite direction and proceeds,

first of all, toward the elimination of all linearity.

7. An unfortunate confusion is often encountered between enunciation properly speaking, the mode of existence of which is that of being what is logically presupposed by the utterance, and the **uttered** (or reported) **enunciation** which is only the simulacrum within the discourse imitative of the *enunciative* doing: the "I," "here," and "now" that we encountered in uttered discourse in no way represents the subject, space, or time of the enunciation. The uttered enunciation is to be considered as a sub-class of utterances which pass for a descriptive (though non-scientific) metalanguage of enunciation.

—ACT, SPEECH; DISENGAGEMENT; COMPETENCE; INTENTION; UTTERANCE

ENUNCIATOR/ ENUNCIATEE

(*énonciateur/énonciataire*)

When considered as the implicit framework which is logically presupposed by the existence of the utterance, the structure of enunciation involves two domains: those of enunciator and of enunciatee. We shall call **enunciator** the implicit sender* of the enunciation (or "communication"), distinguishing it thereby from the narrator*—for example the "I"—which is an actant* obtained through the process of disengagement and is inserted explicitly within the discourse. Similarly, the **enunciatee** corresponds to the implicit receiver of the enunciation, though distinct from the narratee* which is recognizable as such inside the utterance (for example, "The reader will understand that . . . "). So understood, the enunciatee is not only the receiver of the communication but also the discourse-pro-

ducing subject: "reading" is a language act* (a signifying act) in the same way as the actual production of discourse is a language (speech) act. The term "subject of the enunciation," which is often used as a synonym for the enunciator, in fact covers both actantial positions of enunciator and enunciatee.— SENDER

EPISTEME

(*épistémé*)

1. There are at least two possible definitions for the notion of **episteme.** For the first, the word episteme can designate the hierarchical organization of several semiotic systems. This organization, located at the level of deep* semiotic structures, can generate, by means of a combinatory principle and of selective rules* of incompatibility,* the set of manifestations (either realized or potential) included in these systems within a given culture. There must be a new series of selective rules which permit the manifestation to be limited to the surface structures* which are actually realized. It is in this way, for example, that A. J. Greimas and F. Rastier have attempted to construct an episteme by hierarchically organizing the semiotic systems formulating the sexual, socio-matrimonial, and economic relations in the traditional French cultural universe.

2. The episteme can likewise be defined as a meta-semiotics of culture,* that is, as the attitude adopted by a socio-cultural community with respect to its own signs (*cf.* Y. Lotman, M. Foucault). Thus, for example, for medieval culture the sign is essentially metonymic and refers to an underlying totality, whereas for the culture of the Enlightenment, the sign is "natural" and denotes things perfectly. It is in

this perspective that R. Barthes could say that the Saussurian sign is "bourgeois." The episteme, thus conceived, must thereby be considered as a connotative meta-semiotics. —CONNOTATION; SEMIOTICS

EPISTEMIC MODALITIES
(épistémiques [modalités—])

1. **Epistemic modalities** stem from the competence* of the enunciatee* (or, in the case of narrative discourse, of the ultimate sender*) which, after its interpretive* doing, "takes over," assumes (or ratifies) the cognitive* positions formulated by the enunciator (or submitted by the subject). Insofar as the enunciator carries out a persuasive* doing (that is, a causing-to-believe) within the enunciative contract (implicit or explicit), the enunciatee, in turn, completes its interpretive doing by an **epistemic judgement** (that is, by a believing) that it passes on the utterances* of state submitted to it. Account must be taken, however, of the fact that it receives the utterance, whatever its prior modalizations, as a manifestation* (a *seeming* or a *non-seeming*) on the basis of which it must decide concerning the utterance's immanence* (its *being* or its *non-being*). Thus, epistemic judgement, being based on the interpreted phenomenal,* is taking-up of the noumenal.*

2. From the semiotic point of view, we can speak of an **epistemic modal structure** when the modality of believing* overdetermines an utterance of state (having an already-modalized "being" as predicate). Mapping such a structure onto the semiotic square permits the formulation of the epistemic modal category:

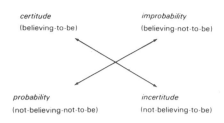

certitude
(believing-to-be)

improbability
(believing-not-to-be)

probability
(not-believing-not-to-be)

incertitude
(not-believing-to-be)

It will be noted that each term of the square can be considered to be a modal value* (named entity) or a modal structure (structurally defined entity).

3. It should be noted that, in distinction, for example, from the alethic* modalities, where the *possible/impossible* distinction corresponds to a contradiction excluding any third term, the epistemic category includes only gradual and relative oppositions, which allow for the manifestation of a large number of intermediary positions. This particular status of the epistemic modalities merely opens a new set of problems, that of **epistemic competence.** Here, epistemic judgement does not depend only on the value of the interpretive doing which is assumed to precede it (that is, on the cognition bearing on the veridictory* modalizations of the utterance), but also— to a degree yet to be determined— upon the wanting-to-believe and on the being-able-to-believe of the epistemic subject.

4. Scholarly ("scientific") discourse in the social sciences is characterized by, among other things, an (over-)abundance of epistemic modalizations, which seem to be there to compensate for the lack of verification procedures. Likewise, such is partially the case in the laboratory sciences and in discourse concerning discoveries,* all of which experience difficulties in verifying

their hypotheses. This is why the concept of acceptability,* set forth by generative grammar,* corresponds really to an epistemic judgment founded on the modality of being-able, which judgment can only be relative (and never absolute).
—BELIEVING; MODALITY

EPISTEMOLOGY
(épistémologie)

1. **Epistemology** is the analysis of the axioms,* hypotheses,* procedures*—even of the results— that are peculiar to a given science. It has, indeed, as its object the examination of the organization and functioning of scientific approaches and of judging their value. Thus understood, epistemology will be confused neither with methodology* nor with the theory of knowledge (or gnoseology)—sometimes also called epistemology—which studies, from the philosophical viewpoint, the relation between subject* and object.*

2. The **epistemological level*** is an essential characteristic of any well-formed theory. By beginning with the material (or language object) studied (considered as level 1), we can locate first of all the plane of description* (level 2), which is a metalinguistic representation of level 1, and that of methodology (level 3), which defines the descriptive concepts.* Epistemology takes place on a hierarchically superior plane (level 4): its task is to criticize and to verify the soundness of the methodological level by testing its coherence and measuring its adequacy* with respect to description; it must evaluate, among other things, the procedures of description and of discovery.*

3. Every theory rests upon a varying number of undefined con-

cepts which are to be included in what is called the **epistemological inventory.** The theory must nonetheless aim at reducing to a minimum the number of these concepts, thanks particularly to interdefinitions (which secure coherency), and must permit the indispensable **epistemological minimum** to be reached (according to the principle that the number of implicit postulates should be the smallest possible).
—THEORY; COHERENCE

EQUILIBRIUM
(équilibre)

1. Put forth by diachronic linguistics, the principle of **equilibrium,** although teleological in nature, accounts for the diachronic transformations of semiotic systems; introduced by Trubetzkoy, it was subsequently taken up by Benveniste and by Martinet.

2. Every structure* is in a relatively unstable state of equilibrium, resulting from the influence of external factors (particularly, of tendencies). If a comparison of two successive states* indeed serves to specify the nature of the intervening transformations,* this is because the principle of equilibrium calls upon another undefined postulate, namely that a disequilibrated system tends to return to a new state of equilibrium (identical or different).

3. In the elementary structure* of signification, the second-generation terms, according to V. Brøndal, can be present either in a state of equilibrium (complex* term) or of disequilibrium. In the latter case, they will be predominantly positive (positive complex term) or negative (negative complex term). Disequilibrium presupposes a syntagmatic trajectory on the semiotic square (creative of new positions).

4. In narrative semiotics, the term **narrative equilibrium** will be used when the schema is articulated by the exchange* structure or, more generally speaking, by the contract* (with its execution by the contracting parties).

—ECONOMY; DOMINANCE; DIACHRONY

EQUIVALENCE
(équivalence)

1. In linguistics, two grammars* are considered **equivalent** when, formulated in two different metalanguages,* they can be formalized* with the help of two formal isomorphic* systems. At a more restricted level, and within the framework of generative* grammar, two sentences are said to be equivalent when there is a relation of reciprocal implication* between them (example: active/passive).

2. From the semantic point of view, **equivalence** corresponds to a partial semic* identity* between two or more recognized units. It authorizes semantic analysis by allowing parasynonymies* to be reduced.* Making the differences* evident, it helps us to understand the metalinguistic functioning of the discourse.

3. In discourse analysis, which postulates several levels (following the schema of the generative* trajectory,*) relations of equivalence are recognized between these levels, which can be accounted for by conversion* procedures (or by vertical transformation* procedures). Beginning with the most abstract level and proceeding toward more concrete levels, new components, (anthropomorphic, figurative, etc.) are added and develop against a background of constant identities.

—IDENTITY; CONVERSION; TRANSFORMATION

ERASING
(effacement)

A term of generative* grammar, **erasing** designates a transformation* which can be assimilated to ellipsis* (as applied in the domain of phrastic syntax).—ELLIPSIS

ETHNO-SEMIOTICS
(éthno-sémiotique)

1. **Ethno-semiotics** is not truly an autonomous semiotics. If it were, it would be in competition with a field of knowledge already established under the name of ethnology or anthropology, whose contribution to the advent of semiotics itself is considerable. Rather, it is a privileged area of curiosities and of methodological exercises. This is due, first of all, to the fact that anthropology appears as the most rigorous discipline among the social sciences, because of the demands that it imposes on itself and because, on the other hand, it has had to attack Euro-centrism and go beyond it, by developing a way to study the universality of cultural objects and semiotic forces as a result of its awareness of the cultural relativism that the very object of its research ceaselessly calls to its attention.

2. Within this discipline, a meeting-place between anthropologists and semioticians has been constituted, under the name of **ethno-linguistics,** which, going beyond the simple description of exotic natural languages, has from its beginnings taken an interest in their semantic particularities (which lent themselves to contrastive and comparative approaches). The development of taxonomic research is probably due to anthropology's own vocation—since it wants to grasp totalities, to apprehend signifying sets. The description—and above all the

methodological elaboration that it presupposes—of **ethno-taxonomies** constitutes an important contribution to general semiotic theory. These taxonomies are, first, grammatical (study of the "conception of time," for example, starting from the description of verbal tense systems), then lexical taxonomies (description of kinship terminologies, permitting the elaboration of a rigorous componential* analysis; description of botanical, zoological, etc., taxonomies), finally, connotative taxonomies (typology of "social languages" distinguished according to criteria of sex, age group, hierarchy, of sacred/profane, etc.).

3. Ethno-semiotics has the merit of having conceived, inaugurated, and founded—beside ethno-taxonomies, which are paradigmatic descriptions—syntagmatic analyses bearing on different genres of ethnic literature, such as folk narratives (V. Propp) and mythic narratives (G. Dumézil, C. Lévi-Strauss). It is thanks to such syntagmatic analyses that the study of literary discourse was taken up in a new way. Since such studies have permitted general semiotics to make rapid progress, it is normal that the latter should now wish to repay, at least partially, its debt by suggesting the possibility of new approaches to ethno-literary discourses.

4. **Ethno-literary semiotics** is thus distinguished from literary* semiotics (in the "noble" meaning of the word "literary"), although the boundary which separates them cannot be strictly established. Among the main criteria that are used to distinguish them, will be noted: (a) the absence (or the implicit presence) of the semantic code* in ethno-literary discourse, which is opposed to its explicitation and to its integration in the literary discourse; (b) the maintaining, as in other semiotic systems, of a specific type of distance between the production of the discourse and its carrying out; (c) the importance of the structures of uttered enunciation,* proper to literary discourse (which can go so far as the "destruction" of the narrative), is the opposite of the effacement of the enunciator* (and of its marks) in ethno-literary discourse. All these differences are but gradual and do not put into question the existence of narrative and discoursive organization common to both ethno-literary discourse and literary discourse.

5. On the other hand, external criteria allow a distinction to be made between ethno-literature, proper to archaic communities (or to relatively closed agrarian societies), and socio-literature, a sort of "sub-literature," characteristic of developed industrial societies.

6. Given that general semiotics authorizes the treatment of non-linguistic (gestual, somatic, etc.) syntagmatic concatenations as discourses or texts, the field of ethno-linguistics can be enlarged to become an **ethno-semiotics;** analyses, still rare, of rituals and ceremonies lead us to suppose that ethnology can become, once again, the privileged locus for the construction of general models of signifying behavior.

—SEMIOTICS; LITERARY SEMIOTICS; SOCIO-SEMIOTICS

EUPHORIA
(euphorie)

Euphoria is the positive term* of the thymic category, which serves to valorize semantic micro-universes* by transforming them into axiologies.* *Euphoria* is opposed to *dysphoria.** The thymic category includes, in addition, as a neutral term, *aphoria.**—THYMIC CATEGORY

EVENT
(événement)

1. In narrative semiotics, **event** can be thought of as the action* of the individual or collective subject, to the degree to which such action has been recognized and interpreted* by a cognitive subject other than the subject of doing* itself and which can be either the observer* actant installed in the discourse (*cf.* the witness) or the narrator,* delegate of the enunciator* (the historian, for example). A structural definition of event seems to us to be necessary due to the fact that certain semioticians, taking their inspiration notably from logics of action, use this term as if it designated a simple and, so to speak, "natural" given. It can be seen, on the contrary, that event is a discursive configuration* and not a simple narrative unit: whence the impossibility of defining the narrative*—as some scholars try to do—as a succession of events.

2. Narrative semiotics distinguishes two dimensions* in narrative discourses: the pragmatic* dimension and the cognitive* dimension. The former is sometimes called the **factual dimension** (literally: **event dimension**) because the concatenations of somatic* behavior are therein represented and described. This distincion cannot be homologated with the one which, in the analysis of historical discourse, opposes factual history (literally: event history) to fundamental history. **Factual history** belongs to the surface* semiotic level and is manifested as a narrated story containing the two dimensions, pragmatic and cognitive, of the syntagmatics of history, whereas fundamental history is located at the level of deep* semiotic structures.
—ACTION; HI/STORY

EVIDENCE
(évidence)

A particular form of certitude —which is the name of the positive term of the epistemic modal category—**evidence** does not require the exercise of interpretive* doing. It is characterized either by the suppression of the distance between referential* discourse and cognitive* discourse which sanctions it thanks to the veridictory* modalities, or by the calling up of what is supposed to constitute a "real" referent.— CERTAINTY; EPISTEMIC MODALITIES

EXCHANGE
(échange)

1. **Exchange** is a performing doing which, located in a binary structure of subjects* (in the relation of one thing given for another), constitutes one of the forms of communication* or of transfer* of objects* of value.

2. As a reciprocal operation involving the doing of S1 and S2, exchange is a twofold performance, following the implicit or explicit establishment of a contract.* Exchange, therefore, involves the pair sender*/receiver. From this point of view, the canonic narrative* schema is dominated by the structure of exchange. The doing of S1 (Receiver) constitutes the performance* component, while the doing of S2 (Sender) constitutes the retribution* or sanction* component (either positive: recompense,* or negative: punishment*).

3. This reciprocal operation presupposes the establishment of competent actants, each of which represents a modal* position at the moment of the narrative pivoting* that exchange is.

4. In this way, hierarchically organized series of exchanges can constitute systems of obligations and of constraints such as those described by, among others, M. Mauss and C. Lévi-Strauss (limited exchange/generalized exchange).
—COMMUNICATION; CONTRACT; NARRATIVE SCHEMA

EXECUTION
(exécution)

When performance, interpreted as the modal* structure of doing,* is located in the pragmatic* dimension, it is called **execution,** by opposition to decision* (where performance takes place in the cognitive* dimension).—PERFORMANCE

EXHAUSTIVITY
(exhaustivité)

1. Bound to the humanistic tradition which makes it a *sine qua non* for research (in scholarship), **exhaustivity** must be linked to the concepts of corpus,* of model,* and of adequacy.* Indeed, it can be understood as the adequation of the proposed models to the total of the elements contained in the corpus.

2. Concerning the description* of linguistic data, L. Hjelmslev makes exhaustivity an integral part of his empiricism principle, all the while noting that, although the requirement of exhaustivity has priority over that of simplicity,* it must give way to the requirement of non-contradiction (or of coherence*). This recourse to exhaustivity is justified insofar as the Danish linguist is concerned with maintaining the equilibrium between the deductive* and inductive* aspects of the analysis.
—EMPIRICISM

EXISTENCE, SEMIOTIC
(existence sémiotique)

1. Since semiotics is given to the study of form* and not to that of substance,* it cannot indulge in making judgments concerning the nature of the objects it analyzes. This fact does not keep these objects from being somehow "present" for the researcher, nor does it prevent the latter from examining either relations of existence or existential judgments (whether implicit or explicit) found inscribed in discourse. Without devoting too much time to this, the researcher must therefore make some sort of pronouncement on that particular mode of existence known as **semiotic existence.**

2. Semiotic theory poses the problem of presence,* that is, of the "reality" of the objects which can be known. Indeed, scientific epistemology as a whole is confronted by this problem. On this level, it can be content with the following operational* definition which puts it under no obligation: the semiotic existence of any entity* is determined by the transitive* relation which binds this entity to the cognitive subject, and at the same time posits it as an object of knowledge.

3. When a given semiotic system is posited as an object of knowledge, Saussurian tradition recognizes in it two modes of existence. The first, **virtual* existence,** characteristic of the paradigmatic axis of language, is an "*in absentia*" existence. The second, **actual existence,** proper to the syntagmatic axis, offers the analyst semiotic objects "*in praesentia*" and seems, by this fact,

more "concrete." The passage from system* to process,* from language to discourse,* is called the process of actualization.*

4. Such a dichotomy was not troublesome as long as a distinction in principle between language and speech and, later, between competence and performance, could be considered satisfactory. Further analysis of these concepts—and the appearance, in the place of speech, of the notions of syntagmatics and above all of discourse—has brought to light the autonomy and the abstractness of the ways in which discourse is organized. Such organization is still very far from the way in which utterance-discourses "are there" as occurrences.* We are thus obliged to recognize a third mode of semiotic existence, which occurs as discursive manifestation,* due to semiosis*: the mode of **realized existence.**

5. The problem of the mode of existence is posed, finally, at another level, within the very semiotic systems under consideration and, most particularly, for the narrative discourses which are supposed to describe "real" situations and actions. While it recognizes that these are only simulacra of actions, in which "paper" subjects are involved, the analysis of such discourses demands that these situations and actions be treated as if they were real. Their diverse modes of existence, the forms of their activities, once described, can indeed serve as models for a semiotics of action* and of manipulation.*

6. This is why an existential definition, properly semiotic in nature, of subjects* and objects* encountered and identified in their discourse, is absolutely necessary. A semiotic subject is said to exist as subject only insofar as at least one determination can be recognized in it, in other words, only insofar as it is in relation with some object of value. Likewise, an object—among the innumerable objects that a discourse contains—is such only if it is in relation, if it is "aimed at" by a subject. Junction* is the necessary condition for the existence of subjects as well as of objects. Prior to their junction, subjects and objects are said to be virtual, and it is the function* which actualizes them. Two types of relations are put together under the name of function. Subjects and value objects in disjunction* is said to be actualized subjects and objects, while after conjunction they are to be realized. By realizing its narrative program,* the subject makes real the value which was only aimed at, and "realizes" itself.

—VIRTUALIZATION; ACTUALIZATION; REALIZATION

EXPANSION
(expansion)

By **expansion** is understood one of the aspects of the discourse's elasticity, in contrast to condensation*: these are two faces of the activity through which utterance-discourses are produced. Interpreted, from the syntactic point of view, as coordination and subordination, and, more recently, as recursivity,* expansion can be compared to paraphrase*: every lexeme can be taken up by a discursive definition, every minimal utterance can give rise, by dint of the expansion of its constituent elements, to a paragraph, etc. Taking the phenomenon of expansion into consideration makes discursive analysis possible; at the same time it complicates enormously the semiotician's task.—ELASTICITY OF DISCOURSE

EXPECTATION
(attente)

1. **Expectation** may be considered as the result of temporalization,* effected by imperfective* aspectuality, of the modality* of "wanting to be": this is no more than a provisional definition, since the configuration* of expectation has not yet been fully described.

2. Expectation designates the signified* of one of the terms of the prosodeme intonation,* which is homologous with the melodic curve of interrogative utterances.

3. In American pragmatics, expectation is a non-defined concept* which helps to characterize, in certain conversational situations, the actant* of communication.*

4. In German aesthetics of reception (H. R. Jauss), the expression **horizon of expectation,** inspired by Husserl, designates the extent to which forms of discursive organization can be foreseen. Thus understood, the horizon of expectation is the narrative and discursive competence* of the readers which enables them to judge the originality of the new discourse offered for their reading.

5. The concept of rhythm can also be defined in terms of expectation (C. Zilberberg, following P. Valéry).

EXPLICIT
(explicite)

1. In a first attempt at definition, the qualifier **explicit** seems to be a para-synonym of manifested*: an utterance (sentence or discourse) is said to be explicit insofar as it is the product of semiosis* (joining together the expression* and content* planes of language). The explicit has meaning only in contrast to the implicit—or presupposed unsaid in every communication* act—the **explicitation** of which appears to be one of the principal tasks of contemporary linguistics. Indeed, the so-called pragmatic* (in the American meaning) conditions, as well as the deep structures* of the utterance, belong to the implicit, and their explicitation is the equivalent, in this sense, of the elaboration of the fundamental components of semiotic* theory.

2. At the metalinguistic level of the construction of theory, the term explicitation is used with the meaning of formalization*: thus, generative* grammar intends to be explicit, that is, formulated in terms of formal* language.
—IMPLICIT

EXPRESSION
(expression)

1. Following L. Hjelmslev, we designate by **expression plane** the Saussurian signifier taken in the totality of its articulations, as the recto of a page whose verso would be the signified. We do not take it in the meaning of "acoustic image," as a superficial reading of Saussure has led others to interpret it. The expression plane is in a relation of reciprocal presupposition with the content* plane, and their union, in the language act, corresponds to semiosis.* The distinction between these two planes of language is, in Hjelmslevian theory, logically anterior to the division of each into form* and substance.* The expression form is thus phonology*'s object of study, whereas the expression substance belongs to phonetics.*

2. In scientific meta-semiosis,* **expression** designates a sequence of symbols* of a given alphabet,* obtained through the application of formulation (or of production) rules,

belonging to a finite set of rules. A sememe* or a phoneme,* for example, can be considered as expressions consisting of a series of semes or of phemes, through the application of the formation rules of the content plane or of the expression plane. By "well-formed expression" is meant a given series of symbols, resulting from the strict application of the rules.
—SIGNIFIER; CONTENT; FORM; SUBSTANCE

EXPRESSIVE FUNCTION
(expressive [fonction—])

In the triadic schema of linguistic communication, proposed by the psychologist K. Bühler (and taken up and expanded upon by R. Jakobson), the **expressive** function (also called emotive)—opposed to the referential* (relative to what is being spoken about) and conative (centered upon the Receiver*) functions—is the one which, bound directly to the Sender,* "aims at a direct expression of the speaker's attitude toward what he is talking about" (Jakobson, p. 354).—FUNCTION; COMMUNICATION

EXTENSION
(extension)

In traditional logic, by **extension** is meant the set of objects, real or ideal, to which an element of knowledge (concept or proposition) applies. Semiotic objects being studied independently from the external referent,* it is incorrect to speak, for example, of the extension of a sememe* as applying to a greater or lesser number of objects (*cf.* B. Pottier's "seats"). However, it can be useful to count the occurrences* of a graphic word, which constitute its extension. Likewise, the extension of

a seme* will be judged by counting the lexemes* (which belong to the linguistic "referential" area) within which it can be recognized. In other words, the objects which define the extension of another object must be—in semiotics—of the same nature this latter object.—COMPREHENSION

EXTEROCEPTIVITY
(extéroceptivité)

For the purpose of finding criteria for the classification of the semic* categories which articulate the semantic universe* considered as coextensive with a culture* or with a given human being, appeal can be made to a certain psychology of perception, which distinguishes **exteroceptive** properties, as coming from the exterior world, from interoceptive* data which have no correspondence in that world and which are presupposed, on the contrary, by the perception of the former. Finally, these will be distinguished from proprioceptive* elements, which result from the perception of one's own body. Such a classification, intuitively justified as it may seem, suffers from being entirely based on extra-semiotic criteria and presuppositions. Therefore we have attempted to substitute another terminology and other definitions for it. We designate by the name of semiological* level (or inventory) the set of semic categories which, while belonging to the content* plane of natural languages,* can appear as categories of the expression* plane of natural* semiotics (or semiotics of the natural world*), opposing it to the semantic* (*stricto sensu*) level, where such a transcoding* is not possible. While this new definition, intra-semiotic in character, seems to us to constitute an undeniable step forward, on the contrary the choice of name is defective, for it introduces polysememy* and ambiguity into the use of the qualifiers semiological and semantic. It seems to us, that when speaking of the semic categories and inventories of this plane, the word figurative* can be substituted for exteroceptive and semiological.—FIGURE

EXTRACTION
(extraction)

1. Once the corpus* has been established, it is the analyst's job to retain only the elements* which are pertinent to the chosen level of description,* leaving aside therefore all the other givens (which will then be qualified as stylistic*). This selection is carried out either by the procedure of **extraction** or of elimination, according to whether the remaining part of the corpus is qualitatively larger or not than the part to be excluded.

2. For L. Hjelmslev such an operation is not scientific, for it contradicts, in its very principle, the analyst's* procedure (which goes from the whole to the parts, or inversely). It is indeed clear that these procedures run the risk of reflecting only the descriptor's subjective viewpoint; nonetheless, it seems to us that they can be justified on the pragmatic and tactical plane, if they are considered solely as provisional tools, instrumental* in character. —PERTINENCE

ABCDE**F**GHIJKLMN
OPQRSTUVWXYZ

FACTITIVENESS
(factitivité)

1. Traditionally the factitive modality* is tentatively defined as a *causing-to-do*, that is, as a modal structure constituted by two utterances* ("causing" and "doing") in hypotactic relation, which have identical predicates* ("causing" is a type of "doing") but different subjects ("*doing*, such that the other *does* . . .").

2. Such a definition is blatantly insufficient. Let us consider successively the two utterances: the modalized utterance ("the doing by the other" as modalized subject) and the modalizing utterance (the "causing to be" performed by the modalizing subject). It is clear that the modalized utterance is not a simple utterance, but a syntagm, the subject's narrative trajectory, which can be broken down into performance* (the "causing-to-be" performed by this *other* subject) and competence* (logically presupposed by every doing, and which contains an autonomous modal investment). As for the

modalizing utterance ("causing to") its doing does not aim—at least directly—at another doing, but at the establishment of the second subject's narrative trajectory and, first of all, at the establishment of that subject's competence. In short, the modalizing subject "does something" such that, as a result of this "doing," the modal subject is instituted as a competent subject. The doing of the modalizing subject is consequently a *causing-to-be* as well, that is, a performance—but strictly cognitive* in nature—which necessarily raises the question of the cognitive competence of the modalizing subject itself (a competence which will first of all consist in the knowing* which bears upon the virtualities of the competence of the subject to be modalized).

3. From this, it can be seen that, far from being a simple hyperotactic relation between two utterances of doing—as tradition suggests—the locus where **factitiveness** is exercised is to be interpreted as a contractual* communication (involving the transmission of the modal investment) between two subjects, each of which is endowed with its own narrative* trajectory. It can likewise be seen that the problem of factitive modalization encompasses that of efficient communication.* This requires that we take into account the two domains of the enunciation, respectively characterized by a persuasive* doing and an interpretive* doing: both are necessary for the factitive transmission. Thus, the apparently simple structures of the exercise of factitiveness (causing-to-make a suit, for example) unfold into complex configurations of manipulation.
—MODALITY; COMMUNICATION; MANIPULATION

FACULTATIVENESS
(facultativité)

Facultativeness is the name of one of the terms of the deontic modal category, the syntactic definition of which is the modal structure of "not-being-obliged-to-do." It presupposes the existence of prescription,* of which it is the contradictory* term.—DEONTIC MODALITIES; HAVING-TO-DO or TO-BE

FALSENESS
(fausseté)

The name **falseness** designates the complex term* which includes the terms *non-being* and *non-seeming,* situated on the axis of subcontraries* in the semiotic square of the veridictory modalities. It will be noted that the "truth values" of the false, as of the true, are situated *within* the discourse, and that they are to be considered as terms resulting from veridiction operations: thus, any reference to (or any homologation with) the non-discursive world is excluded.—VERIDICTORY MODALITIES; SQUARE, SEMIOTIC

FALSIFICATION
(falsification)

In the framework of the confrontation between a theory* (of a hypothetico-deductive* type) and the "given" of the object presumed knowable, **falsification** is a logical procedure which complements that of verification.* It consists in showing that there exists at least one case where the hypothesis* set forth (or the model* constructed) does not conform to the data of the experiment. When a model is not verifiable, it can still be submitted to falsification, which permits a judgment to be made concerning its adequacy. Thus, in linguistic practice, when a model is projective (able to account for a set of facts larger than the set from which it was constructed), it can be falsified by counter-examples (or counter-cases). Such is the game often indulged in by the supporters of generative* grammar.—VERIFICATION

FEAR
(crainte)

Opposed to desire, **fear** is not, from a semantic perspective, a non-wanting, but a contrary wanting,* which can be interpreted only within a syntactic structure which postulates the reciprocity of antagonistic subjects (subject/anti-subject).—DESIRE

FIDUCIARY CONTRACT, RELATION
(fiduciaire [contrat, relation—])

1. The **fiduciary contract** involves a persuasive* doing on the sender's* part and, as counterpart, the receiver's adhesion. Thus, when the object of the persuasive doing is the enunciator's* veridiction (the saying-true), the counter-object which is expected to be gained consists in a believing*-true that the enunciatee grants to the status of the utterance-discourse. In this case, the fiduciary contract is an enunciative contract (or veridiction contract) which guarantees the validity of the uttered discourse. When the fiduciary contract sanctions a narrative program* within the discourse, the term utterative contract will be used.

2. The **fiduciary relation** is the relation established between the two planes of being* and seeming* when, thanks to the interpretive* doing, one moves from one plane to the other by asserting successively the one and the other of these modes of existence.
—VERIDICTION; VERIDICTORY MODALITIES; BELIEVING; EPISTEMIC MODALITIES

FIELD, SEMANTIC
(champ sémantique)

In lexical semantics, the name **semantic field** (or, depending on the authors, **notional** or **conceptual** field) is given to a group of lexical units that are considered, as a working hypothesis, to have an underlying structural organization. This notion of "Begriffsfeld," borrowed from J. Trier, can be used at best as an operational* concept. It enables us to establish intuitively and as a starting point, a lexematic corpus* whose semantic structuring* can then be undertaken through semic analysis. By playing on the addition of new lexemes* and the elimination of others, we can arrive at the description of a semantic micro-universe.*—SEMANTICS

FIGURATIVE
(figuratif)

1. Contrary to the term figure (which is polysemous) from which it derives, the qualifier **figurative** is only used in connection with a given content* (of a natural language, for example) when that content corresponds to something on the expression* level of the natural* semiotic system (or semiotics of the natural world). In this sense, in the context of the generative* trajectory of discourse, discursive semantics* includes, with the thematic (or abstract) component, a **figurative component.**

2. In this same perspective, **figurative trajectory** will be used for an isotopic concatenation of figures,

correlative to a given theme.* This concatenation, founded on the association of figures—proper to a determined cultural universe—is both partially free and partially constrained, in the measure to which, when a first figure is posited, it only elicits certain other figures, exclusive of all others. Given the many possibilities of figurativizing one and the same theme, this theme may underlie different figurative trajectories; thus variants* can be accounted for. For instance, the theme of the "sacred" can be taken up by several figures, such as those of the "priest," the "sacristan," or the "beadle." The figurative unfolding of the sequence will be affected by this diversity of figures. The modes of action, the places, and the times where the sequence must be realized, each time conforming to the initially chosen figure, will be different from each other in the same proportions. Conversely, the polysemy* of the first figure which is posited can potentially open onto several figurative trajectories corresponding to different themes: whence the phenomenon of plurisotopy* which develops significations superimposed on each other in a single discourse.

—FIGURE; WORLD, NATURAL; FIGURATIVIZATION; VARIANT

FIGURATIVIZATION
(figurativisation)

1. When it is decided to take on the task of classifying all discourses into two large classes—figurative and non-figurative (or abstract) discourses—one soon notices that almost all texts called literary and historical belong to the class of figurative discourse. It remains understood, however, that such a distinction is somewhat "ideal," that it seeks to classify forms (figurative and non-figurative) and not discourse-occurrences, which practically never present an "unalloyed" form. In fact, what interests the semiotician is understanding what the **figurativization** of discourses and of texts—a sub-component of discursive semantics*—consists in, and what the procedures, which are put into place by the enunciator* to figurativize the utterance,* are. Thus, the construction of a model of discourse production—which we call the generative* trajectory—proves to be useful if only because it permits the constitution of the general framework within which one can seek to inscribe, in an operational* and tentative manner, subject to invalidations and reconstructions, the **figurativization procedures** of a discourse posed first as neutral and abstract.

2. It is perhaps helpful to give a simple example of what we mean by figurativization. Let there be, at the outset of a discourse-utterance, a subject disjoined from the object, which is but a goal sought by it:

$$S \cup 0.$$

This object, which is only a syntactic position, stands invested with a value* which is, for example, "power," that is, a form of the modality* of being-able* (to do/to be):

$$S \cup 0_v \; (: \;\; power).$$

From there, the discourse can move into gear: the narrative program* consists in joining the subject with the value it seeks. Yet there are a thousand ways to tell such a story. The discourse is said to be figurativized at the moment when the syntactic object (0) receives a semantic investment* which will permit the enunciatee* to recognize it as a **figure**,* as an "automobile," for example:

$$S \cup 0 \; (: \;\; automobile) \; v \; (: \;\; power).$$

The discourse which expresses the quest* for the automobile, the exercise and, possibly at the end, the recognition* by another of the power which it allows to be manifested, is a figurative discourse.

3. This example, despite its simplicity, shows well that figurativization is but rarely manifested by a single point. It is true that figures of rhetoric can operate in the framework of a lexeme* or of an utterance.* However, it is most often the whole trajectory of the narrative* subject which is figurativized. The installation of the figure "automobile" affects the set of processes by changing them into actions,* confers figurative outlines on the subject which becomes an actor,* undergoes a spatio-temporal anchoring,* etc. It is then said that figurativization installs figurative* trajectories and, when these are coextensive with the dimensions of the discourse, that it causes figurative isotopies* to appear.

4. The study of **figurativity** is only at its beginning and, consequently, any hasty conceptualization is risky. The main difficulty lies in the implicit apriorism according to which every semiotic system (literature or painting, for example) is a "representation" of the world and possesses iconicity* as its prime given. Although literary discourse is considered as a "fiction," its fictional character does not bear on the words—which are supposed to represent things—but, in the first place, on the arrangement of the described actions, so that the lexemes inscribed in the discourse do not install semiotic figures there, but readymade "images of the world." It is the same in pictorial semiotics, where a painting is naturally treated as a collection of nameable icons, referring to the world "as it is" and, at the same time, to the world as verbalized. By contrast, all this changes when the text* is considered as the outcome of the progressive production of meaning, in the course of which structures and semiotic figures come into place, detail by detail, by successive strokes, and where the discourse can at every moment diverge towards manifestation* either under an abstract* form, or in a figurative formation, without for all that attaining a kitsch iconicity. Therefore it is necessary to distinguish, from now on, at least two levels in figurativization procedures: the first is that of **figuration,** that is, of the setting-up of semiotic figures (a sort of phonological level); the second would be that of **iconization,** which aims at decking out the figures exhaustively so as to produce the referential* illusion which would transform them into images of the world.

5. Even now, one can note the particular role which, among figurativization procedures, the **onomastic** sub-component is called upon to play. Figurativization is characterized by the specification and the particularization of the abstract discourse insofar as it is grasped in its deep structures, and by the introduction of anthroponyms,* of toponyms,* and of chrononyms* (corresponding respectively, on the plane of discoursive syntax,* to the three procedures constitutive of discoursivization: actorialization,* spatialization,* and temporalization*), that can be inventoried as going from the generic ("king," "forest," "winter") to the specific (proper nouns, spatio-temporal indices, dates, etc.). As such, figurativization is supposed to confer the desirable degree of re-

production of the real upon the text.
—FIGURE; ICONICITY; DIS-
COURSIVIZATION; GENERA-
TIVE TRAJECTORY

FIGURE
(figure)

1. The term **figure** is used by L.
Hjelmslev to designate non-signs,*
that is, units which separately constitute either the expression* plane or
the content* plane. Phonology* and
semantics* are thus, in the
Hjelmslevian sense, descriptions of
figures and not of signs.*
2. Beginning from this position,
it is expedient to limit somewhat the
meaning of the word figure. If we
consider that the two planes of language have the figurative (phemic
and semic) categories as minimal
units, the name of figures can be
kept for only those combinations of
phemes or of semes which are
phonemes* or sememes,* as well as,
potentially, for the different organizations of the latter. From the terminological point of view, when we
are dealing with non-linguistic*
semiotic systems, the use of the
names "sememe" and, above all, of
"phoneme" is evidently inappro-
priate. It is better then to speak of
figures of the expression and **figures of the content.**
3. In discursive semantics* the
definition of figure can be made
more precise, by reserving this term
solely for the figures of the content
which correspond to the figures of
the expression plane of the natural*
semiotic system (or of the natural
world*). Thus, the **nuclear figure**
covers only the figurative part of the
sememe, exclusive of the recurrent
contextual* semes (or classemes*).
Such a conception of figure brings it
close to that of the Gestalt in form
theory and to the Bachelardian fig-

ure, with this exception nonetheless,
that the **semiotic figure** is to be
considered as a second-degree unit,
divisible into those simple units that
are the terms of the figurative categories (phemes or semes).
4. Taken in the overall generative* trajectory, the figurative level*
of the discourse appears as a domain
characterized by new investments—
installations of the figures of the
content—being added onto the
abstract level and the figurative level
of the discourse. Such a definition,
although it is far from exhausting
the inventory of figures of classical
rhetoric, nonetheless shows the different nature of the two meanings
—semiotic and rhetorical—of this
term. It is indeed clear that the
points of view are different and that,
in our perspective, it is difficult, for
example, to distinguish **rhetorical
figures**—which would be properly
"stylistic," corresponding to more or
less stereotyped procedures* of the
enunciator*—from the figures of
language such as Bréal was led to
integrate into his system in order to
account for semantic changes in
natural languages. Furthermore, the
problem of the dimension of figures
arises, according to whether these
figures are considered—in the case
of tropes*—on the lexematic level
(bound then to a given word of the
sentence) or to the transsentential,*
discursive, level. In this second
case, figures can appear as isotopic
connectors* or, in a broader sense,
as relations between terms or levels,
losing by this very fact their "stylistic" specificity. Finally, it will be
noted that rhetorical figures, so it
seems, go beyond the problem of
natural languages alone. The fact
that the cinema, for example, has
metaphors and metonymies, shows
at least that, in the framework of the
generative* trajectory of the dis-

course, figures belong to the semiotic "common stem," prior therefore to any manifestation* in a particular substance* of the expression.
—FIGURATIVIZATION; METAPHOR

FOCALIZATION
(focalisation)

1. Following G. Genette, the term **focalization** serves to designate the delegation made by the enunciator* to a cognitive* subject, called observer, and the latter's installation in the narrative discourse. This procedure thus allows either the whole of the narration, or simply certain pragmatic* programs, to be apprehended from the "point of view" of this mediator. Different types of focalization—which is an actantial disengagement* procedure—can be distinguished according to the mode in which the observer is manifested. The observer sometimes remains implicit or, in other cases, appears, in syncretism with one of the actants* of the communication (the narrator,* for example) or with one of the actants of the narration (a pragmatic* subject, for example). Yet it will be noted that this concept of focalization which, with putting into perspective,* completely encompasses the former notion of "point of view," is still only provisional. It does not take account of all the modes of the observer's presence (in the case, for example, of aspectualization*), nor does it explain the constituting of partial cognitive* spaces, characterized by the presence—within the pragmatic programs —of two cognitive subjects in communication with each other.

2. **Focalization** is also the name given—but here the focalized object, not the focalizing subject, is taken into account—to the procedure which consists in inscribing (or in circumscribing), by successive concentric approximations, an actor* or a narrative sequence* into more and more precise spatio-temporal coordinates. To do this, the enunciator has at its disposal not only the possibilities offered by spatio-temporal localization, but also and above all an embedding procedure thanks to which a punctuality* or a duration can be inscribed in another duration, a space* in another space.
—OBSERVER; PERSPECTIVE; LOCALIZATION, SPATIO-TEMPORAL; EMBEDDING

FORM
(forme)

1. The diverse and varied uses of the word **form** reflect practically the whole history of Western thought. Thus the status attributed to this concept in one or the other semiotic theory (or, in a more limited way, in linguistic theories) lets its epistemological foundations be recognized easily. Indeed, the notion of form has inherited its eminent position in the theory of knowledge from the Aristotelian tradition. Opposed to the matter which it "informs" (to which it gives form) at the same time it "forms" the knowable object, form is what guarantees the permanence and the identity of the knowable object. Taken in this fundamental sense, form is close to our conception of structure (*cf.* Gestalt).

2. When the concept of form is applied to "thought objects," the matter it informs is interpreted progressively, via semantic drift, as the "meaning," the "content," giving rise thus to dichotomies established by daily use. From this point of view, the word form comes close to and becomes almost synonymous with expression. The "base meaning,"

considered as unvarying, is submitted to variations on the phonetic, syntactic, or stylistic planes. Contrariwise, when meaning is considered as something which exists but concerning which nothing can be said (Bloomfield), form is valorized. It alone can be submitted to linguistic analysis (*cf.* American structuralism*).

3. F. de Saussure's affirmation that language is a form resulting from the union of two substances* must be understood in this context. Being neither "physical" substance nor "psychic" substance, but the locus of their convergence, form is a signifying structure (*cf.* Merleau-Ponty). The ontological independence of semiotic form which is thus affirmed confers a status of autonomy on linguistics (which has as object the coherent and exhaustive description of this form).

4. L. Hjelmslev's interpretation of the Saussurian conception of form permits a refining of the mechanism of semiotics, a mechanism which is both epistemological and methodological. While the monist formulation of signifying form (which applies, *stricto sensu,* only to the prosodic* categories of natural languages) is not called into question, it is broadened by postulating the existence of a form proper to each of the two substances: the **expression form** and the **content form** must be recognized and analyzed separately, prior to their joining, which produces the semiotic schema.*

5. Recognition of two forms proper to each of the two planes of language has, within a general theoretical framework, allowed the resituation of both phonology, the expression form, and of phonetics, the study of substance (*cf.* -emic, -etic). It has also authorized the transposition of the same distinction to the content plane, thereby opening the way to the elaboration of a formal semantics.*
—STRUCTURE; EXPRESSION; CONTENT; FORMAL

FORMAL
(*formel*)

1. As an adjective derived from form,* **formal** reflects the different meanings that this concept has received successively as well as in parallel fashion.

2. According to the traditional distinction which opposes "form" to "meaning" (or to "content"), any organization or structure deprived of signification* is qualified as formal. Thus, by opposition to semantics, phonology and grammar are considered to be formal disciplines.

3. Beginning with the distinction established by F. de Saussure between form and substance* and which, in excluding substance of "physical" as well as of "psychic" nature from linguistics's concern, defines language as a form, linguistics and, more generally speaking, semiotics, insofar as they are studies of forms, are presented as formal disciplines (on the same basis as logic or mathematics).

4. Independently of developments in linguistic theory, from the end of the 19th century on, research bearing on **formal systems** (sometimes also called **formal languages**) appeared in mathematics and in logic. The formal character of these systems comes primarily from the fact that they claim to be explicit.* It is the scholastic meaning of the word "formal" which is thus opposed to intuitive,* vague, and implicit.* Furthermore, a formal system is conventional, *i.e.,* it is based on a set of formulas called axioms, which are

arbitrarily declared to be demonstrated. Such a system is characterized by an alphabet* of symbols,* by a set of rules* which permit the construction of well-formed expressions,* etc. It institutes and authorizes, by that very fact, a **formal calculus,** independent of any exterior intervention (of any consideration of the substance). Thus elaborated, the formal system, coinciding with the Saussurian conception of form, is characterized by one of the properties essential to every language (semiotic system*).

5. Yet a formal system is distinguished from a semiotic system because it denies that the forms which it makes explicit and manipulates are signifying forms. Leaving aside the use that can be made of these formal systems in view of a formalization of semiotic theory, the problem of their status as semiotic system (language) inevitably arises. From this point of view, it can be considered, following L. Hjelmslev, that they are monoplanar* semiotic systems (constituted by the sole expression plane) and that, just as the phonemes *b* and *p* in "bin" and "pin" which are differentiated only by the implicit presence of, so to speak, negative and discriminatory* meaning, the symbols of formal semiotic systems are empty of signification. It is, however, no less evident that every semiotic system—and, *a fortiori*, every grammar—is based on a set of universal semantic categories (*cf.* **universals**). Thus the real problem is that of getting rid of meaning in the construction of a formal system, and not that of its being summoned up *a posteriori*, to be used for interpretation,* as in generative* grammar.

—FORM; THEORY; AXIOMATIC; FORMALIZATION; INTERPRETATION

FORMALISM
(formalisme)

1. By **formalism**—in the neutral, but often pejorative, meaning —is understood a scientific attitude which seeks to formalize conceptual theories or to construct formal models to account for the data of experience and, more particularly, which uses formal* systems founded upon an axiomatic* system.

2. The term formalism becomes clearly pejorative when it qualifies research carried out in the human sciences, which uses formal procedures* in its methodological machinery. Thus, semiotics is often accused of being formalist and of "dehumanizing" the object of its research. In fact, semiotics has not yet succeeded in formalizing its analyses and is only at a stage of pre-formalization.

3. **Russian formalism**—which dominated the linguistic and particularly the literary research carried out in Russia in the 'twenties—well illustrates the term's ambiguity. Accused of formalism, because not manifesting enough interest in the ideological content of literary works, this research was not formalist in the neutral meaning of that term, for it aimed at circumscribing the signification of forms* (in the almost-Saussurian meaning of this word). It must be added that Russian formalism is but one particular manifestation of a European episteme common at the time, since one can speak just as well of German formalism (research on the baroque, for example) or of French formalism (discovery and formulation of romanesque art by Faucillon and his collaborators). This tradition was taken up again after the war, with a different expression, by what is called French structuralism.*

FORMALIZATION
(formalisation)

1. **Formalization** is the transcription of a theory into a formal* language (using an appropriate formal system). It thus presupposes the existence of an already-elaborated theory which, even if it is not completed, already has a body of interdefined and hierarchized concepts.* Any hasty formalization—a procedure which is only too frequent these days—is but its caricature.

2. Thus, formalization is not a description* procedure.* It is still less a scientific doing that is an end in itself (for whatever reasons may have been adduced). Intervening only at an advanced stage of the construction of a theory, it serves essentially to test its coherence and to compare two or several theories dealing with the same object of knowledge.

3. For purposes of evaluation, generative* grammar, which is presented as a formalized theory, can be compared only with other grammars of the same sort. However, every formal system can be interpreted.* Thus, once interpreted and brought, so to speak, to the status of a conceptual theory, generative grammar can be compared to other semiotic theories and questioned concerning its epistemological foundations and its capacity to resolve the essential questions asked of every theory of language, as well as concerning its manner of doing so.

4. As can be suspected, semiotic theory is not yet at a stage at which its formalization can be envisaged. When it is recognized that semiotic theory is in the state of **pre-formalization,** it is clear that research should be concentrated on the elaboration of its metalanguage* and of the appropriate representation* systems.
—GENERATION; INTERPRETATION; THEORY

FORMANT
(formant)

By **formant** is understood, in literature, a part of the chain of the expression* plane, corresponding to a unit of the content* plane, and which—at the moment of semiosis*—permits it to be constituted as a sign* (morpheme* or word*). The formant is thus not a syntagmatic* unit of the expression plane considered in itself (as the pheme, the phoneme, or the syllable are, for example). It is, properly speaking, "the formant *of* . . . ," and belongs to use* and not to structure.* L. Hjelmslev foresaw, within linguistics, a particular place for the "theory of formants," independent of phonematics and of morphematics.—SIGN

FUNCTION
(fonction)

While the term **function** is frequent in linguistics and, more generally, in semiotics, it is often employed—sometimes even within the same theory—with at least three different meanings: (A) with a utilitarian or instrumental meaning; (B) in an organicist meaning; (C) finally, in a mathematico-logical sense.

(A) **Instrumental interpretation.**

1. For A. Martinet, the principal function of language is the **communication function,** language being a "communication instrument." Such a conception, which claims to attenuate the formalism* of structural linguistics,* in fact restricts the scope of linguistic theory. Even if language is communication,*

it is also production of meaning, of signification.* Linguistic theory with such a restricted scope can no longer be extrapolated and applied to other semiotic systems (with the possible exception of "true" communication systems, such as the signals used to regulate traffic). **Functional linguistics,** as Martinet conceives of it, is a "realist" linguistics.

2. It is with this same instrumental meaning that the expression **functional definition** is used when it contains information concerning the use or the finality of the described object or behavior (cf. "a chair . . . is to be sat in"). The semantic analysis of lexemes of this type makes explicit either instrumental values* or instrumental programs* that these imply.

(B) **Organicist interpretation.**

1. E. Benveniste uses the concept of **function** with a meaning inspired by biology. For him it is an element necessary for the definition of structure: "What gives the character of a structure to a form is the fact that the constituent parts fulfill a function." This effort at conciliating structure and function allows him to reinterpret the diachronic linguistics of the 19th century, but also to justify the conception of the sentence* as a structure the constituent parts of which are charged with syntactic functions.

2. By **syntactic function** is traditionally understood the role that such or such an element, defined beforehand as a morphological* unit (adjective, verb, etc.) or syntagmatic unit (nominal, verbal syntagm), plays within all that a sentence is. Subject, object, predicate, for example, are names of particular functions. Even if the inventory of syntactic functions does not take into account the hierarchy* of the elements (the subject and the epithet are not situated

at the same level of derivation), this dimension of syntactic organization is still pertinent and can give rise to new reformulations in the framework, for example, of our actantial syntax. Generative* linguistics, which started from a division of the sentence into syntagmatic classes,* has itself been obliged to reintroduce this level of analysis under the guise of syntagmatic markers,* where the subject is defined, for example, as the nominal syntagm immediately dominated by Σ.

3. It is in the framework of an epistemological reflection that certain psychologists (K. Bühler) or linguists (R. Jakobson) have been led to separate the **functions of language** (sorts of spheres of action working together toward the same goal) the set of which would exhaustively define linguistic activity. Thus, Bühler recognizes three principal functions in language: **expressive,* conative*** (summons), and **referential*** (representation*). Setting out these functions along the axis of communication,* R. Jakobson adds three more to them: **phatic,* metalinguistic,*** and **poetic.*** Such a distinction has the advantage of giving a suggestive general view of the different sets of issues concerning language: it would be risky to see anything else there. This schema cannot be considered as an axiomatic* system on the basis of which a whole theory of language could be elaborated, by way of deduction.* Nor is it a taxonomy of utterances. At the very most one could see therein possibilities of connotations* of the "denotative" messages, of the postulations of connotative signifieds* whose markers would need to be recognized on the level of the discourse. Philosophy of language no longer seeks to determine the functions of language on the basis of a general reflection

on its nature, but on the level of the speech act,* inscribed in the framework of intersubjectivity. A pragmatic* approach succeeds in constituting lists of "functions" (of the type "request," "wish," "order," "expectation," etc.) which, while renewing the way the problems of communication are treated, still appear, at the present moment, as so many unscientific paraphrases,* and do not constitute a coherent set.

4. In his *Morphology of the Folktale,* V. Propp designates by the name of **functions** syntagmatic units which remain constant despite the diversity of narratives, and whose ordered sequence (31 in number) constitutes the tale. Such a conception, which provides the possibility of postulating the existence of a principle of organization underlying whole classes of narratives, has served as starting point for the elaboration of different theories of narrativity.* As for the notion of function, still vague in Propp, it can be made more precise and reformulated in terms of narrative utterances.*

5. G. Dumézil uses the term function to account for the tripartite division of society itself into three classes (priests, warriors, and farmers-cattle-raisers). The tripartite articulation of the **ideological functions** permits the attribution of a particular semantic field (a sovereignty sphere) to each of the functions, at the same time that it establishes a hierarchical relation between them.

(C) **Logico-mathematical interpretation.**

1. Conscious of the difficulty, if not the impossibility, of totally excluding from linguistics the organicist meaning of function (which reflects, imperfectly to be sure, the productive and dynamic aspect of

the activity of language), L. Hjelmslev has tried to give to this term a mathematico-logical definition. For him, function can be considered as "the relation between two variables," and he adds that this relation is to be envisaged as "a dependance which fulfills the conditions of the analysis," for it participates in the network of reciprocal interrelations, constitutive of every semiotics. Such a relation, named function, is established between the terms, called *functives.* It can be seen that Hjelmslevian linguistics is indeed functional, but in a very different sense from that of Martinet.

2. A synthesis of the two conceptions of function—those of E. Benveniste and of L. Hjelmslev— seems possible for a definition of the elementary utterance. Keeping the name of **function** solely for the "syntactic function" called predicate, and designating as actants* other syntactic functions which, as functives, represent the end terms of the relation constitutive of the utterance, its canonical formulation can be given: $F(A1, A2, \ldots)$. Minimal semantic investments of function as thus defined can permit the subsequent establishment of a first typology of elementary utterances. Thus, at first, it has seemed economical to distinguish between, on the one hand, utterances constituted by a function and, on the other, those the predicate of which would be a qualification* (corresponding to existence propositions in logic). The application of this opposition to narrative analysis opened the way to two types of research. While the **functional model** accounted for the ordering of narrative utterances defined by their functions (= "functions" in the Propian sense), the qualification model provided the possibility of describing the manner of being of semiotic ob-

jects, considered in their taxonomic aspect. However, the proposed distinction was in contradiction to the structural postulate according to which a relation,* whatever kind it be, can be installed (or be recognized) only between at least two terms* (in this case, between two actants). But qualificative utterances are precisely presented as single-actant utterances. It has thus proved necessary partially to rework the definition of the elementary utterance, assimilating qualificative utterances to utterances of state* (characterized by junction* between the subject and the object) and opposing them to ut-terances of doing* (having transformation* as function). In this perspective, function can then be defined as the constitutive relation for every utterance.

3. L. Hjelmslev calls **semiotic function** the relation which exists between the expression* form* and the content* form. Defined as reciprocal presupposition* (or solidarity*), this relation is constitutive of signs* and, by this fact, is creative of meaning* (or, more precisely, of meaning effects*). The speech act consists essentially in the establishment of the semiotic function.
—UTTERANCE

ABCDEFGHIJKLMN OPQRSTUVWXYZ

GAP
(écart)

1. The notion of **gap** is closely linked to the fate of stylistics* of which it has often appeared to be one of the fundamental concepts. It seems to originate, in large part, in F. de Saussure's remarks about speech* (viewed as the set of gaps between the various individual uses of a natural language*). A misunderstanding was thus created because scholars wanted to institute a linguistic discipline, starting from speech, based upon study of and calculation concerning these gaps: this is a misunderstanding because for Saussure speech was only a catchall concept which permitted a negative definition of language, the only goal of linguistics.

2. The notion of gap is also linked to that of norm.* Thus, literary language would be defined by the gap which would exist between it and normal, "everyday" language. But the normality of everyday language—sometimes designated signifier,* due to the influence of certain psychoanalytic theories—is from both the linguistic and the semiotic point of view, a veritable aberration. When, on the syntactic plane, an attempt is made to grasp

and to verify this "normality," with the help of the concept of grammaticality* (the use of which in practice is so problematic), the determination of the semantic anomalies (*cf*. T. Todorov's research) can only rest upon a particular, positivist, conception of rationality. But the semiotician knows that the natural languages are reservoirs, *loci* of manifestation and of construction for numerous and varied semiotic* systems.

3. The introduction into linguistics of rigorous statistical methods (replacing stylistic gaps, with their intuitive character, by gaps in signification which are objectively calculated) may have given —for a moment—the illusion of a rebirth of stylistic research. This illusion came from confusing the undisputable rigor of statistic calculation with the rigor of the conceptualization and construction of the models on the basis of which the gap could be calculated. For instance, the gap in signification in the use of adjectives by a given author did not appear as any very surprising datum which could nourish stylistic reflection. The most convincing result— obtained by the linguistic statistician Ch. Muller—is the homology recognized in Corneille's work between, on the one hand, tragedy and comedy, and, on the other hand, the frequency of the prepositions "à" and "de." This is indeed a most interesting finding: since it is located on the level of the universals* it permits a reflection leading to something else to be begun. Similarly, the establishment of lists of key words can also be quite suggestive.

4. As practiced, the calculation of gaps, in the absence of at least an implicit* semantic theory, still remains linked to the atomistic conceptions of last century. Thus it is

better to substitute for it the concept of coherent deformation of structures—as proposed by M. Merleau-Ponty. On the basis of this concept one can envision, although with caution, the possibility of calculating semantic originality.

—STYLISTICS; ORIGINALITY, SEMANTIC

GENERALIZATION
(*généralisation*)

1. According to L. Hjelmslev, in the case where an object (01) has a given property and where another object (02) has this property, but other characteristics as well, the **generalization principle** consists in applying to the second object the property of the first, by bracketing out the specific determinations of 02. Thus, for example, if an utterance admits of a reading and if another utterance admits of two, the isotopy* will retain solely, by generalization, the reading which is common to both utterances.

2. In a more general manner, **generalization** is defined as the procedure by which the properties or determinations recognized in a limited number of entities* are attributed to a whole class.*

3. Generalization is characteristic of the inductive approach which is carried out in an interpretation* when one begins from the semiotic manifestation. According to the hypothetico-deductive* procedure which we propose, generalization must involve the construction of a model hierarchically superior to and more extensive than the recognized phenomenon, and of which this phenomenon is but a variable.* The French imperfect tense, for example, in order to be compared with the German imperfect, must be interpreted in the framework of a

model which accounts for the whole of the past tenses. The model thus constructed can subsequently be invalidated, confirmed, or revised.

4. The categories* used for the construction of such models are called *general,* by contrast to the universal categories.

—INDUCTION; UNIVERSALS

GENERATION
(génération)

1. The term **generation** designates the act of engendering, of producing, whether it be taken in the biological or in the epistemological sense. It is this second meaning, current in mathematics (where the generation of a volume or of a number, for example, is spoken of), which was taken over by N. Chomsky in linguistics and which has been extended to semiotics.

2. The **definition*** **by generation** of a semiotic object—which explains the object by the way it is produced —must be distinguished from its taxonomic* definition (which, at least in its traditional form, determines it by genre and species). The **generative approach** is to be radically contrasted to the genetic approach. The latter considers the genesis of an object as situated on the temporal line and as being carried out in a series of successive forms, most often in relation with the exterior circumstances which may have conditioned its development. Thus, the study of the process of language learning (or, in another domain, the psychoanalytic approach) belongs to genetic, not generative, methods. The same distinction is required, again, for the analysis of scientific discourse. Whereas the history of a science— which retraces its advances, its detours, and its dead-ends—represents

a genetic approach, scientific discourse considers itself as a scientific state, produced by a generating algorithm.*

3. Once introduced into linguistics, the concept of generation has given rise to the constitution of a theory known as generative grammar.* (The simultaneous introduction of the transformational model often leads to a confusion between these two aspects of this theory.) Two principal characteristics mark this grammar as specifically generative (we follow closely here the interpretation given by J. Lyons): any grammar can be called generative, if it is projective (or predictive) and explicit.*

4. A grammar is projective if a set of rules, describing—explicitly or implicitly—a limited corpus of sentences, considered as a sample of a vaster set of sentences, can be projected onto that set. It is called predictive if the sentence representations that it gives are applicable not only to the realized sentences, but also to the possible ones. It is important to note, as J. Lyons remarks, that most grammars known in the history of linguistics are "generative" in this first sense of the term, yet on the condition that the "prediction" or forseeableness due to the rules, which results from the structure (or the schema*) of the language, be distinguished from their prescriptive or normative* character, which belongs to use.* A grammar is said to be explicit if it is entirely formalized,* that is, transcribed in a language conforming to the demands of formal* systems.

5. It follows that a theory can be generative (in the projective meaning of the term) without necessarily being entirely explicit and, on the other hand, that a grammar* can be generative without being trans-

formational: actually, this is the case of the semiotic* theory we are attempting to construct.
—GENERATIVE GRAMMAR; GENERATIVE TRAJECTORY

GENERATIVE GRAMMAR
(générative [grammaire—])

1. Developed by N. Chomsky and a group of American linguists, **generative** and **transformational grammar** is a complex theory that it is impossible to present briefly without deforming it. Foregoing a detailed outline—which can easily be found in other works—we shall concentrate only on those most fundamental characteristics whose place in a comparative semiotic approach is clear.

2. Generative and transformational grammar purports to give a description of all the sentences,* realized or possible (linked to the creativity* of the speaking subject*), of all natural languages.* It is thus a sentence-level linguistics (whence its inadequacy for discourse* analysis), universal in scope. Its project is to determine syntactic, semantic, and phonological universals,* even though its examples, so far, have come primarily from occidental languages, especially from English. It considers natural language not as a social entity (F. de Saussure) but as belonging to the subject's activity: whence the Chomskyian dichotomy *performance/competence,* which corresponds to the epistemological point of view adopted. This type of grammar—which deals with utterance,* but not with enunciation*—claims to be the expression of ideal competence,* conceived in a programmatic manner (in the "cybernetic" sense).

3. Properly logical in nature, generative and transformational grammar is presented in a strictly formal mode*: it is a syntactic* approach, which presupposes—at least at the outset—the rejection of meaning.* In its first stage, indeed, it totally leaves content* aside, aiming only at accounting for the grammaticality* of utterances, independently of their semanticity.* Only later does it give a semantic interpretation* to the formal structures earlier disclosed: the semantic component will thus be "hooked on" to the deep structures.* It is said, for example, that transformations* are purely formal rules, which do not cause—with the exception of a few stylistic* variations—any modification of the contents. This *a priori* position borrowed from logic, and according to which interpretation consists of attributing a content to a form which otherwise would be devoid of content, clearly cannot be reconciled with the Saussurian approach, which excludes the opposition of "content" and "form."

4. Chomskian grammar is called generative from two points of view: it is explicit,* because it can be formulated in a system or formal* language, and predictive (or projective) in that the descriptions it proposes apply not only to realized sentences, but also to possible ones (*cf.* **generation***). On the other hand, in fact, it reintroduces the notion of corpus* even though it claims to have eliminated it in its deductive* procedure (which gives priority to the metalanguage* over the object-language), for indeed its updating of the rules is necessarily carried out thanks to a corpus, however restricted it may be (*cf.* all the "mini-corpora" that generativists adduce in their discussions). The concepts of exhaustivity* and of adequateness,* bound to that of corpus, are then abandoned for others, hardly more

valid; those of acceptability* and of grammaticality,* which are founded on the speaking subject's intuition* (since the linguistic object is considered as being no longer empirically observable).

5. When the model (of a Markovian type) involving a finite number of states is left aside—a model that Chomsky himself has set aside because it excludes any sort of hierarchy* and leads to a dead end as far as the analysis of any natural language goes—two types of "grammars"—syntagmatic and transformational—can be distinguished in generative grammar, the second of which is a prolongation of the first, yet without having the same nature.

6. **Syntagmatic grammar,** which was at first called non-contextual, then later integrated contextual rules in order to protect grammaticality in certain cases, permits, on the basis of an analysis into immediate constituents,* a structural description* of the sentence, which can be represented in the form of a tree* diagram. Such a description is based on a certain number of postulates: (a) the sentence can have only one syntactic form; (b) its organization is binary: the subject/predicate structure, expressed with the help of a new terminology (nominal/verbal syntagms), which goes back to Aristotle (for whom every utterance is, basically, attributive), is declared to be universal and innate; (c) derivation,* founded on the concept of substitution* (the role of which in logic is well known) sets up, as categorial* sub-components of the base,* syntagmatic classes* (nominal, verbal syntagms) in which are introduced morphological* classes (verb, noun, adjective, article, etc.), but loses methodological homogeneity* in the process. As for the morphological classes themselves, they are taken over from traditional grammar, without any prior critical analysis. By contrast with what certain generativists claim, taxonomic* description in linguistics is far from being completed: a fact which explains a blatant weak point in generative grammar; (d) the system of rewriting rules* and the tree diagramming are clearly linked to the principle of linearity,* even if the transformational portion of the generativist project has made several corrections (but also raised new problems) on this point.

7. Since syntagmatic grammar seemed to be unable by itself to resolve a certain number of difficulties (discontinuous constituents, certain types of ambiguity, relation of active to passive, problems of agreement, etc.), Chomsky had to resort to another set of procedures, called **transformational grammar.** In this new perspective, analysis is no longer situated at a single level* of description, but on the two planes of deep* structures and of surface* structures, between which take place transformations* (formally defined as operations which, carried out on a syntagmatic indicator,* transform it into another tree) which permit additions, subtractions, permutations, and substitutions to be made on the sequences to be transformed. As J. Lyons notes, insofar as transformational grammar attributes thus a deep structure and a surface structure to a given sentence while linking them together systematically (according to rules), it can be equated —except for its aspect of explicitation—to traditional grammars.

—GENERATIVE TRAJECTORY; GENERATION; INTERPRETATION; CORPUS; SEMANTICS, GENERATIVE; COMPETENCE; PERFORMANCE

GENERATIVE TRAJECTORY
(génératif [parcours—])

1. We use the expression **generative trajectory** to designate the general economy* of a semiotic (or simply linguistic) theory,* that is, the way in which its components fit together. We say this from the viewpoint of generation*; since every semiotic object can be defined according to its mode of production,* we postulate that the components that enter into this process are linked together along a "trajectory" which goes from the simplest to the most complex, from the most abstract* to the most concrete.* The expression "generative trajectory" is not in common use: generative* grammar uses the term "model*" with a comparable meaning when it speaks, for example, of the standard model or of the enlarged (or extended) model. The term "model" having various other uses, we prefer to present under this rubric of "generative trajectory," the set of problems concerning the general setting-out of a theory.

2. **Generative linguistics** has successively proposed three schemas representing what we call the generative trajectory. The first two, of purely syntactic inspiration, are based essentially on the distinction between deep* structures and surface* structures. While deep syntactic structures are generated by the base* component, surface structures result from the operations (formulated as rules) of the transformational system. To these two levels are then connected the semantic and phonological components: the former concern semantic, the latter phonological, interpretation.* The semantic component (thanks to the lexicon,* in the sense

generativists give that word) is associated with deep structures, whereas the phonological and phonetic component is situated on the level of surface structures. The location of the two non-syntactic components makes for the originality of this standard model; it has also provoked the strongest objections. The arrangement whereby semantics is "hooked-up" to the deep structures, and phonology to the surface structures, is based on the hypothesis formulated by N. Chomsky (following Katz and Postal), according to which surface structure is not pertinent* for semantic interpretation, and deep structure is not pertinent for phonologic interpretation. From the semantic point of view, this is the same as saying that a series of syntactic transformations adduces no supplement of signification (other than stylistic) and that, consequently, a surface form is semantically equivalent to a deep form. The hypothesis not being proven and even being contrary to common (intuitive) sense, the standard model has been broadened by Chomsky himself, who has agreed to situate semantic interpretation all along the transformational trajectory and, more precisely, on the two levels—deep and superficial—of syntactic structures.

3. The progressively more important role granted to the semantic component, in the American type of generative linguistics, ends in a sort of paradox: semantics, having been excluded for a time, not only rises up to the surface, as has been noted, but it succeeds, even more, in further "deepening" the deep structures, the analysis of which uncovers increasingly abstract* semantic levels of "representation," going back down to elementary logical organi-

zations. This leads **generative semantics*** to reconsider the whole of the generative trajectory: which done, the deepest generative domains appear to be constituted by logico-semantic forms (permitting the elimination of the concept of interpretation) which, once transformed, generate surface forms. The intervention, at this level, of the phonological component, brings about the phonetic representation of the utterance. Yet this model is only approximative, since generative semantics, despite numerous and diverse investigations, has not yet succeeded in constructing a general theory of language.

4. The semiotic theory which we are seeking to elaborate, although generative in inspiration, cannot easily be compared to generativist models: this is so because what it proposes to do is different. Founded on the theory of signification, it aims at accounting for all semiotic systems (and not only the semiotics of natural languages) and at constructing models capable of generating discourses (and not only sentences). On the other hand, considering that all categories,* even the most abstract (including syntactic structures), are semantic in nature and thereby are signifying, it has no trouble in distinguishing, for each domain of the generative trajectory, syntactic and semantic (*stricto sensu*) subcomponents.

5. Such a semiotic theory distinguishes three autonomous general areas that it considers as loci of meta-semiotic* interpretation and construction: **semio-narrative structures, discursive structures,** and **textual structures.** However, whereas the first two forms can be considered as two superimposed levels of depth, the set of problems concerning textualization* is quite different. Indeed, textualization, as a putting-into-text that is linear (temporal or spatial, according to the semiotic system involved), can intervene at any point in the generative trajectory. Not only are figurative or non-figurative discourses (more or less deep, considered within discoursive semantics*) textualized, but the most abstract logico-semantic structures (in formal* languages, for example) are themselves textualized, from the moment they are put on paper. The textual structures, the formulation of which will give rise to semantic representation*—this latter being able to serve as the deep level for the linguistic structures which generate the surface linguistic structures (according to generative grammar) —constitute consequently an autonomous area of research (so-called textual linguistics, among others, is carried out there), but they are situated, in fact, outside of the generative trajectory, properly speaking.

6. The semio-narrative structures, which constitute the most abstract level, the starting point of the generative trajectory, are present under the form of a **semiotic and narrative grammar** which contains two components—syntactic and semantic—and two levels of depth, a **fundamental syntax*** and a **fundamental semantics*** (on the deep level), a **narrative syntax** and a **narrative semantics** (on the surface level). As for their semiotic mode of existence,* these structures are defined by reference to the concept of "language" (Saussure and Benveniste), as well as to that of narrative "competence" (a Chomskian concept, broadened to the dimension of the discourse), for they in-

clude not only a taxonomy,* but also the set of elementary syntactic operations.

7. The discursive structures, less deep, are charged with taking up for themselves the surface semiotic structures and with "putting them into discourse" by having them pass through the domain of the enunciation.* They are still, at the present, much less detailed than semiotic structures: thus we can point out certain of their components only as areas under investigation. For the moment we will distinguish the syntactic component—or **discoursive syntax**—charged with the discoursivization* of the narrative structures and comprising the three sub-components of actorialization,* temporalization,* and spatialization* (fields which temporal and spatial logics are already exploring in part), and the semantic component—or **discoursive semantics**—with its sub-components of thematization* and of figurativization,* aiming at producing abstract or figurative discourses. It can be seen that, with the production of figurative discourses, the generative trajectory reaches the terminal structures, which does not mean that every generative process seeks to produce figurative discourses, but that this process must be considered as the most concrete and, syntactically, the most detailed, form of the articulations of signification. The textualization* and the manifestation* of the discourse—as we have already insisted—are able to intervene at any moment of the generation. Thus considered, the generative trajectory is an ideal construction,* independent of (and anterior to) the natural languages or of (to) the natural worlds where one or the other semiotic system can, thereafter, be invested so as to be manifested.

8. The following table visualizes the distribution of the diverse components and sub-components of this "trajectory":

GENERATIVE TRAJECTORY			
		syntactic **component**	**semantic** **component**
Semiotic and narrative structures	**deep** **level**	FUNDAMENTAL SYNTAX	FUNDAMENTAL SEMANTICS
	surface **levels**	SURFACE NARRATIVE SYNTAX	NARRATIVE SEMANTICS
Discoursive structures		DISCOURSIVE SYNTAX Discoursivization actorialization temporalization spatialization	DISCOURSIVE SEMANTICS Thematization Figurativization

—DISCOURSE: NARRATIVITY

GENRE
(genre)

1. **Genre** designates a class of discourse, and is recognizable by sociolectal* criteria. These can originate either in an implicit classification* which is based, in oral traditional societies, on a particular categorization* of the world, or in a "genre theory" which, for a number of societies, takes the form of an explicit taxonomy* of a non-scientific nature. Such a theory, clearly stemming from cultural relativism and based upon implicit ideological postulates, has nothing in common with the typology of discourses* the establishment of which is being attempted, and which starts from a recognition of the specific formal properties of the discourses. The study of the **genre theory** which characterizes a given culture* (or cultural area), is of interest only insofar as it can explore an axiology* the underlies the classification; it should be compared with the description of other ethno- or socio-taxonomies.

2. In the European cultural context, modern genre theory—which is different from medieval theory—seems to be constructed along two distinct axes: (a) a "classical" theory, which is based on a non-scientific definition of the "form" and the "content" of certain classes of literary discourse (for example, comedy, tragedy, etc.); (b) a "post-classical" theory, which is founded on a certain conception of "reality" (of the referent*), allowing it to distinguish, from that starting point, either different "possible worlds," or narrative concatenations more or less conforming to an underlying norm (cf. the fantastic, marvelous, realist, surrealist, etc., genres).

3. It should be noted that, in addition to a theory of literary genres, the same cultural context can serve as a basis, for example, for a classification of religious genres. —DISCOURSE

GESTUALITY
(gestualité)

1. As a specific research field, **gestuality** has been introduced into semiotic reflection only progressively and hesitantly, appearing at one time as a circumscribed and autonomous domain of significations, analyzable as a **gestual language,** at another as omnipresent, spilling out over the still imprecise borders of particular semiotic systems that are in the process of being constituted.

2. Gestuality has been—and still is—considered as a paralinguistic* phenomenon which has an auxiliary function in intersubjective communication.* This **accompaniment gestuality** has been judged, a bit too hastily, as "meager"—because it was incapable of producing disengaged* utterances and of transmitting objective contents; certain scholars would, therefore, reduce its role to that of simple emphasis.* Yet upon closer examination, it can be defined as **frame gestuality,** *i.e.,* as gestuality framing the enunciation. The categories that it can utter are abstract* categories that take the form either of modal utterances (assertion, negation, doubt and certitude, etc.) or of utterances of quantification (totalization, division) and of qualification (euphoric and dysphoric states), or, above all, of phatic* utterances (reception and rejection, openness to the world and closure of self, etc.) that transform communication into intersubjective communion.

3. Some scholars have tried to study gestuality as a language* by

applying the Saussurian formula of "sign system" to it. The signs would be recognizable through commutation* tests; the system would be used for communication. Unfortunately, the inventories of communication gestures that have been established (*cf.* the gestures of the North American Indians) could not be structured into systems: they correspond to no "phonological" structure and belong to no semantic organization (other than that of "centers of interest"). Therein are lumped together, pell-mell, accompaniment gestures, icons, and, above all, fixed gestual syntagms, desemanticized and conventionalized, in short the whole Peircean classification in haphazard order. The existence of an autonomous "gestual language" seems, thus, far from being assured.

4. Another approach to gestuality consists in starting this time, not from gestures considered as signs, but from **gestual texts** (folk dances, ballet, acrobatic numbers, pantomime, etc.). The interest of this type of research is multifold. The approach is, first of all, analytic: the segmentation* of the text* raises, of course, the problem of gestual units of more or less large syntagmatic dimensions, but also that of the pertinence of the gestual features that characterize them. It is thus not surprising that this type of investigation should lead, on the one hand, in the area of the expression* plane, to making evident the need for a language of description (the drawing-up of systems of symbolic notation* of gestures has already made quite a lot of progress and raises new questions relating to their metalinguistic coherency). On the other hand, it has led to raising the problem of the signification of these gestual discourses, which appear both as programmed texts, thus undergirded by

an implicit intentionality*, and as theatrical utterances, produced in function of a reader-observer* and, consequently, doubly significant; by themselves, and for others.

5. An examination of gestual texts leads not only to a distinction between signifying gestuality and meaningless gesticulation, but also makes obligatory a definition of "gestual substance" as that which is expressed by means of that particular matter that the human body is, as "volume in motion." Gestuality is not limited merely to the gestures of the hands and the arms or to facial expression, it is an integral part of people's somatic behavior and, in the long run, constitutes only one of the aspects of what can be called their **somatic* language.** But whereas gestual texts, previously mentioned, appear to be processes of constructed (or artificial) somatic semiotic systems, there exists, alongside them, one suspects, one or more "natural" semiotic systems which account for human behavior programmed as signifying practices.* An analysis of narrative discourses allows us, precisely, to distinguish a pragmatic* dimension of the discourse, made up of descriptions of signifying somatic behavior and organized into programs and which are simultaneously designated as events for the reader. We have sought to define gestual texts by means of these two characteristics. Whence it can be seen that the narrative models constructed to account for pragmatic behavior "on paper," can be transposed for the formulation of a natural "pragmatic" semiotic system.

6. It will immediately be noted that "somaticity," as well as gestuality, are not concepts easily described: "speaking" or "singing" are behaviors quite as somatic as "walking" or

"gesticulating." It can thus be said, finally, that the diverse semiotic* systems are embedded into each other in their "natural" state (cf. different rituals and ceremonies, for example) as well as in their "constructed" state (theater, opera, circus, etc.), and that, most often, we have to deal with syncretic* semiotic systems whose constitutive elements and their interconnections are to be disentangled.
—PROXEMICS; PRACTICES, SEMIOTIC

GIFT
(don)

1. A discursive figure* of the communication* of objects* of value, the **gift** represents the transformation* which brings about a concomitant attribution* and renunciation.* Therefore, on the narrative plane it simultaneously corresponds to a transitive* conjunction* and to a reflexive* disjunction. It is thus paradigmatically opposed to the test* (which implies a reflexive conjunction and a transitive disjunction). Furthermore, by contrast with the test, which is centered upon a subject-hero,* the gift takes place between a sender* and a receiver.

3. A syntagmatic chain composed of two renunciations, implying two reciprocal attributions of the same object to two subjects, can be designated as a **reciprocal gift.** Gift and "counter-gift" thus constitute two transformations, the second of which nullifies the effects of the first and re-establishes the preceding equilibrium.* The reciprocal gift (among other things) is distinguished from exchange* because it involves a single identical object. By contrast exchange calls for two objects which are judged to be equivalent.

GLORIFYING TEST
(glorifiante [épreuve—])

A discursive figure* linked to the narrative* schema, the **glorifying test** is situated in the cognitive* dimension; such is not the case for the qualifying* and decisive (or main) tests, which it presupposes. It appears in the narrative when the decisive test has been carried out in the secret* mode. As a cognitive performance* (and persuasive* doing) of the subject, it calls for—on the corresponding plane of competence*—a *being-able-to-cause-to-know* figurativized by the mark.* As the sender's* cognitive sanction,* within the contractual component of the narrative schema, it is the equivalent of recognition.—TEST; RECOGNITION; NARRATIVE SCHEMA

GLOSSEMATICS
(glossématique)

1. **Glossematics** (from Greek *glossa*, language) is the term that L. Hjelmslev proposed to give to the linguistic theory that he developed in collaboration with his friend H. J. Uldall. It is characterized, in his opinion, by four specific features: (a) an analytic procedure, prior to (and presupposed by) synthesis; (b) an insistence on form*; (c) a taking into consideration not only of the expression* form, but also of the content* form; (d) a conception of language as one semiotic system among others.

2. Glossematics has been a stimulant, even if it has not been generalized; by contrast, the language theory set forth by L. Hjelmslev can be considered as the first coherent and complete semiotic theory: it has been a decisive factor in the formation of semiotics in France.

GRAMMAR
(grammaire)

1. The old term of **grammar,** which was pejorative not long ago (insofar as it referred to normative grammar), was recently rehabilitated by generative* grammar. This term, grammar, used to designate all of linguistics.* Now it designates only one of its components. By grammar is generally meant the description* of the modes of existence and of functioning of a natural language* or, possibly and more generally, of any semiotic* system. It will nonetheless be noted that the meaning of this word often varies from one theory to another.

2. If one considers, in the broadest sense, that grammar accounts for the "articulation of words together into sentences," two domains can then be distinguished: morphology and syntax.* Morphology deals with the study of words* and of word classes, whereas syntax handles the study of "sentence articulation." The respective importance that each of these two branches has depends in large part on the natural languages under study. Thus, morphological studies predominate in the comparative grammar of the Indo-European languages, which possess very well-developed case systems. On the contrary, contemporary linguistics, more theoretical in character, founding its empirical validity on the "native speaker" (speaking a non-morphological language), favors the syntactic dimension. Thus the choice made by generative grammar, taking as its starting point the taxonomy* (or the morphology) drawn up by distributional* analysis, and taking into account only syntagmatic classes,* exclusive of morphological classes and of syntactic functions*

(which it surreptitiously reintroduces, however: see **category**), does not seem very successful and does not justify assertions to the effect that the stage of taxonomic description in linguistic research is past. This having been said, the construction of artificial languages* (documentary language, for example) shows the existence of a compensatory relation between morphology and syntax: an elaborate taxonomy only requires the establishment of a relatively limited number of syntactic relations, and—inversely—with a complex network of syntactic relations it is enough to have a rudimentary morphology. It can be seen, moreover, that modern use tends to confuse, if not indeed to confound, the terms grammar and syntax.

3. The meaning of the word **grammar** varies, on the other hand, according to the extension given to this concept. Thus when grammar is assigned the task of constructing a formal model, capable of accounting for and/or of producing all the utterances* of a natural language, one must define what is meant by "all the utterances." If this phrase only refers to all the classes and all the types of utterances, grammar leaves aside two autonomous disciplines: semantics* and phonology.* If, on the contrary, this phrase refers to the production of all possible utterance-occurrences, then semantics and phonology are to be considered as simple components, that can be linked to syntax, of a grammar which covers the totality of the linguistic field being studied. In this sense, grammar is close to our conception of semiotics.*

4. In our theoretical project, **semiotic grammar** corresponds to the semio-narrative structures.* It has as components,* on the deep*

level, a fundamental syntax* (called surface syntax) and a narrative semantics.*

—GENERATIVE GRAMMAR; GENERATIVE TRAJECTORY

GRAMMATICALITY
(grammaticalité)

1. In generative* linguistics, a sentence is said to be grammatical if it can be described by a given grammar*: the **grammaticality** of an utterance, its possible agrammaticality, and—between the two—the **various degrees of grammaticality,** are recognizable only in terms of the competence* of the enunciatee* (which is invited to make an epistemic* judgment), a competence which varies according to the cultural community to which that enunciatee belongs ("He ain't saw nuthin'" is grammatical in "lower-class" American, and agrammatical for a normative grammar).

2. By grammaticality can be meant the relation of compatibility that two elements* maintain on the syntactic level, and thanks to which these elements can be present* together in a hierarchically higher entity: this is one of the criteria not only for the recognition of (syntactic) acceptability, but also for the determination of the interpretation.*

—COMPATIBILITY; INTERPRETATION; COMPETENCE; ACCEPTABILITY; IMPLICIT; NORM

GRAMMEME
(grammème)

Some linguists (such as B. Pottier) designate by the term **grammeme** grammatical morphemes, by opposition to lexemes (understood, then, as lexical morphemes).—MORPHEME; LEXEME

ABCDEFGHIJKLMN OPQRSTUVWXYZ

HAVING/TO HAVE
(avoir)

The verb **to have** serves to attribute "accidental" properties to the subject,* properties which are interpreted, at the level of semantic representation, as objective values in junction* with the subject of state.*
—OBJECTIVE

HAVING-TO-DO or TO-BE
(devoir)

1. **Having-to-(do or be)** is one of the possible predicates* of the modal* utterance which overdetermines and governs either an utterance of doing,* or an utterance of state.* The semantic investment of this predicate cannot be defined in itself but only in the framework of interdefinitions of the modalities chosen for an axiomatic* system. In simpler (or more philosophical) terms, having-to seems to constitute with wanting* a kind of *a priori* stage (the minimal conditions for a doing or for a state). On the plane of the production* of the utterance, having-to appears as a stage at which an utterance of doing or of state is virtualized.

2. When, for simplicity's sake, we designate the modal utterance the predicate of which is the modality having-to by the name "having-to," the utterance of doing by the name "to-do," and the ut-

terance of state by the name "to be," *having-to-do* and *having-to-be* can be viewed as two modal structures which are identical in terms of the modalizing utterance that they have and are distinct in terms of the modalized utterance.

3. When one takes into account the fact that the modal utterance as well as the utterance it commands can each have its own contradictories, the modal structure of *having-to-do* can be characterized by projecting it onto the semiotic square* and by simultaneously giving an appropriate and arbitrary name to each of the terms* thus obtained:

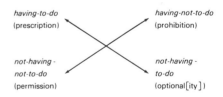

having-to-do (prescription)

having-not-to-do (prohibition)

not-having-not-to-do (permission)

not-having-to-do (optional[ity])

The naming procedure—which here involves converting a verbal and syntactic formulation into a nominal and taxonomic expression—has the effect of transforming, by condensation,* the two predicates into a single modal value. The modal category, thus obtained by naming, clearly belongs—with a few slight modifications—to the set of deontic* modalities used in logic. Therefore we can keep the name **deontic modal category** for it.

4. The same procedure of projection onto the semiotic square in order to make the category appear can be applied to the modal structure of *having-to-be:*

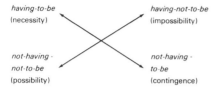

having-to-be (necessity)

having-not-to-be (impossibility)

not-having-not-to-be (possibility)

not-having-to-be (contingence)

The modal values thus named can easily be homologated to the set of alethic* modalities used in logic. Therefore we term this category the **alethic modal category.**

5. The modal structure of *having-to-do* clearly involves close semantic connections with the modal structure of *wanting-to-do,* so much so that one often wonders whether or not it would be possible and appropriate to reduce them to a single virtualizing modal structure. The difficulty is then that one needs to choose either to reduce *having-to-do* to *wanting-to-do* or conversely. Those who favor a psychologizing attitude are then tempted to see in the subject's *having-to-do* a transfer of the sender*'s wanting. Those who favor logic are rather inclined to interpret *wanting-to-do* as a self-oriented *having-to-do.* It is better to let this issue remain in its present state as long as a complete reexamination of the field of the modalities has not been carried out.

6. By contrast, the modal structure *having-to-be* is related to that of *being-able-to-be,* as is shown by the fact that they have some names in common—which results from intuitive semantic homologations. Thus, for instance, necessity* is the name corresponding both to *having-to-be* and to *not-being-able-not-to-be,* and impossibility* is the name for both *having-not-to-be* and *not-being-able-to-*

be. The gap between the logical approach and the semiotic approach grows wider at this point. Whereas logic postulates *a priori* a set of alethic modalities made up of names, semiotics seeks to provide a foundation for the names on the basis of syntactic definitions. In so doing semiotics makes certain distinctions which seem to suggest a number of lacunae in modal logics. It is as if, for instance, *having-to-be,* a virtualizing modal structure which is positive and closely related to the enunciator* subject, was distinct from *not-being-able-not-to-be,* which is an actualizing structure which operates by negating the contingencies and by giving a value to the object. It is thus as if the name necessity designated two modal values and two types of modalization.

—MODALITY; DEONTIC MODALITIES; ALETHIC MODALITIES

HELPER

(adjuvant)

Helper designates the positive auxiliant when this role is assumed by an actor* other than the subject of doing: it corresponds to an individualized being-able-to-do which, under the form of actor, brings its help to bear on the carrying out of the subject*'s narrative program.* It is paradigmatically opposed to the opponent* (which is the negative auxiliant).—AUXILIANT

HERMENEUTICS

(herméneutique)

Hermeneutics generally designates the interpretation, in the common, and not semiotic, meaning, of essentially philosophical and religious texts. It is a discipline relatively close to semiotics (from which it often takes many elements) insofar as it articulates a general theory of meaning with a general theory of text (as P. Ricoeur says). It will nonetheless be noted that the domain of its exercise is very specific and, on the other hand, that it puts into play the relation of the text to the referent,* being linked particularly to the extra-linguistic data of the discourse and to the conditions of their production and of their reading. As distinct from the semiotic approach by which, for example, the enunciation can be reconstructed according to a logico-semantic model built up from the text alone, hermeneutics brings in the socio-historic context, including that of contemporary understanding, and tries—by this complex interplay—to separate out the receivable meanings: it thus presupposes a philosophic reference position as evaluation criterion.

HERO
(héros)

1. The term **hero** can be used to name the subject actant* when this actant is in a certain position on its narrative* trajectory, endowed at that moment with corresponding modal values.* The subject becomes a hero only when it has come into possession of a certain competence* (being-able and/or knowing-how-to-do). Within the narrative's pragmatic* dimension, the **actualized*** **hero** (before its performance*) will thus be distinguished from the **realized*** **hero** (possessing the object of the quest). In the cognitive* dimension, the **hidden hero** should be distinguished from the **revealed hero** (after the sender's cognitive sanction,* or recognition*). That is, hero is the name of a specific actantial* status.

2. In a narrower meaning, particularly in studies of oral or classical literature, the term hero is given to the subject actant as defined above, but endowed, in addition, with moralizing euphoric* connotations,* which oppose the hero to the villain* (disphorically* connoted).
—ACTANTIAL ROLE; STATUS; NARRATIVE TRAJECTORY; MORALIZATION

HETEROGENEITY
(hétérogénéité)

A set* is said to be **heterogeneous** if its constitutive elements* have differing properties such that they cannot be placed into one and the same class.*—HOMOGENEITY

HETEROTOPIC SPACE
(hétérotopique [espace—])

In contrast to topic space* (the reference space which is the place of performances* and of competences*), **heterotopic** space designates the surrounding places (the "behind" and "in front" spaces), the "elsewhere" (by contrast with the "here"/"there" that characterizes topic space).—TOPIC SPACE; LOCALIZATION, SPATIO-TEMPORAL

HEURISTIC
(heuristique)

1. A working hypothesis is said to be **heuristic** if the discourse which develops it has the effect of producing and of formulating a discovery procedure. It is thus the hypothesis, neither true nor false, but preceding the establishment of the procedure,* which is heuristic. Discovery procedures, once formulated, are able in turn to facilitate the drawing up of new hypotheses, the whole process constituting scientific praxis.

2. In a more general and vaguer fashion, a scientific attitude is sometimes qualified as heuristic: the structural approach, for example,

which aims in the first place at grasping relations* and requires, by this very fact, that the potential positions of the terms* of a category* be forseen (terms the manifestations of which are not evident at first glance), can, in this sense, be called heuristic.
—HYPOTHESIS; DISCOVERY

HIERARCHY
(hiérarchie)

1. Itself defined as the class* of classes, **hierarchy** is, for L. Hjelmslev, the term which defines all semiotic systems. Such a definition, which seems exaggerated at first glance, can be understood if the fact that Hjelmslev postulates the unity of morphology* and of syntax* is taken into account. Hierarchy thus appears as the organizing principle of the elementary structure* of signification, where the category,* as the totality, is hierarchically superior to the terms which constitute it and which are its parts; but hypotactic relations, essential for syntax, are equally productive of hierarchy.

2. Hierarchy, conceived as formal organization and based on the principle of logical presupposition,* must be distinguished from the use of this term to designate the relation of superiority/inferiority (or of dominating/dominated), which is axiological* in nature and is based on the modality of being-able* (cf. for example, G. Dumézil's three functions*).

HISTORICAL GRAMMAR
(historique [grammaire—])

The term **historical grammar** was used, in parallel with that of comparative grammar, to designate comparative linguistics, which was constituted progressively through the nineteenth century.—COMPARATIVE LINGUISTICS

HI/STORY
(histoire)

The term **hi/story** (the French term comprises the meanings of both "history" and "story") is ambiguous and covers contents quite different the one from the other.

1. By hi/story (history) is understood a semantic universe considered as an object* of knowledge, the intelligibility of which, postulated a priori, is based on a diachronic* articulation* of its elements. In this sense, "history" can be considered as a semiotic system as object (or as a set of semiotic systems taken prior to their analysis*) the approach of which is determined beforehand by certain postulates.

2. Hi/story (as story) corresponds, on the other hand, to the narration or to the description of actions the veridictory of which status is not fixed (they can be declared to be past and "real," imaginary, or even undecidable). From this viewpoint, hi/story is to be considered as a narrative discourse (as "historical narration," after E. Benveniste, or simply as "narration").

3. If semio-narrative structures* (as deep and general forms of organization) are distinguished from discursive structures (characteristic of the manner in which the 'hi/story' (as story) is recounted), **historical discourse** appears, on the surface level, as a temporalized* discourse (where the transformation-predicates are converted* into processes*). It is in this sense that one can speak of **historical anchoring,** meaning thereby the inscription of the narrative programs* within spatio-temporal coordinates, figurative* in nature.

4. When the narrative discourse (see 2 above) serves as a mode of articulation for the hi/story (as his-

tory in meaning 1), it is called **historiographical** (or, more often, historical). At that point, the problem of the scientificness* of such a discourse—and that of its constructed metalanguage*—is automatically posed. **Historical linguistics** solved it as comparativism* does, that is, by interpreting diachrony as the logical transformation* recognizable between two given language states,* but at the cost of throwing out historicity (or the temporal dimension) itself. In more recent times, the attempts coming from logical philosophy, to establish ordered utterance sequences corresponding to successions of historical events, are far from having been crowned with success.

5. Within a general discourse typology, which semiotics strives for, and in the framework of the models for narrativity* that semiotics proposes, it is not impossible to imagine research programs the goal of which would be to determine the specificity of historical discourse. A preliminary distinction between **event history,** situated on the level of surface narrative syntax,* and **fundamental history,** understood as the set of transformations of deep structures, logico-semantic in nature, then appears as a preamble to such research.

—DIEGESIS; EVENT

HOMOGENEITY
(homogénéité)

1. A set* is said to be homogeneous if all its constituent elements* have the same properties in common. As distinguished from the concept of isotopy,* reserved for the internal analysis of narrative, **homogeneity,** much broader and relatively imprecise (recognized as undefinable by L. Hjelmslev),

applies essentially to the constitution of corpora,* bringing into play, among other things, extra-linguistic conditions.

2. In a more restricted sense, homogeneity can be based on a choice of elements of the same level,* of units of the same dimensions, of relations of the same type (Hjelmslev). From this point of view, it is comparable to pertinence*; nonetheless, whereas the latter belongs to the analyst's viewpoint (or operation), the former would concern, rather, the "immanent" nature of the materials under study.

HOMOLOGATION
(homologation)

1. **Homologation** is an operation of semantic analysis, applicable to all semiotic domains, which is a part of the general procedure of structuration.* It is to be considered as a rigorous formulation of reasoning by analogy.* Given the structure

$$A : B : : A' : B'$$

A and A' are said to be homologous by comparison with B and B'. From the semiotic point of view, such a homology can be affirmed only if three conditions are fulfilled: (a) the terms, represented by the capital letters, must be sememes* that can be broken down into semes*; (b) the terms A and A' on the one hand, and B and B' on the other, must have at least one common seme; (c) the relation between A and B on the one hand, and between A' and B' on the other, is identical and can be recognized as one of the elementary logical relations (contradiction, contrariety, complementarity).

2. Thus defined, homologation is complementary, in semantic analysis, to reduction.* Indeed, an

inventory of parasynonymic occurrences* can be reduced to a single descriptive sememe only if each of them finds its opposed term (contrary or contradictory) in the parallel inventory (or inventories), and if each category* thus established is homologable with the other categories of the parallel inventories.

3. As a constraint imposed on analogical reasoning, the importance of which for research must not be underestimated, homologation is a general procedure which goes beyond the limits of semantics (in the restricted meaning of this term). For example, it is used to establish the rules of conversion* between levels,* to determine correlations in comparative* methodology, to formulate semiotic constraints (syntactic or semantic), etc.
—STRUCTURATION; ANALOGY

HOMONYMY
(homonymie)

Homonymy is the identity* relation, situated on the level of the signifier and recognzied between two or more morphemes or words* whose signifieds* are considered distinct. Homonyms can be **homophones** ("too," "to," "two") or **homographs** ("batter": the person who is to hit the ball; "batter": the dough mixed with the other ingredients). Two lexemes* are considered independent and homonymous if their sememes* do not contain any common nuclear* figure.—POLYSEMY

HYPONYMIC/ HYPERONYMIC
(hyponymique/hypéronymique)

By the double adjective **hyponymic/hyperonymic** is designated the relation* established between the semic category and one of its constituent terms* (situated on the axis of contraries*). This relation is two-directional: what appears as a hyponymic relation from the interpretive* point of view, will be considered hyperonymic from the generative point of view (following the trajectory that goes from the *ab quo* point toward the *ad quem* point). Solely from the interpretive* point of view, the **hyponym** is the term manifested in the place of the semic category, and **hyperonym** is the category in the place of one of the semic terms. Through these semantic distinctions, more basically, it is the relation of **selection** (a unilateral presupposition* according to L. Hjelmslev) that is being considered, as it functions within a single semic category. The hyponymic/hyperonymic relation allows metonymy* to be defined in the narrower meaning (*pars pro tota*).

HYPOTACTIC/ HYPEROTACTIC
(hypotaxique/hypérotaxique)

1. In general, by **hypotactic** relation is meant, in linguistics, the hierarchical* relation* linking two terms* situated at two different stages of derivation* (example: the relation between main and subordinate clauses, between modified and modifier, etc.). L. Hjelmslev has sought to define it in interpreting selections*—in logical terms—as the relation between a presupposed term and a presupposing term (unilateral presupposition*). Insofar as it is hierarchical in nature, **hypotaxis** is opposed to **parataxis** (which establishes no relation of dependence between two contiguous terms).

2. As distinguished from the hyponymic* relation which defines the position of the semic terms of a single category* invested within the

semiotic square,* the **hyperotactic** relation indicates the formal positions of the terms prior to any semantic investment.* Thus, on the square, hypotaxis could be identified, for example, with implication,* which is a relation of unilateral presupposition between one of the prime terms and the negation of the contrary term (between s1 and $\overline{s2}$).

HYPOTHESIS
(hypothèse)

1. Any cognitive activity of the subject is based on an (implicit or explicit) anterior knowing, and consequently presupposes a certain cognitive competence.* In this perspective, the **working hypothesis** appears as the explicitation* of this competence in view of the projected performance* which will take the form of discourse with a scientific aim. As an explicitation posited prior to the research discourse itself, the working hypothesis can be assimilated to a contract* proposed to the enunciatee (*i.e.,* the scholarly community) by the enunciator the performance-discourse of which is supposed to constitute the realization of that contract. This is to say that the hypothesis is neither true nor false, and that its truth value will only appear *a posteriori,* if it transforms the discourse made about it into a discovery* procedure. From another viewpoint, knowing and knowing-how-to-do, the partial explicitation of which constitutes the working hypothesis, are not given *ex nihilo,* but belong to an episteme* and to different theoretical conceptualizations. Thus explicit theories have an important role in the formulation of hypotheses.

2. By **hypothetico-deductive** method is meant the procedure concerning the construction of a theory, which consists in positing, at the outset, a certain number of undefined concepts or propositions that do not yet have truth values, so that the deductive discourse developed from these postulates may *a posteriori* demonstrate its efficacy by producing, as a logical consequence, utterances which can be viewed as discovery procedures. Such a way of proceeding, frequent in mathematics and in physics, has recently been introduced into semiotics (L. Hjelmslev, N. Chomsky).
—PROCEDURE; DISCOVERY; DEDUCTION

ABCDEFGHIJKLMN
OPQRSTUVWXYZ

ICONICITY
(iconicité)

1. By **icon** is meant, following C. S. Peirce, a sign* defined by its relation of resemblance to the "reality" of the exterior world. It is opposed both to index* (characterized by a relation of "natural contiguity") and to symbol* (based on simple social convention). If one considers—as we do—that the definition of the sign by what it is not is not pertinent semiotically and that, on the other hand, semiotics becomes operational only when it situates its analyses on levels both higher and lower than the sign, the proposed classification, without being troublesome, offers but little interest.

2. This is not the case when the concept of **iconicity** is called up to define one semiotic system or another—or its expression* plane—as a whole. To recognize that the visual semiotic system (painting, for example, considered as a typical case) is an immense analogy* of the natural world,* is to get lost in the labyrinth of positivist presuppositions, and is also to declare that one knows what "reality" is, that one knows the "natural signs" the imitation of which would produce such or such a semiotic system, etc. By the same token it is also to negate visual semiotics as such: in this perspective, the analysis of an articulated plane surface will indeed consist of identifying the iconic signs and of lexicalizing them in a natural language. It is not surprising, then, that research carried out on the organization principles of signs thus recognized should lead to the confusion of these organization principles with that of their lexicalization. Consequently, it is not surprising that the analysis of a painting, for example, should be transformed into an analysis of a discourse concerning the painting! The specificity of a visual semiotic system is then diluted into these two micro-semiotic* systems that the natural world and the natural languages are.

3. It is clear that the problem of iconicity concerns, first of all, visual semiotic systems, since it is there, in the domains of the cinema, of painting, of photography, etc., that what is at stake in the discussion appears to be of greatest consequence, whereas one cannot see why the visual signifier would be more "iconic" than the auditive or olfactory signifier, for example. Yet if, instead of taking the problem of iconicity as proper to visual semiotic systems, it were formulated in terms of intertextuality (between fabricated semiotic systems and natural semiotic systems), and if it were broadened to include literary* semiotic systems, for example, then

it could be seen that iconicity has for equivalent what is designated by the phrase "referential* illusion." Referential illusion can be defined as the result of a set of procedures put in place to produce the meaning effect* of "reality." It appears, therefore, as conditioned both by the culturally variable conception of "reality" and by the realist ideology assumed by the producers and the users of such or such a semiotic system. The referential illusion, far from being a universal phenomenon, is found only in certain text "genres," and its distribution is just as unequal and relative. To generalize: iconicity, while it is engendered by a set of semiotic procedures which can be formulated, is not part of semiotics; it does not belong, as Hjelmslev would say, to "denotative" semiotic systems, its base is to be found in the system of the social connotations* which underly the set of semiotic systems.

4. This set of considerations leads us to introduce the term of **iconization** to designate, within the narrative trajectory of texts, the last stage of the figurativization* of discourse, wherein we distinguish two phases: **figuration** proper, which accounts for the conversion* of themes* into figures,* and iconization, which, taking up the figures already constituted, endows them with particularizing investments,* capable of producing the referential illusion. —SIGN; FIGURATIVIZATION; IMAGE; REFERENT; SEMIOLOGY

IDENTITY
(identité)

1. The concept of **identity**, an undefinable one, is opposed to that of alterity* (as "same" to "other") which cannot be defined either. Yet, this pair is interdefinable by a relation of reciprocal presupposition,* and is indispensable for founding the elementary structure* of signification.

2. In contrast to equality, which characterizes objects possessing exactly the same qualitative properties, identity serves to designate the features or the set of features (in semiotics: semes* or phemes*) that two or more objects have in common. Thus, when a categorial opposition—for example *person/non-person*—is suspended, the semantic axis* which joins the two terms reappears and is valorized, and its manifestation induces an identification effect. Whence it can be seen that the recognition* of the identity of two objects, or their **identification,** presupposes their alterity, that is, a semic or phemic minimum which at first makes them distinct. From this point of view, identification is a metalinguistic* operation which requires, beforehand, a semic or phemic analysis*; far from being a first approach to the semiotic material, identification is one operation among others in the construction of the semiotic object.

3. Identity also serves to designate the principle of permanence which permits the individual to remain the "same," to "persist in its being," all through its narrative existence, despite the changes that it provokes or undergoes. In this way one refers to the concept of identity when the permanence of an actant* is brought up, despite the transformations* of its modes of existence* or of the actantial* roles that it assumes along its narrative* trajec-

tory. This is equally the case for the permanence of a discursive actor* all through the discourse in which it is inscribed: at this level, it is the procedure of anaphorization* which permits the identification of an actor with all the moments of that actor's discursive existence.

4. By identification is also understood one of the phases of the enunciatee*'s interpretive* doing, namely when the enunciatee identifies the universe of the discourse (or a part of that universe) with its own universe. For example, one says that a young (female) reader identifies herself with the personage of Joan of Arc. Understood in this sense, identification is still not well enough studied.

—ALTERITY; INDIVIDUALIZATION

IDEOLOGY
(idéologie)

1. Given the richness of the semantic field covered by the concept of **ideology** and the numerous ambiguities which result from its different possible interpretations and definitions, it can be hoped that the semiotic approach might make the concept a bit more precise.

2. Thus, it seems advantageous to distinguish two fundamental forms of organization of the universe of values*: their paradigmatic* and syntagmatic* articulations. In the first case, the values are organized in systems* and are presented as valorized taxonomies* which can be designated by the name of axiologies.* In the second case, their mode of articulation is syntactic* and they are invested in models which appear as potentialities of semiotic processes.* When these models are set in opposition to the axiologies, they can be considered as **ideologies** (in the restricted, semiotic, meaning of this word).

3. Values, participating in an axiology, are virtual* and are the result of the semiotic articulation of the collective* semantic universe*; they thereby belong to the level of deep* semiotic structures. By being invested in the ideological model, they are actualized* and are taken up by an individual or collective subject which is modalized* by *wanting-to-be* and, subsequently, by *wanting-to-do*. This is to say that an ideology belongs to the level of surface* semiotic structures, and thus that it can be defined as an actantial structure which actualizes the values that it selects within axiological systems (of a virtual order).

4. An ideology is thus characterized by the actualized status of the values that it takes up. The realization* of these values (that is, the conjunction of the subject* with the object* of value) abolishes, *ipso facto,* the ideology as ideology. In other words, ideology is a permanent quest* for values, and the actantial structure which informs it must be considered as recurring* in every ideological discourse.

5. Considered as a domain of the generative* trajectory taken as a whole, the ideological organization presents values, that it takes up, under their abstract or thematic* form. However, ideological discourse can, at any instant, be more or less figurativized* and be thus converted into mythological discourses.

—AXIOLOGY

IDIOLECT
(idiolecte)

1. The **idiolect** is an individual*
actor*'s specific semiotic activity
which produces and/or reads significations*—or the set of texts relative
thereto—while this actor participates
in a given semantic universe.* In the
practice of the natural languages,*
individual variations* cannot be too
numerous nor can they constitute
too large gaps: they would run the
risk of interrupting interpersonal
communication. Thus these individual variations are generally viewed
as surface* phenomena, affecting
first of all the phonetic and lexical
components of the language. In its
pure state, the idiolect belongs to
pathological psycholinguistics and
could be identified with the notion
of autism.

2. When it is located on the
level of deep* structures, the problem of the idiolect is to be compared
to the notion of style.* From this
perspective, the idiolect can be considered as the taking up, by an individual actor, of the individual
semantic universe (as it is constituted
by the category* *life/death*) that
he/she can endow with particularizing hypotactic* investments, and of
the collective universe (articulated by
the category *nature/culture*) the terms
of which he/she can use in his/her
own way by homologating it with the
individual universe. Clearly these
are only a few suggestions, relative
to a particularly difficult set of
problems.
—UNIVERSE; STYLE; SOCIO-
LECT

ILLOCUTION
(illocution)

As distinguished from locution*
and perlocution,* **illocution** (in J. L.
Austin's terminology) corresponds to
enunciation insofar as it is a speech
act which influences the relations
between interlocutor* and interlocutee, and which can be paraphrased
by a performative* utterance
(example: "Do the dishes"="I order
you to do the dishes"). Such is the
case of a command, a piece of advice, a promise, a questioning, etc.,
in which a direct effect is produced
by saying—as distinguished from
perlocution, wherein an indirect effect is produced by the fact of saying. As can be seen, illocution, like
perlocution, belongs essentially to
the domain of verbal communication* and refers to the cognitive
competence* of the locutor-subjects.
—ACT, SPEECH; ENUNCIA-
TION; COMMUNICATION

IMAGE
(image)

In visual semiotics, **image** is
considered as a self-sufficient manifestation* unit, as a comprehensive
signification unit, which can be analyzed. Starting from this common
remark, two distinct attitudes can be
discerned. Whereas semiology of the
image (operating in the context of
communication* theory) generally
considers it as a message constituted
by iconic signs, for planar* semiotics
the image is above all an occur-
rence-text (comparable, in spite of
the bi-dimensional specificity of its
signifer,* to other semiotic systems)
which analysis can account for by
constructing it as a semiotic object.
Similarly, whereas, for semiology of
the image, the iconicity of the signs
is a part of the very definition of the
image, planar semiotics considers
iconicity as a veridictory connotation
effect, relative to a given culture,
which judges certain signs to be
"more real" than others and which
leads the producer of the image,
under certain conditions, to submit

to the rules for constructing a cultural "pretending."—ICONICITY; REFERENT; VERIDICTION; SEMIOLOGY

IMMANENCE
(immanence)

1. The autonomy of linguistics —justifiable by the specificity of its object, insisted upon by Saussure— has been reaffirmed by Hjelmslev under the form of the **immanence principle.** Since the object of linguistics is form* (or natural language* in the Saussurian sense), any recourse to extra-linguistic facts must be excluded, because it breaks down the homogeneity* of the description.*

2. The concept of immanence participates, as one of the terms, in the *immanence/manifestation* dichotomy. The manifestation logically presupposes the manifested, that is to say the immanent semiotic form. The affirmation of the immanence of semiotic structures raises then a problem, ontological in nature, relative to their mode of existence. In times past, the question was asked, *à propos* of dialectics, whether it was inscribed "in things" or "in minds." Similarly, the knowledge of semiotic structures can be considered either as a description,* that is to say as a simple explicitation of immanent forms, or as a construction,* if the world is only structurable, that is to say capable of being "in-formed" by the human mind. In order to exclude any metaphysical quarrel from semiotic theory, we deem it appropriate to limit ourselves to setting up certain operational* concepts, by calling semantic universe* (the "there is meaning") any semiotic* system prior to its description, and semiotic object* its explicitation with the help of a constructed metalanguage* (and of constructed representation* languages).

3. It is in the same spirit, which aims at avoiding taking any metaphysical position, that we name, arbitrarily,* and with a minimal semantic investment,* the two axes of the category of veridiction*: the one of being* we name **immanence axis,** and the other, that of seeming,* manifestation axis. This designation presupposes that further investments can give rise to interpretations of immanence as "latency" or as "numenality," for example (just as the modality of "wanting" is neither "will" nor "desire," the two latter names corresponding to additional semantic investments).

4. The opposition *immanence/ transcendence* can be used, on the other hand, to account for the difference in status of the subject and of the Sender,* in the framework of the narrative* schema. The subject is inscribed in an **immanent universe** where it accomplishes its narrative* trajectory by acquiring competence* and by carrying out performances* (by "realizing" itself). Yet a relatively large subclass of narrative discourses also posits subject as the Reciever of a transcendent Sender which establishes it as subject by means of participative communication* (permitting the communication of the objects of value under the form of gifts, without by that fact depriving the Sender thereof; just as, for example, the queen of England keeps her absolute "power," all the while she delegates it almost entirely to Parliament).
—MANIFESTATION; TRANSCENDENCE; CONSTRUCTION

IMPERFECTIVENESS
(imperfectivité)

Imperfectiveness designates the aspectual seme* which corresponds to the durative* aspect and which actualizes* at the same time the absence of a relation of presupposition with the terminative* aspect. The imperfective aspect is also called **unaccomplished.**—ASPECTUALIZATION

IMPLICATION
(implication)

1. Like all fundamental concepts of logic, **implication** has given rise to diverse interpretations. Its application to semiotics constitutes a further difficulty: therefore we will limit ourselves to giving a single definition, conforming to that of another fundamental concept, presupposition.

2. Considered as an act of implying, implication consists, for us, in the assertive calling up of the presupposing term, having as its effect the appearance of the presupposed term. The presuppositional relation is thus envisaged as logically prior to implication: the "if" would not find its "then," if the latter did not already exist as the presupposed.
—PRESUPPOSITION; SQUARE, SEMIOTIC; ASSERTION

IMPLICIT
(implicite)

1. If the explicit* is viewed as constituting the manifested part of the utterance (sentence or discourse), the **implicit** corresponds to the non-manifested part, although it is presupposed directly or indirectly by the utterance produced. The explicit in the utterance can be compared to the visible part of an iceberg, because of the considerable amount of information that any communication seems to carry implicitly. The positivist approach, which tended to treat natural languages* as pure denotations* and

words as transparent labels permitting the things that they name to be clearly seen, is definitively called into question by research which aims at making the implicit explicit.

2. From the semiotic point of view, the implicit can be spoken of only insofar as one simultaneously postulates the existence of a relation, of a reference, binding any element of the manifested utterance to what is outside of it, but which the utterance contains virtually* or actually* and which can, by this very fact, be realized with the help of a paraphrase* (or of additional information). In other words, the implicit —within a given semiotic system—is never anything other than what can be made explicit.

3. To be clearer: the **intrasemiotic implicit** (which can be made explicit within a natural language) can first of all be distinguished from the **intersemiotic implicit** (where the explicit utterance, formulated in a semiotic system, refers back to an implicit and/or an explicit which belong to other semiotic systems). It is only by pure abstraction that the habit has arisen of viewing linguistic communication as an object of study in itself, treating as implicit—or "understood"— the elements called paralinguistic* (gestuality, "body language") as well as the significations coming from the "extralinguistic context" or from the "situation," that is to say, from nonlinguistic* natural* semiotic systems. If, on the contrary, it were postulated from the beginning that intersubjective communication is the product of a syncretic semiotic system, wherein several manifestation languages concur (*cf.*, for example, opera or cinema), the intersemiotic implicit would have a natural explanation as a network between several parallel or interlocking expressions.*

4. By holding to the conventional position of an autonomous linguistic communication, the field of the implicit can be sought in the verbal or verbalizable unsaid. The common procedure of implicitation is what is called ellipsis,* while the parallel and inverse procedure of explicitation, is termed catalysis.* The well-known example, proposed by Hjelmslev, is that of the Latin preposition *sine*. Its mere presence allows the explicitation of the element which is logically bound to it, an element which can be expressly defined as *ablative + category of number + category of gender + root + nominal class*. It can be seen that what is implicit, in the case under examination, is the set of grammatical data which characterize the syntagm in question by reflecting therein the "immanent structure" of the language.

5. From that point, this observation can justifiably be generalized by our saying that what is valid for the syntagmatic* implicit is valid also for the paradigmatic* axis of the language. Thus any explicit element of the utterance, viewed as an entity of a paradigmatic class, exists in signification only because it presupposes implicitly the entire class. Eventually it can be maintained that every grammar, insofar as it seeks to account for the mode of production of the utterances, is but the implicit of these utterances made explicit (with more or less success). Thus one can affirm that the deep* structures, for example, are the implicit of the surface* structures, etc. It is essential to note that the implicit can be grasped only as a relational network and, more exactly, as a network of logical presupposeds (O. Ducrot). It is in this, as well as in the metalogical character which is at the base of every semiotic structure, that the concept of grammaticality* can be located, rather than in the "grammatical feeling" of the speaking subjects.

6. Applying these remarks to the semantic dimension of language is clearly a more delicate operation. Nonetheless, the principle itself, that is to say the definition of the implicit as a logical presupposed which can be made explicit, can be maintained at all the levels of the analysis. Thus, for example, the domain of the enunciation* can be defined as the utterance's implicit. A trivial example, taken from narrative semiotics, can give an idea of the practical use which can be made of this concept. The narrative utterance "victory of S1" presupposes paradigmatically the implicit utterance "defeat of S2"; it presupposes at the same time, syntagmatically, the utterance "confrontation of S1 and S2," which does not need to be manifested in order that the conditions necessary for the establishment of a narrative sequence be fulfilled. There is no need to note that the consequences of the application of this explicitation procedure are quite important for an understanding of narrativity.

IMPOSSIBILITY
(impossibilité)

As a name, **impossibility** designates the modal* structure which, from the viewpoint of its syntactic definition, corresponds to the modal predicate of *having-to (being-obliged)* which governs the utterance of state *not-being. Having-not-to-be,* named impossibility, is the contrary of *having-to-be,* called necessity.* Used in logic, the term impossibility remains semiotically ambiguous, for it also designates the modal structure of *not-having-to-be.*—ALETHIC MODALITIES

IMPROBABILITY
(improbabilité)

The contradictory term for probability* and the contrary term for certainty* on the semiotic square* of the epistemic modalities, **improbability** is the name of the modal structure of *believing-not-to-be.*—EPISTEMIC MODALITIES

INCHOATENESS
(inchoativité)

Inchoateness is an aspectual seme* which shows the beginning of a process*: it is part of the aspectual configuration *inchoateness/durativeness/terminativeness,* and its appearance in the discourse allows the realization of the entire series to be foreseen or expected.—ASPECTUALIZATION

INCOMPATIBILITY
(incompatibilité)

Incompatibility can be considered as the impossibility, for any two semiotic elements,* to contract a relation* (to be present* together in a hierarchically higher unit, or in a contiguous position on the syntagmatic* axis). Incompatibility is either **intra-categorical** (two terms in a relation of contradiction*), or **extra-categorical**: in the latter, it is a case of mutual exclusion, characterizing two micro-systems (semic or phemic): in Latin, for example, "ad" and the ablative exclude each other reciprocally. **Phonological, syntactic,** and **semantic incompatibilities** can be distinguished.—COMPATIBILITY; ACCEPTABILITY; AGRAMMATICALITY; ASEMANTICITY

INDEX
(indice)

1. In his classification of signs, C. S. Peirce opposes **index** both to icon* (which involves a relation of resemblance) and to symbol* (based on a social convention). For him, the index sets up a relation of "natural" contiguity, linked to a fact of experience not provoked by human beings.

2. For L. Prieto, who emphasizes the mechanism of indication (under all its possible forms), the index is to be understood, in a much broader sense, as "an immediately perceptible fact which causes us to know something about something else which is not perceptible." From his point of view, the signal* is only a particular form of the index.

3. If it be admitted, as in Saussurian linguistics, that the exclusion of the referent* is an *a priori* which is necessary for the exercise of any semiotics, then it must be acknowledged that the index—in the two meanings indicated above—is in the category of non-signs.

4. In his concept of narrative, R. Barthes has proposed an opposition of index and informant. While the informant is a "realistic operator," which serves to authentify the referent's reality (for example, the exact age of a person), the index is constituted by a set of notations (for example, the notations relative to a personality type, to a sentiment) which, rather than being immediately signifying data (as in the case of the informant), have only "implicit signifieds." Thus, for example, the description of a landscape, of an object, is sometimes used to inform us indirectly concerning the psychology or the destiny of a character. As is clear, this meaning converges with the common use of the word index.
—SIGN

INDIVIDUAL
(individuel)

1. The semantic universe is said to be **individual** when it is articu-

lated by one of the basic semantic categories,* *life/death;* it is thus opposed to the collective universe founded on the opposition *nature/culture.*

2. An actant is said to be **individual,** as distinguished from a collective actant, defined as a collection of individuals endowed with a common modal competence* and/or doing.*
—COLLECTIVE; PSYCHOSEMIOTIC; UNIVERSE; ACTANT

INDIVIDUATION
(individuation)

1. In philosophy, **individuation** is "the realization of the general idea in a given individual" (Lalande). According to Leibnitz, the individuation principle is that which brings it about that a being possesses not only a specific type, but a singular existence, determined in time and in space.

2. In narrative and discoursive semiotics, the concept of individuation is part of the problems connected with the actor*—be it individual (a character) or collective (a group)—insofar as the actor is defined as made up, at a given moment of the generative* trajectory, of structural properties which are both syntactic and semantic in nature. Then, another principle, that of identity, insures that the actor constitutes a permanent "individual," recognizable all through the discourse (thanks in particular to the procedures of anaphorization*), despite the transformations of actantial* and thematic* roles which can affect him/her. Since the name of the actor (endowing it with an anthroponym* or designating it by a thematic role: example, "the sovereign") does not suffice to individuate it, it must be defined empiri-

cally by the set of pertinent traits which distinguish its doing* and/or being* from those of other actors: individuation will then be characterized as a meaning effect,* reflecting an underlying discriminatory* structure. Since the Leibnitzian definition —according to which individuation is explained by singular existence, determined in space and in time— accounts for the actor's unicity, but not for its permanence, we have been led to consider actorialization* as an autonomous component, independent of temporalization* and spatialization* procedures.
—IDENTITY; ACTORIALIZATION; ACTOR

INDUCTION
(induction)

Induction is a series of cognitive operations, carried out at the moment of description* (or of the construction* of a model), which consists in passing from a component to a class, from a particular proposition to a more general proposition, etc. The **inductive process** is considered by its partisans as closer to the data of experience, as better reflecting "reality." Nonetheless, even if it can account for an autonomous semiotic object, induction does not provide a satisfactory basis for comparative* or typological* doing. If the description of a language or of a language state allows it, for example, to build up the concepts of "subjunctive" or of "imperfect," these are not thereby generalizable and cannot be applied to other languages or language states. Thus it does not seem possible to use the inductive process for other than limited operations, and its results must be inscribed in a deductive framework of greater generality.—DEDUCTION; GENERALIZATION

INFORMANT
(informateur)

The **informant,** often called into play by narratives (such as in the case of the messenger who informs Oedipus that the man he killed is his father, the woman he married, his mother), represents, under the form of an autonomous actor,* a cognitive* subject, endowed with a knowing (partial or total) by the enunciator* and installed by the latter, in the discourse, in a position of mediator vis-à-vis the enunciatee.

INFORMATION
(information)

1. In information theory, the term **information** is used to designate any element that can be expressed with the aid of a code.* When the choice is between two equally probable units, the information brought forth will be said to be equivalent to one bit (binary digit); when it is made between four or eight equally probable units, the information will be of three or four bits, etc. In this case, the quantity of information, measured in bits, is equal to $\log_2$ of the number of elements considered. Exclusive of the hypothesis of equal probability, one can have to deal with contexts of probability or of improbability. From this point of view, the quantity of information is said to be inversely proportional to the probability of the units, with the information diminishing as their foreseeableness rises.

2. Any reduction of information—linked to syntagmatic constraints, to repetitions, etc., in the framework of the message*—corresponds to the redundance to which recourse is had in order to reduce the negative effects of noise.

3. Information theory seeks to account for the modalities of the transfer of messages (as sequences of signals* organized according to a code*) from a source* to a destination,* exclusive of the contents* therein invested. Thus it takes up only the plane of the signifier,* the transmission of which it seeks to optimize. In the domain of natural languages, for example, it will be noted that what is transmitted is a succession of phonemes or of graphemes, and not signification (which belongs to the received, not to the transmitted).

4. The **information schema** (and the communication* schema) includes: (a) a source and a destination (which can be identical with the Receiver*); (b) a channel, that is, a material or sensory support which serves to transmit messages from one point to another; (c) a message which is a sequence of signals, obeying predetermined rules.* Between the source and transmission (in the strict sense of the term) are located the encoding* operations by which the message is constructed; between transmission and reception by the Receiver, the decoding* operations allow the constitutive elements of the message to be received and identified. All along the information trajectory, up to and including the encoding and/or decoding operations, noise can intervene, the effects of which one can attempt to reduce by means of redundance.

5. Information theory exercised at one time (particularly in the 1950s) a rather considerable influence on linguistics by simplifying excessively the problems of the discipline. It will be noted that this theory is situated basically in a mechanistic perspective which makes of the source or of the destination,

for example, empty entities (different in this from semiotics, which considers the Sender and the Receiver as subjects endowed with a particular competence* and inscribed in a process of becoming).
—COMMUNICATION; INFORMATIVE DOING

INFORMATIVE DOING
(informatif [faire—])

In a given narrative, knowing* can be simply **informative:** someone makes something known and the course of events changes. Here it is a case of an operational* concept set out in view of the analysis.* We make the supposition, in the interest of simplicity and of economy (at least in a preliminary stage) that **informative doing** is not modalized by the veridictory* categories, even if an utterance such as "the earth is round"—which seems to be an unalloyed statement—includes at least one affirmation* modalization. Taking into account the schema of communication,* and knowing that it concerns the simple transfer of the object of knowing, it can be foreseen immediately that informative doing —as opposed to persuasive*/ interpretive* doing, which modalizes the communication of the object of knowing—is expressed in two possible manners: it is either **emissive*** or **receptive***; the receptive can, in turn, be envisaged as **active** or **passive** (*cf.* the oppositions "to listen"/ "to hear"; "to see"/"to look").—DOING CAUSING; COGNITIVE

INJUNCTION
(injonction)

1. **Injunction** is the name of the axis of contraries, subsuming the two values—prescription* and interdiction*—of the deontic modal category.

2. The concept of injunction can have two distinct uses. Applied to an axiology* belonging to the transcendent* universe (at times represented, in the narrative discourse, by the Sender*), injunction transforms it into a normative system. From another point of view, considered as a particular modalization of the Subject's competence,* injunction is therein confronted with the volitional modalities: the compatibility (or the incompatibility) between these conjoined modal categories then determines the nature of the **injunctive contract** that the Subject accepts from or refuses to its Sender.
—DEONTIC MODALITIES

INTENTION
(intention)

1. The concept of **intention** is usually introduced in order to account for communication* as act. Supposedly, intention motivates and justifies the act of communication. In our view this notion is open to criticism in that communication is thereby considered to be both a voluntary act, though it is certainly not always so, and a conscious act, a view which presupposes a rather simplistic psychological conception of human beings.

2. It is for these reasons that we prefer the notion of intentionality, the roots of which are plainly phenomenological. While not being identified with either motivation or finality, this concept subsumes both. Thus the act* can be conceived as a tension which is inscribed between two modes of existence*: the modes of virtuality* and of realization.* The semiotic formulation that we would like to give to this concept approximates that of modal competence.
—ENUNCIATION;   COMPETENCE

INTERCALATION
(intercalation)

Normally we mean by **intercalation** the insertion of a micronarrative into a narrative.*—EMBEDDING

INTERDICTION
(interdiction)

1. As the name for the negative term of the deontic modal category, **interdiction** involves as its syntactic definition the modal structure *having-not-to-do*. Together with its contrary term, prescription,* it constitutes the axis of injunction.*

2. In the field of narrative semiotics the use of the concept of interdiction (or **prohibition**) is confusing. At the time of our first study of the narrative schema proposed by V. Propp, we interpreted the pair of Proppian functions "interdiction" *vs** "violation" as a breaking of the contract,* that is, as a negative contractual structure. From this point of view interdiction corresponded to the Sender*'s factitive* doing and the Proppian syntagm appeared to be a structure of manipulation.* Currently, a more exact modal analysis enables us to identify the transgression of interdiction as a problem of the Subject's modal competence.* Interdiction is defined as a conflictual structure that is the result of an incompatibility between two modalizations of the Subject: the modalizations of *having-not-to-do* and *wanting-to-do*. This incompatibility could only result from the Sender's manipulatory doing. In other words, interdiction belongs in the first instance to the axiological* system of the Sender and, in the second, to the modal organization of the Subject's competence.
—DEONTIC MODALITIES; HAVING-TO-DO

INTERLOCUTOR/ INTERLOCUTEE
(interlocuteur/interlocutaire)

As a simulated representation of the structure of communication* within discourse, dialogue presupposes two actants*—sender and receiver—which together are labeled **interlocutors** or, individually, **interlocutor/interlocutee** (for the purpose of fitting this category, as a pair, into the paradigm sender*/receiver, enunciator*/enunciatee and narrator*/narratee).—DIALOGUE; SENDER/ RECEIVER; DISENGAGEMENT

INTEROCEPTIVITY
(intéroceptivité)

1. The set of semic categories* which articulates the semantic universe* taken to be co-extensive with either a given culture or individual may be classified in terms of the classematic category *exteroceptivity/ interoceptivity* according to whether or not they have corresponding elements within the semiotic system of the natural world.* Unduly influenced by psychology, names for this category have at times been replaced with *semiological/semantic,* which itself creates certain ambiguities. In the homologation*

exteroceptivity : interoceptivity
: : semiological : semantic : :
figurative : non-figurative

we propose to designate those categories which are interoceptive as **non-figurative** (or abstract).

2. Thus the semantic field encompassed by the term interoceptivity is that place where the theoretical issue of language universals is located.
—EXTEROCEPTIVITY

INTERPRETATION
(interprétation)

1. The concept of **interpretation** is used in semiotics in two very

different ways according to the fundamental postulates which ground semiotic theory as a whole and, more specifically, the notion one has, either implicitly or explicitly, of semiotic form.*

2. According to the classical concept which contrasts form with content (or "subject matter"), a notion which is found as well in the metalogic of the Polish and Viennese logical schools, every system of signs may be described in a formal* way that does not take into account the content and is independent of possible "interpretations" of these signs. When we render this epistemological point of view into Hjelmslevian terms we may say that every "system of signs" (and therefore every natural language) is viewed as an "expression* system" which can, in a second moment, receive a **semantic interpretation.** In a broad sense this is the meaning that generative* grammar gives this term.

3. The epistemological tradition upon which Saussurian linguistics—and in other domains the phenomenology of Husserl and the psychoanalytic theory of Freud—is based is completely different. This epistemological tradition insists that the sign* be defined in the first place by its signification* and, in a broader fashion, postulates semiotic forms to be signifying forms. Within this perspective **interpretation** is no longer a matter of attributing a given content to a form which would otherwise lack one; rather, it is a paraphrase* which formulates in another fashion the equivalent* content of a signifying element within a given semiotic system or the translation* of a signifying unit from one semiotic system into another. This corresponds to the notion of **interpretant** in the sign theory proposed by Charles S. Peirce.

4. For generative grammar the transformations* which result in the manifestation of base forms as surface* structures are purely formal rules and do not involve modifications of the content. At most they introduce only stylistic* variations (this view is open to criticism from a Saussurian perspective which holds that any change in the expression plane entails a change in the content plane). Consequently, the deep structures, to which the semantic interpretation must be "attached," contain all of the necessary information (at least in the standard theory), just as in a parallel way the **phonetic interpretation** (along with the phonological and phonetic features) is "attached to" the surface structures. **Interpretive semantics** therefore has the task of spelling out the rules* which assign a semantic interpretation to the deep structures, which are syntactic in nature (that is, void of signification). These rules can only be based upon the epistemological concepts of grammaticality* and acceptability* which are already greatly over-extended. The procedures proposed by Katz and Fodor, for example, show that generative grammar is not well equipped to deal with semantic problems. Thus we see that generative semantics,* which postulates the logico-semantic character of base forms, is able to by-pass the concept of interpretation.

5. According to Hjelmslev the issue of interpretation is not pertinent to semiotic theory. The distinction that he establishes between schema* (or structure) and use* (its investment within any sort of substance*) allows him to say that no semiotic system in principle is interpreted but rather that all systems are interpretable. Here the meaning of interpretation is similar to that given

it in semiotics that go by the name "aesthetics" (for instance, the interpretation of a musical work or a play) and which may be defined as the act of selecting and attributing a use to a given semiotic form.

6. Since the concept of interpretation is not pertinent to semiotic systems endowed with an expression* plane and a content* plane, Hjelmslev is led to raise the question of what he calls "non-languages" or "symbolic systems" (for example algebra, chess, as well as formal syntax, for example, by the generativists). While remaining interpretable like other semiotic systems, these systems are characterized by the fact that both the expression plane and the content plane stand in a relation of conformity* to one another: they involve both isomorphic* and isotopic* articulations (elements having the same syntagmatic dimensions). In other words, the semantic interpretation given for these systems reproduces the same articulations and can be represented in accordance with the same rules as the interpreted form. These considerations offer a possible semiotic definition of formal* languages.
—GENERATIVE GRAMMAR; FORMAL; INTERPRETIVE DOING

INTERPRETIVE DOING
(interprétatif [faire—])

1. One of the forms that cognitive doing* takes is that of **interpretive doing.** It is linked to the instance of enunciation* and consists in the enunciatee's summoning up of those modalities* which are necessary for accepting the contractual* propositions that it receives. To the extent that every received utterance* appears as a manifestation, the role of interpretive doing is to confer the

status of immanence (of being* or non-being) upon the utterance.

2. Thus, it appears that the modal category of veridiction constitutes the general framework within which interpretive activity is carried out by appealing to different alethic modalities and by soliciting the intervention, whether progressive or all-at-once, of the epistemic subject. Interpretive doing appears then to be the principal mode by which epistemic competence* functions.

3. As a type of cognitive doing, interpretation is capable of expansion*; it often takes the form of complex cognitive programs and can even encompass an entire discourse (such as commentaries, critiques, certain forms of scientific discourse).
—COGNITIVE; VERIDICTION; VERIDICTORY MODALITIES; COMMUNICATION; FACTITIVENESS

INTERTEXTUALITY
(intertextualité)

1. Introduced by the Russian semiotician Bakhtin, the concept of **intertextuality** has engendered a lively debate in the West because the procedures which it implied seemed able to provide a methodological replacement for the "influence" theory upon which research in comparative literature was for the most part based. However, this concept's lack of precision has given rise to a variety of extrapolations which range all the way from a discovery of intertextuality within a given text (because of the transformations of content taking place within it) to dressing up old views of "influence" with a refurbished vocabulary (for example, in the study of quotations with or without quotation marks).

2. A. Malraux's affirmation that the work of art is not created on the

basis of the artist's vision but on the basis of other works opens up the possibility for a better understanding of the phenomenon of intertextuality. This phenomenon implies the existence of autonomous semiotic systems (or "discourses") within which more or less explicit processes of construction, reproduction, or transformation of models take place. However, to claim, as some do, that intertextuality exists between different text-occurrences, when it is only a matter of semantic and/or syntactic structures common to one type (or "genre") of discourse, is tantamount to denying the existence of social discourses (and semiotic systems transcending inter-personal communication).

3. Nonetheless it appears that a proper use of intertextuality, such as it is rigorously practiced in linguistics and in the study of mythology could restore hope to comparative literature studies. Since the days of Saussure and Hjelmslev we know that the problem of Indo-European languages, for example, is not a matter of "families" but of systems of formal correlations. Similarly, C. Lévi-Strauss has clearly shown that the myth is an intertextual object. At present, a comparativism with a typological goal appears to us to be the only methodology capable of helping intertextual research in progress.
—COMPARATIVISM; CONFIGURATION

INTONATION
(intonation)

1. **Intonation** constitutes one of the dimensions of prosody.* It is likened in a rather imprecise way to the "melody" or "modulation" of the oral utterance; it is considered by some to be an oral gestuality* added

on to the utterance and by others as a constituent* part of the utterance, that is, as a fundamental element of the utterance. This kind of uncertainty in the interpretation of supra-segmental* units of natural languages having oral signifiers* comes from the ambiguous status of these units that are both articulations recognizable on the expression* plane (for example, *rising inflection* and *falling inflection*) and articulations having grammatical value on the content* plane *(suspension/conclusion)*: that is, as morphemes* of a particular sort which organize the linguistic syntagmatic system at the level of the signs* that belong to a very different principle of articulation. Consequently we can understand, for example, the reasons which force semiotics of the theatre to consider the prosodic dimension as an autonomous signifier distinct from the verbal signifier of the theatrical text.

2. Just as the utterance may be reduced to a sign* ("yes"), intonation may be considered, in the final analysis, as a prosodeme having the dimensions of an onomatopoeia (for example, of a "cry" or a "hmmm"), void of any linguistic signification. Reduced in this way to a "pure" state, intonation still seems capable of becoming a bearer of meaning, especially by being articulated, as some maintain, in semantic categories such as *euphoria/dysphoria* or *approval/refusal*.
—PROSODY

INTUITION
(intuition)

Defined in philosophical terms as a form of immediate knowledge which does not involve cognitive operations, **intuition** could be considered a component of the subject's cognitive competence* which is manifested the moment a working hypothesis is elaborated. If the latter is based essentially upon a knowing* and a previous knowing-how-to-do, a specific intervention of the subject must be anticipated, which consists: (a) in the formulation of a hypothesis which in a certain way makes it adequate for an object of knowledge; and (b) in the certainty* (a type of evidence*) which eventually establishes the wanting-to-do of the subject which wants to verify *a posteriori* the already-formulated hypothesis. Without diminishing the importance of research discourse, it appears indispensable that we take intuition into account in the analysis of discourse about discovery.— HYPOTHESIS; HEURISTIC

INVARIANT
(invariant)

A term is labeled **invariant** if its presence* is the necessary condition for the presence of another term in relation* with which it stands, and which itself is said to be variable. This involves a reformulation of the concept of presupposition*: the invariant is the presupposed term in the relation of presupposition.— VARIABLE; PRESUPPOSITION; PRESENCE

INVENTORY
(inventaire)

By **inventory** is understood a set of semiotic units* which belong to the same paradigmatic class, that is, to the same paradigm. For natural languages* we can make a distinction between **limited** inventories, which are made up of grammatical morphemes,* and **unlimited** inventories of so-called lexical morphemes. The frequency rate of those morphemes belonging to limited inventories is quite high in discourse and their recurrence, in part, constitutes its grammatical isotopy.*— CLASS; PARADIGM

INVESTMENT, SEMANTIC
(investissement sémantique)

1. **Semantic investment** is a process by which a given syntactic structure has previously defined semantic values* attributed to it. Insofar as the analysis of an utterance (sentence or discourse) enables us to recognize, specify, and organize semantic units of all sizes (semes, sememes, themes, etc.), thereby authorizing us to speak of an autonomous semantic component that is relatively independent of the syntactic component, a reverse process may be considered from a generative perspective. By beginning with deep, abstract structures* the generative* trajectory can be thought of as containing, in each domain or on each level of depth, syntactic structures and semantic investments which are parallel to and congruent with them.

2. The notion of a semantic charge that determines a state is close to that of investment (which designates an operation). We should take particular note of the fact, fraught with consequences, of the unequalness of the distribution of the semantic charge within the utterance. The charge may be condensed at times on the subject* ("The seamstress is at work"), at other times on the predicate* ("She is sewing"), etc. At the same time this enables us to distinguish between the semantic content properly speaking and those semantic categories* that are used as grammatical categories. It also enables us to consider a different distribution of the semantic

charge by constructing, for instance, thematic roles* or thematized processes that bring together by themselves alone all of the semantic properties of the utterance.
—CHARGE, SEMANTIC

ISOGLOSS
(isoglosse)

1. In the field of dialectology, an **isogloss** is defined as that line which circumscribes a geographic region characterized by the identical manifestation of common linguistic (phonetic, syntactic, or semantic) features. By comparing several features of this sort we observe that the boundary lines of their geographical expansion are not precisely the same, rather they form bundles of isoglosses which allow us approximately to delimit dialectical areas.

2. More specifically, within ethno-literary semiotics, this procedure could be utilized for establishing semio-cultural areas, where we observe the absence of any concomitance between linguistic frontiers and expansion zones of narrative forms.

3. Similarly, we can go about segmenting a text by establishing isoglosses, when several non-concomitant criteria for segmentation are available: the sequence* could then be compared to an isoglossic area.
—CULTURE; SEGMENTATION

ISOMORPHISM
(isomorphisme)

Isomorphism is the formal identity* between two or more structures which connect different semantic planes or levels.* It is recognizable because of the possible homologation of the relational networks out of which they are constituted. Thus, an isomorphism may be

recognized between the articulations of the expression* plane and the content* plane through the homologation of

phemes : semes :: phonemes : sememes :: syllables : semantic utterances.

Obviously such an isomorphism does not account for the dimensions* of the units of the sign* plane within which the structures of expression and of content are realized at the moment of manifestation (the formant* of a sememe* is generally constituted of several phonemes*). Conformity* between language's two planes enables us to define a given semiotic system as monoplanar.* However, the isomorphism between the planes of expression and content is disputed by advocates of double articulation (A. Martinet).—HOMOLOGATION

ISOTOPY
(isotopie)

1. A. J. Greimas has borrowed the term **isotopy** from the fields of physics and chemistry and has transferred it to semantic analysis by giving it a specific signification in view of its new field of application. As an operational concept, isotopy at first designated iterativity* along a syntagmatic* chain of classemes* which assure the homogeneity of the utterance-discourse. From this point of view it is clear that the syntagm* joining together at least two semic figures* may be considered the minimal context* necessary for establishing an isotopy. Such is the case for the semic category that subsumes the two contrary* terms. Taking into account the trajectories to which they can give rise, the four terms of the semiotic square* are called **isotopes.**

2. With regard to the generative* trajectory of the discourse and

the distribution of its components, we distinguish between the **grammatical isotopy** (or syntactic isotopy, understood in semiotic terms) with the recurrence* of categories pertaining to it, and the **semantic isotopy,** which makes possible a uniform* reading of the discourse as it results from the partial readings of the utterances making it up and from the resolution of their ambiguities* which is guided by the search for a single reading. At the junction of syntactic and semantic components, the actor*s' plane will give rise to a particular isotopy, the **actorial isotopy,** as it is manifested as a result of anaphorization.* From another point of view, if we take into account the dimensions of the isotopy we will contrast **partial isotopies** (B. Pottier's "isosemies"), which can disappear in the condensation* of a text, with **isotopies of the whole,** which are maintained however much the discourse may be extended, given its elasticity.*

3. In the second place, the concept of isotopy has been expanded. Instead of designating only the iterativeness of classemes, it is defined as the recurrence of semic* categories, be they thematic* (or abstract) or figurative (which, in older terminology, produced an opposition between **semantic*** **isotopy** —in a narrow sense—and **semiological*** **isotopy**). From this point of view, by being grounded upon the recognized opposition (within the context of discursive semantics*) between figurative and thematic components, the correlative distinction is made between **figurative isotopies** underlying discursive figurations,* and **thematic isotopies,** located at a much deeper level, in conformity with the generative* trajectory: (a) in some cases the figurative isotopy corresponds to nothing at all on the thematic level. Thus, a cooking recipe, which is situated on the figurative plane and refers to a very general isotopy of the "culinary art," is not bound to any specific theme; (b) elsewhere, on the contrary, it happens that a thematic isotopy will correspond to a figurative isotopy. Thus, the isotopy *supplier/consumer* is illustrated by a set of somatic behaviors of the Ogre and Tom Thumb. This is the most common case; it testifies to the normal process of the generation* of discourse (as passage from abstract to figurative). Indeed, we may claim that a deeper isotopy presupposes the surface isotopy, and not the reverse; (c) it happens sometimes that several figurative isotopies correspond to one single thematic isotopy. The Gospel parables, related as they are to a common theme, are a good illustration of the point, just as are certain works by the obsessed, with their recurrent thematic isotopies; (d) in the case of pluri-isotopy* (which sets up connectors*), several co-occurrent figurative isotopies will correspond, for example, to as many thematic isotopies. In Mallarmé's poem *Salut,* the figurative isotopies (banquet, navigation, writing) as described by F. Rastier, are easily attached to corresponding thematic isotopies (friendship, solitude/escape, creation).

4. With comparisons we encounter a co-manifestation of isotopies, generally a **bi-isotopy.** Thus in the sentence: "This man is a lion," a classematic category (of the sort "both human and animal") appears, both terms of which can be manifested along the length of the syntagmatic chain.What we have here is a **complex isotopy** which can be expressed in different ways: (a) the terms may be in a state of equilibrium*: if, for example, the ut-

terance: "This man is a lion," is emitted in an ancient society of lion-men; (b) in other instances the positive* term prevails. In our cultural universe when we say of someone: "This man is a lion," we totally assume the term *human* and only partially the term *animal*; (c) elsewhere it is perhaps the negative* term which dominates (the qualifications of "positive" and "negative" indicate only formal positions on the semiotic square* and imply no value judgment). The complex isotopy is inserted within the discourse and is thereby linked to the problem of the text's linearity,* even though it is paradigmatic in some aspects. Because of this linear linkage, the development of the two isotopies takes place only upon the syntagmatic axis.

5. As an utterance* governing another utterance (either of doing or of state), modality* defines an isotopic plane which frames hierarchically inferior elements on which it bears (*cf.* the phenomenon of integration pointed out by R. Barthes). Thus, for example, in the case of the veridictory* modalities the interplay of being* and seeming* as the cognitive positions to which it gives rise, determines an isotopic plane within the discourse. Given the fact that the categories *true, false, secret,* and *lie* merely constitute a system of relations, the "truth values" are relative to the universe that they modalize (the world of "common sense" and the world of the "marvelous," both of which play upon veridiction,* are very different with respect to their determination of what is "true"). Here we come to the "logic of possible worlds" (the same text may be read on different isotopies), like the problem of the "fantastic" or of "utopias," with the whole question of the impossibility of deciding between two or more possible readings.

6. From the point of view of the enunciatee,* the isotopy constitutes a reading* grid which makes the surface of the text homogeneous since it makes the elimination of ambiguities possible. It happens nonetheless that disambiguization* takes place, as it were, in reverse: as for example in the case of an "intertextual" reading (M. Arrivé) in which a text is nested within a larger discourse. On the other hand, it happens that different readings may be possible without their being thereby compatible with one another. Finally, let us add that for a given text it does not seem that the number of possible readings can be infinite; the number is linked to the polysemic* nature of the lexemes, the possibilities for exploitation of which are finite in number.

7. Theoretically, as others after us have underscored (M. Arrivé, F. Rastier), nothing stands in the way of transposing the concept of isotopy, developed and restricted up until now to the content* plane, to the expression* plane. Thus, poetic* discourse, from the point of view of the signifier,* could be conceived of in terms of a projection of isotopic phemic* bundles, wherein we recognize symmetry and alteration, consonance and dissonance, and ultimately significative transformations of sound groups. F. Rastier's views fit best: he has proposed a definition of isotopy as the iterativeness of linguistic units (whether manifested or not) which belong either to the expression plane or the content plane; or, more generally, as the recurrence of linguistic units (this formulation runs the risk of introducing even greater confusion).

—PLURI-ISOTOPY; CONNECTOR, ISOTOPIC; METAPHOR; READING; SEMANTICS

ITERATIVENESS
(itérativité)

1. **Iterativeness** is the reproduction along the syntagmatic* axis of identical comparable entities* which are situated at the same level* of analysis. Iterativeness is to be distinguished therefore from recursiveness; the latter is characterized by the repetition of the same entities located at different levels of a common hierarchy.*

2. The repetition of the same entities located within a temporal interval may be understood as a specific characteristic of duration. Iterativeness appears then to be one of the aspectual categories and is contrasted to durativeness.* Perhaps it would be preferable to speak in this sense of **discontinuous durativeness** by contrasting it to continuous durativeness.

—REDUNDANCE; DURATIVENESS; RECURENCE; RECURSIVENESS; DURATIVENESS

ABCDEFGHIJKLMN OPQRSTUVWXYZ

JUNCTION
(jonction)

1. **Junction** is defined as that relation* which joins subject* with object.* It is the constitutive function of utterances* of state.* Taken as a semantic axis* this category is expanded in terms of the semiotic square*:

The position of the object* of value along the syntactic trajectory enables us to distinguish, for example, between disjunction* (the object which has never been possessed) and non-conjunction (which presupposes syntagmatically that the object has already been possessed).

2. We reserve the expression **syntagmatic junction** as the name for a sequence of two junctive utterances (conjunction and disjunction, or vice-versa) which have the same subject and are linked by a relation of simple presupposition.* By **paradigmatic junction** is understood the logically necessary concomitance of two utterances of conjunction and disjunction affecting two distinct subjects which are concerned with the same object.

—FUNCTION; CONJUNCTION; DISJUNCTION

JUSTICE
(justice)

1. **Justice** designates the competence* of the social Sender* which is endowed with the modality of an absolute *being-able-to-do*: such a Sender which is responsible for carrying out sanctions is therefore called a judge.

2. By justice is also understood a form of negative retribution* (or punishment) carried out within the pragmatic domain by the social Sender, in contrast to vengeance* which is carried out by an individual Sender.

—SANCTION; PUNISHMENT

ABCDEFGHIJ**K**LMN OPQRSTUVWXYZ

KERNEL (or NUCLEUS)
(noyau or nucleus)

1. **Kernel, nucleus, nuclear** sentence or phrase refer to the minimal constitutive linguistic unit of the sentence* or the "primitive" elements making it up. By tradition (which extends back to Aristotle) as much as by foregone conclusion, the structure* of the utterance is most often held to be binary,* to be made up of subject* and predicate,* a nominal syntagm and a verbal syntagm, a topic and a comment, etc.

2. In semantics we designate the invariable part of a lexeme* as the kernel or nucleus, which, through the addition of contextual* semes, produces one or more sememes.* The constitutive semes* of the kernel often belong to the exteroceptive* order, whence comes the name *nuclear figure*.

—UTTERANCE; FIGURE

KNOWING
(or KNOWLEDGE)
(savoir)

1. Communication* may be considered, from a certain point of view, as the transmission of **knowledge** from one domain of enunciation to the other. Such a transfer of knowledge (about which little can be said, except that it may be intuitively compared to the concept of signification*) first presents itself as a transitive* structure: it is always knowledge about something, it is inconceivable without the **object of knowledge.** This, already, allows us to recognize in the very unfolding of discourse a particular dimension in which objects of knowledge are disposed; these objects can be formulated in terms of descriptive* utterances, and constitute the bases for what can be called the pragmatic* dimension. On the other hand,

knowledge is also presented as an object in circulation. We are therefore dealing with the production and acquisition of knowledge, its presence or absence (not-knowing), and even degrees of knowing. As an object, knowledge refers to the domain of enunciation where knowing subjects exercising cognitive* activities are located: the cognitive dimension of discourse is thus superimposed upon the pragmatic dimension.

2. This return to the domain of enunciation* allows us to conceive of discourse as such either as a doing, *i.e.*, as a cognitive activity, or as a being, *i.e.*, a state of knowing/knowledge. Consequently, **knowing-how-to-do** seems to make this activity possible; it appears as a cognitive competence (that can be interpreted as a "syntagmatic intelligence," as the ability to organize narrative programming). And **knowing-how-to-be** seems to sanction knowledge concerning objects and to insure the modal quality of this knowledge; in other words, it seems to be an epistemic* competence. According to the definition we have given for modalization, knowing appears as a modality* having a very broad scope.

3. If knowing involves, as we have seen, the domain of enunciation as a whole, the procedure of disengagement,* accounting for the insertion of the structures of "uttered enunciation" within the uttered discourse, explains the profusion of different types of cognitive simulacra and mechanisms found therein. Different cognitive subjects such as narrator* and narratee, informer* and observer,* which are set up by delegation, can be found in the discourse. These subjects can take on autonomous actorial* positions, enter into actorial syncretism* with different actants* of the narration, or they can simply be identified with implicit positions. Once they have been set up within discourse, cognitive subjects exercise diverse activities: for example, simple emissive* or receptive* doing, or, more often, more complex cognitive doings (persuasive* and interpretive) which can develop entire programs and can even fill up the whole of certain discourse dimensions. Finally, cognitive subjects may manipulate objects of knowledge (utterances of doing* and of state*) by attributing to them various veridictory* statuses, etc.

—COGNITIVE; META-KNOWLEDGE; RECOGNITION; POINT OF VIEW

ABCDEFGHIJKLMN
OPQRSTUVWXYZ

LABEL
(*étiquette*)

In the metalinguistic tree-diagram representation, each branch is called a node* and is provided with a **label,** that is, an arbitrary name* or symbol. Graphic representations, in the form of trees or of parentheses, generally serve to represent relations,* whereas labels, used in the one case as well as in the other, designate structural terms.*
—TREE

LACK
(*manque*)

1. Among the Proppian functions,* **lack**—associated with the "misdeed," which produces a lack through the efforts of a villain* from outside—occupies a central place in the unfolding of the narrative; for, as Propp himself said, this is what gives the tale its movement: the departure of the hero,* the quest,* and the victory will indeed make it possible for the lack to be fulfilled and the misdeed rectified.

2. In the canonic narrative schema as derived from Propp, the lack is the figurative expression of an initial disjunction* between the subject* and object* of the quest: the transformation* which brings about their conjunction* (or realization*) plays a pivotal narrative role (making possible the passage from a state of lack to its liquidation) and corresponds to the decisive* test (or performance*). Thus we see that the **lack** is not actually a function* but a state* which, admittedly, is the result of a prior operation of negation (situated at the deep* level).
—NARRATIVE SCHEMA; QUEST; NEGATION

LANGUAGE, NATURAL
(*langue*)

1. We call **natural language** a type of macro-semiotic* system whose specificity, while obvious in appearance, does not make for an easy definition. Qualified by the term "natural," language is intended to be contrasted with "artificial" languages in that the former characterizes "human nature" while transcending the individuals who use it. It appears as an immanent* structural organization dominating the speaking subjects who are unable to alter it, though it is in their power to construct and manipulate artificial semiotic systems (languages). Natural languages are to be distinguished from other semiotic systems by their combinatory* power which is due to what is called double articulation* and to the processes of disengagement.* This leads to a quasi-unlimited possibility for forming signs* and relatively flexible rules which govern the construction of

syntagmatic units—such as discourses*—of great length (L. Hjelmslev). A two-fold superiority derives from this: all other semiotic systems may be translated, whether poorly or not, into natural language, whereas the reverse is not true; on the other hand, natural languages can function as a base, with their signifiers* as much as with their signifieds,* for the construction of other semiotic systems (for example, artificial semiotic systems [languages]). This **translatability** must not, however, serve as a pretext for postulating that signifieds exist only to the extent that they can be named and verbalized. To take such a position would be to reduce other semiotic systems to the state of being derivative of natural languages and would, for instance, transform pictorial semiotics into an analysis of discourse about painting.

2. Within the Saussurian tradition **natural language,** as opposed to **speech,*** may be identified as a semiotic system* to the exclusion of the semiotic process.* Established by Saussure with the goal of providing a formal, self-sufficient definition of the linguistic object by separating this object from individual, material and, more generally, non-structural contingencies, this distinction clearly makes a positive and decisive contribution. Nonetheless, the distinction has unfortunately made it possible for many linguists to give standing to an overly paradigmatic conception of natural language (which is reduced then to a pure taxonomy*). It is becoming necessary today to bring the concepts of natural language and of competence* together. This rapprochement seems to demand an explicit integration of syntactic structures in the definition of natural language.

3. While keeping the properties which are credited it by definitions no. 1 and no. 2, natural language appears to be a socio-linguistic* concept as well. The intrinsic criteria enabling a natural language to be distinguished from a dialect often lack coherence and vary from one case to the next. A natural language (the definition of which is applicable as well to "dialects") is raised to the dignity of "natural language" only on the basis of a "linguistic sensitivity" proper to the community. Thus, we are led to consider the hierarchy of "natural languages," "dialects," "regional speech," etc. as a nonscientific taxonomy that belongs to a system of social connotations* underlying the functioning of natural languages.

—SEMIOTIC SYSTEM AND PROCESS; SEMIOTICS; SYSTEM; WORLD, NATURAL

LEVEL
(niveau)

1. By **level** is understood a horizontal plane which presupposes the existence of another plane parallel to it. What we have here is an abstract* figurative* sememe* which serves as a concept operational in linguistics and in semiotics and which in general use is often taken as interchangeable with plane, stage, dimension, rank, axis, etc. The different levels may be enumerated or evaluated starting from the horizontal plane, along the vertical axis, either in the direction of height or of depth: in the one case we speak of **metalinguistic levels** (metasemiotic, metalogical); in the other, the level of deep* structures is distinguished from that of surface* structures. Any euphoric or dysphoric connotation that is added to this belongs to the metaphysical or ideological

order and, as such, is not pertinent to semiotics.

2. In structural linguistics the concept of level is precisely defined. Given that a natural language is a semiotic system and that every semiotic system may be described as a hierarchy,* level (for Benveniste) or rank (for Hjelmslev) is made up of derived units of the same degree. The units are defined by the relations that they maintain among themselves (according to Benveniste, distributive relations) and with the elements of a superior level (integrative relations). It can be seen that the concept of level is fundamental for establishing descriptive* procedures and that it enters into the definition of semiotic pertinence.* Given the complexity of the structural relations of a semiotic object, no coherent analysis would be possible without this distinction between levels of analysis.

3. With generative* grammar, where the need for distinguishing among levels is maintained, the concept of a level of the real becomes operational*: here, the space which separates the plane of deep structures from that of surface structures is conceived of as a generative* trajectory marked out by **levels of representation,** the number of which cannot be predetermined.

4. As a result of its analyses of narrative discourses, semiotics has been progressively brought to recognize the existence of a common semiotic core that is invariant and independent of its manifestations in individual languages (natural languages or non-linguistic* semiotic systems), whence comes the distinction, made in the framework of the generative* trajectory, that we propose between the (deep) **semiotic level** and the more superficial **discoursive level.** This common core is

able in turn to include levels of differing depths. Thus, for the semiotic level alone a distinction is made between the plane of deep semiotic structures (fundamental syntax* and fundamental semantics*) and that of surface semiotic structures (narrative syntax and narrative semantics). Such distinctions are both hypothetical* and operational.* They reflect the state and general economy of semiotic theory at a given moment of its development. While permitting more subtle constructions and more precise formulations of the levels of representation considered separately, they allow for the possibility of eventually reducing or multiplying the number of levels.

5. In its turn, semiotic theory must be considered as a language, that is, a particular semiotic system. Its study and development cannot do without a recognition of levels to be treated separately. A distinction is therefore made between (a) the **level of the object language*** (a signifying set* which is grasped intuitively and upon which the analytic procedures will be applied), (b) the **descriptive level** (where the object language is paraphrased in the form of a semantic representation), (c) the **methodological*** level (where the concepts and procedures that make possible the construction of the level of representation are elaborated), (d) and the **epistemological level** (where the coherence* of the body of concepts is tested and the description and discovery procedures are evaluated).

6. In semantics, considerations on the nature of the semes* that are constitutive of the content form have led us to distinguish within the signifying universe (= the semiotic system considered as the paradigmatic system of the content) between the **semiological*** level and the **seman-**

tic* **level** (in the narrow sense). The semiological level is made up of minimal content units which correspond in the semiotic system of the natural world* to the minimal expression units; the semiological level units are thus distinguished from those of the semantic level, whose content units are abstract* and necessary for the functioning and/or construction of any semiotic system. As usage more and more reserves the term "level" for the syntagmatic axis of semiotic systems, it can be replaced here by the term component.* Moreover, since the terminology previously proposed no longer appears adequate, it is desirable to name the semiological level the "figurative component" and the semantic level the "abstract component" of the content form.

7. In discoursive semiotics it is useful to distinguish sometimes between **discoursive levels,** which function either as levels in the structural sense insofar as they are conjoined and linked together in an organic fashion, or autonomously, as discourses.* We are provided with the simplest illustration in the organization of discourses that are made in the human sciences (= humanities and social sciences). In this case we very often observe the presence of three discoursive levels: an objective level, which describes the objects of knowing and the manipulations that they undergo; a cognitive level, which is logically prior and hierarchically superior to the objective level; and finally a referential level, which supports and justifies the objective discourse. Each of these three levels may be articulated into two hypotactically connected stages: a stage wherein the "facts" are simply noted and a modal* stage. Obviously, what we call here the "discoursive level" will correspond elsewhere to a complete and perfectly autonomous discourse. Thus the objective level often includes a given scientific discourse; in the literary domain the referential level allows the opposition between what is "real" and "fictitious" (according to the veridiction* internal to this type of discourse) to be justified; finally, the cognitive level may become practically independent in cognitive* discourses.

8. In socio-linguistics the phrase **language level** is used to designate the realizations of a natural language which vary according to the social classes or strata that use them. This set of problems does not belong to language as a semiotic system but to a system of social connotations.* The term "level" therefore introduces further confusion here; the term "register*" would seem preferable.

9. Hjelmslev speaks of levels in order to designate different aspects under which a semiotic substance* (expression substance or content substance) may be grasped for the purpose of description. For example, the phonic substance is apprehended in successive stages at the **physiological level** (that of articulation), the **acoustic level** (in physical terms) and at the **psycho-physiological level** of perception. In this case the term domain* seems preferable to that of level.

10. Other uses of level relate most often to the utilization of natural language.

LEXEME
(lexème)

1. Among the minimal signs* —or morphemes* (monemes,* according to A. Martinet)—of a manifested semiotic system, a distinction is usually made between lexical

morphemes and grammatical morphemes. Lexical morphemes are often called **lexemes** in order to contrast them with morphemes properly speaking (or grammemes,* according to B. Pottier).

2. It is easy to criticize such a conception of the lexeme. Even though the lexeme as a sign possesses a formant* which delimits it on the expression* plane, the content* of the lexeme (or of the word, in its common meaning) is not autonomous, for the utterance* constitutes a signifying whole which is not reducible to the sum of its lexemic parts.

3. Thus, it is preferable, at first, to consider the lexeme as belonging solely to the content plane, by continuing to name morphemes (or monemes) the minimal units of the sign plane. In this case the lexeme would be a unit of the content (a figure,* in L. Hjelmslev's sense of the term) which, owing to its coverage by a single formant, can, once inscribed within the utterance, give rise to one or more content elements called sememes*.

4. Two different representations of the lexeme are possible, depending on whether it is grasped at the moment of its realization* or in its virtual* state. The lexeme is realized at the moment of semiosis,* that is, of the conjunction of the formant and of the semic nucleus* (or node) that it covers. But its syntagmatic realization is also its inscription within the utterance from which it receives the contextual* semes that enable it to be constituted as a sememe and that select for it the unique trajectory (or several trajectories in the case of pluri-isotopy*) of its manifestation of signification. Obviously when considered as a potentiality—therefore prior to enunciation* in the *hic et nunc*—the

lexeme appears as a set of possible discoursive trajectories which, setting out from a common nucleus and encountering different contextual semes, lead each time to just as many realizations in the form of sememes. The realization of the lexeme in the form of one particular sememe therefore defines its linguistic functioning. But each specific realization leaves suspended a set (often quite large) of unexploited sememic virtualities; they are ready to be actualized at the least obstruction encountered by the linear realization of the signification. It is the presence of these underlying potentialities which produces as a meaning effect, the words' "thickness" or "bursting forth."

5. As a consequence the lexeme is neither a unit which can be delimited at the level of signs nor a unit, properly speaking, of the content plane. As a configuration which brings together different sememes more or less accidentally, the lexeme appears as the product of history or use* rather than of structure.*
—SEMEME

LEXIA
(lexie)

1. L. Hjelmslev has proposed to designate **lexia** that unit* which is the first to admit of an analysis by selection*: as in the case of a sentence which can be divided into main (or selected) and subordinate (selecting) clauses.

2. R. Barthes introduced the term lexia in order to designate "reading units" of various sizes which constitute intuitively, for the reader, a whole. What we have here is a pre-operational concept which grounds a provisional segmentation* of the text for the purpose of analyzing it.

3. B. Pottier has chosen the term lexia to designate units on the content* plane which are of different sizes ranging all the way from simple lexemes ("dog") to fixed syntagms ("shoe-tree") in order to find a replacement for "word".* It appears impossible to give a general definition that is broad enough for the latter term. Such units—which could fall under the heading of lexia—could be defined paradigmatically by their substitution* possibility within a class of given lexemes* (for example, "goober," "pea-nut," "ground nut") from which we derive the term paralexeme* that we have proposed elsewhere. Syntagmatically they can be defined by a type of lexical recursivity* where the units of a hierarchically superior level can be reproduced at the lexematic level. Only the intersection of these two criteria could account for those lexias which extend beyond the limits of the lexeme. B. Pottier proposes a distinction among three types of lexias: **simple lexias** (lexemes and affixed lexemes, such as "horse" and "unconstitutional"); **compound lexias** ("horse-power") and **complex lexias** ("to take into account").

4. The pertinence of lexical studies which make use of the lexia as a unit for counting and describing depends in the final analysis upon the definition of the lexeme (of which the lexia is, indeed, only the prolongation) and its place within semantic theory.

—LEXEME; WORD

LEXICALIZATION
(lexicalisation)

1. Since every language* is a relational network, we can designate by the name **lexicalization** the attribution of lexical labels to the terms which are the points of intersection of these relations.*

2. Since the content* plane of a language is made up of semantic units called sememes*—which can appear as a more or less greater number of lexemes—lexicalization consists in the passage from the sememic level to the lexematic level of discourse, and more specifically, for each sememe, in the choice of the lexeme (linked to its own context) in which it will be called upon to be invested.

3. In a more limited sense, lexicalization is the durative* process which a natural language* undergoes and which has as an effect the transformation of a syntagm made up of free morphemes* into a closed syntagm (or lexia) which from a paradigmatic point of view is commutable within a lexematic class.

—TERM; LEXEME; LEXIA

LEXICOGRAPHY
(lexicographie)

1. **Lexicography** is a branch of applied linguistics, the goal of which is the production of dictionaries.*

2. As a technical procedure, lexicography presupposes a particular competence which, for its part, is made up of a practical and intuitive knowing-how-to-do that resembles the Lévi-Straussian concept of "bricolage" ("do-it-yourself" work; "knocking something together" [for example, an alphabetical classification of "words," the arrangement of "meanings," illustration of the "meanings" noted, etc.]). At the same time lexicography requires a theoretical knowledge (a definition of lexical elements, a typology of definitions and, more generally, the selection of one semantic theory or another) which depends upon a lexical semantics* (or a semantic lexicology*).

LEXICOLOGY
(lexicologie)

1. **Lexicology** is traditionally defined as the scientific study of the lexicon,* but it is also the theoretical reflection upon its application to lexicography.*

2. Before semantics* was recognized as an independent component of grammar* (or of semiotics), lexicology alone was concerned with problems of signification in linguistics. Lexicological research thus developed along two lines: first, statistical lexicology was concerned with introducing statistical methods into linguistics; secondly, semantic* lexicology inaugurated the description of semantic fields* by alternately applying semasiological* and onomasiological* approaches. The development of semic* (in France) or componential (in America) methods of analysis tends to transform lexicology into a lexical semantics, primarily characterized by taxonomic* concerns.
—CONTENT

LEXICON
(lexique)

1. The **lexicon** is the exhaustive list of all the lexias of a particular state of a natural language. The operational value of this concept must be judged in function of that of lexia and, particularly, in function of the appropriateness of taking lexia as the basic element for semantic analysis.

2. The lexicon is oftentimes contrasted with the vocabulary, as an inventory of virtual units is contrasted with the set of realized units in a corpus* (or, in what amounts to the same thing, in a text).

3. In the field of generative grammar* the lexicon is considered as one of the two sub-components

(the other being the categorial subcomponent) which form the base* of the syntactic component. In the framework of this conceptualization the lexicon is radically distinguished from its traditional definition (no. 1 above): on the one hand it is a part of the grammar* and, on the other, the units which make it up are not conceived of as units which belong solely to the content* plane; rather they are characterized by features which are at one and the same time semantic, phonological, and syntactic. Here, as elsewhere, the problem is the very definition of the lexical unit.
—LEXIA; LEXEME; VOCABULARY

LIE
(mensonge)

The term **lie** designates, in the semiotic square* of the veridictory modalities, the complementary* term which subsumes the terms *non-being* and *seeming* located on the negative deixis.*—VERIDICTORY MODALITIES; SQUARE, SEMIOTIC

LIFE
(vie)

1. **Life** is the positive* term of the *life/death* category which we propose to view as hypothetically universal, since we judge that it can provide a first articulation of the individual semantic universe,* corresponding to the *nature/culture* category (for the social semantic universe). In this sense, *life/death*, the semantic axis* of which can be called "existence," is to be viewed as a thematic elementary structure.*

2. The *life/death* category can be connoted by the thymic* category. Their canonical homologation consists in coupling the positive terms

life + euphoria and the negative ones, *death + dysphoria,* but the ideolectal* appropriation of these categories allows us to envisage a combinatory arrangement of possible homologations (*life + dysphoria* or *life + aphoria,* for example) which determine semantic originality.*
—UNIVERSE; ORIGINALITY, SEMANTIC; THYMIC CATEGORY; STRUCTURE; UNIVERSALS

LINEARITY
(linéarité)

1. For Saussure, **linearity** is one of the characteristics of the syntagmatic manifestation* of natural languages,* according to which, signs,* once produced, are arranged one after another in either a temporal (spoken natural language) or spatial (written natural language) order.

2. This phenomenon of the manifestation of certain semiotic signs has been hypostasized to the point of being considered within certain theories to be a universal* feature of all language. The most frequent confusion consists in considering linearity as a property of each semiotic process or syntagmatic system. But Hjelmslev has shown how the opposition between paradigmatic and syntagmatic axes* rests solely upon a formal distinction: the "either . . . or" relation is constitutive of the paradigmatic axis, the "both . . . and" relation, of the syntagmatic axis. Within this perspective it can be seen that a planar* semiotic system involves a syntagmatic system which has a spatial manifestation that is not necessarily linear.

3. When the concept of linearity is limited in this way (it concerns only the plane of signs and only affects certain semiotic systems) the major difficulties relative to it disappear (for example, the existence of discontinuous constituents,* suprasegmental phonemes, syntactic and semantic ambiguities, and the like). Neither of language's planes—those of expression* and of content,* which must be analyzed separately, —is subject to the constraints of linearity. To ask, for example, whether phonemes* or sememes* (combinations of phemes* or of semes*) are linear or not makes no sense. Phemes and semes do not have a linear organization; they are manifested in bundles. Similarly, the existence of pluri-isotopic* texts contradicts the linearity of signification at the level of the content.

4. Locating its description on the sign plane, distributional* analysis preserves the principle of linearity as a fundamental property of the utterance* and makes possible an examination of the elements' environments and their linear distribution. For this reason it is to be distinguished from glossematics*: whereas for distributional linguistics, segmentation of the sentence into nominal and verbal syntagms is based upon pure linear succession, glossematics recognizes the existence of a logical relation of presupposition* (the linear manifestation of which is but one variable proper to certain natural languages). Generative* and transformational grammar takes over for its own purposes the principle of linearity of the sentence, which it takes to be one of the rules* for tree* formation.

5. As a limited constraint that is localizable in different ways depending upon the language under study (for example, contiguity with or without order of succession of determinant and noun), linearity is to be distinguished from the order* of obligatory succession, which corresponds to a grammatical morpheme (equivalent, for example, to

case opposition). Thus, in the sentence "Peter hits Paul," word order functions as a category of the expression enabling us to distinguish between subject and object.

6. Since linearity is the property of the text when the latter aims at manifestation, **linearization** is a necessary procedure on each occasion when one is forced to manifest this or that level of analysis, this or that semiotic system. This operation, which, in the context of the overall generative* trajectory, belongs to textualization,* consists in rewriting the hierarchical organization, the substitutable segments, the concomitant structures, and the like so as to form temporal or spatial contiguities (according to the nature of the signifier which will ultimately be used). Thus, when it comes to textualizing the elements of the narrative grammar, one is forced, for example, to place in linear succession two narrative programs* that are supposed to be unfolding at the same time, to insert a cognitive narrative program within a pragmatic narrative program, to establish a pluri-isotopy enabling us to speak of several things at once, etc. From this point of view linearization appears to be a constraint which conditions the textual organization and which determines in a negative fashion the discursive competence* of the enunciator.*
—SYNTAGMATIC; DISTRIBUTION; TREE; TEXTUALIZATION

LINGUISTICS
(linguistique)

1. **Linguistics** may be defined as a scientific study of language as semiotic* system and of natural languages.* Theoretical reflection upon language (which is integrated into a more general semiotic theory) concentrates upon the nature, function,

and procedures for describing natural languages and is nourished at the same time by the results of their analysis.

2. Present-day linguistics is the result of a long historical trajectory and its scientific algorithm* is marked by two revolutions: (a) the first corresponds to the invention of writing* (implying, at least for a certain number of natural languages, an implicit phonematic analysis), which inaugurated a historical period that could be designated generally as that of the philosophy of language; (b) the second gave rise to the development of comparative grammar (presupposing the prior analysis of the word* into morphemes*), starting at the beginning of the nineteenth century. The period that it covers could be characterized as that of the elaboration of linguistic calculus. F. de Saussure's work, whereby he formulated a synthesis of **comparative* linguistics** (developed throughout the nineteenth century and otherwise designated as comparative and historical grammar) and laid out the theoretical bases for **structural linguistics,** marks the advent of linguistics as a scientific discipline. It is a discipline involving both a theory* and an operational* praxis; it is the only social science that can lay claim to the name "science" (C. Lévi-Strauss).

3. On the basis of a limited number of general postulates formulated by Saussure, the establishment of structural linguistics became possible through an affirmation of the autonomy of its object, its formal character, and the setting up of formal procedures* that could account for them. Structural linguistics is to be distinguished, however, from logic by the fact that the metalanguage* that it develops is not an end in itself but is meant to serve the

description* of these formal objects (or signifying linguistic forms) that the natural languages are. Structural linguistics developed along parallel tracks in Europe (Prague and Copenhagen Schools) and in the United States (the distributionalism of L. Bloomfield and of Z. Harris). Generative* and transformational grammar (which has established itself regionally in contrast to American structuralism*) is normally registered as a tendency or particular theoretical attitude in the further development of linguistics (which no longer needs to be qualified as structural since it is such by definition). The same applies to **discoursive linguistics,** which, while opposed to **phrase-structure linguistics**, does not for all of that deny its structural heritage.

4. If in the first instance the task of epistemological and methodological reflection could be entrusted to **general linguistics,** it is becoming ever more difficult to do so because of the development of the broad and autonomous fields of **psycholinguistics,* socio-linguistics,*** to say nothing of **applied linguistics,** or the application of linguistics to an ever-larger number of fields. Reflection upon language as a semiotic system joins up with semiology, that "general theory of signs" hoped for by Saussure.

LISTENER
(auditeur)

In the same way as the reader,* the **listener** designates the domain of the reception of a message or discourse, the only difference being in terms of the substance—graphic or phonic—of the signifier* used. In semiotics, it is preferable to use the more general term enunciatee.— ENUNCIATEE

LITERARINESS
(littérarité)

1. If we admit—and this is not in and of itself obvious—that literary* discourse constitutes an autonomous class within a general typology of discourses, its specificity may be considered either as what will be ultimately established (through progressive stages) by a research metadiscourse or as an *a priori* postulate enabling us to circumscribe in advance the targeted object of knowledge. According to R. Jakobson, who has opted for this second attitude, "the object of literary science is not literature but literariness," that is, that which warrants a distinction between what is literary and what is non-literary.

2. But in spite of its superficiality, the attention that linguists give to so-called literary texts is sufficient to persuade them that what are called "literary forms" (figures, procedures, discursive and/or narrative organizations) have nothing that is specifically "literary," because these forms are to be found in other types of discourse as well. Given the impossibility of recognizing the existence of laws or even of simple regularities which would be proper to literary discourse, we are thus led to consider the concept of **literariness** (in the framework of the intrinsic structure of the text) as void of meaning and to grant it, on the other hand, the status of social connotation* (which, as we know, varies according to culture and epoch: as Lotman and others have insisted, a text which is recognized as being religious in the Middle Ages is viewed as literary today). This is to say that literariness must be integrated into the set of problems concerning ethno-theories of genres (or of discourse).

—DISCOURSE

LITERARY SEMIOTICS
(littéraire [sémiotique—])

1. **Literary semiotics** (or, if one considers it as a semiotic process,* literary discourse) is a field of research the boundaries of which seem to have been established more by tradition than by objective, formal criteria. Thus it cannot be characterized by a content* peculiar to itself as is the case with other semiotic systems, for example, legal or religious discourse. It does not matter what content it manifests; in fact, its content plane is coextensive with the semantic universe* encompassed by a given natural language.* As for the expression plane, the "literary forms" which are responsible for its organization become identified, broadly speaking, with discursive linguistic articulations. Therefore, literary discourse seems to be the best illustration of the non-scientific meta-language* responsible for the syntactic organization of transphrastic signs* (or texts). Instead of defining the specificity of their discourse, "literary forms" seem rather like a vast repertoire of discursive universals.*

2. A certain tradition would like to define literary discourse as a "fiction" in contrast, for example, to the "reality" of historical discourse: it characterizes literary discourse by a relation with that which it is not, *i.e.,* with the extra-linguistic referent.* The referent of literary discourse would be "imaginary" and that of historical discourse "real." Numerous studies have shown conclusively that, as it unfolds, each discourse constitutes its own internal referent. In fact, the question of veridiction, of truth-telling, which is peculiar to each discourse, must be substituted for the question of reality. It is tempting, for example, to define literary discourse as advocating the false in order to obtain the true, as flaunting its "seeming" in order better to communicate and to have its "being" accepted. However, such a point of view is still marked by cultural relativism. It is known, for example, that for certain African communities the true discourse is the mythical narrative, whereas the account of daily events is a part of the genre "for the fun of the thing." Variations bearing upon the referential illusion belong after all to a typology of social connotations* and say nothing about the nature of the discourse that they connote.

3. A final criterion, that of figurativity,* can be suggested. By contrast to non-figurative (or abstract*) discourse—such as scientific or philosophical ones—literary discourse can be included in the vast class of figurative* discourses, where it will stand next to historical discourse. These two discursive forms participate in the transmission of culture. Such a dichotomy—*figurative/non-figurative*—seems to us fruitful even though it remains simply theoretical (there are, of course, no perfect discursive realizations). While questioning the specificity of literary discourse (its literariness*), this dichotomy opens it up to other discourses (mythological, folkloric, etc.) and frees it from its isolation, thus making it share in a general typology of discourses.

4. The opening up of literary semiotics to "sub-literary" or "non-literary" discourses poses new problems of delimitation. By making use of extrinsic criteria, we distinguish between an **ethno-literary semiotics,** which takes as its concern the discourses performed by micro-societies of an archaic type (or of surviving groups), and a **socio-**

literary semiotics, which studies social discourses (transcending social differentiations) of industrial macro-societies (such as detective stories, westerns, lovelorn columns, horoscopes, etc.).

—REFERENT; CONNOTATION; POETICS; DISCOUSE; ETHNO-SEMIOTICS; SOCIOSEMIOTICS; VERISIMILITUDE

LOCALIZATION, SPATIO-TEMPORAL
(localisation spatio-temporelle)

Taken individually, spatial and temporal **localizations** consist of the inscription of narrative programs* within given spatial or temporal units. This is an operation which is accomplished through the process of disengagement. We note, however, that the positions so obtained are static and only represent utterances of state* of the narrative structures. As for utterances of doing,* they must be interpreted as **passings** from one space* to another, from one temporal interval to another. A different representation of the spatio-temporalization of narrative programs can be proposed by introducing the concept of **movement**, which, in a way that is parallel to the organization of the loci of space and time, would make use of the directionality of the movements. The category *sender/receiver*, which is utilized only for determining a certain type of actants,* could thus serve to designate spaces and times of origin and destination, with the doing* identified at the figurative* level with the "becoming" of beings and things. This is still but one possible route for analysis. Research is rarely carried out along this line.

(A) **Spatial Localization**

1. **Spatial localization** is one of the procedures of spatialization* (in the broad sense of the term). It may be defined as the construction of a system of references which enables us to situate spatially in relation to one another the discourse's different narrative programs, with the aid of spatial disengagement* and a certain number of semantic categories.* Disengagement installs within the utterance-discourse an **elsewhere** space (utterative space) and a **here** space (enunciative space) which can maintain between themselves the relations established by the processes of engagement.* Considered as zero spatial positions, the discursive elsewhere and here are then points of departure for establishing a three-dimensional topological category which sets off the axes of **horizontality, verticality,** and **prospectivity** (in front of/behind). This constitutes a very simple (indeed, perhaps too simple) model of the spatial localization of narrative programs and their actants which, as a result of particular semantic investments, have become actors.*

2. It is to be noted that narrative semiotics, which uses this model of spatial localization, essentially utilizes the axis of prospectivity, by seeking to establish a linear display that can be homologated with the narrative trajectories* of the subjects and the circulation of objects* of value. This explains in part the meager yield of this model when we try to extrapolate it, for example, by application to visual semiotics (attempts made to establish a visual syntax that conforms to the trajectory of the spectator's gaze are far from convincing).

3. The partial spaces which are juxtaposed along the axis of prospectivity are then named according to the nature of the actants installed there and the performances* they accomplish there. Thus, in the purely Proppian tradition, the space

of folk-tale is articulated in terms of **familiar space/alien space**: the former is considered the place of origin where both the (narrative) subject and the enunciator* are recorded. In this instance we have to do with the **here** space (or enunciative space); the narrative begins in a certain sense with the hero's passing to the **elsewhere** space, that is, the alien space. It appears, nonetheless, that a spatial mechanism such as this, belonging to a particular type of ethno-literature, cannot be generalized.

4. Without straying too far away from the Proppian model, we have proposed another spatial distribution, but which articulates only the **utterative space** (the elsewhere). In a way that is parallel to temporal localization, where the zero time ("the time of the narrative") is held to be concomitant with the realization of the basic narrative program* (the decisive test* in the narrative* schema), spatial localization must first of all choose a space of reference for itself—a zero space starting from which the other partial spaces could be ordered along the axis of prospectivity. This reference space is called **topic space** while the surrounding space (those spaces "in front of" and "behind") are qualified as **heterotopic**. A sub-articulation of topic space often seems necessary: it distinguishes between **utopic** space, a place where the human doing surmounts the permanence of being, a place of performances* (which in mythical narrative is oftentimes underground, underwater, or in the heavens), and **paratopic** spaces, where competencies* are acquired.

(B) **Temporal Localizations**

1. Along with temporal programming* and aspectualization, **temporal localization** is one of the procedures of temporalization,* that is, of the construction of a reference system which, when inserted within the discourse, enables us to locate temporally the different narrative programs in relation to one another.

2. The system of temporal references is made up first of all of a double temporal disengagement* which establishes two zero temporal positions within the discourse: the *then* time (or utterative time) and the *now* time (or the enunciative time). The topological category which belongs to a logical and non-temporal order—

—is then applied to the two zero times, thus establishing in both cases a network of temporal positions. The different narrative programs of the discourse may then be localized in relation to this reference system. These different temporal logics, which are being developed at the present time, utilize—with varying degrees of success and breadth—such a concept of temporality.

3. When it comes to temporalization of the (relatively simple) narrative schema, the then time, which constitutes the temporal reference point, is identified with the realization of the basic narrative program (or decisive* test) and may be considered the "narrative present." It is on the basis of this position that the narrative which precedes appears to be *anterior* (a "past"); for these same reasons the gloryifying* test of the Proppian narrative is only optional. Alongside of this type of temporalization (when the then time, as a narrative present, is located in the enunciator*'s "past"), there obviously exist prophetic or premonitory narratives which refer to the enunciator's "future." How-

ever, far from being a temporal position, the future belongs instead to the modalities* of *wanting-to-be* or of *having-to-be* by means of which the enunciator modalizes its discourse. For this reason we have opted for the topological category *anteriority/ posteriority* and not the articulation *past/present/future* which logicians prefer. The narratives which encompass the enunciator's "present" are obviously only an illusion; this present, mobile as it is, cannot serve as a reference point. Thus the procedures of disengagement* serve to create the illusion of a possible identification of the discourse with the domain of the enunciation.*

4. When it is no longer a matter of temporalization of the narrative schema but rather of the establishment of relations of consecution between narrative programs, temporal localization consists in interpreting every presupposed narrative program as anterior and every presupposing narrative program as posterior. Such an ordering of narrative programs in temporal sequence already belongs to another component of temporalization—temporal programming.*

5. **Nesting** procedures, grounded upon the concept of concomitance,* constitute the immediate prolongation and the complement to spatial and temporal localizations. —DISENGAGEMENT; SPACE; SPATIALIZATION; TEMPORALIZATION; NESTING

LOCUTION
(locution)

The term **locution** refers to the speech act by which utterances* are produced in conformity with the rules of grammar* and on the basis of a given lexicon.* This notion is of interest only to the extent that in the terminology of J. L. Austin it is opposed to illocution* and perlocution.* These different names are to be compared to pragmatics* (in the American sense of the term) since all of them deal with the conditions of linguistic communication (which point to the cognitive competence of the subjects as speakers).—ACT, SPEECH; ENUNCIATION

ABCDEFGHIJKLMN OPQRSTUVWXYZ

MACRO-SEMIOTICS
(macro-sémiotique)

We propose to use the term **macro-semiotics** for each of the two broad signifying sets* that constitute the area of natural semiotics: the set which encompasses what we call the natural world* and the set of natural languages.*—SEMIOTICS

MAIN TEST
—DECISIVE TEST

MANIFESTATION
(manifestation)

1. In the tradition of Saussure, expanded upon by Hjelmslev, the term **manifestation** (as a part of the dichotomy *manifestation/immanence*) served at first as a contrast for enhancing the term immanence. The principle of immanence,* which is essential for linguistics (and, by extension, for semiotics as a whole), is both the postulate that affirms the specificity of form* as linguistic object and the methodological demand that all extra-linguistic facts be excluded. Within this perspective semiotic form is considered to be that which is manifested; its substance* is that which manifests it (is its manifestation) in purport* (or meaning).

2. Taking into account solely the logical anteriority of immanence over manifestation has, as a consequence, permitted the somewhat shaky homologation of this dichotomy with those of *manifest/latent* or *explicit/implicit*. The opposition of the manifest plane and the immanent plane of language could thus appear as a Hjelmslevian formulation, which can be assimilated to the later distinction, established by the generativists, between surface and deep structures.

3. But such is not at all the case, for manifestation, conceived as making the form* present in the substance,* presupposes semiosis* (or the semiotic act) as an *a priori* condition. It brings together both the expression* and content* forms even in advance, as it were, of their material realization (purport). Manifestation is, therefore, before all else the formation of the sign* level or, to put it otherwise, (and trivially), the postulating of the plane of expression at the time of the production of the utterance* and, conversely, the attribution of the plane of content at the time of its reading. The immanent analysis of a semiotic system is then the study of each of the two planes of language taken individually.

4. This results in the two opposing pairs *immanence/manifestation* and *depth/surface*. They can neither be homologated nor superimposed. The different levels* of depth that we can distinguish are articulations*

of the immanent structure of each of the two language planes (expression and content) taken separately, and mark out their generative* trajectory. Manifestation is, by contrast, an event, an interruption, and a deviation, which demands that any given domain of this trajectory be constituted into a plane of signs. When linguists, analyzing deep structures, wish to account for them with the aid of any particular system of representation,* they stop, freeze the generative trajectory at a given moment and then manifest the immanent monoplanar structures with the aid of a linkage of bi-planar signs (or of interpretable symbols). Likewise, a distinction between abstract and figurative discourse can be made when account is taken of the interruption, followed by the manifestation, of the generative trajectory at two distinct moments in the production process.

5. In the context of the veridictory* modalities, the **schema of manifestation** is that of *seeming/non-seeming,* in opposition to and complementary with the schema of immanence *(being/non-being)*—although such names in no way imply an ontological assumption.
—IMMANENCE; DEEP STRUCTURE; SURFACE STRUCTURE; VERIDICTORY MODALITIES

MANIPULATION
(manipulation)

1. In contrast to operation* (as an action of humans upon things), **manipulation** is characterized as an action of humans upon other humans with the goal of having them carry out a given program. In the first instance, what we have is a "causing-to-be," in the second a "causing-to-do." Both forms of activity, one of which is inscribed in

the pragmatic* domain and the other in the cognitive* domain, thereby correspond to modal structures of a factitive* sort. When projected upon the semiotic square,* manipulation as a causing-to-do gives rise to four possibilities:

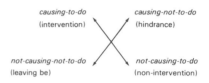

2. As a discursive configuration,* manipulation is undergirded at one and the same time by a contractual structure* and a modal structure. We have, in effect, a communication* (intended to cause-to-know) in which the sender-manipulator pushes the receiver-manipulatee toward a position wherein freedom is lacking (not-being-able-not-to-do), to the point that the latter is obliged to accept the proposed contract. What is at stake at first glance is the transformation of the receiver-subject's modal competence*: If the latter connects *not-being-able-not-to-do* with *having-to-do,* we would have provocation or intimidation; if the subject adds a *wanting-to-do* to *not-being-able-not-to-do* it would be instead a case of seduction or of temptation.

3. Situated syntagmatically between the sender*'s wanting and the receiver-subject's actual realization of the narrative program* (proposed by the manipulator), manipulation plays upon persuasion and thus articulates the persuasive* doing of the sender and the interpretive* doing of the receiver.

(a) The manipulator can exercise its persuasive doing by relying upon the modality of being-able*: on the pragmatic* side it will propose either positive objects (cultural values) or negative objects (threats) to the one manipulated. In other instances the manipulator will persuade the receiver with the help of knowing*: on the cognitive* side it will bring the receiver to know what the manipulator thinks of the former's modal competence, in the form of positive or negative judgments. Thus it appears that persuasion in terms of being-able characterizes temptation (where a positive object of value is proposed) and intimidation (presentation of a negative gift); persuasion in terms of knowing is peculiar to provocation (with a negative judgment: "You are incapable of . . . ") and seduction (manifesting a positive judgment).

(b) The one manipulated is led correspondingly to perform a pragmatic doing and necessarily to choose, either between two images of its own competence (positive in the case of seduction, negative in the case of provocation), if it is a manipulation in terms of knowing; or between two objects of value (positive in the case of temptation, negative in the case of intimidation), if the manipulation plays upon being-able. (Of course, such an elementary typology of the forms of manipulation is only tentative; at least it sketches out an avenue of research.)

4. At the level of the receiver's modal competence, and taking into account only the modality of being-able-to-do we can anticipate four separate positions:

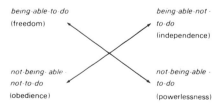

being-able-to-do
(freedom)

being-able-not-to-do
(independence)

not-being-able-not-to-do
(obedience)

not-being-able-to-do
(powerlessness)

On the basis of this approximate lexicalization (as indicated between the parentheses) of the modal structures, we can propose names (within our socio-cultural universe) for the types of sub-codes of honor that the manipulation puts into play (that is, from the receiver-subject's point of view): the codes of "sovereignty" (freedom + independence), "submission" (obedience + powerlessness), "pride" (freedom + obedience), and "humility" (independence + powerlessness). The action that the receiver-manipulatee will carry out following manipulation by the sender thus becomes a simple, practical narrative program* for that receiver; its primary narrative program is conjunction with honor (in the case of a manipulation on the plane of knowing) or with a given object of value (if the manipulation is based upon being-able.)

5. As a causing-to-do, it appears that manipulation must be recorded as one of the essential components of the canonical narrative* schema. The system of exchange* or, more precisely, the contract* that is registered there, is taken over, as it were, at a hierarchically superior level by the structure of manipulation. In this case, indeed, the relation between Sender and Receiver is not one of equals (as in the simple operation of exchange, which calls for two subjects of comparable competence), but of superior to inferior. Moreover, the manipulation effected by the Sender will call for sanction* by the Sender-judge; both operations are located on the cognitive dimension (in contrast to the performance* of the receiver-subject carried out on the pragmatic plane).

6. Even if, as we have noted, manipulation is just beginning to be analyzed, we can nonetheless foresee, by transposing it from the plane of narratives to that of somatic practice,* the development of a true

semiotics of manipulation (corresponding to a semiotics of sanction and a semiotics of action); at the very least we know how important a place it holds in human relations. Such a semiotics must be establishable on the basis of the initial Sender*'s narrative trajectory and account not only for the manipulation of the subject (some possible forms of which we have just mentioned) but also that of the anti-subject (with the strategy of the trick which makes possible operations of "cooptation" and "infiltration," for example).
—MODALITY; FACTITIVENESS; PERSUASIVE DOING; NARRATIVE SCHEMA; NARRATIVE TRAJECTORY

MARK
(marque)

1. In the most general sense of the term, **mark** is the inscription of a heterogeneous, supplementary element* upon (or within) a unit or set, and serves as a sign of recognition.* With this meaning, we will speak, for example, of marks of enunciation* within the utterance.*

2. In linguistics the opposition *marked/non-marked* is widely used. Phonology uses the concept of mark in order to distinguish between elements according to whether they are characterized by the presence* or absence* of a distinctive feature* (where *b* is voiced and *p* is non-voiced then we can say, from this point of view, that *b* is marked and *p* non-marked). The **mark of correlation** is that which enables us to distinguish between several pairs of phonemes* (the voiced series *b, d, g, v, z,* is opposed to the non-voiced series *p, t, k, f, s*). In phrase structure syntax the mark is thus largely used in the study of certain grammatical categories* such as gender (French

"joli," masculine and non-marked; "jolie," feminine and marked) and number (the singular is non-marked, the plural marked).

3. Following V. Propp in the narrative analysis of discourse, we understand mark to mean a material sign (such as object or wound) which in the Sender's eyes attests to a decisive* test that is carried out in a secret* mode by the hero.* From this point of view, within the narrative* schema, recognition* presupposes the attribution of a mark that makes possible the passage from the secret to the revelation of the true.* As a sign of recognition the mark is inscribed therefore in the cognitive* dimension and sets into play the veridictory* modalities: indeed the mark is "what appears" in the veridictory position of secret (being and non-seeming) and constitutes the necessary condition for the transformation of the secret into the truth.
—RECOGNITION

MARKER,SYNTAGMATIC
(indicateur [ou marqueur] syntagmatique)

1. N. Chomsky gives the name of **syntagmatic marker** ("phrase marker") to both the structural description* of the sentence* and to its tree representation.* Along these lines, N. Ruwet proposes to distinguish **underlying** syntagmatic markers, which result from the application of the syntagmatic rules alone, from **derived** markers, which come from the application of one or more transformations.*

2. Under the guise of syntagmatic marker, generative grammar reintroduces, but with a new name, the classical concept of syntactic function.* Indeed, according to generative grammar, the lexicon*

includes **syntactic markers** corresponding to the traditional grammatical categories* (noun, verb, preposition, etc.), without submitting them in advance to any critical analysis. Moreover, it will be noted that the passage from syntagmatic classes* to morphological classes is given no justification. This heterogeneity* cannot but be problematic at the level of the theory's coherence.*

3. In its lexicon, generative grammar uses, in parallel with syntagmatic markers, **semantic markers,** that is, semantic categories (such as *animate/inanimate, human/non-human,* etc.) which play the role of classemes.*

4. E. Benveniste gives the name marker to that which is generally designated by the name of deictic.
—TREE; GENERATIVE GRAMMAR; DEICTIC

MATRIX
(matrice)

The **matrix** is one of the possible modes of representing* the taxonomic* data of an analysis: it is a rectangular form divided into vertical columns and horizontal lines; it serves the same function as a tree diagram or as ordered parentheses.

MEANING
(sens)

1. Although it is a property common to all the different semiotic systems, the concept of **meaning** is undefinable. Intuitively or naively, two approaches to the problem of meaning are possible: it may be considered either as that which permits the operation of paraphrasing* or transcoding,* or as that which grounds human activity as intentionality.* Before its manifestation in the form of an articulated signification,* nothing can be said about meaning, unless metaphysical presuppositions full of implications are introduced.

2. L. Hjelmslev proposes an operational definition of meaning, by identifying it with the primary "material" or "support" by which any semiotic system, as form,* is manifested. Meaning thus becomes synonymous with "matter" (the term "purport" covers both words): "meaning" and "matter" are used interchangeably when speaking of the two "manifestants" of the expression plane and of the content* plane. The term substance is then used to designate meaning as it is assumed by a semiotic system; this allows us to distinguish the content substance from the expression substance.
—PURPORT; SUBSTANCE; SIGNIFICATION; PARAPHRASE; INTENTION

MEANING EFFECT
(effet de sens)

Meaning effect (an expression borrowed from G. Guillaume) is the impression of "reality" produced by our senses in contact with meaning, that is to say, with an underlying semiotic system. It can be said, for example, that the world* of common sense is the meaning effect produced by the encounter of the human subject and the world as object. Likewise, an "understood" sentence is the meaning effect of a particular syntagmatic organization of several sememes.* Thus, when it is affirmed, for example, in the Bloomfieldian tradition, that meaning exists but that nothing can be said about it, the word "meaning" must be understood as "meaning effect," the sole graspable reality, but one which cannot be apprehended directly. As a result, semantics is not description of meaning, but it is the construction which, aiming at producing a representation* of signification,* will be validated only to the extent to which it can give rise to a comparable meaning effect. Located in the domain of reception, meaning effect corresponds to semiosis,* this latter being an act situated at the enunciation level, and to manifestation, constituted by the discourse-utterance.—MEANING; SIGNIFICATION

MESSAGE
(message)

1. In information* theory, the **message,** transmitted from a source* to a destination* by means of a channel,* is a sequence of signals,* organized in accordance with the rules of a code.* It thus presupposes encoding* and decoding* operations. In the limited area of linguistic communication, for example, the message corresponds to the utterance* considered from the sole point of view of the expression* plane (or of the signifier*), exclusive of any invested contents.*

2. In the six-function communication schema proposed by R. Jakobson, the code/message dichotomy can be considered as a reinterpretation of Saussure's *natural language/speech* opposition; in this case the message appears as the product of the code (without, for all that, taking the production process into account in any way).

3. The **message's situation,** as the speech act*'s here and now, can be reformulated in terms of enunciation.* In this case, message becomes a synonym of utterance, therewith including both signifier and signified.*
—COMMUNICATION

META-KNOWLEDGE
(métasavoir)

In contrast to knowledge, which has to do with the pragmatic* doing of a given subject, **meta-knowledge** is the knowing that a subject has about the knowledge of another subject. Meta-knowledge may be either transitive* (when it concerns the knowledge S1 has about the knowledge of S2 bearing upon the doing of S2) or reflexive* (if it concerns the knowledge S1 has about the knowledge of S2 relative to the pragmatic doing of S1).—KNOWLEDGE

METALANGUAGE
(métalangage)

1. The term **metalanguage** was introduced by the logicians of the Vienna school (R. Carnap) and, particularly, by those of the Polish school, who have shown the need "for distinguishing clearly between the language that we speak about from the language that we speak" (Tarski). The concept so created was subsequently adapted to the needs of semiotics by L. Hjelmslev, and of linguistics by Z. S. Harris. The morpheme "meta-" serves therefore to distinguish between two linguistic levels*: that of the object-language* (semiotic system) and that of metalanguage.

2. It suffices to observe the function of natural languages,* to discover that they have the peculiarity of being able to speak not only of "things" but of themselves as well; to see that, according to R. Jakobson, they have a **metalinguistic function.*** The existence of a multitude of metalinguistic expressions within natural languages raises at least two kinds of problems: (a) On the one hand, when this set of expressions is

brought together, could it constitute a metalanguage?* In other words, would it possess the fundamental characteristics that define a semiotic* system?* (b) On the other hand, would the exclusion of all metalinguistic sentences permit us to obtain a pure language of denotation?*

It is difficult to give a positive reply to these questions. What we can affirm, with some certainty, is the extremely complex character of natural languages: they can embrace a number of micro-universes* that produce diverse and quasi-autonomous* discourses.

3. Once Z. S. Harris had recognized the richness and importance of the metalinguistic elements of natural languages, he postulated the possibility that a given language has of describing itself, and the possibility as well for the linguist to construct a grammar* as a **metalanguage** with the aid of materials found within the object-language (semiotic system). Such an attitude has no doubt left its mark upon American linguistics and explains a certain indifference on the part of generative* semantics, for example, to a rigorous conceptualization of the descriptive* language that it uses.

4. Benveniste as well holds metalanguage to be "the language of grammar"; but the consequences that can be drawn from such an affirmation are quite different. If we wanted to take over completely the heritage of comparative* grammar instead of constructing new linguistic theories *ex nihilo*, then reflection upon the conditions of comparability of these languages would force us to admit that grammatical concepts used to this end must necessarily transcend the natural languages being compared. The possibility of comparison raises, for its part, the

problem of the existence of language universals.* In this case metalanguage can only be external to the object-language; it must be conceived of as an artificial language that contains its own construction rules. It is in this sense that we must interpret the theoretical efforts of L. Hjelmslev, for whom metalanguage is a semiotic system, that is, a hierarchy,* not of words or sentences, but of definitions* which can take the form of a semiotic system* or semiotic process.* The hierarchical construction leading to the inventory of the latter, non-definable, concepts (which we can consider to be hypothetical* universals) enables us then to construct an axiomatic* system on the basis of which deduction* will to some extent produce linguistics* as a formal* language, that is as a "pure algebra."

5. Metalanguage as conceived appears then to be a descriptive language (in the broadest and most neutral sense of the term). As such it may be represented in the form of several superimposed **metalinguistic levels.** Each level is meant (in the Polish school tradition) both to question and to found its immediately inferior level. We have in the past proposed a three-level distinction: descriptive,* methodological,* and epistemological.* The epistemological level controls the elaboration of procedures* for and construction of models*; the methodological level in turn supervises the conceptual tools used in the description *stricto sensu*.

6. It is equally fitting to maintain a distinction between metalanguage and the **language of representation*** which we use in order to manifest the metalanguage. We know that different modes of representation—such as the use of parentheses,* tree* diagrams, re-

writing,* etc.—are homologous; they merely offer different ways of representing the same phenomenon or "reality." It is as if these languages of representation were, with respect to the metalanguage, in a relation comparable to that of Latin, Greek, or Arabic alphabets with respect to the natural written languages that they translate.

7. The set of problems concerning metalanguage, as summarized above, is inscribed within a limited framework; it concerns only natural languages taken as object-languages, and the metalanguage we are concerned with here is more or less coextensive with grammar (or grammatical theory). Semiotics* as a theory of the set of "signification systems" has no choice but to go beyond this framework. It is certainly banal, for example, to say that natural languages are able to speak not only about themselves but also of other semiotic systems (painting, music, etc.) as well. In this case it is obvious that certain regions within natural language must be considered metalinguistic, or rather metasemiotic, with respect to the semiotic systems of which they speak. The problem of **non-scientific metalanguages** then arises in semiotics concurrently with the elaboration of a **metalanguage** with a **scientific*** aim, which semiotics needs. The set of relations between linguistics and general semiotics (or semiology*) is thus once more called into question.
—LEVEL; REPRESENTATION; SEMIOTICS; UNIVERSALS

METAPHOR
(métaphore)

1. As a term belonging to rhetoric,* **metaphor** designated one of the figures* (called tropes*) which "modify the meaning of words."

Now this term is used in lexical or phrastic semantics to name the result of the substitution* of one lexeme by another performed in a given context on the basis of semantic equivalence.* Since the studies devoted to the area of metaphor could fill up a library by themselves, we cannot even pretend to sketch an overview of this literature here. We shall therefore limit ourselves to some remarks concerning its role and the way it functions in the framework of discursive semiotics.

2. When it is considered from the point of view of the reception structures, metaphor appears as a foreign body (as an "anomaly" in the generativist perspective). Its readability is always equivocal even when it is guaranteed by the discursive trajectory in which the metaphor is inscribed (the contextual* semes, by integrating it into the discursive trajectory, make it into a sememe*). Indeed, the metaphoric lexeme proposes itself as a virtuality of which the readings* are multifold but suspended by the discursive discipline. It is this virtuality, this number of suspended readings which produces a meaning effect of semantic "richness" or "thickness." For example, the rose which is substituted for "young woman" is, of course, read as "young woman," yet it also manifests for a moment the virtualities of color, form, scent, etc.

3. From the point of view of its origins, metaphor it obviously not a metaphor but a common lexeme. Separated from its context it should be viewed as a "nuclear"* figure* possibly bringing with it, when it is transferred, some but not necessarily all of the semes belonging to its original context. For example, in the above case of the transfer of "rose," this lexeme does not keep the contextual seme *plant*. This transferral

of lexematic figures accounts for the fact that the discourse in which the metaphor is inserted tends to develop into a figurative* discourse.

4. In the perspective of the generative* trajectory of the discourse we are primarily interested in **metaphorization** (and not with metaphor) as a procedure of discursive production. R. Jakobson rightly emphasized the paradigmatic* character of this procedure. Indeed, metaphorization, as the substitution of one semiotic entity for another, presupposes the existence of a paradigm of substitution. In this sense it can be said that all the sememes of a natural language which share at least one common (or identical) seme virtually constitute a paradigm of substitutable terms. (This is what allowed F. Rastier to say that this iterative seme constituted an isotopy.*) Yet—and it is at this point that Jakobson's thesis becomes dubious—the paradigmatic relations are meaningful precisely only insofar as they create meaning, in other words, insofar as they create differences* by means of oppositions, in the framework of each paradigm, between what is kept by the discourse and what is excluded by it. The creation of differences is indeed the only way, since F. de Saussure, to conceive of the production and/or perception of signification.* By contrast, Jakobson's "poetic function" consists of exploiting, by the substitution procedure, paradigms of resemblances, and not paradigms of differences. In fact this amounts to abolishing meaning (Is it not to this totalizing of meaning, to this return of articulated signification to original meaning that the Baudelairian "correspondences" tend?). It is possible that poetic discourse aims, by its redundances, at abolishing meaning. Yet it cannot do so, thanks to

(or because of) the syntagmatic* axis, which maintains signification unaltered, through the elaboration of figurative isotopies.

5. Metaphorization can thus be interpreted as a paradigmatic substitution of figures, which substitution is obtained, on a common semic basis, by the neutralization of the other semes of the same figure. This interpretation of metaphorization also permits an account to be made of the other "anomalies" of the utterance's semantic functioning. As is well known, a seme is not an atom of meaning, but is the term* of a semic category.* Consequently, the substitution procedure which, instead of taking up the same seme, aims at imposing the contrary (or contradictory) seme belonging to the same semic category, produces an antiphrasis.* For example, one says, "Big deal!," to express contempt for the pettiness evidenced by someone else. Similarly, the semes participate in hypotactic* constructs, called sememes. If, during the substitution procedure, the seme chosen as the operator of the substitution is replaced by a hypotactic* (or hypertactic) seme belonging to the same sememe, then the result of the operation can be called metonymy* (a kind of deviant metaphor). Of course, these are not "real" definitions, but suggestions that semantics can offer concerning the way of formulating answers to the problems raised by the figures* of rhetoric.

6. From the perspective of discoursive semiotics, these procedures of semantic substitutions are primarily of concern to us as isotopic connectors. While the metaphor usually functions in the framework of a sentence and can be apprehended and described in this context, it becomes a discoursive fact only when it is prolonged, that is,

when it constitutes a transsentential figurative isotopy. In this case, the procedures of paradigmatic substitution that we have discussed above present themselves as initiators of isotopies, and then, at regular intervals, as maintainers or isotopic connectors, linking isotopies together. The figurative isotopies refer either to other figurative isotopies, or to more abstract thematic isotopies. Taking as starting point a semantic isotopy, viewed as the basic isotopy, one can then designate, according to the nature of the connection—metaphor, antiphrasis, metonymy, etc.—the other isotopies of the discourse as metaphoric, antiphrastic, metonymic, etc. —FIGURE; ANALOGY; POETICS; ANTIPHRASIS; ISOTOPY; CONNECTOR, ISOTOPIC

META-SEMEME
(métasémème)

In contrast to sememes,* which contain a semic figure* and a classematic base, **meta-sememes** manifest only combinations* of contextual semes (*cf.*, at the lexical level, the conjunctions *and, or* and the relational adverbs *more, less,* etc.).— CONTEXT

META-SEMIOTIC SYSTEM
(métasémiotique)

Within pluri-planar* semiotic systems L. Hjelmslev distinguishes connotative* (non-scientific) semiotic systems from **meta-semiotic systems** (which are scientific semiotic systems). The semiotic system which functions as a plane of the latter can be either (a) **scientific** (such as logic, mathematics, linguistics): such systems belong to the issues concerning metalanguage; or (b) **non-scientific**; in this case, Hjelmslev speaks of semiologies.* Metasemiotics with a non-scientific semiotics as object corresponds to our definition of semiotics.—SEMIOTICS; METALANGUAGE; SEMIOLOGY

METATERM
(métaterme)

Every relation* which is taken as a semiotic axis* is made up of a category containing at least two terms.* However, the relation considered in and of itself may be taken as a term. By forming a relation with another term of the same kind it constitutes a category at a hierarchically superior level the relation-terms of which we can call **metaterms** so as to distinguish them from simple terms. Thus, the relations of contrariety which characterize the axes of the contraries and sub-contraries* are **contrary metaterms,** constitutive of a category of contradiction.* Similarly, the relations of complementarity by which the positive and negative deixes* are defined are **complementary metaterms** constitutive of a category of contraries. —SQUARE, SEMIOTIC; CONTRARIETY; COMPLEMENTARITY

METHOD
(méthode)

1. By **method** ordinarily we understand a programmed series of operations* the goal of which is to obtain a result in conformity with the demands of the theory. In this sense the term method is quasi-synonymous with procedure. Particular explicit* and well-defined methods which have a general value approximate discovery* procedures.

2. **Methodology**—or the **methodological level** of semiotic theory—consists in an analysis the goal of which is to test the internal coherence of the operational concepts*

(such as element, unit, class, category, etc.) and procedures* (as identification, segmentation, substitution, generalization, etc.) which have served to produce the semantic representation* of a scientific object. Methodology must be distinguished from epistemology, which is designed to test methodological language.
—THEORY; SEMIOTICS; EPISTEMOLOGY

METONYMY
(métonymie)

1. Traditionally, the rhetorical figure* known as **metonymy** (which includes the more specific instance of synecdoche) designates the linguistic phenomenon in which a given sentential unit is substituted for another unit to which it is "linked" (in a relation of container to contained, of cause to effect, of part to whole, etc.).

2. Interpreted within the context of discursive semantics,* metonymy is the result of a substitution* procedure by which a given seme, for example, is replaced by another hypotactic (or hypertactic) seme; both semes in question belong to the same sememe.* From this perspective we may consider metonymy a "deviant" metaphor. C. Lévi-Strauss has remarked that within mythic thought "every metaphor ends in metonymy", and that all metonymy is by nature metaphorical. His remark is easily interpreted if we take into account that in both of these rhetorical figures a substitution phenomenon is indeed produced on the basis of a semantic equivalence.
—METAPHOR

MICRO-UNIVERSE
(micro-univers)

Since it is impossible for semantics* to describe the semantic universe in its totality (the semantic universe, in effect, would have to be co-extensive with the entire culture* of an ethno-linguistic community), we are forced to introduce the operational* concept of **micro-universe.** We mean by this term a semantic set which can be articulated at its base by a semantic category* such as *life/death* and sub-articulated by other categories which are hyponymically* or hypotactically* subordinated to the former. A micro-universe such as this generates discourse within which it finds its syntagmatic expression. This is the notion of isotopy,* understood to be a bundle of categories common to the discourse as a whole, which enables us to establish the correspondence between a micro-universe and the discourse responsible for it. The categories which constitute the isotopy may be identified with those that articulate the micro-universe taxonomically.—UNIVERSE

MODALITY
(modalité)

1. Taking as a starting point the traditional definition of **modality,** understood as "what modifies the predicate" of an utterance, **modalization** can be conceived as the production of a so-called modal utterance, which over-determines a descriptive* utterance. An intuitive approach to modalities does not seem very convincing. Since inventories of modal verbs (and, when applicable, of modal expressions) can always be disputed and since

they vary from one language to the other, it is reasonable to consider, in a first stage, that the two forms (declared canonical) of elementary utterances*—utterances of doing* and utterances of state*—can be found either in the syntactic description of descriptive utterances or in the hypertactic description of modal utterances. In other words, the following can be conceived: (a) doing modalizing being (*cf.* performance,* art*), (b) being modalizing doing (*cf.* competence*), (c) being modalizing being (*cf.* veridictory* modalities), and (d) doing modalizing doing (*cf.* factitive* modalities). In this perspective, the modal predicate can be defined first of all by its sole tactic function, by its transitive* aim, which can affect another utterance taken as object.

2. Two consequences stem from this stance. The first relates to the syntactic organization of the discourse-utterance. Whereas phrase-structure grammar considers—and understandably so—that it is essential for the analysis to recognize the levels* of pertinence interpreted as steps (or ranks) of derivation,* we believe that the existence of discoursive levels (or of types of discourse) can be affirmed on the transsentential plane due to the fact of the recurrence* of **modal structures** (a modal stage overdetermining a descriptive stage). A new syntagmatic hierarchy* due not only to the hypotactic structures which link the modalized structures, but also due to a typology of modalizations can then be postulated as one of the principles of the syntactic organization of the utterance-discourses.

3. The second consequence concerns just that typology of modalizations. Since the inductive approach is a not very sure one and

since it is insufficiently general, only a hypothetico-deductive procedure has any hope of finding any sort of order in the confused inventories of the modalities of natural languages. It is true that modal logics provide the example of a comparable approach: after having recognized a problematic modal field, they select from it certain "truth values"— alethic or deontic values, for example—and posit them axiomatically as a starting point for their deductions and calculations. The semiotic procedure is somewhat different, since it is based first of all on a rather large number of concrete analyses which, moreover, are situated on the narrative plane, which transcends the discoursive organizations of natural languages. Such studies have constantly shown the exceptional role that the modal values of **wanting**,* **having-to**,* **being-able**,* and **knowing***—which can modalize being as well as doing—play in the semiotic organization of discourses. On the other hand, the Saussurian tradition in linguistics, which N. Chomsky, moreover, has not contradicted (and which, in philosophy, goes a long way back), has gotten us used to reflecting in terms of modes of existence* and of levels of existence— virtual,* actual,* realized.* These modes and levels constitute, as it were, so many domains marking off a trajectory, which can be interpreted as a tension (G. Guillaume) stretching from the zero point to its realization. Even if semiotics aims, as does its logic, at installing a fundamental modal structure squarely in the middle of its theory by an axiomatic declaration, it is clear that semiotics maintains the hypothetical character of its quest by seeking empirical and theoretical underpinnings for its undertaking.

4. The construction of a model which would allow an account to be made of its fundamental modal structure by subsuming its diverse articulations through successive inter-definitions, is only now beginning. The criteria of inter-definition and classification of modalities should be simultaneously syntagmatic* and paradigmatic*; each modality would be defined on the one hand as a hypotactic* modal structure and, on the other hand, as a category* which could be represented on the semiotic square.* Thus, by taking into consideration the tensional* trajectory which leads to realization, the modalities so far recognized can be put into a schema as follows:

Modalities	virtualizing	actualizing	realizing
exotactic	HAVING — TO	BEING — ABLE	DOING
endotactic	WANTING	KNOWING	BEING

Following M. Rengstorf's suggestion, the modalities which can enter into translative relations (which can link together utterances having distinct subjects) can be designated exotactic. The simple modalities (linking together identical or syncretized* subjects) will be called endotactic.

5. Another criterion of classification, *viz.*, the nature of the utterance to be modalized, permits a distinction between two broad classes of modalizations: the class of doing and that of being. Thus, the modal structure of *having-to-do,* called prescription,* for example, is opposed to that of *having-to-be,* called necessity,* but they keep an indisputable semantic affinity. It can be seen that, in the first case, modalization as a predicative relation bears more on

the subject that it "modalizes" and that, in the second, it is the object (that is, the utterance of state) which is "modalized." Within these two classes of modalizations, it is probably possible not only to foresee modalization processes, which can be formulated as ordered sequences of utterances (an actualizing modality presupposing a virtualizing modality, for example), but also to calculate the compatibilities and incompatibilities within these sequences (*having-to-do* is compatible with *not-being-able-not-to-do,* whereas *wanting-to-do* is not compatible with *not-knowing-how-to-do*). A strategy of modalization, under these conditions, is quite conceivable; it would permit the establishment of a typology of modalized subjects and objects (utterances).

—UTTERANCE; ALETHIC MODALITIES; DEONTIC MODALITIES; EPISTEMIC MODALITIES; VERIDICTORY MODALITIES; FACTITIVITY; BEING-ABLE; KNOWING; HAVING-TO; WANTING; SYNTAX, SURFACE NARRATIVE

MODEL
(modèle)

1. In the meaning inherited from the classical tradition **model** means that which can serve as an object of imitation. The model may then be considered either as an ideal form that is preexistent to any more or less perfect realization, or as a constructed simulacrum which allows a set of phenomena to be represented. It is in this latter sense that the term model is employed in linguistics and, more generally, in semiotics where it designates an abstract, hypothetical* construct which is supposed to account for a given set of semiotic facts.

2. The construction of models takes place in between the object language and the metalanguage.* In relation to the object semiotic system, models are to be conceived of as hypothetical representations* which can be confirmed, invalidated, or falsified.* On the other hand, they belong to general semiotic theory,* on the basis of which they are deduced* and which controls their homogeneity* and coherence.* The elaboration and the use of the model are thus caught, as if in a vise, between the demands of the theory and its necessary adequation* with the object of knowledge. It is this level* that we call methodological-cal*—the level where in principle scientific* doing is essentially located. It is this double conformity of models that gives them their hypothetico-deductive* character.

3. The concept of model, however, is in danger of losing its consistency because of an overly-extended use of the term. Thus, when N. Chomsky speaks of three principal models in linguistics (Markov's model, the syntagmatic and the transformational models), the term model is equivalent to grammar.* Likewise, when the generativists compare either the standard or the expanded model to the generative semantic model we have instead a schema representing the general economy* of a linguistic theory that we for our part designate with the expression generative* trajectory. By proposing to consider the *ab quo* elementary structure* as a **constitutional model** (so specified with the help of a determinant), on the basis of which we can deduce and, progressively, elaborate the elements of a morphology and a fundamental syntax,* we have sought to under-score the constructed and deductive character of semiotic theory.

4. While the term model in this very general sense corresponds approximately to the Hjelmslevian concept of *description,* * partial models can correspondingly be homologated to procedures.* The question which is then raised is that of their "good use." Obviously, models taken as falsifiable hypotheses play a remarkable role to the extent that they are substituted little by little for the intuition* of the subject of the scientific doing. They may just as well render valuable service as long as they satisfy the demand for generalization,* that is, as long as they are constructed in such a way that the explored phenomenon constitutes only a variable of a model that can account for a whole set of either comparable or contrasting phenomena. By contrast, the imitative reproduction of the same models runs the risk of transforming a quest for knowledge into an unimaginative technology. The borrowing of heterogeneous* models and their application to the same object of cognition—which is, alas, only too frequently encountered these days—does away with all theoretical coherence and at the same time all signification of the semiotic project.

MONEME
(monème)

A. Martinet has proposed the term **moneme** as a designation for the minimal linguistic sign,* or morpheme (in the American sense of the term), that is, for the minimal unit of the first articulation (in contrast to the phoneme* which is the minimal unit of the second articulation). —MORPHEME; ARTICULATION

MONOPLANAR SEMIOTIC SYSTEM
(monoplane [sémiotique—])

For L. Hjelmslev **monoplanar semiotic systems**—or symbol* systems—are those which contain only one language plane* or at least those two planes which would be linked by a relation of conformity.—SEMIOTICS; CONFORMITY

MONOSEMEMY (or MONOSEMY)
(monosémémie [ou monosémie])

Monosememy is the characteristic of lexemes* which contain only a single sememe* and, ultimately, of discourse in which lexemes such as these predominate. Monosememy is one of the conditions of a well-constructed metalanguage.—POLYSEMEMY; METALANGUAGE

MORALIZATION
(moralisation)

1. As a thymic* connotation* of actant-subjects of the narration, **moralization** has the effect of homologizing the term *euphoria* with the subject and the term *dysphoria* with the anti-subject (hero*/villain*). So conceived, it characterizes a large number of ethno-literary discourses. Nonetheless, moralization may be shifted from the domain of the text to that of the enunciatee* and consist in the euphoric identification* of that enunciatee* with one of the subjects of the narration. This type of moralization is frequently found in socio-literary discourse (romantic detective stories, bicycle races, etc.).

2. The same thymic connotation bears no less upon the actantial structures than upon the invested content itself, and in this sense it appears as one of the more general aspects of the phenomenon of axiologization (which bears upon the categories of the good and the bad, giving a euphoric value to the positive deixis* and a dysphoric value to the negative deixis).
—THYMIC CATEGORY; AXIOLOGY

MORPHEME
(morphème)

1. According to its traditional definition the **morpheme** is the part of a word (or syntagm) which indicates its grammatical function* (for example the suffix, prefix, preposition, case, etc.), in contrast to the semanteme* understood as the lexical base of a word. It it thus that A. Martinet restricts the use of the term morpheme to grammatical elements and that of lexeme* to the lexical base: for Martinet morphemes and lexemes thereby constitute the class of monemes.*

2. For immediate constituent* analysis as it is practiced in America, morphemes are minimal units of grammatical analysis (units which make up words) or, if one prefers, minimal signs* (=monemes,* according to Martinet's terminology) which carry signification and beyond which one enters into phonological* analysis. In this perspective we can distinguish **lexical morphemes** (often called lexemes) from **grammatical morphemes** (often called grammemes*).

MORPHOLOGY
(morphologie)

1. For nineteenth-century linguistics **morphology** and syntax* were the two components of grammar*: morphology was responsible for the study of "parts of speech," that is, units having the dimensions of words*; syntax was concerned with their organization in larger

units (clauses* and sentences*). Such a division of labor appeared satisfactory as long as the concern was principally for the study of Indo-European languages, which had a developed flexional system where homologations between syntactic functions* and morphological characteristics (predicate and verb, subject and nominative, etc.) were frequent. It is the reexamination of the notion of word as well as the shift in interest toward modern or exotic languages which has moved linguistics more recently toward an elimination of morphology as an autonomous component from its field of preoccupation.

2. However, even though the old-fashioned term morphology has disappeared little by little from linguistic literature, the field of study that it encompasses remains no less with us. It is first of all a matter of grammatical categories,* paradigmatic in nature, which are manifested syntagmatically either in the form of flexional grammatical morphemes* or as closed classes of morphemes (prepositions, conjunctions, etc.); the problem of **morphological classes** is also posed, in the construction of categorical grammars (certain syntagms combine, for example, lexical morphemes with grammatical morphemes, allowing us to anticipate syntagms with zero base and syntagms with zero inflection).

3. Even superficial comparison of certain European languages (Russian and English or, diachronically, Latin and French) is enough to make one recognize the existence of languages that could be called morphologically dominant as well as others, syntagmatically dominant, so as to realize that the same grammatical categories can appear either in the form of case inflections, of free grammatical morphemes, or as realized "prosodically" by an obligatory word order.* However, all of these modes of syntagmatic presence are merely surface phenomena which make explicit the grammatical categories that manifest the paradigmatic aspect of the language. It is interesting to note in this regard that artificial languages (for example, documentary languages) may be divided, from the point of view of their construction, into two large classes: those which contain a developed "morphology" need only a small amount of syntactic relations; and conversely those for which the relational network is particularly thick can make do with a reduced morphological (or taxonomic) base. All this takes place as if it were a phenomenon of compensation.

4. Thus, by proposing to give the form of a fundamental syntax* to *ab quo* semiotic structures* (the starting point for the generative* trajectory), we have distinguished an elementary "morphology" (represented by the semiotic square*) and an elementary "syntax." The former is constituted as a taxonomic network which authorizes the operations of the second as so many summations carried out upon the terms of the base categories. Far from signifying a return to traditional concepts, the archaizing use of the term "morphology" is designed to underscore the "morphological reality" that certain syntagmaticians try to ignore (by speaking, for example, of "alphabets" and not of taxonomies).

5. It is perhaps necessary to point out that for all practical purposes the term "morphology" as V. Propp used it is in a sense botanical and non-linguistic. His description of the Russian folktale, as far as "morphology" is concerned, contains

only a bundle of "dramatis personae" (by interpreting this bundle we have articulated it into actantial structures).

—CATEGORY; SYNTAX

MOTIF
(motif)

1. Used in various disciplines (for example, art history by Panofsky), the notion of **motif** has been set forth in particular by ethno-literary studies, wherein it is traditionally opposed to type (of folktale), without a precise definition of these two notions ever having been made. While type is conceived of as a succession of motifs which obeys a particular narrative and discoursive organization, motif is a constitutive element of type, and has best been described by S. Thompson (known, among other things, for his *Motif Index of Folk-Literature*) as "the smallest element of the folktale which can be recognized as such in the popular tradition." At the level of manifestation its units remain imprecise at best, for, as folklorists themselves recognize, this "unit" may ultimately constitute a perfectly autonomous micronarrative and thereby enter into the class of types.

2. In spite of these difficulties we can ask ourselves all the same whether the recognition, description, and typology of motifs does not constitute a research field within the more general framework of discoursive semantics.* It would then be a matter of proceeding in the real texts to delimiting and analyzing these transsentential figurative units constituted in the form of fixed blocks. Such blocks are sorts of invariants which can move either into different narratives of a given cultural universe, or even beyond the limits of a cultural area, all the while persisting in spite of the changes in context and secondary functional significations that the narrative environments can confer upon them. Thus, within the French folktale, the "marriage" motif occupies different positions and plays different functions (it can, for example, constitute the quest object in a base narrative program* or, on the contrary, serve as an instrumental narrative program).

3. The motif appears as a figurative* type of unit which therefore possesses a meaning that is independent of its functional signification with respect to the narrative as a whole within which it takes place. If we consider the narrative structure of the story—with its narrative* trajectories—as an invariant,* the motifs then appear as variables, and vice-versa. Whence the possibility of studying them for themselves by considering the motifs as an autonomous structural level, parallel to narrative articulations. It is within this perspective that we can assimilate motifs to discoursive configurations as much for their own internal organization (upon the semantic as well as the syntactic plane) as for that which concerns their integration within a larger discoursive unit.

4. Folklorists have not failed to observe the migratory character of motifs, not only from one ethnic literature to another or from one of its narratives to another, but also sometimes within the same folktale: for example, in the case where the subject and anti-subject are successively submitted to the same test,* or where the same motif is used for several instrumental narrative programs located at different levels of derivation.* Whence comes perhaps the possibility of interpreting, in certain cases, the existence of motifs by the process of recursivity.* This is

obviously but one simple suggestion in the face of a particularly difficult set of problems (which remain unexplored), the importance of which is no less decisive for a methodological analysis of the discursive level of semiotic* theory.
—CONFIGURATION

MOTIVATION
(motivation)

1. Within Saussurian theory the arbitrary* nature of the sign (that is, of the relation between signifier* and signified*) is affirmed while at the same time its **motivated** character is denied. The opposition thus formulated goes ultimately back to the problem of the origin of natural languages,* the development of which could be explained, according to some philosophers, by the "imitation of nature's sounds," for which onomatopoeia would be witness in the present state of languages' development. The existence of onomatopoeia indeed poses the problem of the analogy* between language's sound substance* and "natural" noises or cries. The interpretation given them locates the imitation either at the level of perception (*cf.* "cock-a-doodle-do") or sound production ("puffing"). However, the analogy, situated at the level of substance, is transcended at the moment of elaboration of the linguistic form.* Thus the rooster's crow, taken over by one or another phonetic system, is represented by formants* which differ from one language to another. Likewise, the "motivated" morphemes which are integrated within the system of expression* obey general constraints of diachronic transformation and lose their onomatopoeic character. P. Guiraud's approach is more interesting: he goes beyond imitations that

serve to produce isolated morphemes (onomatopoeia) and discloses the existence of morphophonological structures, kinds of figurative nodes of lexemes (of the sort "tick"/"tock") which can produce entire families of words and articulate them at the same time at the semantic level, once their phonetic opposition (/i/ vs.* /o/) is taken into account. What is important to the semiotician is not resolving the problem of the origin of natural languages but determining, with the greatest possible precision, the respective roles of analogy and semiotic form in the economy of semiotic systems.

2. In the preceding remarks we dealt with the extrinsic relations between signs and extra-linguistic reality. Altogether different is the problem of motivation considered as an intrinsic relation between the sign and other elements belonging to the same semiotic system. Certain semanticists (Ullmann) go so far as to classify this kind of motivation into (a) phonetic motivation (in which onomatopoeia is wrongly located but where one could, for example, place the relations between homophones); (b) morphological motivation (families formed by derivation); and (c) semantic motivation (relations between the "literal meaning" and the "figurative meaning"). In this case two different things are confused: the relations thus classified are "normal" structural relations that are constitutive of linguistic semiotics; they are to be distinguished from knowledge regarding the existence of this or that relation, that the speaking subject (or linguistic community) may have at a given moment. It is a matter here of a meta-semiotic phenomenon, of an attitude that a society has with regard to its own signs, a

phenomenon which therefore belongs to a typology of cultures* (cf. Lotman). Motivation, as distinguished from analogy* (dealt with in No. 1 above), should be classified as part of the set of problems regarding social connotations.* Depending on the culture, it is possible to recognize either the tendency to "naturalize" the arbitrary by motivating it or to "acculturate" that which is motivated by intellectualizing it (R. Barthes).
—ARBITRARY

MOVEMENT
(mouvement)

An analysis of spatio-temporal localization which is carried out in terms not only of utterances of state* but also utterances of doing* would permit the introduction of the concept of **movement**. Movement is to be interpreted as the passage from one space to another, or from one temporal interval to another. Movement could be articulated in terms of directionality (movements which lead from a space or time of departure to a space or time of arrival).—LOCALIZATION, SPATIO-TEMPORAL

MYTHICAL DISCOURSE, LEVEL
(mythique [discours, niveau—])

1. The term **mythical** is used to qualify a class of discourse belonging to ethno-literature or an underlying discoursive and anagogic level which is recognizable when its practical level is read (this latter level appears as a narrative of actions along with the actors which are implied within it).

2. In his structural analysis of the Oedipus Myth C. Lévi-Strauss holds that the reading of the practical level (the term practical is not

his) is horizontal (that is, syntagmatic), whereas the interpretation of the mythical level is vertical (that is, of a paradigmatic order). This paradigmatic organization enables us to recognize, because of their recurrence at the textual surface, an organization of the contents* which may be formulated in terms of a correlation* between two binary categories* of contradictory* or contrary* semes.* Such an interpretation has permitted a realization of the existence, at the discourse's deep levels, of semiotic structures containing a fundamental syntax* and semantics.* At the same time it has led to the loss of the specificity of the mythical discourse, for comparable semiotic structures govern poetic discourse, dream discourse, etc. Consequently the practical/mythical dichotomy ceases to be operational; the practical level is identified with the figurative* plane of discourse, while the mythical level corresponds, within the generative* trajectory, to the deep* semiotic organizations.

3. The present state of research in the typology of discourse does not enable us to determine with certainty the characteristics proper to mythical discourse considered as a "genre*." Intuitively it would seem that such a discourse establishes a correlation at the deep level between two relatively heterogenous semantic categories with which it deals as if they were two schemas* of a single micro-universe,* and that its fundamental syntax consists in alternately asserting the two contrary* terms of this universe to be true.
—PRACTICAL; DEEP STRUCTURE

MYTHOLOGY
(mythologie)

1. By **mythology** is understood either the set of myths belonging to

a given ethno-linguistic community or a discipline which seeks to describe, analyze, and compare different myths.

2. Recently, however, mythology as a discipline has found itself caught between the excessive and hasty ambitions of a universal mythology (Frazer) and the affirmation of the uniqueness of each mythology, if not of each myth: a position influenced by esthetic concerns. The constitution of mythology as a scientific endeavor is linked to the elaboration of **comparative mythology** by G. Dumézil (the Indo-European domain) and C. Lévi-Strauss (the Amerindian domain). Use of the mythological tools developed by narrative and discursive semiotics is complementary with and indebted to comparative research.
—COMPARATIVE MYTHOLOGY; COMPARATIVISM; MYTHICAL DISCOURSE, LEVEL

ABCDEFGHIJKLMN OPQRSTUVWXYZ

NAME/NAMING

(dénomination)

1. In myths about the origin of language, **naming** is almost always distinguished from the creation of language. Indeed, from an empirical point of view, naming concerns first of all the objects of the world* or of human experience: it concerns the extra-linguistic referent.* Since **names** are variable from one natural language to another, naming is the basis for the classifications* which are specific to a given society.

2. Naming can also correspond to a form of condensation.* In such a case a name is correlated with a definition* (in expansion).

3. "Natural" names need to be distinguished from "artificial" (or constructed) names. **Natural names,** which are inscribed in discourse, belong to the ordinary functioning of natural languages. Thus, a name such as "discussion" encompasses a very complex narrative and discursive form. When the semantic universe* manifested by a natural language is viewed as subdivided into semantic fields* or zones, a name appears as a kind of internal semantic borrowing which can take at least two forms: (a) **figurative name,** in which a figure* encompasses a class of open derivation* (for instance, the semic nucleus "head" in "pinhead," "nail head," "masthead," etc.); (b) **translative name,** characterized by the transfer of a discursive segment (a lexeme or a syntagm)

from one semantic domain to another, relatively far removed, as "Turk's head" for a type of knot, "knucklehead," for an unintelligent person.

4. **Artificial** (or scientific) **names** belong to the construction of a metalanguage* and, more specifically, of a semantic metalanguage. At this level, the chosen names are arbitrary* and have no other value than the one which is given to them by their prior definition. Nevertheless, when the metalanguage is used, the names must be adequate* (they must involve as much information as possible about what is under investigation). Ultimately it would actually be better to substitute symbols (letters, numbers, etc.) for the lexical names. Yet as semiotic research progresses, these symbols would become too numerous to be easily understood. At any rate, at the present time scientific (or artificial) names remain semi-motivated. Thus during analysis it is necessary to make a clear distinction (if possible, a typographic distinction) between the constructed terms belonging to the metalanguage and the lexemes* of the natural languages which belong to practices of non-scientific paraphrasing.*

—CATEGORIZATION; ETHNO-SEMIOTICS; METALANGUAGE; ARBITRARY

NARRATIVE
(récit)

1. A word in common usage, the term **narrative** is often used to designate narrative discourse of figurative* character (involving personages* which accomplish actions*). Since it is then the narrative* schema (or any one of its segments) already put into discourse and, by this fact, inscribed in spatio-

temporal coordinates, that is being dealt with, certain semioticians define the narrative—following V. Propp—as a temporal succession of functions* (in the sense of actions). Conceived thus in a very restrictive way (as figurative and temporal), narrativity* concerns only a class of discourses.

2. The diversity of narrative forms, it has raised the question of whether the **simple narrative** can be defined. At its minimum the latter is reduced to a sentence each as "Adam ate an apple," analyzable as the passage from a previous state* (preceding the eating) to a later state (which follows the eating), carried out through a doing (or a process*). In this perspective the simple narrative comes close to the concept of narrative program.

3. At the level of the discoursive structures,* the term narrative designates the discoursive unit, figurative in character, situated in the pragmatic* dimension, and obtained by the procedure of utterative disengagement.*

—FIGURATIVIZATION; NAR-RATIVITY; PROGRAM, NARRA-TIVE; UNIT (DISCOURSIVE); DIEGESIS

NARRATIVE SCHEMA
(narratif [schéma—])

1. Reflection upon the narrative organization of discourses originated with the analyses carried out by V. Propp on the corpus of Russian folktales. Whereas Soviet semiotics during the decade of the 1960s strove particularly to expand the knowledge concerning the internal mechanisms of the functioning of the folktales (E. Meletinsky and his group) and American and French ethnologists (A. Dundes, D. Paulme) sought to interpret the Proppian

schema in the light of its application to oral narratives of different ethnic groups (Amerindians and Africans), French semiotics sought from the beginning to develop and perfect a model which could serve as a point of departure for understanding the organizing principles of all narrative discourses. The hypothesis that there exist universal forms of narrative organization has put Propp's research at the very heart of the problems facing newly-born semiotics.

2. More than the succession of the thirty-one functions* by which Propp defined the oral narrative—the logical principles governing the arrangement of which are not readily apparent—it is the repetition of three tests—qualifying,* decisive* and glorifying* which appeared as the regularity, located upon the syntagmatic axis, that revealed the existence of a **canonical narrative schema.** The test could then be considered as a recurrent narrative syntagm* that is formally identifiable; only the semantic investment which is recorded in the consequence* enables us to tell them apart. Subsequently, further analyses and progress made in the construction of narrative grammars have succeeded in reducing the importance of the role of the test, going so far as to view it only as a surface* discursive figure.* This does not alter the fact that the very succession of the tests, interpreted as a reverse order of logical presupposition, appears to be governed by an intentionality* that is recognizable *a posteriori* and comparable to that which can account, in genetics, for the development of an organism. While today the tests appear instead to be figurative ornamentations of deeper* logical operations, they are nonetheless inscribed in the three narrative* trajectories which constitute the

warp of a very general syntagmatic schema. Indeed, the narrative schema constitutes a kind of formal framework within which is recorded "life meaning" with its three essential domains: the qualification* of the subject, which introduces it into life; its "realization,*" by means of which it "acts"; and finally the sanction*—at one and the same time retribution and recognition—which alone guarantees the meaning of its actions and installs it as a subject of being. This schema is sufficiently general to allow for all variations upon the theme: considered on a more abstract level and broken down into trajectories, it aids in articulating and interpreting different types of cognitive as well as pragmatic activities.

3. Other regularities may be recognized by examining the Proppian schemata, which are no longer of a syntagmatic but rather of a paradigmatic nature. Projections of paradigmatic categories upon the syntagmatic axis, they may on first approximation be considered as discontinuous narrative syntagms. Whereas syntagmatic regularities play upon the recurrence of identical elements, paradigmatic regularities are iterations of units with inverted structures or contents. The same applies to the contractual organization of the narrative schema. The subject's three tests are, as it were, framed at a hierarchically superior level by a contractual structure. Following the establishment of the contract* between Sender* and subject-Receiver, the latter goes through a series of tests in order to fulfil the obligations it has assumed and in the end is rewarded by the Sender which likewise keeps its contractual end of the agreement. Upon closer inspection, however, it appears that this establishment of the

contract occurs following a break in the established order (that is, a breaking of an implicit social contract which has just been transgressed). The narrative schema thus appears as a series of establishments, breaks, and reestablishments, etc., of contractual obligations.

4. On the other hand, it is understood that the Proppian narrative had a strong spatial articulation and that the different spaces corresponded to distinct narrative forms (the space where the tests are carried out, for example, is not the same as the space where the contract is instituted and sanctioned). For their part the actants* maintain specific relations with the spaces to which they belong (the subject, for example, can only be realized in a utopic* and solitary space). This spatial articulation of the narrative schema—which we considered, at the start, as having the status of a discontinuous narrative syntagm—has given rise to research that is being pursued in two directions: on the one hand, a deeper examination of the spatial organization leads us to consider spatialization* as a relatively autonomous sub-component of the discoursive structures*; on the other hand, the recognition of correlative variations of spaces and actants leads us to see in the successive disjunctions* and conjunctions* a new paradigmatic principle of narrative organization.

5. A final and perhaps most visible paradigmatic projection corresponds to the recognized relation between the two Proppian functions of "lack*" and "liquidation of the lack*" which makes it ultimately possible to interpret the narrative as a succession of degradations and ameliorations (cf. the work of C. Bremond). At first view it is a case here of no longer taking under consideration

the activity of the subjects but rather of the circulation of objects* of value; the subjects of doing* appear then only as simple operators which are destined to carry out a preestablished schema of object transfers. Only by defining the objects as loci where values are invested (these values being the properties of the subjects of state,* and determining them as to their "being") can we reinterpret the schema of object transfers as a syntax of the communication* between subjects.

6. With this rereading of the Proppian schema, the decisive step was taken in recognizing the polemical* structure underlying it. The folktake is not only the story of the hero/ine and his/her quest, it is in a more or less hidden way the story of the villain* as well. Two narrative trajectories, of the subject and of the anti-subject, unfold in two opposite directions, characterized however by the fact that both subjects seek one and the same object of value. Thus an elementary narrative schema becomes apparent, grounded upon a polemical structure. On closer inspection this conflictual structure is, in the last analysis, one of the opposing poles—the other being the contractual structure—of the confrontation, which characterizes all human communication. Even the most peaceful exchange implies the confrontation of two contrary wantings and the conflict is inscribed within the framework of a network of tacit conventions. Narrative discourse appears then to be a locus of the figurative representations of the different forms of human communication, produced from tension, and of returns to equilibrium.

7. The subject's narrative trajectory, which seems to constitute the nucleus of the narrative schema, is framed on both sides by a tran-

scendent* domain wherein the Sender,* charged with manipulating and sanctioning the subject of the immanent* level (the Receiver), is located. The relation between Sender and Receiver is ambiguous: on the one hand it obeys the principle of communication which we have just evoked; the contractual structure seems to dominate the whole narrative schema. The subject's performance corresponds to the execution of the accepted contractual demands and calls for the sanction as a counterpart. However, the symmetrical relations which are thus established between Sender and Receiver as equals and which make it possible to treat them within the syntactic calculus as subjects S1 and S2 are in part contradicted by the asymmetry of their respective statuses. It makes little difference whether the Sender be the manipulator, charged with transforming the Receiver into a competent subject, or that it be a judge, establishing legitimate being-able* and true knowing. In either case, the Sender performs a factitive* doing which puts it in a position hierarchically superior to the Receiver. But that is not enough to establish a definition. For example, as a discoursive configuration,* flattery establishes a subject S1 which manipulates S2. It is no less true that S2, by definition, is hierarchically superior to S1. It is the preestablished being-able, more than the active being-able, that characterizes the hierarchical status of the Sender; and it is probably through this preestablished being-able of the Sender that it is most fitting to define the transcendent domain in which we have inscribed the Sender.

8. As a descendent of successive generalizations rooted in Propp's description, the narrative schema thus appears to be an ideological reference model which will continue to stimulate all reflection upon narrativity* for a long time to come. But it already enables us to distinguish three autonomous segments of the narrative syntax: the narrative trajectories of the performing subject, the Sender-manipulator, and the Sender-judge, and to envision with confidence the projects of a semiotics of action, a semiotics of manipulation, and a semiotics of sanction. However, it would be wrong to imagine that the simple concatenation of these three trajectories produces a syntactic unity of greater dimensions—but of the same nature as its constituents—that would be the narrative schema. Between the narrative schema on the one hand and the narrative trajectories that are encountered there on the other, there exists—with all due proportions being taken into account—the same distance as between the actantial structures of an utterance and the syntagmatic classes which fill one actantial position or another. Thus the discoursive configuration which is identified as the trajectory of manipulation can correspond to the "function" of the Sender-manipulator, but it will be found just as well within the trajectory of the performing subject (the specific rules for this kind of recursivity* are far from being set out). It could be said that it is the narrative strategy* which orders the arrangements and intertwinings of narrative trajectories, whereas the narrative schema is canonic as a reference model, in relation to which deviations, expansions, and strategic localizations may be calculated.

—NARRATIVE TRAJECTORY; NARRATIVITY; MANIPULATION; SANCTION; PERFORMANCE; COMPETENCE; CONTRACT; COMMUNICATION

NARRATIVE TRAJECTORY

(narratif [parcours—])

1. A **narrative trajectory** is a hypotactic* series of either simple or complex narrative* programs (abbreviated NP), that is, a logical chain in which each NP is presupposed by another, presupposing, NP.

2. NPs are simple syntactic units, and the syntactic actants* (subject of doing or of state, object) which enter into their formulation may be any subjects or objects. As a consequence any narrative segment whatsoever that is recognizable within an utterance-discourse can be broken down into NPs. However, once inscribed in a narrative trajectory, the syntactic subjects may be defined, for each of the integrated NPs, by the positions they occupy (or that the NP to which they belong occupies) in the trajectory and by the nature of the objects of value* into junction with which they enter. In this initial approach to the problem, we give the title of actantial* role to this double definition of the syntactic actant by its position and its semiotic being. The definition of its "semiotic being" corresponds to its status as subject of state* (in junction with modal* values or modes of existence*), whereas the definition by way of its position within the trajectory signifies that the actantial role is not characterized solely by the final NP realized and by the ultimate value acquired (or lost), but that it subsumes the entire trajectory already traveled; it contains in itself the augmentation (or loss) in its being. This two-fold character thus has the effect of making the actants "dynamic" and offering the possibility of measuring, at every moment, the **narrative progress** of the discourse.

3. As a result the narrative trajectory contains as many actantial roles as there are NPs constituting it. Consequently the set of actantial roles of a narrative trajectory may be called actant or, in order to distinguish it from the NP's syntactic actants, functional (or syntagmatic) actant. So defined, the actant is not a concept which is fixed once and for all, but is a virtuality subsuming an entire narrative trajectory.

4. We thus find ourselves in the presence of a syntactic hierarchy in which a definite actantial type corresponds to each unit. The syntactic actants, *stricto sensu*, are constituents of the narrative programs. The actantial roles can be calculated within the narrative trajectories, whereas the functional actants belong to the entire narrative* schema.

5. The best known narrative trajectory at present is the subject*'s. It may be defined as a logical chain of two types of programs: the modal NP (called competence* program) is logically presupposed by the realization NP (called the performance* program), whether the latter be situated in the pragmatic* or in the cognitive* dimension. The functional subject defined by such a trajectory will be divided ultimately into a set of actantial roles, such as the competent subject and the performing subject. Then the competent subject is made up of a cumulative series of actantial roles that can be named according to the last modality acquired: the wanting subject, the able subject, the secret* (non-revealed) subject, the lying subject, etc.; as for the performing subject, it may be victorious (realized*) or defeated, a subject modalized according to the "having-to-want" (in view of the realization of the instrumental NPs), etc. What is essential—as can readily be realized—is not endowing all of the actantial roles with the appropriate names but

having available an analytic tool which permits us to recognize mobile subjects, in narrative progression, in place of the "characters" or "heroes" of traditional literary criticism; it is likewise essential to envisage the possibility of a semiotics of action,* by transposing the issues concerning the subject of the verbal discourses towards social semiotic practices.

6. Taking into consideration only the modal competence of the subjects, we can easily imagine, through a consideration of the four principal modalities, a typology of competent subjects which would be grounded as well upon the choice of the modalities which establish a particular modal trajectory as upon the order of their acquisition. Such a typology (and the contribution J.-C. Coquet has made in this area is particularly interesting) should then be relativized, that is, considered as a set of mechanisms that vary according to cultures* (the typology of which would be facilitated by this supplementary criterion).

7. The performantial segment of this narrative trajectory appears, for its part, in two different ways: either it gives rise to a circulation of the already-existing objects containing sought-after and invested values* (the acquisition of a car, for example, invested with values such as "getting away" or "power") or in a more complex way it necessitates, on the basis of the value sought after, the construction of the object in which it could be invested (for example, on the basis of the previously posed gustative value, the preparation of vegetable soup).

8. Two other anticipated trajectories are presently being determined, but a satisfactory formulation has not as yet been given of them. They are the two domains, transcendent* with respect to the subject's trajectory, the function of which is to frame that trajectory: the first domain is that of the initial Sender*, which is the source of all values and particularly of modal values (that can endow the subject-Receiver with the necessary competence); the second is that of the final Sender which is at one and the same time the judge of the subject's performances, the "doing" of which it transforms into a recognized* "being," and receptor for all the values which this subject is ready to give up. The fact that these two Senders may be found in a state of syncretism* in numerous discourses does not alter the problem. Transposed to the level of social semiotic practices* these two autonomous narrative trajectories—the apprehending of which remains intuitive—could give rise to a semiotics of manipulation* and a semiotics of sanction.*

—ACTANT; PROGRAM, NARRATIVE; NARRATIVE SCHEMA

NARRATIVITY
(narrativité)

1. At first sight we could use the term **narrativity** for a given property that characterizes a certain type of discourse.* On the basis of this property, **narrative discourses** are distinguished from non-narrative discourses. This is the attitude, for example, of E. Benveniste, who opposes historical narrative (or hi/story) to discourse (in the narrow sense) by taking as a criterion the category of person (non-person characterizes hi/story; the person—"I" and "you"—belongs to discourse); and secondly by the particular distribution of verbal tenses.

2. Without here going into the theoretical debate (which belongs to

the set of problems concerning enunciation*), it suffices to note simply that these forms of discourse are almost never found in a pure state. Conversation is prolonged almost automatically into a narrative about something, and the narrative is on the brink of turning into a dialogue at any moment. Thus we can easily side with G. Genette who, instead of distinguishing between two independent classes of discourse, sees in the two types of organization two autonomous discoursive levels: to "narrative," understood to be that which is narrated, he opposes "discourse" (in the narrow sense of the term), which he defines as the way of narrating the narrative. On the basis of the distinctions proposed by Benveniste and Genette we adopt a relatively similar organization: the discoursive level belongs to the enunciation,* whereas the **narrative level** corresponds to what can be called the utterance.*

3. A superficial examination of the narrated part of discourse shows that it frequently contains narratives of events, of heroic or treacherous actions; there is much "sound and fury" here. Let us not forget that narratives, taken as descriptions of connected actions (folkloric, mythical, and literary narratives) were at the base of narrative analysis (Propp, Dumézil, Lévi-Strauss). These different approaches have already shown the existence, under the appearance of figurative* narrated content, of more abstract and deep organizations that have an implicit signification and govern the production and reading of this kind of discourse. Narrativity therefore has gradually appeared as the very organizing principle of all discourse, whether narrative (identified, in the first instance, as figurative discourse)

or non-narrative. For there are only two alternatives: either the discourse is only a simple concatenation of sentences,* and thus the meaning that it bears is due merely to a more or less haphazard succession which is beyond the purview of linguistics (and more generally of any semiotics); or it constitutes a signifying whole, an intelligible speech act that contains its own organization; its more or less abstract or figurative nature is linked to ever greater semantic investments and ever more precise syntactic articulations.

4. The recognition of an immanent discoursive organization (or of narrativity in the broader sense) can only raise the problem of discoursive (narrative) competence. For some time now folklore studies have shown the existence of quasi-universal narrative forms that largely transcend the boundaries of linguistic communities. Even if it is often only intuitive, the approach taken toward literary forms, historical narratives, or religious discourses shows us that there are "genres" or "types" of discourse. All of this means that discoursive activity rests upon a discoursive knowing-how-to-do that is no less a knowing-how-to-do than shoemaking. In other words, a **narrative competence*** must be presupposed if we wish to account for the production and reading of discourse occurrences, a competence which may be considered, somewhat metaphorically, as a kind of syntagmatic intelligence (whose mode of existence would be virtual,* like the Saussurian "langue"—natural language).

5. The recognition of narrative competence enables us to raise more clearly the fundamental question on which the general form of semiotic* theory will depend—namely the relation of dependence between the

two previously mentioned levels (that of **narrative structures** [or, better: semio-narrative structures] and that of **discoursive structures**)—and their conjunction defines the discourse in its totality. If we consider that discoursive structures belong to the domain of enunciation and that this highest domain is dominated by the enunciator,* the producer of narrative utterances, the semio-narrative structures will appear, in this case, subordinate to the discoursive structures, just as the product is subordinate to the producing process. However, we can just as easily assert the opposite—and such will be our position—by seeing in the deep narrative structures the domain which can account for the appearance and development of all (and not merely verbal) signification, which can also assume not only the narrative performances but also articulate as well the different forms of discoursive competence. These semiotic structures, which we continue to call, for lack of a better term, narrative (or better, semio-narrative) structures, are in our view the depository of fundamental signifying forms. They enjoy a virtual existence and correspond, with an expanded inventory, to Saussure's and Benveniste's "langue," a (natural) language which is presupposed by every discoursive manifestation and which at the same time predetermines the conditions of "putting into discourse" (that is, the conditions of the functioning of the enunciation). The semiotic structures (called narrative structures) in our view govern the discoursive structures. The stakes involved in this choice are considerable. Within the framework of a unified theory, it is a question, on the one hand, of reconciling the generative option (which in its Chomskian for-

mulation is merely a theory of the utterance*) with the theory of enunciation (to which American pragmatics* should be joined), on the other. Indeed, generative* grammar leaves the problems of enunciation (considered as "extra-linguistic") outside of its concerns. The analyses of any discourse, which semiotics carries out, continuously raise within the manipulated texts the question of act*—of speech act in particular—and of the competence that the accomplishing of the act presupposes. The problem of discoursive (in the narrow sense) competence and performance belongs, in our view, to general narrative (or semiotic) competence. Instead of undergoing a "pragmatic" treatment, the models of competence can and must be constructed first of all on the basis of competencies "described" within the discourses. Later on, they may be extrapolated in view of a more general semiotics of action* and of manipulation.*

6. Within our semiotic project, generalized narrativity, freed from the restrictive meanings that linked it with the figurative forms of narratives, is considered to be the organizing principle of all discourse. All semiotics may be treated either as system* or as process*; the narrative structures may be defined as constitutive of a deep* level of the semiotic process.
—DIEGESIS; ENUNCIATION; GENERATIVE TRAJECTORY; SYNTAX, FUNDAMENTAL; SYNTAX, SURFACE NARRATIVE

NARRATOR/NARRATEE
(narrateur/narrataire)

When the sender and the receiver of the discourse are explicitly installed in the utterance* (such as

"I" and "you"), they may be called, in G. Genette's terminology, **narrator** and **narratee**. As actants of uttered enunciation,* they are directly delegated subjects of the enunciator* and of the enunciatee. Furthermore, they can exist syncretically with one of the actants of the utterance (or of the narration), such as, for example, the subject of the pragmatic* doing or the cognitive* subject.—SENDER/RECEIVER; ACTANT; DISENGAGEMENT

NATURAL SEMIOTICS
(naturelle [sémiotique—])

Natural semiotics refers to two broad signifying sets* (or macro-semiotic systems): the natural world and natural languages.*—SEMIOTICS

NATURE
(nature)

1. In contrast to that which is artificial or constructed, the term **nature** designates the already-given or the state in which humans find themselves from birth. It is in this sense that we speak of natural languages* or the natural world.*

2. Within the framework of structural anthropology, particularly of the Lévi-Straussian system, the opposition between *nature/culture* is difficult to define insofar as it is inscribed in different semio-cultural contexts where it designates a relation between what is conceived to refer to culture and what is supposed to belong to nature. Within this perspective nature can never be a kind of first given, original and prior to humans, but a nature which is already informed by culture. It is in this sense that we have taken over this dichotomy* by postulating that it can articulate the initial elementary* investment of the collective* semantic universe.
—CULTURE; UNIVERSE, SEMANTIC

NECESSITY
(nécessité)

1. According to L. Hjelmslev **necessity** is an indefinable concept* that is at the same time absolutely indispensable for defining the relation of presupposition.* This position is entirely consistent from the point of view of logic, for which necessity forms a part of the concepts postulated by axiomatic* declaration.

2. From a semiotic point of view, necessity may be considered a name for the modal structure *having-to-be* (where a modal utterance governs an utterance of state). It is therefore in a relation of contrariety with impossibility* conceived as *having-not-to-be*. As a logical concept, necessity is semiotically ambiguous because it also encompasses the modal structure *not-being-able-not-to-be*.
—ALETHIC MODALITIES; HAVING-TO-DO or -TO-BE

NEGATION
(négation)

1. Along with assertion, **negation** is one of two terms of the category of transformation* (which, in turn, is considered as the abstract formulation of the factitive modality*). When, on the other hand, it is defined as one of the two functions of the utterance of doing,* negation governs the utterances of state* by operating disjunctions* between subjects* and objects.*

2. From a paradigmatic point of view, negation is seen to be an operation that establishes the rela-

tion of contradiction* between two terms: the first of these terms (the term which is being negated) is made absent,* whereas the second, its contradictory, acquires an existence* *"in praesentia."*

3. A large number of narrative discourses appear to give priority to the operation of negation by considering it as that which initiates the narrative (*cf.* the transgression of the interdiction* and the establishment of the lack* in the Proppian analysis of narrative). This obviously does not exclude the existence of discourse of destruction (such as tragedy).

—ASSERTION; SQUARE, SEMIOTIC; SYNTAX, FUNDAMENTAL

NEGATIVE TERM, DEIXIS
(négatif [terme, deixis—])

In order to distinguish in their common usage between the two terms* of the axis of contraries*—s1 and s2—they are labeled the positive* term and the **negative term** (without any thymic* connotation being thereby implied). The deixis* to which the negative contrary term belongs is called, correlatively, the **negative deixis**: the latter includes the subcontrary term $\overline{s1}$, which is considered only as regards the deixis to which it belongs and not—given that it is the contradictory of s1—as regards its deixis of origin.

—SQUARE, SEMIOTIC

NESTING
(emboîtement)

Nesting is a procedure which is complementary with spatial or temporal localization. It belongs to the sub-articulation of the category of concomitance.* A punctuality* can be concomitant with another, but also with a temporal or spatial continuity. Two unequal continuities can also be (partially) concomitant. In the case of temporal nesting, a period is included in another period and the narrative program* thus has a twofold localization. The case of spatial nesting seems to be more complex because it deals not only with the inclusion of linearities, but also with the inclusion of surfaces within other surfaces (*cf.* the problem of the frame in planar semiotics) or of volumes within other volumes (for example, in architectural semiotics). The procedures of nesting are thus to be found in all visual and temporal semiotic systems and are therefore not specific to the verbal discursive semiotic system alone.—LOCALIZATION, SPATIO-TEMPORAL; FOCALIZATION

NEUTRAL TERM
(neutre [terme—])

Derived from the elementary structure* of signification, the **neutral term** is defined by the relation "both . . . and" established as a result of previous syntactic operations* by the terms $\overline{s1}$ and $\overline{s2}$ which are located on the axis of the subcontraries.* V. Brøndal must be credited for having defined this term as forming a part of the relational network constitutive of grammatical categories* (and not, for example, as a specific term of the category of gender).—SQUARE, SEMIOTIC; COMPLEX TERM; TERM

NEUTRALIZATION
(neutralisation)

Neutralization designates the suppression of the distinctive* opposition within a semantic category,* which can be produced in a given syntagmatic context,* on the condition, however, that there exists a categorical support that defines the linguistic unit concerned. Thus, for example, in Danish, the opposition *voiced/non-voiced* is neutralized at the end of a word because the maintenance of *occlusive* and *dental* phemes common to the phonemes *d* and *t* makes it possible to recognize a support unit (an archi-phoneme) in spite of this neutralization. Neutralization is to be found as much on the expression plane as on the content plane (*cf.* "they" which subsumes "Mary" and "James," following the neutralization of the category of gender) and can be interpreted semantically as the manifestation of the semantic axis* in place of one of its terms.*—SYNCRETISM; SUSPENSION

NODE
(noeud)

1. In generative* grammar, **node** serves to designate any branching point of the tree at each of the levels of derivation.* The node, therefore, is the representation* of the discriminatory* relation between two immediate constituents,* a relation which is recognizable because of linear contiguity.

2. L. Tesnière defines the node as the relational set made up of the governing term and all of its subordinate terms. For example, the expression "My dear friend" is a node made up on the one hand of "friend" which is the governing term and on the other of "my" and "dear" which are the subordinate terms. In turn this node is represented by a stemma (or tree of a different sort).

3. The difference between these two definitions of the node lies in the fact that for Chomsky the node represents a binary relation based upon the linearity* of the utterance and recognizable at each

level taken separately; whereas for Tesnière the node is a set of hypotactic* relations, of a logical order, encompassing all the levels of derivation. Thus, the **node of nodes,** which is the sentence for Tesnière, corresponds to the structural description* of the sentence, although analyzed according to different criteria.
—TREE

NOISE
(bruit)

Noise is a term from information theory and designates everything which causes a loss of information in the communication* process. From the moment that the message* leaves its source (sender*) to the time that it is received by the destination* (or receiver), noise can intervene at any point, both during the transmission itself and during the encoding* and decoding* operations. To compensate for the negative effect of noise, which is considered as unforseeable and to some extent inevitable, we have recourse to the establishment of redundance* to guarantee the efficiency of the communication.*—INFORMATION

NOMENCLATURE
(nomenclature)

By **nomenclature** we mean the set of monosememic* (or bi-univocal) terms artificially constructed or reduced to monosememy, that serves to designate the objects fabricated (or parts of these objects) and that are part of a sociolect.—TERM; SOCIOLECT

NON-CONFORMITY
(non-conformité)

The term **non-conformity** refers to the relation* which exists between the two planes (expression* and content*) of a semiotic object, when they have different paradigmatic articulations* and/or syntagmatic divisions.* It is such a relation which enables us then to consider this object as a bi-planar semiotic system (or, according to L. Hjelmslev, simply a semiotic system).—CONFORMITY; SEMIOTICS

NON-LINGUISTIC SEMIOTIC SYSTEM
(non-linguistique [sémiotique—])

Oftentimes semiotics* of the natural world (such as "semiotic system of objects," gestuality,* proxemics,* etc.) is qualified by the expression **non-linguistic** in contrast to natural languages* (which are thereby given priority).—WORLD, NATURAL

NON-SCIENTIFIC SEMIOTICS
(non-scientifique [sémiotique—])

According to L. Hjelmslev, a semiotics is **non-scientific** if it does not abide by the empirical* principle.—SEMIOTICS

NOOLOGICAL
(noologique)

1. The set of semic* categories which articulate the semantic universe* may be divided into two subsets by using the category *exteroceptivity/interoceptivity* as a criterion. This is a paradigmatic* classification that enables us to distinguish figurative* categories from non-figurative (or abstract*) ones.

2. From the syntagmatic* point of view, this same category (*exteroceptivity/interoceptivity*) may be considered a classematic* category of a universal nature which, owing to its recurrence, authorizes the making

of a distinction between two classes of discourse (or two dimensions of a single manifested discourse). Therefore a discourse is called **noological** if it is undergirded by the *interoceptivity* classeme and cosmological* if it is endowed with the *exteroceptivity* classeme. However, as far as being theoretically satisfactory, the *noological/cosmological* dichotomy appears at the present stage of semiotic research to be rather weak in operational productivity. Semiotic practice tends to substitute in its place the opposition between the pragmatic* and cognitive* dimensions of discourse.

3. The following example will illustrate the difference between the two operational concepts—the one non-figurative (or interoceptive) and the other cognitive (or noological). The utterance "a heavy bag" is situated in the pragmatic dimension and contains figurative semes; the utterance "a heavy conscience" is inscribed in the cognitive dimension. The latter contains both non-figurative ("conscience") and figurative ("heavy") semes. As can be seen from this, the cognitive dimension is the locus where figurative as well as non-figurative discourses can unfold.
—INTEROCEPTIVITY; COSMOLOGICAL; PRAGMATIC; COGNITIVE

NORM
(norme)

1. In the field of sociolinguistics,* by **norm** is meant a model based upon a more or less rigorous observation of social or individual use of a natural language.* The choice between types of usage for the constitution of the norm rests upon extra-linguistic criteria; religious language, political language, literary prestige, etc. This set of uses

is codified in the form of rules* (prescriptions and interdictions) to which the linguistic community must conform, and takes the name of grammar* (labeled *normative grammar* by nineteenth-century linguists, as opposed to descriptive* grammar, which only seeks to provide an account of the way natural language functions, to the exclusion of any preoccupation with deontic concerns).

2. The need for standardization of usage, which is characteristic of modern societies (teaching, administrations, etc.) often imposes the deliberate choice of a norm for the constitution (or affirmation) of national languages. Thus appears the notion of standard language, that some have sought to ground on statistical criteria (what is normal being identified with the "average") or the criteria of probability (what is normal corresponds to what is expected in a given context). Normative grammar reappears once again: by avoiding the use of its epithet, now grown pejorative, it keeps up the confusion between linguistic structure* and linguistic norm and contributes to the creation of a stylistics of gaps.*

3. The confusion between the socio-linguistic norm (the origin and support of which belong to the exercise of political and/or cultural power) and semiotic **constraints*** (a condition for participation in the semiotic practices* of a social nature) leads some to consider natural languages—with the help of certain ideological* positions—as "castration machines" or as instruments of "fascist power." Such metaphorical excesses are not to be taken seriously.

4. With the criteria of grammaticality* and acceptability,* generative* grammar reintroduces, in a certain fashion, the notion of norm.

A whole set of problems that L. Hjelmslev has sought to elucidate through and analysis of the concepts of schema,* norm, and linguistic use* and act,* crops up again under the cloak of a new terminology. The normative appearance of generative grammar is underscored due to the use of a metalanguage* which operates in terms of rules. It is obvious, however, that in the case of normative grammar the rules are directed toward the one who uses the language, whereas in generative grammar they are destined for the automaton* or, as the case may be, for manual analysis.
—CONSTRAINT; GAP; GRAMMATICALITY; ACCEPTABILITY; RHETORIC

NOTATION, SYMBOLIC
(*notation symbolique*)

Symbolic notation, which uses a set of symbols in the form of a conventional way of writing (geometric figures, letters, abbreviations, initials, etc.) serves as a visual representation* of constituent units of a metalanguage.*—SYMBOL

NOUMENAL
(*nouménal*)

Inherited from the scholastics (as taken up by Kant), the term **noumenal**—as contrasted with phenomenal*—is sometimes used as synonymous with being (in the context of the veridictory* modalization of being and of seeming). Thus the **noumenal plane** is seen as identical with the plane of being.—BEING; IMMANENCE

NUCLEUS

—KERNEL

ABCDEFGHIJKLMN
OPQRSTUVWXYZ

OBJECT
(objet)

1. In the framework of epistemological reflection, **object** is the name given that which is thought or perceived as distinct from the act of thinking (or perceiving) and from the subject who thinks (or perceives) it. This definition—which is not really a definition—suffices to say that only the relation* between the knowing subject and the object of knowledge grounds them as existents and as distinct from one another. This is an attitude which seems totally in conformity with the structural approach to semiotics. It is in this sense that we speak of object language or of semiotic entity,* by insisting upon the absence of any *a priori* determination of the object other than its relation to the subject.

2. Perceived in this way, the object is but a formal position; it is knowable only by its determinations which are, also, relational in nature. The object is constituted through the establishment of relations (a) between it and other objects; (b) between it considered as a whole and its parts; and (c) between the parts, on the one hand, and the set of relations previously established, on the other. As a result of the construction carried out by the knowing subject, the **semiotic object** is therefore reduced, as L. Hjelmslev says, to "in-tersecting points in these networks of relations."

3. The procedure of engagement* enables us to project outside of the knowing subject (or subject of the enunciation*) these fundamental relations of human beings in the world and to "objectify" them. Semiotics* takes on the task of providing the representation* of these fundamental relations in the form of utterances* made up of functions* (that is, relations) and actants* (subjects and objects). As actants, **syntactic objects** are to be considered as actantial positions, that can receive investments either of goals belonging to subjects (we refer to them as **objects of doing**) or their qualifications (**objects of state**).

4. Subjects which are disengaged and installed within the discourse are empty positions which receive their qualifications (or semantic investments*) only after the doing* either of the very subject of enunciation (by way of predication*) or of the delegated subject inscribed within the discourse. These subjects are therefore treated as objects which await their qualifications, which can be either positive or negative (if they are defined as being deprived of uttered attributes). This may be represented in the form of an utterance of state* which signals the junction* (conjunction* or dis-

junction*) of the subject with the object. The object—or **object of value**—is then defined as the locus wherein values* (or qualifications) are invested and to which the subject is conjoined or from which it is disjoined.

—SUBJECT; UTTERANCE; ACTANT; VALUE

OBJECTIVE
(objectif)

1. **Objective values*** are occasionally opposed to subjective* values insofar as the former are considered "accidental" properties attributable by predication* to the subject,* whereas the latter are "essential" to the subject. Such a distinction, one that is inherited from scholastic philosophy, corresponds in certain natural languages to two types of predication: in English the verb "to have" is used in the first instance and the copula "to be" in the second.

2. **Objective discourse** is produced by a maximum exploitation of "disengagement"* procedures. Those of actantial disengagement consist of the effacement of all marks of the enunciator* subject in the utterance* (as is obtained, for example, with the use of apparent subjects of the type "it is obvious" and of abstract concepts in the position of sentence subjects). There are also procedures of temporal disengagement, which enable predication to operate in a temporal present. This kind of discourse generally has a pronounced taxonomic* character.

3. In a certain type of analysis, the goal of which is the description of the utterance alone, by **objectivization** of text is understood the elimination* of the grammatical categories* (person, time, space) which refer to the domain of enunciation.* The elimination of these categories marks the indirect presence of the enunciator within the utterance.

OBSERVER
(observateur)

1. The **observer** is the cognitive* subject which is delegated by the enunciator* and installed by it, through the process of disengagement, within the utterance-discourse. There the observer is to exercise the receptive* doing and, should the occasion arise, the interpretative* doing, which is transitive* in nature (that is to say, bearing upon the actants* and the narrative programs* other than itself or its own program).

2. The modes of the observer's presence in the discourse vary:

(a) It may remain implicit* and is then recognizable only through a semantic analysis which discloses its presence within a discoursive configuration.* Thus, for example, event* is defined as an action* envisaged from the point of view of the observer. Similarly, the aspectual* categories can be explained only by the presence of the observer which implicitly speaks out concerning the subject's doing* at the moment of that doing's conversion into process.*

(b) The observer will oftentimes enter into a syncretic relation with another actant of the communication (the narrator* or narratee) of the narration; the structure of provocation, for example, is most often considered from the point of view of the one manipulated (and the one manipulated at the same time exercises an interpretive doing upon the manipulator's program).

(c) The observer's cognitive doing may be recognized by the ob-

served subject; a new cognitive* space is thereby constituted, which is capable of transforming (deviating or cancelling) the original program of the observed subject. Master Hauchecorne, when he notices that he is being observed at the moment he picks up a piece of string (Maupassant's tale *The Piece of String*), establishes a new narrative program of cognitive simulation by "pretending" to search for and find money. A folk dance put on as a stage performance ceases to be a participative communication* with a collective actant and is transformed into a causing-to-see addressed to the public as observer.
—COGNITIVE; COMMUNICATION; THEATER, SEMIOTICS OF THE

OCCULTATION
(occultation)

1. In the field of narrative semiotics, **occultation** designates the expulsion outside of the text* of all marks of the presence of the subject S1's narrative program,* while the correlated program of S2 is amply manifested, or vice-versa. This operation belongs in part to the constraints imposed by the linear textualization* of the narrative structures, which impedes the setting up of two concomitant programs within the discourse. Occultation must be distinguished, however, from the more general phenomenon of putting into perspective. The latter does not exclude the partial manifestation of S2's correlated programs (S2 appearing as the opponent* or anti-subject of S1's programs). But occultation, by effacing any surface* manifestation, only permits the correlated program to be read insofar as it can be deduced as a contradictory* (or contrary*) of the mani-

fested program, that is, insofar as it is implicitly present at a deeper* structural level. One striking example of occultation is that of the *Two Friends* of Maupassant who remain silent in the face of the ostentatious unfolding of the Prussian officer's program.

2. Occultation, which makes it possible to read the implicit program as the contradictory of the explicit* correlated program, must not be confused with simple implication, which permits the non-explicit, prior programs to be reconstituted, due to the relation of logical presupposition* which links them to the manifested program.
—PERSPECTIVE; IMPLICIT

OCCURRENCE
(occurrence)

1. **Occurrence** is the manifestation* of a semiotic entity* within a syntagmatic* system, or the entity itself considered standing alone in a singular manifestation. This term is commonly used in statistical linguistics where it serves as a counting unit for the enumeration of a corpus,* whereas "words," which are classes of occurrences, are units utilized for counting up the vocabulary.* Yet it must further be noted that "words" thus defined are not words in the common sense; for the verbal forms "going," "goes," "went," for example, are so many "words" in the statistical sense.

2. A linguistic approach (and, more generally, a semiotic approach) which takes as its point of departure the occurrential character of the expression* plane considered in its materiality and which aims at constructing linguistic units* without help of a metalanguage,* here manifests its limits. The reduction* of occurrences into these classes of occur-

rences that "words" are requires that procedures of identification* or of recognition* of this most elementary* level of the analysis* be put into place. Two occurrences are never identical, because of the singularity of the pronounciation or the handwriting. By starting from the expression plane where the "words" are situated, it is impossible, despite what distributionalists think, to pass to the plane of signs* where the words are found (which are biplanar* signs). Thus the construction of the word "going," starting from the collection of its variant words, requires that the whole of the language's morphology be drawn upon.

3. The term occurrence is to be kept to designate, for example, an **occurrence-discourse** considered in the singularity and oneness of its manifestation, when it is a matter of distinguishing it from discourse as class or as mode of enunciation. —RECURRENCE

ONOMASIOLOGY
(onomasiologie)

By **onomasiology** is meant the procedure which in lexical semantics starts from the signified* ("concept" or "notion") in order to study the manifestations on the plane of signs.* It is generally opposed to semasiology.—SEMANTICS; SEMASIOLOGY

ONOMASTICS
(onomastique)

From the point of view of the internal organization of discourse,* one can consider **onomastics** with its anthroponyms,* its toponyms,* and its chrononyms* as one of the subcomponents of figurativization.

Since it is supposed to confer on the text* the desirable degree of reproduction of that which is real, the onomastic component permits a historical anchoring,* the effect of which is to form the simulacrum of an external referent* and to produce the meaning effect "reality." —FIGURATIVIZATION

OPENING
(ouverture)

Correlative with the concept of closing, **opening,** always understood relatively, characterizes any articulated semiotic system where the number of possibilities presented by the combinatory* arrangement greatly exceeds that of the combinations actually realized. Therefore it may be said that the schema* of a semantic universe* is open, whereas its use corresponds to its closing.—CLOSING

OPERATION
(opération)

1. In general, the name **operation** is given to the description* which fulfills the conditions of scientificness* (which L. Hjelmslev calls the empiricism* principle). An ordered series of operations is called a procedure.

2. More narrowly, at the level of fundamental syntax, by operation we understand the passage of a term* of the semantic category from one state to another (or from one position on the semiotic square* to another), accomplished through a transformation* (assertion or negation).

3. Operation is also opposed to manipulation,* when operation is understood as the logico-semantic transformation of the action of hu-

mans upon things, whereas manipulation corresponds to the action of humans upon other humans.
—PROCEDURE; SYNTAX, FUNDAMENTAL

OPERATIONAL
(opératoire or opérationnel)

The adjective **operational** is used with three different but not contradictory meanings.

(a) A concept* or a rule* is said to be operational when, although insufficiently defined and not yet integrated into the body of the concepts and/or into the set of rules, it nonetheless allows apparently effective performance of scientific doing. When applied to concepts, **operational** and **instrumental** are, in this sense, almost synonyms.

(b) At the level of an already formalised* theory, a rule is said to be operational when it is explicit,* well-defined, and can be applied by an automaton.*

(c) A theory*—semiotic* theory for example—in its entirety is considered as operational if it has anticipated the procedures of application.
—EFFICACITY; ADEQUATION

OPPONENT
(opposant)

When the role of negative auxiliant is taken up by an actor* different from the actor of the subject of doing,* it is called **opponent** and corresponds then, from the point of view of the subject of doing, to an individualized *not-being-able-to-do* which, under the form of an autonomous actor, thwarts the realization of the narrative program* in question.—AUXILIANT; HELPER

OPPOSITION
(opposition)

1. In a very general sense, the term **opposition** is an operational* concept which designates the existence of any relation* between two entities, sufficient to allow them to be considered together, even though it is not possible, at this stage, to say anything about the nature of this relation. The symbol *vs** (an abbreviation of the Latin "versus") or the oblique bar (/) are most often used to represent such a relation.

2. In a more precise sense, the term opposition is applied to the relation of the type "either . . . or" which is established on the paradigmatic* axis, between units of the same class which are mutually compatible. The paradigmatic axis is then called the **axis of oppositions** (or axis of selections,* by R. Jakobson) and is thus distinguished from the syntagmatic* axis, which is called the axis of contrasts (or axis of combinations* of the type "both . . . and").

3. In order to avoid any confusion, it is necessary to mention the terminology of L. Hjelmslev, who keeps the term relation for contrast and designates by the name correlation the relation of opposition: since the latter is only discriminating, the Danish linguist has proposed a typology of the specific relations which the paradigmatic units maintain among themselves.
—CONTRAST; CORRELATION

OPTIMIZATION
(optimisation)

1. **Optimization** is the application of the principle of simplicity* to syntagmatic* procedures. It can be displayed at different levels of anal-

ysis: it consists, for example, in the reduction of the number of operations* which a procedure of analysis requires (and because of this, it sometimes implies the choice of a particular model*); it is manifest also at the moment of the choice of the system of meta-semiotic representation* (tree* graph, bracketing,* etc.) considered as the most appropriate to the object of analysis, etc.

2. The expression **functional optimization** can be used to designate the application of the principle of simplicity to the temporal programming of a complex narrative program* as is done in operational research, in applied linguistics, in the semiotics of space,* etc.

3. **Aesthetic optimization** is sometimes spoken of in connection with discursive acts such as the reorganization of the chronological programming of the narrative* schema so as to have it conform to the linearity* of the text. In this sense, optimization is interpreted as the search for an agreement between the textual arrangements and the idiolectal* or sociolectal* structures to which the actor of the enunciation* belongs.

—PROGRAMMING, SPATIO-TEMPORAL; STRATEGY

ORDER
(ordre)

The epistemological concept of **order,** the most general meaning of which is that of a regular series of terms,* can be specified only after successive interdefinitions. It is of interest to semiotics in two of its meanings.

1. Order designates, on one hand, the regularity of the presence or appearance of a phenomenon (of an entity*) within a string of non-

defined phenomena. If it is recognized, this regularity becomes significant and can serve as a starting point for a logico-semantic interpretation of the recurrent phenomenon. Order appears thus as the explanatory principle of the syntactic and semantic organization of every discourse.

2. However, in order that regularity may be identified in the discursive string, the recurrent phenomenon must be manifested, in a certain way, as discontinuous,* and show an asymmetric and transitive relation to the terms of what surrounds it. So, for example, the apprehension of rhythm* presupposes not only the regularity of the appearance of the same phenomenon but also the presence of at least two distinct terms situated in a non-reversible "order" of succession in respect the one to the other. It is in this sense that one speaks of the **order of words** (in the sentence), meaning thereby that it is pertinent and significant (in "Peter hits Paul", order functions as a category of the expression,* allowing the subject to be distinguished from the object). Taken in this meaning, the concept of order is one of the fundamental postulates of distributional* analysis. The main criticism that one can make of it is the confusion that it maintains between logical orientation and the order of the signifier.*

—TRANSITIVITY; ORIENTATION; LINEARITY

ORIENTATION
(orientation)

1. An intuitive concept which is probably not defineable but is necessary in order to establish metalogics or semiotic* theory, **orientation** more or less covers the linguistic no-

tions of transitivity and of rection and partially corresponds to the notion of intentionality* in epistemology.

2. In order to delimit this concept more precisely, one can start from L. Hjelmslev's metaphoric expression: he saw "a logical movement" going from the governing term to the governed term. This "movement" can be defined by the asymmetrical and irreversible character of the relation* between two terms* (transitivity goes, for example, from the subject "toward" the object and not inversely). Such an interpretation determines the conditions necessary for the recognition* of the orientation, while the explanation which logic attempts to give thereof (by the psychological "intensity" of the first term or by the impact of its "trace" in the brain—B. Russell) remains hazier and is no better than Hjelmslev's metaphor.

3. An example will help us to clear up this notion somewhat. Two entities x and y, located on the axis of verticality, are defined by the topological relation which unites them (and which is a symmetrical relation), since the entities can exchange their position without modifying in the least the nature of their relation. However, if, while speaking of these two entities, one says that x is above y, the relation that can be recognized between the two terms is asymmetrical: the entity y has become the starting point of an **oriented relation** (oriented towards x), while the discoursive order goes from x to y. Consequently, it can be said that orientation constitutes a supplementary and restrictive investment which is added to the existing topological relation. It is in the same sense that the **non-oriented transformation** (which

is a correlation* between two units belonging to two systems* or to two different processes*) is distinguished from the **oriented transformation** (genetic or historical), which is irreversible.

—TRANSITIVITY;   ORDER; TRANSFORMATION

ORIGINALITY, SEMANTIC

(originalité sémantique)

1. The notion of **originality**—which does not appear, in the French cultural context, until the first half of the 18th century—is very difficult to encompass. The efforts of stylistics,* which has sought to define it as a gap* by comparison to the norm,* are not at all conclusive, for lack of a clear distinction between the levels* of language. Merleau-Ponty has suggested that style be considered as a "coherent deformation" (Malraux's phrase) of the semantic universe*: we should seek to recognize the gaps no longer as atomistic facts, considered by themselves alone, but as structural gaps. However illuminating this suggestion may be, it has not had any practical effects.

2. In the perspective thus opened up, a first step can be attempted by defining originality, at the level of deep* semantic structures, as the specific response that an individual or a society gives to fundamental questions such as can be formulated with the aid of the categories *life/death* and *nature/culture.* Thus we are led to distinguish an **idiolectal*** **originality,** which specifies an individual actor, and a **sociolectal*** **originality,** which relativizes and particularizes a culture.

3. Along with the two thematic axiologies* mentioned above—individual and collective—within which the structural gap which constitutes originality can be calculated, a third, figurative, axiology which articulates the four figures* of the "prime" elements of "nature" (water, fire, air, earth) must be taken into account and made homologous with the first two. Indeed, the use of these figurative elements by an individual or a society and their particularizing disposition on the semiotic square* (the term *death* is made homologous, for example, by Bernanos with *water* and by Maupassant with *earth*) doubtless constitutes an important criterion for the recognition of "coherent deformation." —UNIVERSE; GAP; IDIOLECT; SOCIOLECT; STRUCTURE

OVERLAPPING
(chevauchement)

By contrast with intercalation, which at the discoursive level designates the insertion of a narrative into a larger narrative, **overlapping** corresponds to the tangling of two narrative sequences: the first is prolonged (on the plane of invested contents, for example) into a part of the second, the syntactic articulation of which, for example, is no less manifest and is relatively autonomous.—EMBEDDING

PARADIGM
(paradigme)

1. A **paradigm** is a class* of elements that can occupy the same place in the syntagmatic* string, or, in other words, a set of elements each of which is substitutable for the other in the same context.* The elements identified in this way by the commutation* test maintain between themselves those relations of opposition* which the subsequent analysis can formulate in terms of distinctive features, the distinctive oppositions allowing them in turn to constitute sub-classes within a paradigm.

2. Traditionally, the term paradigm served to designate the schemas of flexion or of accentuation of words (declension, conjugation, etc.). This concept, enlarged and redefined, is now used for the establishment not only of grammatical classes but also of phonological and semantic classes.

PARADIGMATIC
(paradigmatique)

1. The terms of the dichotomy system*/process,* universal in character, are designated by Hjelmslev, when they are applied to semiotics, **paradigmatic** and syntagmatic.* This dichotomy is essentially and solely based on the type of relation which characterizes each of its axes. The functions between the entities situated on the **paradigmatic axis** are "correlations" (logical disjunctions of the type "either . . . or"), while those which are located on the syntagmatic axis are "relations" (logical conjunctions of the type "both . . . and"). Paradigmatics is thus defined as the semiotic system constituted by a set of paradigms* joined together by disjunctive relations. This gives to it, in a first approximation, the form of a hierarchy,* taxonomic* in character.

2. Paradigmatics can be considered as the reformulation of the Saussurian concept of natural language,* with this exception, however, that the Hjelmslevian system is not constituted by simple correlations between paradigms and terms of each paradigm, but of correlations between categories* (defined at the same time by their mode of syntagmatic behavior). While for Saussure, "making sentences by putting words together" belongs to speech,* the simultaneously paradigmatic and syntagmatic definition of category brings Hjelmslevian paradigmatics close to Chomskian competence* (which contains the rules of sentence formation).

3. Literary* semiotics places great emphasis on the **projection of the paradigmatic axis** upon the syn-

tagmatic axis, a procedure which, as R. Jakobson claims, characterizes the mode of existence of a large number of poetic* discourses. The fact is that the terms in paradigmatic disjunction can appear in conjunction (co-presence) on the syntagmatic axis (for example, an antiphrasis* can be manifested under the form antithesis*). The generalization and more rigorous formulation of this principle intuited by Jakobson has brought to light the role of paradigmatic projections in the organization of narrative discourses, particularly in the narrative* schema.
—PARADIGM

PARALEXEME
(paralexème)

The units of the content* plane, the syntagmatic* dimensions of which, on the expression* plane, are larger than those of the lexemes,* but which paradigmatically* are substitutable within a class of suitable lexemes ("color-bearer," "coffee-grinder") can be called para-lexemes. This term is in competition with that of lexia proposed by B. Pottier.—LEXIA

PARALINGUISTIC
(paralinguistique)

Entities* belonging to non-linguistic* semiotic systems are considered paralinguistic when they are produced concomitantly with the oral or graphic messages of natural languages.* Generally included under this label are, on the one hand, the phenomena of intonation,* gestuality,* bodily postures, etc., and, on the other, choice of fonts, page design, etc. The term paralinguistic (or even paralanguage) indicates a narrowly linguistic point of view which, while recognizing the existence of other semiotic

practices, considers them as secondary or subordinate.—SYNCRETISM; SEMIOTICS

PARAPHRASING
(paraphrase)

1. **Paraphrasing** is a metalinguistic* operation which consists in producing, within one and the same discourse, a discursive unit which is semantically equivalent to another unit previously produced. In this sense, a parasynonymy,* a discursive definition,* a sequence can be considered as paraphrasings of a lexeme,* an utterance,* or any other discursive segment. This operation is both an intralinguistic translation* and an expansion* (which belongs to the elasticity* of discourse).

2. Paraphrasing is seen as a "natural" (that is to say, non-scientific) activity of substitution* (which is one of the bases of logical and linguistic calculating), and, as such, it belongs to the paradigmatic* dimension of language. A set of paraphrasings constitutes, in a certain way, a paradigmatic class of "sentences." However, contrary to what occurs at the time of the constitution of morphological, syntactic, or syntagmatic classes*—where the criteria of substitutability chosen are either distribution* or previously recognized grammatical categories* —a class of paraphrases has a more or less intuitively postulated semantic equivalence as common denominator. In this perspective and with the objective of accounting for semantics with the aid of syntax, it can be seen how generative* grammar can envisage a **grammar of paraphrasings.** This would be a class of paraphrasings characterized by a single deep* structure, which would permit the generation of a set of corresponding paraphrasings as so

many surface* structures, resulting from the interplay of the different transformations.* In a strictly semantic perspective, an analogous result could be obtained by postulating a logico-semantic representation* common to all the paraphrasings.

3. It would be helpful to distinguish two kinds of paraphrasing: (a) **substitutive** (or denotative*) **paraphrasings,** which aim at direct equivalence with the paraphrased utterance; (b) **oblique** (partly connotative*) **paraphrasings,** the content of which disambiguates the prime utterance (by reference either to the context of the utterance or to the domain of the enunciation*).

4. In more general way, paraphrasing is to be conceived as one of the two modes of the production and recognition of signification, and, more precisely, as the paradigmatic mode, by contrast to the syntagmatic mode, which would consist in its apprehension as intentionality.* —ELASTICITY OF DISCOURSE; DEFINITION

PARASYNONYMY
(*parasynonymie*)

Parasynonymy (or quasi-synonymy) is the partial identity* of two or more lexemes* that is recognizable because of their substitutability only in certain contexts. Total synonymy can be postulated only at the level of sememes.*—SYNONYMY

PARATOPIC SPACE
(*paratopique*)

As a sub-component of topic* space, and contrasted with utopic* space, where the performances* are realized, **paratopic space** is that in which the preparatory or qualifying* tests take place, in which competen-

cies* in both the pragmatic* dimension and in the cognitive* dimension are acquired.—LOCALIZATION, SPATIO-TEMPORAL

PERFECTIVENESS
(*perfectivité*)

Perfectiveness is the aspectual seme* corresponding to the terminative* aspect of the process* and simultaneously actualizing* the presupposed (durative*) term. The opposition perfectiveness/imperfectiveness is entirely homologable to the dichotomy accomplished/unaccomplished.—ASPECTUALIZATION

PERFORMANCE
(*performance*)

1. In Chomskian theory, the concept of **performance** forms a counterpart to that of competence* in order to establish a dichotomy comparable to that of Saussure's language/speech. The term performance is supposed to cover the domain of realization* of the competence in its double task of production* and interpretation* of utterances. Like the Saussurian concept of speech* (negatively defined as everything which does not belong to natural language,* the sole object of linguistics), which gave free range to all sorts of interpretation and speculation, performance is quite equivocal and remains perplexing. Looked at from a strictly linguistic point of view, the study of performance presupposes the previous knowledge of competence (in this case, of the finished grammar of a natural language): one might as well say that this is only a project for the future. Considered as the production of utterances "in the real conditions of communication," *i.e.,* as the set of realizations as they occur, per-

formance resists being formulated in linguistic models. On the contrary, performance requires the introduction of factors and of parameters extra-linguistic in nature, psychological or sociological in character, (which thus destroys the unity of the linguistic object). Consequently it is understandable that the problematic field of the performance is more and more invaded by conceptualizations dealing with speech act* or enunciation,* both completely foreign to generative* grammar (which is a theory of the utterance only).

2. For semiotics, linguistic performance is first of all inscribed as a particular case in the general set of problems of comprehension and of formulation of human activities that it encounters, depicted in innumerable instances and in diverse forms in the discourse which it has to analyze. Thus envisaged, performance is identified, in a first approach, as the human act* which we interpret (in poor English) as a "causing-to-be" and to which we give the canonical formulation of a modal* structure, constituted by an utterance of doing* governing an utterance of state.* Performance appears, then, independently of every consideration of content (or of domain of application) as a transformation* producing a new "state of things." It is conditioned, however, i.e., over-modalized, on the one hand, by the type of competence with which the subject-performer is endowed and, on the other, by the modal grid of *having-to-be* (of necessity* or of impossibility*) which is called upon to filter the values destined to enter into the composition of these new "states of things" (cf. the concept of acceptability*).

3. Generally speaking, two kinds of performances are distin-

guished, in terms of the nature of the values* on which they bear (and which are inscribed in the utterances of state). First are those performances the goal of which is the acquisition of modal values (i.e., performances the object of which is the acquisition of competence,* of a knowing-how-to-do; for example, learning a foreign language). And second are those which are characterized by the acquisition or the production of descriptive* values (the making of vegetable soup, for example).

4. By further restricting the meaning, the term performance will be reserved to designate one of the two components of the subject's narrative* trajectory; the performance, understood as the acquisition and/or production of descriptive values, is opposed to (and presupposes) competence considered as a programmed series of modal acquisitions. In this case the restriction imposed is twofold. Performance will be spoken of only if (a) the subject's doing bears on descriptive values, and if (b) the subject of doing and the subject of state are inscribed syncretically* in a single actor.* It will then be noted that **narrative performance** is presented as a specific kind of narrative program. The syncretism of subjects, characteristic of the performance, is far from being a general phenomenon: the configuration of the gift,* for example, distinguishes between the sender as subject of doing and the receiver as subject of state.

5. Performance, considered as the narrative program of the competent subject, one that acts (by itself), can serve as a starting point for a semiotic theory of action*: it is known that every narrative program is capable of expansion under the form of instrumental narrative pro-

grams which presuppose each other in the framework of a base program. Interpreted, on the other hand, as a modal structure of doing, the performance—called **decision** when it is located in the cognitive* dimension, and **execution** in the pragmatic dimension*—allows us to envisage further theoretical developments.
—PSYCHO-SEMIOTICS; ACT; NARRATIVE TRAJECTORY; PROGRAM, NARRATIVE; SYNTAX, SURFACE NARRATIVE

PERFORMATIVE VERB
(performatif [verbe—])

1. In J. L. Austin's terminology, by contrast to constative verbs (which have, according to him, only the function of describing a situation, an action, etc.), **performative** verbs would be those which not only describe the action of the one who uses them, but also, and at the same time, which involve this action itself. So, the formulas "I recommend that you," "I swear that . . .," "I order you . . .," would realize the action that they express at the very moment of enunciation.* E. Benveniste has taken over and used this thesis.

2. Austin recognizes that this definition given to performative verbs applies just as well to non-performative expressions, for example, in the case of an order ("Do the dishes") or of a question. Here the imperative or interrogative form would constitute a speech act.* This is why, although continuing in the restricted framework of verbal communication* alone and of the conditions in which it is carried out, Austin has been led to broaden the field of this investigation by introducing the concepts of illocution* and perlocution.*

3. It will be nonetheless noted that the performative aspect—in whatever form that Austin thought

he recognized it—is not bound, in fact, to a particular linguistic form. It depends essentially on certain extra-linguistic conditions relating to the nature of the enunciative contract* and to the modal competence* of the subjects implied in the communication.
—STATEMENT; FUNCTION

PERIODIZATION
(périodisation)

1. **Periodization** is the segmentation* of duration, accomplished with the aid of extrinsic and arbitrary criteria. The segmentation into "reigns" or "centuries" thus constitutes linear temporalities, by contrast with cyclical temporalities such as, for example, "months" or "days."

2. Periodization also designates the conversion,* at the moment of temporal programming,* of doings* into durative* processes* and their linear arrangement in terms of basic narrative programs.* The performance of a complete program (the construction of an automobile, for example) requires the attribution of a period, calculated in terms of the final result, to each instrumental narrative program.
—TEMPORALIZATION; PROGRAMMING, SPATIO-TEMPORAL

PERLOCUTION
(perlocution)

Opposed, in J. L. Austin's terminology, to locution* and illocution,* **perlocution** is directly connected neither to the particular content* of the utterance* nor to its linguistic form. Perlocution relates, rather, to a secondary effect, such as the effect of enthusiasm, conviction, or boredom, produced by a political campaign speech. The same is true for the effect produced when one asks someone either to embarrass him, or on the contrary, to help him. Contrary to illocution, where one produces an effect by saying something, perlocution produces an effect (on the interlocutor or interlocutee) by the very fact of speaking. For us the notion of perlocution belongs partly to cognitive* semiotics and partly to a semiotics of emotions. In certain aspects, it can be compared with pragmatics (in the American sense), insofar as perlocution is linked to the conditions of linguistic communication.—ACT; SPEECH

PERMISSIVENESS
(permissivité)

1. **Permissiveness** is the name of one of the terms of the deontic modal category,* the syntactic definition of which is the modal structure of *not-having-to-do*. It presupposes the existence of interdiction,* of which it is the contradictory* term.

2. When, within the modal competence* of the subject, there exists a compatibility between its *wanting-to-do* and the *not-having-not-to-do* or the *not-having-to-do* suggested by the Sender,* the relational structure between the Sender and the subject-Receiver is designated **permissive contract*** (a somewhat incorrect name, for it also covers the facultative* modality) by contrast with the injunctive* contract. —DEONTIC MODALITIES

PERMUTATION
(permutation)

Permutation is a procedure* comparable to that of commutation, except that the relation noted between the changes which occur on the two planes of language does not concern changes between para-

digmatic terms but transpositions within syntagmas.*—COMMUTATION

PERSONIFICATION
(personnification)

Personification is a narrative procedure which consists in attributing to an object (a thing, abstract entity, or non-human being) properties which allow it to be considered as a subject. In other words, personification consists in endowing the object with a narrative* program within which it is able to perform a doing.* Personification seems to characterize a certain type of ethno-literary discourse (the fairy tale, for example, wherein one meets magical objects, helpful animals, etc.).—REIFICATION

PERSPECTIVE
(perspective)

1. Contrary to point of view, which requires the mediation of an observer,* **perspective** plays upon the relation enunciator*/enunciatee* and depends upon procedures of textualization.*

2. Based upon the polemical* structure of narrative discourse, **putting into perspective** consists, for the enunciator, in the choice which it is led to make in the syntagmatic organization of the narrative programs,* making allowance for the constraints of the linearization* of the narrative structures. So, for example, the narrative of a hold-up can emphasize either the narrative program of the robber or of the person robbed; likewise, the narrative as defined by Propp gives preference to the hero's* program at the expense of the villain's.*

3. Whereas occultation has the effect of totally eliminating the manifestation* of the subject's narrative

program to the benefit of that of the anti-subject (or vice-versa), perspective preserves the two opposed programs, while giving priority—as measured from the receptive domain of the enunciatee—to one of the programs which is then quite explicitly expressed, at the expense of the other, which is only manifested fragmentarily.

—POINT OF VIEW; FOCALIZATION; OCCULTATION

PERSUASIVE DOING
(persuasif [faire—])

1. One of the forms of cognitive* doing, **persuasive doing** is linked to the domain of enunciation* and consists in the convocation, by the enunciator,* of all sorts of modalities* seeking to make the enunciatee accept the proposed enunciative contract* and thus to make the communication* effective.

2. In this perspective, persuasive doing can be considered as an expansion of the modality called factitive; this expansion can produce more and more complex modal narrative programs.* Since factitiveness* can sometimes be directed at the being of the subject to be modalized, and at other times at its potential doing, it is under these two aspects that persuasive doing will be considered.

3. In the case of modalization of the subject's being, persuasive doing is interpreted as a cognitive doing which seeks to have the enunciatee grant the status of immanence* to the semiotic process (or to any one of its segments), a process which cannot be received by the enunciatee except as a manifestation.* Persuasive doing seeks to make the enunciatee infer the noumenal* from the phenomenal.*

From the schema of the manifestation (seeming/non-seeming) one can foresee, in a first attempt, four trajectories capable of leading to the schema of immanence (being/non-being). By starting from seeming, one can demonstrate either being or non-being; by starting from non-seeming, sometimes being and sometimes non-being. These are, quite evidently, trajectories of ontologization, aimed at transforming semiotics into "ontologics." Within these trajectories the more or less complex modal programs of persuasion, of varying complexity, are constructed.

4. In the second case, that of persuasion seeking to provoke the doing of others, persuasive doing inscribes its modal programs within the framework of the structures of manipulation.* The two types of persuasive doing nonetheless have one thing in common: manipulatory persuasion can establish its procedures and its simulacra only as manifestation structures, called upon to affect the enunciatee in its being, *i.e.,* in its immanence. (a) There are, first of all, discourses which are explicitly persuasive (discourses of conviction and of manipulation). (b) There are forms which proclaim another end (for example, the quest for or the communication of knowledge). Yet these discourses contain, inscribed more or less explicitly, narrative programs* of persuasion with models of believing* and of acting (scientific or didactic discourse). (c) Finally, there are forms of persuasive discourse which include, under the forms of uttered enunciations,* more or less autonomous persuasive sequences.

5. Discursive analysis should be able to succeed in distinguishing

different forms of persuasive discourse without too much difficulty.
—FACTITIVENESS; MANIPULATION; VERIDICTION; VERSIMILITUDE; RHETORIC

PERTINENCE
(pertinence)

1. The concept of **pertinence,** connected as it is to developments in phonology,* was made indispensable to linguistics by the Prague School. It first designates the property of a linguistic element (the phoneme*) which distinguishes it from other comparable elements and makes it suitable, by that very fact, to serve for communication (A. Martinet). This characteristic is then called a **distinctive** feature (=pheme*).

2. The recognition of the principle of pertinence introduces a difference in nature between the phonic substance* in which a language is realized and the phonic form,* which is linked to an apprehension of the difference* between two or more given realizations—whence comes the distinction between phonetics* and phonology. Henceforth freed from its attachments to substance, the concept of pertinence sees its range of application expand to cover the whole of semiotics.

3. In this general sense pertinence can be defined as a rule of scientific description* (or as a condition which a constructed semiotic object must satisfy) according to which, among the numerous determinations (or distinctive* features) possible for an object, only those determinations which are necessary and sufficient in order to exhaust its definition* must be taken into account. In this way, this object will not be confused with another of the same level, nor will it be overloaded with

determinations which, in order to be discriminatory, are only to be taken up again on a hierarchically inferior plane. The definition of pertinence that we thus propose is intimately connected, as can be seen, to the conception of levels* of language (Benveniste) as well as to the conception of semiotics* considered as a hierarchy* (Hjelmslev).

4. In a less rigorous, but didactically acceptable, sense, by pertinence will be understood the deontic rule adopted by the semiotician, of describing the chosen object only from a single point of view (R. Barthes), consequently retaining, with a view to the description, only the features that concern this point of view (which, for the semiotician, is that of signification). It is according to this principle that, in the first stage, for example, one will either extract* elements (beginning with the given corpus*) considered relevant for the analysis, or, on the contrary, eliminate* what is judged non-relevant.
—ISOTOPY

PHATIC
(activity, function)
(phatique [activité, fonction—])

To Malinowski belongs the credit for being the first to seek to delineate the notion of **phatic communion.** In his eyes the communication* of information, such as it takes place during verbal* exchanges between human beings, is secondary to the desire to establish and maintain intersubjective solidarity and, more generally, social cohesion. This solidarity and cohesion are the foundation for phatic communion, thanks to which one can "speak of nothing and everything." Following him, R. Jakobson attempted to present this aspect of communicability by formulating it as a particular function,* the **phatic function** of language. The phatic function is acceptable as long as it is considered as a general property of language; but it seems more debatable when it must be integrated into the structure of communication. Instead of speaking of the phatic function as one of the functions of communication, it would be better to say that it is the **phatic intention** which, on the contrary, lays the foundation for communication, and that the **phatic act** must be considered first of all as a somatic* act (comparable to the glance or to gestures of greeting or of welcome), and, as such, capable of being integrated into proxemics (in the broader sense of the term).—COMMUNICATION; PROXEMICS

PHEME
(phème)

1. B. Pottier has suggested the use of the term **pheme** to designate the distinctive* feature of the expression* plane, in contrast to the seme,* a feature of the content* plane. This new name is simpler and allows a useful distinction to be established between the units of the two planes* of language.

2. A pheme is nevertheless only the end term of the relation which constitutes a **phemic category.*** That is why it cannot be considered as a minimal unit* except on the plane (which is a constructed one) of the metalanguage,* and does not belong to any substance* (any "reality"). In other words, a phemic category is nothing other than a semantic category used with a view to the construction of the expression plane (or, more precisely, of its form).

3. This abstract character of the phemic categories allows R. Jakobson to postulate the existence of phonological universals* (as well as the hierarchic structure of these categories). Twelve binary phemic categories such as *compact/ diffuse, grave/acute,* etc., are sufficient to account for the articulation of the expression plane of every natural language. Jakobson's postulate, in spite of the multifold criticism to which it has been subjected (the categories are not necessarily binary; they could be redefined in a simpler way, etc.) remains valid in our view, if only as a working hypothesis,* for it permits a better understanding of the principles which seem to govern semiotic organizations.
—PHONOLOGY; PHONEME

PHENOMENAL
(phénoménal)

Inherited from the scholastic tradition (revived by Kant) the term **phenomenal**—opposed to noumenal*—can be used as a synonym for seeming* (vs. being*) in the framework of the veridictory* modalities. In this manner the **phenomenal plane** is assimilated to the plane of seeming.—SEEMING; MANIFESTATION

PHILOLOGY
(philologie)

1. Currently, by **philology** is understood the combination of procedures which have for their object the establishment of a text, *i.e.,* its dating, its deciphering, the establishment of its variants, its endowment with a referential apparatus aiding the reader and with a critical apparatus guaranteeing its authenticity. It concerns, then, a considerable and indispensable task which constitutes a preamble to an eventual analysis of the corpus.*

2. Historically, philology has played a particularly important role, having been constituted in the Renaissance as the first of the human sciences. Since the 19th century the term philology has served, together with grammar, to name what we consider today as historical and comparative* linguistics.

PHONEME
(phonème)

1. As a linguistic unit of the expression* plane, the **phoneme** is a minimal unit, due to the fact that it is indivisible (or non-segmentable) at the level of the syntagmatic manifestation* (that is to say, following the semiosis* by which the two planes of language are united). On the other hand, as a figure* of the expression plane, it can be analyzed into smaller units called phonological features or phemes.* Although in origin the phoneme is a unit constructed on the basis of considerations concerning the sound signifier* of natural languages, the procedures for its elaboration have a general value and can, if the need arises, be applied to other types of signifiers (graphic, for example) and to other semiotic systems.

2. Prague School linguists (N. Trubetzkoy, R. Jakobson) and others, such as A. Martinet, give the phoneme a paradigmatic* definition: the procedure of commutation* permits them to constitute the paradigm* as a class of phonemes ("bait," "pate," "fate," "weight," etc. constitute a paradigm of commutable consonants). The latter are further differentiated thanks to the partial oppositions recognized between them and which are interpreted as distinctive* features characterizing each particular phoneme (*b* and *p* in "bait" and "pate" are differentiated by the feature *voiced/non-voiced*).

3. The Copenhagen School (L. Hjelmslev, K. Togeby) proceeds somewhat differently. It begins with the unit of maximal expression, the syllable, in which it identifies these two types of units or categories* which are the vowels and consonants each of which constitutes a commutation class but which are not commutable among themselves (a vowel, for example, is not commutable, in the same environment, with a consonant). The phoneme is thus endowed with a definition that is both paradigmatic and syntagmatic.

4. Distributional* analysis reaches just about the same results by examining different distributions of phonemes: beginning with a given corpus, the environments of each occurrence have to be recognized and these diverse realizations have then to be organized into a finite number of sets. It is then noted that these different phonemes possess different distributions and that the same phoneme can belong to different sets, etc. This is a syntagmatic approach, that pays no attention to that with which the Prague School is concerned.

5. These diverse methodologies aim at the analysis of the expression plane considered in itself, and seek to give an account of it either under the form of a phonological system* and/or, eventually, of a syntagmatic phonological system (the syllable can be considered as an "utterance" of the expression plane). However, the problem is posed differently if the expression plane is envisaged solely from the point of view of the role that it plays during semiosis, where it provides the formants* which permit the constitution of signs* (and first of all of morphemes*).

Whence it is understood that generative* grammar, for which phonogy and semantics are only "servants" of syntax, is interested in the phonological component only insofar as it is able to provide it with the formants which permit the realization of the lexical morphemes engendered by the syntactic component. Everything happens, then, as if the generative theory could do without the concept of the phoneme, by proposing that the formants be represented as matrices of distinctive features where each phoneme "location" is characterized by the presence or absence of the pertinent phonological features. The concept of phoneme is therein hidden, but not excluded.

—PHONOLOGY

PHONETICS
(phonétique)

1. **Phonetics** is the linguistic* discipline dedicated to the study of the expression* plane of natural languages.* As the analysis of the expression substance,* it is contrasted to phonology (which studies the expression form*). Sustained by a very rich past, it has been able to develop its methodology in the framework of historical and comparative* linguistics. Present-day phonetics has been completely renewed thanks in particular to technical progress which has provided it with improved and varied experimental tools. The triumphant ascension of syntactic research, such as was seen in the 1960's, produced the (completely false) impression that phonetics was "traditional" and worn out. On the contrary, it is a field of living research, insufficiently known by semioticians.

2. According to the different domains* where phonetic events are apprehended, a distinction is made between: (a) **articulatory** or physiological **phonetics,** which is interested in the modes of production of sounds in language, considered as processes of articulation*; (b) **acoustic phonetics,** which seeks to produce definitions of the articulations of sound in terms of physical acoustics; and (c) **auditive phonetics,** which apprehends the same phenomena, but at the level of perception.

Barely begun, the homologation of these processes and of their definitions poses fundamental problems regarding semiotic theory and risks calling into question certain of its postulates.

3. According to the nature of the phonetic units studied, **segmental** (or phonematic) **phonetics,** working with units corresponding to the dimensions of the phonemes,* can be contrasted with **suprasegmental** (or prosodic) **phonetics,** which handles the sound matter of larger syntagmatic units.

—PHONOLOGY; PROSODY

PHONOLOGY
(phonologie)

1. **Phonology** is the linguistic discipline which has as its object the analysis of the expression* plane of natural languages. As the study of the expression form,* it is to be contrasted with phonetics, which is interested in the expression substance.* As a simultaneously theoretical and practical elaboration of Saussurianism, phonology can be considered as one of the most significant enterprises accomplished in the framework of European structuralism.* It has served as a model for structural-type semantics* but also for the rigorous formulation of

certain dimensions of social anthropology (*cf.* the elementary structures of kinship studied by C. Lévi-Strauss). The effectiveness of the phonological model has not yet been exhausted, and it continues to play its role in the elaboration of particular semiotic systems.

2. Phonology works principally with two types of expression units: phonemes, which are syntagmatic classes obtained by paradigmatic commutation,* and phemic categories, that is, semantic categories,* few in number, which establish and specify the relations of opposition between member phonemes of each paradigm. Phonemes are presented then as the end terms of the phemic categories or, better, as intersection points of the various relations which constitute these categories. It can be seen that the **phonological system** (at the phemic and phonemic levels) is indeed an articulation of the expression-form, and that at no moment is it to be defined by the substance of sound itself, the object of phonetics. That is to say that the phonological model is entirely independent of its manifestation in a given language or a given semiotic system.

3. Phonology is divided into phonematics (or segmental phonology) and prosody (the study of supra-segmental phonemes).
—PHONETICS; PHEME; PROSODY; PHONEME

PIVOT POINT, NARRATIVE
(*pivot narratif*)

1. In the syntagmatic* organization of a narrative* or a sequence,* by **narrative pivot point** can be designated that which occupies a central place among the various successive narrative programs due to the fact that it involves others by way of consequence. Thus, for example, the acquisition of a knowing* bearing upon an antecedent pragmatic* program can set in motion, by the cognitive* competence* which it establishes, a new narrative program (which is produced on the pragmatic or cognitive* dimension). Likewise, in the framework of the tests,* the polemical confrontation* can be considered as a narrative pivot point, insofar as it is may bring about the domination* of one of the protagonists (the domination leads in turn to the attribution of the object* of value).

2. In any case, the narrative pivot point can be revealed as such only by reading backwards, which restores the axis of presuppositions* by first considering the axis of consecutions established by temporal programming.* The concept of narrative pivot point, as is clear, seeks to elucidate on a logical basis a hierarchy* of narrative programs through the analysis of a (segment of a) given narrative.

PLANAR SEMIOTICS
(*planaire* [*sémiotique*—])

Within the framework of the conceptual reorganization which general semiotics* is presently carrying out, we are beginning to distinguish within visual semiotics a **planar semiotics** which is characterized by its use of a two-dimensional signifier* (as distinguished from the semiotics of space,* for example, which uses a three-dimensional signifier). Planar semiotics deals with photography, advertising signs, paintings, comic strips, architectural plans, calligraphic writing, etc. Certain semiologies are based essentially on analogy* and on the iconicity* of the image.* They give, in the final analysis, only a linguistic transcription of the image. There is now an attempt to distinguish, at least for a time, planar semiotics from these, by establishing specific visual categories* at the level of the expression* plane before considering their relation to the content* form. In this perspective the analysis of the still image, for example, is reduced neither to a problem of naming (a verbal translation of the objects "represented" which often has recourse to the dichotomy *denotation/connotation*) nor to a simple apprehension of possible trajectories linked to the prospective dimension (attempts to establish a "visual syntax" conforming to the trajectory of the observer's glance are far from convincing). The interest of such an approach is that it brings to light the general constraints that the nature of such an expression plane imposes on the manifestation of the signification. Its interest also lies in that it disengages the minimal semiotic forms (relations, units) common to different visual areas (partially listed above) previous to the ready-made postulates (bearing on iconicity or upon the nature of visual signs, for example) that aesthetic theories or the tradition of each of the "genres" in question are always ready to bring forward.—ICONICITY; IMAGE

PLANE
(*plan*)

A spatial, figurative* term, **plane** (since F. de Saussure and L. Hjelmslev) serves to designate separately the two terms of the dichotomy *signifier/signified* or *expression/content* which the semiotic function* connects. The recognition of the planes of language is one of the postulates for a definition of semiotics*

(for Hjelmslev, only bi-planar* semiotic systems are "true" semiotic systems).—PLANAR SEMIOTICS

PLURI-ISOTOPY
(*pluri-isotopie*)

By **pluri-isitopy** is meant the superposition of different isotopies in the same discourse. Introduced by isotopic connectors,* it is linked to the phenomenon of polysememy*: a pluri-sememic figure which virtually poses several figurative* trajectories can give rise to different and simultaneous readings,* on the condition, however, that the figurative units, at the level of the manifestation, be not contradictory.*—ISOTOPY; READING; SEMANTICS, DISCOURSIVE

PLURI-PLANAR SEMIOTIC SYSTEM
(*pluriplane [sémiotique—]*)

By **pluri-planar semiotic system** L. Hjelmslev understands a biplanar semiotic system at least one of the planes* of which is a semiotics (called semiotic-object). Such is the case with connotative* semiotic systems (which are not scientific) and meta-semiotic systems (of scientific character).—SEMIOTICS

POETICS
(*poétique*)

1. In its common usage, **poetics** designates either the study of poetry or, by integrating it with prose, the "general theory of literary works." This last meaning, which goes back to Aristotle, has been recently revived by the theoreticians of "literary science" (*Literaturwissenschaft*) who seek to broaden the scope of this study, for a long time treated within the Greco-Roman tradition as a sort of "ethno-theory." Such theoreti-

cians also seek to make clear at the same time the specificity of this form of linguistic activity. Thus R. Jakobson,—with Russian formalism* of which he is the heir and representative—serves as mediator between literature and linguistics by distinguishing, among the principal functions* of language, the **poetic function** which he defines as "the emphasis . . . put on the message for its own sake." Such an integration of poetics into linguistics has given peace of mind to poetic research compromised by romanticism. The imprecision of this concept in turn has permitted some to reintroduce, under a rejuvenated name, aesthetic preoccupations which they do not dare—such is fashion—to present openly.

2. From the point of view of semiotics, literary texts are the manifestations, as occurrences,* of literary discourses* which, in turn, belong to a general typology of discourses. To state as initial postulate the literariness* or the **poeticity** of a particular class of discourses is to put the cart before the horse. There is a common stock of properties, articulations, and forms of organization of discourse which it is necessary to explore before attempting to recognize and determine the specificity of a particular type. Thus poetics, considered as an a-priori discipline certain of the characteristics of its object, cannot be placed within the framework of semiotic theory.

3. Such is not the case when it is a question of the **poetic phenomenon** in the strict sense, *i.e.,* of an autonomous semiotic area based on the recognition of parallel and correlative articulations which involve simultaneously the two planes of discourse—expression* and content.* This "double articulation" (in a non-Martinetist sense)—the loose

and distended form of which is recognizable thanks to the prosodic regularities of the versification, and which attains a degree of exacerbated condensation in so-called symbolist poetry (or in certain sacred texts)—is not sufficient, however, to define poetic discourse. The well-known intuition of Jakobson, according to which poetic discourse would correspond to the projection of the paradigmatic axis (of selection) upon the syntagmatic axis (of combination), has given a new impulse to poetic research ("The Cats" of Baudelaire by R. Jakobson and C. Lévi-Strauss is a milestone). The suspension, at the time of the reading, of the hypotactic* relations governing the discourse, to the benefit of the emphatically underlined taxonomic* relations, has allowed us to envisage possible definitions of units* and of poetic isotopies* situated on both language planes. At the same time other research has shown the existence of a poetic narrativity* and of transformations* articulating poetic discourse at its deepest* level. Thus the paradoxical status of poetic discourse is specified: syntactically, it is an abstract* discourse which, therefore, is comparable to discourses carried on in logic and in mathematics; semantically it is a figurative* discourse, and, as such, a guarantee of great communicative effectiveness. It is consequently not surprising that the meaning effect* which emanates from it, as in the case of sacred discourse, is that of truth.

—LITERARY SEMIOTICS; METAPHOR; UNIT, POETIC

POINT OF VIEW
(point de vue)

The phrase **point of view** generally designates a set of procedures utilized by the enunciator* in order to vary the light in which the narrative is seen, that is, in order to diversify the reading which the enunciatee will make of the narrative taken as a whole or of certain of its parts. This idea is intuitive and very complex. Successive theoretical efforts have attempted to isolate certain definable articulations, such as putting into perspective and focalization. A better knowledge of the cognitive* dimension of narrative discourse also has led us to anticipate the installation of a cognitive subject, called observer, within the discourse.—PERSPECTIVE; FOCALIZATION; OBSERVER

POLEMIC
(polémique)

1. At the level of the utterance,* the multiplication of concrete analyses of narrative discourses has highlighted the existence of a genuine **polemic** principle on which the narrative organization is based. Human activity, conceived in the form of confrontations,* in large measure characterizes the products of human imagination. Even in the case where narrativity* is not organized as a direct opposition of two contrary* (or contradictory*) narrative programs* setting forth together a subject* and an anti-subject, the figure of the opponent* (animate or inanimate) always appears as a metonymic manifestation of the anti-subject. It is in this sense that one can speak of the **polemical structure,** characteristic of a very large number of discourses, figurative as well as abstract.

2. At the level of the enunciation,* the structure of intersubjective communication,* which rests upon an implicit contract between the participants, discloses the existence of a virtual typology of "attitude," that is to say, of enunciative modal competencies* which goes from "benevolent" contractual structures (such as mutual agreement, obedience, etc.) to "constraining" polemical structures (in the case of provocation or of extortion, for example).

3. The recognition of this type of structures in semiotics permits a more precise articulation and formulation of the more general set of problems—proper to the whole of the social sciences—within which two almost irreconciliable conceptions of sociability are opposed: social life as (class) struggle and as competition, and society founded on exchange and social cohesion.
—CONSTRAINT; CONTRACT

POLYSEMEMY (or, traditionally, POLYSEMY)
(polysémémie; polysémie)

1. **Polysememy** corresponds to the presence of more than one sememe within a lexeme. Polysememic lexemes are thus opposed to monosememic* lexemes, which involve only a single sememe (and which characterize specialized lexicons—technical, scientific, etc.). Polysememy exists however—excepting the case of pluri-isotopy*—only in a virtual state ("in a dictionary"), for the manifestation of a lexeme of this kind, by writing it in the utterance,* disambiguates* it, by realizing only one of its sememes.

2. Lexicography traditionally opposes polysememy to homonymy, considering as homonyms morphemes* or words distinct in their signifieds* and identical in their signifiers.* According to the substance of the signifier, they are called homophones (Eng. "holy," "wholly") or homographs (Eng.

"light," luminescence, and "light," not heavy). In practice this distinction between a polysemic lexeme and two or more lexemes which are homonyms is difficult to maintain, since its justification most often belongs to the way they are used.* From a theoretical point of view, nonetheless, it can be considered that two or more lexemes are distinct but homonyms when their sememes do not possess (or no longer possess) any common nuclear* figure.

—SEMEME; LEXEME; HOMONYMY

POSITION
(position)

1. In linguistics, **position** designates the place that an element occupies in the syntagmatic* string and which confers certain additional properties on it. It can be that, once set up as a general procedure, the study of the positions of linguistic elements corresponds to that of the distributions,* which characterizes Bloomfield's school. In attempting to reconcile the paradigmatic and syntagmatic points of view (morphology and syntax), L. Hjelmslev introduced the notion of position into his definition of linguistic category.*

2. In poetic semiotics, **positional analysis,** advocated by J. Geninasca, has brought to light the possibility of a semantic study of texts based on the recogntion of positional articulations (rhyme,* rhythm*) of the signifier.*

3. Narrative semiotics defines the actantial* role by its modal investment together with its position in the subject's narrative* trajectory. Because of that, the characters, far from being unchangeable and defined once and for all, turn out to be

relative: the hero* or the villian* are such only in defined narrative positions.

—ORDER; SYNTAGMATICS

POSITIVE (term, deixis)
(positif [terme, deixis—])

The two terms* of the axis of contraries*, s1 and s2, are called respectively **positive** and negative even though these qualificatives do not involve a thymic* connotation, euphoric, or dysphoric. Likewise, the two deixes* to which they belong are designated, simply for discrimination's* sake, **positive deixis** and negative deixis. Furthermore, the subcontraries* which each belong to a different deixis will be called positive $(\overline{s2})$ and negative $(\overline{s1})$ according to the deixis to which they are attached (and not because they are contradictories,* according to their deixis of origin).—SQUARE, SEMIOTIC

POSSIBILITY
(possibilité)

Considered as a technical term, **possibility** designates the modal structure corresponding, from the point of view of its syntactic definition, to the modal predicate of *not-having-to-do* governing the utterance of state *not-being*. In the framework of the alethic modalities, on the semiotic square* it presupposes the existence of impossibility,* of which it is the negation. As a term in logic, possibility denotes also the modal structure of *being-able-to-be,* which makes it semiotically ambiguous.

—ALETHIC MODALITIES; HAVING-TO-DO

POSTERIORITY
(postériorité)

Posteriority is one of the two terms* of the logico-temporal category *anteriority/posteriority* which permits the construction of the framework of the temporal localization of narrative programs,* during temporalization of the discourse.— LOCALIZATION, SPATIO-TEMPORAL

PRACTICAL
(pratique)

In the reading of a mythical narrative, the term **practical** qualifies the surface* discoursive level, which is presented as a simple narration of actions concerning the actors which are installed there. This is in contrast to the deeper mythical* level underlying the former and which, once made explicit, appears as bearer of abstract* significations (which articulate the fundamental preoccupations of humans and of the culture within which they live). The term *figurative* is progressively being substituted for the term practical, which is open to confusion.
—COSMOLOGICAL DIMENSION; MYTHICAL DISCOURSE, LEVEL; FIGURE

PRACTICES, SEMIOTIC
(pratiques sémiotiques)

1. Proceeding from the definition of meaning* as oriented intentionality* and taking into account the fact that semiotic organizations are constituted within the two macro-semiotic systems (natural languages* and the natural world), we will call **semiotic practices** the semiotic processes that can be recognized within the natural world and that can be defined in a way comparable to discourses* (which are "verbal practices," that is, semiotic processes located within natural languages).

2. Semiotic practices (which can be qualified as social practices just as well) are manifested as signifying series of organized somatic behavior, the realizations of which go from simple social stereotypes up to the programmations that are algorithmic* in form (and that can permit, where it is called for, recourse to an automaton*). The modes of organization of these behaviors can be analyzed as (narrative) programs* the finality of which is recognizable, in extreme cases, only *a posteriori*. Subsequently, the methods and procedures of discoursive analysis are used, insofar as they are applicable. In this sense, certain descriptions of rituals and ceremonies are rather conclusive. The concept of semiotic practice covers, among other things, gestual* discourses and proxemic* strategies, still very little studied. The study of semiotic practices constitutes perhaps only the prolegomena to a semiotics of action.*
—WORLD, NATURAL; DISCOURSE

PRAGMATIC(S)
(pragmatique)

1. The study of narrative discourses has led us to distinguish, at a superficial level, the cognitive* dimension and the **pragmatic dimension,** the latter serving in a way as an internal referent* for the former. The pragmatic dimension, recognized in narratives, corresponds roughly to the descriptions which are made there of signifying somatic* behaviors, organized into programs and taken by the enunciatee* as "events" independently of their possible utilization at the level of knowing.* **Pragmatic objects** are recognizable as descriptive* values (such as objects which can be stored up or consumed) by contrast to modal* values. In this sense, prag-

matics would be homologated with the third function* of G. Dumézil. It is under this meaning that one will distinguish correlatively **pragmatic doing*** and cognitive doing, **pragmatic subject** and cognitive subject, **pragmatic performances** and **competences** and cognitive ones.

2. One sees the gap which separates our conception—which takes into account the set of human activities such as they are described in discourses, by interrelating them according to the dichotomy pragmatic/cognitive—from that which has developed in America, beginning in particular from the works of Ch. W. Morris. **Pragmatics,** in the American sense, essentially seeks to set out the conditions of (linguistic) communication* such as, for example, the way in which two interlocuteurs have an effect on each other. For us, this "pragmatics" of language which has reference to the characteristics of its utilization constitutes one of the aspects of the cognitive dimension; for it concerns in fact the cognitive competence* of the communicating subjects, such as it can be recognized (and its simulacrum reconstructed) within the utterance-discourse. Thus, persuasive* doing and interpretive* doing do not constitute "extra-linguistic" parameters, as a certain mechanical conception of communication would have it understood, but they enter totally into the process of communication—as it is envisaged by semiotics—where the addressor* and the addressee, for example, are not empty domains (such as sender* and receiver) but are competent subjects. It is self-evident that, in the very perspective of American "pragmatics," a semiotics of "genuine" communication (as a describable object) can be drawn up by extrapolating in particular the models

of cognitive semiotics, which have sprung from the analysis of narrative discourses.

—COGNITIVE; DISCOURSE; COMMUNICATION; DOING; KNOWING

PREDICATE
(*prédicat*)

1. The **predicate** is traditionally considered as one of the syntactic functions* constitutive of the utterance.* As a syntactic class,* the predicate more or less corresponds (without being identified therewith) to the verb (defined as a morphological class) or to the verbal syntagm (considered as a syntagmatic class). The nesting of these three types of linguistic units into each other constitutes one of the most difficult problems for every grammatical theory.

2. The definition of the predicate and the place which is accorded it in the economy of the utterance depends on the conception of the structure of the elementary utterance which a given linguistic theory axiomatically declares as true. The binary conception, the most tenacious, goes back to antiquity and in spite of the terminological variations (subject/predicate; theme/rheme; topic/comment, etc.) rests in the aggregate in a semantic opposition between "that of which one speaks" and "that which one says about it." As a result, for all grammars of the utterance (which do not take enunciation into account), **predication** appears as one of the essential elements of the speech act.

3. The *a priori* choice of the binary nature of the utterance is most often accompanied by another hypothesis, more or less implicit, bearing upon the oneness of the elementary utterance, *i.e.*, upon the convic-

tion that all utterances, whatever they may be, are reducible to a single elementary form. It is in this way that classical logic reduces the set of utterances to the sole attributive form ("Peter is sleeping"). More recent linguistic theories—distributionalism* (followed in this by generative* grammar) just as well as glossematics*—attempted to get rid of this problem either by constructing a syntax based on syntagmatic classes, or by desemanticization of the tie which links predicate to subject, that is, by maintaining the sole abstract relation of presupposition.*

4. Following L. Tesnière and H. Reichenbach, we conceive of the predicate as the relation constitutive of the utterance, *i.e.,* as a function the end terms of which are the actants*: by the same token we distinguish two types of elementary utterances (and two types of predicate-relations constitutive of these utterances); utterances of doing* and utterances of state.*
—CLASS; UTTERANCE

PRESCRIPTION
(prescription)

Prescription (the positive term of the deontic modal category*) includes, as its syntactic definition, the modal structure of *having-to-do*. With the contrary term, interdiction,* it constitutes the axis of injunction.* In deontic logic the term prescription is often replaced by obligation; but this involves semantic inconsistency: obligation, including interdiction as well as prescription, would be considered as the parasynonym of injunction.*—DEONTIC MODALITIES; HAVING-TO-DO

PRESENCE
(présence)

1. The concept of **presence** belongs to the theory of knowledge and carries by this fact strong metaphysical implications (presence "in" perception, or "disclosed" by perception, presence "in spirit," etc.). Its ontological definition is to be excluded from semiotic theory.

2. In a semiotic perspective presence ("being-there") is considered as a determination attributed to an entity* which transforms it into an object of knowing* of the cognitive subject. Such a meaning, essentially operational,* established in the theoretical framework of the transitive* relation between the knowing subject and the knowable object, is very extensive: all possible objects of knowing are present in this case; and presence is identified in part with the notion of semiotic existence.*

3. The categorial opposition *presence/absence* appears then as a possible way of distinguishing two modes of semiotic existence. Thus, the recognition of a paradigm, for example, implies—beside a term present (**in praesentia**) in the syntagmatic chain—an absent existence (**in absentia**) of the other constitutive terms of the paradigm. The "in absentia" existence, which characterizes the paradigmatic* axis, corresponds to a virtual* existence, whereas the "in praesentia" existence, syntagmatic in nature, is an actual* existence. In all this, it is evidently a question of modes of existence of units and of syntagmatic classes and not of those of a "real" word-occurrence, for example, which manifests, under the form of

a spelling, only the substance of its signifier.

—EXISTENCE, SEMIOTIC; PRE-SUPPOSITION

PRESUPPOSITION
(présupposition)

1. In common usage, the term **presupposition** is ambiguous, for it designates either the act of presupposing or a certain type of relation between terms, or one of the terms (the presupposed) to which the relation leads. Utilized moreover in logic and linguistics, this concept has recently given rise to wide and deep developments, which it is impossible to recount here. We limit ourselves to specifying only the contribution of this concept to a typology of fundamental relations.

2. Keeping the name presupposition solely for the relation,* we will specify that it designates the relation that the **presupposing** term* contracts with the **presupposed** term. By presupposed term is understood that term, the presence of which is the necessary condition for the presence of the presupposing term, while the presence of the presupposing term is not the necessary condition for the presence of the presupposed term. The now classic example given by L. Hjelmslev is that of the relation of presupposition recognized between (in Latin) *ab* (presupposing) and the ablative (presupposed); the presence of the ablative does not require that of *ab*.

3. This example can aid us in distinguishing presupposition from implication* (which is a relation of the type "if . . . then"). Latin *ab* implies the ablative; by this we understand that, as logically anterior, it is a condition for the presence of the ablative. Conversely, the ablative presupposes *ab*, for, as presupposed

term, it is logically anterior to *ab*, the presupposing term. It can therefore be said that the two types of relation are oriented,* but in opposite directions. It will be noted, on the other hand, that the relation of implication presupposes the relation of presupposition which is anterior to it; insofar as the ablative is the presupposed, and as such necessary, term the implication "if . . . then" can function fully. If such were not the case, implication would be aleatory.

4. Besides **simple presupposition**, which we have just evoked, **a double presupposition** (also called **reciprocal presupposition**) is recognized, in which the two terms are at once presupposing and presupposed. The absence of presupposition between two terms gives them back their autonomy.* The relation which they will contract between themselves will be then either that of combination,* on the syntagmatic axis, or that of opposition, on the paradigmatic axis.

5. In narrative semiotics, back-reading of the narrative* permits, for example, in conformity to the narrative* schema, the disclosure of a logical order of presupposition between the different tests.* The gloryifying* test presupposes the decisive test*, and the latter in its turn presupposes the qualifying* test. In other words, the logic of the narrative is oriented and runs "upstream" and not inversely as certain people might be tempted to believe. In this perspective and from the point of view of the production* of narrative discourse, the conversion* of the **axis of presupposition** into the axis of consecution, which characterizes temporal programmation,* is one of the components of the performance of the enunciator.*

—PRESENCE; SQUARE, SEMIOTIC

PROBABILITY
(probabilité)

As the name for the modal structure of *not-believing-not-to-be*, **probability** is one of the terms of the epistemic modal category, which is contrasted with improbability* as its contradictory term and uncertainty* as its sub-contrary term.—EPISTE-MIC MODALITIES

PROCEDURE
(procédure)

1. In the Hjelmslevian tradition, by **procedure** is understood an ordered series of operations* which seeks exhaustively to describe* a semiotic object according to the chosen level of pertinence.* Such a theoretically irreproachable definition is too general to be useful. Thus the term procedure is usually applied to series of limited and/or localized operations corresponding to a domain, to a segment, or to a given micro-universe,* that one is seeking to subject to description.

2. Two major types of procedures* will be distinguished: **analytical*** (or descending) **procedures** start from a semiotic object considered as a whole and aim at establishing relations between the parts and the whole; **synthetic** (or ascending) **procedures** generally start from elements considered as indivisible, recognizing that they are part of larger units.

3. In the American tradition an attempt is made to distinguish **description*** **procedures** from **discovery*** **procedures.** Two kinds of sets of problems, epistemological in nature, and often not distinguished, can be seen here. Description procedures belong to reflection on the construction of metalanguages* and of systems of representation* of scientific doing, while discovery proce-

dures pose problems relating to the value of theories* and the efficacity of methodologies.*

4. It is in this last perspective that Chomskian linguistics opposes to discovery procedures (considered as non-pertinent for founding and justifying grammatical theories) **evaluation procedures,** which can judge them according to the principle of simplicity.
—DESCRIPTION; DISCOVERY; METALANGUAGE; SIMPLICITY; REPRESENTATION

PROCESS
(procès)

1. In attempting to make the Saussurian dichotomy of natural language/speech more precise, L. Hjelmslev has interpreted it as a particular case of a more general approach by which the knowing subject comes to know the object by envisaging it either as a system* or as a **process.*** The **semiotic process,** which takes up only a part of the determinations of the very hazy concept of speech* designates, then, in Hjelmslev's terminology, the syntagmatic axis* of language, and is opposed to the semiotic system, which represents its paradigmatic axis.

2. In discoursive semiotics, the term process serves to designate the result of the conversion* of the narrative function of doing,* a conversion which is effected thanks to the complementary investments of the temporal and, mainly, aspectual categories. Such a process can then be lexicalized either under a condensed form (a simple verb, for example), or an expanded form (expansion*) (sentence, paragraph, chapter, etc.).
—SYNTAGMATICS; ASPECTU-ALIZATION; TEMPORALIZA-TION

PRODUCTION
(production)

1. In the framework of human activities, **production**—understood as the operation* by which humans transform nature or things—can be opposed to communication,* which deals with intersubjective relations and which, by this fact, is dependent on manipulation* (as it implies a causing-to-believe and a causing-to-do).

2. In semiotics, production is semiotic activity, considered as a whole, and which, situated in the domain of the enunciation,* results in the formation of the utterance* (sentence or discourse). Usage has a tendency to confuse the terms production and generation (or engendering). According to generative* grammar, generation is dependent upon the competence* of the speaking subject (who is both, and indistinctly, sender* and receiver*), whereas production, characteristic of the performance,* belongs only to the enunciation.*

3. Often **grammars of production** are contrasted with grammars of recognition: while the latter are situated ideally in the enunciatee's place and carry on the analysis of a corpus* of utterances, the former adopt the enunciator's point of view and proceed by synthesis,* seeking to construct grammatical sentences beginning from the elements.

—OPERATION; COMMUNICATION; GENERATION; ENUNCIATION; ACT, SPEECH; RECOGNITION

PROGRAM, NARRATIVE
(programme narratif)

1. The **narrative program** (abbreviated NP) is an elementary syntagm* of the surface narrative syntax,* composed of an utterance of doing* governing an utterance of state.* It can be represented* under the following forms:

$$NP = F [S1 \rightarrow (S2 \cap Ov)]$$
$$NP = F [S1 \rightarrow (S2 \cup Ov)]$$

where:
F	=	function
S1	=	subject of doing
S2	=	subject of state
O	=	object (which can undergo a semantic investment in the form of v : value)
[]	=	utterance of doing
()	=	utterance of state
$\rightarrow$	=	function of doing (resulting from the conversion* of the transformation*)
$\cap \cup$	=	junction (conjunction or disjunction) indicating the final state, the consequences of the doing.

Note: for purposes of clarity the function "doing" is represented pleonastically by the two symbols: F and →. The narrative program is to be interpreted as a change of state effected by any subject (S1) affecting any subject (S2). On the basis of the utterance of state of the NP, considered as a consequence, figures* such as text,* gift,* etc., can be reconstituted on the discursive level.

2. A typology of NPs could be established by taking successively into consideration the following criteria: (a) the nature of the junction: conjunction or disjunction (corresponding to the acquisition* or the deprivation* of values); (b) that of the invested value: modal or descriptive* values (and, within the latter, pragmatic* or cognitive* values); and (c) the nature of the subjects present together: these are either distinct (taken in charge, in this case, by two autonomous actors*), or present by syncretism* in a single actor:

in this latter case the NP is then called performance.*

3. The narrative program will sometimes be made complex for the purpose of emphasis,* *i.e.,* in order to produce the meaning effect "difficulty," "urgency" of the task. Two procedures of emphasis are relatively frequent, especially in ethnoliterature: duplication (when the NP is repeated, the failure of the first being followed by the success of the second), noted symbolically NP (x2), and triplication* (where three successive NPs are differentiated only by the increasing "difficulty" of the task), indicated by NP (x3).

4. A simple narrative program will be transformed into a complex NP when it requires the preliminary realization of another NP; for example, the case of a monkey which in order to get the banana must first fetch a stick. The general NP is then called **base NP** while the presupposed* and necessary NPs are called **instrumental NPs.** The latter programs are indefinite in number, depending on the complexity of the task to be accomplished. They are noted as NP (iNP 1, 2 . . .); using parentheses,* as in 3 above, to note the optional character of the expansion.

5. The instrumental NP can be realized either by the subject itself or by another subject as delegated by the first. In this latter case the term **annex NP,** symbolized by NP (aNP) will be used. The annex NP will be recognized as belonging to a lower level of derivation. (The installation of the delegated* subject of doing —human being, animal, or automaton—poses the problem of its competence*.)

6. The actualized* form of the total NP, destined to be put into discourse that is, to begin with, temporalized, in view of its realization,* depends on the chosen base NP, that is, essentially on the final value aimed at. Thus it can be seen how a NP is transformed into operative programming by the establishment of a few procedures of complexification (which can be formulated as rules*). It will be noted that at the discourse level the NPs can be explicit* or remain implicit*: their explicitation is required by the surface narrative syntax.

7. Whether it concerns a simple NP or an ordered series of NPs including the instrumental NP and, if there are any, annex NPs, the syntagmatic set thus recognized corresponds to the *performance* of the subject,* on condition, however, that the subjects of doing and the subjects of state be syncretized in a given actor and that the subjects of the annex NPs be identical with the subject of the principal doing or, at least, delegated and governed by that subject. The NP called performance presupposes another, that of competence* (the subject of the "causing-to-be" must previously be modalized, for example as subject of *wanting-to-do* or of *having-to-do*). From this point of view, competence appears as an instrumental program, characterized nonetheless by the fact that the values aimed for by it are modal* in nature. Performance presupposing competence, a new syntactic unity develops, which results in their logical linking together and which is hierarchically superior to them. We call it **narrative trajectory.**

—SYNTAX, SURFACE NARRATIVE; NARRATIVE SCHEMA; NARRATIVE TRAJECTORY

PROGRAMMING, SPATIO-TEMPORAL

(programmation spatio-temporelle)

From the point of view of the production of discourse and in the framework of the overall generative* trajectory, **spatial and temporal programmings** appear as sub-components of the procedures of spatialization* and of temporalization* (themselves integrated into discoursivization*), thanks to which the conversion* of narrative structures into discoursive structures, among other things, is carried out.

(A) **Spatial Programming.**

1. In discoursive semiotics, by **spatial programming** is understood the procedure which, following the spatial localization* of narrative programs,* consists in organizing the process through which partial spaces are syntagmatically strung together.

2. In the semiotics of space,* spatial programming is carried out by putting the programmed components of the subjects (of their narrative programs) into correlation with the segmented spaces that they use (*cf.* kitchen + dining room; bedroom + bathroom). Such programming is called functional when it aims at optimizing* spatial organization in function of stereotyped narrative programs.

(B) **Temporal Programming.**

1. The principal characteristic of **temporal programming** is the conversion of the axis of presuppositions,* which represents the logical order of the stringing together of narrative programs, into the axis of consecutions, thus bringing about the temporal and pseudocausal spreading out of the actions as recounted. Thus, given a complex narrative program (abbreviated **NP**) (for example, the preparation of vegetable soup), the narrative order consists, starting from the base NP (attribution of soup to the guests), in going by a string of logical presuppositions, from one instrumental NP to another all the way back to the initial state (characterized by the non-existence of the soup and the project of preparing it). Temporal programming has the effect of "chronological" order which rearranges the instrumental NPs in temporal sequence.

2. Sometimes, temporal programming cannot be reduced to the sole arrangement of the diverse NPs on the temporal line according to the category *anteriority/posteriority.* It implies, further, a measuring of time in the form of duration (by thus introducing aspectualization,* which transforms the doings* into processes*). All the instrumental NPs are evaluated as durative* processes so as to be inscribed in the temporal program in such a way that the terminative* aspect of each process corresponds to the moment of the integration of each sub-program into the overall program. This is therefore a procedure of periodization* of the instrumental NPs in terms of the realization of the base NP.

3. Given that temporalization puts into play not only the relational category *anteriority/posteriority,* which connects the NPs situated on a single line, but also that of *concomitance,* which identifies temporally two parallel NPs, temporal programming makes allowance for the possibility of programming two or more NPs concomitantly. The procedure utilized then is that of temporal nesting,* which permits the inscription of a shorter duration or a punctuality* into a longer duration. An NP established in duration either leaves a "waiting" lapse, that is to say, a lapse of non-doing, which allows an NP to be carried out, or else permits the parallel installation of a delegated* subject (an assistant cook, for example) simultaneously executing the NP2.

4. Temporal programming thus having been put into effect offers a chronological representation of narrative organization. But chronology is not necessarily rational; it often involves stereotyped syntagmatic programs which are preserved unchanged notwithstanding the change of the base NP. In that case, it is possible to conceive of procedures of functional optimization* of temporal programmings such as are carried out in operational research, but also are carried out, although still imperfectly, in applied linguistics, procedures which make explicit the concept of simplicity* in syntagmatics.

5. Temporal programming, which results in the establishment of a chronology, must not be confused with textual programming (in the framework of textualization*), which the enunciator* carries out by obeying the constraints of and profiting from the liberties coming from the linear nature (temporal or spatial) of the text.* If the enunciator is constrained, for example, to program concomitances as successions, it has at its command, nonetheless, a margin of freedom to reorganize the chronology at will (by producing anachronizations, and by arranging things so that they dangle). Very tentatively one could perhaps speak here by analogy of an aesthetic (idiolectal or sociolectal) optimization.
—SPATIALIZATION; TEMPORALIZATION; LOCALIZATION, SPATIO-TEMPORAL

PROPOSITION
(proposition)

In logic, by **proposition** is meant an utterance that can be labeled true or false. Such a definition is restrictive, for it excludes interrogative sentences and imperatives and does not permit the use of the term clause as a synonym for utterance.—SENTENCE; UTTERANCE; CLAUSE

PROPRIOCEPTIVITY
(proprioceptivité)

A complex* or (neutral*) term of the classematic category* *exteroceptivity/interoceptivity*, **proprioceptivity** helps to classify the set of semic categories which denotes the semanticism* resulting from the perception which humans have of their own bodies. This term, which comes from psychology, is to be replaced by thymia, which bears psychophysiological connotations.— THYMIC CATEGORY; EXTEROCEPTIVITY

PROSODY
(prosodie)

1. A subcomponent of phonology and/or phonetics* (both are then called supra-segmentals), **prosody** is devoted to the study of the units of the expression* plane which go beyond the dimensions of the phonemes.* These supra-segmental units are generally called **prosodemes.** The inventory of prosodic categories* is far from completed (all sorts of phenomena such as accentuation, intonation,* noise, pauses, delivery, rhythm, etc., are included). This field of research, as yet insufficiently explored, could be one of the places for bringing together poetic and musical semiotics.

2. The status of prosodemes is not clear; but it is evident that the sole discriminatory* function, which characterizes phonemes, is not sufficient for them. Some among them appear as syntactic categories (intonation, for example, can be considered as a sentence constituant*),

morphosyntactic categories (the place of the accent, depending on the language examined, can have a function of demarcating syntagms), or morphologic categories (whether the accent falls on the first or the second syllable of the English "insult" determines it respectively as a noun or a verb).

3. Their properly semiotic status is an equally thorny problem, for prosodemes do not seem to be figures* in the Hjelmslevian meaning of the term, that is to say, units of the expresion* plane, but indeed rather semi-motivated biplanar signs.* Thus, for example, if one distinguishes in French intonation (on the expression plane) an opposition of the type *rising/falling,* this opposition is correlated with another, located on the content plane, that can be designated as *suspension/conclusion.* The prosodic categories are thus to be likened to gestural or pictorial categories, for example.
—PHONOLOGY

PROTO-ACTANT
(proto-actant)

Since structure* is the mode of elementary semiotic existence, every actant can be projected upon the semiotic square and can be expressed thus in at least four actantial positions (actant, antactant, negactant, negantactant). With respect to the actantial category* which is thus established, it will be called **proto-actant.** It will be said, for example, that the subject* or the sender* are proto-actants when they manifest in discourse certain of their actantial positions such as subject and anti-subject, sender and anti-sender.—ACTANT; SQUARE, SEMIOTIC

PROXEMICS
(proxémique)

1. **Proxemics** is a semiotic discipline—or rather a project for a discipline—which seeks to analyze the arrangements of subjects* and of objects* in space, and, more particularly, the use that the subjects make of space in order to produce signification. Thus defined, it appears as a problematic area of semiotic* theory which intersects in part with semiotics of space but also with natural* semiotics, theatrical* semiotics, discourse semiotics, etc.

2. The contours of this field still remain very uncertain. In a first approach, proxemics seems to be concerned with the spatial relations (proximity, distance, etc.) which the subjects maintain between themselves, and with the non-verbal significations which they draw from it. Sometimes when it is no longer a question of natural semiotic systems (that is to say, "real" behavior in the world) but of artificial or constructed semiotic systems (theater, liturgy, ritual, town-planning, etc.) and when one is led to foresee a domain of enunciation,* the arrangements of the objects become bearers of meaning as much as do those of the subjects.

3. Proxemics should not be limited merely to the description of spatial arrangements, formulated in terms of utterances of state.* It must also consider the movements* of subjects and the "displacements" of objects, which are not less meaningful, for they are spatio-temporal representations of the transformations* (betwen states). Such being the case, proxemics has overflowed the borders that it drew and sees itself obliged to integrate gestural

languages as well as spatial languages into its field of analysis.

4. Independently of the limits that proxemics will set up on its own, the procedures of **proxemization** must be integrated here and now into that component of discourse semiotics known as spatialization. —SPATIALIZATION; GESTUALITY

PSYCHO-SEMIOTICS
(psycho-sémiotique)

1. It is best to note, at the outset, that neither the term **psycho-semiotics** here proposed, nor the area that it might be supposed to cover, exist, and that they only are a pious wish on the part of semioticians. Only one particular semiotic system, linguistics, has been linked to psychology for some time; this is **psycho-linguistics,** which has been considered as an autonomous discipline since the 1950s.

2. This bringing together of two disciplines which were constituted independently, was aimed at producing a new autonomous scientific field. Yet this attempt is based on the illusion of interdisciplinarity. Indeed, if it be admitted that a science is defined by its methods of approaching problems and not by its object or area of application, one would have to be quite naive to claim that two separately constructed methodologies can be considered to be compatible and homologatable. Actually, it should even be said that two linguistic theories (and *a fortiori,* two psychological theories) cannot be viewed as compatible and homologatable, because they cannot be translated into a coherent and single formal* language. It is well known that a study undertaken by J. P. Boons, aimed at homologating a dozen reports by scholars from different disciplines of the human sciences and all bearing on one and the same village in Brittany, showed that the maximum convergence of the concerned disciplines was on a word common to them, the qualifier "important"; this is an infallible sign of a high degree of non-scientificness of these discourses. It is evident that an alliance between psychology and linguistics can only have as an effect the domination of one discipline over another, which gives rise to research focused either on the *psychology* of language, or on psychological *linguistics.*

3. In a first phase, psycholinguistics appeared as a rather successful alliance of behavior psychology (behaviorism) and American structuralism, which at least have asemanticism in common. The second period, which extends to the present moment, begins with the rise of generative* grammar, which has as a partner a much more classic and tolerant psychology (treating perception, memory, personality, etc.). Generative linguistics indeed had something to offer psychology: keeping the area of linguistic competence* (the description of which constructs the grammar of a language) for its own, it abandoned to psycholinguistics the area of performance* without the least regret. Psycholinguistics was then expected to define a double model of language production and of perception, a model which would account for the speaking subject's taking over the model of competence. Thus, just like F. de Saussure who, after having defined (natural) language* as linguistics' sole object, threw speech* as a sop to psychological and sociological appetites, N. Chomsky takes competence as his area of study, leaving performance to the most heterogeneous interpretations.

4. Two other psychological theories—Piaget's genetic psychology and Freudian psychoanalysis—do not seem to have been sufficiently exploited by psycho-linguistics. The importance—which seems excessive to us—attached to problems of "innateness" has left no room (or very little) for the methodologically fundamental confrontation of the two approaches: the genetic approach (which characterizes these two forms of psychology) and the generative approach (which is the approach of the dominant sort of linguistics).

5. As for the relations between psychology and semiotics, they seem to be characterized, on both sides, by epistemological and methodological certitudes which only admit the integration (partial or total) of the neighboring area in the other, without conceiving the possibility of a lasting collaboration. This is particularly clear in the case of psychoanalysis. Although Freud's *The Meaning of Dreams* is a remarkable example of semiotic analysis before the development of the term, and although Lacan's borrowings from linguistics (and from semiotics) are not slight, psychoanalysis considers itself as an all-encompassing field of knowledge, which can interpret and absorb the data and the methodological approaches that it encounters on its path. In this area it takes no back seat to semiotics, which, full of the "anti-psychologism" that it inherited from Saussure, is only too ready to be lavish with its "advice" and to offer its methodological services to any taker. The situation thus created is, in sum, perhaps healthier and clearer than that of a false interdisciplinarity. In this case the "psychology of language" and "psychological semiotics"

remain distinct, each one maintaining its own positions.

6. Semiotics is constantly led to encroach on the ground traditionally reserved for psychology. Thus, on the semantic plane, since semiotics has to define the semantic universe* as a given which exists prior to any analysis, it cannot dispense with distinguishing the individual* universe by opposing it to the collective* universe. And thus it cannot dispense with hypothetically foreseeing elementary axiological structures* (such as the categories *life/death* and *nature/culture*) which permit description to be undertaken. Such universes, considered as objects, can be taken on and interpreted by individual or collective subjects,* giving rise to particularizing interpretations that are the idiolectal* and sociolectal* universes. The individual and the social, the psychological, and the sociological are thereby organized into operational concepts, for the needs of semiotics.

7. On the syntactic plane, on the other hand, recent developments in actantial grammar—which clarify the dynamism of actantial* roles and the various modalizations* of subjects—have led semiotics to conceive of the "inner life" of the actor called "person" as a field of syntactic exercises where a rather high number of (syntactic) subjects coexist, confront each other, carry out trajectories, and participate in tactical and strategic manoeuvres. This way of envisaging things can be compared to the way psychoanalysis sees things (with its "egos," its "superegos," and its "ids").

8. There remains, lastly, a still unexplored semiotic area—which was only suggested by Hjelmslev—that of individual connotations,* that is, of a connotation system (giving

rise, probably, to connotative processes) which, in parallel with social connotations, underlies our discourses. Such a connotation system would constitute, a bit like the characterologies of the past, an immanent typology of ways of being, registers, voices, and timbres. Here is where a **psycho-semiotics,** taking on such semiotic systems with their syncretic* mode of manifestation, could find an open field for experimentation.

PUNCTUALITY
(ponctualité)

1. **Punctuality** is the aspectual seme* which is paradigmatically opposed to that of durativeness.* It characterizes process* by the absence* of duration. *Punctuality/durativeness* thus constitutes an aspectual category.*

2. From the syntagmatic point of view, punctuality can mark either the beginning of the process (it is then called inchoateness*) or its end (then it will be called terminativeness*). With durativeness it constitutes an aspectual configuration.* The absence of duration in a process neutralizes the opposition between inchoateness and terminativeness. —ASPECTUALIZATION; DURATIVENESS

PUNISHMENT
(punition)

Inscribed in the canonic narrative* schema, **punishment** is the negative form of retribution* (which, on the pragmatic* dimension, belongs to the contract,* explicit or implicit, passed between the Sender and the subject-Receiver) by contrast to its positive form, which is recompense.* Two modes of punishment—justice* and vengeance*—are distinguished, depending upon whether the negative pragmatic sanction is performed by a social or an individual Sender.— RETRIBUTION; SANCTION

PURPORT
(matière)

In order to designate the raw material on the basis of which a semiotic system, as an immanent form,* is manifested, L. Hjelmslev uses the terms **purport** (in French: matière) or meaning by applying them at the same time to the two "manifesteds" of the expression* plane and the content* plane. His concern not to engage in metaphysical debate is obvious here. Semioticians may therefore choose as they please between a "materialist" or an "idealist" semiotics.—MEANING; SUBSTANCE

ABCDEFGHIJKLMN
OP**Q**RSTUVWXYZ

QUALIFICATION
(qualification)

1. In a first stage of research, we proposed a distinction between two types of predicates*: **qualifications,** corresponding to states* and determinations of actants,* and functions,* understood as process.* This opposition was based upon the category* *static/dynamic.* In this perspective the analysis was carried out in two directions and permitted us to elucidate, in a parallel and complementary way, a **qualificative model** (taxonomic* type) and a functional model (narrative in character), which can be converted the one into the other.

2. However, the qualificative elements thus recognized were presented as utterances* having a single actant* each (contrary to functional statements,* which establish a relation between actants), thus contradicting the general postulate according to which no relation* can exist except between at least two terms.* A re-examination of the concept of elementary statement having become necessary, we can now assimilate qualificative utterances to utterances of state (specified by the junction* of subject* and object*), qualification being then considered as the value* invested in the actant-object.

3. In the framework of the narrative* schema, qualification is the consequence* of the qualifying* text and is seen to be the same as the acquisition of modal competence* (or, more precisely, of the actualizing* modalities* of knowing-how-to-do and/or being-able-to-do).
—FUNCTION; UTTERANCE; TEST

QUALIFYING TEST
(qualifiante [épreuve—])

A discoursive figure linked to the narrative schema, the **qualifying test**—situated on the pragmatic* dimension—corresponds to the actualizing modalities of *knowing-how-to-do* and/or of *being-able-to-do.* It is logically presupposed by the decisive* test. From the point of view of the surface narrative syntax,* the qualifying test can be considered as an instrumental narrative program* in comparison to the base narrative program, corresponding to the performance.*—TEST; COMPETENCE; NARRATIVE SCHEMA

QUEST
(quête)

The **quest** is the figurative* term which designates both the tension between the subject* and the object of value sought, and the displacement of the former toward the latter. It is a spatial representation of actualization (which corresponds to a relation of disjunction* between subject and object) under the form of "movement" and in a durative* mode. More particularly, it is a representation of the modality of wanting.* The terminative* aspect of the quest corresponds to realization* (or conjuction* between subject and object).—OBJECT; ACTUALIZATION

ABCDEFGHIJKLMN OPQ**R**STUVWXYZ

READER
(lecteur)

Reader designates the domain of message or discourse reception. While it is a convenient term, it is not general enough. It competes with listener* and lends itself to metaphorizations that can be misleading (for example, the "reader of a chart"). It would be better therefore to appeal to the notion of **enunciatee.**—ENUNCIATEE; READING

READING
(lecture)

1. As a first approximation, **reading** is understood to be the process of recognizing* graphemes (or letters) and their concatenation, which results in transforming a sheet of paper covered with figures into the expression* plane of a text.* By extension, the term reading is used in connection with other than graphic substances* of the expres-

sion: **tactile reading** is practiced by the blind who make use of books with raised print; **optical reading** designates the computer's deciphering of written characters, etc.

2. While asking ourselves whether reading understood in this manner—that is, as the reconstituting of the textual signifier* without recourse to its signified*—is possible, we must recognize that it is first and foremost a semiosis,* a primordial activity the effect of which is to correlate a content* with a given expression and to transform a chain* of the expression into a syntagmatic system of signs.* Right off it appears that such a performance* presupposes a competence* on the part of the reader which is comparable to, though not necessarily identical with, that of the one who produces the text.

3. Whereas at the moment of ordinary reading the receptive* and interpretive* doing of the enunciatee*-reader remains implicit, the

process of making it explicit in the form of procedures of analysis, established in view of reconstructing the meaning* (informed and mediated by the signifier), constitutes the task of textual (narrative and discoursive) semiotics. Within this perspective, by reading is understood a syntactic and semantic construction of the semiotic object, which accounts for the text as sign.

4. The question which is often posed with respect to reading is how to determine whether a given text is open to a single, a multiple, or a **plural reading** (R. Barthes). The question is often raised in literary* semiotics, since "practical" texts (such as cooking "recipes") or texts are proposed as monoisotopic (legal texts, for example), while they inevitably contain ambiguities* at the level of the utterances, most often offer as well means for remedying this problem by proposing the discourse-context as the place for their disambiguation.* We must also exclude from these considerations the variable psycho-physiological conditions of the readers (to which we sometimes refer by speaking, for example, of the "poetic sense" or the "musical sense" of such and such an individual). The enunciatee* is by definition an actant* which is conformed to the text and not an inexhaustible class of individual actors.* Having said that, we must admit that the same text may contain several reading isotopies.* But, to state that a plural reading of texts is possible, that is, that a given text offers an unlimited number of readings, seems to us to be a gratuitous hypothesis, all the more so in that it is unverifiable. The impression of the text's infinite "openness" is often produced by partial readings: this or that sequence of the discourse taken separately may in effect contain a large number of isotopies which, however, remain in suspension due to the incompatibility with the sequences which follow and which have as one of their functions the disambiguation of the poly-isotopic sequence by allowing only a restricted number of possible readings to exist for the whole text. To the constraints written within the text itself we can add others from the surrounding socio-cultural milieu: the textual competence of the reader is inscribed in and conditioned by the episteme* which presupposes a given semio-cultural state.

—ISOTOPY

REALIZATION
(réalisation)

From the point of view of the modes of existence,* semiotics has been led to substitute the ternary articulation *virtual/actual/realized* for the category *virtual/actual,* so as better to be able to account for narrative organization. Prior to their junction,* subjects and objects are in the virtual* position. With the junctive function*—and in the framework of utterances of state*—two types of relations are established: either there is a disjunction* between subjects and objects, and in this case it will be said that the latter are actualized; or else there is a conjunction,* and they are realized. Therefore by **realization** is understood the transformation* which, from a previous disjunction, establishes conjunction between the subject and the object. According as the subject of doing at the actorial level is different or not from the beneficiary, it will have either a transitive* realization (figurativized by attribution*) or a reflexive* realization (appropriation*). A **realized value** will be the value invested in the object at the moment (*i.e.*, in the syntactic position*) when the latter is in conjunction with the subject.—EXISTENCE, SEMIOTIC; ACTUALIZATION; VALUE; NARRATIVE SCHEMA

RECEIVER²
(récepteur)

1. In information* theory, the **receiver** (as opposed to the sender) designates the domain in the process of communication* where the message* is received. In this sense the receiver is not necessarily the one to which the message finally must be transmitted.

2. In semiotics, and for any type of communication (verbal or non-verbal), the term addressee* (taken from R. Jakobson) is used with a comparable meaning. In the particular case of verbal* communication, the receiver (to which can be linked the concepts of reader* and listener*) will be called enunciatee.*

3. Beyond a simple question of terminology, the difference between communication theory and the semiotic point of view resides, in the first case, in that the receiver represents an empty position (this is consistent with a mechanistic perspective), whereas, in the second case, the addressee corresponds to a subject endowed with competence* and apprehended at a given moment of its becoming, in a more "dynamic" perspective (this underlines the more "humanist" point of view adopted by semiotics). —SENDER/RECEIVER¹

RECEPTIVE DOING
(réceptif [faire—])

In the transmission of knowledge,* the informative **receptive doing** characterizes the activity of the receiver* (or the enunciatee*), in contrast to emissive* doing, which the sender* (or the enunciator*) performs. Receptive doing—which is either **active** or **passive** (*cf.* the oppositions of the kind "hearing"/"listening," "seeing"/"looking at")—is opposed from the modal* point of view to interpretive* doing, which puts into play the epistemic* and veridictory* modalities.—INFORMATIVE DOING; KNOWING (or KNOWLEDGE)

RECIPROCAL PRESUPPOSITION
(réciproque [présupposition—])

Presupposition is called **reciprocal** when the presence* of each of the two terms* is necessary for the other. In the terminology of L. Hjelmslev it is called solidarity.*— PRESUPPOSITION

RECOGNITION
(reconnaissance)

1. In the most general sense, **recognition** is a cognitive operation by which a subject establishes a relation of identity* between two elements, one of which is present* and the other absent* (elsewhere or past), an operation which involves identification procedures enabling the subject to discern identities and alterities.* An example of this is when identification is accomplished by memory.

2. J. Lyons distinguishes production* grammars (such as generative grammar) of a synthetic type (which proceeds from the grammar to the lexicon) from **recognition grammars** (or descriptive grammars), which, based on the analysis of a corpus of utterances, attempt to delineate the formal properties which the utterances manifest. These two types of approach, operating from surface to depth, or

vice-versa, are judged by him to be complementary.

3. Located on the cognitive* dimension of narrative discourses, recognition is a discursive figure* which has often been defined, since Aristotle, as an informative* utterance having to do with the transformation* of non-knowledge into knowledge.* However, if it is examined more closely, it can be seen that what was designated as ignorance in a given narrative is not really an absence of knowledge about events or things, but a knowledge which is not "correct" (a misunderstanding), a knowledge which consists, for example, in considering things which are only appearances* (such as a mirage) as existing (in the order of being*), and vice versa. The narrative pivot* point, cognitive in nature, which is called recognition is not the passage from ignorance to knowledge but the passage from a certain (erroneous) knowledge to another (true) knowledge. In the canonical narrative* schema, recognition—which occurs thanks to a mark* previously attributed to the hero—corresponds to the Sender's cognitive sanction.* It is an identification between the narrative program* executed by the hero-subject and the axiological* system of the Sender (which judges the conformity of the action of the subject-Receiver. From the point of view of the hero, this recognition corresponds to the glorifying* test.

—KNOWING (or KNOWLEDGE)

RECOMPENSE
(récompense)

In the canonic narrative* schema, **recompense** is the positive form of retribution (which, on the pragmatic* dimension, belongs to the contract*—implicit or explicit—passed between the Sender and the subject-Receiver) by contrast to the negative form, which is punishment.*—RETRIBUTION; SANCTION

RECURRENCE
(récurrence)

Recurrence is the repetition of occurrences (which can be identified one with another) within a syntagmatic process* which strikingly manifests the regularities used for the organization of the utterance-discourse. The recurrence of a certain number of semic categories, for example, establishes an isotopy.* The recurrence in the discourse of modal utterances which always, in given conditions, govern descriptive (or declarative) utterances, permits the construction of an autonomous modal discoursive level.* The term recurrence is to be distinguished both from redundance (which indirectly implies a lack of information*) and from recursivity (which specifies recurrence as it is carried out, within a hierarchy,* at different levels of derivation*).—OCCURRENCE; ORDER; REDUNDANCE; RECURSIVITY

RECURSIVITY
(récursivité)

Recursivity is a property of natural languages (and possibly of other semiotic systems) according to which a given syntagmatic unit* can be recognized as such within a single hierarchy* at different levels of derivation* (for example, "the color of the leaves of the trees of the yard of the neighbors"). According to generative* grammar, recursivity is theoretically infinite at the level of competence* but is limited—due to different degrees of acceptability*

—on the performance* plane. The concept of recursivity is still relatively unused in discoursive semiotics. It is, however, in its framework that an attempt could be made to interpret motifs, for example.—ELASTICITY OF DISCOURSE

REDUCTION
(réduction)

Reduction is one of the operations of semantic analysis which is part of the more general procedure of structuration. It consists in transforming an inventory of sememic occurrences,* parasynonymous* in nature, into a constructed class, which is endowed with an arbitrary* or semi-motivated name at the level of the language of description. Reduction can be effected only parallel to homologation, which governs the way in which each of the concerned occurrences belongs to the class being constructed. The construction of this class is done by categorizing it, that is, by seeking to recognize the contradictory and contrary terms, which would belong to one and the same structure, the description of which is sought.—STRUCTURING; HOMOLOGATION

REDUCTIONISM
(réductionisme)

1. In a strictly scientific perspective, the semiotic approach postulates the need to perform reductions in the manipulation of the materials studied, which allow the establishment of homogeneous levels* of analysis conforming to the principle of pertinence.* For this reason, a loss of semantic substance takes place, (which, however, can be taken care of when complementary analyses are carried out). Here the semiotician can be compared to the botanist, whom no one would criticize for bracketing out in his work the aesthetic or economic aspects of the flowers which he studies.

2. Thus the charge of **reductionism,** often addressed to semiotics on the pretext that it is incapable in its analyses of exhaustively accounting for the totality of the lived or of the real, is absolutely not pertinent on the scientific plane, for it ontologically presupposes a knowledge of what the "living" or the "real" is. Those who make such objections, moreover, are not ashamed to use for themselves other reductions just as inadmissable, as is the case for the reviewer of *Masques* by C. Lévi-Strauss, who ends his article with the declaration that "what Lévi-Strauss seeks is his mother."

3. Semiotics refuses to account for all the material under study and all its components, for it retains only what is pertinent to the object which it takes for its own. As for "totalizing perception," "plenitude," such concepts cannot belong to scientific research (analytic by nature), siding as they do with interpretive syntheses, the need for which—as we are well aware—is equally felt. —REDUCTION

REDUNDANCE
(redondance)

1. A term in information theory, **redundance** designates, for a given quantity of information, the difference between the minimal number of signs* (or encoding* and decoding* operations) necessary for its transmission and the generally higher number of signs (or operations) actually used. The signs that are superfluous because they are repeated are considered as **redundant.** Nonetheless, the redundance is justified because it facilitates the reception of messages* in spite of the interference of noise.

2. From the semiotic point of view, the iteration of given elements in the same discourse seems significant, for it manifests the regularities which serve its internal organization. Thus the more neutral term, recurrence, seems preferable to that of redundance.

—INFORMATION; NOISE; RECURRENCE

REFERENCE
(réfénce)

1. Commonly, **reference** designates the oriented, and in most instances undetermined, relation which exists (or is recognized) between any two entities.*

2. Traditionally, the term reference designates the relation oriented from a semiotic entity toward a non-semiotic entity (the referent) belonging, for instance, to the extra-linguistic context.* In this perspective, reference, which links a sign* of a natural language to its "referent" (an object of the "world") is termed arbitrary* in Saussurian theory, and motivated* (through resemblance, contiguity, etc.) in C. S. Peirce's view. If the world as perceived by common sense is defined as a natural* semiotic system, reference is then viewed as a correlation* among previously defined elements of two semiotic systems.

3. In linguistic semiotics, references are found both within the utterance* (namely through the process of anaphorization) and in the relation between utterance and enunciation* (for example, deictics do not point to fixed elements of the natural world: their meaning is related to the circumstances of the enunciation). When reference is established between different discourses, it is termed intertextuality.*

—REFERENT; WORLD, NATURAL

REFERENT
(référent)

1. Traditionally, the term **referent** is used for the objects of the "real" world which the works of the natural languages* designate. The term "object" being clearly inadequate, referent came to be understood as including qualities, actions, real events. Furthermore, as the concept of "real" world is itself too narrow, the referent must also involve the "imaginary" world. The one-to-one correspondance between the linguistic universe and the referential universe, which is thus metaphysically presupposed, is nevertheless incomplete. On the one hand, certain grammatical categories*—and especially logical relations—do not have valid referents. On the other hand, some deictics* (for example, personal pronouns) do not have a fixed referent: each time they point to different objects. This is to say that as long as positivistic presuppositions, held as self-evident, are the starting point, it is impossible to construct a satisfactory theory of the referent which could account for all the phenomena under consideration.

2. It is nevertheless in the above context that two attempts to integrate the referent in broader theories are to be located: (a) Ogden and Richards conceive the referent in terms of the Saussurian theory of the sign.* They propose a triangular model aimed at accounting for the structure of the sign: the symbol* (or signifier*) is linked to the referent not directly but through the intermediary of the **reference** (or signified*). In this interpretation, the reference, instead of being viewed as a relation,* is reified and is transformed into a concept—a hybrid entity, neither linguistic nor

referential—the expansion of which includes a class of referents; (b) R. Jacobson conceives the referent in terms of communication theory. For him the referent is specifically the aspect of context* in the structure of communication. It is necessary for making the message explicit and can be apprehended by the receiver.* It is either verbal* or capable of being verbalized (*i.e.*, it can be made explicit* by means of language). R. Jakobson thereby acknowledges the existence of a **referential function*** of language (following K. Bühler's concept of representation): the discourse-utterance, after being disengaged (expressed in the third person), is used for describing the world, *i.e.*, the referent.

3. Thus the linguistic context —either verbal* or capable of being verbalized—becomes the locus of the text's reference and the specific elements of this context are then called referents. In this sense the term referent is then synonymous with what is anaphorized.* At this point and in this way it appears that the question of the reference* needs to be addressed so as to describe the network of references both within the utterance* and also between the utterance and the domain of the enunciation.

4. In order to establish a compromise between the autonomy of language (proclaimed by F. de Saussure) and the self-evidence of the "real" world, which is emphasized by the positivists, it is sometimes proposed that the referent be defined as constituted by "'things' in so far as they are 'named,' or 'signified,' by words" (J. Lyons), *i.e.*, not things in and of themselves, but things named or capable of being named. Such a view is not without contradictions. If, indeed, the principle of the categorization* of the world by lan-

guage is accepted (*cf.* E. Benveniste and especially Sapir and Whorf), *i.e.*, if the view that natural languages structure the world and constitute it into distinct "objects" is recognized, how then can one call upon this world (which, in part, results from linguistic activity) in order to define the signs which make up these languages?

5. In our opinion, another solution seems possible. First, one needs to note that the extralinguistic world (the world according to "common sense") is given form by human beings and constituted by them as signification.* Such a world, far from being the referent (*i.e.*, the denotative* signified of natural languages) is itself, on the contrary, a bi-planar* language,* a natural semiotics* (or a semiotics of the physical world*). The problem of the referent is then reduced to the question of the correlation between two semiotic systems (for example, natural languages and natural semiotics; pictural semiotics and natural semiotics). This is a problem of inter-semioticity (*cf.* intertextuality*). Conceived thus as a natural semiotic system, the referent loses its need to exist as a linguistic concept.

6. In such a perspective, the question of the referent of literary discourse can be circumscribed. Literary discourse is often defined as lacking a referent or as having a fictive or imaginary referent: the term fiction is even used in order to designate this textual genre. On the one hand, the impossibility of defining the "real" discourse (*i.e.*, a discourse the signs of which would correspond to objects of the world), excludes the definition of the fictive discourse. These two types of discourse can only be characterized by veridiction,* which is an intrinsic property of the saying and of the said. On the

other hand, any discourse (literary discourse as well as legal or scientific discourse, among others) builds its own **internal referent** and establishes for itself a **referential discoursive level*** which provides a basis for its other discoursive levels.

7. When one wants to deal with discourse from a generative perspective, the problem which needs to be addressed is not that of a referent given *a priori*, but rather the problem of the **referentialization** of the utterance. And this implies the study of the procedures through which is constituted the **referential illusion** —the meaning effect "reality" or "truth," proposed by R. Barthes. Among these procedures, which have not yet been systematically studied, one can note, for example, spatio-temporal anchoring* (the use of toponyms* and/or of chrononyms* providing the illusion of "reality") or internal disengagement* (which referentializes the discoursive segment on the basis of which the disengagement is performed: *cf.* the passage from dialogue* to narrative* or conversely).
—LANGUAGE, NATURAL; ENGAGEMENT; VERIDICTION; WORLD, NATURAL; CONTEXT; ICONICITY; DISENGAGEMENT

REFLEXIVITY
(réflexivité)

In contrast to transitivity, **reflexivity** is a concept of discoursive semiotics, used to designate the syncretism* of several actantial* roles when the latter are invested in a single actor.*—TRANSITIVITY

REGISTER
(registre)

Out of a concern for clarity and in order to avoid additional confu-sion in the concept of level, the term **register** (which in the 18th c. corresponded to style* in the typology of discourses) will be reserved to name what socio-linguists generally call **language level,** that is, the realizations of a natural language* which vary depending upon social class. The question of registers is not directly linked to natural language as semiotic system. It refers rather to the problem of social connotations. —LEVEL; SOCIO-SEMIOTICS

REIFICATION
(réification)

Reification is a narrative procedure which consists in transforming a human subject into an object by inscribing it in the syntactic position of object* within the narrative program* of another subject. This program can be merely in a state of actualization* (*cf.* the problem of the "woman as sex object") or completely realized* (*cf.* the capture of the two friends in the Maupassant story of the same name). In the latter case reification deprives the subject (which has become an object) of its doing and transforms it from an agent into a patient in either the pragmatic* or cognitive* dimension or in the two together.—PERSONIFICATION

RELATION
(relation)

1. **Relation** can be conceived of as a cognitive activity which concomitantly establishes both the identity* and the alterity* of two or more entities* (or objects of knowing) or indeed as the result of this act. Such a meaning, however, is only an inter-definition which articulates semiotic universals among themselves, for the terms identity and alterity require for their own defini-

tion the presence of the non-definable concept of relation. This latter concept is no less fundamental for semiotic theory: it is the establishment (production* and/or recognition*) of relations and of relational networks which ground objects and semiotic universes. The organization and the construction of such objects or of such universes will then depend upon the typology* of relations that semiotic theory will choose and posit as a preliminary to its practice.

2. Thus, the two fundamental axes* of natural language—the paradigmatic* axis and the syntagmatic* axis—are defined by the type of relation which characterizes them: the "either . . . or" relation (called opposition* or correlation* by L. Hjelmslev, or selection* by R. Jakobson) for the paradigmatic axis; and the "both . . . and" relation (called combination* or relation in the strict sense by Hjelmslev, or contrast* by Martinet) for the syntagmatic axis.

3. Another typology of relations which constitute the semantic category* (considered as a minimal semiotic unit) is being superimposed on the preceding one: these are the relations of contrariety,* contradiction,* and complementarity,* which, when represented on the semiotic square, permit the foundation of a fundamental syntax* and a fundamental semantics.* These are presented on the two axes of language. Thus, for example, antiphrasis,* a paradigmatic figure articulated according to contradiction, appears as antithesis,* a syntagmatic figure of the same nature. These two terms, instead of excluding each other, are present together.
—STRUCTURE; SQUARE, SEMIOTIC; SYNTAX, FUNDAMENTAL

RENUNCIATION
(renonciation)

Located on the figurative* level, **renunciation** characterizes the position of the subject* of an utterance of state* when it deprives itself of the object of value. It corresponds therefore to the reflexive* disjunction* of the object of value, effected at any moment whatsoever of the narrative* trajectory. With dispossession,* renunciation is one of the two forms of privation which can be considered, by virtue of the consequence,* as sub-components of the test.*—ACTUALIZATION; DEPRIVATION

REPRESENTATION
(représentation)

1. **Representation** is a concept of classical philosophy which, when utilized in semiotics, suggests in a more or less explicit way that language* would have as a function being there in the place of something else; that is, a function of representing a different "reality." It is clear that this is the origin of the conception of natural language as denotation.* Words, then, are only signs, representations of things of the world.* The denotative or referential* function* of language is, in R. Jacobson's terminology, only the **function of representation** of K. Bühler in more modern dress.

2. Linguistic and, more generally, semiotic theories use the term representation with a more precise technical meaning. Thus by **semantic** or **logico-semantic representation** the construction of a description language for a semiotics as object is meant, a construction which consists, very approximately, in joining semantic investments* to concepts that are inter-defined and

monitored by the theory* (or in interpreting* the symbols* of a formal* language). The domain which must receive a logico-semantic representation—deep* structures or surface* structues, for example—depends on the way in which each theory conceives the total generative* trajectory.

3. It can be seen, however, that the same meta-linguistic* level can be represented in different ways (tree* graph, matrix*, parenthetization*, rewriting rules*, etc.) and that these diverse **systems of representation** can be homologated, translated the one into the other. It would be advisable, therefore, to maintain a distinction between the metalanguage and its different possible representations.
—REFERENT; METALANGUAGE

REPRESENTATIVITY
(représentativité)

When used as a criterion for the selection of a corpus, **representativity** enables the describer better to satisfy the principle of adequacy, without having to submit to the requirement of exhaustivity.* Representativity is obtained either by statistical sampling or by saturation of the model.*—CORPUS

RESEMANTIZATION
(resémantisation)

Contrary to desemantization, **resemantization** is the operation by which certain partial content* units, having previously been lost (often by being subsumed into a more comprehensive signified* of a broader unit of discourse), once again find their initial semantic value. Thus, in *Two Friends* (by Maupassant), the title "Mister," which in the beginning of the tale places the characters Sauvage and Morissot in their usual social status (the term is therefore desemanticized), is used at the end of the tale both by the Prussian officer (in order to underline—but unwillingly and unknowingly—their excellent human qualities) and by Sauvage and Morissot themselves (while speaking to each other) as a sign of mutual recognition of their own value.—DESEMANTIZATION

RESEMBLANCE
(ressemblance)

1. **Resemblance** is the intuitive* grasping of a certain affinity between two or more entities,* allowing an identity* relation to be recognized between or among these entities, under certain conditions and with the help of appropriate procedures. However, this relation (as well as the underlying identification operation) presupposes a pre-existant alterity* (which is but a formulation of their difference in terms of categories). The complex and simultaneous grasping of both resemblance and difference thus constitutes the epistemological condition permitting meaning to appear.

2. From an intuitive point of view, collecting and recording of resemblances and differences is the first step of any comparative* approach.
—DIFFERENCE; IDENTITY

RESTRICTION
(restriction)

Unlike generalization,* **restriction** consists in limiting the scope of a rule, a procedure, etc., by certain particular conditions of usage; this term can be compared with the somewhat broader term "constraint."—CONSTRAINT

RETRIBUTION
(rétribution)

Retribution is a figure* of discourse belonging to the pragmatic* dimension. It is a component of the contract structure that characterizes the narrative* schema, *i.e.*, the compensation given by the Sender to the subject-Receiver, once the latter has acomplished the performance* agreed upon (explicitly or implicitly) within the framework of the initial contract.* If the compensation is positive, we speak of recompense*; if it is negative, punishment.* In both cases, it is a matter of re-establishing narrative equilibrium.*
—SANCTION

REVALORIZATION
(révalorisation)

After realization* (*i.e.*, the conjunction* of subject* and object* within a given quest*), an object may at times acquire a new value* due to the modality of knowing,* for example, in the case of someone who is preparing to hold on at all costs to an object which someone else plans to take from him/her. **Revalorization,** brought about by cognitive* doing, is thus directly related to a new *wanting** and can generate a new narrative program.*

REWRITING SYSTEM
(réécriture [système de—])

In generative grammar,* the **rewriting system** is a mode of representation* of the process of derivation* and ends in a structural description* of the sentence which puts into effect the axioms and the rules for the construction of well-formed expressions.* Thus the rewriting rule "$\Sigma \rightarrow NP + VP$" is to be read as an operation of substitution* in which the symbol Σ is repalced by the series "$NP + VP$."—RULE

RHETORIC
(rhétorique)

Rhetoric, rooted in the Greco-Roman tradition (Aristotle, Quintilian), was consecrated by being integrated into the medieval trivium along with grammar and dialectics; it was officially included in school curricula up to the 19th century. It is presented as a sort of prescientific theory of discourse, marked by the cultural context within which it developed. The present-day renewed interest in rhetoric can be explained by the reappearance of concerted study of the discourse, brought on by semiotics. Even though, for reasons which are evident, certain theoretical fields of old-style rhetoric cannot be integrated as such into discoursive semiotics, they nonetheless correspond to areas of contemporary concern and merit an examination.

1. Taking into consideration the discourse as a whole, recognizing the "parts of speech" (or the discourse) and its syntagmatic organization ("dispositio"), correspond to our concern for segmentation* and definition of discoursive units* (larger than the sentence*). However, defined from its beginnings as an "art of speaking well," as an "art of persuading," rhetoric is concerned only with one class of discourse, persuasive* discourse. In addition, since it has assumed the task of setting out "rules of the art," it has a pronounced normative* character (*cf.* normative grammar, which is parallel with it).

2. A part of rhetoric, called "inventio," hitherto neglected, would warrant serious study. Looked down on as a collection of "commonplaces," "inventio" could be reexamined as a storehouse "in language" both of the principal discoursive themes* and of the most

general discoursive configurations,* that is, as a "topics," as a fundamental semantic taxonomy.

3. As for "elocutio," it is a sort of locus for a possible taxonomy of rhetorical figures,* the dimensions of which are no longer those of the discourse, but those of the sentence or of the word. This is the part that people are now trying to rejuvenate, first of all, by integrating it into discoursive and textual semiotics as a stylistic* component. Despite the interest of this undertaking, its dangers are evident. As a result of centuries-old accumulations, the inventory of the figures cannot claim to have the status of a coherent taxonomy. Only its complete reevaluation, founded on linguistics, will permit its integration into the theory of discourse. Such a reexamination has been undertaken very recently by the Liège Group, which, taking Hjelmslev's linguistic theory as its base, aims at constituting a new **general rhetoric.**
—FIGURE; DISCOURSE

RHYME
(rime)

In poetic semiotics, **rhyme** corresponds to the recurrence,* at regular intervals, of a segment of expression* (identical or simply comparable), a segment that is part of two formants* involving two distinct content* units (lexemes); for this reason, semantic difference is given prominence. Therefore, rhyme is not merely a particular articulation* of the expression* plane, but a phenomenon stemming from prosody and engaging both planes of language—it is a prosodeme that emphasizes the identity of the signifiers* only to underline better the difference between the signifieds.* By thus establishing the rhyme or-

ganization of poetic discourse (due to these "strong positions"), rhyme allows us to foresee the construction of a sort of positional syntax (*cf.* J. Geninasca).—PROSODY; POSITION

RHYTHM
(rythme)

Rhythm may be defined as an expectation* (C. Zilberberg, following P. Valéry), *i.e.,* as the temporalization* (aided by the aspect of inchoateness*) of the modality of *wanting-to-be* as applied to the recurrent interval between groups of asymmetrical elements, reproducing the same formation. Contrary to the usual meaning given this term (understood as a particular arrangement of the expression* plane), we prefer a definition of rhythm that considers it to be a signifying form, and therefore, as having the same character as the other phenomena of prosody.* Such a conception frees rhythm from its bonds with the auditory signifier* (this allows us to speak of rhythm in visual semiotics, for example) and even from its bonds with the signifier itself (rhythm may then be acknowledged on the content* level, for example).
—PROSODY

ROLE
(rôle)

1. The concept of **role** is all the more difficult to define as there are numerous meanings given to it, depending on its areas of use. We shall retain here, for the sake of comparison, only one point of view, that of psycho-sociology, which uses this term to designate an organized model of behavior, bound to a determined position in society, the manifestations of which are largely predictable. It is probably possible to

associate with this conception the "narrative roles" proposed by C. Bremond (even though the initial definition he gives is much broader).

2. In narrative and discoursive semiotics, the role is of a more formal nature and becomes a synonym of "function" (in the usual sense of the term); partially desemanticized, it is always used with a determinant. Thus, **actantial roles** constitute the paradigm of modal syntactic positions that the actants* may assume along the narrative trajectory.* In a parallel manner, **thematic roles** are the actantial formulation of themes or thematic trajectories.

—ACTANTIAL; THEMATIC

RULE
(règle)

1. A **rule** is the metalinguistic* expression of a deontic* modal structure (as a *causing-to-have-to-do*) which presupposes any sort of subject (or neutral subject) giving instructions to another subject (human or machine) in order that it carry out certain cognitive operations generally consisting in the passage from one state to another.

2. Take, for example, the case of taxonomic* doing which segments* a syntagmatic unit (such as the sentence) into its immediate constituants.* The results of this doing can receive a double representation at the metalinguistic level: (a) they can be considered as a state* resulting from an analysis* and can be represented as a structural description* of the taxonomic type ($\Sigma = NP + VP$); (b) but the metalanguage used can just as well aim at constructing the simulacrum of this taxonomic doing by representing it as a derivation* process. In this case, the representation will then take the form, for example, of a **rewriting** **rule** ($\Sigma \to NP + VP$). The operation of dichotomization with its symbol ($\to$) corresponds to the relation of inclusion, symbolized by ($=$).

The two modes of representation are thus comparable; they correspond to the two meanings of the word description which sometimes designates descriptive doing and sometimes its result.

3. The formulation of the rule implicitly underlies an actantial structure* of manipulation,* containing two subjects (joined together by a relation of the type "teacher"/ "student"). The epistemological problem is knowing what conditions of scientificness* must be satisfied in order that the two subjects of this modal structure may be set up as concepts, that is to say, installed as actants* simultaneously abstract and competent. The first subject—the scientific subject—is supposed to represent a certain knowing*-how-to-do; and it is there that the problem summarized by L. Hjelmslev under the name of the empiricism principle is met once more. The second subject must be any sort of subject (human or machine), which can perform correctly and reproduce endlessly the instructions received. Such is the case of the automaton.*

4. Taxonomic doing, which can be represented in the form of rules, is dominated by programmatic doing, which syntagmatically organizes the first into an ordered series of rules, called algorithms.*

—NORM

ABCDEFGHIJKLMN OPQR**S**TUVWXYZ

SANCTION

(sanction)

1. **Sanction** is a figure of discourse, correlative to manipulation,* which, when inserted into the narrative* schema, occupies a place in both the pragmatic* and cognitive* dimensions. Inasmuch as sanction is exercised by the final sender, sanction presupposes that this sender has an absolute competence.*

2. **Pragmatic sanction** is an epistemic judgment, passed by the judge-Sender, concerning the conformity of the behavior and, more precisely, of the narrative program* of the performing subject.* It is made with respect to the axiological* system (justice, "good manners," esthetics, etc.), implicit or explicit, such as it was actualized at least in the initial contract.* From the point of view of the subject-Receiver, pragmatic sanction corresponds to retribution.* As such, it is the result of another function in the structure of exchange: it is the counterpart called for by the performance* carried out by the subject conforming to its contractual obligations. This compensation may be positive (recompense*) or negative (punishment*); in the latter case, depending on whether the punishment is given by an individual or social sender, negative retribution is called vengeance* or justice.* These different types of retribution permit the reestablishment of narrative equilibrium.*

3. As a judgment concerning doing,* pragmatic sanction is opposed to **cognitive sanction,** which is an epistemic judgment of the being* of the subject and, more generally, of the utterances of state that it overdetermines thanks to veridictory* and epistemic modalities. (Here could be placed the concept of acceptability,* used in generative grammar and presented as an epistemic judgment, comparable to cognitive sanction.)

From the point of view of the subject-Receiver, cognitive sanction is equivalent to the recognition* of the hero* and, negatively, to the foiling of the villain. Recognition on the part of the Sender is the compensation resulting from the glorifying* test, taken on by the subject-Receiver.

4. By transposing sanction, viewed as a narrative* trajectory, to the level of social semiotic* practices, we can foresee the elaboration of a **semiotics of sanction** (correlated to a semiotics of manipulation and a semiotics of action*).

—NARRATIVE SCHEMA; NARRATIVE TRAJECTORY

SCHEMA
(schéma)

1. We use the term **schema** to designate the representation* of a semiotic object reduced to its essential properties.

2. L. Hjelmslev thus introduced the expression **linguistic schema** as a substitute for Saussure's natural language* (*langue*), by opposing it to linguistic use, which more aptly replaces, in his opinion, the concept of speech* (*parole*), judged theoretically unsatisfactory. This dichotomy, applied only to natural languages, can be extended to other semiotic systems: in this case, schema (or form,* as understood by Saussure) is opposed to substance.*

3. We have tried to make use of the schema/usage dichotomy in general semantics: if we designate by the term schema the open semiotic combinatory* principle at the disposal of a culture as a set of virtualities, then the term use will serve the purpose of naming the closed, restricted combinatory principle, that is, the set of sememic combinations (or expressions*) such as they are indeed produced.

4. In the strict sense, schema is used to designate one of the dimensions* of the semiotic square, the one that connects two contradictory* terms. We differentiate between a **positive schema** (whose first term belongs to the positive deixis*) and a **negative schema** (whose first term is located on the negative deixis). The name chosen is semi-motivated, since it refers to semiotic form as made up of exclusion, presences, and absences.

—USE; NARRATIVE SCHEMA; SQUARE, SEMIOTIC

SCIENTIFIC SEMIOTICS
(scientifique [sémiotique—])

For L. Hjelmslev, a semiotics is **scientific** when it is an operation (or description*) conforming to the principle of empiricism; with respect to this criterion, he distinguishes between scientific semiotics and nonscientific semiotics.—SEMIOTICS; EMPIRICISM

SCIENTIFICNESS
(scientificité)

1. Scientific research is one particular form of cognitive* activity, characterized by several deontic* precautions (conditions of **scientificness**) that the knowing subject assumes in order to proceed with scientific research and, more specifically, to carry out the program undertaken. Consequently, the scientific attitude is to be considered as an ideology,* *i.e.*, as a quest* for knowledge, followed by the gift of this object* of value or, rather, by the renunciation* of this object in favor of its transmittal to the sender (in this case, society). The subject of this quest—as of any ideological quest— is equipped with the modalities of *wanting-to-do* and *having-to-do*, the latter taking on the form of a scientific deontology.* What distinguishes scientific research from other cognitive activities is not so much its submission to a particular deontics, but the specific content of the *having-to-do*.

2. Scientific research is expressed in the form of scientific discourse; little does it matter whether this discourse is "interior" or manifested (oral or written). As discourse, it can be submitted to semiotic anal-

ysis in order to recognize its specificity. It will be noted that if, as a cognitive* doing, it is defined as a process productive of knowing, then as a causing-to-know it will be submitted, if the case should arise, to an enunciatee* and will thereby change status in order to be presented as a referential* discourse (which, after an epistemological* evaluation, can be used as a basis for a new cognitive discourse, and so forth). The individual subject of research is thus inserted into a syntagmatic chain that transcends that subject and that thereby presents itself as a social scientific discourse. Nevertheless, this latter discourse is not defined as an historical development (its genetic interpretation), but as an algorithm* that has been finalized *a posteriori*, collective referentiality being the reconstruction of an ideal approach.

3. Scientific practice, which we have outlined very briefly, has a weak point: it is the time and the place where individual discourse attempts to insert itself into social discourse, the moment when it is submitted to epistemological evaluation before being approved/sanctioned and declared "dignus intrari" (worthy of being admitted). Analyses, still very partial, of biological discourse have already shown that the essential element in intercommunication among scientists who work on partial programs consists in questioning the degree of probability* or certainty* of the results obtained. It is this locus of uncertainties that is covered by theoretical reflection concerning the conditions of scientificness.

4. One of these conditions consists in giving scientific discourse such a form that the scientific subject, having a place within the uttered discourse, may function as any subject whatsoever (which, as an actant,* includes an indefinite class of substitutible actors*): it may eventually be capable of being replaced by an automaton.* In order to do this, the subject must implement a "clean" language (or metalanguage*) the terms of which are well defined* and unequivocal*; in addition, the subject must be equipped with a knowing-how-to-do (*savoir-faire*) formulated in terms of procedures and/or rules* that can be put into algorithmic* strings, etc.

5. All these precautions are supposed to guarantee the proper functioning of scientific discourse: scrutiny and organization constitute one of the tasks of the general epistemology* of the sciences and of the theories of every field of research. However, they bear upon only certain aspects of scientificness; they are satisfactory conditions for the coherence* of discourse, but they cannot, for example, resolve problems dealing with the adequation* of the methods used as concerns the object under study (this is one of Hjelmslev's concerns in his principle of empiricism*). These precautions leave open especially the problems of the relations between the discourse of discovery* and that of research, and between hypotheses* of an intuitive* character and the verification* of these same hypotheses.
—THEORY; METALANGUAGE; EMPIRICISM

SECRET
(secret)

In the semiotic square of veridictory modalities, we use **secret** to designate the complementary* term that subsumes *being* and *not-seeming*, located on the positive deixis.*—VERIDICTORY MODALITIES; SUSPENSION; SQUARE, SEMIOTIC; MARK

SEEMING
(paraître)

By **seeming** is meant the positive term* of the schema* of manifestation* on the semiotic square* onto which the modal category of veridiction is projected. The term *seeming* is in a relation of contrariety with that of *being* (understood, in this sense, as the positive term of the schema of immanence*). The double operation, which has the effect of asserting the terms of *seeming* and *being,* produces the complex veridictory term named *truth* (characterizing a state of which one says that it "seems" and that it "is" at the same time).—VERIDICTORY MODALITIES

SEGMENTATION
(segmentation/découpage)

1. By **segmentation** is understood the set of procedures for dividing a text into segments, that is, into provisional syntagmatic units which, while entering into combinations among themselves (by relations of the "both . . . and" type), are distinguished from each other by one or more segmentation criteria without specifying for all that to which level of pertinence* these syntagmatic units belong. In other words, segmentation, syntagmatic in nature, does not by itself permit recognition* of linguistic (or, more generally, semiotic) units. Thus procedures of the paradigmatic sort, such as commutation* or substitution,* are called upon in phrase-structure linguistics (and particularly in phonology*). This twofold approach guarantees the definition of units proper to each language level. It will be nonetheless noted that the units obtained by segmentation are not the only possible linguistic units. There exist discontinuous units

(such as the French negation "ne . . . pas", or the English emphatic verbal form "I do not see"). Furthermore, phonology is even divided into **segmental** phonology (which deals with phonemes*) and suprasegmental* phonology (or prosody*).

2. In discoursive linguistics, segmentation is to be considered as a first empirical step, aiming at tentatively dividing the text* into entities* that can be handled more easily. The sequences* thus obtained are not thereby established discoursive units,* but only textual units. Segmentation can proceed by searching for demarcators* (the disjunctive conjunction "but," for example), which are kinds of signals that indicate the existence of a frontier between two sequences. But the most effective procedure seems to be to recognize categorical disjunctions* where one of the terms of the category* under consideration characterizes the preceding sequence and the other the following one. Thus, different disjunctions can be recognized: spatial (here/elsewhere), temporal (before/after), thymic* (euphoria/dysphoria), topical (same/other), actorial (I/(s)he), etc. The inventory of segmentation criteria is far from exhaustive, and the degree of certitude of the operation itself rises with the number of concomitant disjunctions. Nevertheless, the latter are not necessarily located at the same place, and two sequences thus disjoined can often appear as areas of isoglosses,* comparable to dialectal zones within a language.

3. If, from the perspective of reading* or of analysis,* segmentation is an operation which thus isolates textual units, then it can be considered, from the point of view of the generative* trajectory, as one of the textualization* procedures which cuts the discourse up into

parts, which establishes the textual units (sentences, paragraphs, chapters, etc.) and sets them out in succession, and which proceeds to anaphorization,* etc., while, of course, taking the elasticity* of the discourse into account.

4. The term segmentation (here=découpage) is also used at times to designate the categorization of the world and/or of experience, as it is carried out in different ways by the various natural languages. Thus, C. Lévi-Strauss uses in this sense the phrase "conceptual segmentation" to refer to a paradigmatic type of organization.
—CATEGORIZATION; TEXTUALIZATION; SEQUENCE

SELECTION
(sélection)

Selection is the term that L. Hjelmslev gives to unilateral presupposition when this presupposition is recognized in the syntagmatic* string. This term tends to be generalized in actual usage; it is applied as well to paradigmatic* relationships.—UNILATERAL PRESUPPOSITION

SEMANTEME
(sémantème)

1. The term **semanteme** used to belong to a terminology now abandoned, in which it designated the lexical basis of a word, in opposition to morpheme* (carrying grammatical information). In this meaning, it has been replaced by lexical morpheme (or lexeme*). In order to speak of the semantic investment* of a morpheme or of an utterance* before having analyzed* it, it is preferable to use the term **semanticism.**

2. The term semanteme has recently been revived by B. Pottier; in his system it refers to a subset of specific semes* that, with the classeme* (subset of generic semes) and the virtueme (subset of connotative* semes), constitutes the sememe.*

SEMANTIC INVENTORY (or SEMANTIC LEVEL)
(sémantique [inventaire, niveau—])

Unlike the semiological* inventory of semic categories* which, stemming from the content* plane of natural languages, correspond to figures* of expression* in natural* semiotics, a **semantic** inventory (in the strict meaning of the term) is made up of categories that have no relation with the outside world as it is perceived, and that are even presupposed by the categorization* of the world. In order to avoid terminological confusion, we suggest the use of the qualifier **figurative***to replace semiological, and **nonfigurative** (or **abstract**) to replace semantic.—INTEROCEPTIVITY

SEMANTICISM
(sémantisme)

By the term **semanticism** we designate the semantic investment of a morpheme* or utterance,* before it is analyzed.—INVESTMENT, SEMANTIC

SEMANTICITY
(sémanticité)

For generative* and transformational linguistics, the **semanticity** of an utterance corresponds to its capacity to receive a semantic interpretation (which brings into play an epistemological* evaluation of the enunciatee*). By contrast, we understand semanticity, from an operational* point of view, as the relation of compatibility maintained by two elements* at the semantic level (for example, two semes* or two sememes*). As a consequence of this relation, the two elements may be present together within a hierarchically superior unit. Semanticity is not only a criterion of acceptability,* but also of semantic interpretation.— COMPATIBILITY; ACCEPTABILITY; INTERPRETATION

SEMANTICS
(sémantique)

1. Sometimes opposed to the couple phonetics/phonology, sometimes to syntax (especially in logic), **semantics** is one of the components of the theory of language (or of grammar*).

2. During the nineteenth century, linguistics dealt principally with the elaboration of phonetics* and morphology*; in the twentieth century, as if by a reversal of trends, it has especially undertaken the development of syntax* and semantics. Indeed, it was not until the end of the last century that M.Bréal first formulated the principles of a diachronic semantics; its main task was to study changes of word meaning, by adapting to the social dimension of natural languages the tools of ancient rhetoric (especially tropology) and of nineteenth-century stylistics.

3. In abandoning the diachronic dimension of research in favor of a synchronic description of occurrences of signification, semantics, during the first half of the twentieth century, took on the task of recognizing and analyzing semantic (or notional, or conceptual) fields.* Beginning with the work of J. Trier, who also made use of semasiological* and onomasiological* approaches, it received the name of lexicology (G. Matoré). Nevertheless, such a **lexical semantics** maintains the word* as the basic unit of analysis, and is close to the

hypothesis of Sapir and Whorf, concerning the categorization* of the world with the help of the lexical mechanism of natural languages. This approach, with its taxonomical* goal, only produced partial and limited results, for lack of criteria stemming from the immanent structure of language.

4. It was in the 1960's that the use of the phonological* model (based on the more or less explicit postulate concerning the parallelism of the two planes* of language) opened the way to what is commonly called **structural semantics.** Considering the expression* plane to be made up of differential gaps and considering these gaps of the signifier* to correspond to gaps of the signified* (interpreted as distinctive* features of signification), this new approach thereby possesses a means to analyze explicit lexical units (morphemes or comparable units), by decomposing them into smaller underlying units (sometimes called minimal units), *i.e.,* semantic features or semes.* Whatever may be the theoretical presuppositions of those linguists engaged in this research (to give a few names, U. Weinrich, B. Pottier, A. J. Greimas, Apresjan, Katz and Fodor), and without considering the diversely satisfying results obtained by these linguists individually, structural semantics undeniably constitutes a decisive step forward: its methodological experience has made possible new reflections on the theory of signification and has opened the way to semiotics.

5. As it exists today, semantics seems to have dismissed the apprehensions of a good many linguists, condensed in Boomfield's famous formula: meaning does exist, but we cannot say anything meaningful about it. Indeed, al-

though the "materiality" of the signifier* serves as a sort of guarantee for its scientific description, the plane of the signified*—which can only be presupposed—resisted a positive approach. In order for semantics to be admitted and recognized as a constructed language capable of describing an object-language, a revolution of thought had to take place. It is a matter of replacing the certitude of a description of "facts" of language by the idea that linguistics is but a theoretical construction, seeking to account for phenomena that are otherwise elusive (and that cannot be seized directly). Even then, one must realize that the status of semantics as a metalanguage* creates a division among semanticians, of which they are more or less conscious. In addition to the demanding project of developing a scientific metalanguage (a project in which we are involved), semantic language is often considered as a mere paraphrase into natural language.

6. Among those problems that have been left unanswered and that semantics should resolve, let us first point out the problem of semic production. We can theoretically imagine that some twenty binary semic categories,* considered as the taxonomical basis of a combinatory* system, can produce several million sememic combinations; at first glance, this number is quite sufficient to encompass the semantic universe coextensive with a given natural language. Leaving aside the practical difficulty of setting up such a basic set of semantic universals,* we run into another problem, just as difficult, when we attempt to define rules of semantic compatibility and incompatibility,* which govern not only the construction of sememes,* but also broader syntagmatic units

(utterance, discourse). It is therefore clear that semic* (or componential) analysis obtains satisfying results only when it produces limited taxonomic descriptions (which can be extended to the structuration* of more open semantic fields). It is also clear that the idea that we have matrices at our disposal (for the purpose of semantic interpretation), that are comparable to those that phonology can furnish for its own interpretation, must be abandoned; finally, **linguistic semantics** (generative or logical, *cf.* O. Ducrot) is limited to clarifying only possible universals. Thus, the great illusion of the 1960s—*i.e.,* the possibility of providing linguistics with the necessary means for an exhaustive analysis of the content plane of natural languages—had to be abandoned, since linguistics had gotten engaged, often without realizing it, in the extraordinary project of a complete description of all cultures, even embracing all of humanity.

7. In order to move beyond the development phase we have briefly outlined, semantics—as we have set out to develop it within the *Groupe de Recherches sémio-linguistiques*—must satisfy, it would seem, at least three main requirements: (a) it must be **generative,** in the form of progressive investments of content, situated on successive levels, leading from the most abstract* investments toward the most concrete* and figurative,* in such a way that each level may receive an explicit metalinguistic representation*; (b) it must be **syntagmatic,** and not simply taxonomical, in order to explain, not particular lexical units, but the production and reception of discourse. Concerning this point, the importance given to contextual* semes in the construction of sememes allows us to postulate the following hy-

pothesis: the deepest semantic investments correspond to syntagmatic units having the broadest dimensions and serving as a base for establishing isotopies of discourse; in this way, additional layers of semantic investment will give rise to making contents more specific, breaking discourse down into smaller syntagmatic units in order, finally, to arrive at sememic combinations; (c) Semantics must be **general:** natural languages,* just like natural worlds,* are loci where many different semiotic systems appear and are produced; it is therefore necessary to postulate the unicity of meaning and to recognize that meaning may be manifested by different semiotic systems at the same time (in the case of theater, for example). That is why semantics stems from a general theory of signification.*

8. Within the framework of semiotic grammar* as we conceive of it, two complementary components —syntactic and semantic—are to be distinguished; these two components can be articulated at two different levels of depth. The generative process of discourse thus presents two semantic domains at the semiotic or narrative level: (a) **fundamental semantics,** equipped with an abstract logical representation; and (b) a **narrative semantics,** the investments of which are inscribed within the molds of the surface narrative syntax.* The resulting semantico-syntactic representation is that of semiotic structures, which can be assumed by the domain of the enunciation for the purpose of producing discourse.
—CONTENT; SEMANTICS, DISCOURSIVE; SEMANTICS, GENERATIVE; SEMANTICS, FUNDAMENTAL; SEMANTICS, NARRATIVE; GENERATIVE TRAJECTORY

SEMANTICS, DISCOURSIVE
(sémantique discursive)

1. The putting into discourse (or discoursivization*) of semiotic and narrative structures can be defined, from the syntactic point of view, as a set of three types of procedures: actorialization,* temporalization,* and spatialization.* Concomitantly, from the semantic point of view, new investments accompany this syntagmatic reorganization; such investments are distributed among several levels. A very simple example may help to elucidate our thought. Let us suppose that, on the level of the narrative structures, there exists a narrative program* the object actant of which is invested with the value* "freedom" (a value belonging to the modal structure of being-able). This object being inscribed as disjoined from the subject, the value "freedom" will constitute the goal of the subject's narrative* trajectory. That being the case, the inscription of such a trajectory in the discourse can give rise, for example, to its spatialization, and the trajectory of "freedom" can thereby be thematized as a trajectory of "escape." Yet escape is still an abstract* trajectory; new investments can figurativize it by presenting it, for example, as a setting out for faraway places. We thus say that a narrative trajectory can be converted, at the time of its discoursivization, either into a thematic* trajectory or, at a later stage, into a figurative* trajectory. A distinction is thus made —taking into account the two procedures, of thematization* and of figurativization*—between two broad classes of discourses: non-figurative (or abstract) and figurative.

2. The distance separating the two discoursive levels (the figurative

and thematic levels) is thus the locus of semantic conversions,* the complexity of which is variable. Thus, a given discourse can implement a thematic trajectory by converting it successively into several figurative trajectories. This is a frequent case, an instance of which are the Gospel parables. Another discourse, instead of setting the figurative trajectories out sequentially, superimposes them simultaneously one upon another. This happens in the case of pluriisotopy,* which gives rise to multiple readings* of a single discourse. It is likewise at this level that the discourse's taking charge of the numerous discursive figures* and configurations* (often iterative and migratory in nature) is inscribed. All of these phenomena constitute a very large field for study, so far relatively unexamined, a field belonging to **discoursive semantics.**

3. Within the figurative area of the discourse, the two levels of figurativization and of iconization* should be distinguished. Figurativization consists in putting a set of figures into place throughout the discourse (*cf.* nuclear* figures, G. Bachelard's schemata, children's drawings, etc.). By contrast, iconization consists, at a more advanced state, in "dressing up" these figures, in making them resemble "reality"; it thus consists in creating the referential* illusion. It is likewise at this figurative level that the onomastic* procedures take place. These procedures, which involve anthroponymy,* chrononymy,* and toponymy,* correspond, on the semantic level, to the three principal syntactic principles of discoursivization (actorialization, temporalization, spatialization).

4. In the present state of semiotic research, it is clearly impossible to determine the general economy of discoursive semantics with any certainty. Thus here we can indicate only the outlines of a project based on a certain number of postulates. Since the generative* trajectory of the discourse goes from the abstract toward the concrete and the figurative, it is methodologically most proper to break it down into as many semi-autonomous domains as are needed so as to apprehend, at each stage, its particular modes of production. On the other hand, the generative process as a whole, together with the semantic investments recognized on each level, constitute just so many restrictions* and specifications of the discourse (or discourse about discoursive semantics) we are trying to generate. The set of successive options and of the selections that will ensue therefrom will then serve as a basis for a typology of discourses.

—SEMANTICS, NARRATIVE; THEMATIZATION; FIGURATIVIZATION; CONFIGURATION; GENERATIVE TRAJECTORY

SEMANTICS, FUNDAMENTAL
(*sémantique fondamentale*)

1. **Fundamental semantics** is complementary to narrative semantics, and constitutes, with the latter, the semantic component* of semiotic grammar (*i.e.*, at the level of semiotic structures). It is defined by its abstract* character as well as by the fact that—along with fundamental syntax*—it corresponds to the starting point of the generative* trajectory of discourse. Its units are the elementary structures* of signification: they can be formulated as semantic categories* and can be articulated on the semiotic square* (giving them a logico-semantic status and making them operational).

2. As a rule, it is thought that one semantic category alone is sufficient to set into order and produce a micro-universe* of discourse, as a result of investments* successive to each generative domain. However, two distinct semantic categories, taken as schemata* in the semiotic square, can, just as well, generate an innovative discourse (analytic or synthetic-mythic). The existence of discourses that are incoherent or that lack a closing does not contradict such a conception: just as a two-voiced discourse (dialogue*) or a discourse with several voices (a group debate) may constitute but one discourse universe and may owe its fundamental organization to only one category (or to a couple of intersecting categories), so may a single manifested discourse be incoherent and belong to several universes of discourse. Under certain specific conditions, we can also foresee the case in which a single category (or two intersecting schemata), governing a micro-universe, dominates other categories that are subordinate to it or simply coordinated with it. Such a mechanism has a hierarchical form; when it governs a given cultural universe, it is called an episteme.*

3. Given the fact that a semantic universe* can be articulated in two ways—either as an individual* universe (a "person") or as a social universe (a "culture")—it is possible to suggest, as a hypothesis, the existence of two types of semantic universals*: the category *life vs. death,* and that of *nature vs. culture.* The operational efficiency of these two categories seems indisputable.

4. Fundamental semantics appears, at this level, as an inventory (or a taxonomy?) of semic categories, which can be used by the subject of enunciation,* as so many virtual axiological* systems. These systems have values that are actualized only at the narrative level, at the moment of their junction with subjects. Such an elementary axiological structure, paradigmatic* in nature, can be syntagmatized by syntactical operations that cause their terms to move along predictable trajectories on the semiotic square: the semantic structure is then capable of receiving, on this plane, a syntagmatic representation.

—GENERATIVE TRAJECTORY; SEMANTICS; STRUCTURE (B: Elementary structure of signification); EPISTEME; UNIVERSE, SEMANTIC

SEMANTICS, GENERATIVE
(sémantique générative)

1. **Generative semantics** needs to be understood by contrast with generative grammar. In its earliest stages, generative grammar endeavored to locate the semantic component at the level of deep structures alone. But since syntax and semantics were thereby separated totally, an effort was made to reconcile these two components by locating semantics along the entire transformational trajectory. Generative semantics reversed the particulars of the problem by postulating that the starting point of the generative* trajectory is made up of logico-semantic forms from which surface forms are generated through an interplay of transformations*. Just as, for instance, the phonological component allows a phonetic representation of the utterance to be made. And thereby the problem of semantic interpretation,* a thorny one in generative grammar, was solved.

2. The exclusion of a purely formal approach, making more room for a truly semantic option, brings generative semantics nearer to French semiotics. Even if the model given is still only approximative, it can be compared, for example, to our own conception of the generative trajectory, and its organization of deep structures may partially correspond to the deep level of our semiotic grammar.*

3. However, even if generative semantics shows a positive interest for universals,* its area of research, at present, seems to be very localized, especially lacking a general theory of signification. Furthermore, unlike our scientific project, generative semantics seems to refuse (or at least show indifference for) descriptive metalanguage.
—GENERATIVE TRAJECTORY; GENERATIVE GRAMMAR

SEMANTICS, NARRATIVE
(sémantique narrative)

1. In the economy of the generative* trajectory, **narrative semantics** is to be considered as the domain of the actualization* of values. Indeed, although the fundamental level, where we find fundamental syntax* and fundamental semantics,* has the role of articulating and giving categorical form to the micro-universe* that can produce discursive significations, this organized universe still remains that of virtual* values as long as it is not assumed, taken on, by a subject. The passage from fundamental semantics to narrative semantics, then, consists essentially in selecting available values—positioned on the semiotic square(s)*—and actualizing them by their junction* with subjects of the surface narrative syntax. Whereas

the deep level is presented as an axiological mechanism, that can serve as a basis for the generation of a typological spectrum of possible discourses, the narrative level of semantics is where we find restrictions imposed on the combinatory system; it is also where the type of discourse to be produced is decided, at least in part.

2. The syntactic mold where the investment of selected values takes place is the utterance of being, an utterance describing a state.* Independently of the nature of the value (modal,* cultural, subjective,* or objective*), its inscription in the object-actant in junction with the subject defines the latter in its "being." The subject, the "being" of which is constantly redefinable, then can be mobilized for the narrative program* that will transform it. Just as the actualization of values sets narrative programs up into signification, the narrative* trajectory constitutes the syntactic framework for the accumulation of values (not only by a process of addition, but also through "memory," as thematic roles show, at the level of discoursive semantics).
—SEMANTICS, FUNDAMENTAL; SYNTAX, SURFACE NARRATIVE; GENERATIVE TRAJECTORY; ACTUALIZATION

SEMASIOLOGY
(sémasiologie)

In lexical semantics, the term **semasiology** designates the approach that aims at describing significations,* taking minimal signs* (or lexemes*) as a starting point. Semasiology is usually opposed to onomasiology.—ONOMASIOLOGY; SEMANTICS

SEME
(sème)

1. **Seme** commonly designates the "minimal unit" of signification (comparable to the pertinent*—or simply distinctive*—features of the Prague School). Located on the content* plane, it corresponds to the pheme,* the unit on the expression* plane. By maintaining the parallelism between the two planes of language, we can say that semes are elements constituting sememes,* just as phemes are elements constituting phonemes.* It can also be said that a semantic system may be postulated, hypothetically,* so as to account for the content plane of a semiotic* system, comparable to the phonological system, the articulations of which constitute the expression plane.

2. The seme is not an autonomous, atomistic element; it exists only because of the differential gap that opposes it to other semes. In other words, the nature of semes is purely relational and never substantial, and the seme cannot be defined as the end-term* of the relation* that one sets up and/or grasps with at least one other term of the same relational network. Thus, we acknowledge that **semic categories** (= semantic categories* that constitute the content plane) are logically anterior to the semes that make up these categories and that semes can be apprehended only within the elementary structure* of signification. It is by giving a precise logical status to constituent relations of such a structure (contradiction,* contrariety,* implication*) that the concept of seme can be determined and made operational.*

3. Because semes are only terms, *i.e.,* points of intersection and of meeting of signifying relations (only rarely corresponding to lexical realizations in natural language), they must be named arbitrarily* during the procedure of analysis: *verticality/horizontality,* for example, are denominations of a metalinguistic* type, to which we should give a coherent organization; we are not dealing here with mere paraphrases* in natural language. This is a theoretical position that opposes semioticians (such as ourselves) to generative semanticists (and even to B. Pottier): semic* analysis is for us a metalinguistic construction.

4. The approximative definition of the seme as the "minimal unit" of content must be challenged, not only in its status as a unit,* but also as being "minimal": (a) Theoretically, it is easy to imagine that a combinatory* system of some twenty semic categories (a number compatable with the number of phemic categories used by a given natural language) may produce as many sememes as necessary for the needs of a natural language or any semiotic system. These semic categories, once an inventory has been made of them, would probably contain the universals* of language. This is what we mean when we speak of semes as minimal units of meaning. However, without a complete inventory of "primitive" semes, no semic analysis can operate; (b) Therefore, the "minimal" character of the seme must be understood in a very relative sense, as minimal with respect to a chosen field of inquiry. Thus, faced with a given terminology of kinship or with a syntagmatic class of determinatives in an enclosed paradigm, semic analysis will call upon only the minimal number of differential features (or semic categories) necessary to exhaust all oppositions among the morphemes being studied. The same situation obtains for

the analysis of the semantic component of one or several discourses. The minimal nature of the seme (we must not forget that the seme is a construct) is, therefore, relative and is based on the criterion of the pertinence* of the description.

5. An examination of different semic categories allows us to distinguish several classes: (a) **figurative*** **semes** (or exteroceptive* semes) are entities* on the content plane of natural languages, corresponding to elements of the expression* plane of the semiotics of the natural world,* *i.e.,* corresponding to the articulations of the sensory classes, to the perceptible qualities of the world; (b) **abstract*** **semes** (or interoceptive* semes) are content entities that refer to no exteriority, but which, on the contrary, are used to categorize* the world and to give it meaning: for example, the categories *relation/term, object/process;* (c) **thymic semes*** (or proprioceptive* semes) connote semic micro-systems according to the category *euphoria/dysphoria,* thus setting them up as axiological* systems.

6. Two types of organization of semic sets may be distinguished: (a) **taxonomic** (or systematic) structures representing the organization of homogeneous semic categories as hierarchies* (based on hyponymic* relationships); (b) **morphematic** structures resulting from the integrating articulations originating in different semic categories and micro-systems and appearing as figures* (possessing diverse elements in hypotactic* relationship).

The distinction set up by B. Pottier between **generic semes** and **specific semes** stems from a taxonomic conception and a semic organization; our own conception of semic figures (constituting sememic kernels*) is based on morphematic organization.

7. The establishment of the semic combinatory system produces a large number of semes. These are not, however, mere collections of semes, but hypotactic constructions, obeying a set of formation rules. Within a sememe, we may distinguish **contextual*** **semes** (which the sememe possesses in common with the other elements of the semantic utterance) and **kernel*** **semes,** that characterize the sememe (and, possibly, the lexeme it belongs to) in its specificity.

—SEMIC ANALYSIS; STRUCTURE; SQUARE, SEMIOTIC; SEMEME

SEMEME
(sémème)

1. In B. Pottier's terminology, the **sememe** is defined as the set of semes* identifiable within the minimal sign (or morpheme*). This unit of signification thus delimited is composed of three semic sub-sets: the classeme* (generic semes), the semanteme* (specific semes), and the virtueme* (connotative* semes).

2. With respect to this definition, our own conception of the sememe is different in several fundamental aspects: (a) Whereas Pottier attributes to the sememe the totality of investments* of the signified* of a morpheme, the sememe —for us—corresponds to what everyday language calls an "acceptation" or "particular meaning" of a word. Pottier's sememe, then, corresponds to our lexeme,* the latter being made up of a set of sememes (a set that may even be monosememic*) that are held together by a common semic kernel.* For example, the lexeme "table" possesses, in addition to the sememe given by dictionaries as "a flat surface held up by one or several legs,"

other identifiable sememes in expressions such as "table talk," "water table," "table of contents," " multiplication table," etc. The lexeme, as a set of sememes, is the result of the historical development of a natural language, whereas the sememe is a structural phenomenon, a unit on the content plane; (b) The semanticism* common to several sememes included in the same formant,* but distinct from the semic investments of contiguous sememes of a same string,* constitutes the kernel of the sememe (cf. Pottier's specific semes, or semantemes). This kernel—or semic figure—is peculiar to the sememe, everything else coming from the context* (usually from the minimal contextual unit, made up of at least two sememes) and constituting its classematic* base. In other words, the sememe is not a unit of meaning delimited by the dimensions of the minimal sign; "in language" it is only a semic figure. It is only at the moment of its manifestation in a discourse that this figure is joined with its classematic base (made up of contextual semes) and thus selects a **sememic trajectory** which actualizes it as a sememe, excluding other possible trajectories which remain virtual, capable of producing other sememes of the same lexeme in other discourse contexts. Where Pottier decomposes the sememe into

sememe = semanteme + classeme,

we would prefer to substitute another break-down:

sememe = semic figure +
classematic base

These two formulations are based on different theoretic foundations. (The problem of the virtueme remains to be solved.); (c) The distinction made between lexeme (bound to its formant) and sememe (the unit resulting from the articulation of the

content plane alone) frees the semantic analysis from the constraints of the sign* and allows us to uncover similar or comparable sememic contents under different lexematic covers. By defining in advance the level of analysis considered pertinent, and by suspending (see suspension*) those semic oppositions judged non-pertinent, it is possible to go from the para-synonymy* of sememes to the recognition of their synonymy,* and, thereby, to constitute classes of sememes (or of **constructed sememes**), joining together many occurrences of sememes dispersed throughout a discourse and belonging to different lexemes; (d) Finally, the sememe cannot be considered as a collection of semes, the product of a mere combinatory system. It is a syntactic* organization of semes; semic figures often contain, implicitly, actantial structures (for example, "to give" implies the presence of at least two actantial positions) and/or more or less complex thematic configurations* ("to moan" = "to make a low, prolonged sound, while in pain or in sorrow").
—SEME, SEMIC ANALYSIS

SEMIC ANALYSIS
(sémique [analyse—])

1. **Semic analysis** and **componential analysis** are most often placed together, despite their different origins (one is European, the other American), and despite their autonomous development and their divergent goals (the first seeking to account for the semantic organization of a lexical field, the second to describe as economically as possible the terminology of kinship). They have in common the fact that they are taxonomic* procedures that attempt to expose the paradigmatic*

organization of linguistic phenomena on the semantic* plane, by establishing distinctions with the help of pertinent* features (oppositions of semes* in one case, of "components" or constitutive elements in the other).

2. **Semic analysis** may be correctly considered as the extension of distributional* analysis, but with the contribution of the tools of semantics. For example, the class of noun determinatives, once it has been established thanks to their distributions,* will be treated as a closed paradigm,* made up of sub-classes such as articles, demonstratives, possessives, etc., and which can only be defined by semic oppositions; a later analysis of these sub-classes, considered one by one, permits their articulation into grammatical categories,* etc.

3. The complexity grows if we want to treat open classes (nominal or verbal radicals) in the same way. The criteria chosen to determine the limits of a sub-class made up of lexemes are weak and often intuitive (for this reason, B. Pottier, who inaugurated this type of analysis with a taxonomy of types of "seats," makes reference to the vague concept of "field of experience," the fragility of which he recognizes); in addition, the nature of the semes establishing the necessary distinctions (for "seats": "to sit in/on," "with or without arms," "with or without a back," etc.) is problematic. Such an approach involves the risk of passing, without realizing it, from the analysis of a semantic field to that of a field of experience (psychological), ending up finally with the description of a field of "reality" (physical). The example of Pottier's classification of means of transportation, for example, following upon his "seat"

taxonomy, proves this point very well.

4. **Componential analysis,** at the outset, takes as its object of study a microsystem within natural languages that is constituted by kinship terminology. The strange, unique character of this microsystem—the functioning of which can be compared only to that of the category of person—presents as many advantages as disadvantages for analysis. The main advantages, which guarantee for componential analysis its homogeneity* and rigor, are the purely paradigmatic nature of this code* and its purely arbitrary* and semantic character (the ego, which serves as a reference point for the whole system, cannot be identified with any referential human being). By using only a small number of semic categories—*consanguinity/marriage, lateral relationship/vertical relationship, close relationship/distant relationship* (for the calculation of degrees of kinship), etc.—componential analysis succeeds in building an almost perfect taxonomic model. But its major disadvantage lies in the restricted nature of its field of applicability: attempts at extrapolation outside of this immanent microsystem—for example, for the study of botanical or zoological ethnotaxonomies in ethnolinguistics—run into difficulties comparable to those present in semic analysis.

5. Semic and componential analysis, inasmuch as it is defined as a clarification of paradigmatic relationships and an establishment of taxonomies considered as results of the combinatory* principle alone, appears to be an autonomous discipline with its own specificity and, as an indirect consequence, with a limited domain of application. The broadening of this field of research

depends largely on the progress of semantics* itself, which is slow in developing. Indeed, semantics, built upon the phonological* model, is finding it difficult to introduce into its analyses the principles of syntagmatic and syntactic organization of the semantic universe.*

—SEME; TAXONOMY; CLASSIFICATION; COMBINATORY (principle or arrangement); SEMANTICS; ETHNO-SEMIOTICS

SEMIOLOGICAL LEVEL
(sémiologique [niveau—])

In an earlier formulation, the **semiological level,** in opposition to the semantic* level, was considered as made up of semes* forming kernel figures,* whereas the semantic level furnished discourse with contextual* semes; together, the two levels composed the signifying universe. The useless ambivalence of the term "semantic"—the semantic universe being identified with the signifying universe taken as a whole, and the semantic level taking into account only the interoceptive* categories of this universe—has led us to correct this terminology: the "figurative* component" of the clearer concept of semantic universe replaces the former "semiological level."

SEMIOLOGY
(sémiologie)

1. The term **semiology** is used, concurrently with that of semiotics,* to designate the theory of language and its applications to different signifying sets.* It goes back to F. de Saussure, who used this label when he called for constituting the general study of "systems of signs." As for the fields of knowledge (or wanting-to-know) that these two terms cover,

they were first constituted in France in the 1960s, within the framework of what is called French structuralism (Merleau-Ponty, Lévi-Strauss, Dumézil, Lacan, etc.), influenced in the area of linguistics by the heirs of Saussure: L. Hjelmslev and, to a lesser degree, R. Jakobson. Of the two terms (used interchangeably for a rather long time), "semiotics" was finally favored: hence, the name of the International Association for Semiotic Studies (in French, *l'Association Internationale de Sémiotique*). Despite this institutionalization, the term "semiology," solidly in place in France (among the disciples of R. Barthes and, partially, those of A. Martinet) and in other Latin countries, continues to be widely used, and it was not until the 1970s that the methodological content of semiology and of semiotics was progressively differentiated, making the distinction between the two designations significant.

2. The semiological project was quickly reducd to almost nothing since it was developed within the limited framework of Saussure's definition (and outside of any contact with the epistemology of the human sciences of the period). The concept of "system," in this project, excludes semiotic process and, at the same time, the most diverse signifying practices; the study of "signs," inscribed in the theory of communication,* consists in the almost mechanical application of the model of the "linguistic sign," etc. Semiology was thus reduced to the analysis of a few artificial, supplementary, codes (*cf.* the analyses of Prieto and Mounin), making semiology appear as a discipline appended to linguistics.

3. In order to discover the reasons for the decisive impact of F. de Saussure on the development of

semiological studies, we should turn, not to the aforementioned narrow formulation, but to the theory of language (of which Saussure outlined the basic dimensions), considered in its entirety. Thus, it is in its Hjelmslevian formulation (*cf.* R. Barthes' *Elements of Semiology* and A. J. Greimas' *Sémantique structurale*) that Saussurianism entered for good into French semiology. However, Hjelmslev, while keeping Saussure's term, endows it with a precise definition: by *semiology* he means the scientific meta-semiotics,* the object-semiotics of which is not scientific. Thus, he excludes from the domain of semiology, on the one hand, connotative semiotic systems (*i.e.,* languages of connotation*) and, on the other hand, meta-semiotic systems that have scientific semiotic systems (logical languages, for example) as their object-semiotic systems.

4. These terminological subtleties may appear futile, but to us they seem necessary, as they serve as a reference point, allowing us to locate basic options that were present during the progressive differentiation between semiology and semiotics. Thus, with respect to the Hjelmslevian definition of semiology, R. Barthes' first "disloyalty," even before *Elements of Semiology,* was his interest in the connotative dimension of language (*cf.* his *Mythologies*), a domain excluded by Hjelmslev from the definition of semiology but which we place within socio-semiotics* (for social connotations) and psycho-semiotics* (for connotations at the level of the individual). Obviously, this was not an act of disloyalty, but a fundamental attitude regarding signs and languages, and one may remember the shock effect produced by the originality of this approach, as well as the almost immediate result—the rec-

ognition of the establishment of such a semiology. However, this oblique approach to language left too much to the intuition of the describer (or Barthes' "scriptor"): since the signifier* of connotative languages is disseminated along the whole length of discourse, inaccessible for any direct structuration, it could only be approached by a preliminary and arbitrary postulation of the signified.* Inasmuch as it was no longer supported by an imagination subjected to a rigorous conceptual discipline, semiological analysis of a connotative nature could only succeed in producing a redundance of commonplaces, unless it were to seek a foundation elsewhere, either in a certain form of psychology (at which time the object-semiotic system, not analyzed, becomes the "signifer" for the psychoanalyst) or in a certain sociology (at which time semiology becomes the *post facto* justification of a theory of ideologies). As soon as we let signifieds choose their own signifiers (a consistent connotative approach could proceed in no other way), we abandon the basic postulate of semiotics—the reciprocal presupposition of the signifier and the signified, which constitutes the force and specificity of semiotics.

5. The reverse "disloyalty"— still with respect to the Hjelmslevian definition of semiology—consisted in an interest in meta-semiotics whose object-semiotic systems were already scientific semiotic systems (*i.e.,* scientific discourse and formal languages), a domain that Hjelmslev had left to logicians and mathematicians. It was obviously not a question of taking the place of these two groups (although the difference between the semiotic and logical points of view could possibly reveal their complementarity), but to see how they treated a particularly difficult

problem, that of descriptive metalanguages.* This encounter with the Viennese School of logic and its Anglo-American continuation (which defines semiotics as the union of two components: syntax and semantics), as well as with the Polish School of mathematics (which developed the issue of the hierarchy of metalanguages), only confirms Hjelmslev's requirement of a "scientific" metalinguistic description. It must be said—from this point of view—that semiology (in the restricted sense that we are beginning to give to this term) was never very interested in the problems of semantics; for it, the description of the signified was a mere problem of paraphrase.* However, to avoid an unverifiable subjectivity, the paraphrase must be regulated and the paraphrastic description of the signified plane (of the semiotic system) must be submitted to analysis; if the description is recognized as a construction, the analysis must be coherent and adequate. It is not, as some would claim, a question of an unwarranted domination of linguistics over semiology, but of general conditions under which any activity having a scientific calling is exercised. A gap therefore divides semiology (for which natural languages serve as instruments of paraphrase in the description of semiotic objects) and semiotics* (the main task of which is the construction of an appropriate metalanguage).

6. Finally, the last point of contention lies in the evaluation of the relations between linguistics and semiology/semiotics. Semiology seems to challenge the primacy of linguistics, by insisting on the specificity of signs and organizations recognizable within non-linguistic semiotic systems, semiotics is considered tightly bound to the methods of linguistics. In reality—and this is particularly clear in the field of visual semiotics (see planar* semiotics)—semiotics more or less explicitly postulates the mediation of the natural languages in the process of reading signifieds belonging to non-linguistic semiotic systems (pictures, paintings, architecture, etc.), whereas semiotics challenges this mediation. Beginning with *Système de la mode,* the most Hjelmslevian of Barthes' works, in which, in order to describe the semiotics of clothing, he makes use of the mediation of "written fashion" (considering, however, that it was simply for convenience sake, and not required by methodology), the semiology of painting came to be conceived as the analysis of discourse on painting. The misunderstanding goes back to the period when linguistic theoreticians such as R. Jakobson, fighting against the psychologism of "thought," expressed by the "tool" of language, openly affirmed the indissoluble interconnection of these two "entities." Recognizing that there is no language without thought, nor thought without language, does not imply that we have to consider natural languages as the only receptacle of "thought": the other, non-linguistic, semiotic systems are also languages, that is, signifying forms. Consequently, the felt and the experienced—terms by which we designate, for exmple, the hold that architectural forms have over us—are but the signifieds of these forms, that a constructed, more or less adequate, but arbitrary, metalanguage is supposed to account for.

—SEMIOTICS; SIGN; ICONICITY; CONTENT

SEMIOSIS
(sémiosis)

1. **Semiosis** is that operation which, by setting up a relationship of reciprocal presupposition* between the expression* form* and the content* form (in Hjelmslev's terminology)—or the signifier* and the signified* (Saussure)—produces signs: in this sense, any language act* implies a semiosis. The term is synonymous with semiotic function.

2. By semiosis can also be meant the semic category* of which the two constituant terms are the expression form and the content form (or, the signifier and the signified).

—SIGN; FUNCTION

SEMIOTIC SYSTEM AND/OR PROCESS
(langage)

1. **Langage** (English **"language"**), a term of the natural language, French, was disentangled in a definitive way from its quasi-synonymy with *langue* (English "natural language*") only in the 19th century. Only then did it become possible to contrast **"semiotic"** language (or language in the broad sense of the term) and "natural language." This distinction, which would be very useful, is once again put into question when inserted within the international context, where numerous natural languages (as English) possess only a single word for both French terms. Consequently this term is either naturalized (we say either "metasemiotics" or "metalanguage") or reasserted pleonastically (when "language" is opposed to "natural language"). For its technical sense, we use here in English, **semiotic system and/or process** for French *langage*.

2. We may say of semiotic systems that they are the object of knowing sought after by general semiotics* (or semiology). An object such as this is not definable in and of itself but only in terms of the methods and procedures which permit its analysis and/or construction. Any attempt, therefore, to define semiotic systems and/or processes (whether as human faculty, as social function, or as means of communication, etc.) reflects a theoretical attitude which disposes the set of "semiotic facts" in its own way. The least compromising procedure is perhaps that of substituting the expression **signifying set*** for the term **semiotic systems.** On the basis of the intuitive conception of the semiotic universe* taken to be the world which can be apprehended in its signification prior to any analysis, we can justifiably postulate that this universe is an articulation of signifying sets or semiotic systems which are juxtaposed with or superimposed upon one another. We can just as well try to indicate some of the characteristics which seem applicable to the set of semiotic systems. For instance, all semiotic systems are bi-planar, which is to say that the means by which they are manifest is not to be confused with what is manifested. Spoken language is made up of sounds but its purpose is not to speak of sounds. The whistling noises produced by dolphins signify something other than the sounds they emit, etc. Furthermore, every semiotic system is articulated. As a projection of the discontinous* upon the continuous,* it is made up of differences* and oppositions.*

3. While the study of language (as semiotic system) belongs to semiotic theory, the study of particular languages belongs to a variety of semiotics. A typology of these

semiotics is nowhere near at hand and initial attempts in this direction are based upon criteria which are not at all certain or are improductive (such as classifications made according to the "nature" of the signs in terms of their relation to the referent,* after the substance* of their signifier* or—which is to say the same thing—after the transmission canals,* or, finally, according to the number of planes of the language which enter into the composition of a given semiotic system). We shall take the time here only to examine a few traditional distinctions.

4. **Human** semiotic systems are opposed to **animal** semiotic systems; the latter number nearly six hundred and constitute the object of zoosemiotics.* Lang**uage** has for a long time been considered one of the fundamental characteristics of the human species. The threshold between animal and human communication is made up of particular natural language properties such as double articulation,* elasticity* of the discourse, or disengagement* (which makes it possible for humans to speak of something other than themselves). Progress in the sphere of animal psychology and zoosemiotics raises some question about age-old certainties, by replacing the concept of limit by that of gradation.

5. Likewise, **natural** semiotic systems are to be distinguished from **artificial** semiotic systems. We thereby emphasize that the semiotic structures which govern the organization of the former are immanent* and that the human subject participates in them only as user and as patient, whereas by contrast the latter are constructed by humans who can manipulate them. In this first category we place not only the natural languages but also that which we understand as the semiotics of the natural world.* However, the dichotomy thus established is not as sharp as one would hope. If classical music is indeed an artificial, constructed semiotic system ("language"), what are we to say of popular songs which, while possessing the same fundamental principles of semiotic organization, appear nonetheless "natural"? The same applies to the invention of writing*: while it is an artificial construct, it is not thereby a conscious construct. Artificial semiotic systems are numerous and varied. An attempt is being made to classify them following the criteria of "transposition" or of transcoding,* according to which their origin would be either natural languages or the semiotics of the natural world, by consequently subdividing them into "transpositions" of the signifier (writing, morse code, braile; photography, music) or the signified (ideography, romantic nature "poetry," etc.), or both at the same time (documentary languages, for example). Presently there does not appear to exist an overall effort to produce a general taxonomy of semiotic systems.

6. The distinction between **languages** (in the technical sense) and **meta-languages*** is just as subtle. Every predication*—or, at least, every attributive predication—may ultimately be considered a metalinguistic operation. A paraphrase* is none other than a discourse upon a semiotic system. The boundary between what is linguistic and metalinguistic is nearly impossible to draw. At the other extreme, all scientific discourse, indeed every science, may similarly be considered metalinguistic in nature.

—SEMIOTICS;   LANGUAGE, NATURAL

SEMIOTICS
(sémiotique)

The term **semiotics** is used in different meanings, depending on whether it designates (A) any manifested entity* under study; (B) an object of knowledge, as it appears during and after its description*; and (C) the set of ways that make knowledge about this object possible.

(A) Semiotics as object

1. Clearly, the standard definition of semiotics as a "system of signs" is not appropriate for meaning (A), for it already presupposes a recognition* of the signs.* By using the expression "system of significations," we would introduce the broader concept of "signification," and, further, by replacing "system" —which is a limitative, precise, and theoretic notion—by "set,*" we can propose to define, at least temporarily, a given semiotics as a signifying set that we suspect, at least hypothetically,* possesses an organization, *i.e.,* an autonomous* internal articulation.* It may also be said that any signifying set, as soon as one proposes submitting it to analysis,* can be designated as an **object-semiotics**; this definition is tentative, since it is valid only within the framework of a descriptive project and therefore presupposes a metasemiotics* that, theoretically, encompasses it. Furthermore, the concepts of signifying set and object-semiotics are not coextensive: the results of the analysis sometimes show that only one part of the signifying set is embraced by the constructed semiotic system, or, on the contrary, the latter sometimes accounts for more entities than those initially thought to be part of the signifying set (see semantic field).

2. These preliminary remarks, apparently idle, assume their importance when we have to deal with the status of the so-called natural* semiotic systems and with the pertinence of the dichotomy between what is "natural" and what is "constructed": moreover, such a problem involves semiotic theory as a whole.

By **natural semiotic systems** we mean two vast signifying sets: on the one hand, natural languages,* and on the other, "extra-linguistic contexts*" that we consider as semiotics of the natural world.* They are called "natural" because they impose themselves upon human beings rather than being constructed by them—people are immersed in their mother tongue and are projected, from birth, into the world of "common sense." However, the boundary between what is given "naturally" and what is constructed, is blurry: literary discourse uses a given natural language, and logic finds its origin in natural languages; yet, unquestionably, they are genuine constructions. The semiotics of space* experiences the same difficulty in distinguishing between "built" space and "natural" space: a "natural" countryside is obviously a cultural concept and has meaning only with respect to space formed by humans. Contrary then to F. de Saussure and L. Hjelmslev, for whom natural languages are semiotic systems among others, natural languages and the natural world appear to us as vast reservoirs of signs, as the place where numerous semiotic systems are manifested. Furthermore, the concept of construction* must also be revised and reasserted from this point of view: inasmuch as construction implies the existence of a constructing subject, room must be made for collective* subjects, alongside of individual subjects (ethno-literary or ethno-musical discourses, for example, are constructed discourses, whatever may be the status the genetic anthropology may attribute to subjects producing such discourses). Consequently, it would seem desirable to substitute for the opposition *natural/constructed* (or "artificial") the opposition *scientific semiotic systems/non-scientific semiotic systems;* here, by scientific semiotic systems—in the broad sense of "scientific"—we understand an object-semiotics treated within the framework of a semiotic theory, explicit* or implicit* (the construction of a documentary language, for example, is built on a theory, even if the latter is only barely scientific).

3. It consequently becomes indispensable to define the status of these **macro-semiotic systems,** in which particular semiotic systems are organized. These macro-systems, *i.e.,* natural languages and natural worlds, are "natural" only in the sense that "nature" is perceived through "culture," which makes them relative and permits the use of the plural. In the first place, it is necessary to record the correlations* that exist between the two sets: thus, the affirmation that the natural world is translatable into natural language has to be interpreted as the correspondence that can be established between units stemming from two types of semiotic systems (phemes* of the natural world correspond, on the figurative* plane, to semes* in natural languages; somatic activities—behavior—are "described" as linguistic processes,* etc.). The result of this is a certain interpenetration of segments stemming from the two semiotic systems, recognizable on the syntagmatic plane: linguistic deictics* refer to the natural context, gestural segments replace verbal syntagms, etc. In the second place, the affirmation that natural languages are the only languages into which the other semiotic systems are translatable (while the reverse is impossible) can be explained two ways: first, because figures of the natural world are coded semantically in natural languages; secondly (and especially), because only natural languages can lexicalize and manifest abstract (or universal*) semantic categories* that generally remain implicit in other semiotic systems.

4. For us, the macro-semiotic systems—natural languages and natural worlds—are the loci where all other semiotic systems are manifested.

—LANGUAGE,   NATURAL; WORLD, NATURAL

(B) **Semiotic typology**

1. While, in meaning (A), the term "semiotic" serves to designate a signifying set prior to its description, in a different acceptation it is used to refer to an object of knowledge that is being or is already constituted; we are then dealing with an object-semiotics considered either as a project of description, or as already having undergone analysis, or finally as a constructed object. In other works, we can speak of semiotics only if there is a point of encounter between the object-semiotics and the semiotic theory that apprehends it, gives it form, and articulates it.

2. Following the tradition of L. Hjelmslev, who was the first to propose a coherent semiotic theory, we can accept the definition that he gives for semiotics: he considers it to be a hierarchy* (*i.e.,* a network of relations, hierarchically organized) endowed with a double mode of existence, paradigmatic and syntagmatic (and therefore which can be grasped as a semiotic system* or process*), and provided with at least two articulation planes*—expression* and content*—the union of

which constitutes semiosis.* Present research, focusing on analyses of discourse* and of semiotic practices,* seems to favor the syntagmatic axis and semiotic processes; but does not at all modify Hjelmslev's definition. One can envision a later phase of research being devoted to the systematization of established results.

3. To these common characteristics, let us try to add some other, more specific, features, in order to open the way for a **typology of semiotic systems.** At the present time, two types of classifications are implicitly or tacitly accepted: a distribution of semiotic systems, based on channels* of communication,* and another, based on the nature of the recognized signs. Neither of them, however, corresponds to our definition of semiotics. The classification according to the channels of sign transmission (or according to the orders of the senses) depends on our taking into consideration the expression substance*: but the latter is not pertinent for a definition of semiotics (which is, first and foremost, a form*). Moreover, a distribution according to the nature of the signs is based on relations that these signs (symbols,* icons,* indices,* etc.) maintain with respect to the referent.* Such a criterion, because it infringes upon the principle of autonomy* (or of immanence*) of semiotic organizations, established by F. de Saussure, cannot be accepted, for it also is not pertinent. In any case, one can wonder whether, given the present state of semiotic research, any such classification is not premature.

4. The typology of semiotic systems as proposed by L. Hjelmslev in his *Prolegomena* is of a very different nature. In order to avoid confusion, we shall first present it concisely,

adding our own remarks afterwards. This typology is based on two criteria of classification: (a) scientificness* (a semiotics is called scientific when it is a description conforming to empirical principles), and (b) the number of (language) planes* that constitute a given semiotics. It is, therefore, possible to differentiate **monoplanar semiotic systems** (or systems of symbols,* in Hjelmslev's terminology) that are also scientific or not, and **pluriplanar semiotic systems** which are biplanar semiotic systems of which at least one of the planes constitutes a semiotics (called an object-semiotics)—the case in which only one of the two planes is an object-semiotics is by far the most frequent. Pluriplanar semiotic systems are subdivided according to whether (a) they are scientific or not, and (b) their object-semiotics is scientific or not. The following schema represents this distribution:

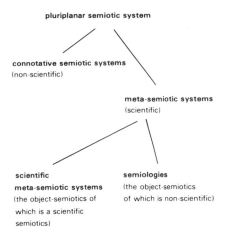

pluriplanar semiotic system

connotative semiotic systems
(non-scientific)

meta-semiotic systems
(scientific)

scientific
meta-semiotic systems
(the object-semiotics of
which is a scientific
semiotics)

semiologies
(the object-semiotics
of which is non-scientific)

To this classification are added two other categories: a **meta-semiology** and a **meta-semiotic of connotative semiotics,** that examine, respectively, semiologies and connotative semiotics.

5. To understand, interpret, and evaluate such a typology, several remarks are necessary: (a) With respect to the classifications given above (in par. 3), that of Hjelmslev is differentiated first by the introduction of the criterion of scientificness, that is, by the absolute necessity of having an explicit theory* (when speaking of semiotics) that is to account for it; in addition, Hjelmslev's classification differs from the previous ones, by the utilization, as a criterion, of the planes of language (signifier* and signified* taken as a whole), a criterion already part of the definition of semiotics and, therefore, homogeneous with it (whereas substance or referent introduce suplementary and heterogeneous variables). This forces us to consider the proposed typology as being part of a theory taken as a whole; it is possible to reject the entire theory, but not the classification by itself; (b) In order to obtain a homologous terminology, we should note that our definition of semiotics corresponds, in Hjelmslev's typology, to the **meta-semiotics** called **semiology:** every signifying set treated by semiotics (semiotic theory) becomes a semiotic system; (c) Scientific meta-semiotic systems are linked to the issues concerning metalanguages,* issues common to logic, mathematics, linguistics, and semiotic theory; (d) The creation of a separate category for **mono-planar semiotic systems,** which Hjelmslev considers as systems of symbols not having the status of "semiotics," does pose a problem. The definition that he gives for mono-planar semiotic systems—they should be identifiable by the conformity* of the two planes, by their isomophism* and their isotopism,* by the one-to-one correspondance of their units—does not necessarily mean that they involve only a single plane of language, but that they are manifested as a signifying form* (in the Saussurian, and not Hjelmslevian, sense). Moreover, a distinction could be established between such monoplanar semiotic systems, depending on the type of conformity recognized. Formal* languages (or systems of symbols) would be, in this sense, "elementary." This is because each element, taken separately, is recognizable either on the expression plane, or on the content plane (in this latter case it is called "interpretable"), since the differentiation is based on nothing other than discrimination* (which allows us to identify these languages on the expression plane alone). By contrast with formal languages, then, there are "molar" or semi-symbolic languages, characterized not by the conformity of isolated elements, but by the conformity of categories.* Prosodic* and gestural categories, for example, are signifying forms—"yes" and "no" correspond, in our cultural context, to the opposition *verticality/horizontality* (nodding *vs.* shaking the head)—as are the categories recognized in abstract painting or in certain musical forms. Thus, what is at stake in the distinction between interpretable monoplanar semiotic systems and those that are signifying is considerable; (e) The handling of **connotative semiotic systems** (linked with that of dcnotation*), lcft outside the field of scientificness, is problematic. It is easy to see that the difficulty of a rigorous description of these languages of connotation* resides in the fact that by proceeding from their expression plane, it is impossible to predict connotations (which have as signifier a peculiarity of pronunciation, or the choice of a lexeme, or a syntactic turn of

phrase, etc.). It is even more difficult to propose a hierarchical distribution of these connotations (*i.e.*, a connotative semiotic system). For these reasons, R. Barthes' *Mythologies*, however ingenious and refined they may be, are but connotative fragments and do not succeed in even suggesting an underlying system.

From this we conclude that a directly opposite approach to languages of connotation must be attempted, one that would begin by establishing a theory of connotation, from which a description of connotative systems could be undertaken, based on the content plane. We have barely outlined this theory, by dealing with social connotations that are presented in the form of connotative taxonomies ("profane" and "sacred" languages, "internal" and "external" languages, "masculine" and "feminine" languages, etc.) in ethno-semiotics,* or in the form of connotative syntaxes (corresponding to a typology of discourses) in socio-semiotics.* Research in this field has barely begun; in addition to social connotations, Hjelmslev suggests that there are also individual connotations (more or less corresponding to ancient and modern characterology), connotations of which we have scarcely a vague idea; (f) Present usage tends to differentiate between **linguistic semiotic systems** and **non-linguistic semiotic systems,** with reference to the two privileged loci of manifestation of semiotics that we call (perhaps improperly) **macro-semiotic systems:** natural languages and natural worlds. This can be done only by postulating a separate, specific status for macro-semiotic systems— contrary to Hjelmslev for whom a natural language is one semiotic system like another (having, however, a

privileged character). These macro-semiotic systems must be considered capable of containing and developing autonomous semiotic systems (for example, a number of recent analyses concerning religious and legal discourse justify this last point).

Immediately, however, another problem comes to mind, that of the transgression of the boundary that we have just established, in the form of **syncretic*** **semiotic systems,** the existence of which is obvious at once. The expression plane of these systems is constituted by elements belonging to several heterogenous semiotic systems. If opera and film are presented at the outset as preemptory examples of syncretic discourses, one might wonder whether natural language—and oral discourse in particular—constitute only one, although essential, element of communication, beside other paralinguistic* or proxemic* elements; in this case, communication itself is syncretic; (g) Other distinctions may also be proposed, taking into account the generative* trajectory of discourse. Thus, we may oppose figurative* and non-figurative (or abstract) discourse, and, at the same time, **figurative** and **non-figurative semiotic systems,** depending on the level of depth that is textualized* and manifested.* The difference between discourse and semiotic system lies in the fact that the former is nothing else than the apprehension of the latter as process.

All these distinctions and reorganizations, even if they sometimes are a source of confusion within the semiotic field, should be considered as a sign of health and vitality for a semiotics that proposes itself both as a project for research and as already on-going research.

—PSYCHO-SEMIOTICS; SOCIO-

SEMIOTICS; ETHNO-SEMIOT-
ICS; LITERARY SEMIOTICS;
THEATER, SEMIOTICS OF;
PLANAR SEMIOTICS

(C) **Semiotic theory**

1. In definition (B), semiotics
was conceived as the adequate* superimposition of an object-semiotics
and a descriptive language. Here we
view it not only as (a) the locus for
the elaboration of procedures,* for
the construction* of models,* and
for the choice of systems of representation,* governing the descriptive* level (*i.e.,* the methodological
metalinguistic level), but also as (b) a
locus for the verification of the
homogeneity* and coherence* of
these procedures and models, as well
as (c) the locus for the explicitation
(in an axiomatic* form) of undefinables and of the foundation of this
entire theoretical construction (this
is the epistemological* level, strictly
speaking). From this point of view,
semiotics will be taken either as **general semiotics,** thus insisting on the
requirement imposed upon it, that it
account for the existence and functioning of all the particular semiotic
systems, or as **semiotic theory,** inasmuch as it is called upon to satisfy
conditions of scientificness proper to
any theory,* and inasmuch as it is
defined, therefore, as a metalanguage* (both as scientific meta-
semiotics and metasemiology, in
Hjelmslev's terminology).

2. In principle, several semiotic
theories—just as several generative
grammars—may be elaborated: only
their formalization would possibly
allow them to be compared and to
be evaluated with respect to one
another. Such a comparative approach is at the present time absolutely impossible, since no semiotic
theory worthy of its name yet exists;
on the one hand, we find intuitive
theories having no operational* procedures (often replaced by
peremptory "professions of faith")
and, on the other hand, procedures
that are sometimes formalized, but
which are not based on any explicit
theory. This authorizes us to limit
ourselves here to a brief account of
what we consider to be the general
conditions of a semiotic theory,
while, at the same time, referring to
our theoretical project.

3. Semiotic theory must be presented, first, for what it is, *i.e.,* as a
theory of signification. Its first concern, therefore, is to render explicit
the conditions for the apprehension
and production of meaning; this is
to be done in the form of a conceptual construction. Thus, by being
situated in the Saussurian and
Hjelmslevian tradition (according to
which signification is the creation
and/or apprehension of "differences"), it will have to bring together
all those concepts that, while being
themselves undefinable, are necessary in order to establish the definition of the elementary structure* of
signification. This conceptual explicitation then gives rise to a **formal
expression** of the concepts retained
by the theory. Considering structure
as a network of relations, semiotic
theory will have to formulate a
semiotic axiomatics that will be presented essentially as a typology of
relations (presupposition, contradiction, etc.). This axiomatics will permit the constitution of a stock of
formal definitions, such as, for
example, semantic category* (minimal unit) and semiotics itself (maximal unit). The latter includes, following Hjelmslev, the logical definitions of system (the "either . . . or"
relation) and of process ("both . . .
and"), of content and expression, of
form and substance, etc.

The next step consists in setting
up a minimal **formal language.** The

distinction between relations-as-states (for example, contradiction) and relations-as-operations (for example, negation) allows us to postulate symbol-terms and operator-terms, thus opening the way for the calculation of utterances.* It is only then that the theory will have to be concerned with the choice—or free choice—of the **representation systems** in which it will have to formulate its procedures and models (for example, the semiotic square* or elementary utterance*).

These few remarks are meant to give only a general idea of the approach that appears to be necessary for the construction of a semiotic theory. The elements of our semiotic project are scattered throughout this work.

4. To these general features of a semiotic theory, we must also add other, more specific, options upon which the articulation of its total economy will, nevertheless, depend. The first of these options is the **generative form** which, we believe, is suitable for its unfolding. By that, we mean, in a very broad sense, seeking out the definition of the semiotic object, viewed from the angle of its mode of production. This approach, leading from the most simple to the most complex and from the most abstract to the most concrete, has the advantage of allowing us to introduce, at appropriate intervals, a certain number of established items from linguistic theory, such as issues relative to "language" (Benveniste) or "competence" (Chomsky), but also the articulation of structures into levels according to their modes of existence*: virtual, actual, or realized. Thus, the semiotic generation of a discourse will be represented in the form of the mapping of a **generative* trajectory** involving a good

number of levels and components, distinctions that are perhaps only temporary and operational, but that allow us to situate the different fields of exercise of semiotic activity with respect to one another.

5. The second of our options consists in introducing into semiotic theory the questions of **enunciation,*** the putting of language into discourse (Benveniste) and of the specific, definable conditions that surround it, a problem treated, although differently, by American pragmatics. To the deep semiotic structures, located "in language" and in which "competence" finds its source, we have added discourse structures that are less deep, in such a way that they are constructed by passing through the filter constituted by the phenomenon of enunciation.

Semiotic theory must be more than a theory of the utterance—as is the case for generative grammar—and more than a semiotics of enunciation; it must reconcile what appears at first to be irreconcilable, by integrating them into a general semiotic theory.

—SCIENTIFICNESS; THEORY; GENERATIVE TRAJECTORY; ENUNCIATION; DISCOURSE; SEMIOLOGY

SENDER/RECEIVER
(destinateur/destinataire)

1. The terms **sender** and **receiver** (usually written with a small first letter)—taken over from R. Jakobson's schema of linguistic communication*—designate, in their most general sense, the two actants* of the communication (also called in information* theory source and receptor, but in a mechanical and non-dynamic perspective). When they are viewed as logically presup-

posed implicit actants of every utterance,* they are called enunciator* and enunciatee. When, by contrast, they are explicitly mentioned and are thereby recognizable in the utterance-discourse (for instance, "I"/"you") they are called narrator* and narratee. Finally, when the discourse reproduces the structure of communication by simulating it (*cf.* dialog*), they are called interlocutor* and interlocutee. In these last three cases it is clear that we are dealing with an act of delegation* originating from the sender and the receiver.

2. Considered as narrative. actants, Sender and Receiver (in this case usually written with a capital letter) are actantial domains characterized by a relation of unilateral presupposition (between Sender as presupposed term and Receiver as presupposing term). Consequently the communication between them is asymmetric. Paradigmatically, the Sender is in a hyperonymic* relation with the Receiver, while the latter is in a hyponymic* position. This asymmetry is amplified in the syntagmatization of these two actants, when they appear as two subjects concerned with a single object. This is what happens, for instance, in the case of participative communication.* Sender and Receiver are stable and permanent narrative actants, whatever might be the roles of communication actants that they can assume. Thus the subject-Receiver communicates, as sender, knowledge about its own performances.

3. Often posited as belonging to the trancendent* universe, the Sender is the one which communicates to the subject-Receiver (belonging to the immanent* universe) not only the elements of modal competence,* but also the set of values at stake. The Sender receives the communi-

cation concerning the results of the subject-Receiver's performance; it falls to the Sender to sanction* this performance. From this point of view and in the framework of the narrative* schema, the **manipulatory Sender** (the initial Sender) can be opposed to the **judicatory Sender** (the final Sender).

4. Given the polemical* structure of the narrative, the presence of a subject* and an anti-subject presupposes the existence of a Sender (S1) and of an anti-Sender (S2). This axis of contraries* can then—according to the semiotic square*—unfold and produce as contradictories* two new actantial positions: the position of non-Sender ($\overline{S1}$) and that of non-anti-Sender ($\overline{S2}$). It happens, for instance, that S1 assumes, on the pragmatic* dimension, the role of active and performing Sender (as communicating the elements of modal competence) in the framework of the positive deixis,* while $\overline{S2}$ is, on the cognitive* dimension, the passive Sender (receiving the knowledge about the subject-Receiver's doing and sanctioning it) and thus belongs to the negative deixis. In such a case the active Sender is inchoate, promoting movement and action (it is then related to the manipulation*); the passive Sender is conclusive, gathering in the fruits of the action (in the framework of the sanction*). Yet it is not sure that this organization of these actants on the semiotic square is actually part of the narrative structure properly speaking.

5. During the analysis of narratives it is sometimes necessary to make a distinction between **individual Sender**—as manifested in the case of vengeance*—and **social Sender,** called on to render justice.* Each of these two actants may manifest a having-to-do either compatible

or incompatible with that of the other.
—NARRATIVE SCHEMA; NARRATIVE TRAJECTORY

SENTENCE
(phrase)

1. Traditionally, a **sentence** is defined as a unit of the syntagmatic string,* characterized semantically by the relative autonomy of its signification and phonetically by the presence of prosodic* markers (pauses and modulations, capital letters and punctuation marks). It is clear that the semantic definition is intuitive (a sentence can contain several meaning units, several phrases) and that the phonetic criteria remain uncertain. These two approaches indeed try to define the sentence by something other than what it is: a syntactic unity.

2. Structural linguistics gives its syntactic independence to the sentence. So, for Bloomfield, the sentence, although being put together with the aid of constituent* elements, is not itself a constituent of any other, larger, unit. For his part, L. Hjelmslev defines the sentence as the largest syntactic unit, having an iterative character within the infinite text, and he considers it alone as capable of undergoing analysis.* Whether the approach is ascending and begins with minimal elements (Bloomfield) or whether it is descending and proceeds by segmentation (Hjelmslev), the result in the two cases is comparable: the sentence appears as a totality covering a syntactic hierarchy.* As a superior unit, beyond which one cannot go, the sentence imposes its limits on grammar which, by this fact, cannot be other than a **phrase-structure** grammar.

3. More than the dimensions of the sentence, it is its internal organization which both defines it and poses a problem. The binary structure is not necessary in the "nature of things," although it goes back to Aristotle (with the distinction subject/predicate) and is solidly maintained even now (Hjelmslev, Bloomfield, Chomsky); this is even more the case in that syntax is considered today as a language constructed on the basis of an axiomatics.* In other words, the definition of the fundamental structure of the sentence (its binary or ternary character) comes from an *a priori* choice. Thus, the determination of the elementary structure of the utterance is today replacing the set of problems concerning the sentence.
—UTTERANCE

SEQUENCE
(séquence)

1. In narrative semiotics, it is desirable to set aside the term **sequence** to designate a textual unit, obtained by the procedure of segmentation, thus distinguishing it from syntagms, located at a deeper* level.

2. The discrete quality of a sequence is guaranteed by the presence of demarcators* that serve to determine its boundaries. Comparison with the sequences that precede and follow makes possible the establishment of contrastive disjunctions,* allowing us to recognize either its formal properties or its identifiable semantic characteristics. This is done, in the first case, by distinguishing descriptive, dialogue, narrative sequences, etc., and, in the second, sequences such as "a walk," "a dance," "a hunt," "a dream," etc. Names of the first type aim at constituting a typology of discursive units, those of the second type are given as approximate summaries, of a thematic nature, that help in giv-

ing an idea of the general economy of the discourse being studied.

3. A sequence may be subdivided into smaller textual units*—segments—thus revealing the existence of an internal organization. The goal of such a division* is the identification of discourse units the dimensions of which will not necessarily correspond with a segmentation into sentences or paragraphs, but which will permit the discovery of underlying narrative utterances or syntagms. A purely operational* concept, the sequence thus does not coincide with narrative syntagm. —SEGMENTATION; SYNTAGM; OVERLAPPING

SET
(ensemble)

1. In mathematical terminology, a **set** is a collection of elements* (finite or infinite in number) which can be logically related among themselves or with elements of other sets.

2. In semiotics, it seems that its use can only be justified when it has the imprecise meaning of universe* or of micro-universe.* This is because the mathematical sense of this term, by the fact that it gives priority to the elements (or discrete units) over the relations, seems to be in contradiction with the structural approach, which never establishes the terms before the relations which define them, and for which only the latter are significative. For the sake of coherence, it is generally preferable not to use the concept of set.

3. It may nonetheless be useful, at times, to introduce the rather vague notion of **signifying set** to designate the union of the signifier* and the signified.* —SEMIOTIC SYSTEM; SEMIOTICS

SHIFTER
(shifter)

Shifter is an English word introduced by R. Jakobson and rendered in French as *embrayeur,* engager, (N. Ruwet). Further analysis of this concept, with respect to enunciation,* has led us to distinguish two different procedures, which are here rendered as engagement and disengagement.— ENGAGEMENT; DISENGAGEMENT

SIGN
(signe)

1. The **sign** is a unit* of the manifestation* plane constituted by the semiotic function,* *i.e.,* by the relation of reciprocal presupposition* (or solidarity*) that is established between entities* on the expression* plane (or signifier*) and on the content* plane (or signified*) during the language act.

2. For F. de Saussure, who raised the issue of the **linguistic sign,** the latter results from the union of signifier and signified (which, in his first analysis, he identifies with acoustical image and concept). Although, in developing his theory, he was consequently led to refine these two notions by considering the signifier and the signified only inasmuch as they serve to constitute linguistic form* (like the front and back of a sheet of paper), the term sign was commonly identified for a long time—and still is today—with the **minimal sign,** *i.e.,* with the "word" or, more rigorously, the morpheme* (or moneme* for A. Martinet). It is in this sense that the all-purpose definition of language as "system of signs" is used.

3. The contribution of L. Hjelmslev to the theory of the sign is

twofold: (a) by presenting the sign as the result of semiosis* taking place at the time of the language act, he demonstrates that the dimension* of the units of manifestation is not pertinent for the definition of the sign; in other words, in addition to minimal signs ("words"), we can also speak of utterance-signs or discourse- signs; (b) by postulating for each of the two planes of language (expression and content) the distinction between form* and substance,* he is led to specify the nature of the sign as the union of the form of expression and the form of content (thus, on the expression plane, it is the phonological,* and not the phonetic,* structure that enters into the constitution of signs).

4. The use of language produces, then, semiotic manifestation in the form of strings of signs. The analysis of signs, produced by the articulation of the form of expression and that of content, is possible only if the two planes of language are first disassociated the one from the other in order to be studied and described, each one separately. In other words, if the analysis of manifestation (aiming at the recognition and establishment of minimal signs) constitutes a necessary first step, semiotic exploration actually begins with the study of units smaller than the minimal sign, and must be pursued separately for each language plane, where the constituent units are no longer signs, but figures.*

5. The extra- or para-semiotic meaning of the term **sign** does nonetheless exist and is sometimes introduced into semiotic or linguistic literature. In this case, **sign** commonly designates "something that is there in order to represent something else." As used in semiotics, it then denotes any form of expression assigned to translate an "idea" or a "thing"—corresponding to the concept of formant.* Such a use of the term presupposes a particular conception of language,* *i.e.,* as a stock of "labels" to be attached to preexistent objects, as a pure and simple nomenclature (Hjelmslev).

6. Anglo-American linguistics, influenced by behaviorism, has either been scarcely interested in the issue of the sign, or else it has, under the influence of positivism, sought to introduce the notion of referent* into the definition of sign, by constructing a triangular model of its interpretation (Ogden and Richards, following Charles S. Peirce). The three terms of the model consist of: (a) the symbol (= the signifier, or representamen for Peirce), (b) the reference (= the signified, or interpretant for Peirce), and (c) the referent (the denoted "reality," or object according to Peirce). Saussurian linguistics, as we know, considers the exclusion of the referent as the necessary condition of the existence of linguistics.

7. The problem of the referent broadens even more the gap that continues to separate two conceptions of linguistics, and especially of semiotics. Whereas the analysis of signs is for European semiotics but one step toward a description of the articulation network of forms, American semiotics (T. Sebeok) tends to stop at the level of signs and to proceed to a classification of these signs, based for a large part on the type of relation existing between the sign and the referent (for example, the icon* is defined by a relation of resemblance, the index* by a relation of "natural" contiguity, the signal* by an artificial relation, etc.).

8. Another distribution of signs, of an intrinsic nature, seems possible; it would specify signs according to whether they belong to a

given type of semiotic* system (monoplanar, biplanar, pluriplanar). —SIGNIFIER; SIGNIFIED; ARTICULATION; SEMIOLOGY; REFERENT; SOCIO-SEMIOTICS

SIGNAL
(signal)

1. In information* theory, **signal** refers to any unit that enters into the composition of a message* by obeying rules of a code*; in the specific case of linguistic communication, it can be seen that the signal might be equivalent to, for example, those units on the expression* plane that we call phonemes.*

2. For L. Hjelmslev signals are the minimal units of manifestation of the monoplanar semiotic systems, whether they are scientific (for example, algebra) or non-scientific (for example, games).

3. For some (L. Prieto), the signal is part of the more general category of indices*; it would then be defined by the fact that it is produced to serve as an index (and not by chance) and by the fact that the person to whom the indication is destined may recognize it as such. Among the examples often used, let us cite road or marine navigational signs and signals.

4. If we acknowledge, with the Saussurian linguistic tradition, that the exclusion of the referent* is a necessary condition for the exercise of any semiotics, then we must also recognize that the signal, like the index, enters into the category of non-signs.
—MESSAGE; INDEX; SIGN

SIGNIFICATION
(signification)

1. **Signification** being the key concept around which all semiotic theory is organized, it is not surprising to see that it has a place in the different positions of the area of study that semiotic theory hopes to delimit. The term signification became progressively excluded from its initial delimitations because of the definitions and names that were set up incorporating it. Nevertheless, it kept its parasynonomous uses in everyday language. We shall note some of these.

2. Like all nouns of this subclass (*cf.* description, operation, etc.), signification may sometimes designate a doing (signification as a process), sometimes a state (that which is signified), thus revealing a dynamic or a static conception of the underlying theory. From this point of view, signification may be paraphrased either as a "production of meaning" or as "meaning already produced."

3. We arrive at a first delimitation of the semantic field embraced by "signification," by opposing it to "meaning," *i.e.,* by saving the latter term for that which is anterior to semiotic production. We will thus define signification as articulated* meaning. That means that the term "signification" is sometimes used to designate the "purport" in the Hjelmslevian sense, but this acceptation ought to be excluded from semiotic metalanguage.

4. Conjointly with the term meaning, signification is still used to denote the content* substance.* As the content substance has already been selected with signification in mind and as it presupposes the existence of the content form, use of the term "signification" is not incorrect; it is superfluous. We have the same situation when signification is employed as synonymous with the signified* of the sign or with the content plane in general.

5. Signification is also used as a synonym for semiosis* (or the act of signifying) and is then interpreted either as the union of the signifier* and the signified* (constituent of the sign*), or as the relation of reciprocal presupposition* that defines the constituted sign.

6. Since these uses of the term are already provided with particularizing semantic labels, we reserve the term signification for what appears essential to us, *i.e.,* for "difference"—the production and reception of gaps—that defines, according to Saussure, the very nature of language. Understood in this sense as the construction and perception of relationships, signification is established as "articulated meaning" in the *meaning/signification* dichotomy and, as a general concept, subsumes at the same time all the acceptations presented above.

7. To this axiomatizing definition of signification, we must add another one, of an empirical character, bearing no longer on its "nature," but on the means of apprehending it as a knowable object. We then realize that signification can be grasped only during its manipulation, when, pondering over it in a given language and text, the enunciator is led to operate transpositions and translations* from one text to another text, from one level of language to another, and, finally, from one semiotic system to another semiotic system. This paraphrasing* activity may be considered as the representation of signification as a producing act, uniting in one domain the interpreter-enunciatee (as signification is not an *ex nihilo* production) and the producer-enunciator. As a programmed cognitive activity, signification is then supported and sustained by intentionality,* which is another manner of para-

phrasing signification.

—MEANING; STRUCTURE (B: Elementary structure of signification); CONTENT

SIGNIFIED
(signifié)

1. In the Saussurian tradition, by the term **signified** is designated one of the two planes* of language (the other being the signifier*), the union of which (or semiosis*) constitutes signs as bearers of signification,* during the language act.* The signifier and the signified are defined by a relationship of reciprocal presupposition.* This acceptation of the term, of an operational* character, is satisfactory for semiotics, since the latter abstains from making any ontological judgment concerning the nature of the "signified."

2. Different readings of Saussure's *Course in General Linguistics* have given rise to diverse interpretations of the sign. Proceeding in a didactic way, Saussure begins by representing the sign as constituted by an acoustical image (= signifier) and by a concept (= signified). If one stops at this point, it appears that the sign is to be identified with the morpheme* and the signified with the lexeme*—that would reduce the Saussurian innovation to next to nothing. A continued reading of the *Course* leads to a totally different representation of language, developed in a metaphorical form with a sheet of paper whose front side would be the signifier and whose back side would be the signified; the arabesque designs that are traced on the paper would give an idea of the way in which linguistic form* should be conceived. This second formulation insists on the indissoluble character of the bond between signifier and signified and

on the fact that they incorporate the totality of the text (and not only words taken separately). It is on the basis of this second formulation, the heart of Saussurian theory, that L. Hjelmslev adopted the signifier/signified dichotomy, but in terms of language planes,* by calling the signifier the expression plane, and the signified the content plane.
—CONTENT; SIGN; SIGNIFIER

SIGNIFIER
(signifiant)

1. By **signifier** is meant one of the two constituent terms of the category of semiosis,* in which two entities* are necessary during the language act in order to produce a semiotic manifestation. Such a definition is formal: only the relation of reciprocal presupposition* (or solidarity*) defines, respectively, the two terms in question—signifier and signified—excluding any other semantic investment.

2. Historically, and depending on how one reads F. de Saussure, signifier sometimes means one of the constituent entities of the minimal sign* (or morpheme*), corresponding, in Saussure's own first approximation, to the "acoustical image." At other times it means a language plane,* considered as a whole and incorporating in its articulations* the totality of signifieds. It is from this second conception of the Saussurian signifier that L. Hjelmslev, by calling it the expression* plane, defined it as one of the two constituent planes of any semiotics (or of any language).

3. We can follow Hjelmslev when he says that the concepts of signifier and signified, by the very presence of the formal relation that constitutes them, are interchangeable, especially when we are dealing

with pluri-planar* semiotics. Nevertheless, in the case of biplanar semiotics (such as natural languages), the signifier is perceived by relation to the signified, as the external plane of language, as exterior to humans, stemming from the natural universe and manifested by its perceptible qualities. Thus, whether it be at the level of perception (hearing, reading, viewing) or at the level of emission by the subject constructing his/her utterance, the signifier finds itself referentialized and appears as belonging to the world. Only a deeper analysis of the expression plane succeeds in showing that the signifier is also the result of a construction that is semantic in character.

4. This "material" aspect of the signifier can only suggest a classification of different semiotic* systems according to the nature of the substance* of the signifier, *i.e.,* according to the sensorial orders (or communication channels*) by which the perceptible qualities of the world are arranged. In this sense, we can, for example, speak of visual, olfactive, or tactile semiotics. Such a classification does not, however, inform us about the mode of existence and organization of the signifier: natural languages, musical semiotics, and the language of noises cannot be sufficiently defined by the sound signifier that they have in common, and their specificity, even on this plane alone, must be sought for elsewhere, in the articulation* mode of the form* of the signifier.

5. The term signifier is used by non-linguists (the most often in texts inspired by psychoanalysis) to designate "everyday language" (a most confusing notion). As such, this use cannot be placed in an homologous relation with the semiotic definition of the signifier; at the very best the

signifier might be considered as a sort of "meta-signifier" inasmuch as everyday language, taken as a whole, might play the role of signifier on a new plane of the signified. This, however, would be possible only if natural languages were really denotative,* *i.e.,* did not develop within themselves secondary semiotic systems (religion, law, morals, etc.).
—SIGNIFIED; EXPRESSION; SIGN

SIMPLICITY
(simplicité)

1. L. Hjelmslev considers **simplicity** as one of the three criteria —along with coherence* and exhaustivity*—for the scientificness of a theory.* From the postulate of simplicity, he deducts two other principles—those of reduction* and economy*—which scientific activity must obey.

2. In semiotic practice, the application of the principle of simplicity is translated by "simplification," *i.e.,* by the optimization of syntagmatic procedures, which can itself be manifested either by the reduction of the number of operations that an analysis procedure requires, or by the choice of particular systems of metalinguistic representation,* etc.
—EMPIRICISM; SCIENTIFICNESS; OPTIMIZATION; PROGRAMMING, SPATIO-TEMPORAL

SIMULATED TEST
(simulée [épreuve—])

When camouflage*—which, starting from the true,* consists in negating the term *seeming* and thereby in producing a state of secret*—is followed by a performance,* the syntagmatic unit that is constituted in this way is called **simulated test.** Such is the case

when, for example, the role of the anti-subject is taken on by the sender* or its delegate (example: in the Bible, the wrestling with the Angel, in which Jacob confronts God).

The simulated test seems to affect above all the qualifying* test.
—CAMOUFLAGE; VERIDICTORY MODALITIES; TEST

SOCIOLECT
(sociolecte)

1. As opposed to both idiolect,* which designates the semiotic activities of an individual actor, and to dialect,* which refers to the differentiation of these same activities considered from a social point of view (the differentiation is due to a geographical distribution of human groups), **sociolect** characterizes semiotic activity in its relations with social stratification. If the organizations of a given society are viewed as extra-semiotic phenomena, the semiotic configurations that correspond to them constitute the signifying face of these organizations, for they reveal how society, classes, and social strata or groupings are distinguished from one another. Sociolects are thus sorts of sub-languages, recognizable by the semiotic variations that oppose them to one another (their expression* plane) and by the social connotations* that accompany them (their content plane*). Sociolects are constituted as social taxonomies, underlying social discourse. The study of sociolects stems from a particular discipline, socio-semiotics.*

2. Sociolectal variations can be pinpointed either on the lexical surface level (*cf.* nomenclatures,* terminologies,* etc.) or on the level of discourse organizations (writing* can be assimilated to a sociolectical act, as opposed to style,* which is of an idiolectical order). At the level of

deep* semantic structures,* the **sociolectal universe** is characterized both by a particular use of the *nature/culture* category (by providing the collective* semantic universe* with specific hypotactic investments) and by its articulation of the *life/death* category, which allows it to interpret the individual* semantic universe in its own fashion. In the long run, it is a matter of accounting for the attitude that a socio-cultural community adopts with respect to fundamental issues that it faces.

—UNIVERSE, SEMANTIC; PSY-CHO-SEMIOTIC; IDIOLECT; SOCIO-SEMIOTICS

SOCIO-SEMIOTICS
(socio-sémiotique)

1. In a field that might be encompassed by the term **socio-semiotics,** only **socio-linguistics** can claim the status of a somewhat established discipline. The attempt to bring together two disciplines— sociology and linguistics—the methodologies of which are heterogeneous, has given rise to inquiries that can briefly be grouped under two main aspects: (a) research dealing with the co-variations of linguistic structures and social structures, and (b) research concerned with the social context of linguistic communication.

2. The study of co-variations, irreproachable in itself, does indeed present problems when the nature of the retained variables is examined a little more closely. As long as one relates the traditional social classes (aristocracy, bourgeoisie, workers) on the one hand, and to the registers* of language on the other, this comparison is generally accepted as self-evident. But the criteria used to establish the social stratification of our industrial societies (such as "life-styles": behavior regarding clothing, cooking, habitat, etc.) appear, for the semiotician, to stem from signifying practices* that belong to what he considers as the vast domain of semiotic systems and processes called non-linguistic.* Correlating them with linguistic practices is then, for him/her, a question of semiotic intertextuality* and not of socio-linguistic interdisciplinarity. Furthermore, linguistic structures, which constitute the second variable of the correlation, have nothing that allows us to consider them as "structures": the marks by which one can recognize the speech of "white collar workers" or the New York City dialect are disparate, stemming from all planes and levels of language. Since they cannot be structured, they are rather dispersed indices that refer to something other than the language under consideration, *i.e.,* to a language of social connotation.*

3. Similar remarks may be made concerning a comparison between social context and linguistic communication. Semiotics cannot be satisfied with the concept of communication,* developed within the framework of information theory, in which the two domains, of the source and of the destination, would be considered as automatons* in charge of neutral information. Communication brings into play complex semiotic syncretisms,* in which somatic attitudes, gestuality, and spatial proximity play an important role. Its participants are not automatons, but competent* subjects; the logical presuppositions and implications that can be drawn from an analysis of the exchanged messages show them to be equipped with much know-how (knowing-how-to-do), possesssing numerous cultural codes. That being the case, one can wonder whether the information

(probably insufficient, but sure) that an analysis of the utterance offers us does not enlighten us more about the nature of enunciation* than do the sociological parameters, drawn somewhat haphazardly and in indefinite numbers as if from a magician's hat. In both cases—whether we are dealing with structural correlations or with the status of communication—methodological coherence seems preferable to interdisciplinary ambitions, especially since this coherence will be better maintained by inscribing linguistic problems within a more general semiotic framework.

4. In order to provide a firm grounding for its first steps, semiotics has to postulate the existence of a semantic universe,* considered as the totality of significations prior to analysis; it thus encroaches on the "sociological" by arbitrarily distinguishing between the collective* universe and the individual* universe. By next proposing on a hypothetical basis the elementary categories* of *culture/nature* and *life/death* as capable of articulating these two universes (in a first approximation), semiotics can contemplate defining the *sociolect** as the specific way (distinctive for each society) of interpreting and assuming both the collective universe and the individual universe (*i.e.*, of defining what each society means by culture and nature, life and death). It can be seen that such an *a priori* conceptualization is aimed at giving a representation of culture* identified with "society as signification" and, at the same time, of accounting for a possible typology of cultures as ambient cultural relativism.

5. The universality of culture and cultural specificities form together one of the subjects of research in semiotic theory, which seeks to elucidate them and systematically analyze them through the diversity of semiotic systems and processes than can be understood as axiologies* or as ideologies,* and which can be defined as models of action* or manipulation.* For socio-semiotics—insofar as such a terminological distinction may be of some use—would be reserved the vast domain of social connotations*; we shall briefly indicate some of the dimensions of the latter.

6. A first level of connotation corresponds to what we could consider as a "mythical epistemology," made up of the attitudes that a given society adopts with regard to its own signs (Y. Lotman, M. Foucault) and which can be detected just as well in discourses that speak of signs as in those that analyze or interpret them, from myths of the origin of language to the most recent philosophies of language. We know, for example, that medieval signs are metonymic and refer to a totality of meaning, that eighteenth-century signs are "natural" and that the Saussurian sign is called "bourgeois" by R. Barthes. Some of these interpretations can be questioned; others can enrich semiotic theory. Whatever the case may be, it should be noted that, within the field of linguistics, scientific activity in the strict sense of the term is relatively independent of the sign theories to which this activity is, nonetheless, attached. Everything happens as if scientific research, having attained a degree of maturation, were progressively liberating itself of the gnoseological variations that are thought to give it a basis.

7. Another level of connotation, rather closely connected to the first, seems to subtend discourses and establish the mode and degree of veridiction* that a society attributes to

them: what is "reality" and what is only "fiction," what is a "true story" and what is only a "joke" (criteria for a classification of literary "genres" and for a typology of "possible worlds") stem from a cultural ontology of a connotative order.

8. As long as we are dealing with archaic or traditional societies, it is easy to add to the above a taxonomy of social languages, based on ten or so differentiating categories (such as as "sacred"/"profane," "external"/"internal," "masculine"/ "feminine," "superior"/"inferior," etc.), that embrace a stable social morphology. When macro-societies develop, these rigid frameworks break up into a large number of social discourses (sacred language, for example, turning into religious, philosophical, poetic discourse, etc.) corresponding to "users' guilds" (with their entry dues). At the same time the closed connotation morphologies of these discourses (by which speaking subjects are bound to their languages) are transformed into flexible connotative syntax (each individual being relatively free to choose his/her own language according to the circumstances). Furthermore, these morphologies are transformed into real communication strategies in which connotative investments win out over denotative contents. What frequently appears at the surface as a democratization of society by language is, in fact, but the construction of a new Tower of Babel, all the more dangerous as it gives people the impression that they speak one and the same language.

9. As if in order to fill the void left by the proliferation of languages and also by the disappearance of the whole of folk literature, new semiotic forms are developing, forms that tend to reinforce the weakened social cohesion. They are manifested in the form of a **socio-literature,** the genre theories of which (detective stories, westerns, advice to the lovelorn, horoscopes, etc.) have yet to be established. They are also manifested by various "socio-spectacular" semiotic systems (sports events, horse races, bicycle races, etc.) that are close to the complex syncretic objects that used to exist (such as poetry that was sung and danced at the same time). Thus is opened a vast domain that socio-semiotics, interested in both the means (*i.e.,* media) and their social finality, could undertake to identify and organize.
—SEMIOTICS; CONNOTATION; ETHNO-SEMIOTICS

SOLIDARITY
(solidarité)

L. Hjelmslev introduced the term **solidarity** to name reciprocal presupposition as recognized in the syntagmatic string.* Use tends to apply this concept to paradigmatic* relationships as well.—PRESUPPOSITION

SOMATIC
(somatique)

1. The adjective **somatic** is generally used to qualify a figurative* actor (character), located and acting in the pragmatic* dimension of discourse. **Somatic doing*** is either pragmatic (if it refers to a programmed bodily activity) or communicative (the human body being able to signify by gestures, attitudes, miming, etc.). It will therefore be useful, in the latter case, to distinguish between somatic communication* and verbal* communication.

2. Under certain conditions that remain to be determined (when a pragmatic narrative—for example,

a miracle narrative in the Gospel—is inserted into another, broader, narrative), somatic doing is related (or accomplished) not only with respect to an assigned goal (a healing, for example), but also in regard to an actant observer* (usually implicit) which is supposed to read and interpret this narrative (or this behavior) constructed as signification. Such a somatic doing, both pragmatic and communicative, brings about a meaning effect of "irreality" and is read on the cognitive* dimension of discourse.

—PRAGMATIC; GESTUALITY

SOURCE
(émetteur)

1. In information* theory, the source, opposed to the destination,* designates the domain (person or apparatus) in the process of communication* which is the origin of the message.*

2. In semiotics, and for all kinds of communication (and not merely verbal communication) the term sender* (borrowed from R. Jakobson) is most often used with a partially comparable meaning. In the more specific case of linguistic communication (whether oral or written), the source is called enunciator.*

3. This terminological difference is linked to the difference between communication theory and semiotics. While the source represents an empty position (in a fundamentally mechanistic perspective which aims at using simple automatons), the sender is a subject endowed with a specific competence and considered at a given point of its becoming—this corresponds to the more "humanizing" point of view adopted by semiotics.

SPACE
(espace)

1. The term space is used in semiotics with different meanings, the common denominator of which is that space is considered as a constructed object (having discontinuous elements)—constructed on the basis of area, this latter being envisaged as a full, filled-up, seamless entity. The construction of the space-object can be examined from the geometrical point of view (every other property having been excluded), from the psycho-physiological point of view (as a progressive emergence of spatial qualities out of primordial confusion), or from the socio-cultural point of view (as the cultural organization of nature; example, a town as inhabited and organized space). When all the different metaphorical uses of this word are added together, one can see that the use of the term space requires great prudence on the semiotician's part.

2. Insofar as semiotics wants to account for the subject considered as producer and as consumer of space, the definition of space implies the participation of all the senses, requiring that all sensible qualities (visual, tactile, thermic, acoustic, etc.) be considered. The space-object is then viewed as partially identical with the object of the semiotics of the natural world* (which treats not only of the significations of the world, but also of those which are connected with the somatic behavior of human beings), and the exploration of space is but the explicit* construction of such a semiotic system. Semiotics of space is nonetheless distinguished therefrom by the fact that it seeks to account for the transformation which the natural semiotic system undergoes due to

human intervention. Such an intervention, by producing new relations between subjects and "fabricated" objects (invested with new values), substitutes—at least in part—artificial semiotic systems for the natural semiotic system.

3. In the more restricted meaning of the word, space is defined only by its **visual properties.** It is thus that architectural semiotics (and at times even the semiotics of urbanism) deliberately limits its object to the sole consideration of forms, volumes, and of their reciprocal relations. However, since it is proper to account for the human subjects who are the users of spaces, their programmed behavior patterns are examined and related to the use they make of space. This inscription of narrative programs* in segmented spaces makes up spatial programmation,* functional in nature, which so far seems to be the component of spatial semiotics that has acquired a certain operational* efficiency. When its functional character is left aside, this programmation corresponds approximately to the models of spatial distribution used in the analysis of narrative discourses.

4. With an additional restriction, space stands defined solely by its **tri-dimensionality,** wherein one of its axes, prospectivity (*cf.* perspective in painting) is valorized. This axis corresponds, in narrative discourse, to the text's linearity, which follows the subject's trajectory. For its part, **planar semiotics** (bi-dimensional) is led, beginning from a surface which is but a set of configurations and of colored areas, to account for the putting in place of the procedures which allow the subject (located facing the surface) to be given the illusion of a prospective space. The fact that scholars have

been concerned with understanding the construction of the prospective dimension perhaps partially explains why planar semiotics is not as developed as it could be.

5. In addition to the concept of spatialization* and of spatial localization, narrative and discursive semiotics uses also the concept of **cognitive* space,** which allows an accounting to be made of the inscription in space of cognitive relations (such as: seeing, hearing, touching, coming closer in order to hear, etc.) between subjects.

—WORLD, NATURAL; SPATIALIZATION; LOCALIZATION, SPATIO-TEMPORAL; COGNITIVE; DISENGAGEMENT

SPATIALIZATION
(*spatialisation*)

1. Despite the favor in which the notion of space* is held at present, the semantic field embraced by this term remains ambiguous and uncertain. Various semiotics use this term in their own way; but as yet there has ensued no comparative and overall effort of reflection.

2. In the overall generative* trajectory, **spatialization** appears as one of the components of discoursivization* (*i.e.,* the putting into discourse of deeper semiotic structures). First, it comprises procedures of spatial localization,* which can be interpreted as operations of disengagement* and engagement,* carried out by the enunciator* in order to project out from itself and apply onto the utterance-discourse a more or less autonomous spatial organization that serves as a framework for the inscription of narrative programs* and their concatenations. Spatialization also includes procedures for spatial programming,* thanks to which a linear disposition

of partial spaces (obtained through localizations) is realized; this disposition conforms with the temporal programming of the narrative programs.

3. Spatial localization, located in the pragmatic* dimension of discourse, is to be differentiated from **cognitive spatialization,** which consists in investing with spatial properties (*cf.* "seeing," "hearing," "saying," "touching," etc.) the cognitive relations between various actants (between subjects, but also between subjects and objects). Discursive analysis, which seeks to identify and organize such occurrences of spatiality, is justified, in return, in instituting a cognitive* dimension, superimposed on the pragmatic dimension, but unable to enter into a homologous relationship with it.

4. The notion of cognitive spatialization introduces the issue of proxemics,* a discipline the project of which is situated outside discoursive semiotics. By seeking to analyze the disposition of subjects and objects in space (from a point of view that is no longer that of the description of spatiality, but of the exploitation of space carried out with a view to signification), proxemics poses the problem of spatial languages that use spatial categories in order to speak about something other than space.

—SPACE; DISCOURSIVIZATION; DISENGAGEMENT; LOCALIZATION, SPATIO-TEMPORAL; PROGRAMMING, SPATIO-TEMPORAL; COGNITIVE; PROXEMICS

SPEAKER
(locuteur)

Instead of the term **speaker,** which is used to designate actants within dialogue,* we prefer the term interlocutor, which has the advantage of bringing to mind the intersubjective structure of communication.*—INTERLOCUTOR

SPEECH
(parole)

1. In the Saussurian dichotomy **speech** is opposed to natural language* without it being a well defined concept for all that. Indeed, as this dichotomy was posited and developed by F. de Saussure only in order better to circumscribe the notion of natural language (for him the sole object of linguistics), speech appeared from its origin as a kind of catchall notion; but its suggestive force has nevertheless been considerable during the subsequent development of linguistics. The underlying set of problems split up subsequently into a series of conceptualizations, variable from one theory to another, so that today the concept of speech has ceased to be operational.*

2. The following concepts can be considered as partial reinterpretations of speech (in the Saussurian sense): (a) **Process** (opposed to system*), which is for L. Hjelmslev one of the two ways of being of the structured (or structurable) universe, and **syntagmatics*** (opposed to paradigmatics*), defined as semiotic process covering one of the aspects of speech, in the sense of an arrangement of the elements of speech in view of the construction of sentences; (b) **Message*** (opposed to code*) considers speech, in communication* theory, as the product of the code (but without taking account of the process of production*); (c) **Discourse** (opposed to natural language), conceived by E. Benveniste as natural language assumed and transformed by the

speaking subject, occupies in his analyses a place comparable to that of speech in Saussure's theories. However, his insistence on the role of the subject which assumes natural language provides a new dichotomy, that of enunciation* and of utterance,* which are two complementary aspects of speech for Saussure; (d) **Performance*** (opposed to competence*) corresponds in generative* theory to the term speech insofar as it insists on its aspects of realization* (contrary to natural language, which is virtual*). By the same token it situates the activity which forms sentences on competence's side; (e) **Use*** (opposed to schema*), according to Hjelmslev, corresponds to the "psycho-physical mechanism" of speech according to Saussure, and, by subsuming everything which in language belongs to substance, is opposed to the linguistic schema considered as form.* Thus, syntagmatics, as form, is placed alongside of schema; (f) **Stylistics*** (opposed to linguistics) seeks, finally, to exploit everything which in speech concerns individual use (and not the activity of the enunciator* considered as "speaking subject") or, indeed, collective use.
—PERFORMANCE; LANGUAGE, NATURAL

SQUARE, SEMIOTIC
(carré sémiotique)

1. By **semiotic square** is meant the visual representation* of the logical articulation of any semantic category.* The elementary structure* of signification, when defined—in a first step—as a relation between at least two terms,* rests only on a distinction of opposition* which characterizes the paradigmatic axis of language. It is, consequently, adequate for the establishment of a paradigm* composed of *n* terms, but it does not thereby allow for the distinction, within this paradigm, of semantic categories founded on the isotopy* (the "family relations") of distinctive* features which can be recognized therein. A typology of relations is necessary, which will make it possible to distinguish intrinsic features, those which constitute the category, from those which are foreign to it.

2. The linguistic tradition which sprang up in the 1920s and '30s has imposed the binary* conception of category. In the wake of comparative research into morphological categories, it was rare for linguists (such as V. Brøndal, for example) to uphold the existence of multipolar structures containing as many as six inter-linked terms. However, even R. Jakobson, one of the defenders of binarism, was obliged to recognize the existence of two types of binary relations: the first, of the type A/Ā, characterized by the resultant opposition of the presence* and absence of a definite trait, and the second, of the type A/non-A, which manifests to some extent the same trait, present twice in different forms. On the basis of this knowledge, the result of linguistic doing, it has been possible to establish a typology of intercategorial relations.

3. **The first generation of categorial terms.** It is sufficient to start with the opposition A/non-A, and, while considering that the logical nature of this relation remains undetermined, to call it the **semantic axis,** in order to realize that each of the terms of this axis may separately enter into a new relation of the type A/A. The representation of this

group of relations is then given the form of a square:

It remains for us to identify these various relations one by one: (a) The first—A/Ā—defined by the impossibility for two terms to be present together, is known as the relation of **contradiction,*** which is its static definition. From the dynamic point of view, it can be said that this is the operation of negation,* carried out on the term A (or non-A), which generates its contradictory Ā (or $\overline{\text{non}}$-Ā). Thus, starting with the two primitive terms, it is possible to generate new contradictory terms (terms of the first generation); (b) The second operation is that of **assertion***: carried out on the contradictory terms (Ā, $\overline{\text{non}}$-Ā), it can be presented as an **implication*** and may cause the two primitive terms to appear as presupposed elements of the terms asserted (Ā ⊃ non-A; $\overline{\text{non}}$-Ā ⊃ A). If, and only if, the effect of this double assertion is to produce these two parallel implications, we are right in saying that the two presupposed primitive terms are the terms of one and the same category and that the chosen semantic axis is constitutive of a semantic category. On the contrary, if Ā does not imply non-A and if $\overline{\text{non}}$-Ā does not imply A, the primitive terms—A and non-A—with their contradictories, are dependent on different semantic categories. In the first case, the operation of implication established between the terms (Ā and non-A) and ($\overline{\text{non}}$-Ā and A) is a relation of **complementarity***; (c) The two primitive terms are both presupposed terms; characterized moreover by the fact that they can be present concomitantly (or, in logical terms, that they

can be true or false together—a criterion which is difficult to apply in semiotics), they are said to enter into a relation of **reciprocal presupposition*** or which comes to the same thing, a relation of **contrariety.***

It is now possible to give a definitive representation of what we call the semiotic square:

where:
   ◄——► : relation of contradiction
   ◄----► : relation of contrariety
   ——► : relation of complementarity
   S_1 - S_2 : axis of contraries
   $\bar{S}_2$ - $\bar{S}_1$: axis of sub-contraries
   S_1 - $\bar{S}_1$: positive schema
   S_2 - $\bar{S}_2$: negative schema
   S_1 - $\bar{S}_2$: positive deixis
   S_2 - $\bar{S}_1$: negative deixis

There remains, however, one point which requires clarification; that of the existence of binary semantic categories *stricto sensu* (whose constitutive relation is not contrariety, but contradiction), such as, for example, *assertion/negation*. There is nothing to prevent such categories from being represented in a square:

It is clear from this that the negation of a negation is equivalent to assertion. Generalizing, it can be said that a semantic category may be called contradictory when the negation of its primitive terms produces tautological implications. Such a definition, taxonomic* in nature, satisfies traditional logic, which can operate substitutions* in both directions (non-oriented) by replacing *assertion* with *negation,* or inversely. In linguistics, things happen differently: discourse retains the traces of previously carried out syntactic operations

"yes"   "no"

↑

"certainly"

The term "certainly" is, of course, the equivalent of "yes," but at the same time it contains, in the form of an implicit presupposition, an operation of prior negation. Thus, it is preferable in semiotic descriptions to use—even for the contradictory categories—the canonical representation in square form.

4. **The second generation of categorial terms.** It has been shown how two parallel operations of negation, carried out on the primitive terms, enabled two contradictory terms to be generated, and how, following this, two implications established relations of complementarity by determining, at that same time, the relation of contrariety which thus has become recognizable between the two primitive terms. We will not take the time to go through, beginning with the network thus constituted, the same operations which, by the negation of the subcontraries, establish a reciprocal presupposition between them. It is important now to derive the first consequences of the relational model* thus constructed: (a) Clearly, the four terms of the category are not defined in a substantial manner, but only as points of intersection, as the results of relations: this satisfies the structural principle laid down by F. de Saussure, according to which "in language, there are only differences"; (b) It will also be noted that, starting from the projection of the contradictories, four new relations have been recognized within the square: two relations of contrariety (the axis of the contraries and of the subcontraries), and two relations of complementarity (positive and negative deixes); (c) Given that every semiotic system is a hierarchy,* it is established that the relations contracted between terms may serve, in their turn, as terms establishing between themselves hierarchically superior relations (functions* playing the role of functives, in L. Hjelmslev's terminology). In this case it is said that two relations of contrariety enter into the relation of contradiction between themselves, and that two relations of complementarity establish the relation of contrariety between themselves. The following example illustrates this finding:

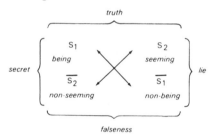

It can thus be seen that *truth* and *falseness* are **contradictory metaterms,** whereas *secret* and *lie* are **contrary metaterms.** The metaterms and the categories they constitute are considered as terms and categories of the second generation.

5. **The third generation of categorial terms.** The problem so far not tackled is that of the third generation of terms. In fact, the comparative research of V. Brøndal has shown the existence, within the network which articulates the grammatical categories, of **complex** and **neutral** terms which are a result of the establishment of the relation "both . . . and" between contrary terms. The complex term is seen as

the joining of the terms of the axis of the contraries ($S_1 + S_2$), whereas the neutral term results from the combination of the terms of the axis of the subcontraries ($\bar{S}_1 + \bar{S}_2$). Some natural languages may even be able to produce **positive complex terms** and **negative complex terms**, depend on which of the two terms constituting them dominates.

Various solutions have been proposed to account for the formation of such terms. While not wishing to put forward yet another hypothesis, we consider that until more precise and more numerous descriptions are furnished, the problem area remains open. For all that, the importance of the problem is inescapable: we know that discourses of a sacred, mythic,* poetic,* etc., nature manifest a particular predilection for the use of complex categorial terms. The solution becomes difficult since it implies the recognition of highly complex and probably contradictory syntactical trajectories, which culminate in this kind of formation.

6. The semiotic square can be usefully compared to the hexagon of R. Blanché, and to the groups of Klein and Piaget. It is dependent, however, both on the epistemological question which deals with the conditions of existence and the production of signification, and on methodological doing applied to concrete linguistic objects. In this it is distinguished from logical or mathematical constructions, which are independent, as formulations of "pure syntax," from the semantic component. Under these conditions, any hasty identification of the semiotic models with the logico-mathematical models can only be hazardous.
—STRUCTURE

STATE
(état)

1. The term **state** can be homologated with that of continuous* (as noun); the discontinuous, which introduces a break, is the locus of transformation.*

2. To account for diachronic* transformations, linguistics uses the concept of **language state** (or linguistic state); the intervening transformations can be described only by first postulating the existence of two successive language states. These language states are defined in different ways: (a) either as two synchronic* cross-sections, made in the continuum of history and separated by a certain length of time (this is an empirical and trivial approach); (b) or as two achronic* linguistic structures belonging to a typology of natural languages (L. Hjelmslev); (c) or, finally, as two states of relatively unstable equilibrium,* where the tendencies which are recognizable in the first state—thanks to this comparison—appear as solutions realized in the second (E. Benveniste).

Of course, these linguistic approaches can be applied to the study of the transformations of semiotic systems in general.

3. Discourse and, more particularly, narrative discourse, can be considered as a series of **states,** preceded and/or followed by transformations.* The logico-semantic representation of such discourse must thus introduce **utterances of state,** corresponding to junctions* between subjects and objects, and utterances of doing, which express the transformations.

—DIACHRONY; UTTERANCE; SYNTAX, SURFACE NARRATIVE

STRATEGY
(stratégie)

1. Borrowed in part from game theory, the term **strategy** is being introduced little by little into semiotics, where it incorporates a set of problems the perimeters of which are still very vague. It would first be necessary to differentiate **discourse strategy** (that is, that of the subject of enunciation* engaged in putting narrative structures into discourse or discoursivization*) from **narrative strategy** (which aims at elaborating narrative* schemas from which the generation of discourse can be envisaged).

2. Narrative strategy seems to comprise, on the one hand, programming* in the broad sense of the term (that is, the establishment of complex narrative programs* that bear on the construction, circulation, and destruction of objects* of value, as well as the institution of delegated subjects, responsible for executing annex narrative programs), and, on the other hand, manipulation* in the strict sense of the term (that is, the exercise of "causing-to-do" which leads the anti-subjects to construct and realize narrative programs desired in reality by the subjects). In these two directions, strategy encroaches on the domains of narrative syntax,* dealing with the setting up and functioning of narrative trajectories.* It would perhaps be best to reserve this term for the highest and last domain of narrative organization, by locating at that level the examination of the modes of inter-articulation of these syntactic units, known as broad narrative* trajectories.
—NARRATIVE TRAJECTORY

STRING
(chaîne)

String or **spoken string** is the common traditional term used to designate the syntagmatic axis of language. It has the advantage of evoking stringing together—and not simple linearity—which governs the organization of this axis.—SYNTAGMATIC; AXIS

STRUCTURALISM
(structuralisme)

1. **Structuralism** designates either, in the American sense, the achievements of the Bloomfieldian School, or, in the European sense, the continuation of the theoretical effort of the Prague and Copenhagen Schools, based on Saussurian principles. The fundamental incompatibility between these two perspectives derives from the way the problem of signification* is considered. Whereas for Bloomfield syntax is only a continuation of phonology (phonemes form morphemes, morphemes form sentences) without meaning* intervening at any point, European structuralism, following Saussure, differentiates between the signifier* plane and the signified* plane, the conjunction (or semiosis) of which produces manifestation. One can understand that the attacks formulated by N. Chomsky against formalism,* for example, do not apply to the European conception of structuralism.

2. Structuralism is presented especially (and perhaps wrongly: see Language, natural) as a taxonomy,* which Chomsky seems to consider as already completed in linguistics. It is nonetheless obvious that the tax-

onomical foundations are insufficient in generative* grammar.

3. Under the name **French structuralism,** is generally arranged a whole set of research activities inspired by linguistics, carried out during the 1960s, that bear on the various areas of the human sciences. Because of its success, it has unfortunately become very rapidly a sort of fashionable philosophy; as such, it has been attacked, accused of totalitarianism, of reductionism,* of being static, etc.

4. As a scientific attitude, structuralism's value remains. It is characterized either by the search for immanent* structures, or by the construction of models*; in both cases, it maintains the principle according to which the object of knowledge under scrutiny is relation* (or structure*), and not terms* or classes.* The heuristic* value of structuralism remains intact, and the attitude that distinguishes it is comparable to the one that animates the natural sciences, for example.

It is from the structuralist movement that semiotics* was able to develop, at the very time when it was extending beyond the overly restrictive framework of linguistics.* —SEMIOLOGY

STRUCTURE
(structure)

(A) General meaning

1. Without entering into the philosophical and ideological controversies that the notion of **structure** continues to provoke, it is appropriate to specify the constituent elements of the definition of this concept, by placing it within the framework of structural linguistics,* which has succeeded in giving it an operational* character. By borrowing the broad lines of the formulation that L. Hjelmslev has given it,

we will consider structure as an autonomous entity of internal relations,* set up into hierarchies.* In order to explain this definition, let us take a look at each one of its elements: (a) Such a conception implies that priority has been given to relations at the expense of elements*: a structure is first of all a network of relations, the intersections of which constitute terms; (b) The network of relations that defines structure is a hierarchy, that is, an entity* that can be divided into parts that, while being bound to one another, maintain relations with the totality that they constitute; (c) Structure is an autonomous entity, which means that, while maintaining relations of dependance and interdependence with the broader set of which it is a part, it is equipped with an internal organization of its own; (d) Structure is an entity, that is, its ontological status does not need to be questioned, but must, on the contrary, be put between brackets, so as to render the concept operational.

Thus, the question of whether structures are immanent* to the object examined or whether they are constructions* resulting from the cognitive activity of the knowing subject, is to be excluded from properly semiotic concerns, however fundamental this question may be from a philosophical point of view. Likewise, the philosophical presuppositions that underly the conception of structure (and which are manifested especially in the way in which one considers the relations between structure and function* and defines the latter), by giving it at times a slightly mechanistic (Bloomfield) or phenomenological (Hjelmslev) tint, and at other times a somewhat organicist (Benveniste) hue, rather enrich the epistemological-methodological tools, without harming their operational character.

2. Such a conception of structure constitutes a background for semiotic* theory, a "scientific attitude" from which the approaches that the researcher makes can be sketched out. Considered in itself, structure is not the specific property of semiotics, nor even of the human sciences taken as a whole. With a few adjustments, one could say that it is implied in any project or approach with a scientific aim. What especially led linguistics, at a critical moment of its growth, to make explicit the principles upon which is grounded its own doing, was the difficulty experienced by the human sciences in moving from the stage of "opinions" to that of "disciplines." Let us add, moreover, that such a definition of structure is not directly operational: being too general, it applies to any set that one suspects of being organized or that one intends to organize. Defined as a network of relations, structure refers to the concept of relation* and, in order to be semiotically efficient, presupposes a typology of relations. Considered as a network, it does not give us any information concerning either its amplitude or its complexity: the problem of minimal structural organizations, of *elementary* structures, is posed quite naturally, for only these structures can permit us to understand the modes of existence and of functioning of more complex sets.

—RELATION; HIERARCHY; FUNCTION

(B) Elementary structure of signification

1. If we accept the definition of structure as a "network of relations," thinking about elementary structure must first consider only one relation, considered as a simple relation. By positing, within the same definition framework, that "objects of the world" are not knowable in themselves, but only by their determinations (or their properties) and that, in addition, the latter can be recognized only as values* (that is, as they relate one to another), we are led to postulate that relation alone institutes "properties"); these properties, in turn, serve as determinations for objects and render them knowable. Such a relation, called elementary,* is nonetheless present in a double aspect: it gives the basis for "difference" among values, but difference, in order to have meaning, can only rest on the "resemblance" that situates values with respect to one another. Interpreted in this way, the relation that sets up the elementary structure includes the two definitions of the syntagmatic* axis (the "both . . . and" relation) and of the paradigmatic* axis (the "either . . . or" relation) of language. Defined as a relation that establishes at least two value* terms, elementary structure is to be considered, on the one hand, as a concept uniting the minimal conditions for the apprehension and/or the production of signification,* and, on the other hand, as a model* containing the minimal definition of any language (or, more generally, of any semiotic* system or process) and of any semiotic unit. It is thus presented as a locus of convergence of gnoseological reflection and of epistemological postulation for a subsequent axiomatic* system.

2. The concept of elementary structure can become operational only if it is submitted to a logical interpretation and formulation. It is the typology of elementary relations (contradiction,* contrariety,* complementarity*) that opens the way to new generations of interdefined terms, and which allow us to give a

representation* of the elementary structure in the form of the semiotic square.*

3. Formulated in such a way, elementary structure may be considered as a constitutive model,* and this for two reasons: as an organization model of signification (its morphological* or taxonomical aspect) and as a production* model (its syntactic* aspect). As deep* structure, it is the basis for the level of fundamental syntax.*

4. Elementary structure must, in addition, be viewed as a locus of (semantic) investment* and of formation (that is, putting into a form) of contents. These contents, syntactic or semantic (*stricto sensu*), projected upon the square, may be articulated in foreseeable positions and constituted in semantic categories.* Thus, for example, any actant* may be "split open" and give rise to an actantial category (actant, antactant, negactant, negantactant). Once a semantic category has been thus obtained, it may serve as a basis for a set of hypotactic* sub-articulations, each one more narrowly defined; and for that very reason, it may incorporate a semantic micro-universe,* (that is, a generator of discourse). Certain categories— abstract and very general—may hypothetically* be considered as semantic universals,* that is, as **elementary axiological structures;** it will be said that the category *life/ death* articulates individual* universes, and that the category *nature/ culture* articulates collective* universes. To these two elementary structures can be added, because of its large degree of generality, the **figurative* axiological structure** which articulates, in the form of a square, the four "elements of nature" (earth, air, fire, water).

5. The elementary structure, as an articulatory model, has its main application at the level of deep and abstract structures. There it plays the role of description* procedure (and, possibly, of discovery* procedure), allowing semiotic phenomena to be represented prior to their manifestation* (and, in the case of natural languages, prior to their lexicalization*). Thus, the almost mechanical application of this model to surface phenomena ususlly constitutes but a caricature of semiotic procedures. However, that does not mean that elementary articulations do not appear at the surface,* at the level of morpheme-signs, for example; but at that level the categories rarely lexicalize the set of their possible terms: in manifestation these categories present various forms that may be grasped as binary articulations (masculine/feminine, for example), ternary articulations (love/ hate/indifference, for example), etc.
—SQUARE, SEMIOTIC

(C) Structural forms

1. In addition to the precise meaning that we have just acknowledged for the term structure, common usage has imposed a more general meaning which more or less corresponds to the one attributed to articulation, organization, device, mechanism, etc., and which emphasizes the relational character— supposed or established—of the semiotic sets of objects being considered. Therefore, in order to introduce more clarity into the presentation of the lexical items of this dictionary, we have found it preferable to bring together here a rather ill-sorted set of expressions currently used, providing each one with a few summary explanations and cross-references (which will allow a more in-depth examination).

2. *Actantial and actorial structures.*
The distinction between actant* and
actor,* derived from the intuitive
notion of character (or from Vladimir Propp's *dramatis persona),* has
had not a few repercussions on the
whole of semiotic theory. The actant, a syntactic unit of the surface
narrative grammar, once it is placed
on the narrative trajectory* was divided into a set of actantial* roles;
the actor, a unit of discourse, has
been redefined as the incarnation,
the locus of semantic investment,
within discourses, of at least one actantial role and, at the same time, of
at least one thematic* role. Consequently, the actantial mechanism—
the set of actants taken on by the
narrative grammar for the purpose
of generating discourse—has proven
to be not isomorphous with respect
to the actorial organization such as it
is constituted at the discourse level
of the same text (the modality of
being-able-to-do, for example, may be
presented in the form of an independent actor, such as a magic object, or it may be integrated into the
subject-hero, as an intrinsic property). Proceeding from such observations, we may speak of **actorial
structures,** characteristic of such and
such a type of discourse. The actorial structure is objectivized (and
socialized) when the actorial mechanism is characterized by the establishment of a large number of independent actors; on the other hand, it
is said to be subjectivized (or
psychologized) if the number of actors present in the discourse is reduced and is, in certain cases, summarized within one actor subsuming
a large number of actantial roles
(yielding an interiorized, intense
dramatization, well known in
psychoanalysis).
—ACTANT; ACTANTIAL ROLE;
ACTORIALIZATION; ACTOR

3. *Aspect structures and category
structures.* Located at the deep
semiotic level, narrative grammar
uses a categorial logic, based on the
discrete* character of units* and on
the discontinuous character of
states* (an object of the world is
either "black" or "not black," without
transition). When narrative structures are thus formulated, they are
temporalized during discoursivization* and consequently receive
complementary aspectual investments; therefore, to logical transformations* at the deep* level
correspond, at the discourse level,
diachronic "changes" which we can
account for with the help of aspectual categories (articulating semes of
punctuality,* durativity,* inchoativ-
ity,* perfectivity,* etc.). Such a conception of **aspectual structures** consequently allows us to reconcile
"story" and "structure" and to conceive of conversion* mechanisms of
category structures as aspectual
(temporal) structures, and vice versa.
—TEMPORALIZATION; ASPEC-
TUALIZATION

4. *Modal structures.* A somewhat
deeper examination of modal categories (wanting to, having to,
being-able to, knowing) has shown
that their character as "governing
term" would not permit them to be
formulated independently of the
"governed term"; in other words, it
was not possible to speak of *wanting*
or of *being able,* but only of
wanting-to-do or *wanting-to-be,* of
being-able-to-do or *being-able-to-be,* etc.
Since the modality* is an integral
part of the utterance of doing* or
the utterance of state* which it
overdetermines, it is appropriate, in
syntagmatics,* to speak of **modal
structures,** whereas in paradigmatics
modalities may be considered as
modal categories.*
—MODALITY

5. *Narrative structures and discoursive structures.* This distinction corresponds to two levels of depth which we consider as the fundamental domains of the overall generative* trajectory, which ends in the production of discourse. The expression **narrative structures** or, more accurately, **semio-narrative structures,** is then to be understood in the sense of deep* semiotic structures (which preside at the generating of meaning and bear general forms of discourse organization); they are distinct from **discoursive structures** (in the narrow sense) are located at a more superficial level and which, beginning with the domain of enunciation,* organize the discoursivization* (putting into discourse) of narrative structures. In addition, by narrative structures (in the narrow sense) is often meant simply the surface narrative syntax*—this confusion stems from the fact that certain "grammars" or "logics" of narrative conceive of the deepest level of narrativity in a more or less comparable form.

—NARRATIVITY; SURFACE NARRATIVE; SYNTAX; GENERATIVE TRAJECTORY

6. *Polemic structures and contract structures.* Different textual analyses have come to the conclusion—which can seemingly be generalized—that all discourse at least implicitly carries with it a confrontation* structure, bringing together at least two subjects. This confrontation often takes the form of a somatic or cognitive clash (we can then speak of **polemic structures**); or it may take the form of a transaction, in which case the structure organizing the discourse can be called **contractual**. These two forms, which, as can be seen, correspond to the level of sociological theories, to the concepts of "class struggle" and "social contract," can

be found together in the structures of manipulation.* In addition, the polemico-contractual structure of discourse which has but one enunciator* allows us to understand and interpret dialogue* communication as a discourse having two voices.

—POLEMIC; CONTRACT

7. *Deep structures and surface structures.* The distinction between **deep* structures** and **surface* structures** is totally relative, since semiotic theory can, depending on its needs, foresee along the overall generative* trajectory as many levels* of depth as it wants. Thus, for us discourse structures appear as surface structures with respect to semio-narrative structures, which are deeper. However, we use this dichotomy especially in order to establish a distinction, among semiotic structures (to which we give the form of a grammar*), between two levels of depth: between the fundamental (deep) grammar and the narrative (surface) grammar in the strict sense (superficial), the former having a logico-semantic nature, the latter having an anthropomorphic* nature.

—DEEP STRUCTURE; SURFACE STRUCTURE; GRAMMAR; GENERATIVE TRAJECTORY

8. *Semio-narrative structures.* The fact that semiotic theory has only been developing in a progressive and sometimes meandering way has been the source of certain terminological confusions. Such is the case, for example, for the concept of narrativity* which, first applied solely to the class of figurative* discourses (narratives*), has proved to be an organizing principle of all discourse. Consequently, the content of the expression "narrative structures" has been transformed so as finally to designate, in opposition to discourse structures, the deep generative

trunk which is in principle common to all types of semiotics* and to all types of discourse, the locus of a general semiotic competence. A slow terminological substitution is therefore taking place; little by little the expression **semio-narrative structures** is replacing "narrative structures" in the broad sense.
—NARRATIVITY; GRAMMAR; GENERATIVE TRAJECTORY

9. *System structures and morpheme structures.* At first glance the semic organization of the semantic universe* takes on two different forms: on the one hand, that of semic systems (that is, hyponymic* sub-articulations of a paradigmatic character, bearing only homogeneous semes) and, on the other hand, that of semic morphemes which appear as organizations of signifying objects (comparable to sememes*), utilizing heterogeneous semes* (that is, stemming from several semic systems), and bound together by hypotactic* relations of a syntagmatic nature. This distinction seems sufficiently important to us to be mentioned here, since it probably allows us to account for the functioning of the figures* of metaphor* and metonymy,* as of the relationship of contiguity.

STRUCTURING
(structuration)

Structuring is one of the procedures of semantic analysis that entails, on the one hand, the reduction of parasynonomous sememic occurrences into classes, and, on the other hand, the homologation of the identified sememic categories* (or sememic oppositions). Based on the postulate according to which the semantic universe* is structuralizable (or possesses an underlying immanent* structure), structuring re-

quires the preliminary establishment of homogeneous* levels* of analysis and must include the interdefinition of structured elements in terms of logical relations.*—REDUCTION; HOMOLOGATION

STYLE
(style)

1. The term **style** belongs to literary criticism and it is difficult, if not impossible, to give it a semiotic definition. Whereas, in the eighteenth century, style was associated with a sociolectal* approach and corresponded, in the typology of discourses, to the sociolinguistic concept of register,* in the nineteenth century it became the personal characteristic of a writer and was not far from the present-day conception of idiolectal universe.

2. In his early writings, Roland Barthes sought to define style by opposing it to writing. According to Barthes, style was the idiolectal universe, governed and organized by our thymic* category *euphoria/dysphoria* (= a set of attractions and repulsions) which underlaid it. While the notion of writing enjoyed a well-known success, the notion of style does not seem to have been exploited and deepened since then.
—IDIOLECT; WRITING

STYLISTICS
(stylistique)

1. **Stylistics** is a field of research that is part of the tradition of rhetoric,* but which was not constitued as a distinct area in France until the end of the nineteenth century. Sometimes drawing its inspiration from linguistics, at other times from literary studies, stylistics has not succeeded in getting organized as an autonomous discipline. It gen-

erally endeavors to recognize and classify **stylistic devices,*** textual phenomena comparable to rhetorical figures.* However, it is the very interpretation of these devices that creates difficulties and gives rise to divergences within stylistics itself: (a) Stylistic devices may be studied synchronically and brought together into a "system of means of expression of a given language"; this "system" then is proposed as underlying the linguistic manifestation of the phenomena of sensibility or affectivity. This is a **linguistic stylistics,** such as conceived by Ch. Bally. (b) Starting from the conception of style* as an "author's style," we may consider the set of devices catalogued and analyzed within a work, as accounting for the "world view" of its author; such an interpretation already gives an idea of what a **literary stylistics** can be, as represented by L. Spitzer, for example.

2. Both these approaches, however, encounter a major methodological difficulty at the level of the recognition*—no longer intuitive—of stylistic devices, and of their evaluation (making it possible to distinguish the significant, or the more "important" ones). A descriptive stylistics, based on the definition of the device as a gap* (in relation to the norm*), is thus created. The gap may be identified either by statistical methods applied to several texts (mainly with respect to vocabulary*) —P. Guiraud's **statistical stylistics**—or by trusting the "normal" reader-informer ("the average intelligent Frenchman," as M. Riffaterre has proposed, concerning a reading of the poet Baudelaire). Since **gap stylistics** has been incapable, in the present state of research, of defining the norm of a literary discourse, thereby producing disappointing results, it has been abandoned by its own promoters who are now attempting to elaborate a **structural stylistics** (M. Riffaterre), closer to semiotic concerns.

3. In semiotics, we will call structural phenomena **stylistic** (whether they stem from the content* form or from the expression* form of a discourse) when they are located beyond the level of pertinence* chosen for the description* (which thus does not take them into consideration). Indeed, given the complexity of organization, both syntactic and semantic, of texts (especially literary texts), the analyst, for strategic reasons, is obliged to adopt a single point of view and thereby limit the description, leaving aside at least temporarily a vast number of other textual phenomena. The boundary between semantics and stylistics is consequently of an operational* nature, and not a categorical one.

—STYLE; DEVICE, STYLISTIC; EXTRACTION

SUBCONTRARIETY
(subcontrariété)

Subcontrariety designates the relationship of contrariety* between the contradictory* terms ($\overline{s1}$ and $\overline{s2}$) of the two primitive contrary terms (s1 and s2) in the framework of the constitutive* model. From the point of view of the **axis of subcontraries** which is thus constituted, the two contradictory terms are then called **subcontrary** with respect to one another.—SQUARE, SEMIOTIC

SUBJECT
(sujet)

1. Located at the crossroads of different traditions (philosophical, logical, and linguistic), the concept of **subject** is difficult to handle and gives rise to numerous ambiguities.

Hence, we will retain here just two points of view from which it is most often considered:

(a) The subject is often spoken of as being that which is (etymologically) "sub-jected" to thought or observation, or as that with which we are dealing, as opposed to that which is said about it (the predicate*). Such is the common meaning of the term in classical logic, in which the subject is located within an objectivized utterance and treated as an observable entity* that can receive the determinations that the discourse attributes to it. The extrapolation and application of such a **logical subject** in linguistics gives more or less adequate results. Indeed, linguistics must introduce, in addition to the logical subject, an **apparent subject** (for example, "It is true that . . . ") and a **grammatical subject** (for example, in the sentence "Nothing is beautiful but truth," "truth" being the logical subject, we must postulate for "nothing" the status of grammatical subject), etc.

(b) For another, more philosophical, tradition, the term *subject* refers to a "being," to an "active principle" capable not only of having qualities, but also of carrying out acts. This is the meaning that is conferred on it in psychology or in sociology, and to which we can join the notions of **speaking subject** in linguistics and of **knowing** (or **epistemic**) **subject** in epistemology. However, by excluding individual particularities that can characterize the subject in the here and now, epistemology attempts to define it as an abstract* locus where we find the set of necessary conditions guaranteeing the unity of the object* that it is able to constitute. Such a conception is at the basis of linguistics's view concerning the subject of enunciation* (or its simulacrum, installed within the discourse).

2. Certain linguists (Tesnière) and logicians (Reichenbach) have attempted to go beyond these two points of view (mutually incompatible) by inverting the issue: instead of beginning with the subject in order to endow it afterwards with determinations and activities, they have postulated the priority of the relation* ("verb" or "function") of which the subject is to be but one of the end-terms. In this perspective, it is useless to define the subject "in itself," since its value is determined by the nature of the function* that constitutes the utterance.* An actantial grammar thus shows itself able to go beyond the subject as substance, since it renders the status of the subject relative.

3. Within the framework of the elementary utterance, the subject then appears as an actant* the nature of which depends on the function in which it is inscribed. The development of discourse linguistics, however, forces us to postulate, in addition to this **phrastic subject,** the existence of a **discoursive subject** which can occupy, within sentence-utterances, diverse actantial positions (*i.e.,* those of non-subject as well) but which can also succeed in maintaining its identity* throughout the discourse (or throughout a discoursive sequence), thanks especially to procedures of anaphorization.*

4. This inadequacy between phrastic subjects and discoursive subjects (and, more generally speaking, between actants of these two types) is one of several reasons that leads the semiotician to construct a logico-semantic representation* of the functioning of discourse. This representation, in the form of canonic elementary utterances, can

account for phenomena that are both phrastic and discoursive. Consequently, there correspond to the two types of elementary utterance (the utterance of state* or being, and the utterance of doing*) two types of subjects: the first type consists of **subjects of state,** characterized by a relationship of junction* with objects* of value (to be compared with the definition in terms of substance in 1(a) above) the second type consists of **subjects of doing,** defined by the relationship of transformation* (closer to the notion of subject suggested in 1(b) above).

5. The identification of two distinct dimensions* leads us, moreover, to establish a distinction between **pragmatic* subjects** and **cognitive* subjects.** They are specified by the nature of the values* that defines them as subjects of state, as well as by the mode of doing that is theirs—somatic and pragmatic on the one hand, cognitive on the other. This opposition seems all the more operational* as it can account for the existence of a particular category of actants (called, for lack of a better term, "cognitive subjects") which the enunciator* often delegates and installs in pragmatic discourse (represented by the pronoun "they"—in French, "on"—designating public opinion, for example, or being in syncretism* with certain actants of the narration, thereby endowed with a particular knowing*).

6. The type of syntax* called narrative syntax is not to be confused with the narrative schema*; narrative syntax gives rise to **syntactic subjects** (so defined and temporarily classified, until progress in discourse semiotics introduces more refined distinction) and makes it possible to identify broader syntactic units called narrative programs* and narrative configurations.* In contrast, the narrative schema is a hypothetical model of the general organization of narrativity* that attempts to account for the forms by which the subject conceives its life as a project, realization, and destiny. Such a subject—which we will call a **semiotic subject**—is inevitably divided paradigmatically, as any proto-actant,* into at least the four positions of the semiotic square.* Indeed, the narrative schema is at first defined as a polemical* and/or contractual* structure, implying the presence (adjacent to, or rather opposite to, the **subject**) of an **anti-subject** which the subject has to confront. Moreover, the narrative schema provides, for any **performing* subject,** a domain for the acquisition of competence,* which is modal* in nature. Thus, a typology of **competent subjects** will be possible, depending on the nature of the competence they are endowed with. For example, J.-Cl. Coquet uses the following symbols to denote the four subjects corresponding to the four positions of the semiotic square: "je + ," "je - ," "on," and "ça" (the pronouns "I + ," "I - ," "one" or "they," and "it" or "that"); such a typology of subjects, which is only at its beginning, seems particularly promising.

—ACTANT; OBJECT; VALUE

SUBJECTIVE VALUE
(subjective [valeur—])

The term **subjective value** is used for the "substantial" properties of the subject,* which are attributed to it by predication* with the help of the copula "to be,"* as opposed to objective, "accidental" values, attributable, in numerous natural languages, by the verb "to have" and its parasynonyms.—OBJECTIVE

SUBSTANCE
(substance)

1. In L. Hjelmslev's terminology, by **substance** is understood "purport" or "meaning" inasmuch as they are taken on by the semiotic form* for the purpose of signification.* Indeed, purport* and meaning,* which are synonyms for the Danish linguist, are exploited in only one of their aspects, as "supports" for signification, in order to serve as semiotic substance.

2. "Meaning" attains signification as a result of its articulation* in two distinct forms, corresponding to the two planes* of language; the expression* plane thus is composed of an expression form and an **expression substance,** and the content* plane involves a content form and a **content substance.**

3. With respect to semiotic form, which is invariant,* semiotic substance must be considered as a variable,* which is the same as saying that a form can be manifested by several substances (phonic or graphic, for example), whereas the inverse is not true. So as to clear up any misunderstanding, we will say that a single phonic "purport," for example, can serve as a semiotic substance having several forms (verbal and musical languages, for example); this excludes the possibility for one substance to avail itself of several forms at the same time.

4. A given substance, as a knowable object, contains several domains* of apprehension and analysis; for this reason the expression substance is apprehended either at the level of physiological articulation, at the acoustical level, or at the level of psycho-physiological hearing. The same is true for the content substance, which, for simplicity's sake, may be considered as located at the level of the enunciator* or at that of the enunciatee.

5. If, for Hjelmslev, form is a constituent of the semiotic schema,* substance, viewed as "the set of habits of a society," is included in the concept of semiotic (or linguistic) use.* In drawing the ultimate consequences of the Hjelmslevian conception of connotation* languages, we could say that social connotations are but semiotic articulations of a given substance. In this perspective, we would thus account for "interpretations" of the expression-substance, such as when we speak of "vowel symbolism" or "texture" as a category of so-called concrete painting.

6. It must, however, be emphasized (and Hjelmslev himself insists on this point) that the distinction between form and substance is quite relative and depends, in the long run, on the level of pertinence chosen for the analysis. This opposition, undeniably fruitful, must not be hypostatized, for then it would lead to a differentiation between two irreconcilable semantics, one based on form, the other on substance.
—FORM; MEANING; PURPORT; DOMAIN

SUBSTITUTED TEST
(substituée [épreuve—])

By **substituted test** is meant that test in which a violent confrontation, for example, is replaced, by common accord, by a lesser combat (for example, the struggle of David and Goliath, instead of a battle between their respective armies), or by means of a simply symbolic combat (for example, a chess game instead of a real battle, as in the Mahābhārata); or the inverse may take place. Such a substitution changes nothing in the narrative organization.—SUBSTITUTION; TEST

SUBSTITUTION
(substitution)

1. Commutation* rests on the principle according to which to any change on the expression plane must correspond a change on the content plane, and vice versa; **substitution** may be defined as the contrary of commutation, that is, an exchange among the elements of the paradigm of one of the two planes of language does not bring about a parallel exchange on the other plane. Substitution thus allows us to identify variables* within the framework of a structure of invariance; it is also thanks to substitution that the problem of synonymy* and parasynonymy* may be adequately addressed on the content plane.

2. Logical calculation may be said to be tautological, precisely because it rests on the principle of substitution, such as it is used, for example, by N. Chomsky in the procedure of derivation* for the structural description* of sentences.

3. In narrative semiotics, substitution phenomena are encountered whether we are dealing with the substitution of objects or the **substitution of subjects** (either within the syntagmatic collective* actant, in which different subjects take turns in carrying out a single narrative* program, or between two correlated and inverted narrative programs, which makes it possible to account for a "reversal of the situation").

—COMMUTATION; SUBSTITUTED TEST

SUPRASEGMENTAL
(suprasegmental)

The terms **suprasegmental phonology*** and **suprasegmental phonetics*** are used to designate the parts of these respective disciplines that are devoted to the study of phenomena belonging to the expression* plane that go beyond the limits of the units of this plane, which units are obtained by segmentation* (phonemes* and, possibly, syllables), for example, intonation or accentuation. Suprasegmental phonetics and/or phonology are more generally called prosody.—PROSODY

SURFACE STRUCTURE
(surface [structure de—])

1. The notion of **surface** was intuitively chosen because the utterance is first perceived only as a surface, but beneath which can be found a deeper* underlying organization (which can account for the perceptible superficial articulations). However, this notion is not a very happy coinage, since the precise definition that generative* grammar gives for **surface structures** is far from this first intuition. It is an example *par excellence* of a poorly motivated* name* which, despite recognition of the arbitrary character of any naming, adds to the confusion, especially among those who use the notion paralinguistically.

2. Surface structure can be defined only with respect to deep structure, and a surface sentence is the form that results from a transformation* (or a string of transformations) carried out upon its deep organization. We see then, for example, that for the two sentences: "The police arrested the bandit" and "The bandit was arrested by the police" (between which is located a "passive" transformation), the first stems from the deep structure, and the second from the surface structure, whereas in the first meaning (1 above) both sentences are "on the

surface." Moreover, to say that these sentences "belong" to one structure or another, simply means that only their syntactic* organizations (and not the realized* sentences themselves) belong to structural types called "deep" and "surface," and this prior to the phonological interpretation that makes semiosis* possible. Surface must therefore not be confused with manifestation.

3. The concept of surface is correlative to that of depth. When, for example, generative* semiotics excludes the level of deep structures while postulating, in their stead, the existence of logico-semantic forms that generate utterances, then the concept of surface structure disappears as well.

4. In semiotics, we use the terms surface and depth in their relative meaning simply to designate the degree of progress along the generative* trajectory,* which goes from elementary* structures of meaning to the production of the discourse-utterance. Thus, the level of anthropomorphic* syntax is closer to the surface than is the level of underlying logico-semantic structures; likewise, the thematic* level is deeper than the figurative* level.
—LEVEL; DEEP STRUCTURE; GENERATIVE TRAJECTORY

SUSPENSION
(suspension)

1. As a figure in ancient rhetoric, **suspension** consists in the creation of a gap between the topic of the utterance, which is delayed until the end of the utterance, and the initial, allusive presentation of the topic, located at the beginning of the utterance.

2. For semiotics, suspension appears as one of the elements of "dramatic tension" of narrative dis-course. Although the theory of suspension is far from developed, it would seem that it is manifested first as the projection of paradigmatic categories* on the syntagmatic axis of discourse. Thus, for example, the appearance, in narrative, of the Proppian function* of "creation of a lack" produces suspense, an expectation* of the function "liquidation of the lack." This procedure seems even more refined and complex when, for example, the suspension of epistemological modalization manifests, at a given time, a neutral informative* doing, thus provoking "anxiety" on the part of the enunciatee,* which is left in ignorance regarding the veridictory status of the received knowledge. In other cases (in the case of the isotopy of secret,* for example), the difficulty resides in the identification of marks* of the secret, *i.e.,* marks of an allusion that insinuate that the *non-seeming* nevertheless hides a *being*; it is obvious that without these marks, the secret would not exist.

SYMBOL
(symbole)

1. For L. Hjelmslev, the **symbol** is an entity* of monoplanar* semiotics, which can receive one or several interpretations.* By contrast with bi-planar* semiotic systems, the Danish linguist thus reserves the name of **symbol systems** to monoplanar semiotic systems. As a non-sign, the symbol is thus differentiated from the sign, which is an entity of bi- or pluri-planar semiotic systems.

2. One may retain the expression **molar symbol** (also termed by Hjelmslev—but improperly it would seem—**isomorphic symbol**) in order to designate, in the sense Saussure gives to symbol, an entity (possibly

inscribed in a biplanar semiotic text, but having its own autonomous status) which, in a given socio-cultural context, can yield only one interpretation and which, contrarily to the sign, does not allow for subsequent analysis into figures* (for example, the scale, symbol of justice). Such symbols may be catalogued, but they do not, strictly speaking, constitute symbol systems.

3. It is with a similar meaning that C. S. Peirce defines the symbol as founded on social convention, as opposed to the icon* (characterized by a relationship of resemblance with the referent*) and to the index* (based on a relationship of "natural" contiguity). Ogden and Richards, on the other hand, attempt a clumsy synthesis between the Saussurian conception of the sign* and the traditional definition of the symbol; in their triangular model, the symbol corresponds to the Saussurian signifier,* the reference to Saussure's signified,* whereas the referent* denotes "reality."

4. In its non-linguistic and non-semiotic uses, the term of symbol accepts multiple and varying definitions, such as "that which represents something else by virtue of an analogical correspondence," or "absence made presence," etc. In all these cases, its sign nature is not challenged, since the complementary determinations which are added thereto refer at times to the pluri-isotopic* character of the discourse, and at other times they refer to the still ill-examined mechanisms of connotation,* etc. The use of this syncretic term is ambiguous and should, provisionally, be avoided in semiotics.

5. In scientific metasemiotic* systems, a symbol is a conventional type of drawing (using geometrical figures, letters, etc.) which is used to name univocally a class of entities,* a type of relation* and/or of operation.* **Symbolic notation** is to be considered as a visual mechanism for representing* constituant units of a metalanguage.* In the narrower sense, the term symbol applies, in the first place, to the representatives of the entity classes. Thus it is said that a finite set of symbols (from a to z, for example) constitutes the alphabet* (which more or less corresponds to traditional "morphology"). Algebraic and logical notation had accustomed us to using letters as symbols of classes, whereas figures (equal signs, multiplication signs, etc.) are reserved for representing relations and operations: these figures are sometimes called **operational symbols.** In the case of tree* representation, **non-terminal symbols** are used to label the nodes* of all the levels, except for the final level, the **symbols** of which, called **terminal,** can be replaced by lexical items through the application of the rules of lexical insertion. The tree's branches are assimilated to operational symbols, charged with representing the operations of concatenation and of derivation.* It is thus clear that Hjelmslev's definition of the symbol as a unit of a monoplanar semiotic system (par. 1 above) can be identified with the definition of the entities of a scientific meta-semiotic system.

—SIGN; REPRESENTATION

SYNCHRONY
(synchronie)

1. The term **synchrony** was proposed by F. de Saussure, in opposition to diachrony, in order to designate simultaneity as a criterion for gathering together a set of linguistic phenomena which thus constitute a state* of language; this for the purpose of a systemic study of

language.

2. Synchrony was an operational* concept, inasmuch as it made possible the creation of the concept of linguistic system* (conceived as a relational hierarchy,* the functioning of which is insured by its own internal organization). Although the concept of synchrony was useful in order to conceive the idea of system, it is no longer useful for the analysis of system. Indeed, this notion is as imprecise as that of "present," for example. Is a metaphor, invented by the speaking subject at the very moment in which s/he is speaking, a synchronic or diachronic phenomenon? A state of language—therefore, a synchrony—lasts several hundred years and embodies many various internal transformations* (called conversions* by L. Hjelmslev). Linguistics today operates in achrony, the concept of synchrony no longer being operational.

—DIACHRONY; ACHRONY

SYNCRETISM
(syncrétisme)

1. **Syncretism** may be considered as the procedure that consists in establishing, through superimposition, a relation between two (or among several) heterogeneous terms or categories, by encompassing them with the help of a semiotic (or linguistic) entity* that brings them together; it may also be considered as the result of this procedure. Thus, when the subject of an utterance of doing* is the same as that of an utterance of state* (which is the case for the narrative program* of acquisition, in opposition to attribution,* where the two subjects correspond to different actors*), the actantial role that brings them together is the result of a syncretism. In the sentence "Eve gives a fruit to Adam," the phrastic subject "Eve" represents the syncretism of two actants, subject and sender. The resulting syncretism is closely tied to the establishment of a linguistic unit (phrastic subject) that belongs to a more superficial level of generation than the actantial one; we are thus dealing with an **a posteriori syncretism.** On the other hand, when the enunciation domain, for example, is defined as the locus of original indistinction among "I-here-now," enunciation* is to be considered as an **a priori syncretism.**

2. In a broader sense, different semiotic systems—such as opera or cinema—will be considered **syncretic** when they implement several manifestation languages. Similarly, verbal communication is not only of a linguistic kind, since it also includes paralinguistic* elements (such as gestuality or proxemics), sociolinguistic elements, etc.

—NEUTRALIZATION; SUSPENSION; SEMIOTICS; IMPLICIT

SYNONYMY
(synonomie)

1. **Synonymy** generally refers to the relation of identity* that two or more entities* of the content plane (which are then called **synonyms**) may contract. This relation, between two lexemes* for example, can be verified by the substitution* test. In that case, the two lexemes can be substituted in any context, thus showing that the contextual* semes—which enter into the composition of their sememes*—are identical. However, numerous verifications, which can be generalized until the contrary is proved, attest the existence of only **partial synonymy**; two verbs ("to fear" and "to dread," for example) can be substituted for each other in certain con-

texts, and not in others. At the lexeme level, we can therefore only speak of para-synonymy,* which, moreover, corroborates F. de Saussure's declaration, according to which in language there are only differences.

2. The problem of synonymy is different at the level of those semantic units called sememes.* If one considers that a lexeme may have as many sememes as there are possible contextual trajectories (or different contextual semes), then we are right to maintain, using the same example, that if the lexemes "to fear" and "to dread" are not synonyms, there exists at least one sememe of "to fear" identical to at least one sememe of "to dread" (since these two lexemes may be substituted in one class of contexts). While yet remaining faithful to the Saussurian principle, semantics can thus free itself of the constraints forced upon it by the diversity of formants (which include the lexemes) and can conceive of sememes as content units, that can be manifested in different lexemes. Although we encounter only para-synonymy in lexemes, at least *sememic synonymy* exists.

—SEMEME; LEXEME; PARA-SYNONYMY

SYNTAGM
(syntagme)

1. The term **syntagm** is used to refer to a combination* of elements co-present in an utterance* (sentence or discourse). These elements can be recognized because they have a "both ... and" type of relation; they can be further defined by relations of selection* or solidarity* that they maintain among themselves on the one hand, and by the hypotactic* relation that links them to the superior unit that they constitute. The

syntagms are recognized by the segmenting* of the syntagmatic string, since the establishment of relations between the parts and the segmentable totalities results in the transformation of this string into a syntagmatic hierarchy.* Syntagmatic analysis is completed when the last constitutive elements of a syntagm are no longer segmentable and can no longer be considered as syntagms. Paradigmatic analysis then takes up where syntagmatic description leaves off.

2. The concept of syntagm, with a purely relational definition, is applicable to all planes of language and to units of diverse dimensions. Thus, for example, the syllable is a syntagm on the expression plane, where the syllabic kernel is considered as the presupposed element in relation to the presupposing, peripheral elements. Similarly, we speak of **narrative syntagms,** made up of several narrative utterances* that presuppose each other (for example, as in the test*). However, common usage tends to limit the application of this term to the syntagmatic domain alone. In the framework of distributional* analysis, the syntagm is used to designate the immediate constituents* of the sentence, which are respectively called noun syntagm (noun phrase [NP]) and verb syntagm (verb phrase [VP]).

—SYNTAGMATIC

SYNTAGMATIC
(syntagmatique)

1. When any knowable object is semiotic in character, it can be perceived either as system* or as process*—its two fundamental aspects. In such a case, the term **syntagmatic** is used to designate the process. In opposition to the para-

digmatic* axis (which is defined by relations of the type "either . . . or") that identifiable entities have among themselves, the **syntagmatic axis** is characterized, in a first approach, by a network of relations of the type "both . . . and."

2. We should emphasize the purely relational nature of syntagmatics in order to remove all ambiguity from this concept that suffers from unfortunate confusion. When it is identified with Saussurian speech, syntagmatics is considered as the realization* of language, *i.e.*, as provided with a different mode of existence,* more "real" than paradigmatics; but such is certainly not the case. In addition, syntagmatics is often defined by linearity.* But this is only one mode of manifestation, either temporal or spatial, of the logico-relational structure—and is, therefore, atemporal and aspatial— that syntagmatics is. The "both . . . and" relationship is further confused with the notion of "material" contiguity, whereas it should be interpreted only as the co-presence of entities within an utterance (sentence or discourse). As for contiguity (word order*), it corresponds to one of the regulated constraints concerning the expression plane (*i.e.*, the plane of suprasegmental* phonology). We already know the important role played by the syncretism of the notions of linearity and contiguity in distributional* analysis.

3. It is against this background, established by the relational network of co-presence (or of combinations*), that more precise and more restrictive syntagmatic relations are worked out. Thus, Hjelmslev distinguishes three types of possible relations by recognizing, in addition to mere combination, relations of selection* (by which the presence of one term presupposes that of the

other, but not inversely) and of solidarity* (by which two terms mutually presuppose each other). Such an elementary typology then leads to the identification and formulation of syntagmatic units* (or syntagms*), definable by the relations that the constituent elements maintain among themselves and with the unit that subsumes them. Consequently, syntagmatics appears as a hierarchy* of relations, a hierarchy arranged into successive levels* of derivation.*

4. Since every process presupposes the existence of a semiotic system, it is not possible to speak of different semiotic systems that are purely syntagmatic, for the simple reason that all types of discourse, although they possess a syntagmatic organization, are inscribed in intertextuality* and are therefore in correlation with other discourses. At present, the difficulty in establishing a typology* of discourse comes from the limitations of our knowledge; but from this gap, we cannot infer the absence of paradigmatic networks.

—SYNTAGM; PARADIGMATIC; LINEARITY; AXIS

SYNTAX
(syntaxe)

1. In logic, **syntax** is opposed (and complementary) to semantics. In semiotics, syntax and semantics* are the two components* of semiotic grammar.*

2. From the point of view of linguistics, syntax is traditionally considered as one of the two parts (the other being morphology*) that constitute grammar. From this angle, morphology is the study of units that make up sentences,* whereas syntax seeks to describe their relations and/or to establish the rules of their construction.

3. This conception of syntax was changed drastically when the status of morphology* in grammatical systems was challenged. Since the Indo-European languages, with which linguistics was mainly concerned during the last century, are flectional in nature, morphological classes (nouns, verbs, adjectives, etc.) held an important place in linguistics and could easily be considered as basic units for syntactic descriptions. The broadening of the field of studies to other types of natural languages revealed the existence of three sorts of classes which could be taken as units for syntactic calculation; in addition to morphological classes, we indeed find "syntactic" classes (or syntactic functions,* such as subject, predicate, epithet, etc.) and "syntagmatic" classes (noun and verb groups, determinant/determined, etc.). Consequently, two solutions became available to theoreticians. The first was an attempt at synthesis in order to try to construct syntactic units provided with determinations satisfying the requirements made necessary by the existence of three types of classes (this is essentially what L. Hjelmslev did). The second solution is to opt, at the outset, in constructing a grammatical theory, for a given type of basic unit, even if that entails attempting to resolve problems posed at a hierarchically inferior level by the other classes. Thus, we encounter syntagmatic grammars (and syntaxes) (for example, generative* grammar, which has opted for syntagmatic distributional* classes), categorial grammars (working with morphological classes) developed by logicians such as Ajdukiewicz, Bar-Hillel, etc., and syntactic grammars proper (cf. Tesnière's structural syntax, but also our own actantial syntax).

4. The status of a given syntax can be determined only with respect to the semantics with which it makes up a semiotic system (or a grammar). A superficial observation makes it possible to differentiate between semantic relations and syntactic relations within the same clause. Thus, in the syntagm "the top of the hill," syntactically "top" governs "hill," whereas semantically it is the reverse, so to speak. In other words, syntactic (here, hypotactic) relations are established among syntactic classes, independently of their semantic investment and thus constitute an autonomous organization (a syntactic structure).

Another problem then comes up, as to whether syntactic relations are semantic in nature (*i.e.*, whether they are meaningful) or whether they are void of meaning. In this respect, there are two opposing attitudes. **Formal syntaxes** are developed without any reference to meaning; the symbols of a formal* language (a, b, c) are distinguished from each other only in a discriminatory* way, and their discrete* character is based on a "negative meaning" (a is not b). Just like the organization of the phonemes* of a natural language, a formal syntax may be considered, all things considered, as stemming from the expression form (in the Hjelmslevian meaning of the term). On the contrary, **conceptual syntaxes** recognize syntactic relations as being meaningful (as stemming from the content form), even if they are abstract and can be equated with logical relations. For semiotic theory, that is a fundamental option: whereas the symbol-units of a formal syntax constitute an alphabet* (*i.e.*, any kind of inventory, sometimes improperly called "structure") which is then governed by a set of operational rules,* the units of conceptual syntax are organized into a taxonomy* (a sort of elementary morphology) within which syntactic operations are carried out. The semiotic syntax that we put forward is both actantial (and therefore syntactic, in the strict sense) and conceptual.

5. Syntax, both traditional and recent (with its generative and transformational extensions) is essentially a sentence syntax, studying only the combinations, substitutions, and equivalences located within this syntagmatic unit that has limited dimensions. However, research on narrativity* has demonstrated not only the existence of broader, trans-sentential syntagmatic organizations, but also their universality, since these organizations turn out to be characteristic of all ethno-linguistic communities. From another point of view, transformational grammar has indeed shown—but without drawing all the conclusions therefrom—that, for example, two or more deep level sentences may correspond to one surface sentence. This means that the dimensions of the sentence do not constitute impassable limits in the exploration of syntagmatic organizations. Finally, the generative approach makes it possible to conceive of syntax as a many-storied construction, each floor having its own syntactic formulation and its own conversion* rules (a particular form of homologation*) allowing us to move from one floor to another. All this establishes favorable conditions for a diversity of research projects, aiming at developing a **syntax** that is no longer phrastic, but **discoursive.**

6. The present state of development in semiotic research—analyses of specific objects and theoretical reflection—allows us to conceive of semiotic grammar as a project well on its way. Although its different components may still be unequally developed, the general framework and the contours of such a theory are sufficiently precise. Thus, we differentiate between a **syntactic component** and a semantic component.* Each one can be formulated on two levels of depth. Semio-narrative syntax, then, involves a deep level, that of **fundamental syntax,** and a surface level, where **narrative syntax** (in the strict sense) is located.
—MORPHOLOGY; FUNCTION; GRAMMAR; GENERATIVE TRAJECTORY; SYNTAX, FUNDAMENTAL; SYNTAX, SURFACE NARRATIVE; SYNTAX, DISCOURSIVE; SYNTAX, TEXTUAL

SYNTAX, DISCOURSIVE
(syntaxe discursive)

Since **discoursive syntax** is presently in the process of development, it is impossible to determine exactly and definitely the status of the units and operations that it involves. Therefore, we prefer to present the general outline in the form of procedures that are implemented, at the level of the domain of the enunciation,* during the production of discourse. These procedures, which we term **discoursivization,** lead, by means of engagement* and disengagement,* to the constitution of discoursive units* the typology and interrelations* of which will have to be thoroughly studied. We have identified three sub-components in discoursivization: actorialization,* temporalization,* and spatialization,* which, as procedures, make it possible to inscribe the narrative structures (of a logical character) within spatio-temporal coordinates and to invest the actants into discoursive actors. Such an articulation of discoursive syntax—even if it is only provisional—has the advantage of determining where issues are situated and where research is to be carried out. Thus, we may, for example, profit from the experience (and, perhaps, from some of the acquired knowledge) of those who construct temporal logical systems in order to formulate more precisely the temporal component of this syntax (and thereby avoid the confusion of scholars who see temporal categories used inappropriately). Similarly, the spatial subcomponent certainly constitutes a meeting point for different approaches relative to spatiality, and scattered over the whole of the semiotic field (for example, spatial languages, proxemics, gestuality, semiotics of space, etc.).— DISCOURSIVIZATION; GENERATIVE TRAJECTORY

SYNTAX, FUNDAMENTAL
(syntaxe fondamentale)

1. **Fundamental syntax,** with fundamental semantics,* constitutes the deep level of semiotic and narrative grammar.* It is supposed to account for the production, functioning, and understanding of syntagmatic organizations, called discourses, that belong to different semiotic systems, linguistic as well as non-linguistic. It thus represents the domains wherein the generative* trajectory of these discourses originate.

2. Such a syntax contains a taxonomic* sub-component (that corresponds to the alphabet* of formal* languages) and an operational sub-component (or syntactic sub-component, in the strict sense). These two aspects of a syntax that attempt to account for both the mode of existence and the mode of functioning of signification can be

illustrated with a somewhat simplistic example: the term "contradiction" designates at one and the same time a relation between two terms and the negation of one term, which induces the appearance of the other.

3. The taxonomic model corresponds to the epistemological conditions that are necessary for the identification of the elementary* structure of meaning. At the same time, it is formulated in terms of qualitative logic (or logic of comprehension*) and finds its representation* in the form of the semiotic square* (other modes of representation are just as possible). It thus constitutes a sort of organized space, containing interdefined terms on which syntactic operations may be carried out, operations that give rise either to new organizational combinations (derived and complex terms) or to ordered syntactic strings.

4. Fundamental **syntactic operations,** called transformations,* are of two types: negation* and assertion.* While negation is used essentially to produce contradictory* terms, assertion can bring together terms located on the axes of contraries* and of subcontraries.* The taxonomic model, as a preexistent schema of relations, makes it possible to circumscribe the field where operations (for the production and/or reception of meaning) are carried out. These operations form strings, not only in the sense of their being oriented,* but also due to their "memorizational" capacity (denial,* for example, is not a mere negation, but the negation of a previous assertion). We are, then, dealing with an essential feature that distinguishes semiotic syntax from logic syntax.

5. Conceived in this way, fundamental syntax is made up purely of relations and is both conceptual

and logical. The term-symbols of its taxonomy are defined as intersections of relations; operations, on the other hand, are only acts* establishing relations. Consequently, fundamental syntax is logically anterior to surface narrative syntax,* formulated in terms of utterances containing actants* and functions.*
—SQUARE, SEMIOTIC; ASSERTION; NEGATION; SYNTAX, SURFACE NARRATIVE; GENERATIVE TRAJECTORY

SYNTAX, SURFACE NARRATIVE
(syntaxe narrative de surface)

1. **Surface narrative syntax** (or narrative syntax, properly speaking) is a domain of the generative* trajectory, derived from fundamental syntax by means of a set of procedures (that can be formulated as rules). The problem of constructing this level is twofold: we must both predict what the general form of this domain will be, and account for its homologation with fundamental syntax which, alone, will make it possible to specify the rules of conversion* from fundamental syntax to narrative syntax.

2. By contrast with fundamental syntax (in which we deal with a set of operations carried out on terms), the general form of surface syntax is that of a manipulation of utterances.* Through an analogy that is only partially accurate, we could say that the movement from the deep syntactic level to the surface one corresponds roughly to the movement from logic of classes to propositional logic.

3. The construction of a syntactic model implies a certain number of theoretical options (epistemological and methodological) on which its form depends, in the last

analysis. The first of these options resides in the choice of the units that the syntax will have to manipulate. Whereas categorial grammars use morphological classes* and transformational grammars use syntagmatic classes (borrowed, moreover, from distributional analysis), we have opted for syntactic classes (traditionally called syntactic functions*). We consider them hierarchically superior to morphological and syntagmatic classes. These are accounted for and integrated at more superficial syntactic levels (such as those of discoursivization* and textualization*).

4. The second option is just as important. It involves conceiving the most simple syntactic structure and thus defining the form to be given to the elementary utterance.* Contrary to the tradition that goes back to Aristotle and that postulates the binarity* of the elementary structure (subject/predicate, noun phrase/verb phrase), our conception of the utterance is relational. By following Hjelmslev (but also taking into account the work of Tesnière and Reichenbach, among others) we consider the utterance as a relational expansion of the predicate.* As a function, the predicate projects the "functives" (which we designate as actants*) as the end-terms of the relation. We thus define the elementary narrative utterance as a function-relation between at least two actants.

5. Such a conception of the elementary utterance then makes it possible to formulate the principle on which are based the procedures for conversion from fundamental syntax to narrative syntax. To the relations (which constitute the taxonomic base of the deep syntactic structure) and to the transformation-operations (that are carried

out on this base), correspond, at a more superficial level, "states*" and "doings," formulated as **utterances of state*** and **utterances of doing**.* The latter govern the former, just as transformations operate on relations.

6. The structure that consists of an utterance of doing governing an utterance of being is called a narrative program* (NP). It is considered the elementary* operational* unit of narrative syntax. The NP may be somewhat clumsily interpreted as the "causing-to-be" of the subject, as the calling forth of a new "state of things" into semiotic existence. Thus the NP can be viewed as the generation (that can be apprehended both at the moment of production and of reception) of a new "semiotic state." The distinction that is next established, betwen pragmatic doing* and cognitive doing, makes it possible to split the NPs by placing them either in the pragmatic dimension* or in the cognitive dimension of narrativity.

7. Narrative programs, which may be simple or complex (possibly integrating an indefinite number of instrumental NPs, in which case they are called base NPs) are made more complex due to the identification of **modal utterances** that govern utterances of doing. When the narrative program, as a "causing-to-be" of the subject, is considered as that subject's performance,* then the modalities (such as those of *wanting-to-do* and *being-able-to-do*) appear as necessary conditions for the realization of this performance, thus constituting what can be designated as the subject's modal competence.* Consequently, we see that every NP of doing logically presupposes a modal NP, just as every performance presupposes competence. Such a broadened program (which

can integrate other optional elements) is then called the subject's narrative trajectory.

8. The identification of the polarized (*i.e.,* polemic or contractal) structure of narrative discourse imposes upon narrative syntax the necessity of taking into account, and of accounting for, the presence and mutual relations of at least two subjects, with their own narrative programs and trajectories. Such a syntax then appears as a **communication* syntax** between subjects (or as a syntax of object transfers, since pragmatic, cognitive, or modal acquisitions of one of the subjects may be considered as so many losses for the anti-subject).

9. Obviously, the aforementioned are but some of the elementary forms of narrative syntax, such as we conceive of it in its present state of development in semiotic research. The narrative organization forms of discourse are certainly more complex, although not yet well known. It is clear that narrative syntax will have to develop the theoretical bases of a strategy* of narrative programs and trajectories, which, alone, will make it possible to manipulate "narrative masses" of broader dimensions and greater complexity. Strangely enough, the final goal seems to consist in filling (with the help of a typology of strategic programs) the gap that separates the already recognized elementary forms from the narrative* schema developed—through successive generalizations—as a sort of canon, beginning with V. Propp's discoveries.

10. Some time ago, we emphasized the anthropomorphic* character of narrative syntax, which distinguishes it from fundamental syntax, which is logical and abstract.* Indeed, if we consider the concep-

tion of the elementary utterance (which is but the syntactic formulation of the fundamental relation of subject-human to object-world), or that of narrative programs that are interpreted as transformations of things by humans (who, by that very fact, are themselves transformed), or if we consider the communicative* dimension of narrativity (that corresponds to the general concept of intersubjective exchange), then everything seems to show that, genetically, surface narrative syntax is the originating source of any semiotic process. It is strict adherence to the genetic conception that forces us to consider that domain as closer to the surface than fundamental syntax. —UTTERANCE; FUNCTION; ACTANT; PROGRAM, NARRATIVE; PERFORMANCE; COMPETENCE; NARRATIVE TRAJECTORY; NARRATIVE SCHEMA; SYNTAX, FUNDAMENTAL; GENERATIVE TRAJECTORY

SYNTAX, TEXTUAL
(syntaxe textuelle)

It is possible to bring together under the term **textual syntax** the set of procedures of **textualization** (*i.e.,* putting the discourse into text). Textualization can intervene at any moment of the generative* trajectory (deep or surface levels, figurative or non-figurative discourse, etc.). Since textualization consists of the union of discourse (located on the content* plane) with the expression* plane that is attributed to it (a union called semiosis*), discourse is necessarily subject to constraints that are imposed upon it by the spatial or temporal nature of the signifier being used. Among the procedures that stem from these constraints, let us mention linearization,* segmentation* (constitutive of the textual

units* of paragraph and sentence), anaphorization,* etc.—TEXTUALIZATION; GENERATIVE TRAJECTORY

SYNTHESIS
(synthèse)

As contrasted with analysis, which begins with the semiotic object to be described, (considered as a meaningful whole, *cf.* signification*) **synthesis** is understood—in the Hjelmslevian tradition—as the procedures that take this semiotic object first as a constitutive part of a hierarchically* superior unit or as an individual element belonging to a class*; these procedures also recurrently seek progressively to reach the totality of the set containing it. Thus, those procedures that first posit discrete* elements, in order to obtain their combinations* or their expressions,* are called **synthetizing** (or ascending), in opposition to analytic (or descending) procedures.— ANALYSIS

SYSTEM
(système)

1. **System** is one of the two modes of existence (complementary to that of process*) of structured or structurable universes. For L. Hjelmslev this concept has a universal range and surpasses not only the framework of linguistics, but also that of semiotics; he therefore terms semiotic systems paradigmatic.*

2. For F. de Saussure, the term system makes it possible to define the concept of language* (= "sign system"), inasmuch as it traditionally refers to a coherent whole the elements of which are interdependent. Saussure enriched the concept of language-as-system by considering it first as a set of associative fields (now reformulated in terms of para-

digm*) the terms of which maintain mutual "associative relations," thereby emphasizing the resemblances that unite them and the differences that oppose them. Each term of a paradigm is, then, defined negatively by all that it is not, by being opposed to the set of the other terms. But what holds together all the terms of a paradigm and establishes the resemblances is only a differential feature by which the paradigm as a whole is opposed to another paradigm. The concept of system is then refined: language ceases to be a set of interdependent elements and becomes a **system of relations** (differential and oppositional). In passing, we see that there are two possible readings of Saussure. The first consists in gathering and organizing the concepts that are used as a point of departure for his thinking (for example, "language is a system of signs"; the signifier and the signified are the two sides of a word-sign). The second consists in drawing all the consequences, sometimes implicit, from this thinking.

3. Given the fact that language, as system, constitutes a stratified set, that is, it contains two planes* (expression* and content*), and that each of these planes, in turn, displays levels of articulation (the levels of phonemes* and of phemes,* of sememes* and of semes*), we can identify within language relatively autonomous **sub-systems** that are called, respectively, phonological and phemic, sememic and semic systems. It can be seen that Saussure's initial definition, concerning language as a sign system, concerns only the most apparent stratum, that of morpheme*-signs.

TAXONOMY
(taxinomie)

1. In the past, **taxonomy** was traditionally conceived of as a "theory of classifications." Now this term is used to designate classification* itself, *i.e.,* the procedures of systematic organization of observed and described data.

2. Because N. Chomsky too hastily identified the taxonomic approach with a certain, outdated, conception of science (the ultimate goal of which seemed to be the observation and classification of facts, as in traditional botany or zoology), he protested against distributional* linguistics, accusing it of being purely taxonomic and, through its procedures, of aiming only at the hierarchical classification of linguistic units. This criticism certainly enjoyed a great deal of notoriety in its time. But, although it is not false, it rests both on a narrow, restrictive conception of taxonomic activity and on the lack of breadth in the scientific project of distributional analysis itself, enclosed within its formalistic certainties.

3. The analysis of discourse with a scientific goal (in the social sciences) has revealed that the cognitive activity found therein consists mainly in **taxonomic doing.** This sort of doing involves constructing semiotic objects (elements,* units,* hierarchies*) with the help of recognized identities* and alterities.* This taxonomic construction constitutes a genuine prerequisite for the development of a scientific metalanguage.* Moreover, the study of this type of discourse has clearly demonstrated that the degree of progress of one discipline or another is a function of the taxonomic progress already realized. Consequently, Chomsky's criticism cancels itself out and can be turned against generative* grammar, which will then be blamed for its taxonomic insufficiencies, its lack of interest for preliminary semantic analysis of the concepts utilized, as well as its lack of rigor as far as its metalanguage is concerned. This deficiency is also found both in generative semantics and in philosophical logic. However, if the generativist criticisms addressed to distributional analysis are pertinent, they are, nonetheless, wrong in considering it one of the main achievements of linguistics. The constitution of hypothetical models for the purposes of explanation and which can be substituted for taxonomical procedures was often successfully practiced by comparative* linguistics.

4. Taxonomical procedures such as those which were examined and criticized by Chomsky were in fact applied, in the framework of distributional analysis, essentially on

the syntagmatic* axis of language. Hierarchical classification was based on the distribution,* *i.e.,* positional order, of linguistic units. But taxonomy is, first of all, a principle of paradigmatic* organization, neglected by the distributionalists. This explains why semic* analysis—or, in America, componential* analysis— or ethno-taxonomic studies (which have undergone a real development in cultural anthropology) have developed without any contact with generative and transformational grammar. Yet, this whole set of research areas together with their procedures constitute the field of **taxonomic research** properly speaking.

5. In ethno-linguistics, certain American anthropologists (for example, H. C. Conklin) use the term taxonomy in a restricted sense, to designate a paradigmatic hierarchy which is constituted by nodes* made up of the lexemes* that are indeed realized in the natural language being described and which takes into account only the relations of purely discriminatory* oppositions* among lexemes of the same level and the relations of inclusion among lexemes of different levels. Such a taxonomy is therefore a classification that aims at describing a corpus* of lexemes and that can use only lexemes from this corpus as labels* of the tree* that is used to represent this classification.

6. Unlike lexical taxonomies, **semic taxonomies** are hierarchies elaborated not by taking into account the lexematic categorization* of the world, but the network of semic* oppositions (or of distinctive* features) underlying linguistic manifestation. A semic taxonomy is presented as a combinatory* arrangement of which only certain expressions* (or certain nodes in the tree

representation*) are manifested at the level of linguistic signs. A semic taxonomy has therefore the advantage —invaluable in our opinion— that it can serve as a model* for the comparative study of several ethnotaxonomies.

—CLASSIFICATION; ETHNO-SEMIOTICS; SEME; SEMIC ANALYSIS

TEMPORALIZATION
(temporalisation)

1. Together with spatialization* and actorialization,* **temporalization** is one of the sub-components of discoursivization (or of discoursive syntax), and belongs, as they do, to the implementation of the mechanisms of engagement* and disengagement* which concern the domain of the enunciation.*

2. Temporalization consists of a set of procedures that may be grouped into several sub-components:

(a) **Temporal programming** is primarily characterized by the conversion* of the axis of presuppositions* (the logical order of the string of narrative programs*) into an axis of consecutions (the temporal and pseudo-causal order of events).

(b) **Temporal localization** (or temporalization, in the strict sense), uses the procedures of temporal engagement and disengagement, segments and organizes temporal succession(s) by establishing the framework in which the narrative structures* are inscribed.

(c) **Aspectualization** transforms narrative functions* (of a logical nature) into processes* evaluated from the point of view of an observer* actant located within the utterance-discourse.

3. Temporalization consists, as its name implies, in producing the

meaning effect "temporality" and in thus transforming a narrative organization into a "story."
—ENGAGEMENT; DISCOURSIVIZATION; PROGRAMMING, SPATIO-TEMPORAL; LOCALIZATION, SPATIO-TEMPORAL; ASPECTUALIZATION

TENSIVENESS
(tensivité)

Tensiveness is the relation contracted by the durative* seme of a process* with its terminative* seme, producing the meaning effect of "tension" or "progression" (for example, the adverb "almost," or the aspectual expression "to be about to . . ."). The aspectual relation overdetermines the aspectual configuration and, in a way, makes it dynamic. Tensiveness is paradigmatically opposed to detensiveness.*—ASPECTUALIZATION

TERM
(terme)

1. When we take into consideration the fact that any semiotic system is simply a network of relations* (or that a natural language, for example, is made up only of differences), then **terms** can be defined only as intersection points of various relations. Thus, a study of the elementary structure* of meaning clearly demonstrates that any term of the semiotic square* is an intersection point of the relations of contrariety,* contradiction,* and complementarity.* Moreover, the representation* of a relational network in the form of a tree* reveals that the terms corresponding to the junction points are at the same time both the "end-terms" of the relations and the relations themselves which, considered at a hierarchically higher level, are presented as terms (Hjelmslev's

functions playing the role of functives). Only the **terminals** of a taxonomy* are simply terms in the strict sense.

2. Terms, as intersection points of relations, may be lexicalized (*i.e.,* given labels* that designate them) or not. A natural language, as a semiotic system, offers huge possibilities of lexicalization, due to the fact that it is a combinatory* arrangement.

A second definition of **term** is then possible: a term is the name* (label) of an intersection point of relations (or an intersection within a relational network), a name that results from the procedure of lexicalization.

3. The lexicalization of terms is called "natural" (for example, in the case of ethno-taxonomies) or "artificial." In the latter case, label-terms constitute either a terminology* of a metalinguistic* nature or a nomenclature.*—RELATION; SQUARE, SEMIOTIC, TREE; LEXICALIZATION

TERMINAL
(terminal)

1. We call **terminal** those symbols that, according to syntagmatic analysis, denote morphological classes* (or "lexical" classes, such as noun, verb, adjective, etc.), belonging to the last level of derivation.

2. We sometimes call **terminal** those lexemes* located on the lowest level of a taxonomic* hierarchy* of a paradigmatic order, and indeed realized in the natural language under study.
—SYMBOL; TERM

TERMINATIVENESS
(terminativité)

Terminativeness is an aspectual seme indicating the completion of a process.* It is part of the aspectual configuration *inchoateness/durativeness/terminativeness*; when it is recognized, one can presuppose the existence of the entire configuration. At the level of surface* semiotic syntax, *terminativeness* may indicate the realization* of a doing.*—ASPECTUALIZATION

TERMINOLOGY
(terminologie)

1. **Terminology** refers to a set of terms, more or less defined, that partially constitutes a sociolect. A terminology which has interdefined terms and explicit* construction rules can be transformed into a metalanguage.

2. In anthropology, the expression **terminology of kinship structures** is used to distinguish between (a) the taxonomy* of lexicalized terms (= lexemes*) that designate the set of roles constituting kinship structure in a given linguistic community and (b) the taxonomy that may be constructed from the analysis of social discourse about these roles (or the analysis of observed somatic behavior). The two taxonomies—that of explicitly named roles and that of implicit thematic* roles—are not necessarily homologous, since the latter may have undergone an historical recategorization.
—TERM; NOMENCLATURE; METALANGUAGE; SOCIOLECT; TAXONOMY

TEST
(épreuve)

1. Analysis of the Proppian functions* has pointed out the recurrence in the folktale of the narrative syntagm* to which the **test** corresponds, in its three forms: qualifying,* decisive,* and glorifying* tests. This recurrence, by authorizing a comparison, guarantees their formal identification.

2. The test must be distinguished from the gift.* The latter simultaneously implies transitive* conjunction* (or attribution*) and a reflexive* disjunction* (or renunciation*), and is situated between a sender* and a receiver.* In contrast, the test is a discursive figure* of the transfer* of objects of value, which implies a reflexive conjunction (or appropriation*) concomitant with a transitive disjunction (or dispossession*), and which characterizes the doing* of the subject-hero in quest* of the object of value.

3. As a reflexive conjunction, the test corresponds, on the level of surface narrative syntax,* to a narrative program* in which the subject of doing* and the subject of state* are invested in one and the same actor.* As a transitive disjunction, it at least implies the existence of an anti-subject seeking to carry out an inverse narrative program—or even the manifestation of this program. The test thus emphasizes the polemic* structure of the narrative.

4. From the point of view of its internal organization, the test is constituted by the concatenation of three utterances that, on the discursive level, can be expressed as confrontation,* domination,* and consequence* (acquisition* or privation*). The axis of presupposition* can be substituted for this axis of temporal sequence; in this case a sort of "reverse" logic appears (consequence presupposes domination, which in turn presupposes confrontation) such that if in a given narrative only the consequence is manifested, this utterance alone will permit the encatylization* of the entire test.

5. Though the three tests— qualifying, decisive, and glorifying

—have the same syntactic organization, they are distinguished nevertheless, in the canonic narrative schema,* by their semantic investment, manifested in the consequence. Thus the qualifying test corresponds to the acquisition of competence* (or of the modalities* of doing), the decisive test corresponds to performance,* the glorifying test to recognition.* This sequence of the three tests (the first two being located in the pragmatic* dimension, the last in the cognitive* dimension) in fact constitutes a reverse linking, in which recognition presupposes performance, and this presupposes the corresponding competence. There cannot be a glorifying test except in order to ratify the prerequisite decisive test, and likewise the decisive test cannot be carried out without there having been (implicitly or explicitly) the qualifying test.
—NARRATIVE SCHEMA

TEXT
(texte)

1. Taken as an utterance,* **text** is opposed to discourse,* as concerns the substance* of their expression* (graphic for the former, phonic for the latter) which is used in the manifestation of the linguistic process. According to certain linguists (for instance, R. Jakobson), oral expression (and, consequently, discourse) is the first given; writing* would then be but a derivative, a translation of oral manifestation. For others (such as L. Hjelmslev), on the contrary, the genetic point of view is not pertinent, since a semiotic form can be manifested by different substances.

2. The term text is often used as a synonym of **discourse,** primarily because of terminological mixing with natural languages that do not possess the equivalent of the word discourse (as between French and English). In that case, textual semiotics is theoretically not distinguished from discursive semiotics. The two terms—text and discourse—may be indifferently applied to designate the syntagmatic axis* of non-linguistic* semiotic systems; a ritual, a ballet may be considered as text or as discourse.

3. L. Hjelmslev uses the term text to designate the totality of a linguistic string, unlimited because of the system's productiveness. It is the identification and choice of units* having maximal dimensions and recurrent in the text that make it possible to undertake their analysis* and to determine for example, the type of linguistics (or grammar) that can be constructed. If the recurrent unit adopted is the sentence,* then the type of linguistics that is developed to account for it is called phrastic; the choice of discourse* as the maximal recurrent unit of text gives rise to the construction of a discursive linguistics.

4. The term text is sometimes used in a narrow sense, when the nature of the chosen object (the work of a writer, a set of known documents or collected accounts) imposes limits on the term. In this sense, text becomes synonymous with corpus.*

5. In meanings (3) and (4), text designates an entity* prior to its analysis.* However, we already know that analysis always presupposes the choice of a level of pertinence* and seeks to recognize only certain types of relation,* excluding those which could just as well be determined (substance* or form,* syntax or semantics,* etc.). The outcome of this is a new definition, according to which a text is made up only of those semiotic elements fitting the theoretical goal of the description.*

It is in this sense that we can speak, for example, of the utterative text (obtained after the elimination* of the marks* of enunciation*). It is also in this sense that it is possible to interpret "text as productivity" (J. Kristeva), a concept that subsumes the set of operations of production* and transformations of the text, and which attempts at the same time to account for the semiotic properties of enunciation and utterance.

6. When the generative* trajectory is interrupted, it leads to textualization* (linearization* and junction with the expression plane). The text obtained through this procedure is the equivalent of the semantic representation of the discourse. From the point of view of generative grammar, the text, as semiotic representation, can then serve as the deep* level* for the linguistic structures which generate surface* linguistic structures.
—DISCOURSE; UNIT TEXTUAL; TEXTUALIZATION

TEXTUALIZATION
(textualisation)

1. **Textualization** is the set of procedures (making up textual syntax*) the end product of which is a discursive continuum, constituted prior to the manifestation of discourse in any given semiotic system (and, more precisely, in any given natural language). The text* thus obtained, provided it is manifested as text, is then a semantic representation* of the discourse.

2. Insofar as the text is a semantic representation, the modes of semiotic manifestation* that are logically subsequent to it do not alter the text. Thus, the text of a comic strip, for example, takes the form of either "captions" or "illustrations." Likewise, the text of an ethno-literary corpus is homogeneous even if its manifestation has a multilingual character, provided, of course, that this corpus corresponds to an identifiable cultural area. The theatrical text, for its part, subsumes the set of manifestation languages (intonation, gestuality, proxemics, lighting, etc.) to which it has recourse.

3. The text is thus defined with respect to the manifestation that it precedes, and only with respect to it; it is not the end product of the total generative* trajectory, considered as the movement from the simple to the complex, from the abstract to the figurative.* On the contrary, textualization is a pause in this trajectory, at any given moment of the process, and deviates it towards manifestation. Thus, when we want to give a representation of one or another of the levels of the generative trajectory (of the deep grammar, of the surface grammar, of the figurative domain, etc.), we necessarily proceed to the textualization of this level (*i.e.,* of the data that an analysis of this plane would provide).

4. At the time it is carried out, textualization encounters a certain number of constraints and benefits from advantages that the characteristic properties of the text itself confer upon it. The main constraint seems to be the linearity* of discourse, but that is in a way compensated for by the text's elasticity.* The linearity of the text is determined by the nature of the signifier* that it encounters during the manifestation. The signifier may be temporal (in the case of oral languages, for example) or spatial (writing, painting, etc.). The elasticity of the text, for its part, is defined by the discourse's aptitude for flattening out semiotic hierarchies, *i.e.,* its aptitude

for arranging in succession segments stemming from very diverse levels of a given semiotic system. A debate, for example, may be expressed in discourse in the form of the lexeme "discussion," but may also be expressed by means of a complex sentence or of a dialogue sequence. There is textualization in the strict sense of the term when either the linearity or the elasticity of the discourse are used to the best of their possibilities.

5. The linearization of the text is to be distinguished from its temporalization.* It is known, for example, that algebraic calculation, which is not temporal in nature, has to be linearized for the purposes of its manifested representation. Without going that far, we can distinguish **textual programming,** properly speaking (by which two concomitant narrative programs* are necessarily placed in linear succession), from temporal* programming (or the arrangement in chronological order of diverse programs). These two types of programming do, however, leave some room for manoeuver in the organization of discourse and belong to the discoursive competence* of the enunciator.* Furthermore, the same is true concerning the use of the elasticity of discourse, which is related to the same type of competence. These two forms of intervention on the part of the enunciator constitute, then, the procedures of textualization (in the broad sense of the word), procedures to which we can add, for example, anaphorization,* and which, from a certain point of view, appear more or less coextensive with the concerns of classical rhetoric.*
—GENERATIVE TRAJECTORY; LINEARITY; ELASTICITY OF DISCOURSE

THEATER, SEMIOTICS OF THE
(théâtrale [sémiotique—])

1. In a narrow sense—that presently adopted by the "semiology of the theater"—theater discourse is first of all the text,* a sort of director's score that is open to various performances; it is also a discourse having several voices, a succession of dialogues, considered as a literary genre. From this perspective, **semiotics of the theater** is a part of literary* semiotics, with which it shares many concerns. The narrative organization underlying the dialogic form obeys the same principles, and the surface discoursive structure alone is held to constitute the specificity of the theater text.

2. At the other extreme, there is another conception of theatricality that is just as exclusive, according to which the semiotics of the theater covers anything that happens on the stage during a performance, *i.e.,* it covers all the manifestation languages that work towards the production of meaning, with the exception of the verbal text itself. This overall approach seems more promising. However, we do not see what justifies the elimination of one of the manifestation languages, that of natural language.

3. But this second conception of theatricality raises a difficulty that is both theoretical and practical. It involves the necessity of reconciling the presence of multiple signifiers* with one and only one signified.* For indeed theatricality involves many manifestation languages: oral gestuality (intonation), visual gestuality (mime, comportment, gestures), proxemics (the position on the stage of actors, props. backdrops), chromatic programming (lighting,

etc.) and, finally, verbal discourse (from various actors). Is it necessary to analyze each of these manifestation languages separately and then to proceed to bring together the results obtained through these partial analyses*? Or, on the contrary, should we carry out a segmentation* in terms of the simultaneousness of the complex theater discourse? Does each manifestation language possess an autonomous signified, or does each only help in the articulation of a common, overall signification through a partial contribution? Semiotics of the cinema can serve as a cautionary example, to show what is at stake in these preliminary choices, in that it hypostatizes visual manifestation at the expense of the other languages that are concomitant with the visual.

The hypothesis held in some on-going research is that of the possibility of a construction of the theatrical object which, if located at the level of underlying semiotic structures,* might be able to account for and/or to generate the "show" manifested by all the languages involved.

4. The term **show,** which we use to designate theater discourse, includes, however, a much broader semiotic field. In addition to theater, properly speaking, it also includes opera and ballet (all these three traditionally subsumed under the heading of "performing arts," and referring to "high" culture), circus, races, sports matches, street corner performances, etc. The definition of show, then, includes, from an internal point of view, characteristics such as the presence of a closed tridimensional space,* proxemic* distribution, etc., whereas, from an external point of view, it involves the presence of an observer* actant (excluding from this definition ceremonies, mythical rituals, for example, in which the presence of spectators is not necessary).

General semiotics is at present in a process of reorganization, by progressively liberating itself from former habits and conventions. We can see that there is clearly room for a **semiotics of show** in the reorganized conceptual field of general semiotics.

—PROXEMICS; GESTUALITY; COMMUNICATION

THEMATIC
(thématique)

1. Within the framework of discoursive semantics,* the **thematic trajectory** is the isotopic* but disseminated manifestation of a theme,* reducible to a thematic role.

2. By **thematic role** is meant the representation, in an actantial* form, of a theme* or thematic trajectory (for example, the trajectory "fishing" may be condensed or summarized by the role of "fisherman"). A thematic role is obtained both by (a) the reduction of a discoursive configuration* to a single figurative* trajectory (either realized or realizable in the discourse) and, beyond that, to a competent agent that subsumes it in a virtual manner; and (b) by the determination of its position* in the trajectory of the actor, a position that makes it possible to establish a precise isotopy for the thematic role (an isotopy taken from among all those on which it may be inscribed). The conjunction of actantial* roles and thematic roles defines the actor.*

3. The concept of **thematic recategorization,** proposed by Louis Panier (in his research on Biblical semiotics), may be used to designate content* transformations undergone by thematic roles (socio-taxonomic in character) of a narrative discourse

during its unfolding. Thus, for example, unlike what happens in the folktales studied by Propp in which the actors' thematic trajectories remain, until the end, conformed to their roles (roles by which these actors are often designated: "father," "son," "king," etc.), the Gospel texts introduce at the beginning social, religious, or family roles which, during the narrative progression, have to undergo a thematic "recategorization" that manifests their true being accompanied by the loss of their initial seeming.
—THEME; THEMATIZATION; SEMANTICS, DISCOURSIVE; ROLE; ACTOR

THEMATIZATION
(thématisation)

1. In discoursive semantics,* **thematization** is a procedure—still relatively unexamined—which first takes over the values* (of fundamental semantics*) that are already actualized (in junction with subjects) by narrative semantics. It then, in a way, spreads them out, with various degrees of concentration, in the form of themes,* in the narrative* programs* and trajectories. Thematization thus opens the way to possible figurativization* of themes. Thematization may either be more focused upon the subjects,* objects,* or functions,* or else be equally spread out over the different elements of the appropriate narrative structure.

2. As a procedure of semantic conversion,* thematization also makes it possible to formulate a given value differently, always in an abstract* way. For example, the value "freedom" may be thematicized—as regards the procedures of spatialization* and temporalization* of discoursive syntax*—either as "spatial escape" (and

figurativized, in a later stage, as taking off for faraway seas), or as "temporal escape" (with the figures* of past, childhood, etc.)
—THEME; THEMATIC; SEMANTICS, DISCOURSIVE

THEME
(thème)

1. In discoursive semantics,* **theme** may be defined as the dissemination, along narrative programs and trajectories, of values* that have already been actualized (i.e., values that are in junction* with subjects*) by narrative semantics.

2. From the point of view of the analysis, a theme may be recognized in the form of a **thematic trajectory**, which is a syntagmatic spreading out of partial thematic investments concerning the different actants and circumstantials of this trajectory (the dimensions of which correspond to those of the narrative programs). The thematization carried out may either be more focused on subjects, objects, or functions, or more or less equally spread out over the elements of the narrative structure.

3. If we succeed in gathering together the semanticism* that is disseminated along the thematic trajectory and if we condense it, with the help of an appropriate name, as the set of properties of the subject following this trajectory (for example, the trajectory "fishing" is summarized in "fisherman"), we then obtain a thematic* role which is simply the thematization of the doing subject, which is in control of its own narrative program.
—THEMATIZATION; THEMATIC

THEORY
(théorie)

1. By the term **theory** is usually meant a coherent set of hypotheses,

which can undergo verification. Hypothesis,* coherence,* and verification* are the key terms for a definition of the concept of theory, and they are used as identification criteria for distinguishing what is really theory from what is simply presented as such.

2. A theory is supposed to "account for" an object of knowledge. In this respect we adopt the point of view of C. Bernard, who opposed the notion of theory to that of system.* Whereas the latter is subjected to logical coherence alone, theory, in addition, must be submitted to verification (which corresponds, for C. Bernard, to experimentation). Indeed, the notion of verification may vary from one theory to another (for example, procedures of falsification* or the requirements of adequation may be substituted for it); nevertheless, the confrontation between what is "formulated" and what is "given" is a *sine qua non* condition for any theory.

3. The fact that a theory is a set of hypotheses is no justification for scattering these hypotheses among different concepts. On the contrary, a theory attempts to gather them together into a body of general hypotheses, going as high (or as low) as possible, through successive presuppositions,* in such a way that its postulates account both for the considerations of gnoseology (the theory of knowledge, in the philosophical sense of this term) and for the requirements of scientific epistemology* which aids in formulating these hypotheses into a simple axiomatic* system (in the form of elementary structures* of meaning, for example, in the case of semiotic theory). Since semiotics does deal with the theory of knowledge, semiotic* theory refers to the fundamental relationship between the knowing subject and the object of knowledge, and seeks to specify the general conditions of the reception and production of meaning.

4. The vast area in which a theory is constructed between, on the one hand, this set of hypotheses that are not demonstrable but are declared demonstrated (or, what amounts approximately to the same thing, the body of non-definable, fundamental concepts) and, on the other hand, the locus for the confrontation of the theory with the given (or of its adequation, during its application). The initial approach, mostly intuitive, consists in first elaborating a description* language —beginning with an object posited as knowable (the object-language, in semiotics)—and then in justifying it with the help of a methodological* language in order finally to arrive at the epistemological* level, where undefinable concepts and non-demonstrable hypotheses must be organized into an axiomatic system. Such operations make the theory explicit and give it the form of a **hierarchy of metalanguages.*** It is only then that the second phase of the elaboration of a theory may begin, that of formalization,* *i.e.,* the transcription into a formal* language. Beginning with the already-formulated axiomatic system, it goes through the process in the opposite direction through deduction, thus guaranteeing the theory's coherence and testing its adequateness. This second approach gives the theory its **hypothetico-deductive** status.

5. Although the formalization of a theory seems to be a good means to test its coherence, it intervenes, in principle, only afterwards, at a time when the theory has already been conceptualized. It is therefore necessary to distinguish the test of coherence from the cohe-

rent construction of the theory itself, which takes place through procedures of interdefinition of concepts and through the superimposition of the metalinguistic levels that question, analyze, and test each other. In particular, the construction of different logics is characterized by the axiomatic apriorism that often makes them unfitted for use in semiotics.

6. As a result of all that, it can be said that a theory is a constructed language of a peculiar kind, which can become the object of a semiotic analysis; we can imagine, for example, a typology of theories according to their mode of construction. If theory is considered as a hierarchy of concepts and of their definitions, it is acknowledged that they take on either the form of systems,* or that of semiotic processes.* In the first case, theory will resemble a taxonomy* (the concepts are interdefined through specifications and inclusions). In the second case, the syntactic (or syntagmatic) form and the interconceptual relations stem from presupposition.* The movement from one formulation to the other is conceivable under certain conditions: generative* grammar's use of distributional* analysis is one example of this movement.

7. In paragraph (4) we presented the construction of a theory as a two-step approach, since conceptual and metalinguistic construction is presupposed by formalization. In practice—and, more precisely, in the domain of linguistics—things are not as clear. Many efforts at theorization usually remain at the intuitive* stage of preconceptualization; others stop at preformalization; still others, putting the cart before the horse, hurry to construct a formalized theory, caring little for the elaboration and expla-

nation of the concepts. The construction of a theory is a painstaking task—it took comparative* linguistics a hundred years or so, from Bopp to Saussure, to develop into a coherent theory.
—METALANGUAGE; FORMALIZATION; HYPOTHESIS

THYMIC CATEGORY
(thymique [catégorie—])

1. A **thymic category** is a classematic* category* the name of which is motivated by the sense of the root—**thymia**—"a condition of mind and will" (Webster's *Third New International Dictionary*). The thymic category is used to articulate the semanticism* that is directly bound to the perception that humans have of their own bodies. As a complex* (or neutral*) term, it enters into the articulation of the category that is hierarchically superior to it, that of *exteroceptivity/interoceptivity*, used to classify the set of semic categories of a semantic universe.*

2. In turn, the thymic category is articulated into *euphoria/dysphoria* (with *aphoria* as the neutral term) and plays a fundamental role in the transformation of semantic microuniverses into axiologies. By connotating one deixis* of the semiotic square* as euphoric, and the opposite deixis as dysphoric, the thymic category provokes the positive and/or negative valorization of each of the terms of the elementary structure* of meaning.
—PROPRIOCEPTIVITY; EXTEROCEPTIVITY; AXIOLOGY

TOPIC SPACE
(topique [espace—])

With respect to a given narrative program,* defined as a transformation* located between two stable narrative states,* we may consider as **topic** space the place in which this transformation is manifested syntactically, and as heterotopic space the places that surround it, by preceding and/or following it. A sub-articulation of topic space can differentiate, as the need arises, between utopic space (where performances* are carried out) and paratopic space (reserved for the acquisition of competences*). To "here" (topic space) and "there" (paratopic space) is thus opposed "elsewhere" (heterotopic space). —LOCALIZATION, SPATIO-TEMPORAL

TOPONYM
(toponyme)

Toponyms, as designations of space* by proper nouns, are part of the onomastic sub-component of figurativization. Together with anthroponyms* and chrononyms,* they make possible a historical anchoring* aimed at constituting the simulacrum of an external referent and at producing the meaning effect "reality."—ONOMASTICS; FIGURATIVIZATION; REFERENT

TOTALITY
(totalité)

1. In philosophy, **totality** is considered as one of the fundamental concepts of thought; for this reason, Kant classifies it, under the heading of quantity, among the twelve categories of understanding.
2. In semiotics, totality may be viewed first as an undefinable concept that belongs to the epistemological* inventory of universals.* It is used, for example, to define the universe* as the totality of all that exists, and also to define, in a first approximation, discourse as a meaningful whole, etc.

3. Considered as being part of the general semantic articulation of quantity,* totality may be treated either as a category* which, according to V. Brøndal, is articulated in the two contrary terms of integral *(totus)* and universal *(omnis)*, or as a sub-articulation of the first of these terms, which can then be formulated as the complex* term, making it possible to apprehend totality under both aspects at the same time: as a discreet entity, distinct from everything that it is not *(unus)* and as a whole entity, understood in its indivisibility *(totus)*. Nevertheless, it is necessary to acknowledge that the semantic research concerning quantitative universals still needs further development.

TRAJECTORY
(parcours)

Scarcely used until now in semiotics, the term **trajectory** ought to be extended in use progressively until it implies not only a linear and directed disposition of the elements between which it occurs but also a dynamic perspective suggesting a progression from one point to another by way of intermediate domains. In this way we speak of a **narrative trajectory** of the subject or of the Sender, of a **generative trajectory** of discourse (which is established between the *ab quo* and the *ad quem* structures), of the **thematic** and **figurative trajectories.**—GENERATIVE TRAJECTORY; NARRATIVE TRAJECTORY; THEMATIC; FIGURATIVE

TRANSCENDANCE
(transcendance)

From the point of view of the (subject*-) Receiver, the state of **transcendance** corresponds to its participation in the very being of the Sender.* In the context of the folktale, the Sender is posited as established in a **transcendant universe** (where gifts are never supposed to diminish the quantity of available goods, postulated as inexhaustible), in opposition to the subject-Sender belonging to the immanent universe. By the same token, given the asymmetry of the Sender/Receiver relation, the transmission of objects* of value between them no longer obeys the principle of closed value systems (where what is acquired by one is so acquired at the expense of another), but rather it obeys the principle of participative* communication.—IMMANENCE

TRANSCODING
(transcodage)

We may define **transcoding** as the operation (or set of operations) by which an element or a meaningful set* is transposed from one code* into another, from one language* into another language. If transcoding obeys certain rules of construction which are determined according to a scientific model, it can then be the equivalent of a metalanguage.—TRANSLATION; METALANGUAGE

TRANSFER
(transfert)

Located at the figurative* level, **object transfers** correspond, on the surface narrative syntax plane, to operations of conjunction* and disjunction.* Object transfers may be interpreted as a syntax of communication among subjects, since these transfers call for the intervention of doing* subjects and, consequently, since they give way to acquisitions* and, correlatively, to privations (for, in a closed value system, what is given to one is done so at the expense of another, and what is taken from one is done so to the profit of another).

TRANSFORMATION
(transformation)

1. By **transformation** can be meant, in a very general way, the correlation* (or the establishment of a correlation) between two or among several semiotic objects: sentences, textual fragments, discourses, semiotic systems, etc.

Because of its origins, the term transformation, in the European tradition, refers to linguistic comparativism,* whereas, in the American context, it refers to procedures developed in mathematics; whence, especially in semiotics, frequent confusions and misunderstandings occur.

2. From the point of view of their field of application, we can distinguish, independently of their intrinsic nature, **intertextual transformations** (established between two or among several autonomous* semiotic objects—be they paradigmatic or syntagmatic) and **intratextual transformations.** The latter are of two kinds: (a) transformations located at the level of deep semiotic structures,* and (b) those that are established or identified between the deep* levels and the surface* levels of a semiotic object. For simplicity's sake, and following T. Pavel's example, we shall designate intertextual transformations as **L-transformations** (formulated and used by Lévi-Strauss and his disciples), horizontal intratextual transformations as **G-transformations** (which it is our task to define in paragraph 5 below), and vertical intratextual transformations as **C-transformations** (Chomskian and post-Chomskian).

3. Among intertextual transformations, we should first set aside the Proppian transformations. After having described the "morphology" of the Russian folktale, V. Propp tried to place his narrative model back into the historical dimension, attempting to identify the transformations that the model can undergo in the course of its evolution. These transformations are described by Propp with the help of parameters of historical evolution. But Propp's parameters have a very dubious character, since, according to them, the magical comes before the rational, the heroic comes before the humorous, the coherent before the incoherent. Propp's transformations are thus **oriented transformations.** In addition, the transformations described by Propp are local (they affect only one class of equivalences corresponding to a sub-segment of his concept of "function"), isolated (the transformation produced in one place in the text does not affect the other syntagmatic positions), and superficial (they are located at the level of surface variants). One example will suffice to make us realize the imprecision and ineffectiveness of such "transformations": the house of the donor, represented at the surface level as a thatched cabin in the forest, having chicken legs on which it turns around, is "transformed" into a thatched cabin which, all other things remaining equal, does not turn around. Even from an atomistic point of view, such "transformations" cannot be compared with the historical changes described, in the 19th century, in the form of "phonetic laws."

4. The concept of transformation, such as it was progressively developed and applied by C. Lévi-Strauss, possesses on the contrary a definite heuristic* value. Since it is applied to very complex and diverse linguistic phenomena, it cannot receive a precise and homogenous formulation, as its author admits. Therefore, we can give only its main characteristics. The Lévi-Straussian transformation falls within the framework of a linguistic comparativism* which would have been carried to its final conclusions:

(a) Thus, myth, for example, is defined by Lévi-Strauss neither as an ideal form, nor as a prototype that is historically or logically prior to all its variants, but as a **structure of transformations** (or of formal correlations) that undergirds all the variants of the myth, whether the variants be known or unknown, realized or not. The Freudian interpretation of the Oedipus myth is thus but one of the variants of this myth and is in a transformation relation with the other variants.

(b) Defined in this way, myths maintain, at a higher level, transformation relations with other myths (myths about the origin of fire are "transformed" into myths about the origin of water; those dealing with fire for cooking are "transformed" into myths about the origin of edible meats, etc.) in order, finally, to constitute "mythical systems" that are closed and circular (a continuous reading of the mythical transformations brings the reader back to the point of departure).

(c) These transformations are neither local nor isolated (as with Propp), but concomitant. A transformation affecting one segment of text (stemming from a paradigmatic class of equivalences*) brings about, under conditions that remain to be specified, a concomitant transformation of another textual segment (belonging to another class of equivalences). It is clear that the noted concomitance makes it possible to imagine the possibility of a formal definition of the narrative syntagm.*

5. As far as we are concerned, the transformations that we acknowledge, in the framework of narrative semiotics, are intratextual and syntagmatic: they complement Lévi-Straussian transformations, without contradicting them, since the latter are intertextual and paradigmatic. When located at the level of deep semiotic structures,* transformations are considered as logical operations.* On the logico-semantic plane, they are defined as the shifting from one term of the semiotic square* to another, carried out through the operations of negation* and assertion.* On the narrative plane, closer to the surface, transformations correspond to operations of conjunction* and disjunction* between subjects of being (see state*) and objects of value: these are elementary transformations. If we conceive of narrative discourse—and perhaps discourse in general—as "something that happens," *i.e.*, as a trajectory leading from an initial state to a final state, then a **transformation algorithm*** should be able to account for this trajectory: discourse then appears as a string of transformations.

While keeping the term transformation for these **horizontal** logical operations, and in order to avoid any ambiguity, we use the term conversion* (conversions are similar to Chomsky-type transformations, but cannot be identified with them) to refer to the **vertical** reformulations of structures, created by the shifting from one level of semiotic depth to another.

6. In the typological framework that is thus constituted, we can try to locate the transformations of generative* grammar. Setting aside their more or less formal* character and considering them only from the point of view of conceptual theory,* we may say that they are intratextual, vertical, oriented (going from deep* structures to surface* structures), and paradigmatic (indeed, they are located within the paradigmatic class of the sentence). As a conversion of deep structures into surface structures (or the shifting from one syntagmatic indicator* to another, derived, indicator), transformations are here presented in the form of rewriting rules,* that intervene only after the syntagmatic rules and are carried out on strings produced by syntagmatic rules (obviously, inasmuch as they allow for transformations, as determined by their structural analysis). Traditionally, there is a differentiation made between **optional** and **obligatory** transformations on the one hand, and, on the other hand, **single** and **binary** ones (the latter are generalized, in the case of embedding* and coordination), depending on whether they concern one or two strings generated by the base.*

The status of Chomskian transformations is difficult to define, and for several reasons: (a) they are "supplementary" rules with respect to the syntagmatic rules; (b) they are often heterogeneous in nature (a rule that is syntagmatic in itself may become "transformational" simply by its position in the grammar); (c) the very order of the rules (or their being placed into an algorithm) is sometimes a problem, as J. Lyons has pointed out, and the deep structures have to be disrupted so that the transformational system may be safeguarded.

—SYNTAX, FUNDAMENTAL; ASSERTION; NEGATION; DOING

TRANSITIVITY
(transitivité)

1. In traditional grammar, a verb is called **transitive** when, as a predicate, it can have an object, or, in other words, when the verb is but the locus of a transition going from the subject to the object. Whatever may be the difficulty in interpreting and giving a name to this "process" concept (it may usefully be compared to orientation* in logic or to intentionality* in philosophy), the existence of a "dynamic" relation, bearing the strict minimum of semantic investment constitutive of any utterance,* must necessarily be postulated, before proceding to construct any actantial syntax. It is by first positing the **relation of transitivity** that, by complementary investment, we may next proceed to differentiation between predicates of transformation* and junction,* as well as to the establishment of two canonic forms of elementary utterances: utterances of doing* and utterances of being* (*cf.* state*).

2. On the discoursive* plane (where the actorial structures are found), the term **transitive,** in opposition to reflexive,* is used to distinguish the actantial autonomy of the actors* from their actantial syncretisms.* Thus, in the sentence "Peter walks his dog," we have two actants,* subject and object, invested in two distinct actors: the relation between the actants is then called transitive. On the other hand, in the utterance "Peter's walk" the two actants—subject and object—are syncretized within a same actor (Peter takes himself for a walk): the relation is here termed reflexive. Similarly, the relation of knowing* is called transitive or reflexive depending on whether or not the subjects between whom communication is established are distinct actors (for example, we can thus differentiate between knowledge about others and knowledge about oneself).
—ORIENTATION; INTENTION

TRANSLATION
(traduction)

1. By **translation** is meant the cognitive activity that brings about the passage from a given utterance* to another utterance considered as equivalent.

2. Translatability stands as one of the fundamental properties of semiotic systems and as the very cornerstone of the semantic approach. Indeed, translation comes in between the existential judgment "there is meaning" and the possibility of saying something about it. "To speak of meaning" is both to translate and to produce signification.*

3. We generally grant natural* languages a privileged status with respect to the other semiotic systems, since they alone can be used as languages *into* which all other semiotic systems may be translated, whereas the opposite is only rarely possible. Thus, it can be said that natural languages are macro-semiotic* systems into which these other macro-semiotic systems (the natural worlds*) are translated; this holds as well for the semiotic systems constructed from natural worlds (such as painting, music, etc.). Moreover, as natural languages are translated into each other, they also provide the necessary material for the metalinguistic* constructions that allow them to speak of themselves (*cf.* paraphrase*).

4. Such considerations, however valid they may be in principle, have nonetheless led to hypostatization of natural languages and sometimes to the affirmation, more or less explicit, that if natural languages provide us with signifieds, these

signifieds are in fact signifieds from other semiotic systems which are themselves but pure signifiers (the world and painting, for example, are then understood as signifying only inasmuch as they can be verbalized). The acknowledgement of the privileged status of natural languages does not authorize their reification as loci of the "constructed meaning": signification is first an activity (or an operation of translation) before being the result of this activity.

5. It is in its role as semiotic activity that translation may be broken down into a doing interpretative* of the *ab quo* text and a doing productive of the *ad quem* text. By differentiating between these two phases, it is possible to understand how the interpretation of the *ab quo* text (or the implicit or explicit analysis of this text) can lead either to the construction of a metalanguage* that attempts to account for it, or to the production (in the literal sense of this term) of the *ad quem* text that is more or less equivalent, due to the non-adequation of the two figurative* universes, to the first.

TRANSPHRASTIC
(transphrastique)

An utterance* is called **transphrastic** when it exceeds the limits of one sentence.*

TREE
(arbre or *graphe arborescent)*

1. The **tree** is a graphic representation* of the results of the analysis (or structural description*) of a semiotic object: the tree provides a visual representation of the hierarchic relations* and the levels of articulation (or of derivation*) of the semiotic object. The point of bifurcation, at each of the levels represented, is called the node,* and is endowed with a label* (a symbol* or name*). While the tree clearly shows, thanks to the horizontal contiguity of the nodes, the existence of relations regarded as existing between them at each level, it does not provide any information on the nature of these relations. This explains the great diversity of types of trees and the difficulties in interpreting* them. It is also important that the rules* for formation of the trees be made clear each time.

The representation by a tree usually accounts for the taxonomic* activity which to a large extent characterizes scientific discourse. Depending on which of the two fundamental axes of language and which of the two types of relational networks is recognized therein, it is possible to distinguish paradigmatic and syntagmatic trees.

2. **Paradigmatic trees** are particularly useful in semic* or componential analysis and in the elaboration of various ethno-taxonomies. Essentially, they represent hierarchies characterized by hyponymic* relations and provide a visual representation of the complex interconnections which result from the interweaving of partition criteria.

3. **Syntagmatic trees** are used primarily for the representation of syntactic* descriptions. The best known—the stemma of L. Tesnière and the syntagmatic indicator* of generative* grammar—already show some of the possible uses to which trees can be put.

4. In its restricted and currently more frequent meaning, the tree is used in linguistics for the representation of immediate constituent* analysis. This analysis is the basis of transformational grammar, which considers it as the best structural description of the sentence.* Since it is

only a representation, the tree cannot be of any greater value than the theory on which the description is based: in the present case, it underlines the presupposed, debatable principles of the underlying theory which include, among others, the principle of the linearity* of the sentence and the claim for the binarism* of structural relations.

5. The tree is to be considered as one of the possible forms of the representation of a semiotic object and, as such, must be evaluated in terms of its yield and simplicity.* Thus, one and the same sentence, for example, can be represented in equivalent manner by means of a tree, by the use of labelled parentheses,* or by a matrix.* In the same way, the representation of rewriting rules (the use of an arrow, a meaning attributed to the left-right orientation, the coupled juxtaposition of symbols) is homologous to representation in tree form.

The tree is a precise, useful tool that should not be confused with a simple diagram or sketch.
—GENERATIVE GRAMMAR; REPRESENTATION; CLASSIFICATION

TRICKERY
(tromperie)

In contrast to camouflage,* which aims at displacing the sender* from the cognitive* position of true* to that of secret,* **trickery** tends to bring the sender from true to lie*: it therefore corresponds to the discursive configuration* known as the deceptive test.—DECEPTION

TRIPLICATION
(triplication)

Within the narrative schema,* the **triplication** of a same narrative program* is a procedure frequently found in ethno-literature. The program thus tripled is often submitted to figurative* variations,* but in principle involves a gradation of difficulties, making it possible to interpret it as an emphatic expression of totality. Triplication generally intervenes at the moment of the acquisition of competence* by the subject. Since it is only a mechanical device, triplication must not be confused with the succession of three narrative programs that aim at obtaining distinct modalities* (those of *wanting-to-do, knowing-how-to-do,* and *being-able-to-do*).—DUPLICATION

TROPE
(trope)

In rhetoric,* by **tropes** are traditionally meant the figures located on the lexematic level, such as metaphor or metonymy.* To these "figures of words" are opposed, among others, "figures of thought" (litotes, antiphrasis,* etc.), "of diction" (diaeresis, spoonerisms. . .), or "of construction" (parataxis, ellipsis, etc.).—FIGURE; METAPHOR

TRUTH
(vérité)

Truth designates the complex* term which subsumes the terms *being* and *seeming* situated on the axis of contraries* within the semiotic square of veridictory modalities. It might be helpful to point out that the "true" is situated within the discourse, for it is the fruit of the veridiction operations: this thus excludes any relation (or any homologation) with an external referent.*—VERIDICTORY MODALITIES; VERIDICTION; SQUARE, SEMIOTIC

TYPOLOGY
(typologie)

1. By **typology** is understood a set of procedures which permit the recognition and establishment of correlations* between two or more semiotic objects, or their result (which takes the form of a constructed correlational system). This concept can be put together with that of classification,* with, nonetheless, a difference: whereas classification aims at constructing a hierarchy,* typology seeks to bring hierarchies into confrontation with each other.

2. Typologies can be **partial**—when they are based on the choice of a small number of criteria for comparison (correlations among a particular type of units situated on a given level of analysis)—or **general**—when two or more semiotic objects are inter-correlated, following homogeneous analyses, and all the semiotic units, levels, and planes have been taken into account. In this latter case, the **typological model,** subsuming all the correlated objects, produces at one and the same time the finished definition* of each of them and allows each of them to be considered as the transformation* of each other.

3. Already in the nineteenth century, linguistics was concerned with setting up a typology of natural languages. Various attempts were made, based on different compatability criteria.

The best known is the typology founded on the diverse formulations of the morpho-syntactic unit called "word."* Languages where the unit "word" is identical with the bare radical are called isolating; those where the "word" is constituted by a simple juxtaposition of the radical and of one or more affixes, are named agglutinative; finally, those where the "word" can be defined only as the combination of the radical and the flections, are entitled flexional. The criticism of such a typology has already been made: the definition of "word" on which it is based is imprecise and incoherent. Thus, different types of "words" can be found in the same natural language. This typology is, nonetheless, convenient and has remained in current use down to the present.

4. Such typologies can be called **structural** insofar as they are based only on intrinsic and formal criteria and do not take into account the closed nature of the inventories of the compared units. They are thus distinguished from **genetic** typologies which, set up by comparative* linguistics, have particular restrictions.

5. In semiotics, the problem of establishing typologies arises particularly on the level of cultures,* with the result that it can be taken in charge by sociosemiotics,* It also arises on the level of discourses* and of genres,* where the classifications now in use are based on the recognition of social connotations* and not on internal criteria, strictly semiotic in nature.

—CLASSIFICATION; SOCIO-SEMIOTICS; DISCOURSE

UNACCOMPLISHED
(inaccompli)

Some linguists call *accomplished/ unaccomplished* the aspectual semic category* *perfectiveness/imperfectiveness.*—IMPERFECTIVENESS; ASPECTUALIZATION

UNCERTAINTY
(incertitude)

The contradictory* term for certainty* within the epistemic modal category, **uncertainty** is the name of the modal structure of *not-believing-to-be.*—EPISTEMIC MODALITIES

UNEQUIVOCALNESS
(univocité)

1. As opposed to equivocalness or ambiguity,* **unequivocalness** is, in one of its current meanings, the characteristic of a name* when it has but a single meaning, whatever might be the context in which it is found. In semiotics, taking into account the *signifier/signified** dichotomy, we thus speak of **bi-unequivocalness,** proper to mono-sememic terms, which is one of the conditions that are indispensable for the proper construction of a metalanguage* and, more generally, of any scientific discourse.

2. Insofar as it is recognized that a given language has two planes* (expression and content) and that these two planes have the same structure and present an **unequivocal relation** (according to which, in the usual meaning of the term, an element always entails the same correlative) between the functions* and the terms* of one plane and those of the other, it can then be affirmed that these two planes are in conformity* with each other and that we are in the presence of a mono-planar* semiotic system (chess, algebra). In the contrary case, we would have a biplanar* (example: natural language) or pluri-planar* semiotic system.
—MONOSEMEMY; SEMIOTICS

UNILATERAL PRESUPPOSITION
(unilatérale [présupposition—])

Presupposition is called **unilateral** (or simple) if the presence* of one term* is necessary for the presence of the other, but not vice-versa. In L. Hjelmslev's terminology, unilateral presupposition is called selection.*—PRESUPPOSITION

UNIT
(unité)

1. By semiotic (or linguistic) **unit** is understood a class* of entities,* situated on the syntagmatic axis of language, constructed with the help of segmentation* procedures and characteristic of each

plane, level, or degree of derivation of this language. The units, intuitively recognized as occurrences* belonging to the same text, must be recognized as identical* to each other through the substitution* test in order to be declared variants* of one and the same class. Units—considered as classes—are constructed* semiotic beings and therefore no longer belong to the object semiotic system (as is the case with occurrences), but to the descriptive metalanguage. While the occurrences in a text are theoretically infinite in number, the class-units are finite in number and can be used as elements* for new metalinguistic operations. The quite complex procedure that we have just alluded to might appear useless to those social scientists whose disciplines do not raise the question of scientific metalanguage, or to those practicing linguists who live comfortably off the methodological results obtained by the generations which have preceded them. Indeed, if there are several grammatical theories in existence today and if there is a debate going on among them, it is because —although they are based partially on options which favor one or the other type of units—they all recognize as pertinent the question of the construction of the units themselves.

2. There are specific units for each of the planes of language: thus morphemes, for example, are units of the sign* plane, phonemes, of the expression* plane, sememes, of the content plane. Signs or "signifying units" can then be distinguished from phonemes and sememes which, as articulations of a single plane of language, are to be considered as "non-signifying units" (or figures,* in Hjelmslev's terminology). On the other hand, the units of each plane have a hierarchical* or-

ganization and unequal dimensions: the morpheme, a minimal sign, is part of larger signs such as the sentence or the discourse; the phoneme is part of the syllable, etc. The hierarchical dependance of the units in respect to each other is, consequently, part of the definition of the unit.

3. The constructed character of semiotic units authorizes us to define them as discrete* units, that is, as distinct from each other within their syntagmatic combinations,* and as being able to be opposed the one to the other on the paradigmatic axis. Because of this latter characteristic, one can recognize these paradigmatic "units" which the categories* (both phemic and semic) are, even though they are smaller than and of a different nature from the syntagmatic units. Indeed, the opposition between "bat" and "pat" shows that the two entities are not substitutable the one for the other and do not belong, as free variants,* to one and the same class-unit. But this opposition, which creates a difference in meaning, can be interpreted as due to the presence of the phemic category *voiced/non-voiced:* the units *b* and *p*, as phonemes, can therefore be divided (but not syntagmatically) into phemes. Thus, the discrete character of the semiotic unit does not imply its indivisibility. On the other hand, it can be seen that categories are logically anterior to units and that Saussure's postulate, according to which natural language is composed only of differences, is verified in one more way.

4. However, although quarrels between different schools of thought often make syntagmatic and paradigmatic approaches appear irreconcilable as far as a definition of semiotic units is concerned, it is perhaps not impossible to show the cor-

relation which exists between paradigmatic oppositions and the complementary distributions* found on the syntagmatic axis. To return to the example already used, we see that the *voiced/non-voiced* opposition, which defines the opposition between the phonemes *b* and *p*, is linked with the contextual position of these phonemes (in initial position, followed by a vowel—in this case, the vowel *a*) and that a different contextual position (in first position, in certain natural languages, for example) can "neutralize,"* as the expression goes, this opposition. In other words, a subclass of variant-occurrences of a unit, called combinatory variant,* can be endowed with a paradigmatic definition which specifies it, or—to say the same thing—a paradigmatic category appears, in the syntagmatic string, in complementary distribution. Since this remark can be generalized and extended to the other planes of language, one can understand Hjelmslev's concern for the category of complementary syntagmatic determinations. Even more: such a convergent approach—paradigmatic and syntagmatic at the same time—proves to be fertile in the area of comparative* research (not only linguistic, but above all mythological and folkloric, where establishing **narrative units** is particularly difficult). Indeed, quite often a narrative segment can be recognized as the transformation* of another segment only if their mutual substitution initiates the parallel transformation of another segment which 's contextually bound to it.

5. Beginning from the same principle of the complementarity of paradigmatic and syntagmatic articulations, we can attempt to give a more rigorous definition of **poetic unit,** recognizing that it is a question here of a syntagmatic unit of which the hypotactic* relations (those which institute hierarchies within the syntagmatic string) would be bracketed out to the benefit of the paradigmatic relations (taxonomic in nature), which are the only ones retained during reading. The poetic unit would therefore be a sort of paradigmatic emphasis, the effect of which would be to hide the syntagmatic relations. This observation would account for R. Jakobson's intuitive feeling, that what is poetic resides in the projection of the paradigmatic axis onto the syntagmatic axis.

6. The problem of the basic units appears capital in the construction of the syntactic component of grammar* (or of semiotics). Three sorts of class-units—morphological classes, syntactic classes (or functions*) and syntagmatic (in the strict sense) classes—can be chosen as basic elements for syntactic description, and give rise to three distinct types of grammar. Without taking a stance for any one of them, it suffices to note that the principle of distributional* analysis is not necessarily bound to syntagmatic form (taking the distribution classes as units) of syntax: the morphological classes (noun, verb, etc.) and the syntactic ones (subject, predicate, etc.) involve their own distributions and are to be interpreted as combinatory variants.

7. Discoursive semiotics cannot avoid meeting, at some moment in its development, the problem of the establishment of **discoursive units.** These units should not be confused with **textual units.** Segmentation of the texts aims at establishing sequences,* that is, provisional textual units, which allow analysis to be undertaken and permit the analyst to seek to recognize therein the differ-

ent organizational modes and forms (which can belong to narrative structures* as well as to discoursive ones). By contrast, **discoursive units** (the limits of which, on the manifestation plane, can correspond or not to those of the sequences) must be considered as semiotic units, which can be formally defined in conformity to the text's articulations established by discoursivization* (or by putting-into-discourse) of the semiotic structures (narrative in nature). From this point of view, discoursive units are uttered units, recognizable and definable by particular modes of the discoursive enunciation.

8. Literary criticism has long recognized, intuitively, the existence of such discoursive units, by distinguishing, for example, dialogue,* description,* narrative,* free indirect discourse, etc. As far as we know, no attempt at formulating a theory has yet been undertaken so as to provide appropriate definitions for these units and to situate them in the general framework of a description of discourses. Now, a closer examination of disengagement* and engagement* procedures—one of the essential mechanisms of enunciation* and, consequently, of discoursivization—has shown the possibility of establishing a rigorous typology of discoursive units by taking as criteria, on the one hand, the modes or forms of disengagment and engagement and, on the other, the principal types of discourse already recognized. Thus, uttered discoursive units are distinguished according to their mode of production, such as it is carried out either by simple disengagement, by disengagement followed by engagement, by enunciative or utterative disengagement, or, finally, by actantial and/or temporal and/or spatial dis-

engagement and/or engagement. On the other hand, units are recognized by keeping in mind that these different procedures can bear either on the pragmatic* or cognitive* dimension of the discourse, or—in the case of the cognitive dimension—on the persuasive* or interpretive* discourse, or, finally, from the point of view of semantic investments, on the figurative* discourse in general.

9. This rapid inventory of criteria for classifying and defining discoursive units makes no pretense at being exhaustive: it only intends to suggest the possibility of a new dimension for discoursive studies (in the restricted sense of the term). Thus we restrict ourselves to giving in this dictionary only a few definitions of well-known units such as narrative, dialogue, commentary (for more numerous examples, see A. J. Greimas's *Maupassant*). The interest of research in this area does not lie only in the possibility of making a new segmentation of discourse taken as a whole. Thus, discoursive units are not produced in succession and organized in linear fashion, but can be considered as transformations of each other ("dialogue" becoming "narrated discussion," "direct discourse" turning into "indirect free discourse," etc.). In certain cases, a referentialization function can be recognized in them (the "narrative" which develops into "dialogue" constitutes the internal referent* of this dialogue and, inversely, the "dialogue" from whence is set off the "narrative" appears as a situation of referential communication), Likewise, it is perhaps not impossible to seek to establish relations between discoursive and narrative units (the "description" with which Maupassant's *Piece of String* begins, for example, corresponds, on the narrative level, to the construction of

the collective actant*), etc. Finally, it is clear that such a typology, when carried out, would eventually lead to a typology of discourses.

—DISENGAGEMENT; ENGAGEMENT

UNIVERSALS
(universaux)

1. In linguistics, by **universals** is generally understood the concepts, categories, or features that are considered to be common to all existing natural languages. Such a definition is based on an erroneous interpretation of the principle of exhaustivity* and is therefore unsatisfactory: the more than 3000 known languages have not all been described and those that have been, have not been described by using the same methods. On the other hand, such a corpus does not include languages which have disappeared nor those which might arise in the future. Research concerning characteristics common to natural languages is nonetheless not useless, but it aims only at generalization,* without being able to affirm the universality of such or such an element.

2. The problem of universals already arises in a different way with the development of semiotics, due to the fact that it establishes a distinction between **language (semiotic system) universals** and **natural language universals.** The former are common to all semiotic systems, whether linguistic or non-linguistic; the latter, in addition to the properties they have in common with the former, have their own properties (such as double articulation,* linearity* of the syntagmatic string, etc.)

3. While seeking to go beyond the set of problems relating to the immanent* or constructed* character of semiotic structures—namely, whether universals are "discovered"

or "invented" by the semiotician— one cannot avoid noticing a close link between, on the one hand, the necessary and sufficient conditions for the existence of a semiotic system (that one is supposed to find again by "observing" the object of knowledge) and, on the other hand, the concepts used on constructing the semiotic (or linguistic) theory. Thus, generativists have been led, in their work, to note that one can speak of universals only when dealing with the level of deep* structures, whereas analysis of surface structures would have the analyst recognize more and more numerous specific traits and more and more noticeable differences between languages (even between languages as syntactically close to each other as French and English). The rise of generative semantics* is doubly significant from this point of view: on the theoretical plane, this new approach postulates a deep level that is logico-semantic in nature (guaranteeing its universality) and, on the practical level, it organizes linguistic research as a sort of quest for universals.

4. The question of universals is thus a problem of metalanguage.* How is a metalanguage constructed?* What materials, what hierarchies and what certitudes does it involve?* To answer such questions is already to sketch out the general outline of semiotic universals. Thus, when N. Chomsky proposed that **formal universals** (bearing on types of relations and rules) be distinguished from **substantive universals** (concerning elements and categories), he is doing two things at the same time: he is indeed setting forth the problem of universals as a specific problem of formal* metalanguage, and he implicitly poses the necessity of a "meta-meta-language,"

which can analyze the metalanguage. For the criterion which authorizes the recognition of two classes of universals (and which we identify with the category *relation/term* which we consider universal) is hierarchically superior to the metalinguistic level where he situates the universals.

5. All of this happens, then, as if the metalanguage, dwelling place of the universals used by the one semiotic theory or the other (or by such and such a formal, logical, or mathematical language) were dominated by a "meta-meta-language" (or meta-logics) that could examine them, that could, if the case arose, reduce them to simpler categories and that could test their coherence.* The Polish logicians have nonetheless succeeded in showing that such a superposition of "meta-meta-languages" can be carried on, theoretically, to infinity. Consequently, it is necessary to stop the process at a given moment by an axiomatic* procedure. It is curious to note that L. Hjelmslev, whose constructivism was tempered by his fondness for the empirical* principle, could say that "an operation with a given result is called *universal,* and its resultants *universals,* if it is asserted that the operation can be performed on any object whatsoever" (*Prolegomena,* Definition 32). Within a theory, it can be seen—and Chomsky would not gainsay this—that the universals are established by an axiomatizing definition, an act which leaves unresolved the problem of the "meta-universals" such as *assertion/negation,* that the axiomatic act implies.

6. The task of general semiotics is double: it has an obligation to construct the semiotic theory and, in order to do so, to stop the development of the meta-linguistic scaffolding, at a given moment, as abstract and deep as possible. On the other hand, it cannot default on one of its obligations, which is the quest for "meta-universals." It is in this way that some reason can be seen for the apparent paradox, according to which universals, as objects at which semiotics aims, are semantic in nature (and as such can be submitted to semantic analysis) and can simultaneously be considered as formal (desemanticized) and thus serve as materials for syntactic and logical constructions.

7. Following Hjelmslev on this point, we can hold that the semantic analysis of a metalanguage consists, for each concept, in establishing its definition and in then dividing it into a number of more abstract constituent concepts. The definition of each of these new concepts, followed by deeper and more abstract divisions, thus constitutes a conceptual hierarchy which perforce ends, at a given moment, in the recognition of ultimate and non-definable concepts. The epistemological* inventory of the undefinables (such as "relations," "operations") is thus equivalent to a first list of semantic universals. It will be noted, as an example, that this is the procedure that we use to establish the framework for the elementary structure* of signification. It is only in a second stage, through a new procedure, after having isolated a typology of elementary relations (relations of the types "both . . . and" and "either . . . or," contrariety, contradiction, complementarity), that we have declared these relations and operations (assertion/negation) to be universal, thus opening the way to a further formalization procedure.

8. By following the development of such and such a component of semiotic theory, the semiotician can be led to declare (with more or

less certitude*—for this certitude is gradual and not categorical) as universal such and such categories or operations that are proper to the component in question. Thus R. Jakobson proposed that a dozen binary phemic categories be considered as **phonological*** **universals.** Likewise, in order to stimulate the operativeness of the semantic component, we consider as "ad hoc" universal the categories *life/death* and *culture/nature,* judging that they could serve as starting points for the analysis of semantic universes.*

UNIVERSE
(univers)

1. In its general meaning, the term **universe** designates "the set of all that exists." In this sense, the concept of universe includes that of world, which contains a minimum of uttered properties (*cf.* natural world*): the set of possible worlds constitutes the universe.

2. In semiotics, the totality* of significations, postulated as such prior to its articulation,* is called **semantic universe** (*cf.* Saussure's "nebula"). Such a universe has a semiotic existence,* which excludes any ontological judgment, and implies, on the contrary, its inscription (as object under study) in the structure that links the knowing subject to the object of knowledge. From this point of view, the **individual universe** is to be distinguished from the **collective universe.**

3. In a more restricted sense, semantic universe can be defined as the set of the systems of values.* Since the semantic universe can be apprehended as meaningful only by means of differentiating articulations, we are obliged to postulate the existence of elementary axiological structures* which, as universals,* permit the semantic universe to be

described. The individual universe is said to be articulatable, in its foundational domain, according to the category *life/death,* whereas the collective universe can be articulated according to the category *nature/culture.* On this level, these two types of universe remain abstract*: they can be figurativized* by homologating one or another of their basic categories with the elementary figurative structure (that we define as the projection onto the semiotic square* of the four "elements" of nature: fire, air, water, earth).

4. The two universes, individual and collective, whether figurativized or not, can be assumed, interpreted, and articulated in specific ways, either by an individual or by a society. The result of such selective and restrictive productions is called, in the first case, **idiolectal*** **universe** (and corresponds to what is generally understood by "personality") and, in the second, **sociolectal*** **universe** (corresponding to a given "culture"). These definitions are situated on the deep semantic level and can serve as starting point for further semantic analyses which use, for example, the operational concept of episteme* (defined as a closed axiological hierarchy).

5. Since an analysis of the semantic universe insofar as it is manifested in a given natural language (and therefore coextensive with the concept of culture*) is impossible to conceive of in its totality, the concept of semantic **micro-universe,*** considered as including and producing a particular class of discourse, has been substituted for that of universe in semiotic practice. The notion of micro-universe is comparable to that of **discourse universe** (which has its origin in logic), but cannot be identified therewith. The micro-universe is

thought to account for the semantic organization of the discourse, whereas the concept of discourse universe represents the legitimate concern for constituting the whole contextuality (paradigmatic as well as syntagmatic) of an utterance (the dimensions of which are those of the sentence*). The micro-universe is the locus where only the semantic component is at work, whereas the discourse universe contains at the same time the syntactic implications and presuppositions. Finally, the discourse universe includes the references to the "exterior" world, whereas the micro-universe is self-sufficient and allows only intertextualities* and semiotic syncretisms. —TOTALITY; STRUCTURE (B: Elementary structure of signification); IDIOLECT; SOCIOLECT; MICRO-UNIVERSE; PSYCHO-SEMIOTICS

USE
(usage)

1. In attempting to specify the nature of Saussure's distinction language/speech, L. Hjelmslev proposed that language be called linguistic schema and that certain essential aspects of the concept of speech* (wherein Saussure's heirs saw at times the syntagmatic axis of language and at other times individual stylistic manifestations) be called **linguistic uses.** Linguistic use, considered as the set of the linguistic habits of a given society, is then defined as the substance* (of the expression* and of the content* simultaneously) which manifests the linguistic schema (or language).

2. Where any given semantic universe* can be articulated through the rules of a combinatory* principle, the set of the virtual expressions* that it can produce may be considered as the schema of that universe, whereas the expressions actually realized and manifested belong to its use: the schema is then called open, by opposition to use, which is its closing.
—SCHEMA; SPEECH

UTOPIC SPACE
(utopique [espace—])

A sub-component of topic space, and opposed to paratopic* space (where competences* are acquired), **utopic space** is that wherein the hero* accedes to victory: it is the locus where performances* are carried out (a locus which, in mythic narratives, is often subterranean, celestial, or underwater).—TOPIC SPACE; LOCALIZATION, SPATIO-TEMPORAL

UTTERANCE
(énoncé)

1. In the general sense of "that which is uttered," we understand **utterance** to mean any entity* endowed with meaning, belonging either to spoken strings* or to written texts, prior to any linguistic or logical analysis.

2. In contrast to enunciation* understood as a speech act,* the utterance is the state resulting from enunciation, independently of its syntagmatic dimensions (sentence or discourse). So defined, utterance has to do with elements that point us toward the domain of the enunciation. These elements include, on the one hand, personal and possessive pronouns, evaluative adjectives and adverbs, spatial and temporal deictics, etc. (the elimination* of which enables us to obtain an utterative text, that is, one lacking markers* of the enunciation). On the other hand, they include performative* verbs, which are descriptive elements of the enunciation uttered and re-

ported within the utterance, and which may be equally considered as markers which help us to conceive and to construct the domain of the enunciation.

3. Every syntactic theory addresses the problem of the simplest and, at the same time, the most self-sufficient form of the utterance and consequently imposes it by axiomatic* decision. We label this the **elementary utterance.** It is the class that is analyzable into components but which is itself not the component of any class (Hjelmslev). This is the kernel* sentence postulated axiomatically as the prior condition for its structural description* (generative grammar*), etc. However, either with Hjelmslev or with Bloomfield (and Chomsky) the concept of the elementary utterance rests upon two *a priori* principles: (a) there is only one form of the elementary utterance; and (b) the structure of such an utterance is binary.* Both of these principles date back to Aristotle and the absence of a distinction between logic and linguistics. But these principles are neither universal nor necessary. Since the choice of axioms is an open one, rather than a single elementary form of the utterance we can allow for the existence of two or more canonical formulations which depend upon the definition that we give of the constitutive function* of the utterance. Thus, in linguistics (Tesnière) as well as in logic (Reichenbach, for example), it is possible to conceive of and to postulate an elementary utterance the nucleus of which is the verb (or function) definable as a relation among actants (or proper nouns). The structure of such an utterance is then binary, tertiary, etc.

4. For reasons that are both theoretical (conforming to the structural approach that postulates the priority of relations over terms) and pragmatic (a more satisfactory representation of act* and, in a general way, of narrative organization), we have been led to conceive of the utterance first of all as the function-relation constitutive of actant-terms and to formulate it as follows:

F (A1, A2, ...)

The following step postulates a relation of transitivity* and is based both upon the recognition of the symmetrical position of the subject and object actants (which are situated at the same structural level) and upon the possibility of varying the minimal investment of relations. It consists, therefore, in positing the existence of two forms of elementary utterances: (a) **utterances of state,** written in the form "F junction (S;O)." Given that junction* as a category is articulated in two contradictory terms—conjunction* and disjunction*—two types of utterances of being—**conjunctive** (S∩O) and **disjunctive** (S∪O)—are possible; (b) **utterances of doing,** written in the form "F transformation (S;O)," which account for the passage from one state to another.

When an utterance (either of doing or of state) governs another utterance (either of doing or of state) the former is called the **modal utterance** and the latter the **descriptive utterance.**

5. The recognition of the elasticity of discourse,* with its phenomenon of condensation* and expansion,* and the principle of syntactic isomorphism* (at the level of the deep structures) which may be inferred from it, allows us to postulate the elementary utterance as a canonical form that is able to account for the organization of narrative discourses. Thus, to take the Proppian schema as an example, the disjunctive utterance of state corresponds to the "initial lack" and the conjunctive utterance of state to the "liquidation

of the lack"; the utterance of doing which is inserted in between the two accounts for the passage from the initial to the final state:

$$F [S1 \rightarrow (S2 \cap O)]$$

(The transformation* function is indicated by the arrow and the conjunction by the sign ∩).

Consequently we see that the very formulation of the discursive organization in terms of **narrative utterances** (and the "functions" of Propp must first of all be written as narrative utterances) leads to its being drawn up in a "condensed" syntactic form. Nonetheless, it is evident that by a process of substitution* each utterance (or each narrative syntagm) can be replaced with an "expanded" series of utterances. Thus, the utterance of doing will on occasion be replaced with a series of three utterances, which series we label test.* Such substitution operations thus are the first steps toward a calculus of narrative utterances.
—FUNCTION; TRANSITIVITY; STATE; DOING; JUNCTION; TRANSFORMATION; MODALITY; PROGRAM, NARRATIVE; SYNTAX, SURFACE NARRATIVE; DISCOURSE

ABCDEFGHIJKLMN OPQRSTU**V**WXYZ

VALIDATION
(validation)

By **validation** is understood the positive result of the verification* procedures, that is, when the working hypothesis* or the model set up turns out to conform to the data of the experiment. In this sense, this term is synonymous with adequation.* For L. Hjelmslev, who emphasizes the deductive* procedure, there can be no validation on the level of the theory,* for the theory does not depend on the experiment: the "datum" confirms (or disproves) only the applicability of the theory.
—VERIFICATION; ADEQUATION

VALUE
(valeur)

1. The term **value** is used with widely differing meanings in different disciplines: in linguistics, logic, economics, axiology, esthetics, etc. Semiotic theory would like to bring the different definitions closer together and to reconcile them by attributing to them appropriate positions in its general economy.

2. The merit of having introduced the concept of **linguistic value** belongs to F. de Saussure. By noting that meaning resides only in the differences apprehended between words, he raises the problem of signification* in terms of values

which are relative and which are determined by relations among themselves. This has permitted the establishment of the concept of content* form* (L. Hjelmslev) and its interpretation as a set of semic articulations.* In linguistics, value can therefore be identified with the seme* taken within a semantic category* (and representable with the help of the semiotic square*).—It is in a meaning which is relatively close to its linguistic meaning that the term value is used in esthetics (pictorial criticism).—The expression **truth value,** used in logic to designate the character that an utterance has of being true or false, is to be interpreted in the same meaning, as an organization of modal* values in the form of a semantic category. This interpretation, however, is too restrictive, for it applies only to the veridictory* modalities and does not take into account the development of modal logics. In point of fact, every logic is determined by the *a priori* choice of a modal category (deontic,* alethic,* etc.) which serves as its base morphology.*

3. A semantic category, represented by means of the semiotic square, corresponds to the neutral, descriptive state of the invested values. As regards their mode of existence,* it will be said that on this level we are dealing with **virtual* values.** Their axiologization* appears only with the complementary investment of the thymic* category which denotes the positive deixis* as euphoric and the negative deixis as dysphoric. Since this category is of a proprioceptive* order, thymic investment can be conceived only insofar as such or such a value—articulated in the square—is put into relation with the subject.* This is the same as saying that values are axiologized—and, from virtual, be-

come **actualized* values**—only when they are inserted into the frames which are foreseen for them within surface* narrative structures and, more exactly, when they are invested in the object*-actants of the utterances of state.* In this case, values remain virtual as long as they are disjoined from subjects, which then are subjects only according to wanting.* Conjunction* with the object of value, when it has taken place to the benefit of the subject, transforms the actual value into **realized* value.**

4. Two broad categories of values can also be distinguished: **descriptive values** (objects which can be consumed and can be stored up, pleasures and "states of feeling," etc.) and **modal values** (wanting-, being-able-, having-to-, knowing-how-to-be/to-do). While the former belong to G. Dumézil's third function,* the latter belong to the set of problems concerning the two great functions of sovereignty. Descriptive values can be divided, in turn, into **subjective* values** (or "essential" values, frequently conjoined to the subject, in natural languages, by the copula "to be") and **objective* values** (or "accidental" values, often attributed to the subject with the help of the verb "to have" or of its parasynonyms).

5. The recognition of complex narrative programs* has led narrative semiotics to distinguish **instrumental values** from **base values:** the banana that the monkey tries to reach is a base value, while the stick it goes and fetches so as to carry out this program is only an instrumental value for it.

6. Narrative discourse is often seen in the form of a circulation of objects of value. Its organization can then be described as a series of **transfers* of values.** A particular and complex mode of transfer is

that of the exchange of values. Such an operation implies—in the case where the exchanged values are not identical—their preliminary identification; a fiduciary* contract is thus established between the subjects participating in the exchange, a contract which fixes the **exchange value** of the values in question.

VARIABLE
(variable)

A term* is said to be **variable** if its presence* is not the necessary condition for the presence of another term with which it is in relation* and which is said to be invariant (or constant). In this sense, we can recognize the variable term to be the presupposing term, while the invariant is the presupposed term.—INVARIANT; PRESUPPOSITION

VARIANT
(variante)

1. Generally entities* which appear in the same text and which are judged to be identical with each other (when the analyst says intuitively that one is then dealing with the "same" word or with the "same" sentence) are called **variants.** The identification* of variants thus belongs to the procedure of reduction,* which allows linguistic (or, in more general terms, semiotic) units to be constructed as classes,* starting from occurrences.* In principle, variants can be recognized from the fact that their substitution* on one of the planes* of language does not provoke a change on the other plane.

2. Two types of variants are distinguished: **combinatory** (or "contextual," or "bound") **variants** —which Hjelmslev proposes to call **varieties**—are entities which contract a relation of reciprocal presupposition* with those situated on the same syntagmatic string; **free variants** (also called "stylistic" variants), named **variations** by Hjelmslev, are neither bound to the context nor presupposing or presupposed.

3. These distinctions—and the procedures which support them— were first worked out in phonology (where they provoked, among other things, a debate on neutralization*). Introduced subsequently into grammar (where combinatory variants are said to be in complementary distribution*), they were generalized by Hjelmslev, who insisted that they were applicable to the analysis of the content-* figures*: the sememes of a lexeme, for example, could be considered as combinatory variants. In a generative perspective, linguistic units, tending towards manifestation,* would procede first of all to be dispersed into combinatory variants and then be realized as free variants. —CLASS; UNIT

VENGEANCE
(vengeance)

Like justice,* **vengeance** is a form of negative retribution* (or punishment), carried out in the pragmatic* dimension by a Sender* endowed with an absolute *being-able-to-do.* Justice and vengeance are nonetheless different in that the former involves a social Sender, while the latter involves an individual Sender.—PUNISHMENT; SANCTION

VERBAL
(verbal)

1. Complementary and opposed to pragmatic* doing, which concerns the relations of humans with objects of the world, communicative doing* involves intersub-

jective relations and puts either pragmatic objects or cognitive* objects into play. In the latter case, and depending on the channel used, it takes a **verbal** or a somatic form (gestures, mimicking, positions, etc.). In turn verbal communicative doing is subdivided into oral and written communication, depending on the signifier used (phonic or graphic).

2. In narrative discourses, the **verbal plane,** which takes form, for example, in dialogue,* can be considered as a figurative* expression of the cognitive* dimension.

—SOMATIC; DOING/CAUSING

VERIDICTION
(véridiction)

1. Classical communication* theory has always been interested in the "correct" transmission of messages,* that is, in the conformity of the message received with the message sent. The problem of their "truth" was thus only that of their adequation in regard to what they are not, that is, to their referent.* By postulating autonomy as well as the immanent* character of every language and, by this same token, the impossibility of any recourse to an external referent, Saussurian theory has constrained semiotics to make its concerns not the problem of truth, but that of truth-saying, of **veridiction.**

2. The integration of the set of problems concerning truth within the uttered discourse can be interpreted first of all as the inscribing (and the reading) of the marks of veridiction, thanks to which the utterance-discourse shows itself as true or false, lie or secret. This veridictory device, while it insures a certain discoursive coherence on the plane of the utterance-discourse, does not at all guarantee the transmission of truth, which depends exclusively on the epistemic* mechanisms set up at each end of the communication chain, in the domains of the enunciator* and of the enunciatee or, better, on the correct coordination of these mechanisms. As is clear, the *truth-believing (i.e.,* the "believing to be true") of the enunciator is not sufficent for the transmission of truth. The enunciator can say as much as it wants about the object of knowing that it is communicating—for instance, that it "knows," that it is "certain," that the truth is "evident"—there is nonetheless no assurance thereby that the enunciator will be believed by the enunciatee. A *truth-believing* must be installed at the two extremities of the communication channel. We use the term **veridiction contract*** (or utterative contract) for this more or less stable equilibrium, this tacit agreement between two more or less conscious accomplices.

3. It is nonetheless clear that the proper functioning of this contract depends, in the last analysis, on the domain of the enunciatee. Every message received by the latter, whatever may be its veridictory mode, presents itself as a manifestation* on the basis of which the enunciatee is called on to grant the message one or another status on the immanence* level (to pronounce a judgment on its *being* or its *non-being*). Here various collective epistemic attitudes appear, which are culturally relativized and concern the veridictory interpretation of the sign-discourses. Thus, for instance, certain societies exploit the materiality of the signifier* in order to point out the analogical and true character of the signified* (the *recto tono* recitation of sacred texts, the rhythmic distortion of accentuation schemas, for example, suggest the underlying existence of another voice and of a

"true" discourse uttered by this voice). In addition, reification of the signifed (for example, the setting up, in juridicial discourse, of the implicit internal referent,* which produces the impression that juridicial norms are based on a "reality") is presented as a means of valorizing the truth-saying of the discourse. Other discursive procedures contribute, as well, to producing the same effect: thus, dialogue,* inserted in a given narrative discourse, referentializes this discourse, whereas the "fictive" narrative disengaged from this dialogue makes the dialogue's situation "real." It can be seen, therefore, that the creation of referential illusions always serves the production of "truth" meaning effects. What is true for the signifier and the signified taken separately is also true in the case of the metasemiotic interpretation of the truth of the signs* themselves. Thus, the denotative (N. Chomsky) or connotative (R. Barthes) approach to language is based on two "mythologies" and two different interpretations of the relation between language as manifestation (or, as the case may be, "representation") and the immanence (the "true" referent) that it manifests. In the first case, language is supposed to cleave innocently to things, in the second it constitutes a lying screen, destined to hide an underlying reality and truth.

4. Given this cultural relativism which engenders various systems of **veridictory connotations,*** a reformulation of the set of issues concerned with "truth" has begun. Due to the fact that it is no longer considered as the representation of a truth exterior to it, discourse is no longer satisfied with the simple inscription of the marks of veridiction. "Truth," in order to be spoken and assumed, must move toward the domains of the enunciator and the enunciatee. The enunciator is no longer presumed to produce true discourses, but discourses producing a "truth" meaning effect. From this point of view, the production of truth corresponds to the exercise of a particular cognitive doing, of a *causing-to-seem-true* that can be called, without any pejorative nuance, persuasive* doing.

5. Exercised by the enunciator, persuasive doing has a single goal: seeking the enunciatee's adhesion, which is conditioned by the interpretive* doing that the latter, in turn, exercises. By the same token, the construction of the simulacrum of truth, an essential task of the enunciator, is as much linked to its own axiological universe as it is to that of the enunciatee and, above all, to the representation which the enunciatee has of the enunciator's universe. In this light, it can then be understood that, in epistemological reflection, the concept of efficacity* is being more and more substituted for that of truth.

6. It would nonetheless be wrong to link the problems of veridiction to the structure of intersubjective communication. For us, the enunciator and the enunciatee are syntactic actants* which can be (and often are) subsumed syncretically by a single actor, the subject of the enunciation (or the speaking subject). Persuasion and interpretation, *causing-to believe* and *truth-believing* are then only syntactic problems, which can account for an "interior quest of truth," of a "dialectical reflection," whether or not this "interior quest" is to be manifested in the form of discourse having a scientific, philosophical, or poetic aim.

—VERIDICTORY MODALITIES;

EPISTEMIC MODALITIES; PER-SUASIVE DOING; INTERPRE-TIVE DOING; COMMUNICA-TION; SOCIO-SEMIOTICS

VERIDICTORY MODALITIES

(véridictoires [modalités—])

1. When an utterance of state* can overdetermine and modify another utterance of state, the former corresponds to a modal utterance: its existential predicate does not bear on "the state of things" described by the second utterance, but solely on the validity of its predicate, which is the relation of junction.* On the actantial plane, it is necessary to distinguish two independent subjects for each utterance: a modal subject and a subject of state (the subject that produces the utterance of state subjects this utterance to the sanction of another subject). On the actorial plane, a single subject of enunciation,* considered as an actor which syncretizes and subsumes the enunciator* and enunciatee actants, carries out the two acts intermittently.

2. The modal predicate—the being of being—that can be regarded as the disengaged* form of *knowing-to-be,* can be treated as a modal category* and projected onto the semiotic square*:

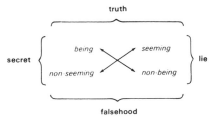

The **category of veridiction** is constituted, as can be seen, by the correlation of two schemas*: the *seeming/non-seeming* schema is called mani-festation*, the *being/non-being* schema is called immanence.* The "truth game" is played out between these two dimensions of existence. To infer from manifestation the existence of immanence, is to make a pronouncement concerning the being of being.

3. The category of veridiction is thus manifested as the framework within which cognitive activity, epistemic* in nature, is carried out. Such activity aims, with the help of various modal programs, at reaching a veridictory position, which can be sanctioned by a definitive epistemic judgment.

—MODALITY; VERIDICTION

VERIFICATION

(vérification)

1. A *sine qua non* condition of every theory* (of the hypothetico-deductive type), **verification** is the set of procedures by which working hypotheses* are confronted with the experimental data. Thus, in the area of the natural sciences, experimentation, to which one has most often recourse in order to observe whether there is conformity or non-conformity between the theory and the "datum," allows the established models* to be confirmed, disproved, or corrected.

2. In the "human sciences," verification often proves to be a problem, all the more so in that certain models are difficult to subject to verification. Whence sometimes a superabundance—in scientifically oriented discourse—of epistemic* modalizations. At the very best, one must be satisfied with the principle of adequation,* which governs the relation between the theory and its application. At the worst, one is forced to fall back on falsification procedures (*cf.* the counter-

examples scattered all through the generativists' discourses).

3. In semiotics, from an operational* point of view, verification can take place either by saturating the model (while one part of the corpus* serves to set up the model, the other serves to confirm it), or by samplings (where only certain portions of the second part of the corpus, intuitively* judged to be representative, are retained).

4. Verification can bear not only on the relation between the "constructed" and the "given," but also on the internal organization of an already established theory. Thus the verification of coherence* can take place on the epistemological* level.

—ADEQUATION; FALSIFICATION; VALIDATION

VERISIMILITUDE
(vraisemblable)

1. As used in literary semiotics,* the notion of **verisimilitude** belongs to the more general set of problems concerning discursive veridiction* (of speaking what is true), and is part of the conceptual apparatus of the theory of non-scientific literature, called upon to account for European literary productions of modern times. From this point of view, its utilization for the analysis of literary discourses, since it goes beyond the cultural context so defined, is to be excluded: this would be the expression of an unacceptable Euro-centrism. Its use within this cultural context can be considered only after a redefinition which would situate verisimilitude as a typological variable in the framework of the general model of discoursive veridiction.

2. As an intra-cultural concept, verisimilitude is bound to the conception of the discourse—and, more generally, of language as a whole—as a representation more or less conforming to sociocultural "reality." This concerns the attitude that a culture adopts with respect to its own signs, a meta-semiotic attitude that is connotative* in nature, which some people consider as one of the principal parameters allowing the scholar to envisage the establishment of a typology of cultures.* Verisimilitude then concerns more particularly the syntagmatic organization of discourses insofar as this organization "represents" stereotypical linkings—expected by the enunciatee*—of events and of actions, of their ends and of their means. Within such a conception, verisimilitude serves as a veridictory criterion for evaluating narrative discourses that are figurative in character (and not merely literary discourses), to the exclusion of normative (legal, esthetic, etc.) discourses, scientific discourses and, more generally, discourses that are principally non-figurative and abstract* (philosophical, economic, etc., discourses). On the other hand, it can be seen that, in this perspective, the verisimilitudinous discourse is not only a "correct" representation of sociocultural reality, but also a similacrum set up *to cause to seem true* and that it thereby belongs to the class of persuasive* discourses.

—VERIDICTION

VILLAIN
(agresseur or traître)

1. In V. Propp's terminology, the **villain** is one of the seven characters of the folktale, whose "sphere of action" includes "villany; a fight or other forms of struggle with the hero." (p. 79) On this ground, this character can be seen as the anti-donor. As distinguished from the

donor, which assumes the role of helper* and gives to the hero* the competence* necessary for the latter's performance, the villain—which can be homologated with the opponent—has the essential function of establishing the lack and thereby of setting off what Propp calls the narrative's "movement": the negative transformation* calling for a positive transformation as counterbalance.—LACK; OPPONENT; DONOR

2. Propp's study of the Russian folktale has shown that the tale is not a homogeneous whole, that it is in reality a double narrative,* organized according to a polemic* structure. Parallel to the tests* realized by the hero,* there is another story, that of the anti-subject, the **villain.** From a properly syntactic perspective, the narrative thus introduces two narrative* trajectories that are opposite and complementary (as in a closed value system where what is given to one person is done so at the expense of another, and where what is removed from one person is done so to the profit of the other). These two narrative trajectories are those of the hero and the villain; they are differentiated in reality only by their euphoric* or dysphoric* moralizing connotation. Thus, the Proppian villain, negatively overdetermined, is in every way comparable to Tom Thumb, who is qualified as hero and who is involved in deceptive* tests.
—SUBJECT; HERO; NARRATIVE SCHEME; MORALIZATION

VIRTUALIZATION
(*virtualisation*)

1. In the framework of the modes of semiotic existence,* the *virtual/actual* category permits a characterization of the relation between system* and process,* between language* and speech.* Contrary to actual existence, which belongs to the syntagmatic axis of language, **virtual existence** characterizes the paradigmatic axis: it is an existence "in absentia."

2. Narrative semiotics has been led to substitute the ternary articulation *virtualization/actualization/realization* for the couple *virtualization/actualization*. From this point of view, **virtualization** corresponds to the act of positing subjects* and objects* prior to any junction* (or, inversely, of purely and simply suppressing this relation). In the framework solely of the utterances of state,* it is the role of the function* to operate their actualization by disjunction* and their realization* by conjunction.*
—ACTUALIZATION; VALUE; EXISTENCE, SEMIOTIC

VIRTUEME
(*virtuème*)

In B. Pottier's terminology, the sememe*—the equivalent of our lexeme*—contains: (a) on the denotative plane, specific semes* (or semantemes*) and generic semes (or classemes*); (b) on the connotative plane, the **virtueme,** defined as the set of connotative semes proper to an individual, a social group, or a society. It seems to us that such a distribution is particularly weak, insofar as it presupposes that the problem of denotation* and of connotation* is already resolved and that, correlatively, the procedures of analysis for the recognition* (not merely intuitive) of these two levels of language have already been established.—SEME; SEMEME; DENOTATION; CONNOTATION

VOCABULARY
(vocabulaire)

The **vocabulary** is the exhaustive list of the words* of a corpus* (or of a text), by contrast with the lexicon understood as the inventory of all the lexias* of a natural language state. However, the term "word" still remains ambiguous, independently of the difficulties raised by its definition. This is why the vocabulary can be either the sum of all the occurrences of words in a text, or the sum of the classes of occurrences* (bringing together all identifiable occurrences), or, finally, the set of label words, subsuming all the different grammatical forms (for example, "going," "goes," "went," "gone" . . .).—LEXICON; LEXIA; WORD

VS
(vs)

An abbreviation of the Latin *"versus"* (=against), **vs** is a conventional symbol,* used to designate the relation of opposition* when it is not yet determined. The oblique bar -/-is likewise used with the same meaning, but more frequently.

ABCDEFGHIJKLMN OPQRSTUVWXYZ

WANTING
(vouloir)

1. **Wanting** is the name chosen to designate one of the predicates of the modal utterance that governs either an utterance of doing* or an utterance of state.* Since it is impossible to define this investment of the predicate, its semantic status can be determined only within a taxonomy of modal predicates and in function of the syntactic organizations in which it can appear. Wanting, just like having-to,* seems to constitute a virtual *a priori* requirement that conditions the production of utterances of doing or of state.

2. According to the type of utterance it governs, the modal utterance of *wanting* is a constituent of two modal structures that can be designated, for short, as *wanting-to-do* and *wanting-to-be*. The categorization* of these structures obtained by their projection onto the semiotic square,* permits the production of two **wanting modal categories,** either:

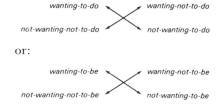

or:

However, whereas the logics that manipulate the modality of having-to—deontic* logics and alethic* logics—employ names already established by use and which correspond, in semiotics, to the different positions occupied on the semiotic square by modal structures of the same nature, there is no **wanting logic** (or bulestic)—although it can be foreseen,—the terminology of which could be used in semiotics. On the other hand, psychoanalysis, the concerns of which correspond best of all to this semiotic project, is well known for its resistance to the development of a scientifically oriented metalanguage.* It would be desirable that semiotic theory take charge of the logico-semantic articulation of this set of problems.

—MODALITY; HAVING-TO-; DESIRE

WORD
(mot)

1. For the semiotician the term **word** is a particularly tricky one in linguistics. Having been unsuccessful in defining the term, linguists have tried many times to expel it from their vocabulary and concerns. But each time it was able to return in another guise and raise the same problems anew.

2. In comparative* linguistics, born of the studies carried out upon Indo-European languages, the word appeared to be a self-evident fundamental datum of natural languages. For this reason it was the object of one of the components of grammar*—morphology*—which took it as part of one or another morphological class* (or part of speech), as bearing the marks of grammatical categories,* as a base element of syntactic combinations, etc.

3. The difficulties began, as it were, only when linguistics was led to take into its purview very different languages, languages other than the Indo-European sort, in which it was difficult to find roughly equivalent correspondences for the word taken as a separate entity. Thus, for so-called "agglutinative" languages there is no boundary between the word and the utterance and we find here what are called "word-sentences"; by contrast, for "isolating" languages the word appears as a root. What is paradoxical is that in order to show that the word is not a pertinent and universal linguistic unit, these languages have, precisely, been defined as having "words" of another sort. The result is nonetheless that the word, although it is a syntagmatic unit, can be grasped as such only within a language or group of particular languages.

4. Today certain linguists are seeking a way to rid themselves of the concept of word by proposing a new syntagmatic unit, the lexia,* to take its place more or less. This new, operational,* concept seems acceptable; nonetheless the definition of lexia sets as a condition, that it be able to be substituted within a class of lexemes* (which brings us close once again to the notion of word as a morphological class).

5. Another way to be able to do without the notion of word consists in building a phrase-structure syntax that is no longer based on morphological classes by instead upon syntagmatic classes which are obtained through distributional* analysis (or by successive divisions of the text into its parts, as is done in glossematics*). An analysis of this sort, which begins with the establishment of syntagms* (nominal or verbal) results, in its final phase, in the estab-

lishment of "lexical classes" (noun, verb, adverb, etc.) without desiring (or being able) to account for the way in which the change of the units from one type to those of another has been managed (J. Lyons). Thus in generative* grammar the concept of word reappears without having been invited.

6. The hiatus that is encountered between both types of phrastic organization—"syntactic" and "morphological"—and which L. Hjelmslev has sought to bridge by providing a new definition for the concept of category,* appears in an even more evident way between semantic structures and lexical structures (the latter still remain very poorly understood). The change from one to another, to which we have given the name lexicalization,* could very well offer a privileged locus for new procedures of generation and transformation that can lead to solutions of the enigma, "word."

—MORPHOLOGY; TYPOLOGY; OCCURRENCE; CLASS; CATEGORY; LEXICALIZATION

WORLD, NATURAL
(monde naturel)

1. We take **natural world** to mean the seeming by which the universe appears to humans as a set of sensible qualities endowed with a certain organization which occasionally brings it to be designated as the "world of common sense." In relation to the "deep" structure of the universe, which belongs to the physical, chemical, biological, etc. order, the natural world corresponds, as it were, to its "surface structure." On the other hand it is a "discursive" structure, for it appears within the framework of the subject/object relation: it is the "utterance" constructed by the human subject and decipherable by that subject. Thus

we see that the concept of natural world which we propose aims at nothing other than giving a more general semiotic interpretation to the notions of referent* or of extra-linguistic context,* which appear in strictly linguistic theories.

2. The qualifier **natural** which we use on purpose to underscore the parallelism between the natural world and natural languages* serves to indicate its anteriority in relation to the individual: the latter is inscribed from birth within a signifying world made up of both "nature" and "culture," and is progressively integrated therein through experience. Nature,* therefore, is not a neutral referent; it is strongly culture-bound—"If a person grew up all alone would he or she know how to make love?" was sometime ago the theme of a well-known debate in which the responses from the anthropologist and the psychologist were negative—By the very same token, nature is relativized (ethnotaxonomies provide different "world views", for example). This amounts to saying that the natural world is the place for working out a vast semiotics of cultures.*

3. It is clear that the relationships between natural worlds and natural languages are close: natural languages give form to, especially, and categorize* the external world by going about its segmentation. It would be mistaken, however, to adopt the extreme attitude which affirms that the natural world is a "spoken world" and that it exists as signification only through the application of linguistic categories to it: zoo-semiotics* could easily provide many counter-examples. Let it suffice merely to note that, in contrast to natural languages, which alone are capable of making abstract semantic (or universal) categories

explicit, semiotic organizations that are recognized within the natural world are characterized by the implicit* nature of these categories. Moreover, the natural world is a figurative language the figures* of which—which we encounter once again on the content* plane of the natural languages—are made up of the "sensible qualities" of the world and act directly—without linguistic mediation—upon humans.

4. As with all natural languages, the natural world must not be considered a particular semiotic system but rather a place for the elaboration and practice of multiple semiotic systems. At the very most, by supposing the existence of a certain number of properties which are common to all of these semiotic systems, we would be able to deal with them as a macro-semiotic system. It would be pretentious of us to try to sketch out a classification or even make a simple list of the different semiotic systems of the natural world. Nonetheless we can already suggest an initial distinction between "signifying points of view" and "signifying practices," between significations which speak of the world as it appears and significations which are related to humans such as they act and signify both for themselves and others. To the first group would belong ethnotaxonomies, "semiotics of objects," that of "natural" processes (clouds portend rain, a bad smell signals the presence of the Devil, etc) and, finally, but only in part, the semiotics of space,* which is still trying to find its own way. The second group would be made up at least of the large semiotic fields such as gestuality,* proxemics,* and the like, and in a general way by these semiotic practices* that our more or less programmed types of behavior are, behaviors finalized (before or after the fact) and stereotyped, that can be analyzed as "discourses" of the natural world.

WRITING
(écriture)

1. **Writing** is the manifestation of a natural language* by means of a signifier* the substance* of which is visual and graphic (or pictographic) in nature. There is a controversy concerning writing's character as derived from or autonomous of oral expression. Those who hold that writing is derived from oral expression (for example, R. Jakobson) base their argument on the data of the history of writing, whereas those who argue for the autonomy of writing (L. Hjelmslev) direct their research to the establishment of a typology.

2. A still provisional typology of writing systems postulates three types: (a) **narrative** (or syntagmatic) writing, in which each drawing corresponds to a narrative utterance (Eskimos and Alaskan Indians); (b) **morphematic** (or analytical) writing where a morpheme-sign corresponds to a grapheme sign (Chinese, Egyptian, etc., writing systems); and (c) **phonematic** writing, which establishes a correspondence between graphemes and phonemes (for example, Western languages). The history of writing, still insufficiently known, shows, as could be expected, that "pure" writing types are rare if not non-existent.

3. In literary semiotics, the term writing, borrowed from the Goncourt brothers, was introduced and popularized by R. Barthes. A victim of its own success—used as it is in literary criticism (and also in the critical study of other arts) and more recently by the philosophy of language (J. Derrida)—the concept of writing has faded away for the most

part and, despite its promising prospects, retains only an extremely weak operational* usefulness.

As a property of the sociolectal* universe, writing can be opposed to style,* which characterizes the idiolectal* universe, even though the nature of this opposition has given rise to various interpretations. An iterative and stereotyped manifestation of literary forms (classical writing, for example, can be characterized by metaphor), located at the level of the discoursive structures of the text, writing is still apprehended only intuitively and tentatively. —SOCIOLECT; ENGAGEMENT

ABCDEFGHIJKLMN OPQRSTUVWXY**Z**

ZOO-SEMIOTICS
(zoo-sémiotique)

Animal languages (numbering some 600) constitute the domain of research of **zoo-semiotics.** They are characterized in their original forms by communication by means of signals,* yet they can achieve a certain complexity as much in their syntagmatic articulations (for example, among the birds), as in their paradigmatic articulation (among the bees). By integrating studies bearing upon the organization of animal societies, as well as upon experimentation with symbolism among primates, zoo-semiotics is destined to become a genuine semiotic realm, both autonomous and promising.— SEMIOTIC SYSTEM AND PROCESS

APPENDIX
French Head Words with English Equivalents
(* = change from French edition)

absence: absence
abstrait: abstract
acceptabilité: acceptability
accompli: accomplished
achronie: achrony
acquisition: acquisition
actant: actant
actantiel: actantial
acte: act
acte de langage: act, speech* (language act)
acteur: actor
action: action
actorialisation: actorialization
actualisation: actualization
adéquation: adequation
adjuvant: helper
affirmation: affirmation
aggramaticalité: agrammaticality
agresseur: villain* (agressor)
aléthiques (modalités):* alethic* modalities (alethiological)
algorithme: algorithm
alphabet: alphabet
altérité: alterity
ambiguïté: ambiguity
analogie: analogy
analyse: analysis
anaphore: anaphora
ancrage: anchoring
antériorité: anteriority
anthropomorphe (syntaxe–): anthropomorphic syntax
anthroponyme: anthroponym
anti-destinateur: anti-Sender* (–addresser)
anti-donateur: anti-donor
antiphrase: antiphrasis
antithèse: antithesis
antonymie: antonymy
aphorie: aphoria
appropriation: appropriation
arbitraire: arbitrariness
arbre (or *graphe arborescent):* tree
archilexème: archilexeme
armature: armature
articulation: articulation
asémanticité: asemanticity
aspectualisation: aspectualization
assertion: ,assertion
attente: expectation
attribution: attribution
auditeur: listener
automate: automaton
autonomie: autonomy

auxiliant: auxiliant
avoir: having/to have* (to have *only*)
axe: axis
axiologie: axiology
axiomatique: axiomatic*

base: base
binarité: binarity
bi-plane (sémiotique–): bi-planar semiotic systems
bruit: noise

camouflage: camouflage
canal: channel
carré sémiotique: square, semiotic
catalyse: catalysis
cataphore: cataphora
catégorie: category
catégorisation: categorization
certitude: certainty
chaîne: string
champ sémantique: field, semantic
charge sémantique: charge, semantic
chevauchement: overlapping
chrononyme: chrononym
classe: class
classème: classeme
classification: classification
clôture: closure* (closing)
code: code
cognitif: cognitive
cohérence: coherence
collectif: collective
combinaison: combination
combinatoire: combinatory principle *or* arrangement* (c. principle *only*)
commentaire: commentary
communication: communication
commutation: commutation
comparatisme: comparativism
comparative or comparée (linguistique–): comparative linguistics
comparée (mythologie–): comparative mythology
compatibilité: compatibility
compétence: competence
complémentarité: complementarity
complexe (terme–): complex term
componentielle (analyse–): componential analysis
composante: component
compréhension: comprehension
conative (fonction–): conative function
concept: concept
concomitance: concomitance

concret: concrete
condensation: condensation
condition: condition
configuration: configuration
conformité: conformity
confrontation: confrontation
conjonction: conjunction
connecteur d'isotopies: connector, isotopic
connotation: connotation
conséquence: consequence
constante: constant
constituant: constituent
constitutionnel (modèle–): constitutive
   model
construction: construction
contenu: content* (contents)
contexte: context
contingence: contingency
continu: continuous
contradiction: contradiction
contrainte: constraint
contrariété: contrariety
contraste: contrast
contrat: contract
conversion: conversion
co-occurrence: co-occurrence
co-réfénce: co-reference
corpus: corpus
corrélation: correlation
cosmologique: cosmological
crainte: fear
créativité: creativity
croire: believing
culture: culture

débrayage: disengagement* (shifting
   out)
décepteur: deceiver
déception: deception
décision: decision
décisive (épreuve–): decisive test
décodage: decoding
découpage: segmentation
découverte (procédure de–): discovery
   procedure
déduction: deduction
définition: definition
déictique: deictic
déixis: dcixis
délégation: delegation
démarcateur: demarcator
dénégation: denial* (denegation)
dénomination: name/naming*
   (denomination)
dénotation: denotation
densité sémique: density, semic
dóntiques (modalités–): deontic modalities
déontologie: deontology
dépossession: dispossession
dérivation: derivation
désambiguisation: disambiguization

descriptif: descriptive
description: description
désémantisation: desemantization
déséquilibre: disequilibrium
désignation: designation
désir: desire
destinateur/destinataire: sender/receiver*
   (addresser/addressee)
détensivité: detensiveness
devoir: having-to-do or to-be
diachronie: diachrony
dialogue: dialogue
dichotomie: dichotomy
dictionnaire: dictionary
diégèse: diegesis
différence: difference
dimension: dimension
dimensionnalité: dimensionality
discontinu: discontinuous
discours: discourse
discret: discrete* (discreet)
discriminatoire: discriminatory
discursivisation: discoursivation*
   (discursivization)
disjonction: disjunction
disqualification: disqualification
distinctif: distinctive
distinction: distinction
distribution: distribution
division: division
dominance: dominance
domination: domination
don: gift
donateur: donor
duplication: duplication* (test d.)
durativité: durativeness
dysphorie: dysphoria

écart: gap
échange: exchange
économie: economy
écriture: writing
effacement: erasing
effet de sens: effect, meaning
efficacité: efficiency* (efficacity)
élasticité du discours: elasticity of
   discourse
élément: element
élémentaire: elementary
élimination: elimination
ellipse: ellipsis
emboîtement: nesting
embrayage: engagement* (shifting in)
émetteur: source* (sender)
émissif (faire–): emissive doing
emphase: emphasis
empirisme: empiricism
encatalyser: encatalyzing* (to encatalyze)
enchâssement: embedding
encodage: encoding
engendrement: generation

énoncé: utterance* (enunciate)
énonciateur/énonciataire: enunciator/
énonciation: enunciation   enunciatee
ensemble: set
entité linguistique: (entity; *put together*
  with grandeur, entity)
épistémé: episteme
épistémiques (modalités–): epistemic
  modalities
épistémologie: epistemology
épreuve: test
équilibre: equilibrium
équivalence: equivalence
espace: space
état: state
éthno sémiotique: ethno-semiotics
étiquette: label
être: being
euphorie: euphoria
événement: event
évidence: evidence
exécution: execution
exhaustivité: exhaustivity
existence sémiotique: existence, semiotic
expansion: expansion
explicite: explicit
expression: expression
expressive (fonction–): expressive
  function
extension: extension
extéroceptivité: exteroceptivity
extraction: extraction

factitivité: factitiveness
facultativité: facultativeness
faire: doing/causing* (doing *only*)
falsification: falsification
fausseté: falseness
fiduciaire (contrat, relation–): fiduciary
  contract, relation
figuratif: figurative
figurativisation: figurativization
figure: figure
focalisation: focalization
fonction: function
formalisation: formalization
formalisme: formalism
formant: formant
forme: form
formel: formal

généralisation: generalization
génératif (parcours–): generative trajectory*
  (g. process)
génération: generation
générative (grammaire–): generative
  grammar
genre: genre
gestualité: gestuality
glorifiante (épreuve–): glorifying test
glossématique: glossematics

grammaire: grammar
grammaticalité: grammaticality
grammème: grammeme
grandeur: entity

Herméneutique: hermeneutics
héros: hero
hétérogénéité: heterogeneity
hétérotopique (espace–): heterotopic space
heuristique: heuristic
hiérarchie: hierarchy
histoire: hi/story
historique (grammaire–): historical
  grammar
homogénéité: homogeneity
homologation: homologation
homonymie: homonymy
hyponymique/hypéronymique: hyponymic/
  hyperonymic
hypotaxique/hypérotaxique: hypotactic/
  hyperotactic
hypothèse: hypothesis

iconicité: iconicity
identité: identity
idéologie: ideology
idiolecte: idiolect
illocution: illocution
image: image
immanence: immanence
imperfectivité: imperfectiveness
implication: implication
implicite: implicit
impossibilité: impossibility
improbabilité: improbability
inaccompli: unaccomplished
incertitude: uncertainty
inchoativité: inchoateness
incompatibilité: incompatibility
indicateur (or marqueur)
  syntagmatique: marker, syntagmatic
indice: index
individuation: individuation
individuel: individual
induction: induction
informateur: informant
informatif (faire–): informative doing
information: information
injonction: injunction
instance: domain* (instance)
intention: intention
intercalation: intercalation
interdiction: interdiction
interlocuteur/interlocutaire: interlocutor/
  interlocutee
intéroceptivité: interoceptivity
interprétatif (faire–): interpretive* doing
  (interpretative)
interprétation: interpretation
intertextualité: intertextuality
intonation: intonation

intuition: intuition
invariant: invariant
inventaire: inventory
investissment sémantique: investment, semantic
isoglosse: isogloss
isomorphisme: isomorphism
isotopie: isotopy
itérativité: iterativeness

jonction: junction
justice: justice

langage: semiotic system and/or process
langue: language, natural
lecteur: reader
lecture: reading
lexème: lexeme
lexicalisation: lexicalization
lexicographie: lexicography
lexicologie: lexicology
lexie: lexia
lexique: lexicon
linéarité: linearity
linguistique: linguistics
littéraire (sémiotique–): literary semiotics
littérarité: literariness
localisation spatio-temporelle: localization, spatio-temporal
locuteur: speaker
locution: locution

macro-sémiotique: macro-semiotics
manifestation: manifestation
manipulation: manipulation
manque: lack
marque: mark
matière: purport
matrice: matrix
mensonge: lie
message: message
métalangage: metalanguage
métaphore: metaphor
métasavoir: meta-knowledge
métasémème: meta-sememe
métasémiotique: meta-semiotic system
métaterme: metaterm
méthode: method
métonymie: metonymy
micro-univers: micro-universe
modalité: modality
modèle: model
monde naturel: world, natural
monème: moneme
monoplane (sémiotique–): monoplanar semiotic system* (m. semiotics)
monosémémie (or monosémie): monosememy* (monosememia)
moralisation: moralization
morphème: morpheme
morphologie: morphology

mort: death
mot: word
motif: motif
motivation: motivation
mouvement: movement
mythique (discours, niveau–): mythical discourse, level
mythologie: mythology

narrateur/narrataire: narrator/narratee
narratif (parcours–): narrative trajectory
narratif (schéma–): narrative schema
narrativité: narrativity
nature: nature
naturelle (sémiotique–): natural semiotics
nécessité: necessity
négatif (terme, deixis): negative term, deixis
négation: negation
neutralisation: neutralization
neutre (terme–): neutral term
niveau: level
noeud: node
nomenclature: nomenclature
non-conformité: non-conformity
non-linguistique (sémiotique–): non-linguistic semiotic system* (non-l. semiotics)
non-scientifique (sémiotique–): non-scientific semiotic system* (non-s. semiotics)
noologique: noological
norme: norm
notation symbolique: notation, symbolic
nouménal: noumenal
noyau (or nucleus): kernel, nucleus

objectif: objective
objet: object
observateur: observer
occultation: occultation
occurrence: occurrence
onomasiologie: onomasiology
onomastique: onomastics
opération: operation
opératoire (or opérationnel): operational* (instrumental)
opposant: opponent
opposition: opposition
optimisation: optimization
ordre: order
orientation: orientation
originalité sémantique: originality, semantic
ouverture: opening

paradigmatique: paradigmatic
paradigme: paradigm
paraître: seeming
paralexème: paralexeme
paralinguistique: paralinguistic

paraphrase: paraphrasing
parasynonymie: parasynonymy
paratopique: paratopic space
parcours: trajectory* (path *or* process)
parenthétisation: bracketing*
    (parenthetization)
parole: speech
perfectivité: perfectiveness
performance: performance
performatif (verbe–): performative verb
périodisation: periodization
perlocution: perlocution
permissivité: permissiveness
permutation: permutation
personnage: character* (personage)
personnification: personification
perspective: perspective
persuasif (faire–): persuasive doing
pertinence: pertinence* (relevance)
phatique (activite, fonction–): phatic
    activity, function
phème: pheme
phénoménal: phenomenal
philologie: philology
phonème: phoneme
phonétique: phonetics
phonologie: phonology
phrase: sentence
pivot narratif: pivot point, narrative
plan: plane
planaire (sémiotique–): planar semiotics
pluri-isotopie: pluri-isotopy
pluriplane (sémiotique–): pluri-planar
    semiotic system* (p.p. semiotics)
poétique: poetics
point de vue: point of view
polémique: polemic
polysémémie (or polysémie): polysememy
    (*or, traditionally,* polysemy)*
    (polysememia)
ponctualité: punctuality
positif (terme, deixis–): positive term,
    deixis
position: position
possibilité: possibility
postériorité: posteriority
pouvoir: being-able (to do *or* to be)
pragmatique: pragmatic(s)
pratique: practical
pratiques sémiotiques: practices, semiotic
prédicat: predicate
prescription: prescription
présence: presence
présupposition: presupposition
privation: deprivation
probabilité: probability
procédé stylistique: device, stylistic
procédure: procedure
procès: process
production: production
profonde (structure–): deep structure

programmation spatio-temporelle:
    programming, spatio-temporal*
    (spatial and temporal p.)
programme narratif: program, narrative
proposition: clause; proposition* (prop.
    only)
proprioceptivité: proprioceptivity*
    (proprioceptiveness)
prosodie: prosody
proto-actant: proto-actant
proxémique: proxemics
psycho-sémiotique: psycho-semiotics
punition: punishment

qualifiante (épreuve–): qualifying test
qualification: qualification
quête: quest

réalisation: realization
récepteur: receiver
réceptif (faire–): receptive doing
réciproque (presupposition–): reciprocal
    presupposition
récit: narrative
récompense: recompense
reconnaissance: recognition
récurrence: recurrence
récursivité: recursivity* (recursiveness)
redondance: redundance
réduction: reduction
réductionisme: reductionism
réécriture (système de–): rewriting system
référence: reference
référent: referent
réflexivité: reflexivity
registre: register
règle: rule
réification: reification
relation: relation
renonciation: renunciation
représentation: representation
représentativité: representativity
resémantisation: resemantization
ressemblance: resemblance
restriction: restriction
rétribution: retribution
rétro-lecture: back-reading
révalorisation: revalorization
rhétorique: rhetoric
rime: rhyme
rôle: role
rythme: rhythm

sanction: sanction
savoir: knowing (*or* knowledge)*
    (knowing *only*)
schéma: schema
scientificité: scientificness
scientifique (sémiotique–): scientific
    semiotics
secret: secret

segmentation: segmentation
sélection: selection
sémantème: semanteme
sémanticité: semanticity
sémantique: semantics
*sémantique (inventaire, niveau–)semantic
 inventory, level*
sémantique discursive: semantics,
 discoursive* (discourse s.)
sémantique fondamentale: semantics,
 fundamental
sémantique générative: semantics,
 generative
sémantique narrative: semantics,
 narrative
sémantisme: semanticism
sémasiologie: semasiology
sème: seme
sémème: sememe
sémiologie: semiology
sémiologique (niveau–): semiological level
sémiosis: semiosis
sémiotique: semiotics
sémique (analyse–): semic analysis
sens: meaning
séquence: sequence
shifter: shifter
signal: signal
signe: sign
signifiant: signifier
signification: signification
signifié: signified
simplicité: simplicity
simulée (épreuve–): simulated test
sociolecte: sociolect
socio-sémiotique: socio-semiotics
solidarité: solidarity
somatique: somatic
spatialisation: spatialization
stratégie: strategy
structuralisme: structuralism
structuration: structuring*
 (structuralization)
structure: structure
style: style
stylistique: stylistics
subcontrariété: subcontrariety
subjective (valeur–): subjective value
substance: substance
substituée (épreuve–): substituted test
substitution: substitution
sujet: subject
suprasegmental: suprasegmental
surface (structure de–): surface structure
suspension: suspension
symbole: symbol
synchronie: synchrony
syncrétisme: syncretism
synonymie: synonymy
syntagmatique: syntagmatic
syntagme: syntagm

syntaxe: syntax
syntaxe discursive: syntax, discoursive*
 (discourse s.)
syntaxe fondamentale: syntax,
 fundamental
syntaxe narrative de surface: syntax,
 surface narrative* (n. syntax)
syntaxe textuelle: syntax, textual
synthèse: synthesis
système: system

taxinomie: taxonomy
temporalisation: temporalization
tensivité: tensiveness
terme: term
terminal: terminal
terminativité: terminativeness
terminologie: terminology
texte: text
textualisation: textualization
théâtrale (sémiotique–): theater, semiotics
 of the
thématique: thematic
thématisation: thematization
thème: theme
théorie: theory
thymique (catégorie–): thymic category
topique (espace–): topic space
toponyme: toponym
totalité: totality
traduction: translation
traître: villain* (traitor)
transcendance: transcendance
transcodage: transcoding
transfert: transfer
transformation: transformation
transitivité: transitivity
transphrastique: transphrastic
triplication: triplication
tromperie: trickery* (deceit)
trope: trope
typologie: typology

unilatérale (présupposition–): unilateral
 presupposition
unité: unit
univers: universe
universaux: universals
univocité: unequivocalness
usage: use
utopique (espace–): utopic space

valeur: value
validation: validation
variable: variable
variante: variant
vengeance: vengeance
verbal: verbal
véridiction: veridiction
véridictoires (modalités–): veridictory
 modalities

vérification: verification
vérité: truth
vie: life
virtualisation: virtualization
virtuème: virtueme
vocabulaire: vocabulary

vouloir: wanting
vraisemblable: verisimilitude
vs: vs

zoo-sémiotique: zoo-semiotics

SELECTED BIBLIOGRAPHY

prepared by Edward J. McMahon II

Adriaens, Mark
1979   "Isotopic Organization and Narrative Grammar," *PTL*, vol. 4, pp. 501–44.
Ajdukiewicz, Kazimierz
1934   "Das Weltbild und die Begriffsappartur," *Erkenntnis*, vol. 4, pp. 259–87.
1934   "Sprache und Sinn," *Erkenntnis*, vol. 4, pp. 100–38.
1935   "Die syntaktiche Konnexität," *Studia Philosophica*, vol. I.
1974   *Pragmatic Logic*, trans. O. Wojtasiewica (Dordrecht: D. Reidel Publishing Co.).
Alexandrescu, Sorin
1974   *Logique du personnage* (Paris: Mame).
Almeida, Ivan
1978   *L'Opérativité sémantique des récits-paraboles* (Louvain: Bibliothèque de Linguistique).
1980   "L'interprétation en sémiotique et en herméneutique," *Le Bulletin*, no. 15, pp. 58–64.
Apresjan, Ju. D.
1966   "Analyse distributionelle des significations et champs sémantiques structurés," *Langage*, vol. 1, pp. 44–74.
1969   "Semantics and Lexicography: Towards a New Type of Unilingual Dictionary," *Studies in Syntax and Semantics*, ed. F. Kiefer (Dordrecht: D. Reidel Publishing Co.), pp. 1–13.
1973   "A Description of Semantics by Means of Syntax," *Linguistics*, vol. 96, pp. 5–33.
1973   *Principles and Methods of Contemporary Structural Linguistics*, trans. D.B. Crockett (The Hague: Mouton).
Aristotle
1926   *Aristotle: The Art of Rhetoric*, trans. J.H. Freese (London: W. Heinemann; New York: G.P. Putnam's Sons).
1963   *Categories and Interpretations*, trans. J.L. Ackrill (Oxford: Clarendon Press).
1968   *Poetics*, trans. L. Golden (Englewood Cliffs, N.J.: Prentice-Hall).
Arnauld, Antoine and C. Lancelot
1660,   new ed. 1969 *Grammaire générale et raisonnée* (Paris: P. Le Petit).
Arnauld, Antoine and P. Nicole
1662   *La Logique ou l'Art de penser* (Paris: C. Saureux).
Arnold, Madeleine
1979   "La Dissociation des plans de l'expression et du contenu en conception architecturale assistée par ordinateur," *Le Bulletin*, no. 10, pp. 13–21.
1980   "Ordinateur, sémiotique et 'Machine molle,'" *Documents de Recherche*, no. 18 (Paris: EHESS and CNRS).
Arrivé, Michel
1965   "Encore les indéfinis," *Le Français Moderne*, vol. 33, pp. 97–108.
1968   "Aspects de la structure morphologique des déterminants français," *Revue Romane*, vol. 3, pp. 1–7.
1969   "Postulats pour la description linguistique des textes littéraires," *La Langue Française*, vol. 3, pp. 3–13.

1972　"Structuration et destruction du signe dans quelques textes de Jarry," *Essais de sémiotique poétique*, ed. A.J. Greimas (Paris: Larousse), pp. 64–79.

1973　"Pour une théorie des textes poly-isotopiques," *Langage*, vol. 31, pp. 53–63.

Austin, John L.

1961　*Philosophical Papers*, ed. J.D. Urmson and G.W. Warnock (Oxford: Clarendon Press).

1962　*How To Do Things with Words* (Cambridge, Mass.: Harvard University Press).

1962　*Sense and Sensibilia*, ed. G.W. Warnock (Oxford: Clarendon Press).

Bachelard, Gaston

1969　*La Formation de l'esprit scientifique*, 6th ed. (Paris: Vrin).

Bakhtin, Mikhail

1969　*Rabelais and His World*, trans. H. Iswolsky (Cambridge: Cambridge University Press).

1973　*Problems of Dostoevsky's Poetics*, trans. R.W. Rotsel (Ann Arbor, Mich.: Ardis).

Bally, Charles

1939　*Traité de stylistique française* (Paris and Genève, reprinted, Heidelberg: Carl Winter, 1952).

1939　"Qu'est-ce qu'un signe?" *Journal de Psychologie*, vol. 36, pp. 161–74.

1940　"L'Arbitraire du signe," *Le Français Moderne*, vol. 8, pp. 193–206.

1965　*Linguistique générale et linguistique française*, 4th ed. (Berne: Editions Francke).

Bar-Hillel, Yehoshua

1954　"Logical Syntax and Semantics," *Language*, vol. 31, pp. 230–37.

1954　"Indexical Expressions," *Mind*, vol. 63, pp. 359–79.

1964　*Language and Information: Selected Essays on Their Theory and Application* (Reading, Mass.: Addison-Wesley Publishing Co.; Jerusalem: Jerusalem Academic Press, Ltd.).

Baran, Henryk, ed.

1976　*Semiotics and Structuralism: Readings from the Soviet Union* (White Plains, N.Y.: International Arts and Sciences Press, Inc.).

Barthes, Roland

1954　*Michelet* (Paris: Editions du Seuil).

1966　*Critique et vérité* (Paris: Editions du Seuil).

1967　*Système de la mode* (Paris: Editions du Seuil).

1968　*Writing Degree Zero*, trans. A. Lavers and C. Smith (New York: Hill & Wang).

1968　*Elements of Semiology*, trans. A. Lavers and C. Smith (New York: Hill & Wang).

1972　*Critical Essays*, trans. R. Howard (Evanston: Northwestern University Press).

1972　*Mythologies*, trans. A. Lavers (New York: Hill & Wang).

1975　"An Introduction to the Structural Analysis of Narrative," *New Literary History*, vol. 6, pp. 237–72.

1975　*The Pleasure of the Text*, trans. R. Miller (New York: Hill & Wang).

1976　*Sade, Fourier, Loyola*, trans. R. Miller (New York: Hill & Wang).

1977　*On Racine*, trans. R. Howard (New York: Octagon Books).

1977　*Roland Barthes*, trans. R. Howard (New York: Hill & Wang).

1977　*Image, Music, Text*, trans. S. Heath (New York: Hill & Wang).

1978　*A Lover's Discourse*, trans. R. Howard (New York: Hill & Wang).

1979　*The Eiffel Tower and Other Mythologies*, trans. R. Howard (New York: Hill & Wang).

1979   *Sollers écrivain* (Paris: Seuil).
1980   *New Critical Essays,* trans. R. Howard (New York: Hill & Wang).
Bastide, Françoise
1979   *Le Foie Lavé, Documents de Recherche,* no. 7 (Paris: EHESS and CNRS).
1980   "Remarques sur le faire interprétatif du chercheur," *Le Bulletin,* no. 15, pp. 26–36.
Bedier, Joseph, ed.
1923   *Histoire de la littérature française* (Paris: Larousse).
Benveniste, Emil
1964   "Lettres de Ferdinand de Saussure à Antoine Meillet," *Cahiers Ferdinand de Saussure,* vol. 21, pp. 91–130.
1965   "Structure des relations d'auxiliarité," *Acta Linguistica Hafniensia,* vol. 9. pp. 1–15; also in: *Problèmes de linguistique générale II* (Paris: Gallimard, 1974), pp. 177–93.
1965   "Le Langage et l'expérience humaine," *Diogène,* vol. 51, pp. 3–13; also in: *Problèmes de linguistique générale II* (Paris: Gallimard, 1974), pp. 67–78.
1966   "Convergences typologiques," *L'Homme,* vol. 6, pp. 5–12; also in: *Problèmes de linguistique générale II* (Paris: Gallimard, 1974), pp. 113–25.
1966   "Comment s'est formée une différenciation lexical en français," *Cahiers Ferdinand de Saussure,* vol. 22, pp. 15–28; also in: *Problèmes de linguistique générale II* (Paris: Gallimard, 1974), pp. 258–71.
1967   "La Forme et le sens dans le langage," *Le Langage,* vol. 2 (Neuchâtel: La Baconnière), pp. 29–40; also in *Problèmes de linguistique générale II* (Paris: Gallimard, 1974), pp. 215–38.
1967   "Fondements syntaxiques de la composition nominale," *Bulletin de la Société de Linguistique de Paris,* vol. 62, pp. 15–31; also in: *Problèmes de linguistique générale II* (Paris: Gallimard, 1974), pp. 145–62.
1968   "Structuralisme et linguistique," *Les Lettres Françaises,* vol. 1242, pp. 10–13; also in: *Problèmes de linguistique générale II* (Paris: Gallimard, 1974), pp. 11–28.
1969   "Genèse du terme 'scientifique': L'Age de la science," *Aix,* vol. 2, pp. 3–7; also in: *Problèmes de linguistique générale II* (Paris: Gallimard, 1974), pp. 247–53.
1969   "Sémiologie de la langue," *Semiotica,* vol. 1, pp. 1–12, 127–35; also in: *Problèmes de linguistique générale II* (Paris: Gallimard, 1974), pp. 43–57, 58–66.
1970   "L'Appareil formel de l'énonciation," *Langages,* vol. 17, pp. 12–18; also in: *Problèmes de linguistique générale II* (Paris: Gallimard, 1974), pp. 79–88.
1970   "Deux Modèles linguistiques de la cité," *Echanges et communications,* ed. P. Maranda and J. Puillon (The Hague: Mouton), pp. 489–96; also in: *Problèmes de linguistique générale II* (Paris: Gallimard, 1974), pp. 272–80.
1970   "Structure de la langue et structure de la société," *Linguaggi nella società e nella tecnica* (Milan: Edizioni di Comunità), pp. 459–69; also in: *Problèmes de linguistique générale II* (Paris: Gallimard, 1974), pp. 91–102.
1971   "Active and Middle Voice in the Verb," *Problems in General Linguistics,* trans. M.E. Meek (Coral Gables: University of Miami Press), pp. 145–51.
1971   "Analytical Philosophy and Language," *Problems in General Linguistics,* trans. M.E. Meek (Coral Gables: University of Miami Press), pp. 231-38.

1971 "Animal Communication and Human Language," *Problems in General Linguistics,* trans. M.E. Meek (Coral Gables: University of Miami Press), pp. 49-54.

1971 "Categories of Thought and Language," *Problems in General Linguistics,* trans. M.E. Meek (Coral Gables: University of Miami Press), pp. 55-64.

1971 "The Correlations of Tense in the French Verb," *Problems in General Linguistics,* trans. M.E. Meek (Coral Gables: University of Miami Press), pp. 205-15.

1971 "Delocutive Verbs," *Problems in General Linguistics,* trans. M.E. Meek (Coral Gables: University of Miami Press), pp. 239–46.

1971 "The Levels of Linguistic Analysis," *Problems in General Linguistics,* trans. M.E. Meek (Coral Gables: University of Miami Press), pp. 101–11.

1971 "The Linguistic Functions of 'To Be' and 'To Have,'" *Problems in General Linguistics,* trans. M.E. Meek (Coral Gables: University of Miami Press), pp. 163–81.

1971 "A Look at the Development of Linguistics," *Problems in General Linguistics,* trans. M.E. Meek (Coral Gables: University of Miami Press), pp. 17–27.

1971 "The Nature of the Linguistic Sign," *Problems in General Linguistics,* trans. M.E. Meek (Coral Gables: University of Miami Press), pp. 43–48.

1971 "The Nature of Pronouns," *Problems in General Linguistics,* trans. M.E. Meek (Coral Gables: University of Miami Press), pp. 217–22.

1972 "The Nominal Sentence," *Problems in General Linguistics,* trans. M.E. Meek (Coral Gables: University of Miami Press), pp. 131–44.

1971 "The Passive Construction of the Transitive Perfect," *Problems in General Linguistics,* trans. M.E. Meek (Coral Gables: University of Miami Press), pp. 153–61.

1971 "Recent Trends in General Linguistics," *Problems in General Linguistics,* trans. M.E. Meek (Coral Gables: University of Miami Press), pp. 3–15.

1971 "Relationships of Person in the Verb," *Problems in General Linguistics,* trans. M.E. Meek (Coral Gables: University of Miami Press), pp. 195–204.

1971 "The Relative Clause, a Problem of General Syntax," *Problems in General Linguistics,* trans. M.E. Meek (Coral Gables: University of Miami Press), pp. 181–92.

1971 "Saussure after Half a Century," *Problems in General Linguistics,* trans. M.E. Meek (Coral Gables: University of Miami Press), pp. 29–40.

1971 "Semantic Problems in Reconstruction," *Problems in General Linguistics,* trans. M.E. Meek (Coral Gables: University of Miami Press), pp. 249–64.

1971 "Subjectivity in Language," *Problems in General Linguistics,* trans. M.E. Meek (Coral Gables: University of Miami Press), pp. 223–30.

1971 "The Sublogical System of Prepositions in Latin," *Problems in General Linguistics,* trans. M.E. Meek (Coral Gables: University of Miami Press), pp. 113–19.

1971 "Toward an Analysis of Case Functions: The Latin Genitive," *Problems in General Linguistics,* trans. M.E. Meek (Coral Gables: University of Miami Press), pp. 121–27.

1974 *Problèmes de linguistique générale II* (Paris: Gallimard).

Bernard, Christian
  1964 *Esthétique et critique*, 2nd ed. (Paris).
Bertrand, Denis
  1979 "Le Spectacle du savoir," *Le Bulletin*, no. 11, pp. 21–26.
Bertrand, Denis and Jean-Jacques Vincensini
  1980 "La Vengeance est un plat qui se mange cuit," *Le Bulletin*, no. 16, pp. 30–43.
Blanchard, Marc Eli
  1980 *Description: Sing, Self, Desire: Critical Theory in the Wake of Semiotics* Approaches to Semiotics, 43 (The Hague: Mouton).
Blanché, Robert
  1966 *Structures intellectuelles: Essai sur l'organisation systématique des concepts* (Paris: Vrin).
  1967 *Raison et discours* (Paris: Vrin).
  1968 *Introduction à la logique contemporaine* (Paris: A. Colin).
  1972 *L'Epistémologie* (Paris: P.U.F.).
Bloomfield, Leonard
  1914 *An Introduction to the Study of Language*, ed. C. Hockett (New York: Henry Holt & Co.).
  1933 *Language* (New York: Henry Holt & Co.).
  1939 2nd ed. 1961 *Linguistic Aspects of Science* (Chicago: University of Chicago Press).
  1970 *A Leonard Bloomfield Anthology*, ed. C. Hockett (Bloomington: Indiana University Press).
Boons, Jean-Paul
  1971 "L'Importance du jugement d'importance dans le langage des sciences sociales," *Essays in Semiotics*, ed. J. Kristeva et al. (The Hague: Mouton), pp. 204–16.
Bouissac, Paul
  1975 *Circus and Culture* (Bloomington: Indiana University Press).
  1977 *Essays on the Semiotics of Non-Sense* (Toronto: Toronto Semiotic Circle).
Bréal, Michel
  1866 *De la forme et de la fonction des mots* (Paris: Franck).
  1897, 4th ed. 1908 *Essais de sémantique* (Paris: Hachette).
  1964 *Semantics: Studies in the Science of Meaning*, trans. H. Cust (New York: Dover Books).
Bremond, Claude
  1964 "Le Message narratif," *Communications*, vol. 4, pp. 4–32.
  1966 "La Logique des possibles narratifs," *Communications*, vol. 8, pp. 60–76.
  1967 "La postérité américaine de Propp," *Communications*, vol. 11, pp. 148–64.
  1970 "Morphology of the French Folktale," *Semiotica*, vol. 2, pp. 247–76.
  1972 "Le modèle constitutionnel de A. J. Greimas," *Semiotica*, vol. 5, pp. 362–82.
  1973 *Logique du récit* (Paris: Seuil).
  1977 "The Morphology of the French Fairy Tale," *Patterns in Oral Literature*, ed. H. Jason and D. Segal (The Hague: Mouton), pp. 49–76.
  1980 "Comment concevoir un index des motifs," *Le Bulletin*, no. 16, pp. 15–29.
Brøndal, Vigo
  1948 *Les Parties du discours: Etudes sur les catégories du langage*, trans. P. Naert (Copenhagen: Ejnar Munksgaard).
  1950 *Théorie des prépositions* (Copenhagen: Ejnar Munksgaard).

Bühler, Karl
   1928   "Die Symbolik der Sprache," *Kantstudien,* vol. 33, pp. 405–409.
   1931   "Phonetik und Phonologie," *Travaux du Cercle Linguistique de Prague,* vol. 4, pp. 22–53.
   1933   "Die Axiomatik der Sprachwissenschaften," *Kantstudien,* vol. 38, pp. 19–90.
   1934, 1965   *Sprachtheorie* (Jena: G. Fischer).
   1960   "Von den Sinnfunktionen der Sprachgebilde," *Sinn und Sein,* ed. R. Wisser (Tübingen), pp. 95–112.
Butor, Michel
   1972   "L'Usage des pronoms personnels dans le roman," *Répertoire II,* (Paris: Minuit); also in: *Essais sur le roman* (Paris: Gallimard, 1972).
Carnap, Rudolf
   1934   *Philosophy and Logical Syntax* (London: K. Paul, Trench, Trubne & Co.).
   1937   *The Logical Syntax of Language* (New York: Harcourt, Brace, & Co.).
   1942   *Introduction to Semantics* (Cambridge, Mass.: Harvard University Press).
   1967   *Meaning and Necessity,* 5th ed. (Chicago: University of Chicago Press).
Certeau, Michel de
   1979   "L'Absolu du pâtir: Passions de mystiques (16ᵉ–17ᵉ siècles)," *Le Bulletin,* no. 9, pp. 26–36.
Chabrol, Claude
   1971   *Le Récit féminin* (The Hague: Mouton).
   1973   "De quelques problèmes de grammaire narrative et textuelle," *Sémiotique narrative et textuelle,* ed. C. Chabrol (Paris: Librairie Larousse), pp. 7–28.
Chatman, Seymour
   1978   *Story and Discourse: Narrative Structure in Fiction and Film* (Ithaca, N.Y.: Cornell University Press).
Chatman, Seymour, U. Eco, and J. M. Klinkenberg
   1979   *A Semiotic Landscape* (The Hague: Mouton).
Chomsky, Noam
   1957   *Syntactic Structures* (The Hague: Mouton).
   1959–62   "On Certain Formal Properties of Grammars," *Information and Control,* vols. 2–4, pp. 137–67.
   1963   "Formal Properties of Grammars," *Handbook of Mathematical Psychology, II,* ed. R. Bush, E. Galanter, and R. Luce (New York: Wiley).
   1964   *Current Issues in Linguistic Theory* (The Hague: Mouton).
   1965   *Aspects of the Theory of Syntax* (Cambridge, Mass.: MIT Press).
   1966   *Cartesian Linguistics* (New York: Harper & Row).
   1966   *Topics in the Theory of Generative Grammar* (The Hague: Mouton).
   1968   *The Sound Pattern of English* (New York: Harper & Row).
   1969   "Linguistics and Philosophy," *Language and Philosophy,* ed. S. Hook (New York: New York University Press), pp. 51–94.
   1972   *Studies on Semantics in Generative Grammar* (The Hague: Mouton).
   1972   *Language and Mind* (New York: Harcourt Brace Jovanovich).
   1975   *Reflections on Language* (New York: Pantheon Press).
   1975   *The Logical Structure of Linguistic Theory* (New York: Plenum Press).
   1977   *Essays on Form and Interpretation* (Amsterdam: North-Holland).
   1980   *Rules and Representations* (New York: Columbia University Press).
Chomsky, Noam and G.A. Miller
   1963   "Introduction to the Formal Analysis of Natural Languages," *Handbook of Mathematical Psychology, II:* ed. R. Bush, E. Galanter, and R. Luce (New York: Wiley), pp. 325–418.

Combet-Galland, Corina
    1979   "Thèses: J. Escande, Le Récepteur face à l'acte persuasif," *Le Bulletin*, no. 11, pp. 31–34.
Conklin, Harold
    1962   "Lexicographical Treatment of Folk Taxonomies," *International Journal of American Linguistics*, vol. 28, pp. 119–41.
    1964   "Ethnogeneaological Method," *Explorations in Cultural Anthropology*, ed. W.H. Goodenough (New York: McGraw-Hill Co.), pp. 25–55.
Coquet, Jean-Claude
    1968   "Questions de sémantique structurale," *Critique*, vol. 24, pp. 70–85.
    1972   "Poétique et linguistique," *Essais de sémiotique poétique* (Paris: Librairie Larousse), pp. 26–44.
    1973   "La Relation sémantique sujet-objet," *Langages*, vol. 31, pp. 80–89.
    1973   "Sémiotiques," *Langages*, vol. 31, pp. 3–12.
    1973   "Le Système des modalités et l'analyse transformationnelle du discours: *La Ville* de P. Claudel," *Sémiotique littéraire*, ed. J.-C. Coquet (Paris: Mame), pp. 147–256.
    1974   "Sémantique de discours et analyse du contenu," *Connexions*, vol. 11, pp. 93–118.
    1979   *Prolégomènes à l'analyse modale: le sujet énonçant, Documents de Recherche*, no. 3 (Paris: EHESS and CNRS).
    1979   "Thèses: E. de Kuyper, Pour une sémiotique spectaculaire," *Le Bulletin*, no. 11, pp. 40–44.
Coquet, Jean-Claude, and Julia Kristeva
    1972   "Sémananalyse: Conditions d'une sémiotique scientifique," *Semiotica*, vol. 5, pp. 324–49.
Courtés, Joseph
    1970   "La Spiritualité des manuscrits autobiographiques de Thérèse de Lisieux comme système de représentation mythique," *Revue d'Ascétique et Mystique*, vol. 182.
    1971   "Le Dire dans les manuscrits autographiques de Thérèse de Lisieux," *Revue d'Ascétique et Mystique*, vol. 184.
    1971   "Actes 10.1–11.18 comme système de représentation mythique," *Exégèse et Herméneutique*, ed. R. Barthes (Paris: Seuil), pp. 205–12.
    1971   *Nature et culture dans les mythologiques de C. Lévi-Strauss, Documents de Travail*, vol. 1 (Urbino: Centro Internazionale di Semiotica e di Linguistica).
    1972   "De la description à la spécificité du conte populaire merveilleux français," *Ethnologie Française*, vol. 2, 1–2.
    1973   *Lévi-Strauss ou les Contraintes de la pensée mythique* (Paris: Mame).
    1975   "L'organisation foundamentale de la séquence 'mariage' dans le conte populaire merveilleux français," *Structures élémentaires de la signification*, ed. F. Nef (Paris and Bruxelles: Complexe), pp. 73–89.
    1976   "A Sequencia do 'Casamento' no Conto Maravilhoso Popular Frances," *Acta Semiotica et Linguistica* (Sao-Paulo); vol. 1; also in: *Ethnologie Française*, vol. 7, 1977.
    1976   *Introduction à la sémiotique narrative et discursive* (Paris: Hachette).
    1978   "Rhétorique et sémiotique: de quelques divergences et convergences," *Revue des Sciences Religieuses*, vol. 52, pp. 227–43.
    1979–80 "La 'Lettre' dans le conte populaire merveilleux français: Contribution à l'étude des motifs," *Documents de Recherche*, vol. 9, 10, and 14 (Paris: EHESS and CNRS).
    1979   "Note de lecture: A Propos de la formation des discours pédagogiques, par C. Desirat et T. Hordé, in *Langages*, no. 45, mars 1977," in *Le Bulletin*, no. 7, pp. 33–37.

1979   "Quelque Chose qui ressemble à un ordre (Analyse d'un fragment de l'ouverture des *Mythologies* de C. Lévi-Strauss," in *Introduction à l'analyse du discours en sciences sociales* (Paris: Hachette), pp. 61–70.

1980   "Dictionnaire de langue et dictionnaire conceptuel," *Le Bulletin,* no. 13, pp. 16–20.

1980   "Le Motif selon Stith Thompson," *Le Bulletin,* no. 14, pp. 3–14.

1980   "Le Motif, unité narrative et/ou culturelle?" *Le Bulletin,* no. 14, pp. 44–54.

1980   "Notes de Lecture: Michel Martins-Baltar, *La notion de besoin dans une sémantique de l'action,*" *Le Bulletin,* no. 14, pp. 44–45.

1981   "Pour une approche modale de la grève," in *Figures de la manipulation,* ed. A.J. Greimas and I. Darrault (Paris: Editions des Autres).

Courtés, Joseph and A.-J. Greimas

1977   "Cendrillon va au bal," in *Hommage à Germaine Dieterlen* (Paris: Hermann).

Crist, Larry S.

1978   "Roland, héros du vouloir," *Marche Romane (Mélanges Jeanne Wathelet-Willem),* pp. 77–101.

1979   "Du ou Ma Dame: The Polysemic Object of Love in Rudel's 'Languan li jorn,'" in *Marche Romane,* vol. 29, 3-4: Mediaevalia 79, pp. 61-75.

1981   "On Believing as Modalisation in the *Chanson de Roland*," *Oliphant,* vol. 6, pp. 326–38.

Christ, Larry S. and James A. Lee

1980   "L'Analyse fontionnelle des fabliaux," in *Etudes de Philologie Romane et d'Histoire Litteraire offertes à Jules Horrent* (Liège: J.M. d'Heur, N. Cherubini), pp. 85-104.

Culler, Jonathan

1975   *Structuralist Poetics* (Ithaca, N.Y.: Cornell University Press).

Darrault, Ivan

1979   "Thèses: J. Fontanille, La Dimension cognitive dans 'La Semaine Sainte' d'Aragon," *Le Bulletin,* no. 7, pp. 22–26.

1979   "Pour une description sémiotique de la thérapie psycho-motrice," *Le Bulletin,* no. 7, pp. 22–26.

1979   *Pour une approche sémiotique de la thérapie psychomotrice: Documents de Recherche, no. 8* (Paris: EHESS and CNRS).

1979   "Pourquoi?" *Le Bulletin,* no. 12, pp. 3–5.

Delorme, Jean, ed.

1976–81   *Sémiotique et Bible,* nos. 1–23 (Lyon: (Centre pour l'Analyse du Discours Religieux).

Derrida, Jacques

1976   *Of Grammatology,* trans. G. Spivak (Baltimore: Johns Hopkins University Press).

1978   *Writing and Difference,* tran. A. Bass (Chicago: University of Chicago Press).

Détienne, Michel

1962   *Homère, Hésiode et Pythagore* (Bruxelles-Berchem: Latomus).

1979   *Dionysos Slain,* trans. M. and L. Muellner (Baltimore: Johns Hopkins University Press.

Ducrot, Oswald

1966   "Logique et linguistique," *Langages,* vol. 2, pp. 3–30.

1968   "La Notion de présupposition et la classification sémantique des énoncés français," *L'Homme,* vol. 8, pp. 37–53.

1968   *Qu'est-ce que le structuralisme?* (Paris: Seuil).

1969   "Présupposés et sous-entendus," *Langue Française,* no. 4, pp. 33–40.

1972 *Dire et ne pas dire* (Paris: Hermann).
1973 "Les Présupposés, conditions d'emploi ou éléments de contenu?" *Recherches sur les systèmes signifiants,* ed. J. Rey-Debove (The Hague: Mouton).

Ducrot, Oswald and Tzvetan Todorov
1979 *Encyclopedic Dictionary of the Sciences of Languages,* trans. C. Porter (Baltimore: Johns Hopkins University Press).

Dumézil, Georges
1950 "Civilisation Indo-Européenne," *Collège de France, Chaire de Civilisation Indo-Europénne, Leçon Inaugurale.*
1952 *Les Dieux des Indo-Européens. Mythes et Religions,* vol. 29 (Paris).
1953 *La Saga de Hadingus (Saxo Grammaticus I. v–viii): Du mythe au roman* (Paris: Bibliothèque de l'Ecole des Hautes Etudes en Sciences Religieuses, vol. 66).
1954 *Rituels indo-européens à Rome* (Paris: Etudes et Commentaires, vol. 19).
1956 *Déesses latines et mythes védiques* (Brussels: Collection Latomus, vol. 24).
1956 *Aspects de la fonction guerrière chez les Indo-Européens* (Paris: Bibliothèque de l'Ecole des Hautes Etudes en Sciences Religieuses, vol. 68).
1958 *L'Idéologie tripartie des Indo-Européens* (Brussels: Collection Latomus, vol. 31).
1959 *Les Dieux des Germains: Essai sur la formation de la religion scandinave: Mythes et Religions,* vol. 38 (Paris).
1960 *Hommage à Georges Dumézil* (Brussels: Collection Latomus, vol. 45).
1966 *La Religion romaine archaïque* (Paris: Bibliothèque Historique).
1968 *Mythe et épopée: L'Idéologie des trois fonctions dans les épopées des peuples indo-européens* (Paris: Bibliothèque des Sciences Humaines).
1969 *Idées romaines* (Paris: Bibliothèque des Sciences Humaines).

Dundes, Alan
1962 "From Etic to Emic Units in the Structural Study of Folklore," *Journal of American Folklore,* vol. 75, pp. 95–105.
1964 "Texture, Text, and Context," *Southern Folklore Quarterly,* vol. 28, pp. 251–65.
1964 *The Morphology of North American Indian Folktales* (FF Communications, vol. 195) (Helsinki: Suomalainen Tiedeakatemia).

Durkheim, Emile
1898 "Représentations individuelles et représentations collectives," *Revue de Métaphysique et de Morale,* vol. 6, pp. 273–302.

Eco, Umberto
1978 *A Theory of Semiotics* (Bloomington: Indiana University Press).
1979 *The Role of the Reader* (Bloomington: Indiana University Press).

Engeler, Rudolf
1968 *Lexique de la terminologie saussurienne* (Utrecht: Het Spectrum).

Escande, Jacques
1978 *Un Discours évangélique* (Paris: Diplôme de E.P.H.E.).
1980 *Le Récepteur face à l'acte persuasif* (Paris: Thèse de 3ᵉ Cycle EHESS).

Fabbri, Paolo
1979 "Champs de manoeuvres didactiques," *Le Bulletin,* no. 7, pp. 9–14.

Fillmore, Charles J.
1965 *Indirect Object Construction in English and the Ordering of Transformations* (The Hague: Mouton).
1968 "The Case for Case," *Universals in Linguistic Theory,* ed. E. Bach and R.T. Harms (New York: Holt, Rinehart, & Winston).

1968   "Types of Lexical Information," *Working Papers in Linguistics*, vol. 2, pp. 65–103.

Fillmore, Charles J. and T. Langendoen
1971   *Studies in Linguistic Semantics* (New York: Holt, Rinehart, & Winston).

Floch, Jean-Marie
1979   "Thèses: F. Thürlemann, Trois Peintures de Paul Klee," *Le Bulletin*, no. 11, pp. 52–55.
1979   "Thèses: R. Lindekens, Thèse d'Etat," *Le Bulletin*, no. 11, pp. 56–57.
1979   *Des couleurs du monde au discours poétique, Documents de Recherche*, no. 6 (Paris: EHESS and CNRS).
1979   *Problèmes de sémiotique plastique* (Paris: Thèse de 3ᵉ Cycle EHESS).

Fontanille, Jacques
1980   *Le Désespoir, Documents de Recherche*, no. 16 (Paris: EHESS and CNRS).
1980   "Introduction," *Le Bulletin*, no. 15, pp. 3–10.

Foucault, Michel
1971   *The Order of Things* (New York: Pantheon).

Frazer, James
1951   *The Golden Bough: A Study in Magic and Religion* (New York: Macmillan).

Freud, Sigmund
1954–1974   *The Standard Edition of the Complete Psychological Works*, ed. J. Strachey et al. (London: Hogarth Press).

Fried, Vilem
1972   *The Prague School of Linguistics and Language Teaching*, ed. V. Fried (London: Oxford University Press).

Garvin, Paul
1969   *A Prague School Reader in Aesthetics, Literary Structure and Style* (Washington, D.C.: Georgetown University Press).

Gasmi, Laroussi
1977   *Narrativité et production du sens dans le texte coranique: Le récit de Joseph* (Paris: Thèse de doctorat de 3ᵉ Cycle EHESS).
1979   "Vers une sémiotique du texte coranique," *Le Bulletin*, no. 8, pp. 21–25.

Genette, Gérard
1965   "Structuralisme et critique littéraire," *L'Arc*, vol. 26, pp. 30–44.
1966, 1969, 1972   *Figures I, II, III* (Paris: Seuil).
1971   "Langage poétique, poétique du langage," *Essays in Semiotics*, ed. J. Kristeva et al. (The Hague: Mouton), pp. 423–47.
1976   "Boundaries of Narrative," *New Literary History*, vol. 8, pp. 1–15.
1976   *Mimologiques* (Paris: Seuil).

Geninasca, Jacques
1971   *Analyse structurale des* Chimères de Nerval (Neuchâtel: La Baconnière).
1972   "Découpage conventionnel et signification," *Essais de sémiotique poétique*, ed. C. Chabrol (Paris: Larousse), pp. 45–62.
1973   *Les* Chimères de Nerval (Paris: Larousse).
1979   *Du bon usage de la poèle et du tamis, Documents de Recherche*, no. 1 (Paris: EHESS and CNRS).

Geoltrain, Pierre
1979   "Compte-rendu de *Pour une Exegèse structurale* de D. et A. Patte," *Le Bulletin*, no. 8, pp. 42–45.

Godel, Robert
1969   *A Geneva School Reader in Linguistics* (Bloomington: Indiana University Press).

Greimas, Algirdas J.
  1948   *Le Vocabulaire de la mode romantique* (Paris: Thesis Sorbonne).
  1950   "La Méthode en lexicologie," *Romanische Forschungen,* vol. 60, 62.
  1956   "Pour une sociologie du langage," *Arguments,* vol. 1.
  1956   "L'Actualité du saussurisme," *Le Français Moderne,* vol. 24.
  1960   "Idiotisme, proverbes, dictons," *Cahiers de Lexicologie,* vol. 2.
  1960   "Les Problèmes de la description mécanographique," *Cahiers de Lexicologie,* vol. 1.
  1962–1963   "Linguistique statistique et linguistique structurale," *Le Français Moderne,* vol. 30, pp. 241–52, vol. 31 (1963), pp. 55–68.
  1963   "Comment définir les indéfinis," *Etudes de Linguistique Appliquée,* vol. 2.
  1963   "La Description de la signification et la mythologie comparée," *L'Homme,* vol. 3, pp. 51–63.
  1964   "La Signification et sa manifestation dans le discours," *Cahiers de Lexicologie,* vol. 5.
  1964   "Les Topologiques," *Cahiers de Lexicologie,* vol. 4.
  1964   "La Structure élémentaire de la signification en linguistique," *L'Homme,* vol. 4, pp. 5–18.
  1965   "Le Conte populaire russe, analyse fonctionnelle," *International Journal of Slavic Linguistics and Poetics,* vol. 9, pp. 152–75.
  1966   "Eléments pour une théorie de l'interprétation du récit mythique," *Communications,* vol. 8, pp. 28–59. "The Interpretation of Myth: Theory and Practice," also in: *Structural Analysis and Oral Tradition,* ed. P. Maranda and E. Maranda (Philadelphia: University of Pennsylvania Press, 1971), pp. 81–121.
  1966   "Linguistique française. Le Verbe et la Phrase," *Langages,* vol. 3.
  1966   "Equisse d'une morphologie du français en vue de sa description mécanographique," *Linguistics,* vol. 22, pp. 34–59.
  1966   "Préface," *Le Langage,* L. Hjelmslev (Paris: Minuit).
  1966   *Sémantique structurale* (Paris: Larousse).
  1967   "Approche générative de l'analyse des actants," *Word,* vol. 23:1–2–3, pp. 221–38.
  1967   "La Linguistique structurale et la poétique," *Revue Internationale des Sciences Sociales,* vol. 19, pp. 8–17.
  1967   "Le Problème des ad'dad et les niveaux de signification," *L'Ambivalence dans la culture arabe,* ed. J. Berque and J.P. Channey (Paris: Anthropos).
  1967   "L'Ecriture cruciverbiste," *To Honor Roman Jakobson* (The Hague: Mouton), pp. 799–815; also in: *Du sens* (Paris: Seuil, 1970), pp. 285–307.
  1968   "Conditions d'une sémiotique du monde naturel," *Langages,* vol. 10; also in: *Du sens* (Paris: Seuil, 1970), pp. 49–91.
  1968   "Semiotica o Metafisica," *Strumenti Critice,* vol. 2, no. 1.
  1968   *Dictionnaire de l'ancien français* (Paris: Larousse).
  1969   "Eléments d'une grammaire narrative," *L'Homme,* vol. 9, pp. 71–92; also in: *Du sens* (Paris: Seuil, 1970), pp. 157–83. "Elements of a Narrative Grammar," trans. F. Nef, in: *Diacritics,* vol. 7 (1977), pp. 23–40.
  1969   "Des modèles théoriques en socio-linguistique," *International Days of Socio-Linguistics.*
  1970   "Sémantique, sémiotique et sémiologie," *Sign, Language, Culture,* ed. A.J. Greimas et al. (The Hague: Mouton).
  1970   "La Quête de la peur," *Du sens* (Paris: Seuil), pp. 231–47.

1970   "La Littérature ethnique," *Colloque de Palerme sur la littérature ethnique;* also in: *Sémiotique et sciences sociales* (Paris: Seuil, 1976), pp. 189–216.

1970   "Sémiotique et communications sociales," *Annuario 1970* of the Instituto Agostino Gemelli (Milan); also in *Sémiotique et sciences sociales* (Paris: Seuil, 1976), pp. 45–60.

1970   *Du sens* (Paris: Seuil).

1971   "Narrative Grammar: Units and Levels," trans. P. Bodrock, *Modern Language Notes,* vol. 86, pp. 793–807.

1971   "Préface," *Pour une sémiologie esquimaude,* ed. R.D. Collis (Paris: Dunod).

1971   "Transmission et communication," *L'Enseignement de la littérature,* ed. S. Doubrovsky and T. Todorov (Paris: Plon), pp. 71–102.

1972   "Pour une sémiotique topologique," *Colloque sur la sémiotique de l'espace;* also in: *Sémiotique et sciences sociales* (Paris: Seuil, 1976), pp. 129–57.

1973   "Les Actants, les acteurs, et les figures," *Sémiotique narrative et textuelle,* ed. Claude Chabrol (Paris: Larousse), pp. 161–76.

1973   "Description et narrativité dans 'La Ficelle' de Guy de Maupassant," *Canadian Journal of Romance Linguistics,* vol. 1.

1973   "Un Problème de sémiotique narrative: les objets de valeur," *Langages,* vol. 31, pp. 13–35.

1973   "Réflexions sur les objets ethno-sémiotiques," *Congrès International d'Ethnologie Européenne;* also in: *Sémiotique et sciences sociales* (Paris: Seuil, 1976), pp. 174–85.

1973   "Sur l'histoire événementielle," *Geschichte: Ereignis und Erzahlung,* ed. R. Kosellek (Munich: W. Fink); also in: *Sémiotique et sciences sociales* (Paris: Seuil, pp. 161–74.

1974   "L'Enonciator (une posture epistemologique)," *Significacão-Revista Brasileira do Semiotica,* vol. 1, pp. 9–25.

1974   "Entretien," *Le Monde* (June 7).

1974   "Interview," *Discussing Language,* ed. H. Parret (The Hague: Mouton), pp. 55–71.

1974   "Sémiotique," *Encyclopédie Larousse* (Paris: Larousse).

1975   "Des accidents dans les sciences dites humaines," *Versus,* vol. 12, pp. 1–31; also in: *Introduction à l'analyse du discours en sciences sociales* (Paris: Hachette, 1979), pp. 28–60.

1976   "Le Contrat de véridiction," *Langages (Japanese),* vol. 5.

1976   "Entretien," *Pratique 11–12.*

1976   "Entretien avec Frédéric Nef," *Structures élémentaires de la signification,* ed. F. Nef (Brussels: Complexe).

1976   "Entretien" (with B. Vardar), *Dilbilim* (Istanbul), 1.

1976   *Maupassant. La Sémiotique du texte: Exercices pratiques* (Paris: Seuil).

1976   "Préface," *La Structure sémantique,* ed. C. Legare (Quebec: Les Presses de l'Université), pp. vii–viii.

1976   "Semiotica do discurso sientifico: Da Modalidaire," (Sao Paulo: Difel).

1976   *Sémiotique et sciences sociales* (Paris: Seuil).

1976   "Pour une théorie des modalités," *Langages,* vol. 43, pp. 90–108.

1977   "Les Acquis et les projets," *Introduction à la sémiotique narrative et discursive,* ed. J. Courtés (Paris: Hachette), pp. 5–25.

1977   "Le Contrat de véridiction," *Dilbilim 2* (Istanbul), vol. 5.

1979   *La Soupe au pistou: La construction d'un objet de valeur, Documents de Recherche,* no. 5 (Paris: EHESS and CNRS).

1979   "Avant-Propos," to A. Hénault, *Les Enjeux de la sémiotique,* (Paris: P.U.F.).

1979   "Avant-Propos," to Françoise Bastide, *Le Foie Lavé: Approche sémiotique d'un texte de sciences expérimentales, Documents de Recherche,* no. 7 (Paris: EHESS and CNRS).

1979   "Avant-Propos" to *La 'Lettre' dans le conte populaire merveilleux français,* Joseph Courtés, *Documents de Recherche,* no. 9 (Paris: EHESS and CNRS).

1979   "De la modalisation de l'être," *Le Bulletin,* vol. 9, pp. 9–19.

1979   "Pour une sémiotique des passions," *Le Bulletin,* vol. 3, pp. 1–7.

1979   "Pour une sémiotique didactique," *Le Bulletin,* vol. 7, pp. 3–8.

1979   "Rapport d'activités du Groupe Sémio-Linguistique 1977–78 et 1978–79," *Le Bulletin,* vol. 12, pp. 6–34.

1979   *Description et narrativité* et *A Propos du jeu, Documents de Recherche,* no. 13 (Paris: EHESS and CNRS).

1980   ;"Roland Barthes: Une Biographie à construire," *Le Bulletin,* vol. 13, pp. 3–7.

1980   "Notes sur le métalangage," *Le Bulletin,* vol. 13, pp. 48–55.

1981   "La Provocation par défi," *Figures de la manipulation,* ed. A.J. Greimas and I. Darrault (Paris: Editions d'Autres).

A. J. Greimas, ed.
1972   *Essais de sémiotique poétique* (Paris: Larousse).

Greimas, Algirdas J., and J. Courtés
1976   "The Cognitive Dimension of Narrative Discourses," trans. M. Rengstorf, *New Literary History,* vol. 7, pp. 433–47.

Greimas, Algirdas J. and I. Darrault
1981   *Figures de la manipulation* (Paris: Editions d'Autres).

Greimas, Algirdas J., and E. Landowski
1970   "Analyse d'un discours juridique," *Sémiotique et sciences sociales* (Paris: Seuil, 1976), pp. 79–128.

1979   "Introduction: Les Parcours du savoir," *Introduction à l'analyse du discours en sciences sociales* (Paris: Hachette), pp. 5–28.

Greimas, A.J., and E. Landowski, eds.
1979   *Introduction à l'analyse du discours en sciences sociales* (Paris: Hachette).

Greimas, Algirdas J., and G. Matoré
1957   "La Naissance du 'genie' au XVIIIe siècle," *Le Français Moderne,* vol. 4, pp. 256–72.

Greimas, Algirdas J., and F. Nef
1978   "Essai sur la vie sentimentale des hippopotames," *Grammars and Descriptions,* ed. J. Petöfi and T. van Dyck (Berlin: De Gruyter), pp. 85–105.

Greimas, Algirdas J., and F. Rastier
1968   "The Interactions of Semiotic Constraints," *Yale French Studies,* vol. 41, pp. 86–105. "Les Jeux des contraintes sémiotiques," also in: *Du sens* (Paris: Seuil, 1970), pp. 135–55.

Gresset, Philippe
1979   "Vers une sémantique de la représentation architecturale classique," *Le Bulletin,* vol. 10, pp. 28–32.

Groupe d'Entrevernes
1978   *Signs and Parables,* trans. G. Phillips (Pittsburgh: Pickwick Press).

1979   *Analyse sémiotique des textes* (Lyon: Presses Universitaires de Lyon).

Guillaume, Gustave
1929   *Temps et verbe* (Paris: Champion).

1964　*Langage et science du langage* (Paris: Nizet).

1971　*Leçons de linguistique de Gustave Guillaume (1948–49)*, ed. R. Valin (Paris: Klincksieck).

Guiraud, Pierre

1955, 6th ed 1969　*La Sémantique* (Paris: P.U.F.).

1958　*La Grammaire* (Paris: P.U.F.).

1963　"Structures aléatoires de la double articulation," *Bulletin de la Société de Linguistique de Paris*, vol. 58, pp. 135–55.

1965　"Les Structures élémentaires de la signification," *Bulletin de la Société de Linguistique de Paris*, vol. 60, pp. 97–114.

1967　*Structures étymologiques du lexique français* (Paris: Larousse).

1970　*Essais de stylistique* (Paris: Klincksieck).

1971　"The Semic Matrices of Meaning," *Essays in Semiotics*, ed. J. Kristeva et al. (The Hague: Mouton), pp. 150–60.

1973　*La Sémiologie* (Paris: P.U.F.).

Hammad, Manar

1979　"Espaces didactiques: Analyse et conception," *Le Bulletin*, vol. 7, pp. 30–32.

1979　"Définition syntaxique du topos," *Le Bulletin*, vol. 10, pp. 25–27.

Harris, Zellig S.

1951　*Methods in Structural Linguistics* (Chicago: University of Chicago Press).

1954　"Distributional Structure," *Word*, vol. 10, pp. 146–62.

1957　"Co-occurrence and Transformation in Linguistic Structure," *Language*, vol. 33, pp. 283–340.

1962　*String Analysis of Sentence Structure* (The Hague: Mouton).

1965　"Transformational Theory," *Language*, vol. 41, pp. 363–401.

Haudricourt, André G.

1961　"Bipartition et tripartition des systèmes de tons dans quelques langues d'Extrême Orient," *Bulletin de la Société Linguistique de Paris*, vol. 56, pp. 163–80.

1966　"Quelques Etudes de champs sémantiques," *Pensée*, vol. 130, pp. 44–46.

1966　"Récents Travaux de sémantique structurale," *Pensée*, vol. 130, pp. 32–35.

Henault, Anne

1979　"Brèves," *Le Bulletin*, vol. 12, pp. 40–47.

1979　"Platon et la Dynamique des Passions," *Le Bulletin*, vol. 9, pp. 20–25.

1979　*Les Enjeux de la sémiotique* (Paris: P.U.F.).

1980　"La Terminologie du dictionnaire," *Le Bulletin*, vol. 13, pp. 10–15.

Hiz, Henry

1969　"Referentials," *Semiotica*, vol. 1, pp. 136–67.

1969　"Aletheic Semantic Theory," *Philosophical Forum*, N.S., vol. 1, pp. 438–51.

1969　*Referentials* (Philadelphia: University of Pennsylvania Press).

Hjelmslev, Louis

1936　"Essai d'une théorie des morphèmes," *Actes du IVᵉ Congrèss International de Linguistes*, pp. 140–51; also in: *Essais linguistiques* (Paris: Minuit, 1971), pp. 161–73.

1939　"Note sur les oppositions supprimables," *Travaux du Cercle Linguistique de Prague*, vol. 8, pp. 51–57; also in *Essais linguistiques* (Paris: Minuit, 1971), pp. 90–96.

1939　"La Notion de rection," *Acta Linguistica*, vol. I, pp. 10–23; also in: *Essais linguistiques* (Paris: Minuit, 1971), pp. 148–60.

1943   "Langue et parole," *Cahiers Ferdinand de Saussure*, vol. 2, pp. 29–44;
        also in: *Essais linguistiques* (Paris: Minuit, 1971), pp. 77–89.
1944   "Linguistique structurale," *Acta Linguistica* (Copenhagen), vol. IV,
        pp. v–xi; also in: *Essais linguistiques* (Paris: Minuit, 1971), pp. 28–33.
1948   "Structural Analysis of Language," *Studia Linguistica*, vol. I, pp.
        69–78. "L'Analyse structurale du langage," also in: *Essais linguis-
        tiques* (Paris: Minuit, 1971), pp. 34–43.
1953   *Prolegomena to a Theory of Language* (Bloomington: Indiana Univer-
        sity Press).
1954   "La Stratification du langage," *Word*, vol. 10, pp. 163–88; also in:
        Essais linguistiques (Paris: Minuit, 1971), pp. 44–76.
1956   "Animé et inanimé, personnel et non-personnel," *Travaux de
        l'Institut de Linguistique*, vol. I, pp. 155–99; also in: *Essais linguistiques*
        (Paris: Minuit, 1971), pp. 220–58.
1958   "Pour une sémantique structurale," *Proceedings of the 8th Interna-
        tional Congress of Linguists*, pp. 636–54; also in: *Essais linguistiques*
        (Paris: Minuit, 1971), pp. 105–21.
1958   "To What Extent Can Meaning Be Said To Be Structured?" *Pro-
        ceedings of the 8th International Congress of Linguistics*, pp. 636–54.
1961   "Some Reflections on Practice and Theory in Structural Semantics,"
        Language and Society (Copenhagen), pp. 55–63.
1971   *Essais linguistiques* (Paris: Minuit).
1971   "La Forme du contenu de langage comme facteur social," *Essais
        linguistiques* (Paris: Minuit), pp. 97–104.
1971   "Introduction à la linguistique," *Essais linguistiques* (Paris: Minuit),
        pp. 15–27.
1971   "La Structure morphologique," *Essais linguistiques* (Paris: Minuit),
        pp. 122–47.
1971   "Le Verbe et la phrase nominale," *Mélanges de philologie, de littérature
        et d'histoire ancienne offerts à J. Marouzeau*, pp. 253–81; also in: *Essais
        linguistiques* (Paris: Minuit), pp. 174–200.
1971   "La Nature du pronom," *Mélanges de linguistique et de philologie offerts
        à Jacques van Ginneken*, pp. 51–58; also in: *Essais linguistiques* (Paris:
        Editions de Minuit), pp. 201–207.
1971   "Sur l'indépendance de l'épithète," *K DUS Histoirique-Filol Medd.*,
        vol. 36, pp. 1–8; also in: *Essais linguistiques* (Paris: Editions de
        Minuit), pp. 208–19.
Husserl, Edmund
1960   *Cartesian Meditations*, trans. D. Cairns (The Hague: Nijhoff).
1970   *Logical Investigations*, trans. J.N. Findlay (New York: Humanities
        Press).
1970   "Zur Logik der Zeichen (Semiotik)," *Philosophie der Arithmetik*, ed. L.
        Eley (The Hague: Nijhoff).
1973   *Experience and Judgement*, trans. J.S. Churchill and L. Landgrabe
        (Evanston: Northwestern University Press).
Hymes, Dell
1962   "The Ethnography of Speaking," *Anthropological Society of Washing-
        ton*, ed. T. Gladwin and W.C. Sturtevant (Washington: Washington
        Anthropological Society), pp. 15–53.
1972   *Towards Communicative Competence* (Philadelphia: University of Penn-
        sylvania Press).
1974   *Foundations in Sociolinguistics* (Philadelphia: University of Pennsyl-
        vania Press).
Hymes, Dell, ed.
1964   *Language in Culture and Society* (New York: Harper & Row).

Jakobson, Roman
  1957 "The Cardinal Dichotomy in Language," *Language,* ed. R.N. An-
        shen, (New York: Harper).
  1960 "Closing Statement: Linguistics and Poetics," *Style in Language,* ed.
        T.A. Sebeok (New York: Wiley), pp. 350–77.
  1963 *Essais de linguistique générale* (Paris: Minuit).
  1964 "On Visual and Auditory Signs," *Phonetica,* vol. 11, pp. 216–20.
  1965 "A la recherche de l'essence du langage," *Diogène,* vol. 51, pp.
        22–38.
  1966 *Selected Writings IV: Slavic Epic Studies* (The Hague: Mouton).
  1967 "About the Relation Between Visual and Auditory Signs," *Models for
        the Perception of Speech and Visual Form* (Cambridge: Cambridge
        University Press).
  1968 *Child Language, Aphasia, and Phonological Universals* (The Hague:
        Mouton).
  1971 "The Concept of the Sound Law and the Teleological Criterion,"
        Selected Writings I (The Hague: Mouton), pp. 1–2.
  1971 "The Identification of Phonemic Entities," *Selected Writings I* (The
        Hague: Mouton), pp. 418–25.
  1971 "Implications of Language Universals," *Selected Writings II* (The
        Hague: Mouton), pp. 580–91.
  1971 "Linguistics and Communication Theory," *Selected Writings II* (The
        Hague: Mouton), pp. 570–79.
  1971 "Principes de phonologie historique," *Selected Writings I* (The
        Hague: Mouton), pp. 202–20.
  1971 "Proposition au Premier Congrès International de Linguistes,"
        Selected Writings I (The Hague: Mouton), pp. 4–6.
  1971 "Quest for the Essence of Language," *Selected Writings II* (The
        Hague: Mouton), pp. 345–59.
  1971 *Selected Writings I: Phonological Studies* (The Hague: Mouton).
  1971 *Selected Writings II: Word and Language* (The Hague: Mouton).
  1971 *Studies on Child Language and Aphasia,* 2nd ed. (The Hague:
        Mouton).
  1971 "Toward a Linguistic Classification of Aphasic Impairments,"
        Selected Writings II (The Hague: Mouton), pp. 289–306.
  1971 "Two Aspects of Language and Two Types of Aphasic Distur-
        bances," *Selected Writings II* (The Hague: Mouton), pp. 239–79.
  1971 "Zeichen und System der Sprache," *Selected Writings II* (The Hague:
        Mouton), pp. 272–79.
  1971 "Zur Struktur des Phonemes," *Selected Writings I* (The Hague:
        Mouton), pp. 280–310.
  1972 "Verbal Communication," *Scientific American,* vol. 227, pp. 73–80.
  1973 "Postscriptum," *Questions de poétique,* ed. T. Todorov (Paris: Seuil),
        pp. 485–504.
  1974 "Life and Language," *Linguistics,* vol. 138, pp. 97–103.
  1974 *Main Trends in the Science of Language* (New York: Harper & Row).
  1975 "Glosses on the Medieval Insight into the Science of Language,"
        Mélanges linguistiques offerts à Emile Benveniste, ed. M. Dj. Moinfar
        (Paris: Société de Linguistique de Paris), pp. 189–303.
  1975 "Metalanguage as a Linguistic Problem," *The Scientific Study of Lan-
        guage,* ed. A.S. Dil. Abbottabad (Pakistan: Pakistani Linguistic Re-
        search Group of Pakistan).
  1975 *Coup d'oeil sur le développement de la sémiotique* (Bloomington: Indiana
        University Research Center for Language Sciences).
  1976 *Six Leçons sur le son et le sens* (Paris: Minuit).

1979   *Selected Writings V: On Verse: Its Masters and Explorers* (The Hague: Mouton).
Jakobson, Roman, and C. Lévi-Strauss
     1973   "Charles Baudelaire's 'Les Chats,'" *Issues in Contemporary Literary Criticism,* ed. G.T. Polleta (Boston: Little, Brown, & Co.), pp. 372–87.
Jakobson, Roman, and Linda Waugh
     1979   *The Sound Shape of Language* (Bloomington: Indiana University Press).
Jauss, Hans Robert
     1969   *Poetik und Hermeneutik* (Munich: Fink).
     1970   *Literaturgeschichte als Provokation* (Frankfurt-am-Main: Suhrkamp).
Jauss, Hans Robert, ed.
     1960   *Die nicht mehr schönen Kunste. Poetik und Hermeneutik,* 3 (Munich: W. Fink).
Kalinowski, Georges
     1980   "Sur les universaux," *Le Bulletin,* vol. 14, 20–28.
Kant, Immanuel
     1953   *Critique of Pure Reason,* trans. N.K. Smith (London: Macmillan).
Katz, Jerrold J.
     1966   "The Semantic Component of a Linguistic Description," *Zeichen und System der Sprache,* III, ed. G.F. Meier (Berlin), pp. 195–205.
     1966   *The Philosophy of Language* (New York: Harper & Row).
     1971   *The Underlying Reality of Language and Its Philosophical Import* (New York: Harper & Row).
     1972   *Semantic Theory* (New York: Harper & Row).
Klein, Felix
     1921   "Das erlanger Programm," *Gesammelte mathematische Abhandlungen,* vol. I, pp. 460–97.
Koerner, Edward F.K.
     1972   *Bibliographia Saussureana 1870–1970* (Metuchen, N.J.: Scarecrow Press).
Kristeva, Julia
     1968   "Problèmes de la structuration du texte," *Nouvelle Critique,* vol. 10, pp. 55–64.
     1969   "Narration et transformation," *Semiotica,* vol. 1, pp. 422–49.
     1969   *Semeiotiké: Recherches pour une sémanalyse* (Paris: Seuil).
     1970   *Le Texte du roman* (The Hague: Mouton).
     1974   *La Révolution du langage poétique* (Paris: Seuil).
Kuyper, E. de
     1979   *Pour une sémiotique spectaculaire* (Paris: Thèse de 3ᵉ Cycle EHESS).
Laboratoire d'Architecture, No. 1
     1979   "Laboratoire d'Architecture No. 1," *Le Bulletin,* vol. 10, pp. 56–59.
Lacan, Jacques
     1966, 1979   *Ecrits I, II* (Paris: Seuil).
     1968   "The Function of Language in Psychoanalysis," *The Language of the Self,* ed. A. Wilden (Baltimore: Johns Hopkins Press).
Lalandre, André
     1948   *La Raison et les normes* (Paris: Hachette).
     1951   *Vocabulaire technique et critique de la philosophie,* 6th ed. (Paris: P.U.F.).
Landowski, Eric
     1977   *Figures d'autorité: Une Typologie sémiotique, Documents de travail, no. 65* (Urbino: Centro Internazionale di Semiotica e di Linguistica).
     1979   "Introduction," *Le Bulletin,* vol. 9, pp. 3–8.
     1980   "Notes de Lecture," *Le Bulletin,* vol. 14, pp. 41–44.

1980 *L'Opinion publique et ses porte-parole, Documents de Recherche,* no. 12 (Paris: EHESS and CNRS).

1981 *Jeux optiques, Documents de Recherche,* no. 23 (Paris: EHESS and CNRS).

Lauritsen, Laurits
1979 "Discours sur l'inconnu," *Le Bulletin,* vol. 8, pp. 18–20.
1979 "Enonciation, diégèse et passion," *Le Bulletin,* vol. 9, pp. 43–45.
1979 "Relecture de La Possession de M. de Certeau," *Le Bulletin,* vol. 8, pp. 37–41.

Leibniz, Gottfried W.
1923 *Leibniz, Saemtliche Schriften und Briefe* (Darmstadt: Otto Reichl Verlag).

Lemon, Lee T., and M.J. Reis
1965 *Russian Formalist Criticism* (Lincoln: University of Nebraska Press).

Lévi-Strauss, Claude
1955 "The Structural Study of Myth," *Journal of American Folklore,* vol. 68, pp. 428–44.
1963 *Structural Anthropology 1,* trans. C. Jacobson and B. Schoepf (New York: Basic Books).
1965 *Tristes Tropiques,* trans. J. Russell (New York: Atheneum).
1966 *The Savage Mind* (Chicago: University of Chicago Press).
1967 "The Story of Asdiwal," *The Structural Study of Myth and Totemism,* ed. E. Leach (London: Tavistock), pp. 1–48.
1967 *Totemism,* trans. R. Nedham (Boston: Beacon Press).
1968 *Race and History* (Paris: UNESCO).
1969 *Elementary Structures of Kinship,* trans. J.H. Bell and J.R. von Sturmer (Boston: Beacon Press).
1969 *The Raw and the Cooked,* trans. J. and D. Weightman (New York: Harper & Row).
1971 "The Family," *Man, Culture, and Society,* ed. H.L. Shapiro (New York: Oxford University Press), pp. 313–57.
1971 *From Honey to Ashes,* trans. J. and D. Weightman (New York: Harper & Row).
1972 *L'Homme nu* (Paris: Plon).
1976 *Structural Anthropology,* trans. M. Layton (New York: Harper & Row).
1978 *The Origin of Table Manners,* trans. J. and D. Weightman (New York: Harper & Row).

Lévy, A.
1979 *Sémiotique de l'espace: Architecture classique sacrée* (Paris: Thèse de 3e Cycle EHESS).

Lindekens, René
1971 *Pour une sémiotique de la photographie* (Paris: Aimav-Didier).
1977 *Essai de sémiotique visuelle* (Paris: Klincksieck).

Lotman, Yuri M.
1977 "Primary and Secondary Communication-Modeling Systems," *Soviet Semiotics,* ed. and trans. D. Lucid (Baltimore: Johns Hopkins University Press), pp. 95–98.
1977 "Two Models of Communication," *Soviet Semiotics,* ed. and trans. D. Lucid (Baltimore: Johns Hopkins University Press), pp. 99–101.
1977 "Problems in the Typology of Texts," *Soviet Semiotics,* ed. and trans. D. Lucid (Baltimore: Johns Hopkins University Press), pp. 119–24.
1977 "The Structure of the Narrative Text," *Soviet Semiotics,* ed. and trans. D. Lucid (Baltimore: Johns Hopkins University Press), pp. 193–97.

1977   "Problems in the Typology of the Culture," *Soviet Semiotics,* ed. and trans. D. Lucid (Baltimore: Johns Hopkins University Press), pp. 213–21.

Lotman, Yuri M., and A.M. Pjatigorskij
1977   "Text and Function," *Soviet Semiotics,* ed. and trans. D. Lucid (Baltimore: Johns Hopkins University Press), pp. 125–35.

Lotman, Yuri M., and V.A. Uspensky
1977   "Myth-Name-Culture," *Soviet Semiotics,* ed. and trans. D. Lucid (Baltimore: Johns Hopkins University Press), pp. 233–52.

Lyons, John
1963   *Structural Semantics* (Oxford: Blackwell).
1968   *Introduction to Theoretical Linguistics* (Cambridge: Cambridge University Press).

Malinowski, Bronislaw
1956   "The Problem of Meaning in Primitive Languages," in: Charles K. Ogden and I.A. Richards, *The Meaning of Meaning* (London: International Library of Psychology), pp. 296–336.
1962   *Myth in Primitive Psychology* (New York: W.W. Norton).

Malraux, André
1949–50   *The Psychology of Art,* trans. S. Gilbert (New York: Pantheon Books).

Marin, Louis
1971   *Etudes sémiologiques* (Paris: Klincksieck).
1971   *Sémiotique de la passion, topiques et figures* (Paris: Desclée de Brouwer; Aubier-Montaigne).
1973   Utopiques: Jeux d'espaces (Paris: Minuit).
1975   *La Critique du discours* (Paris: Minuit).
1978   *Le Récit est un piège* (Paris: Minuit).

Markov, Andrei A.
1961   *Theory of Algorithms,* trans. J.J. Schorr-Kon et al. (Jerusalem: Israel Program for Scientific Translations).

Martin, Robert
1980   "Universaux du langage et primitifs sémantiques," *Le Bulletin,* vol. 14, pp. 29–40.

Martinet, André
1933   "Remarques sur le système phonologique du français," *Bulletin de la Société Linguistique de Paris,* vol. 34, pp. 191–202.
1952   "Function, Structure, and Sound Change," *Word,* vol. 8, pp. 1–32.
1955   *Economie des changements phonétiques,* 2nd ed. (Berne: A. Francke).
1960   *Eléments de linguistique générale* (Paris: A. Colin); trans. E. Palmer, *Elements of General Linguistics* (Chicago: University of Chicago Press, 1964).
1962   *A Functional View of Language* (Oxford: Clarendon Press).
1966   "Structure and Language," *Yale French Studies,* vol. 36/37, pp. 10–18.
1967   "Syntagme et synthème," *La Linguistique,* vol. 2, pp. 1–14.
1970   *La Linguistique synchronique* (Paris: P.U.F.).

Matejka, Ladislav, and Irwin Titunik
1976   *Semiotics of Art* (Cambridge, Mass.: MIT Press).

Matejka, Lee, and K. Pomorska
1971   *Readings in Russian Poetics* (Cambridge, Mass.: MIT Press).

Matoré, Georges
1953   *La Méthode en lexicologie* (Paris: M. Didier).

Maurand, Georges
1980   "Le Corbeau et le renard: Approche narrativo-discursive," *Documents de Recherche,* no. 17 (Paris: EHESS and CNRS).

Mauss, Marcel
    1954   *The Gift* (New York: Free Press).
    1964   *Sacrifice,* trans. W.D. Halls (Chicago: University of Chicago Press).
Meletinsky, Eleazar M.
    1970   "Problèmes de la morphologie historique du conte populaire," *Semiotica,* vol. 2, pp. 128–35.
Meletinsky, Eleazar, and D. Segal
    1971   "Structuralisme et sémiotique en U.R.S.S.," *Diogène,* vol. 73, pp. 94–116.
Merleau-Ponty, Maurice
    1959   "De Mauss à Claude Lévi-Strauss," *La Nouvelle Revue Française,* vol. 7, pp. 615–31.
    1964   *Signs,* trans. R. McCleary (Evanston: Northwestern University Press).
    1964   *Sense and Non-Sense,* trans. H. and P. Dreyfus (Evanston: Northwestern University Press).
    1968   *The Visible and the Invisible,* trans. A. Lingis (Evanston: Northwestern University Press).
    1974   *Phenomenology of Perception,* trans. C. Smith (New York: Humanities Press).
Miereanu, Costin
    1979   *De la "Textkompositin" au "Poly-Art"* (Paris: Thèse d'Etat EHESS).
Mill, John S.
    1874   *A System of Logic,* 8th ed. (New York: Harper & Brothers).
Morris, Charles
    1938, 9th ed. 1957   *Foundations of the Theory of Signs* (Chicago: University of Chicago Press).
    1971   *Writings on the General Theory of Signs* (The Hague: Mouton).
Mounin, Georges
    1967   *Histoire de la linguistique* (Paris: P.U.F.).
    1971   *Saussure: Le Structuraliste sans le savoir* (Paris: Seghers).
    1972   *Clefs pour la sémantique* (Paris: Seghers).
    1972   *La Linguistique de XXe siècle* (Paris: P.U.F.).
Muntanola, José
    1979   "Sémiotique, épistémologie et pédagogie de l'architecture," *Le Bulletin,* vol. 10, pp. 22–24.
Nef, Frédéric
    1976   "De Dicto, De Re, Formule de Barcan et sémantique des mondes possibles," *Langages,* vol. 43, pp. 28–38.
Nef, Frédéric, ed.
    1976   *Structures élémentaires de la signification* (Paris:: P.U.F.).
Odin, Roger
    1980   "Stratégie du désir dans 'Une Partie de campagne,'" *Le Bulletin,* vol. 15, pp. 49–57.
Odgen, Charles K., and I.A. Richards
    1925   *The Foundations of Aesthetics* (New York: Lear Publishers).
    1938   *The Meaning of Meaning,* 5th ed. (New York: Harcourt, Brace, & Co.).
Oguibenine, Boris
    1979   "Auto-Interview," *Le Bulletin,* vol. 8, pp. 30–36.
    1980   "Notes de lecture: E.M. Meletinski, l'epopée mythologique paléoasiatique," *Le Bulletin,* vol. 16, pp. 55–63.
Osgood, Charles E.
    1971   "Explorations in Semantic Space: A Personal Diary," *Journal of Social·Issues,* vol. 27, pp. 5–64.

Osgood, Charles E., and T. A. Sebeok, eds.
    1965   *Psycholinguistics* (Bloomington: Indiana University Press).
Ostrowetsky, S.
    1979   "Analyse socio-sémantique des formes symboliques con-
            temporaines," *Le Bulletin,* vol. 10, pp. 7–12.
Panier, Louis
    1979   "Sémiotique du discours religieux et sémiotique générale," *Le Bulle-
            tin,* vol. 8, pp. 5–17.
    1979   *Récit et commentaire* (Paris: Thèse de 3ᵉ cycle EHESS).
Panofsky, Erwin
    1955   *Meaning in the Visual Arts* (New York: Doubleday).
    1967   *Studies in Iconology* (New York: Harper & Row).
Patte, Daniel
    1976   *What Is Structural Exegesis?* (Philadelphia: Fortress Press).
    1978   *Organisation Sémantique et Narrativité; Travaux du Cercle
            Méthodologique,* no. 7 (Toronto: Toronto Semiotic Circle).
    1979   "Du Didacticisme de trois ouvrages d'introduction à la sémiotique,"
            Le Bulletin, vol. 11, pp. 13–20.
    1980   *Aspects of a Semiotics of Didactic Discourse; Documents de Travail* (Ur-
            bino: Centro Internazionale di Semiotica e di Linguistica).
    1981   *Carré Sémiotique et syntaxe narrative; Documents de Recherche,* No. 23
            (Paris: EHESS and CNRS).
    1982   *Paul's Faith and the Power of the Gospel: A Structural Introduction to His
            Letters* (Philadelphia: Fortress Press).
Patte, Daniel, ed.
    1976   *Semiology and Parables* (Pittsburgh: Pickwick Press).
    1981   *Genesis 2 and 3: Kaleidoscopic Structural Readings, Semeia,* vol. 18.
Patte Daniel, and Aline Patte
    1978   *Pour une Exégèse structurale* (Paris: Seuil).
    1978   *Structural Exegesis: From Theory to Practice* (Philadelphia: Fortress
            Press).
Paulme, Denis
    1964   *Documents sur la langue kisi* (Université de Dakar: Documents Lin-
            guistiques, vol. 8).
Pavel, Thomas
    1973   "Phèdre: Outline of a Narrative Grammar," *Language Science,* vol.
            28, pp. 1–6.
    1976   *La Syntaxe narrative des tragédies de Corneille* (Paris: Klincksieck).
    1978   *Move-Grammar: Explorations in Literary Semiotics* (Toronto: Toronto
            Semiotic Circle).
    1980   *Modeles génératifs en linguistique et en sémiotique; Documents de Recher-
            che,* No. 20 (Paris: EHESS and CNRS).
Peirce, Charles S.
    1960   *Collected Papers,* eds. C. Hartshorne and P. Weiss, 2nd ed. (Cam-
            bridge, Mass.: Harvard University Press).
    1977   *Semiotic and Significs,* ed. C.S. Hardwick (Bloomington: Indiana
            University Press).
Pelc, Jerzy
    1961   "Semantic Functions as Applied to the Analysis of the Concept of
            Metaphor," *Poetics / Poetika / Poetyka,* no. 1, ed. D. Davie et al. (The
            Hague: Mouton), pp. 305–39.
    1969   "Meaning as an Instrument," *Semiotica,* vol. 1, pp. 26–48.
    1971   "On the Concept of Narration," *Semiotica,* vol. 3, pp. 1–20.
    1971   *Studies in Functional Logical Semiotics of Natural Language* (The
            Hague: Mouton).

1975 "Some Methodological Problems in Literary History," *New Literary History*, vol. 7, pp. 89–96.

Pessoa de Barros, Diana Luz
1978 *Verbos de comunicacão: Estudio sintatico-semantico* (Paris: Thèse de 3ᵉ cycle EHESS).
1979 "C'est arrivé demain: Sur la dissolution de l'Ecole Freudienne de Paris," *Le Bulletin*, vol. 12, pp. 35–39.

Piaget, Jean
1970 *Structuralism*, trans. C. Maschler (New York: Basic Books).

Poppe, E.
1979 *Analyse sémiotique de l'espace spectaculaire* (Paris: Thèse de 3ᵉ Cycle EHESS).

Postal, Paul M.
1964 *Constituent Structure* (Bloomington: Indiana University Research Center for Anthropology, Folklore, and Linguistics).

Pottier, Bernard
1962 *Introduction à l'étude des structures grammaticales fondamentales* (Nancy: Publications de la Faculté des Lettres et Sciences Humaines).
1963 *Recherches sur l'analyse sémantique en linguistique et en traduction automatique* (Nancy: Publications de la Faculté des Lettres et Sciences Humaines).
1964 "Vers une sémantique moderne," *Travaux de Linguistique et Littérature*, vol. 2, pp. 107–38.
1967 *Présentation de la linguistique* (Paris: Klincksieck).
1973 *Le Langage* (Paris: Denoël).
1974 *Linguistique générale: Théorie et description* (Paris: Klincksieck).
1980 "Comment dénommer les sèmes," *Le Bulletin*, vol. 13, pp. 21–29.
1980 "L'Homme, le monde, le langage, les langues et le linguiste," *Le Bulletin*, vol. 14, pp. 3–7.

Prieto, Luis J.
1964 *Principes de noologie: fondements de la théorie fonctionnelle du signifié* (The Hague: Mouton).
1965 "Fonction et économie," *Linguistique*, vol. 1, pp. 1–13, 41–66.
1966 *Messages et signaux* (Paris: P.U.F.).
1968 "La Sémiologie," *Le Langage*, ed. A. Martinet (Paris: Gallimard), pp. 93–144.
1969 "Langue et style," *Linguistique*, vol. 4, pp. 5–24.

Propp, Vladimir
1965 "Les Transformations des contes merveilleux," *Théorie de la littérature*, ed. T. Todorov (Paris: Seuil), pp. 234–62.
1968 *Morphology of the Folktale*, trans. L. Scott (Austin and London: University of Texas Press). First edition (Bloomington: Indiana University Research Center in Anthropology, 1958).
1971 "Fairy Tale Transformations," *Readings in Russian Poetics*, ed. L. Matejka and K. Pomorska (Cambridge, Mass.: MIT Press), pp. 94–115.

Quintilianus, Marcus F.
1920–22 *The Institutio Oratoria of Quintilian*, trans. H.E. Butler (New York: G.P. Putnam's Sons).

Rask, Rasmus K.
1976 *A Grammar of the Icelandic or Old Norse Tongue*, 2nd ed., trans. G.W. Pasent (Amsterdam: Benjamins).

Rastier, François
1971 "Les Niveaux d'ambiguïté des structures narratives," *Semiotica*, vol. 3, pp. 289–343.

1971 *Idéologies et signes* (The Hague: Mouton).
1972 "Systématique des isotopies," *Essais de sémiotique poétique,* ed. A.J. Greimas (Paris: Larousse), pp. 80–106.
1973 *Essais de sémiotique discursive* (Paris: Mame).

Reichenbach, Hans
1938 *Experience and Prediction* (Chicago: University of Chicago Press).
1976 *Elements of Symbolic Logic,* 2nd ed. (New York: Macmillan).

Rengstorf, Michael
1976 "Pour une quatrième modalité narrative," *Langages,* vol. 43, pp. 71–77.

Renier, Alain
1979 "L'Ecole et l'architecture," *Le Bulletin,* vol. 7, pp. 27–29.
1979 "Pour une sémiotique architecturale," *Le Bulletin,* vol. 10, pp. 3–6.

Rey-Debove, Josette
1980 "Du bon usage du jargon," *Le Bulletin,* vol. 13, pp. 31–41.

Ricoeur, Paul
1970 *Freud and Philosophy,* trans. D. Savage (New Haven: Yale University Press).
1976 *Interpretation Theory* (Fort Worth, Tex.: T.C.U. Press).
1977 *The Rule of Metaphor,* trans. R. Czerny (Toronto: University of Toronto Press).
1980 *La Grammaire narrative de Greimas; Documents de Recherche,* no. 15 (Paris: EHESS and CNRS).

Riffaterre, Michel
1966 "Describing Poetic Structures," *Yale French Studies,* vol. 36–37, pp. 200–42.
1970 "The Stylistic Approach to Literary History," *New Literary History,* vol. 2, pp. 39–55.
1971 *Essais de stylistique structurale* (Paris: Flammarion).
1978 *Semiotics of Poetry* (Bloomington: Indiana University Press).
1979 *La Production du texte* (Paris: Seuil).

Ruprecht, Hans-George
1981 *Du formant intertextuel: Remarques sur un objet ethnosémiotique, Documents de Recherche,* no. 23, (Paris: EHESS and CNRS).

Ruprecht, Hans-George et al.
1978 "Pour un projet de '*Théorie de la littérature*'"; *Documents de Travail,* nos. 72–73 (Urbino: Centro Internazionale de Semiotica e di Linguistica).

Russell, Bertrand
1940 *An Inquiry into Meaning and Truth* (London: Allen & Unwin).
1956 *Logic and Knowledge, Essays 1901–1950,* ed. R.C. Marsh (London: Allen and Unwin).

Ruwet, Nicolas
1968 "Limites de l'analyse linguistique en poétique," *Langages,* vol. 12, pp. 56–70.
1969 *Langage, musique, poésie* (Paris: Seuil).
1972 *Théorie syntaxique et syntaxe du français* (Paris: Seuil).
1973 *Introduction to Generative Grammar,* trans. N. Smith (Amsterdam: North-Holland).

Sacré, James
1979 *Pour une définition sémiotique du maniérisme et du baroque; Documents de Recherche,* no. 4 (Paris: EHESS and CNRS).

Sapir, Edward
1929 "The Status of Linguistics as a Science," *Language,* vol. 5, pp. 207–12.

1931   "Communication," *Encyclopedia of the Social Sciences,* vol. 4, pp. 78–80.
1933   "Language," *Encyclopedia of the Social Sciences,* vol. 9, pp. 155–68.
1934   "Symbolism," *Encyclopedia of the Social Sciences,* vol. 4, pp. 492–95.
1949   *Selected Writings of Edward Sapir,* ed. D. Mandelbaum (Berkeley: University of California Press).

Saudan, Alain
1979   "Eléments pour une étude sémiotique de l'analyse spinoziste des passions," *Le Bulletin,* vol. 9, pp. 37–42.

Saussure, Ferdinand de
1966   *Course in General Linguistics* (New York: McGraw-Hill).
1969   *Les Sources manuscrites du Cours de linguistique générale de Ferdinand de Saussure,* ed. R. Godel (Genève: Droz).

Sbisa, Marina, and Paolo Fabbri
1980   *Models (?) for a Pragmatic Analysis; Documents de Travail,* no. 91 (Urbino: Centro Internazionale di Semiotica e di Linguistica).

Scholes, Robert
1976   *Structuralism in Literature* (New Haven: Yale University Press).

Searle, John R.
1969   *Speech Acts* (Cambridge: Cambridge University Press).
1971   "What Is a Speech Act?" *The Philosophy of Language* (Oxford: Oxford University Press) pp. 39–53.
1979   *Expression and Meaning* (Cambridge: Cambridge University Press).

Sebeok, Thomas A.
1972   *Perspectives in Zoosemiotics* (The Hague: Mouton).
1976   *Contributions to the Doctrine of Signs* (Atlantic Highlands, N.J.: Humanities Press).
1979   *The Sign and Its Masters* (Austin: University of Texas Press).

Sebeok, Thomas A., ed.
1977   *How Animals Communicate* (Bloomington: Indiana University Press).

Shomali, Quastadni
1977   *La Morphologie du conte fantastique* (Paris: Thèse de Doctorat de 3ᵉ Cycle-Sorbonne).

da Silva, Ignacio Assis
1980   *Une Lecture de "Vieja Friendo Huevos" de Velasquez; Documents de Recherche,* no. 19 (Paris: EHESS and CNRS).

Smyth, Françoise
1979   "Présentation de la thèse de Laroussi Gasmi: Narrativité et production," *Le Bulletin,* vol. 8, pp. 26–29.

Spitzer, Leo
1961   "Les Etudes de style et les différents pays," *Actes F.I.L.L.M.,* pp. 23–38.
1961   "Quelques Aspects de la technique du nouveau roman de M. Butor," *Arch. Ling.,* vol. 13, pp. 171–95.
1970   *Etudes de style* (Paris: Gallimard).

Starobinski, Jean
1979   *Words upon Words: The Anagrams of Ferdinand de Saussure,* trans. O. Emmet (New Haven: Yale University Press).

Sulowski, Jan. ed.
1976   *Studia z Historii Semiotyki, III* (Warclaw, Warszawa, Kraków, Gdánsk: Zaklad, Narzdowy Imienza Ossolińskich Wydawnic to Polskie: Akademii Nauk).

Tarasti, Eero
1979   *Myth and Music* (The Hague: Mouton).

Tarski, Alfred
    1944 "The Semantic Conception of Truth," *Philosophical and Phenomenological Research*, vol. 4, pp. 341–76.
    1956 *Logic, Semantics, Metamathematics* (Oxford: Clarendon Press).
    1972–74 *Logique, Sémantique, Metamathématique (1923–1944)*, trans. G. Granger (Paris: A. Colin).

Tesnière, Luciene
    1965 *Eléments de syntaxe*, 2nd ed. (Paris: Klincksieck).
    1969 *Eléments de syntaxe structurale* (Paris: Klincksieck).

Thompson, Stith
    1955 *Narrative Motif-Analysis as a Folklore Method* (Helsinki: Suomalainen Tiedeakatemia).
    1955–58 *Motif-Index of Folk-Literature* (Bloomington: Indiana University Press).

Thürlemann, Felix
    1979 *Trois Peintures de Paul Klee: Essai d'analyse sémiotique* (Paris: Thèse de 3e Cycle EHESS).
    1980 *La Fonction de l'admiration dans l'esthétique du XVIIe siècle; Documents de Recherche*, no. 11 (Paris: EHESS and CNRS).
    1980 "Fonctions cognitives d'une figure de perspective picturale," *Le Bulletin*, vol. 15, pp. 37–48.

Todorov, Tzvetan
    1965 *Théorie de la littérature* (Paris: Seuil).
    1966 "Les Catégories de récit littéraire," *Communications*, vol. 8, pp. 125–51.
    1967 *Littérature et signification* (Paris: Larousse).
    1968 "La Grammaire du récit," *Langages*, vol. 12, pp. 94–102.
    1969 *Grammaire du Décameron* (The Hague: Mouton).
    1970 "Comment Lire," *La Nouvelle Revue Française*, vol. 18, pp. 129–43.
    1970 "Les Transformations narratives," *Poétique*, vol. 3, pp. 322–33.
    1977 *Théorie du symbole* (Paris: Seuil).
    1978 *The Poetics of Prose*, trans. R. Howard (Ithaca, N.Y.: Cornell University Press).
    1978 *Les Genres du discours* (Paris: Seuil).
    1978 *Symbolisme et interprétation* (Paris: Seuil).

Togeby, Knud
    1949 "Qu'est-ce qu'un mot?" *Travaux du Cercle Linguistique de Copenhague*, vol. 5, pp. 97–111.
    1965 *Structure immanente de la langue française*, 2nd ed. (Paris: Larousse).
    1967 "Littérature et linguistique," *Orbis Literarum*, vol. 22, pp. 45–48.

Trier, Jost
    1931 *Der deutsche Wortschatz im Sinnbezirk des Verstandes: Die Geschichte eines sprachlichen Feldes*, vol. 1 (Heidelberg: Carl Winter).

Troubetzkoy, Nikolai
    1929 "Sur la morphologie," *Travaux du Cercle Linguistique de Prague*, vol. 1, pp. 85–88.
    1931 "Die phonologischen Systeme," *Travaux du Cercle Linguistique de Prague*, vol. 4, pp. 96–116.
    1969 *Principles of Phonology*, trans. A.M. Baltaxe (Berkeley: University of California Press).

Uldall, Hans J.
    1957 *Outline of Glossematics* (Copenhagen: Nordisk Sprog–Og Kulturforlag).

Uspensky, Boris
   1973 *A Poetics of Composition: The Structure of the Artistic Text and Typology of a Compositional Form,* trans. V. Zavarin and S. Wittig (Berkeley: University of California Press).

Vachek, Josef, ed.
   1964 *A Prague School Reader in Linguistics,* (Bloomington: Indiana University Press).

Vergniaus, A.F.
   1979 "Le Système de l'intégration en architecture," *Le Bulletin,* vol. 10, pp. 33–36.

Weinrich, Harald
   1964 *Tempus* (Stuttgart: W. Kohlammer Verlag).
   1966 "Explorations in Semantic Theory," *Current Trends in Linguistics,* vol. 3 (The Hague: Mouton), pp. 395–477.
   1968 "Semantics and Semiotics," *International Encyclopedia of the Social Sciences,* vol. 14 (New York: Macmillan), pp. 164–69.
   1973 *Le Temps: le récit et le commentaire* trans. Michèle Lacoste (Paris: Seuil).

Whorf, Benjamin L.
   1957 *Language, Thought, and Reality* (Cambridge, Mass.: Harvard University Press).

Winner, Irene Portis, and Jean Umiker-Sebeok, eds.
   1979 *The Semiotics of Culture* (The Hague: Mouton).

Zemb, Jean Marie
   1980 "L'Armistice des universaux," *Le Bulletin,* vol. 14, pp. 8–19.

Zilberberg, Claude
   1972 "Un Essai de lecture de Rimbaud: Bonne Pensée du Matin," *Essais de sémiotique poétique,* ed. A.J. Greimas (Paris: Larousse), pp. 140-54.
   1972 *Une Lecture des Fleurs du Mal* (Paris: Mame).
   1979 *Taches Critiques; Documents de Recherche,* no. 2 (Paris: EHESS and CNRS).
   1979 "Les Passions chez Freud," *Le Bulletin,* vol. 9, pp. 46–48.
   1979 Review: "D. Bertrand, 'Le Joueur' de Dostoievski," *Le Bulletin,* vol. 11, pp. 27–30.
   1980 "Notes de lecture: Phillippe Hamon, 'Narrativité et lisibilité,'" *Le Bulletin,* vol. 14, pp. 45–46.
   1980 "Notes relatives au faire persuasif," *Le Bulletin,* vol. 15, pp. 11–25.

Zumthor, Paul
   1972 *Essai de poétique médiévale* (Paris: Seuil).
   1975 *Langue, texte, énigme* (Paris: Seuil).
   1978 *Le Masque et la lumière: La poétique des grands rhétoriqueurs* (Paris: Seuil).